WATCH IT MADE
IN THE U.S.A.

Praise for *Watch It Made in the U.S.A.*

"Ever wonder how Celestial Seasonings mixes all those herbs for their teas? Or how Hallmark comes up with those cute sayings for their cards? Here's your chance to find out."

—USA Today

"Unusual travel opportunities, and they're closer than you think . . . "
—Good Morning America

"A nifty new book . . . The guidebook gurus give the lowdown on 240 tours, including sightseeing highlights, nearby attractions, directions and tons of freebies."
—Globe

"This is a product that makes you proud to be an American: a guide to all the tourable places that make the products America loves best."
—Daily News, New York's Hometown Newspaper

". . . a fascinating behind-the-scenes look at household names, names that many of us take for granted. . . ."
—Chicago Tribune

"Factory tours are great value vacations."
—Boston Sunday Herald

"*Watch It Made in the U.S.A.* would be right up your assembly line . . . a wealth of information on tours and museums."
—The Philadelphia Inquirer

". . . take time out to visit one of these factories—the whole family will enjoy the tour!"
—Good Housekeeping

"If the mystery of how the fortune gets into the fortune cookie keeps you up at night, thumb through *Watch It Made in the U.S.A.* . . . ."
—SELF

WATCH IT MADE
IN THE U.S.A.

**A Visitor's Guide to the Companies
That Make Your Favorite Products**

Second Edition

Karen Axelrod and Bruce Brumberg

Foreword by Richard S. Gurin
President and CEO, Binney & Smith Inc.
(maker of Crayola products)

**AVALON
TRAVEL**
publishing

The information in this book is subject to change without notice. We strongly recommend that you call ahead to verify the information presented here before making final plans or reservations. (Note: area codes were in flux at press time.) All companies and their logos are included without charge to them. The companies whose photographs appear here have paid a modest fee to help defray publication costs.

Avalon Travel Publishing, 5855 Beaudry Street, Emeryville, CA 94608
formerly published by John Muir Publications

Copyright © 1997, 1994 by Karen Axelrod and Bruce Brumberg
Cover © 2001 by Avalon Travel Publishing
All rights reserved.

Printed in the United States of America.
Second edition. Third printing February 2001.

Library of Congress Cataloging-in-Publication Data
Axelrod, Karen.
Watch it made in the U.S.A. : a visitor's guide to the companies that make your favorite products / Karen Axelrod and Bruce Brumberg.
—2nd ed.
  p.   cm.
  Rev. ed. of: Watch it made in the U.S.A. / Bruce Brumberg and Karen Axelrod. 1994
  Includes indexes.
  ISBN 1-56261-337-5 (pbk.)
1. Industries—United States—Directories. 2. Manufacturing industries—United States—Directories. 3. United States—Tours—Handbooks, manuals, etc. 4. Tour guides (Manuals)   I. Brumberg, Bruce. II. Brumberg, Bruce. Watch it made in the U.S.A. III. Title.
HF5035.B64   1997
338.7'4'02573—dc21   97-11093
                                                 CIP

Editors: Sarah Baldwin, Nancy Gillan
Production: Nikki Rooker
Typesetter: Kathleen Sparkes
Cover Photos: Crayola Factory, featured on page 260.
Back Cover Photos: Boehms Chocolates, featured on page 318, Journal American; BMW, featured on page 282; Hershey's Visitor's Center, featured on page 23.
Printer: Publishers Press

Distributed to the book trade by
Publishers Group West
Berkeley, California

Watch It Made in the U.S.A. is available at special discounts for bulk purchases, sales promotions, fund raising, and educational purposes. For details contact Avalon Travel Publishing, Special Sales.

Dedications

To the American workers, engineers, and managers who have regained their pride by making the best quality products in the world.

To our marriage and the love and times we share together.

Special Second Edition Dedication

To Hilary Dana, the best product we've made—so far.

Hilary Dana Brumberg enjoying the bears with Merilee Woods, owner of Basic Brown Bear Factory in San Francisco.

Contents

Foreword

Remember how it feels to draw with a perfect new Crayola crayon, or to open your first 64-box with the built-in sharpener in the back? Not surprisingly, the wonderful scent of crayons is one of the most recognizable smells in America. With crayons, many of us have our first experiences using color to make pictures and feeling the joy of creation. Common experiences like these connect us to one another in subtle but important ways.

Factory tours and company museums help us appreciate our collective history by giving us insight into familiar brands like Crayola, Coca-Cola, Harley-Davidson, and Louisville Slugger. In these fast-paced times, it is easy to take for granted the products we use every day. Tours and museums provide an inside look at the time, effort, and pride poured into products made in the U.S.A.

Binney & Smith's original Crayola tour program became so popular that there was often a two-year waiting list. To accommodate the growing number of people who wanted to see our Crayola crayons and markers being made, we created The Crayola Factory at Two Rivers Landing (see page 260). Just as the Hallmark Visitors Center helped revitalize downtown Kansas City, Missouri, we wanted The Crayola Factory to contribute to the economic development of downtown Easton, Pennsylvania. Within one year of The Crayola Factory's launch, almost 100 new businesses opened downtown as a result of the added visitors to our town.

Authors Karen Axelrod and Bruce Brumberg guide you to factory tours and company museums around the country where you can discover how your favorite products are made. We know that young and old alike are curious about how a Crayola crayon is formed out of hot wax. Seeing firsthand the skill and pride that go into each guitar made at the Martin Guitar plant, or the cooperation between workers and robots in transforming sheet metal into a Ford Explorer, is a truly memorable experience. The places described in this book provide fun learning tools and history lessons for us all.

I hope all of you will enjoy this book. With each page you'll get a new idea for a family or business trip and gain a new appreciation for the manufacturing of great American products. On every tour you take, American workmanship and pride come through loud and clear.

Richard S. Gurin
President and CEO, Binney & Smith Inc.
Easton, Pennsylvania

Crayola®

Preface

When you were younger, you probably read *Charlie and the Chocolate Factory* or watched the movie version, *Willie Wonka and the Chocolate Factory*. As you may remember, Charlie won the opportunity to visit a chocolate factory by finding a special golden ticket in his Wonka Bar. His luck led to a fascinating journey.

This book is like that golden ticket in Charlie's chocolate bar. With this guide you can visit factory tours and company museums throughout the U.S.A. Whether you're with your family, traveling alone, or on a field or business trip, you'll have fun, discover how well-known products are made, and learn what these companies did to grow and prosper. Along the way, you will receive plenty of free samples and tastes.

Ours is a harried society that just wants to plug it in, mix it with milk, turn the ignition, or open the box. We want you to experience the excitement of watching people and machines make the food we eat, the cars we drive, the musical instruments we play, and the sporting goods we use.

After visiting (by foot or armchair) the nearly 300 companies featured in this book, you'll marvel at the behind-the-scenes processes involved in producing the products we take for granted. You'll be proud of the hardworking American people and companies that make it all possible. We like to say that this book gives you the opportunity to go out and "kick the tires" of the American economy. Watch how American companies have proudly regained their competitive edge and are again perceived as the world leaders in many industries.

To compile the list of companies that offer tours, museums, and visitor centers, we followed many paths and traveled thousands of miles. The book focuses on recognized national or regional companies that make familiar products, whether they be chocolates, cars, clothes, toys, or beer. Each tour or museum either has regular hours or is open to the general public by reservation.

Enjoy the tours. But don't stuff yourself with the free samples like the guests did on the tour of Willie Wonka's chocolate factory!

Second Edition Thoughts

We were delighted by the media coverage that the first edition of *Watch It Made in the U.S.A.* received. The book sold very well and went into three printings. We were interviewed as factory tour experts on "Good Morning America." Print publicity for the first edition included articles in the *Wall Street Journal*, the *New York Times*, *USA Today*, *Business Week*, *Parenting*, *Good Housekeeping*, and *Bottom Line*. Even *Bride's Magazine* featured the book in an article on offbeat honeymoon ideas. We did numerous radio interviews, including those on WBZ-Boston, KABC-Los Angeles, WGN-Chicago, WCBS-New York, and National Public Radio. Microsoft has also added *Watch It Made* to the new version of its CD-ROM called "Automap."

Throughout our numerous interviews, we were asked why we wrote the book. There are many reasons—the short, sound-bite kind and longer ones. We often answered that we're curious people—curious about how the toothpaste gets into the toothpaste tube and how the tea gets into the tea bag. There was no book out there like this one, so we decided to write it before having our first child. For the second edition we traveled, albeit a bit less, with Hilary (who has had her own frequent-flier account numbers since she was three months old). Her first official factory tour was at Creegan Company in Ohio. She even went to meetings with us at such companies as Amway and Binney & Smith (Crayola).

When asked about the best tours, we say that that depends on your interests. Some people like the craftsmanship required to make Fenton art glass and Martin guitars. Others enjoy the high speed of Coca-Cola bottling lines or the robots and welding at automobile plants. We prefer to mention tours that can easily be added onto an existing vacation: If you're traveling between San Francisco and Yosemite National Park, you can tour the Hershey's plant in Oakdale, California. If you're going skiing, hiking, or climbing in the Rockies, you can watch the tea get into the tea bag at Celestial Seasonings Tea in Boulder, Colorado.

For the second edition, we've completely updated all the existing write-ups, and visited many more places. Highlights include information about the new Crayola Factory (cover photo) in Easton, Pennsylvania, and the new Louisville Slugger Museum now in Louisville, Kentucky. Plus, we added full write-ups for 66 new sites! New factory tours in the book include Blaine Kerne's Mardi Gras World in New Orleans, Louisiana, and Bacardi Rum in Cataño, Puerto Rico; and new company museums and visitors centers include SPAMTOWN USA in Austin, Minnesota, and Kellogg's Cereal City in Battle Creek, Michigan. With the increased popularity of agritourism, we've added Amon Orchards, near the world's cherry capital of Traverse City, Michigan, and Kliebert's Alligator Farm in Hammond, Louisiana. We also searched for more furniture sites: two factories in Indiana and the Furniture Discovery Museum in High Point, North Carolina. From our travels with our daughter Hilary, we've added six new tours in Indiana, five in California, four in Louisiana, and six in Michigan. Over 60 percent of states have at least one new tour. Unfortunately, we had to drop 16 sites from the book because the facilities closed, tours were discontinued, or companies didn't want the continued publicity.

Since 90 percent of the tours in this book are free, and many give free samples, factory tours remain the *best vacation value* in America. Enjoy!

Second Edition Acknowledgments

First and foremost Karen would like to thank Bruce for giving her something valuable—her name listed first on the cover.

Together, we want to thank the companies that provide tours and museums, and also the people at those businesses who met with us, answered our numerous questions, verified the accuracy of our information, and gave us encouragement. Convention and visitors bureaus, state tourism boards, and chambers of commerce gave us information and materials, which we appreciated. Twenty years ago this book wouldn't have been needed, as just about all companies gave public tours. Now many forces, including budget cuts, insurance rates, trade-secret protection, and government regulations, have caused companies to end them. But a trend does exist toward opening new visitors centers to replace factory tours. The firms that open their doors to the public have stories to tell about their place in America's heritage and in its economic future.

We also specially thank those companies with photographs in the book. While no company paid for its inclusion in *Watch It Made in the U.S.A.* or for our publishing its logo, companies did pay a modest fee to include black-and-white or color photos. This was a very expensive book to research, write, and produce. Without this small amount of funding the book either would not have been published or its purchase price would have been far beyond what the average person spends for a travel book.

We enjoyed the support from our parents, Elaine and Norman Brumberg (actually, Bruce's parents became supportive once we gave his dad a Harley-Davidson T-shirt and his mom T-shirts from Ben & Jerry's and Wild Turkey), and Harriet and David Axelrod (Karen's mother's love of travel inspired us both to do this book; we wish she were alive to see it in print); strength from our grandmother Franziska Hirschhorn; and guidance from our aunt and uncle, Erika and Larry Casler. Elaine Brumberg and Larry Casler set good examples for us, as they have written books of their own.

Susan Koffman, a friend and colleague, provided writing, editing, computer assistance, and emotional support throughout the two-year marathon to produce the first edition and continued her support for the second edition. Also, Pam Kubbins, who doubles as a flight attendant at Delta Airlines, wrote the most features of any freelance writer for the first edition, gave us constant encouragement, and again helped with the new edition.

Specific to the second edition, we thank Valerie Dumova for writing many of our new West Coast features; and Eve Kaplan, who helped research new companies to add to the second edition and wrote some of these features. Kathryn Schoenbrun came midstream and really moved the book forward through her writing, production, organizational, and follow-through skills. She cheerfully helped flesh out the priorities and strategize finishing the book to meet deadlines. She even joined in and celebrated our triumphs.

Other folks who tangibly helped us (in alphabetical order) include Harriet Brumberg, Rebecca Bunting, Dan Carney, Phil and Betty Comerford, Scott Dimetrosky (who developed our Website at www.factorytour.com), Sam Donisi, Ilyse Kramer, Jessica Lefroy, Kristina Lupariello, Amy and Mark Seiden, Judith

Woodruff (who took care of Hilary so we could work on the book), and Howard Zaharoff.

Unfortunately, we could not list all those friends, relatives, writers, and editorial assistants who helped with research, writing, editing, and word processing of the first edition, and who provided general advice, support, and ideas for both editions—but we do express our heartfelt appreciation to all of them. We appreciate the help with accommodations provided by Jim and Judy Allen, Country Oaks Guest House (B&B), Breaux Bridge (318-332-3093), in the Cajun area of Louisiana; Beatriz O. Aprigliano, Fairchild House (B&B), New Orleans, Louisiana (800-256-8096); and Conrad and Lynette Showalter, The Ol' Barn (B&B), Goshen (219-642-3222), in the heart of northern Indiana's Amish area. We used Jane Ware's *Other People's Business* to locate a few of the new tours in Ohio, and Jack and Eunice Berger's *Inside America* for a few nearby attractions.

Finally, we thank the staff at John Muir Publications for sharing our vision for this book.

Safety Guidelines

Lawsuits are a product we make too many of in the U.S.A. During our research we discovered many companies that have discontinued their tours because of fears of lawsuits from injured guests and increases in liability insurance rates for allowing public visitors. Follow basic safety rules and your common sense to avoid injury.

The authors and publisher of *Watch It Made in the U.S.A.* make no warranty, expressed or implied, regarding the safety of any of the tours in this book and assume no liability with respect to the consequences of using the information contained herein. If you have any special safety concerns, contact the companies directly before you decide to visit.

The factories in this book are all working facilities, not full-time tourist attractions. While many of them provide the kind of space-age excitement you normally see only in the movies, these factories are the real thing, with potentially dangerous machines.

If you are injured, it is likely that the company will completely discontinue its public tours. Please listen to your tour guide and read any safety warnings. Remember the following rules:

1. Do not wander away from your tour guide or away from any specified tour path. Many factory tours have lines painted on the floor. You must stay between them.
2. Parents and adult group leaders should keep a close watch on children. Kids will be very curious about the sights, sounds, and smells, and may be tempted to wander off and touch things that could be dangerous.
3. Wear any protective equipment that you are provided with on your tour. These may include eyeglasses, earplugs, hard hats, or hair nets. If you have trouble wearing any of these items, tell your tour guide immediately.
4. Do not touch anything, including machines, products, parts, or boxes, unless your tour guide specifically hands something to you.
5. Wear closed-toe shoes with rubber soles that have good traction. Do not wear sandals or high heels (many companies will not allow you to go on tour). Wear shoes that will provide protection against sharp objects and that are comfortable for walking. Floors can be slippery. For safety reasons, it is best not to wear shorts.

How Companies Were Selected

Our search for companies to include in *Watch It Made in the U.S.A.* began in stores where their products are sold. We went through supermarkets, department stores, car dealerships, and sporting goods stores, searching for the names of companies that make popular products in the U.S.A. Sometimes store owners thought we were competitors, as we would pick up a box, turn it over to see who made the product, and scribble down the company's address and phone number.

We also searched through directories and magazine ads, hunting down more manufacturers of U.S.A.-made products. We contacted state travel offices, local convention and visitors bureaus, and chambers of commerce looking for names of companies in their areas that gave tours. For the second edition, readers of the book and companies who had started tours also contacted us with suggested additions. These lists, which we continued making and updating throughout our writing and traveling, were only the start of our research.

Then we called . . . and called . . . and then visited most of the sites in the book. We spoke with companies throughout the U.S.A., asking whether they gave tours or had a museum (often called a "visitors center"). We didn't hide the fact that we were writing a book. We wanted to include only those companies that regularly accept public visitors and would talk with us about their history, tours, and products.

No company paid for its written feature in *Watch It Made in the U.S.A.* The companies had to meet the following criteria:

1. **Tours open to the general public.** Throughout our research we found companies that give tours only to buyers, to technical organizations, or upon special request. We did not include these companies or others that had too many requirements for visitors.

2. **Tours available to individuals and families.** Some companies will give tours only to local school groups, senior citizen clubs, boy and girl scout troops, or bus tour companies. To be included in *Watch It Made,* a company had to at least allow individuals and families not affiliated with a group tour to visit. You may need to join a scheduled group tour (or the company may combine individual requests to form a group) and make reservations far in advance, but every facility in this book should be open to you.

3. **Products of general interest that are worth traveling to see made.** Unless you have a technical background or are in a specific industry, we thought that seeing how your favorite everyday products are made would hold the most fascination. In addition to tours of the icons of American business, we sought out small companies that have good products and interesting tours. Most of the companies in the book make consumer-related or widely recognized products. We also selected companies where you could watch the completion of the final product and therefore excluded parts manufacturers.

4. **Company did not object to being featured in book.** Companies generally do not make money from their tours. They give tours as a public and community service, often pulling employees from their regular jobs to conduct the tours. We excluded companies that did not want the calls and tour requests that this wide-

ly distributed book would generate, if the tour was not already mentioned in other public sources. A small number of companies asked not to be included after we had visited them and written our extensive features. In most cases we were able to retain their features after modifying the tour information to meet the companies' concerns. In a few instances we had to drop tours of well-known companies.

We strove to select companies from diverse industries and all areas of the country. We wanted to capture the industries for which different regions are known, such as cheese in Wisconsin and Vermont, glass in West Virginia, movies in Southern California, bourbon in Kentucky, RVs in northern Indiana, Cajun hot sauces in Louisiana, and wood products in the Pacific Northwest. Certain high-tech industries, such as computer manufacturing and biotechnology, do not give regular public tours for proprietary reasons, so they are excluded by their choice. In other industries, such as beer brewing and newspaper publishing, tours are a standard practice; from this group we selected the most high-profile companies or those with interesting processes or histories.

We were surprised that companies in certain states, even though very industrial, do not seem interested in giving public tours. For example, while manufacturing-intensive states such as Pennsylvania, Wisconsin, and Ohio offer a variety of captivating tours, most New Jersey and Connecticut companies remain closed to the public. In contrast, companies in less industrial states such as Kentucky and Vermont have exhibited great pride in opening themselves to the public.

In addition to factory tours, we also included company museums or visitors centers devoted to one company's products and history. Some companies have replaced the public factory tours with educational and entertaining museums that explain how they started, succeeded, and make their products. The Crayola Factory at Two Rivers Landing in downtown Easton, Pennsylvania is a recent example. More companies are now establishing museums to preserve their heritage, instill corporate culture, and tell their story to the public, new employees, and customers. We did not include company museums that are like art exhibits. The museums we selected, like the tours, give you a sense of what the companies are all about.

Going Beyond This Book

We excluded wineries, power plants, chemical factories, meat processors, most service industries, and tobacco manufacturers. The company tours in this book are the easiest ones to join—you either just show up or call in advance to reserve a space. If you are interested in visiting a company not featured here, contact the public affairs or human resources department at the corporate headquarters or local plant. With persistence, you can tour many firms if you're not a direct competitor. Explain your individual request and also ask if the company offers tours for specialized business and technical groups (often for a fee).

No book like this has ever been published before. Although we tried hard to find the public factory tours and company museums currently available, we do not claim that this guide contains all of them. Since we will update this book again, we would like your comments on the sites you visit from this guide and on tours we should consider for the next edition. Please write us at John Muir Publications (P. O. Box 613, Santa Fe, NM 87504) and visit our Website at www.factorytour.com. We hope this book's success will lead more companies to open their doors to the general public.

How to Use This Book

We wanted *Watch It Made in the U.S.A.* to be much more than a directory. Therefore, we *did not* write it by sending surveys out to companies and then publishing a compilation of the responses. We visited most of the companies included here. We took periodic breaks from our regular jobs to travel the U.S.A. in search of its economic soul. For those companies that time did not permit us to visit, we either hired writers to do so or conducted in-depth phone interviews that required companies to send us videos, articles, and tour scripts. After we wrote each feature, we verified its accuracy with the company. Just before press time, we confirmed the information again.

Each company tour or museum feature includes a narrative description and a practical information section. This book is organized alphabetically by state. The features appear in alphabetical order unless positioning of photographs necessitated slight alteration.

Narrative Description

Some of us are awed by fast-moving bottling machines and fascinated by robotic welders or giant presses, while others enjoy the artisanship of a glassblower, woodworker, or potter. The narrative description will help you determine which tours you and your family will enjoy.

Each feature has a three- to five-paragraph write-up that captures the highlights of the tour and some background on the company. The write-ups also provide a basic understanding of how different products are made. We try to give you a sense of being there—what you might see, hear, smell, taste, or even touch; if a company is big or small; and whether you actually visit the factory floor or watch production through glass windows. We wrote this part in a conversational tone so that even the armchair traveler would be able to vicariously experience the tour or museum.

Practical Information Section

The second part of the feature provides basic practical information on location, hours, admission charge, freebies, age and group requirements, disabled access, gift shop and outlet stores, and nearby attractions. The category titles in this section are self-explanatory. The following are some special notes on the different categories in this section:

Cost: Many company tours, visitors centers, and museums are free or have a nominal charge, which makes them a great vacation value. However, charges may change after this book's printing, so call ahead.

Freebies: Many tours give samples, ranging from beer and ice cream to miniature baseball bats. Remember—you're a guest, so be appreciative.

Video Shown: These are often interesting, informative, and even humorous. They provide a close-up view inside machines and show production steps not seen on the tour. If videos are optional, we suggest you view them before going on the tour. They help you understand what you will see.

Reservations Needed: If a company requires reservations, please respect those requirements. *Do not just show up*—you will not get a tour. Make reservations as far in advance as possible. Some companies require individuals and families to join a scheduled group tour that has not reached its maximum size, which this section will note. For these companies, you need to be more flexible in scheduling your visit. Many companies produce a range of products; if you have certain favorites, call ahead to find out what will be in production on the day of your visit.

Days and Hours: These are the hours for the tour or museum, not for the gift shop or outlet store. Hours are subject to change, and factories may shut down (hopefully for expansion construction), so call before your visit to avoid disappointment. Automobile plants, for example, often temporarily discontinue their tours so assembly lines can be reconfigured for major model changes. Many of the companies with regular tour schedules have voice-mail telephone numbers that answer common questions on schedule changes and directions. The hours listed here are the range during which tours are given, unless a frequency is specified. Holiday schedules vary by company. For example, some companies view the day after Thanksgiving as a holiday.

Plan to Stay: We included the amount of time needed for the basic visit, plus additional time for optionals such as the gift shop. The length of time spent on self-guided tours depends on the level of your interest. A short recommended time provides an indication of the company size or the amount you'll see.

Minimum Age: Tours have minimum age restrictions because of safety and insurance requirements. Companies strictly enforce these limits.

Disabled Access: Almost all of the tours in this book are working factories first and not full-featured visitor attractions. They try to accommodate people with disabilities while focusing on the safety concerns of both visitors and workers. Few companies told us absolutely "no" for disabled access. Almost all plants, however, have some limited-access areas, which we tried to note, and some may require advance notice. We are not commenting on the restrooms or compliance with the Americans with Disabilities Act standards, only the ease with which people with disabilities can visit these companies.

Group Requirements: Advance reservations are almost always required for groups, and some companies have maximum group sizes. This section is useful for group tour planners.

Special Information: Re-read the safety rules at the beginning of the book, since we do not repeat them in this section. For worker safety and proprietary reasons, many tours do not allow photography (which includes snapshot and video cameras). "No photography" refers to factory production areas, not gift shops, museums, and display areas. If you or a family member are sensitive to noise, smells, or temperature changes, be aware of these conditions when selecting a tour. However, these shocks to the senses are part of the exciting realism of factory tours.

Gift Shop/Outlet Store: Most gift shops sell logoed items and company products. The real factory outlet stores offer great bargains. Hours are often longer than the tour hours.

Directions: Many companies have maps that they can mail or fax you. While we have made our best efforts to give you accurate narrative directions (double-checked with the companies and often given from two possible directions), a map is always helpful. At the top of each write-up is the street address of the factory or museum.

Nearby Attractions: To round out your day, we list some of the nearby parks, museums, and other activities. We also draw your attention to other nearby factory tours and company museums. These factory tours and museums, which are listed first, are within a larger radius from the plant than the other nearby attractions. In addition to the nearly 300 full-page company features in the book, we list over 150 additional factory tours in this section of the write-ups (phone number included). For reasons of variety, quality, tour restrictions, or time, we decided not to write full features on these other tours.

Trademarks

We have used the commonly known company name rather than the longer corporate name. To the best of our knowledge, all of the product names in this book are trademarks. Throughout the text, we capitalized the first letter of all words that are trademarks. When companies provided us with their logos, we included them at no charge. The logos in no way imply that a company is a sponsor of the book. These logos are also trademarks that cannot be reproduced without a company's express consent.

Advice for Business Travelers

These tours are not merely a new way to grab a free beer during a business trip to Milwaukee or St. Louis. At its core, *Watch It Made in the U.S.A.* is a travel guide to American business. Our business backgrounds led us to write it. When we took a factory tour or visited a company museum, we discovered how that company makes and markets its products, and how the company started and grew. We developed ideas that we couldn't get from any newspaper, magazine, or business book. Sure, you can read a book about Ted Turner, Andy Grove, or Mary Kay Ash—but *Watch It Made in the U.S.A.* tells you how to visit CNN, Intel, or Mary Kay Cosmetics to see the companies in action. Visiting the sites in this book will spice up a business trip with new experiences that may help you in your own work.

Improve Your Understanding of Business News and Trends

The tours offer a new perspective on our economy, workplace productivity, and job creation. After visiting a few of the companies profiled, you'll have a better filter for understanding business and economic news. The concepts of total quality management, re-engineering, just-in-time inventory, or *kaizen* (constant improvement), for example, which just about every company in this book uses in some form, have new meaning when you see how they are adapted to the production of baseball bats, cars, and chocolate. You'll also notice production and product trends before they are reported in the media and appear on store shelves.

Sources of Useful New Ideas

By visiting these companies you will not only experience first-hand how they operate but also expose yourself to new business techniques. Don't think that these tours appeal only to people in manufacturing-related jobs! Many of the tours and museums show you much more than just how the company makes its products; they also reveal its marketing, management, and new-product development approach. To get the most from your visit, make it a point to look for and ask about innovative approaches and solutions that the company has developed, then think about how your business could adopt them. Try to discover what really makes the company successful and admired, then ponder how your firm can emulate it.

The companies' public relations departments may at times shape the tour scripts, but what you see, hear, sense, and ask cannot be totally controlled. The tour guides, especially those who are company retirees or volunteer line employees, can provide great insights and amusing anecdotes. However, while you want to be inquisitive, be careful not to sound like an industrial spy. Companies are very concerned about protecting what they view as proprietary technology, processes, or information. Kellogg's, for example, ended its cereal-factory tours because of suspected spying by competitors. Because of this anxiety, some businesses have limited their tours, replaced them with museums or visitors centers (see Kellogg's Cereal City on page 147), or asked us not to include them in the book.

Don't confine yourself to visiting firms that make products similar to your company's. Trips outside of your own industry can provide stimulus, inspiration, and new techniques. The cross-fertilization of ideas from other industries helps develop business creativity. To have a "Learning Organization," one of the current train-thing, or are they working independently? Do they use machines or small hand tools? Why are the workers wearing aprons, hard hats, or goggles? Do you think the workers are proud of the products they make? Similar questions delving into the history of the company, its products, and its culture can be developed for company museums.

The most important thing to remember on the tour is to *follow the safety directions* on page xxi of this book, as well as any special instructions the company gives you. Children must understand that factories can be dangerous places. Be sure to tell them that when they are on a tour, they must listen to the tour guide, wear any protective gear the guide gives them, and walk only where they are allowed.

After the Tour

After the tour or visit to a company museum, talk about which parts were most interesting, a great topic for long car rides during driving vacations. What did each person learn? Younger children can draw pictures of how products are made or of workers doing their jobs. They can discuss what they found "cool" and share their experiences with their classes at school.

Parents and teachers might also encourage teenagers to imagine being an integral part of a company. Companies need all sorts of people, the innovators and creators, the builders and writers, the people selling on the front line and the ones doing the work behind the scenes. Perhaps they will leave with a new job or career idea. (That goes for adults, too!)

You never know who or what you may see on a factory tour! "Job Switching" *episode of* I Love Lucy, *first aired September 15, 1952* (Photo © CBS Inc.)

Cinram/Disc Manufacturing

4905 Moores Mill Road   ⟶   *music CDs and CD-ROMs*
Huntsville, AL 35811
(205) 859-9042 / (205) 851-0209

If you're reading this book while listening to music from a CD sold by a major or independent recording label such as BMG, Polygram, or Capitol/EMI, the CD was probably manufactured by Cinram/Disc Manufacturing. The CD-ROM you may have used today in your computer from Apple, Hewlett-Packard, or Microsoft may also have come from Cinram's plants in Anaheim, California; Richmond, Indiana; or this one in Alabama. Cinram also replicates the highest quality audio and video cassettes. With five state-of-the-art facilities in North America and three more in Europe, Cinram is the world's largest independent replication company for audio and video tape, CD, CD-ROM, and DVD.

The guided tour shows you the steps in creating a master, duplicating the compact discs, and packaging. The music or computer company supplies a premastered digital audiotape. The tape is reformatted to create a data master. A laser beam recorder cuts a glass master by etching the data codes into glass. A metal stamper is then "grown" from this glass by an electroforming, photographic-like process to create a mold to mass produce the compact discs.

You can peek through windows at the manufacturing part of the process, which occurs in a sterile environment with workers dressed like surgeons. The stamper is inserted into an injection molding press. Small beads of polycarbonate resin, a clear plastic-like material, flow through the press, and out pops a CD. A thin layer of aluminum reflective film is coated onto the disc, followed by a lacquer protection to shelter the digital codes on the plastic disc.

A five-color screen printing press applies the multicolored label directly onto the disc in the final production step. After an intricate visual and automated inspection, the disc and its paper parts are packaged in a jewel case, shrink-wrapped, and shipped to distribution centers. This process continues to the tune of approximately 225,000 compact discs per day, with the production of CD-ROMs the fasting

growing part of the business. The next time you hold one of these silver platters in your hand, you'll think about the neat machines and the complex process used to make something that looks so uncomplicated.

Cost: Free
Freebies: No
Video Shown: No
Reservations Needed: Yes. Individuals and families need to join a scheduled group tour.
Days and Hours: Mon–Fri (based on availability of tour guide and production schedules). Closed holidays and week between Christmas and New Year's.
Plan to Stay: 1 hour
Minimum Age: 18
Disabled Access: Yes
Group Requirements: 2 weeks' advance notice for reservations. Minimum group size needed for a tour is 10 people, with a maximum of 15.
Special Information: No photography. For an interesting comparison to the production of player-piano music rolls, an early form of recorded music, see the feature on QRS Music, Buffalo, New York, on page 223.
Gift Shop: No
Directions: Take Hwy. 231 North (Memorial Pkwy.) and turn right at Hwy. 72 East (Lee Hwy.). Or take I-565 East until it ends at Hwy. 72 East. Turn left at Moores Mill Rd., and the plant is ahead on the left. From Chattanooga, take Hwy. 72 West and turn right on Moores Mill Rd.
Nearby Attractions: U.S. Space and Rocket Center/NASA tour; Alabama Constitution Village; Historic Huntsville Depot; 1879 Harrison Brothers Hardware; Huntsville Museum of Art.

Website: www.discmfg.com

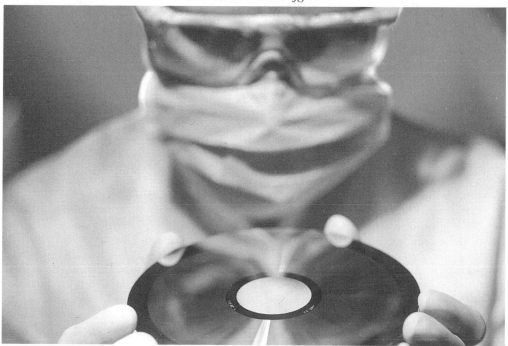

At Cinram/Disc Manufacturing, a technician prepares a glass substrate for the start of the compact disc mastering process.

Thousands of compact discs wait to be packaged at Cinram/Disc Manufacturing in Huntsville, Alabama.

Mercedes-Benz   〜 *cars*

1 Mercedes Drive
Vance, AL 35490
(205) 507-3300

Mercedes-Benz

Most Americans credit Henry Ford with the invention of the automobile. However, as you'll learn from the History Exhibit at the new 24,000-square-foot Mercedes-Benz Visitor Center that opened in June of 1997, the first automobile came to be known as the Mercedes-Benz (invented in 1886).

The Racing Exhibit portrays Mercedes' long and illustrious racing career through photographs of all their famous drivers, historical racing footage, and a historical Mercedes-Benz racing vehicle. Many safety features were first tested in race cars and then incorporated into passenger cars.

Take a short bus ride to the M-Class plant, the company's first outside of Europe. Walk into the huge, futuristic lobby with its high ceilings and large glass wall leading into the factory.

Sheet-metal panels for the M-Class, an all-activity vehicle, come into the plant pre-stamped and subassembled on a just-in-time basis. The panels are welded together in the body shop. The vehicle leaves the body shop complete with four doors, tailgate, and hood, but it's only a colorless shell. Look through windows into the paint shop, where cars enter on the mezzanine level as raw steel precision-shaped bodies. In this clean room, workers wear astronaut-like suits and hair nets. The cars zigzag their way back and forth along the whole length of the paint shop, alternating between dip tanks and oven lines, and come out in front of you in glossy painted colors. The selectivity bank shuffles the cars around into assembly sequence, much like playing checkers.

In assembly, notice that all the work is done without robotics—except for one robot that installs the windshield and back glass. One of the highlights is the "marriage" station on the final line, where the completed chassis is lifted up and team members bolt it to a completed body. You'll wish you had arranged for factory-direct delivery so you could drive your new M-Class vehicle right out of the Visitor Center.

Cost: Adults, $4; children 6–15, $3; children under 6, free.

Freebies: No

Video Shown: 10-minute video overviews body, paint, and assembly.

Reservations Needed: Yes, for factory tour. No, for Visitor Center, except for groups of 10 or more people. Factory tours are limited in size, so call well in advance.

Days and Hours: Factory tour: Mon–Fri 9:00 AM, 11:00 AM, AND 1:00 PM. Visitor Center: Tue–Fri 9:00 AM– 5:00 PM, and Sat 10:00 AM– 5:00 PM. Both closed holidays. Factory closed July 4th week and week between Christmas and New Year's. Mercedes-Benz reserves the right to cancel the factory tour for production or safety reasons.

Plan to Stay: 1 hour each for factory tour and Visitor Center, plus time for Mercedes Boutique.

Minimum Age: 12 for tour; none for Visitor Center.

Disabled Access: Yes

Group Requirements: Groups over 10 people should call in advance at least 1 week for the Visitor Center and 1 month for the factory tour. Maximum group size is 25 people for factory tour.

Special Information: Factory tour program starts in the fall of 1997, so there may be changes as it evolves. No photography in factory.

Gift Shop: Mercedes Boutique sells logoed key chains, caps, and T-shirts, coffee mugs showing the Visitor Center's silhouette, plus other Mercedes-Benz merchandise. Also carries lifestyle items such as hiking equipment and water bottles. Open same hours as Visitor Center. Closed holidays.

Directions: From Birmingham, take I-59/20 West to Exit 89. Turn left over the Interstate. Bear right onto Mercedes Dr. Visitor Center is first building on left.

Nearby Attractions: Tannehill State Park; Tuscaloosa's attractions, including Paul (Bear) Bryant Museum, Mound State Monument, and antebellum homes, about 17 miles away.

See color photos, page 179

Website: www.m-class.mercedez-benz.com

Assembly shop team members scrutinize their work on a Mercedes-Benz vehicle.

The new Mercedes-Benz M-Class All Activity Vehicle manufacturing facility in Vance, Alabama, is the company's first plant outside of Europe.

Robinson Iron ⌒ *architectural ironworks*

Robinson Road
Alexander City, AL 35010
(205) 329-8486

Have you ever taken the New York City subway from Astor Place and admired the cast-iron kiosk entrance? If so, you've already seen Robinson Iron's handiwork. Perhaps you've sat on their benches, which line Pennsylvania Avenue in Washington, D.C., or daydreamed while watching water flow through the 12,000-pound Court Square Fountain in Montgomery. Robinson restored the fountain, as well as the intricate ironwork at Singapore's renowned Raffles Hotel. Although you cannot tour the foundry, where 2,500° molten iron flows like melted butter, you can watch skilled ironworkers turn the raw castings into ornate fountains, urns, lampposts, garden statuary, or perhaps customized railings for subway stations.

As you enter the shop, welding arcs hiss, grinding wheels squeal, and drills buzz, leaving no doubt that you're surrounded by heavy ironworking. Masked welders in the fabrication area wield plasma arc cutters, which produce a light as bright as a laser. A metallic, flinty odor fills your nose. When the sparks clear, you'll find the raw castings have become a 16-foot multi-tiered fountain for a municipal park, or a 400-pound deer, complete with antlers, for someone's backyard.

In the finishing area, workers spray-paint Charleston Green, Gloss White, or Black in a painting booth. An overhead crane lifts the mammoth ornaments into place, so workers can construct shipping crates around them. Before you end the tour, head outside down the path to the Pattern Shop, to see how the whole process starts. Pattern-makers follow blueprints from Robinson's designers to custom-carve, detail, and create a wooden master, which is then used to fashion a plastic or metal working pattern. The foundry uses the pattern to produce a hollow sand mold into which molten iron is poured. The raw casting it creates will go to the workers in the Fabrication Area, where you began. In the Atrium Showroom, finished pieces stand ready for your close inspection, admiration, and purchase.

Cost: Free
Freebies: No
Video Shown: Optional 15-minute video on company's history, by request only.
Reservations Needed: No, except for groups of 8 or more people.
Days and Hours: Mon–Fri 8:00 AM–4:00 PM. Closed holidays. Production decreases during 4th of July week and Christmas week.
Plan to Stay: 45 minutes, plus time in showroom.
Minimum Age: None, although some areas are restricted for children under 5, who might stay in the Atrium Showroom to watch the fountain.
Disabled Access: Yes
Group Requirements: Groups of 8 or more people should call 1 day in advance.
Special Information: Plant can be quite noisy at times.
Showroom: The Atrium Showroom features a representative collection of ironworks from the company's catalog and its Architectural Handbook (both available for purchase in showroom or from above phone number), including small garden statuary, ornamental urns, and animal sculptures. Open same hours as tour.
Directions: From Birmingham, take Hwy. 280 East to Kelleton. Turn left on Business 280 (*not* Bypass 280). In 2 miles, where the road widens, watch on the right for Robinson Foundry. Take the first right after the foundry. Cross the railroad tracks. Robinson Iron is the brown metal building on your right. From Montgomery, take Hwy. 231 North to Wetumka. Turn right on Hwy. 9 North. Turn right on Hwy. 22 East. Turn left onto Hwy. 280 West. In a little over 1 mile, turn right on Robinson Rd. Bear right at the fork, and watch for Robinson Iron on your left.
Nearby Attractions: Russell Corp. clothing manufacturer tour (call 205-329-5307); Martin Lake; Kowaliga Marina; Horsebend National Military Park.

Alaskan Brewing ⟶ *beer*

5429 Shaune Drive
Juneau, AK 99801
(907) 780-5866

Small, family-like Alaskan Brewing Company brews Alaskan Amber (based on a Gold Rush–era recipe from the local extinct Douglas City Brewing Co.), Alaskan Pale, Alaskan Frontier, and seasonal beers. Since its start in 1986, Alaskan Brewing Company's beers have won awards for quality at annual beer festivals. To expand its production space, the brewery took over a golf driving range in the other half of this wooden building (to this day, some golf balls linger in the roof's insulation) and built two new additions.

The tour starts off right—with a glass of Alaskan Pale (their lighter, fruitier beer). Now that you're in the spirit, walk into the newly designed tour hallway. You can look through glass walls into the brewhouse at three 310-gallon kettles known as the mash tun, lauter tun, and brew kettle. If you're lucky, you'll see activity here—a worker transferring mixtures from kettle to kettle or shoveling "spent" (already used) barley. In show and tell, the tour guide hands out malted barley (tastes like Grape Nuts) and hops (a bittering spice). Notice what used to be "Alaska's biggest six-pack," six 10-foot-high stainless steel fermentation tanks stacked in a row. Now there are 11 fermentation tanks (one short of a 12-pack), each 20 times the size of the small ones in the tank area.

Walk outdoors and upstairs to a landing. Through windows, peer inside at the kegging and bottling operation (usually on Wednesdays and Thursdays). As oxygen escapes, foam flows out. The worker hammers in the "bung" (wooden cork), and beer flies everywhere.

In the hospitality room and gift shop, admire the national/international bottle collections on display. Find your home state's beer. If your local brewery is not represented, be sure to send them one for their extensive collection when you get home.

Cost: Free
Freebies: 6-oz. glasses of beer
Video Shown: No

Reservations Needed: No, but preferred for groups larger than 10 people.
Days and Hours: May through September: Mon–Sat 11:00 AM–4:30 PM, every 30 minutes; October through April: Thur–Sat, same time schedule. Closed Thanksgiving, July 4th, Christmas, and New Year's.
Plan to Stay: ½ hour, plus time in gift shop.
Minimum Age: None. However, you must be 21 years old to sample beer.
Disabled Access: Yes
Group Requirements: Prefers 1 day's advance notice for groups larger than 10 people. Groups larger than 35 people will be divided into smaller groups.
Special Information: Best days to see bottling and kegging are Wednesday and Thursday. If your timing is right, you can sample their seasonal beers (usually made in the spring and fall) or one of their R&D brews called "Rough Draft."
Gift Shop: Sells T-shirts, sweatshirts, baseball caps with beer label designs, and embroidered logoed WEK shirts. Offers bottlecap fishing lures with the "Made In Alaska" bear design on a crown and collectible pint glasses. Open same hours as tour. Catalog available. Gift shop displays historical photographs and artifacts of Alaskan breweries from the 1800s to today.
Directions: From Juneau, take Egan Dr. to stoplight at the base of Vanderbilt Hill. Turn only way possible onto Vanderbilt Hill Rd. Turn right onto Anka Dr. Take second right onto Shaune Dr. The brewery is 1½ blocks ahead on the left. You'll smell the strong scent of malt and hops as you approach on brewing days.
Nearby Attractions: Alaska Seafood Co. tour (call 907-780-5111); Mendenhall Glacier; DIPAC (salmon hatchery); Historic Downtown Juneau's attractions include the Capitol building and the Alaskan Bar & Hotel (features their beer on tap); sport fishing.

Musk Ox Farm   *musk oxen*

Mile 50.1 Glenn Highway
Palmer, AK 99645
(907) 745-4151

The name "musk ox" (the Eskimo word is *oomingmak*) is a misnomer—the animals neither have musk glands nor belong to the ox family. Rather, they are short, stocky beasts. Underneath the shaggy carpet of the musk oxen's brown guard hair is a coat of fine, soft, warm hair called "qiviut." In the winter, qiviut protects the musk ox against wind and bitter Arctic temperatures. In spring, the musk oxen shed their qiviut naturally. This "down," or underwool, is combed out of their coats, spun into yarn that is eight times warmer than sheep's wool, and knitted by Eskimo women into beautiful lacy stoles, scarves, and hats. The Musk Ox Farm is a nonprofit organization formed to breed and study musk oxen and to provide a native-run and -owned cottage knitting industry. It is the only herd of domesticated oxen in the world.

At the farm, you see extensive displays describing the history and background of the animals, and the special project of the Anchorage cooperative that sells the knitted qiviut items. Next you are shown where and how the furry beasts are combed. At a fenced-in walkway by the ox pens, the guide describes the animals' lives and habits, both in the wild and in captivity. In the wild, two bulls contest for dominance by banging their heads together. After circling around and challenging each other, they may back away as much as 50 feet and then run straight at one another, crashing their horns together in a sound that can be heard up to a mile away. You probably won't see any headbanging, but these curious creatures, who can weigh as much as 900 pounds, may approach and eat grass from your hand.

Stay as long as you like to observe these unique animals, or venture 50 miles away to the 'Oomingmak' Co-operative in Anchorage. Here you'll see the lacy qiviut items that the Eskimo women made being washed, blocked (stretched on a pattern board to straighten the sides), and packaged at the front table of the small shop.

Cost: Adults, $7; seniors and students 13–18, $6; children 6–12, $5; children under 6 accompanied by an adult, free.

Freebies: No

Video Shown: No

Reservations Needed: No, except for groups larger than 12 people and for winter tours.

Days and Hours: Mother's Day through mid-June, and mid-August through last Sunday in September: Mon–Sun 10:00 AM–6:00 PM. Mid-June through mid-August: Mon–Sun 9:00 AM–7:00 PM. Tours run every 30 minutes. Open summer holidays. Winter tours by appointment only. Call ahead.

Plan to Stay: 30 minutes, plus time in gift shop.

Minimum Age: None

Disabled Access: Yes

Group Requirements: Groups of 12 or more people should call at least 1 day in advance. Groups larger than 50 people will be split into 2 or more staggered-time tours. Group rate is $5.50 per person.

Special Information: The animals are more active in the morning. Early groups on Monday, Wednesday, and Friday mornings can see the oxen being fed.

'Oomingmak' Musk Ox Producers' Co-operative in Anchorage: Watch the final blocking process of caps, scarves, and other knit items with each Eskimo village's signature knitting pattern. Call (907) 272-9925.

Gift Shop: Sells qiviut items such as scarves, hats, and stoles. Also sells musk ox mementos such as stuffed animals, toys, mugs, and T-shirts. Open same hours as tour.

Directions: From Anchorage, take Glenn Hwy. North, through Palmer. About 2 miles past Palmer (at Mile 50.1), turn left onto Archie Rd. Follow signs to Musk Ox Farm, which is about ¼-mile down the road on left.

Nearby Attractions: Reindeer Farm; Palmer Visitors Center; Iditarod Trail Headquarters and Dorothy Page Museum in Wasilla (about 11 miles away); Hatcher Pass; Independence Mine State Historical Park.

Cerreta's Candy ⟿ *chocolates, candy, and*
5345 West Glendale Avenue   *caramel popcorn*
Glendale, AZ 85301
(602) 930-9000

Candy Company

Since 1968, this family-owned company has been producing chocolate candy that's sold at their retail store and in supermarkets throughout the western U.S.A. Because the entire factory is open, your nostrils fill with the sweet smell of cocoa and your ears, hear the loud noises of mixers, enrobers, and conveyors turning chocolate into candy. Cerreta's makes four different types of chocolate candy in this factory: mints, creams, caramels, and clusters. Throughout the factory, you will notice workers hand-pouring and hand-mixing ingredients into oversized copper kettles.

Since this is a self-guided tour, overhead monitors along the walkway help explain the candy-making process. Lean against the waist-high railing to see the action. The long, yellow, automatic molding machine makes French mints. A pale green, minty liquid fills one plastic tray, containing 32 molds, every six seconds. The trays are flipped over to allow the excess to flow out. Once the mint cools, chocolate centers are injected and cooled again before dollops of mint are added, sealing the chocolate inside. Notice the mile-long spiral conveyor in the glass-enclosed chilling room. After the mints travel around and around up the spiral, workers release the candies from their molds, much like removing ice cubes from plastic trays. The released candies travel down twin-lane conveyor belts to the specially designed wrapping machine, which swallows them up and spits them out wrapped at a rate of 1,000 candies per minute.

In the background, watch as a worker pours liquid caramel from a copper cauldron onto a long, refrigerated stainless-steel table. Once solidified, the caramel is cut into long ribbons. The ribbons are fed into an automatic wrapping machine, which individually twist-wraps each caramel in clear cellophane. The caramel and other centers, such as butter creams and peanut brittle, travel to the enrobing machine. There, centers move along a wire conveyor belt and are drenched in chocolate. If they're making caramel popcorn, workers dig into the bowl to scoop and mix the coated popcorn to prevent sticking. It looks like so much fun, you'll want to put on a pair of rubber gloves and help them.

Cost: Free

Freebies: Sample of Cerreta's candy

Videos Shown: Videos on overhead monitors along walkway provide up-close view of the entire chocolate-making process.

Reservations Needed: No, except for groups of 10 or more people who want a special guided tour.

Days and Hours: Mon–Sat 8:00 AM–6:00 PM self-guided viewing; Mon–Fri 10:00 AM and 1:00 PM guided tours. Closed holidays. Even though there is limited production on Saturdays, you can view video monitors and see equipment.

Plan to Stay: 20 minutes for self-guided tour, plus time for retail store.

Minimum Age: None

Disabled Access: Yes

Group Requirements: Groups of 10 or more people should call 1 month in advance to arrange guided tours for special tour times.

Special Information: The tour is offered year-round; do call ahead, however, since limited production on Saturday and in summer. Hot in summer.

Retail Store: Sells entire selection of Cerreta's chocolates, caramels, and French mints. Open Mon–Sat 8:00 AM–6:00 PM. Closed holidays.

Directions: From I-10, take 59th Ave. North to Glendale Ave. Turn right, and Cerreta's will be on the right. You'll recognize the building by its upside-down copper cauldron-like awning.

Nearby Attractions: Karsten Manufacturing (Ping golf club) tour (see page 10); Saguaro Ranch Park; Phoenix attractions include Breck Girl Hall of Fame at Dial Corp. headquarters (call 602-207-2800).

Karsten Manufacturing 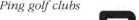 *Ping golf clubs*

2201 West Desert Cove
Phoenix, AZ 85029
(602) 870-5385

Long before Karsten Solheim began playing golf at the age of 43, he had an interest in golf clubs. Solheim, one of the golf industry's most recognizable figures, started perfecting golf clubs with the goal of making a fiendishly fickle game easier to play. The first putter he developed made a loud, shrill "ping" sound; hence, the eventual name for his clubs. When Julius Boros won the Phoenix Open in 1967 with a Ping putter, the popularity of Ping golf clubs increased. That same year Solheim left General Electric as a project engineer to start Karsten Manufacturing Corporation in a small 20-by-40-foot building. Today the company employs about 1,000 workers, and the site covers most of a city block.

Your tour begins after you view the displays of the company's golf clubs, woods, irons, apparel, and bags in the visitors center. The guide, usually a former golf professional, leads you past the original 1967 building. Currently the repair department, it initially served as Karsten's production area, machine shop, reception area, order desk, and shipping department.

Because of the size of the "campus," you walk in and out of buildings based on proximity rather than order of production. Since the iron and putter grinding area is so noisy, the guide explains the process only outside the building. The irons, cast by the off-site foundry, require grinding and tumbling for further shaping.

In the iron, putter, and wood assembly areas, shafts are cut to the correct length and installed into club heads, while clubs wait on shelves for grips. To attach a grip, two-way adhesive tape is wrapped around the shaft. A solvent poured onto the tape turns it into glue, and the grip is slid onto the shaft. The club's lie angle is adjusted for the height and swing habits of its future owner. In the stamping area, the clubs are stamped with individual serial numbers. The last part of your tour takes you to Karsten Engineering, a subsidiary that assists in designing clubs

and other products. See milling machines and examine their handiwork at nearby display tables. After the tour, you'll want to play golf at one of the many golf courses in the Phoenix area.

Cost: Free
Freebies: Information sheets, brochures, key chain, personalized fitting recommendations.
Videos Shown: 3 videos on the history of Karsten and its subsidiaries.
Reservations Needed: Yes
Days and Hours: Tue and Thur 9:30 AM. Call for availability and reservations 1–2 months in advance.
Plan to Stay: 1 hour for tour, videos, and questions.
Minimum Age: 9
Disabled Access: Yes
Group Requirements: Cannot handle group tours larger than 10 people.
Special Information: No photography. Wear comfortable shoes for the ½-mile of walking. Ping golf club owners and people interested in golf will enjoy the tour the most.
Gift Shop: No. Products sold through dealers and area golf courses.
Directions: From I-17, go east on Peoria Ave. Turn left onto 23rd Ave. Turn right on Desert Cove. Turn right on Karsten's Way and park in the lot on the left.
Nearby Attractions: Cerreta Candy tour (see page 9); Metro Center Shopping Mall; Phoenix attractions include over 100 golf courses and Breck Girl Hall of Fame at Dial Corp. headquarters (call 602-207-2800).

Peanut Patch ～ *peanuts*
4322 East County 13th Street
Yuma, AZ 85365
(520) 726-6292 / (800) USA-PNUT

Peanut farming conjures images of Georgia's Jimmy Carter and other southeastern farmers. The Southeast, mainly Georgia and Alabama, produces 51 percent of all the peanuts in the U.S.A. However, Peanut Patch is the largest of the six Arizona growers that together produce two million pounds per year.

Led by one of the young family-member owners, tours begin with a peanut-growing lesson. You may be amazed to learn that peanuts do not grow on the farm's eucalyptus trees. Rather, as legumes, they grow underground; they are planted in March and harvested in August.

During the peanut processing period, tours go through the shelling plant. In one warehouse, five screens "size" peanuts for different uses. For example, large sizes may be sold as "jumbo" in-shell ballpark peanuts, small peanuts will be used for peanut oil, and medium sizes will be planted for next year. Watch a quick-fingered picking crew hand-cull undesirable peanuts by their appearance. On a good day, the plant produces 200 100-pound bags, or 20,000 pounds.

In another Peanut Patch warehouse, which is government-bonded, you may see huge mountains of peanuts stored for the company and the federal government. The government will auction off its peanuts. Come mid-November, it seems like not one more peanut will fit into the warehouse.

Your nose and ears will lead you to the shelling building, where noisy machines remove the hulls (shells) and skins. In the roasting area, 600 pounds of peanuts are dry-roasted at one time. Savor the taste of a warm, freshly-roasted peanut.

In the Farm Store kitchen butter, peanuts, and sugar simmer together in copper kettles. The mixture is poured onto old-fashioned marble slabs for cooling, and later it's broken into pieces of peanut brittle. You will leave with a well-rounded introduction to farming, the peanut industry, and candy-making.

Cost: Free

Freebies: Fudge and peanuts samples

Video Shown: Slide show includes planting, harvesting, processing, and end use of peanuts.

Reservations Needed: No, except for groups larger than 10 people. In addition to scheduled tour times, individuals can join pre-scheduled group tours at other times.

Days and Hours: Open for peanut processing tours October through May only. Tue, Wed, Fri, and Sat 10:00 AM. Call for other days and times. Closed Thanksgiving, Christmas, New Year's and Easter.

Plan to Stay: 1 hour for peanut processing, plus time in gift shop to see fudge- and candy-making.

Minimum Age: None

Disabled Access: Yes

Group Requirements: Call at least 2 weeks in advance for reservations. Minimum group is 10 people. No maximum group size.

Special Information: Tours vary based on the harvesting/processing cycle. Special company outing near Thanksgiving open to public. Shellers are noisy and dusty. On children's tours, kids get to make their own peanut butter.

Gift Shop: Country Store sells peanuts, other nuts, trail mixes, dried fruits, and candies displayed in family-collected antiques. Offers unique Arizona specialties (cactus jellies and other products directly from local farmers). Buy freshly made fudge, just cut from the big slab, peanut brittle, and nut clusters. Mon–Sat 9:00 AM–6:00 PM. Closed June 1–September 30, Thanksgiving, Christmas, and Easter. Catalog available at above number.

Directions: Take I-8 to Yuma. Take Ave. 3E exit. Go south to County 13th St. Turn left for 1¼ miles, and Peanut Patch will be on your left.

Nearby Attractions: Saihati Camel Farm tour (see page 12); Territorial Prison; Yuma Crossing.

Saihati Camel Farm ~

15672 South Avenue 1E
Yuma, AZ 85365
(520) 627-2553

*Arabian camels and
other desert animals*

SAIHATI CAMEL FARM
Desert Wildlife Center

Contrary to myth, the Arabian dromedaries (one-humped camels) at Saihati Camel Farm would never be so impolite as to spit on you when you tour their Arizona desert home. But if they think manager Terrill Standley is taking too long to talk to visitors, they will begin milling around and grumbling. The camels wait eagerly for their "human servants" to hand-feed them hay over the chain-link fence of their pen, ignoring the hay lying on the ground. And because they learn about things by eating them, you may find a camel snacking on your straw hat, your leather jacket, or even your hair.

Standley and owner Abdulwahad Al-Saihati, a native of Saudi Arabia, chose the Arizona desert as the place to conserve, breed, and educate people about Arabian desert animals because it so closely resembles the beasts' native habitat. The camels are sold to people who train them to give rides or use them in movies or commercials, and the profit from their sale helps to fund the conservation of other species, like the endangered Arabian oryx (large antelope), various Arabian wild cats, and the fennec fox.

Visitors can meet all these exotic beasts and almost feel as if they're in Arabia, without having to travel halfway across the world. You learn that although camels do not store water in their humps, which are filled with fat, they can endure long periods of dehydration. You also discover that the dromedaries are not the only comedians at the farm. One male oryx likes to dump out his water bucket and carry it around on his horns, while the ostrich shows off for visitors by strutting around proudly. You leave Saihati Camel Farm with an appreciation for the importance of conserving these nearly extinct animals.

Cost: Adults, $3; children under 3, free.
Freebies: No
Video Shown: No

Reservations Needed: Suggested, though not required.
Days and Hours: Tours October 1 through June 30 only. Mon–Sat 10:00 AM and 2:00 PM; Sun 2:00 PM. Closed Thanksgiving and Christmas.
Plan to Stay: 1 hour
Minimum Age: None
Disabled Access: Limited, because of sand surface.
Group Requirements: Special tour times can be arranged for groups of 20 or more people by calling at least 1 week in advance. Maximum group size is 80.
Special Information: Best time to see animals is in the morning, when they are more active.
Gift Shop: Sells postcards, T-shirts, zoo books, and camel charms. Open in conjunction with the tours.
Directions: From I-8, take exit for Ave. 3E South. Turn right onto County 16th St. Turn right onto Ave. 1E. Farm entrance is 500 feet down the road on left. From Hwy. 95 (Ave. B) South, turn left onto County 15th St. and then right onto Ave. 1E. The entrance is about 1 mile down the road on right.
Nearby Attractions: Peanut Patch tour (see page 11); Cocopah Casino; Rancho del Sol Citrus Packing House and gift shop; Territorial Prison State Park (a 19th-century adobe prison).

Wal-Mart Visitors Center ~ *retail stores*

Visitors Center
105 North Main Street
Bentonville, AR 72712
(501) 273-1329

The Wal-Mart retail empire, with over 500,000 employees (called "associates") and billions of dollars in yearly revenues, began in the building that now houses the Visitors Center. From the outside, it's an exact replica of the first Walton's 5 & 10 opened by Sam and Helen Walton in 1950. The folksy center brings together the history, growth, philosophy, and present-day scope of the company. As you walk on the original checkerboard red and green linoleum tile floor, examining the displays and watching the videos, you're surrounded by a true American business success.

Merchandise from the 1950s and '60s sits in the front window. In the lobby is a cut-out figure of Sam Walton (the store's first manager) next to a huge mural showing a typical 5 & 10 of the early '50s. Family portraits and other murals of the company's operations also hang throughout the center, along with early newspaper ads and memorabilia. The center has over 40 separate displays. The most popular are the laser video programs on the history of the company and on the Walton family. One large exhibit is a timeline that traces the Wal-Mart story from its variety store roots to the present day. Mementos, photos, and products such as old Barbie dolls fill the display. At the push of a button is a narrated, illuminated photomap tracking the nationwide spread of Wal-Mart stores.

The Visitors Center holds many of Sam's prized possessions. The Presidential Medal of Freedom, the nation's highest civilian award, which Sam Walton received in 1992, is proudly displayed. So are his old red pickup truck and original office, complete with the apple crate used as a chair for guests. Other exhibits include Wal-Mart and Wall Street, Community Involvement, Satellite Communi-cations, and Saving the Environment.

The "Buy American" exhibit features a changing display of the American-made products that Wal-Mart sells and the jobs created by this partnership of retailers and domestic manufacturers. The long-range goal of the Buy American program is to re-establish the competitive position of U.S.-made goods. You leave understanding more about the people and heritage behind what has been called "the retailing phenomenon of the century."

Cost: Free
Freebies: No
Videos Shown: Four 8-minute laser video programs on the company, the Walton family, the Medal of Freedom, and conversations between Sam and his brother.
Reservations Needed: No, however, recommended for groups of 10 or more people.
Days and Hours: Mon–Sat 9:00 AM–5:00 PM. Closed Mondays November through February, and Thanksgiving, Christmas, and New Year's.
Plan to Stay: 30 minutes, plus time for videos.
Minimum Age: None, but recommends children be at least 10 to appreciate and enjoy the exhibits.
Disabled Access: Yes
Group Requirements: Groups of 10 or more people should call 2 days in advance.
Special Information: Exhibits change to reflect Wal-Mart developments. You may want to schedule your visit around Wal-Mart Stores, Inc.'s annual meeting (usually first week in June) in nearby Fayetteville. About 15,000 people attend the largest annual meeting in the U.S.A., which features live entertainment, enthused employees, and a real sense of the corporate culture.
Gift Counter: Sells Wal-Mart and Visitors Center logoed items, including mugs, key chains, and T-shirts. Open same hours as Visitors Center.
Directions: Take Hwy. 71 or Hwy. 71B to Hwy. 72. The Visitors Center is on the west side of the square in downtown Bentonville. Look for the big American flag and the building that says "Walton's 5 & 10."
Nearby Attractions: Terra Pottery Studios tour, 20 miles away, in Fayetteville (call 501-643-3185); University of Arkansas; Beaver Lake; Eureka Springs.

Basic Brown Bear Factory ⟶ *teddy bears*

444 DeHaro Street
San Francisco, CA 94107
(415) 626-0781

You'll enjoy playing teddy bear obstetrician on this tour. At this small factory, discover how teddy bears are born and participate in their delivery. One of the few U.S. manufacturers of stuffed bears, Basic Brown Bear (BBB) lets you watch them handmake the cuddly creatures from start to finish.

In the cutting and sewing area, the owner proudly explains her process. First, she draws each pattern on paper and makes a sample animal from the pattern. Workers use bandsaws to slice 24 layers of plush fabric. Seamstresses sew together individual bear parts and outfits, stitching the sections inside-out, then reaching inside to push out the bear legs, ears, and noses. They can make about 35 baby bears or 10 grandparent bears a day, plus their clothes.

You learn that the first stuffed bears had shoe buttons for eyes. Now, grommets snap mushroom-shaped plastic eyes into place. A tour highlight is stuffing bears with polyester from a bright yellow machine used to fill life jackets during WWII. Now you can bring a bear to life by inflating it like a balloon. Wait on a line of yellow paw-prints to push the filler's foot pedal. Out shoots a mixture of air and polyester. Once a bear is cuddly enough, its back is hand-sewn shut.

At the beauty parlor, workers smooth out bear seams with an electric wire brush. A pressurized-air "bear bath" or "bear shower" (depending on the critter's size) removes fur "fuzzies." Children (and adults) giggle when they too receive a "bear shower" or give a bear a "bath." Bears are dressed in their outfits, including company-made wire-rim glasses. Visitors leave with a special affection for the bears they brought to life.

Cost: Free tour. Prices for stuffing your own animal run from $9.50 to $300.
Freebies: No
Video Shown: No
Reservations Needed: No, except for groups of 8 or more people.

Days and Hours: Mon–Sun 1:00 PM. Additional 11:00 AM tour on Saturdays. Closed holidays. Possible additional weekday tours in summer.
Plan to Stay: 30 minutes, plus time for stuffing and showering your own bear, and the gift shop.
Minimum Age: 3
Disabled Access: Yes
Group Requirements: Groups of 8 or more people should call 2 weeks in advance. Maximum group size is 25.
Special Information: Can also partially stuff your own animals at BBB's other store in The Cannery, near Fisherman's Wharf.
Gift Shop: Over 30 styles of stuffed bears (and other animals) and bear clothes, all handmade by BBB, are sold exclusively at this location. Mon–Sat 10:00 AM–5:00 PM and Sun 1:00 PM–5:00 PM. Price list available from (800) 554-1910.
Directions: From the East Bay Bridge, take 9th St./Civic Center exit and get into the immediate left-hand lane, which puts you onto 8th St. Stay on 8th St. until it ends at the traffic circle. Turn right onto Kansas St. Turn left onto Mariposa St. BBB is on the left-hand corner of Mariposa and DeHaro Sts. From the South Bay, take Hwy. 101 North. Take the Vermont St. exit and cross over Vermont St. onto Mariposa St. Stay on Mariposa St. until you reach DeHaro St. (about 4 blocks). BBB is on the left-hand corner.
Nearby Attractions: Anchor Brewery Co. tour (across the street, call 415-863-8350); San Francisco attractions are 10–20 minutes away, including Levi Strauss factory tour (see page 26), Wells Fargo Bank Museum (call 415-396-2619), Chevron U.S.A. Museum (call 415-894-6697), and Fisherman's Wharf.

See color photos, page 184

Bradbury & Bradbury   ∼   *Victorian wallpaper*
940 Tyler, Studio 12
Benicia, CA 94510
(707) 746-1900

The beautiful Victorian wallpaper from the movies *Hook*, featuring Robin Williams and Julia Roberts, *American President,* and *James and the Giant Peach* came from this Victorian wallpaper factory. These movie sets joined Disney World and EuroDisney, as well as countless bed and breakfasts and restored Victorian homes, in using Bradbury & Bradbury's handprinted wall and ceiling papers.

The smell of oil-based paint permeates the printing area, where long sheets of paper lay across six tables, each about 30 yards long and one yard wide. You'll watch as workers repeatedly bend over a table, place the patterned screen onto the specially coated paper, stroke the squeegee through the ink to create the printed design, and then switch on a small overhead fan to quicken the drying. To avoid smudges, the screen is put down only every other pattern length. After doing this for all six tables, the printer scampers back to fill in the missing patterns.

In the art department, you'll learn the strategy behind redesigning ornate nineteenth-century ceiling- and wallpapers. In a process analogous to the design of Lego blocks, the artists meticulously draw the patterns by hand on graph paper and also on a computer design system, striving to create modular patterns that can fit together in any size room. Since B&B is a small company, you can stand next to the printers and artists as they work to reproduce the past.

Cost: Free for individuals as well as school and nonprofit groups. $1 per person for bus tours.
Freebies: No
Video Shown: No
Reservations Needed: Yes
Days and Hours: Mon–Fri 9:00 AM–5:00 PM. Closed holidays.
Plan to Stay: 30 minutes
Minimum Age: None

Disabled Access: The studio is all on one floor, but you must climb a few flights of stairs to reach it.
Group Requirements: Groups should call a day in advance. Maximum group is 44 people. Fee for bus tours.
Special Information: Be sure to ask if they will be in production when you plan to visit. The paint smell may bother some visitors. To make an appointment to see their on-site showroom, call (707) 746-6262.
Gift Area: Nothing formal, but you can look through the samples, purchase a catalog, and place orders. Catalog and design service kit available. Bargin bin offers discontinued wallpaper and seconds at great discounts, sometimes $1 per roll. Open same hours as above.
Directions: The company recommends you call for specific directions since there are many forks in the road. From I-80, take I-780 to the exit for Fifth St. (the last Benicia exit coming from the Bay area). From Fifth St., turn left onto Military East. Follow this road down, around, and under a bridge until it ends on Tyler. Make a right on Tyler. The company is located on the second floor of an old military building occupied by several arts-related companies.
Nearby Attractions: Zellique, Nourot, and Smyers glassblowers studio tours (call 707-745-5710 or 707-745-2614); Old State Capitol Building.

Callaway Golf   *golf clubs*

2285 Rutherford Road
Carlsbad, CA 92008
(619) 931-1771

Many famous professional and amateur golfers attribute their triumphs to Callaway's Great Big Bertha drivers. The popularity of these oversized metal drivers, named after the WWI German cannon Big Bertha, helped position the company as the world's largest golf-club manufacturer. Callaway Golf is Ely Callaway's third successful business venture. After being president of Burlington Industries, he bought and developed a vineyard, later selling it to Hiram Walker & Sons. Callaway started the golf-club industry wars by using a new technology—called "investment casting"—for making metal club heads, resulting in more precise weight calibrations.

Carlsbad, California, is clearly the capital of golf-club production in the U.S., with about 25 club manufacturers in the area. As the largest factory, Callaway sprawls across 450,000 square feet in nine buildings, plus three greens located on 8.1 acres of land that make up their outdoor testing facility. Your tour covers the 80,000-square-foot main plant.

On computerized scales, workers weigh shiny stainless-steel heads, checking for variations of 5 grams (the weight of a nickel). In the quality control area, 50 heads are sorted in ascending order by the amount of epoxy needed to bring them to the desired weight. Walk inside the clean, bright, noisy shaft-cutting room, where cutters slice shafts to correct lengths, and giant pencil sharpeners sandblast their tips for better gluing into the heads.

A shaft, wood, and grip, placed on a scale together to measure their pre-swing weight, are forever mated. These married threesomes travel together through the assembly process on carts in groups of 50. Once glued together with black epoxy, the assembled clubs bake in the long, narrow oven for one hour. An entire cart fits sideways into the oven. With 25 clubs sloping on each side of the cart, this sideways view resembles a teepee.

You'll weave your way through carts of clubs at various stages of production. Notice the laser grip machine: a shooting red light beam helps a worker put the grip onto the club. Look inside the soundproof rattle room. Holding one club in each hand, workers shake and bounce the club heads to hear their different sounds. Once fully assembled, the clubs receive a final cleaning to wipe off all "100" fingerprints from the labor-intensive production process.

Cost: Free
Freebies: VIP button and catalog
Video Shown: No
Reservations Needed: Yes. Groups, see below.
Days and Hours: Mon–Fri 9:30 AM and 1:30 PM. Arrive 10 minutes early to sign nondisclosure waiver. Closed holidays and 1–2 weeks around Christmas and New Year's.
Plan to Stay: 45 minutes
Minimum Age: Children must be able to wear safety goggles. Prefer elementary school–age minimum.
Disabled Access: Yes
Group Requirements: Groups larger than 10 people should call 1 week in advance. Maximum group size is 50. Groups are broken down to 10 people per guide.
Special Information: Wear comfortable shoes for 1 mile of walking. No photography.
Gift Shop: Company store sells logoed key chains, sweatshirts, hats, and mugs. Maps available showing nearby dealers who sell Callaway golf clubs.
Directions: From San Diego, take I-5 North. Take Palomar Airport Rd. exit. Turn right at end of exit. Turn left onto College Blvd. into industrial park. Take first right onto Aston St. At dead end, turn right onto Rutherford Rd. Follow to second to last building on right.
Nearby Attractions: Nearby golf-club manufacturers occasionally give tours: Taylor Made (call 619-931-1991) and Cobra (call 619-929-0377); Aviara golf course; Old Carlsbad; Carlsbad State Beach.

Fleetwood *recreational vehicles*

2350 Fleetwood Drive
Riverside, CA 92517
(800) 326-8633

With its 32 different brands of RVs, Fleetwood is the largest manufacturer of recreational vehicles in the U.S. You can tour the plant that makes the Bounder, the number-one-selling motor home in North America, and the Southwind factory across the street. When introduced in 1985, with its jumping kangaroo logo, the Bounder revolutionized the motor-home industry with its patented basement and affordable price. Wearing a headset, you get to watch just about everything it takes to build an RV, except for the 12-mile road test.

The chassis yard is where production begins. Sitting in the sunny Southern California weather are 5 acres of Ford and Chevy chassis neatly arranged in long rows. These steel chassis are the foundation of Fleetwood's Power Platform. Once you're inside the plant, with its giant horseshoe-shaped assembly line, the Bounder seems to come together like a big puzzle. In fact, when the dash assembly is put over the engine, this marks what's referred to as the "zero point" for the modular construction of the RV.

Observing the Vacubond process used to build the walls, ceilings, and floors is most visitors' favorite part. All the pieces that make up the wall, including the fiberglass outside, the steel frame, and the vinyl interior wallpaper, are placed on a big table. As each layer goes down, glue is automatically sprayed along its surface. These walls-to-be are covered with what looks like plastic bags and locked down to the table. Vacuum hoses suck out all the air for one hour. This intense suction creates a perfect seal between the wall's layers. Fleetwood pioneered Vacubond construction for durability, plus thermal and sound insulation.

Construction of subparts seems to take place everywhere. You move in and out of the basement building, where the flooring layers come together, and see more carpentry at work in the cabinetry area. On another part of the line, a crane hoists the entire floor-and-basement assembly and sets it on the chassis. Workers scamper around to bolt the carriage together. Toward the back end of the horseshoe line, the Bounder enters the paint booths, and soon it moves to final finishing. Although the production takes about four days, RVs move at a pace that allows you to see the Bounder in all production stages.

Cost: Free

Freebies: Product brochures

Video Shown: No

Reservations Needed: Preferred

Days and Hours: Bounder and Pace Arrow plant tour: Wed 1:00 PM. Southwind plant tour: Wed 10:00 AM. Closed holidays and between Christmas and New Year's.

Plan to Stay: 1–2 hours

Minimum Age: None, but children under 11 must be accompanied by an adult.

Disabled Access: Yes

Group Requirements: No maximum group size, but should call 2 weeks ahead for space availability. Special times can be arranged for groups.

Special Information: May also see Flair, Southwind Storm, and Pace Arrow production during tour. No photography. Tours at other Fleetwood RV plants throughout the U.S.A. available. Call (800) 444-4905 for information on other tours. Bounder tours also at Paxinos, PA.

Gift Counter: Sells T-shirts, hats, and other logoed items. Open Mon–Fri 8:00 AM–3:30 PM. Closed holidays.

Directions: From Los Angeles, take 60 Frwy. East. Exit at Market St. in Riverside. Go left at exit onto Market St., right at Viacerro, then right again onto Fleetwood Dr. Park in visitors' spaces at the appropriate plant.

Nearby Attractions: Graber Olive House tour (see page 21); Universal Studios, Paramount Pictures, and NBC Studios tours, approximately 60 miles west (see pages 34, 31, and 29); Lake Perris; Mission Inn; Disneyland, 45 miles west; Knott's Berry Farm, 40 miles west; Palm Springs.

Dreyer's and Edy's Grand Ice Cream

1250 Whipple Road   ~   *ice cream and frozen yogurt*
Union City, CA 94587
(510) 471-6622

William Dreyer and Joseph Edy started Dreyer's and Edy's Grand Ice Cream in 1928 on Grand Avenue in Oakland, California. Just one year later, they became famous by creating the world's first batch of Rocky Road ice cream. Now the company is the number-one premium ice-cream maker in the U.S. and the top exporter of premium ice cream to Japan. While your friendly guide sprinkles the tour with company trivia and industry facts, you'll learn, see, and taste how ice cream is made, from the cow to the cone.

After watching a video in the Double Scoop Depot, walk up marble fudge–colored stairs and take a walk down the Rocky Road to peer through glass windows overlooking the production floor. The assembly lines look like a maze of steel pipes and rapidly moving ice-cream containers. The base mix travels through the flavor vats, continuous flow freezer, and fruit feeders. Workers lift plastic bags of whatever ingredients are required for the flavor in production (perhaps strawberries for strawberry ice cream), pouring their contents into the feeder.

You first see the ice cream as it drops from the container-filler machines into round cartons. The windowed lids then twist down to cover the containers. At this point, the ice cream has the consistency of soft-serve. It moves through the inspection and shrink-wrap stations before resting in the hardening freezer for about seven hours at 40° below zero. This routine continues until workers produce up to 60,000 gallons per day, in some 20 different flavors.

You'll shiver as you quickly pass through the gigantic warehouse and loading dock area, with wind chill temperatures 20–30° below freezing. It's worth being cold for a few brisk moments to see the one million gallons of ice cream and frozen yogurt piled everywhere you look. At the end of the tour, you might run into John D. Harrison, the "Official Taster." The company insured his well-publicized taste buds for $1 million.

Cost: $2 per person

Freebies: Scoops of ice cream and frozen yogurt in your favorite flavors, and a bag of souvenir items that includes coupons, a factory poster, and a paper hat.

Video Shown: 11-minute video entitled "The Cool Facts" provides a close-up view of the ice-cream production process.

Reservations Needed: Yes. Prefers to consolidate individuals and families into a group tour.

Days and Hours: Mon–Fri 9:15 AM, 11:15 AM, and 2:00 PM. Closed holidays and week between Christmas and New Year's.

Plan to Stay: 1½ hours including video, tour, and ice-cream tasting.

Minimum Age: 6

Disabled Access: Yes, except for 5 stairs into the freezer area.

Group Requirements: Maximum group size is 40 people, with reservations recommended approximately 2 months in advance.

Special Information: No photography. Freezer area can be refreshingly chilly, so warm-weather natives should bring a sweater. Wear flat-heeled shoes.

Gift Cabinet: The Double Scoop Depot has a gift cabinet with a small selection of logoed items, including T-shirts and bookcovers. John D. Harrison's 10-minute video on ice-cream making and tasting, entitled "All In Good Taste," is available for purchase. Open after tours.

Directions: Take I-880 to the Whipple Rd. exit. Make a right on Whipple Rd. The factory is about .7 mile ahead on the right.

Nearby Attractions: NUMMI auto plant tour (see page 30); C.F. Kennedy Community Center & Park; Town Estates Park; Oakland and San Francisco attractions about 30 minutes away.

Website: www.dreyers.com

Dreyer's classic striped lids hint of icy treats inside.

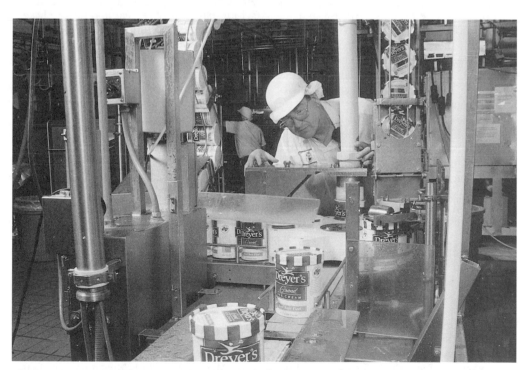

Creamy ice cream fills cartons at Dreyer's and Edy's Grand Ice Cream in Union City, California.

Fortune Cookie Factory   ⟶ *fortune cookies*
261 12th Street
Oakland, CA 94607
(510) 832-5552

Did you ever wonder how the fortune got inside a fortune cookie? Ever want to write your own fortune? What you may think of as great Oriental secrets are revealed at the Fortune Cookie Factory, a 30+-year-old family business. Don't be disappointed, however, when the owner, a UC Berkeley–educated mechanical engineer, tells you that fortune cookies were *not* created in the Orient. An ingenious Chinese restaurant owner invented them in the 1920s as an inexpensive and unique dessert.

Fortune cookies start as a mixture similar to pancake batter, made of whole-wheat flour, cane or beet sugar, water, and powdered whole eggs. Margarine, flavoring, and artificial coloring give the fortune cookies their golden color. A young Chinese worker concocts 100 pounds of batter in a vertical electric mixer, then scurries across the floor to pour it into one of the seven custom-made fortune-cookie machines. You will be mesmerized by the circular, methodical motion of this groaning machine. Batter flows through a spigot into individual 3-inch-diameter waffle irons. The individual plates clamp shut for their four-minute circular journey through the 225° piano-shaped oven. Small, wafer-thin pancakes emerge, cooked on both sides and pressed to squeeze out all air pockets.

With great dexterity the worker seated in front of each oven removes each pancake, randomly grabs a fortune from her lap, places it on the pancake, folds the pancake in half like a taco, and bends it around a metal rod. For cooling, the cookies are placed points-down in a holding tray. Listen to the women chatter in Chinese while they hand-fold 15 to 16 fortune cookies per minute, or 50,000 per day.

Cost: $1 per person
Freebies: Sample bag of fortune cookies.
Video Shown: No
Reservations Needed: No for viewing of the production process from the entrance of the production area. Yes for guided explanation.

Individuals need to latch onto guided group tours.
Days and Hours: Mon–Fri 8:00 AM–4:30 PM, but may want to call to check if English-speaking person is available. Closed major Chinese and some U.S. holidays.
Plan to Stay: 15 minutes for viewing, plus time for gift counter.
Minimum Age: 7, unless with family
Disabled Access: Yes
Group Requirements: Maximum group size is 25 people, which requires reservations 1 week in advance for guided tour.
Special Information: When the owner is there, he will gladly answer questions and tell you about his appearance on "What's My Line," a popular classic TV show; otherwise, look for a 1-page handout on the business and fortune cookie–making process.
Gift Counter: Small retail shop at front of factory sells bags of regular and flavored (i.e., strawberry, lime) fortune cookies, along with sassy and X-rated versions. You can also order customized fortune cookies (various sizes and messages, even with an engagement ring, if desired) and purchase bags of "misfortunes," which are broken fortune cookies. Price information available at above number. Open Mon–Fri 9:00 AM–4:30 PM.
Directions: From north of Oakland, take I-980 South and get off at the 11th/12th St. exit. Make a left onto 11th St. Turn left onto Alice and left onto 12th. Look for the factory storefront on the left side of 12th St. From south of Oakland, take I-880 North to Oak St. exit. Turn right at first intersection. Turn left on 12th. Storefront on left side.
Nearby Attractions: Golden Gate Fortune Cookies, in San Francisco's Chinatown, is a smaller business that has a viewing area near the retail counter (call 415-781-3956); Lotus Fortune Cookies, near city hall, uses an automated system to insert fortunes (call 415-552-0759); Oakland's Chinatown; Madison Park; Lake Merritt; Oakland Museum; San Francisco's attractions are across the Bay Bridge.

Graber Olive House ⟋ *olives*

315 East 4th Street
Ontario, CA 91764
(909) 983-1761

Companies that mass-produce California olives tell you that the black, pitted variety found on pizzas and supermarket shelves are natural and tree-ripened. After visiting the Graber Olive House, you will know what these terms really mean. The C.C. Graber Co. is the oldest olive packer (1894) in the only U.S. state that produces olives.

The cherry-red fruits are carefully removed from the tree by a picker who holds only a few olives in his hand at one time and drops them gently into a felt-bottomed bucket. Mass-produced California "ripe" black olives are green when harvested, and then oxidized a uniform black to hide bruises. Graber olives turn a natural nut-like color in processing.

After viewing pictures of the olives and groves, you're led through the company's production area. In the grading room, smock-clad women face a conveyor belt and carefully pick "culls" (overripe, underripe, or imperfect) out of the olive procession before them. More than one million olives roll by the graders during an eight-hour shift. The perfect olives then move to the vat room where, using the Graber family recipe, they are stirred, soaked, and tended for about three weeks in round cement vats. After the careful curing process removes the olives' natural bitterness, they are ready to be canned.

The pampered olives undergo a thorough canning and sterilization process. Workers, using the "hand-pack filling machine," scoop olives into cans as they pass under a wheel. Paddles on the "Panama-paddle packer" rotate and push a small amount of water out of each can, forming a head space for steam. The machine then hermetically seals each can. In the boiler room, carts filled with sealed cans of olives are rolled into a "retort." The door is closed, and the olives are sterilized with 242° steam from the boiler (like that on an old train) for over an hour. Finally, the cans are labeled with the Graber name familiar to gourmets around the world.

Cost: Free

Freebies: The "hospitality bowl" is filled with free olive samples.

Video Shown: 12-minute video on canning process.

Reservations Needed: No, except for groups of 10 or more people.

Days and Hours: Mon–Sat 9:00 AM–5:30 PM, Sun 9:30 AM–6:00 PM. Lunch break from 12:00 PM–1:30 PM. Last tour at 5:00 PM. Tours are conducted all year, but grading, curing, and canning only take place in October and early November. Closed Christmas, Thanksgiving, New Year's, Easter, and July 4th.

Plan to Stay: 30 minutes for tour, plus time for museum and gift shop. Museum contains an original grading machine made by C.C. Graber and other items related to the olive business. Lawn area available for picnics.

Minimum Age: None

Disabled Access: Yes

Group Requirements: Groups larger than 10 people should call 1 week in advance. Large groups will be split into groups of 20.

Special Information: When the factory is not in production, tour goes through canning plant with a colorful explanation and photographs of the process.

Gift Shop: The Casa del Olivo Fancy Food and Gift Shop sells Graber olives, nuts, dates, fancy foods, gift baskets, candies, toys, cookbooks, and unusual pottery. La Casita sells kitchen supplies and works by local artists. Open Mon–Sat 9:00 AM–5:30 PM and Sun 9:30 AM–6:00 PM. Catalog is available at (800) 996-5483.

Directions: From Los Angeles and Palm Springs, take I-10 (San Bernardino Frwy.) to Ontario. Take the Euclid Ave. exit, then south to 4th St. Turn left onto 4th St. Graber Olive House will be on your left.

Nearby Attractions: Fleetwood Motor Homes factory tour (see page 17); San Antonio Winery tasting room (call 909-947-3995); Claremont Colleges; Griswald Center; Mission Inn.

Herman Goelitz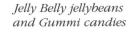

2400 North Watney Way
Fairfield, CA 94533
(707) 428-2838

*Jelly Belly jellybeans
and Gummi candies*

If you question whether former President Ronald Reagan's policies were good for the U.S. economy or for kids, then you should visit this factory that produces millions of jellybeans per day. The publicity surrounding President Reagan's fondness for their gourmet jellybeans ("Jelly Belly") led to increased demand, round-the-clock shifts, a new factory, and amusing tours for children and adults. The Herman Goelitz company has been making candy since 1922, but it was the introduction of the Jelly Belly jellybean in 1976 that spurred its growth.

While you'll see how the company makes a variety of creative candies, such as its line of Pet Gummi candies, the highlight is watching how it makes the Jelly Belly beans in over 40 flavors. From an open-air walkway, you'll view the beans at different stages of their creation. Be prepared for intense aromas. Unlike standard jellybeans, Jelly Belly beans are flavored both in the center and in the shell. Machines pour the special bean-center mixture into cornstarch molds that hold 1,260 centers per tray. Guess the exotic flavors, like strawberry daiquiri or peanut butter, as the bean centers travel by in the distance.

After the centers harden overnight, mechanical arms flip the trays over, and the centers pour into spinning, open copper drums. Here, workers add four layers of flavored syrup and sugars to create the outer shells. Each bean is automatically checked for correct size and color before traveling through the bagging and boxing machines. You'll look down at a hopper filled with a colorful and flavorful sea of jellybeans. The correctly weighed amount of jellybeans drops into plastic packets below. However, workers handpack the Gummi candies because they are too sticky for machines. At the tour's end, you'll stare at large mosaic portraits of famous faces and figures such as Ronald Reagan and the Statue of Liberty, each made of 14,000 jellybeans.

Cost: Free

Freebies: 4-ounce bag of Jelly Belly beans with an official menu matching colors to flavors. Logoed paper hat to wear during the tour. Throughout the tour the guide periodically gives out fresh Jelly Belly beans in various stages of production.

Video Shown: 7-minute video that explains and gives a close-up view of the candy-manufacturing process.

Reservations Needed: No

Days and Hours: Mon–Sun 9:00 AM–3:00 PM. No production on weekends, holidays, and the last week in June through the first week of July.

Plan to Stay: 40 minutes, plus time for video and gift shop.

Minimum Age: None, with 1 adult for every 6 children.

Disabled Access: Yes

Group Requirements: None

Special Information: No photography. 100-year-old North Chicago Goelitz Confectionary factory also gives tours (call 847-689-8950).

Retail Store: Sells more flavors of jellybeans than you can imagine (not only exotic fruit tastes, but also unusual flavors like toasted marshmallow, buttered popcorn, and jalapeño). Look for 2-pound bags of Belly Flops, the factory rejects. Open Mon–Sun 9:00 AM–5:00 PM.

Directions: From the San Francisco/Oakland area, take I-80 East to Hwy. 12 East. Turn right onto Beck Ave., right onto Courage Way, and right onto North Watney Way. From Sacramento, take Abernathy exit left to Hwy. 12 East, then follow the above directions.

Nearby Attractions: Seguin Moreau barrel making tour in Napa Valley (see page 32); Anheuser-Busch (Budweiser) Brewery tour is in same industrial park (call 707-429-7595); Marine World Africa U.S.A.; Old Town Vallejo; Marcel Shurman factory store; Napa Valley wineries and Culinary Institute of America located 20 minutes away.

See color photos, page 182

Hershey's Visitors Center ⌒ *chocolate*

120 South Sierra
Oakdale, CA 95361-9368
(209) 848-8126

 **Hershey Foods Corporation**

"Wow, look at all those Hershey's Kisses!" will be your first words as you enter the only Hershey's chocolate factory in the U.S. that gives public tours. Watch each Hershey's Kiss, one of the most recognizable shapes in the world, receive its own silver evening gown and paper necklace. Hershey Foods Corporation, founded in 1894 by Milton S. Hershey in the small Pennsylvania town later named after him, is the country's largest candy-maker; it makes approximately 33 million Kisses per day.

At one stop on your speedy, sweet-smelling journey, peek through glass walls at rows of 10,000-pound vats called "conch machines." At all major tour stops, the guide plays a taped explanation of what's happening in front of you. You hear, for example, that the conch machines' granite rollers move back and forth on corrugated granite beds to create smooth chocolate paste from a mixture of cocoa butter, sugar, milk, and chocolate liquid.

From an overhead walkway, peer through glass windows at the high-speed computerized production lines that build well-known Hershey products such as the top-selling Reese's Peanut Butter Cups. After the brown paper cups land on a moving belt, they are lined with milk chocolate and then a layer of peanut butter. The top layer of chocolate is air-blown on and vibrated to ensure a smooth surface. In the wrapping and packaging area the peanut-butter cups move so quickly on a sophisticated "freeway" system that they deserve a speeding ticket. You'll leave this tour feeling like Charlie after his visit to Willy Wonka's Chocolate Factory.

Cost: Free
Freebies: Coupon for choice of free candy bar or 10 percent off purchase of single item valued at $5 or more.
Videos Shown: Videos in the visitors center: 13-minute "The Cocoa Bean Story" about the production process and Arts & Entertainment TV's 22-minute Milton Hershey story.

Reservations Needed: No, except for groups of 15 or more people.
Days and Hours: Mon–Fri 8:30 AM–3:00 PM. Closed holidays, including the day after Thanksgiving. Shuttle buses leave the visitors' center for the factory every 15–30 minutes. During peak periods (summer, Christmas and Easter weeks), 1:30 PM is recommended sign-in time for 3:00 PM tour. Call about maintenance shutdowns.
Plan to Stay: 1 hour, which includes tour and shuttle bus ride (a great chocolate smell hits you when you approach the factory). Allow extra time for gift shop and video.
Minimum Age: None, but no strollers.
Disabled Access: Yes, for the first half of the tour. If you are unable to use the stairs, tell a Hershey's Guest Relations Representative before the tour begins.
Group Requirements: Groups of 15 or more people should call (209) 848-5100, ext. 5625, at least 1 month in advance. No maximum group size.
Special Information: See page 263 about the simulated factory tour at Hershey's Chocolate World in Hershey, PA.
Gift Shop: Sells Hershey's candy, T-shirts, and gifts, including teddy bears holding stuffed Kisses. Exhibits include a model 1915 wrapping machine. Open Mon–Fri 8:30 AM–5:00 PM. Closed holidays.
Directions: From San Francisco, take I-580 East to I-205 East. Take Hwy. 120 East to intersection of Hwys. 108 and 120. Go through intersection, travel 1 block, and turn left onto G St. Parking is on right. From Yosemite, take Hwy. 120 West. Continue on Hwy. 108/120 to Oakdale. Turn left onto Yosemite St. Turn left onto G St. Parking is on right. Phone recording has directions.
Nearby Attractions: Western Theme Park; Knights Ferry; Oakdale Museum; St. Stans Brewing Co. tour (call 209-524-BEER); Delicato Vineyard tour (call 209-825-6212); Hershey's Visitors Center has list of additional nearby attractions and events.

See color photos, page 180

Intel ⟶ *computer chips*

Corporate Museum, Robert N. Noyce Building
2200 Mission College Boulevard
Santa Clara, CA 95052-8119
(408) 765-0503

Few U.S. companies embody the computer revolution like the Intel Corporation. At the company's museum, which opened in 1992, you'll learn about Intel's development, innovation, range of products, pride, and also how Intel became the world's largest computer-chip maker.

You're lured inside by shifting green, purple, aqua, and silver lights bouncing off a glass etching of an Intel computer chip. You'll quickly notice a dummy in a "bunny suit." (No, it doesn't have giant ears.) The workers who build computer chips wear this fully enclosed white suit, complete with air packs to filter their breathing. Computer-chip making requires factories thousands of times cleaner than hospital operating rooms. To illustrate this point, in the chip-making exhibit you can walk through an air shower that blows dust particles off your clothes.

The museum's exhibits appeal to all levels of technical knowledge and interest, so don't become discouraged if one display goes over your head. Visitors with technical backgrounds will enjoy exhibits of Intel's key memory products, such as EPROMs (erasable programmable read-only memory) and DRAMs (dynamic random access memory), and descriptions of memory technologies such as magnetic core and semiconductor. These products transformed computers from huge, expensive machines into affordable, powerful desktop systems available to everyone. Intel's microprocessors are displayed, from the Intel 4004 (the world's first, invented in 1971), to the newest processors. The history section includes enlarged circuit diagrams, along with the history of and the design teams behind each chip's development.

Although you cannot tour the factories where Intel actually makes its chips, the museum shows the sophisticated robotic-arm wafer transfer device and the complex steps involved in manufacturing computer chips. One of the most fascinating of the many interactive exhibits deals with "embedded controllers"—the highly integrated microcomputer chips that power everyday products, from answering machines to cars. This extensive, less technical display, featuring a life-size plastic cow wearing a computerized collar, makes you realize how pervasive and important computers have become.

Cost: Free
Freebies: No
Videos Shown: Video interviews with the employees behind Intel's innovations.
Reservations Needed: No, except for scheduled guided group tours.
Days and Hours: Mon–Fri 8:00 AM–5:00 PM. Closed company holidays.
Plan to Stay: About 1 hour, depending on your computer and engineering background and your desire to try the hands-on displays.
Minimum Age: None, but 12 is the recommended minimum. Displays have interactive components, but children should be interested in computers or science.
Disabled Access: Yes
Group Requirements: Maximum group size is 20 people. Contact Intel Museum office (408-765-0662) 1 week in advance to schedule a group tour. Special educational programs available for school groups.
Special Information: Dress appropriately— the museum is located in Intel's corporate headquarters. Various museum displays change quarterly to highlight recent technical developments. Expansion scheduled for 1999, so call for changes.
Gift Shop: No
Directions: Take Rt. 101 to the Montague/San Thomas Expwy. exit. Turn onto Montague Expwy. (left at exit if going south on Rt. 101, right at exit if going north), then turn left onto Mission College Blvd. (look for Mission College sign). Company headquarters is on left; museum is in the lobby of the Robert Noyce Building.
Nearby Attractions: Stanford Linear Accelerator Center tour (call 415-926-2204); Tech Museum of Innovation; The Barbie Hall of Fame (call 415-326-5841); Great America Theme Park.

Website: www.intel.com

You'll learn much about the computer revolution at "The History of Microprocessors at Intel" exhibit at Intel Museum in Santa Clara, California.

The exhibit also identifies the design teams behind each chip's development.

Levi Strauss ⟿ *jeans*
250 Valencia Street
San Francisco, CA 94103
(415) 565-9159

In 1849 the discovery of gold near Sacramento ushered in California's Gold Rush, and hordes of prospectors raced west to seek their fortunes. Long hours in the mines, however, quickly wore out their pants. A young, entrepreneurial German immigrant named Levi Strauss cleverly solved their dilemma. In 1853, using leftover canvas he had hoped to use for tents and wagon covers, he designed the first pair of jeans. Exhausting his original supply of canvas, Levi switched to a sturdy fabric made in Nîmes, France, called "serge de Nîmes" (later shortened to "denim"). They became known as "those pants of Levi's," and quickly grew in popularity. Blue jeans have been an American icon ever since.

Entering the Levi Strauss factory will remind you more of the famous garment shops of early-1900s New York than of the Gold Rush. Smell the fresh-cut fabric and observe the ring of sewing machines. Watch the stages from the initial cutting of the denim to the final preparation for shipping. Large carts whirl past you, carrying jeans in various stages of production. In the smallest and oldest (built in 1906) Levi Strauss factory in the world, approximately 60 workers make Levi's famous 501 jeans.

The presence of the patriarchal founder and the sense of family history pervade the tour. Old looms sit in hallway displays, early advertising posters adorn the walls, and a life-size cardboard cut-out of Levi himself proudly greets visitors to the upper level. Even the shiny wooden floors are a testimonial to the kindness of the family-owned company, which employed workers to improve the factory rather than fire them during the Depression.

You will leave with the feeling that you did not merely watch pants being made, but you witnessed the making of a legendary American product by a respected U.S. company. However, you'll have to go to Asia to buy a pair of the 501s made during your tour. Almost every pair made at this factory ends up in Japan, because the Japanese insist on the high-priced San Francisco originals.

Cost: Free

Freebies: Occasionally a souvenir such as a key chain with a leather Levi Strauss trademark patch or a ballpoint pen.

Video Shown: 8-minute video, usually of classic Levi's commercials.

Reservations Needed: Yes. Individuals and families must latch onto group tours. Individuals should call in advance to check for space availability, as priority is given to tour groups. Groups, see below.

Days and Hours: Tue and Wed 9:00 AM, 11:00 AM, and 1:30 PM. Closed holidays, 2 weeks around Christmas, and 3–4 weeks in July.

Plan to Stay: 1–1½ hours including tour, video, museum, and question-and-answer session at end of tour. Museum has pictures and displays that highlight the history of jeans and the company.

Minimum Age: None

Disabled Access: Yes

Group Requirements: Groups should make reservations as early as possible, since tours fill up months in advance. Maximum group size is 35 people.

Special Information: No video cameras. Tour director is a retiree now but has voice-mail that is checked daily (415) 565-9159.

Apparel Store: Open Tue and Wed 9:00 AM to 4:00 PM.

Directions: Take Hwy. 101 to the Van Ness/Mission St. exit. Go straight onto Duboce Ave. Turn left onto Valencia.

Nearby Attractions: Basic Brown Bear Factory tour (see page 14); San Francisco's attractions include Fisherman's Wharf, Anchor Brewery Co. tour (call 415-863-8350), Wells Fargo Bank Museum (call 415-396-2619), and Chevron U.S.A. Museum (call 415-894-6697).

Los Angeles Times ⟿ *newspaper*

Times Mirror Square
202 West 1st Street
Los Angeles, CA 90053
(213) 237-5757

Los Angeles Times

If you ever wondered how that story in your newspaper got there, you'll enjoy touring the *Los Angeles Times*. The sound of clattering typewriters has given way to the relative quiet of computers in the newsroom. This tour of one of the world's great newspapers begins with a slide show illustrating the history of the *Times* and how it has grown along with the Southern California region. After the slide show, you'll visit the newsroom, where a vast expanse of reporters work busily on late-breaking stories and rush to meet deadlines.

Discover that the Food Department even has a full working kitchen, where staff members carefully taste-test dishes before the recipes appear in the paper. See how the News and Editorial Departments work together, learn about the paper's different editions, and walk by the library (known as the "morgue") and photography areas, containing over 4.5 million negatives. Photography buffs will enjoy the magnificent display of old and new cameras used by *Times* photographers. Huge black cameras with giant flashbulbs recall a time before television, when newspapers were almost exclusively our eyes on the world. In the composing room, every page of the paper is carefully laid out with the news stories and ads before being printed.

The *Times* printing plant, 2 miles away, is open by reservation. You'll see the state-of-the-art pressroom, which extends nearly the length of two football fields, and the newsprint storage area, where robot-like automated guidance vehicles carry 2,500-pound rolls of newsprint. While you'll see very few people, you will hear and see the beeping and flashing robots as they glide around. Visit plate-making, where newspaper pages are converted from photographic negatives to aluminum printing plates, and observe the distribution system that takes newspapers from the press to the delivery truck. It's exciting to watch the newspaper-printing process in this massive, super-automated plant.

Cost: Free

Freebies: *Times* pencil, plus reporter's notepad for those 18 or under.

Video Shown: Possible 7-minute video gives a quick history of the newspaper.

Reservations Needed: Editorial tour: No, except for groups of 10 or more people. Printing Plant tour: Yes. Individuals latch onto group tours.

Days and Hours: Editorial tour: Mon–Fri 11:15 AM. Printing plant tour: see group information below. Closed holidays.

Plan to Stay: 45 minutes to 1 hour for either tour.

Minimum Age: 10, or 5th grade

Disabled Access: Yes

Group Requirements: Groups larger than 10 people need to call 1 month in advance. Group tours are by reservation Mon–Fri 10:00 AM and 1:15 PM for either plant. Call (213) 237-5757 to schedule. Maximum group size is 35 people.

Special Information: The *Times'* Globe Lobby contains circa-1935 murals, a rotating globe of the world, and a historical display.

Gift Shop: No

Directions: Editorial Plant: From Frwy. 101 South heading toward downtown L.A. (past Frwy. 110), take Broadway exit. Turn right onto Spring St. Pass the *Times* entrance at the corner of 1st and Spring Sts. and park in the *Times* garage at 213 S. Spring St. From Frwy. 10 East, exit onto one-way Spring St. Follow directions above. Olympic Printing Plant: directions provided with reservations.

Nearby Attractions: Paramount Pictures, Universal Studios, and Warner Bros. Studios, tours (see pages 31, 34, and 35) are 7–15 miles away; NBC Studios tour (see page 29), about 30 minutes away; Museum of Contemporary Art; The Music Center; Little Tokyo; Olvera Street.

Marin French Cheese   *cheese*

Rouge et Noir

7500 Red Hill Road
Petaluma, CA 94952
(707) 762-6001 / (800) 292-6001

Thousands of miles away from France, this fifth-generation company has been making Camembert, Brie, and other soft-ripened French cheeses under the Rouge et Noir label since 1900. The Thompson family started at their ranch location in 1865, when they hand-dug the original cellar, which is still in use today. Until the 1950s they made their own wooden boxes for the individual cheeses.

While you wait in the cool cellar for your tour you can look at some of this old equipment, including a 1906 box-making machine. Follow your tour guide down the hall to look through windows into each of the small cheese-making rooms.

In the Make Room, the white, chunky, cottage cheese-like curds are poured from buckets into rows of metal cylindrical molds that resemble empty baked-bean cans. As the molds are filled with four inches of curd, white liquid whey pours out. The whey continues to drain out until the curd is only one inch thick. The cheese stays in the molds for approximately 18 hours.

Across the hall in the Salt Room, the cheese, now removed from the molds, soaks in salt brine. The Brie wheels soak the longest. Although you cannot go down to the aging cellars, the tour guide explains that the Camembert and Brie sit in the cellar for about 11 days so the edible mold can develop on the outside of the cheese.

Next, walk upstairs to watch women seated at a table hand-packing the cheese. In the adjacent tasting area are historical photographs of the company's earlier cheese-making methods, awards their cheeses have won, and a display of all their different products. On a red-and-white-checked tablecloth, cheeses for tasting sit invitingly on red-and-black logoed porcelain plates covered by glass cheese domes. After you sample the cheeses, you'll be ready for your own wine and cheese picnic.

Cost: Free

Freebies: Crackers and cheese samples in the tasting area and sales room; recipe brochure.

Video Shown: No (possible in future)

Reservations Needed: No, except for groups larger than 10 people.

Days and Hours: Mon–Sun 10:00 AM–4:00 PM, every hour on the hour. Best time to see production is 1:00 PM, when the curds are poured. No production on weekends. Most production in summer and before Christmas. Closed Thanksgiving, Christmas, and New Year's.

Plan to Stay: 20 minutes for tour, plus time in sales room and on 5-acre grounds, which include duck pond and picnic tables.

Minimum Age: None

Disabled Access: Yes

Group Requirements: Groups over 10 people should call 10 days in advance. No maximum group size.

Special Information: Can rent barbecue area for weddings and parties.

Sales Room: Sells all the Rouge et Noir cheeses (including flavored Bries), wine, bread, sandwiches, and other picnic supplies. Offers gift assortment packs and logoed aprons, wineglasses, T-shirts, and caps. Open Mon–Sun 9:00 AM–5:00 PM. Closed Thanksgiving, Christmas, and New Year's.

Directions: From San Francisco, take Hwy. 101 North to Novato. Turn left onto San Marin Dr., right onto Novato Blvd., and left onto Petaluma-Pt. Reyes Rd. You can't miss the giant cheese-wheel sign ¼-mile ahead on right. From Santa Rosa, take Hwy. 101 South to Petaluma. Turn right onto E. Washington St., left onto Payran St., and right onto "D" St. Continue about 9 miles past the town. Marin French Cheese will be on your right.

Nearby Attractions: Sonoma Cheese self-guided tour (call 800-535-2855); California Cooperative Creamery Store, company used to give tours (call 707-778-1234); Pt. Reyes National Seashore; Bodega Bay; Petaluma Adobe State Historic Park; Petaluma Historical Library; The Great Petaluma Mill.

NBC Studios ⟶ *television shows*

3000 West Alameda Avenue
Burbank, CA 91523
(818) 840-3537

NBC is the only major television network that provides tours to the public. Your tour guide will take you through the life of a television broadcast, from its conception to the building of the set, from the studio taping to your television at home. Visit the actual facilities as shows are taping in the studio next to you. Walk the halls of the stars and keep your eyes peeled for Jay Leno.

Begin your tour in the carpenter shop. Here, carpenters and artists work side by side to build and put the finishing touches on sets for NBC shows and other events, such as the 1996 Olympics Opening Ceremony in Atlanta. Though sometimes huge, the sets are made with lightweight plywood and fiberglass brick so they don't become too heavy. The sets have to be fit together inside the studio due to the size limitations of studio doors.

Walk down the main hallway, cluttered with the sets for "Days of Our Lives." Learn how this daily one-hour show is really a 24-hour-a-day operation. Sets are ever-changing. The show is taped year-round, unlike seasonal shows, which can run repeats in the summer. Peek into the studio if the door is open.

Follow your guide through the midway, where the stars park their cars. Check to see what Leno drove to work that day—he owns around 30 vintage cars and even more motorcycles, including a Stanley Steamer, a classic Duesenberg, and a WWI-era motorcycle.

If the "Tonight Show" is not in session, go into Studio 3. Sit in the audience chairs and watch the bustle of setup onstage. The show is taped live with only about 1½ hours for editing before it is broadcast on the East coast.

On the special-effects set, learn how the blue Chroma Key screen works, while a volunteer plays weatherman or flies like Superman. Your tour ends in the guest relations patio, which you may recognize as the Salem Place Mall from "Days of Our Lives."

Cost: Adults $7; seniors (60 and over) $6.25; children (5–12) $3.75; under 5, free.
Freebies: No
Videos Shown: 6½-minute video on the history of NBC and the tour, plus a behind-the-scenes look at production; 1-minute video on wardrobe and make-up techniques.
Reservations Needed: No, but tickets sold on first-come, first-served basis. Yes, for groups of 15 or more people.
Days and Hours: Mon–Fri 9:00 AM–3:00 PM. July and August also Sat 10:00 AM–2:00 PM. Closed some holidays.
Plan to Stay: 70 minutes, plus time for the gift shop.
Minimum Age: None
Disabled Access: Yes
Group Requirements: Groups of 15 or more people should call NBC Group Services, at (818) 840-3551, at least 2 weeks in advance. Groups over 15 people will be split. Group reservations when available. Reservations difficult between Christmas and New Year's.
Special Information: No photography. Tours will not go into studios during production. Tours before 1:30 will likely include the "Tonight Show" studio. Free audience show tickets available daily at NBC's ticket counter on first-come, first-served basis. Send ticket requests to NBC Tickets at above address or call above number for more information.
Gift Shop: NBC Peacock Shop sells merchandise from NBC shows along with logoed souvenir items. Open same hours as tour.
Directions: From the South, take Frwy. 405 North to 101 East (to LA). From the left lane, merge into Ventura Frwy. 134 East. Exit Buena Vista off ramp. Turn left on Riverside Dr. Turn right on Bob Hope Dr. and follow signs to NBC Studios tour. From the East, take Frwy. 10 West to Frwy. 5 North. Exit Alameda Ave. West. Studio is 2 miles ahead, near St. Joseph's Hospital.
Nearby Attractions: Universal Studios, Paramount Pictures, and Warner Bros. tours (see pages 34, 31, and 35); Gene Autry Western Heritage Museum.

New United Motor Manufacturing

45500 Fremont Boulevard   *Toyota and GM cars*
Fremont, CA 94538   *and pickup trucks*
(510) 498-5649 / (510) 770-4008

Automobile factory tours always offer a special excitement. Because the General Motors/Toyota joint venture (nicknamed "NUMMI") uses this refurbished GM plant, it's a showcase of Japanese manufacturing techniques within the context of U.S. union-management relations. As your electric tram motors more than 1 mile over the factory floor, watch workers (called "team members"), giant machines, and robots build the Geo Prizm, Toyota Corolla, and Toyota Tacoma pickup truck.

Because of the plant's layout, your narrated trip does not follow the exact sequence of building cars and trucks. However, you will see most of the steps in the manufacturing process. Each of the plant's work areas—whether for stamping, body and welding, assembling, or inspecting—manufactures cars and trucks at a measured pace along the plant's 1.2 miles of conveyer belt. For example, as an engine is hydraulically lifted into the overhead car engine compartment, team members scramble to bolt the engine into place within 62 seconds, the scheduled time each unit spends at each workstation in the car-assembly area.

A cacophony fills the air: drilling, crunching, hissing, and buzzing. Since the plant has the largest metal parts–stamping facility on the West Coast, a constant thumping reverberates through part of the plant. Suddenly you may hear music playing. A team member on the assembly line has spotted a quality problem and pulled the Andon Cord. If the problem can't be resolved quickly, production stops on that section of the line, and the music keeps playing until the problem is fixed. (Each area has its own tune.) This cord empowers all team members to guarantee quality in the manufacturing process, what the Japanese call "Jidoka". Even if you're not interested in the details of the Toyota production system, you'll marvel at the movements and flying sparks generated by over 350 computerized welding robots.

Cost: Free

Freebies: Currently no souvenirs

Video Shown: No, but captioned pictures in the tour waiting room explain the different manufacturing steps. Video is planned.

Reservations Needed: Yes. Individuals and families must join a scheduled group tour.

Days and Hours: Tue, Wed, Thur, Fri 9:30 AM and 11:30 AM. Tour content and schedule may change due to the line change for 1998 models. Call for tour times. Closed holidays and week between Christmas and New Year's.

Plan to Stay: Approximately 2 hours, including introductory talk, tour, and wrap-up Q&A session.

Minimum Age: 10. Tours for children ages 10 to 18 require 1 adult for every 10 children.

Disabled Access: Yes

Group Requirements: Maximum group size is 48 people. Tours need to be scheduled 3–4 months in advance for larger groups.

Special Information: No photography. Because tour is by electric tram and you wear a headset, there's not much walking or excessive noise.

Gift Shop: No

Directions: From I-880 North, use the Fremont Blvd. exit just past Mission Blvd. Turn right at first light and take immediate right. Visitor parking on left after three stop signs. If traveling south on I-880, use the second Fremont Blvd. exit, just past Auto Mall Pkwy. (Do not take the earlier Alvarado Niles/Fremont Blvd. exit). Plant is visible from freeway. Upon exiting, stay right to loop back over freeway. Turn right at first light. Follow above directions. Ask for map when making reservations.

Nearby Attractions: Dreyer's and Edy's Grand Ice Cream factory tour (see page 18); Intel Museum (see page 24); Great American Theme Park; Mission Peak Regional Park.

Paramount Pictures   *movies and television shows*

5555 Melrose Avenue
Hollywood, CA 90038
(213) 956-1777

A Paramount Communications Company

Paramount Pictures, founded in 1912, shows the true TV and movie fan current movie-making techniques while retaining its nostalgic charm. The only major studio still located in Hollywood, Paramount provides an exciting behind-the-scenes look at movie and television production. Tours of this original, classic studio are never exactly alike, since old sets are taken down and new projects begin every day.

Your tour guide will point out a number of famous Paramount landmarks along this two-hour walking tour. You will see sets not only for such television shows as "I Love Lucy," "Happy Days," and "Cheers," but also for some of Paramount's best-known movies, such as *The Godfather*, *Star Trek*, and *The Hunt For Red October*. Stroll by the famous Wardrobe Department, as well as a display of Oscars and Emmys on loan from stars who have awards to spare.

As you peer through the old Bronson Gate, the arched gateway entrance synonymous with Paramount Pictures, and gaze upon the famous "Hollywood" sign in the hills, you'll hear the story about this passage being the magic gateway to the Silver Screen for aspiring stars. Carefully study the roof architecture of some of the soundstages to identify the three film production companies located here before Paramount took over the site in 1928.

Notice the B tank, a body of water used for shooting miniatures and special effects, such as the parting of the Red Sea in the 1956 filming of *The Ten Commandments*. The 100,000 gallon–capacity water tower still marks the actual borderline dividing Paramount and RKO Studios, which was acquired by Paramount. Stroll through Production Park, not only the company's business hub, but also one of the most photographed areas in Hollywood. On screen, its buildings double as college campuses, foreign embassies, police precincts, hospitals, and more. At any point on the tour, you may suddenly see your favorite performer.

Cost: $15 per person

Freebies: Complimentary tickets to any of the TV shows filmed daily at Paramount.

Video Shown: No

Reservations Needed: No, except for groups larger than 15 people.

Days and Hours: Mon–Fri 9:00 AM–2:00 PM, every hour on the hour.

Plan to Stay: 2 hours; 4–6 hours if you stay to watch a TV show in production.

Minimum Age: For tour, 10; to watch most of the TV shows, 16.

Disabled Access: Yes

Group Requirements: Admission is $12 per person for groups larger than 15 people. Groups should call at least 1 week in advance to check the shooting schedule, make tour reservations, and arrange for group discount. Maximum group size is 50 people. Call (213) 956-1777.

Special Information: No photography. Check time schedule and ticket availability for the day's TV show filmings by calling above number. Wear comfortable shoes—this is a walking tour.

Gift Shop: Studio Store sells exclusive Paramount and Viacom (MTV, Nickelodeon, etc.) logoed merchandise, including T-shirts, hats, and mugs. Open Mon–Fri 8:30 AM–4:30 PM.

Directions: From Los Angeles, take 101 Frwy. North to Melrose Ave. exit. Turn left onto Melrose Ave. Park in the Bronson parking lot on left. Walk to the second entrance, to studio known as Melrose Walk-On. From San Fernando Valley, take 101 Frwy. South to Gower St. exit. Make a right onto Gower St., go down hill. Turn left onto Melrose. Parking lot is on your right.

Nearby Attractions: Universal Studios, NBC Studios, and Warner Bros. tours (see pages 34, 29 and 35); Frederick's of Hollywood Lingerie Museum (call 213-466-8506); Mann's Chinese Theatre, with famous people's footprints in the forecourt; Downtown Hollywood's famous streets, including Hollywood Blvd., the Sunset Strip.

Seguin Moreau *wine barrels*

151 Camino Dorado
Napa, CA 94558
(707) 252-3408

While everyone knows that Napa Valley wineries offer tours, you may not know that in South Napa you can watch the ancient art of barrel-making. Of 22 cooperages in the U.S. (most make whiskey barrels), only three are in Napa Valley. Seguin Moreau's Napa cooperage is a division of Seguin Moreau, France's oldest cooperage, established in the late 1800s.

As soon as your guide opens the doors to this cooperage built in 1994, you'll smell a pleasant vanilla aroma from the toasting barrels. You stroll along an open-air walkway just a few feet from the action. Brown overhead signs clearly mark all 12 of the production stations. Diagrams along the walkway show you which steps are performed in each of the two large, high-ceilinged rooms. With all the small fires in the first room, you wonder if some ancient witchcraft is brewing. Flames, water, and banging hammers are the key tools for shaping barrels. No glue is used. More modern woodworking machinery is used in the second room to finish the barrels.

American white oak, split from 90-year-old trees, seasons outdoors for two to three years to reduce moisture and tannins. Then the wood is ready to be cut into 37½-inch-long "staves" and arranged in pairs—one wide, one narrow. With great skill, a master cooper "raises a barrel" by vertically arranging 27 to 30 of these alternating-width staves into a "rosette." He lines up the tops of the staves against the inside of a metal hoop, with the bottoms flaring out to form a teepee. If done correctly, the barrel could stand alone without the metal hoop; otherwise, the staves will fall into a tangled pile. To hold them tightly, metal hoops are pounded into place by the cooper circling the barrel in what's known as the "barrel-maker's dance." The staves are bent into the barrel shape with the help of moisture, heat, and an electric winch. The bending process takes approximately 20 minutes.

The barrels then move to the fires, where they are toasted for approximately one hour along a row of 12 small campfires. The coopers turn them over regularly so the insides toast evenly. The toasting releases natural flavors that enhance the taste of the wine that will eventually be put in the barrel. Barrelheads, assembled with wooden dowels and river reed, are toasted in a large oven. A cooper wedges the head into place with a shoehorn-type tool. At station 12 in the second room, the barrel rolls under the sanding belt. Each barrel takes 17 coopers about four hours to make.

Cost: Adults, $2; children, free

Freebies: Great toasting wood smells!

Video Shown: 10-minute video covers company history, where wood comes from, and barrel-making process at Seguin Moreau's French facility.

Reservations Needed: Recommended

Days and Hours: Mon–Fri 10:00 AM and 2:00 PM. Closed week of July 4th and week between Christmas and New Year's.

Plan to Stay: 40 minutes for tour and video.

Minimum Age: None

Disabled Access: Yes

Group Requirements: Groups over 50 people will be split.

Special Information: No video cameras. Due to the flames, cooperage is very hot in the summer.

Gift Area: Sells logoed polos, mugs, and other items. Open Mon–Fri 8:00 AM–5:00 PM.

Directions: From Oakland/San Francisco, take I-80 North to Napa turnoff (Hwy. 37 West). Take Hwy. 29 North. After the Napa Airport on left, you'll pass Seguin Moreau on your right. Turn right onto N. Kelly Rd. and right onto Camino Dorado. Seguin Moreau will be on your right.

Nearby Attractions: Hakusan Sake self-guided tour (call 800-564-6261); Carneros area winery tours include Domain Carneros Sparkling Wine (call 707-257-0101) and Cordorniu Napa (call 707-224-1668). For general information about Napa Valley winery tours, call (707) 226-7459.

Sunset ∿ *magazines and books*

80 Willow Road
Menlo Park, CA 94025
(415) 321-3600

Sunset

Sunset magazine was founded in 1898 by Southern Pacific Railroad Company as a promotional tool to encourage westward travel, and was named after the Southern Pacific's *Sunset Limited* train. The magazine evolved into a gardening, travel, food, and home-improvement magazine for the West. The company now publishes seven monthly regional editions of *Sunset* magazine for 13 Western states. Each edition focuses on that region's needs and interests, particularly in travel and gardening. In 1931 Sunset published its first cookbook. You can take a self-guided walk through their display gardens.

Sunset's adobe-style home was designed by renowned architect Cliff May and opened in 1952. Enter the light, airy main lobby through the thick, hand-carved, 10-foot-tall front doors. Notice some of the interesting interior architectural features, such as the desert-tile lobby floor and the adobe brick walls—each brick is 2 feet deep and weighs 30 pounds!

Outside, stroll through the formal gardens created by landscape designer Thomas Church. This "Walk through the West" features native plants from Southern California to Washington, plus Hawaii. You'll first walk past the Old Man live oak, growing increasingly lopsided as it chases the sun.

Walk along the curved walkway to the Southwest Desert and Southern California section, which features cacti, succulents, and certain perennials that will grow under extreme drought conditions. Notice the large Southern yucca, which is probably 150 years old. Further along the walkway is the Central California area. The lawn here is sometimes mowed into a putting green in the summer. Notice how the sun shines through the "Monterey Peninsula."

Huge coast redwoods reign over the garden's Northern California section. Look up at the magnolia blossom trees. Four Chardonnay and four Cabernet grapevines represent the Sonoma and Napa Valleys. Wet winters and cold temperatures characterize the climate for the Northwest. Here you'll see dogwood, firs, and many types of rhododendron, including azaleas.

After the peaceful, perfectly manicured formal gardens, you visit the organic test garden used for editorial projects. This 3,200-square-foot garden is divided into four test plots. Ever-changing, the beds may contain 30 varieties of gourmet lettuce, or hyacinth and tulips in the spring. Next time you browse through *Sunset*'s brightly colored garden photographs, you'll know where they were taken.

Cost: Free
Freebies: Walking tour map, which includes company history.
Video Shown: No
Reservations Needed: No
Days and Hours: Mon–Fri 9:00 AM–4:30 PM. Closed holidays.
Plan to Stay: 20 minutes
Minimum Age: None, however, children should be interested in horticulture.
Disabled Access: Yes
Group Requirements: None
Special Information: No professional photography allowed. Best times to tour are spring (when the gardens are in full bloom) and Christmas (when crafts projects are displayed in lobby).
Gift Shop: No, however Sunset books are displayed and can be ordered in lobby or by calling (800) 759-0190. Also sells magazines in lobby. Subscribe to *Sunset* magazine by calling (800) 777-0117.
Directions: From San Francisco, take Hwy. 101 South to Willow Rd./Menlo Park West exit. Follow Willow Rd. for approximately 1 mile. Sunset is on your left.
Nearby Attractions: Intel Museum (see page 24); Filoli Estate; Allied Arts Guild; Stanford Linear Accelerator Center tour (call 415-926-2204).

Universal Studios Hollywood

100 Universal City Plaza ⟶ *movies and television shows*
Universal City, CA 91608
(818) 622-3801

Film pioneer Carl Laemmle established Universal Studios in 1915 on a former chicken ranch. In the early days of silent pictures, visitors ate box lunches provided by the studio and sat in bleacher seats watching films being made. With the advent of "talking pictures," the tours stopped.

Largely as an effort to boost the lunchtime business at the Studio Commissary, Universal reopened its doors to the public in 1964. Millions of dollars and visitors later, Universal Studios Hollywood has developed its famed 420-acre studio lot into a first-rate theme park. Attractions provide a fun family experience through which to learn the secrets of motion picture and television production.

Universal Studios Hollywood really is a trip into what it feels like to be in a movie. It's not about what it's like to be an actor in a film, but rather what it's like to be a character in a Hollywood adventure story. While Charlton Heston or Ava Gardner did their *Earthquake!* scenes in hundreds of boring pieces, the tour puts the pieces together and plays them at full speed.

You can enjoy the Backlot tram tour, which visits famous production sets of the world's largest movie studio. This tram ride takes you past renowned sets from *E.T.—The Extraterrestrial, Twins, City Slickers, Animal House,* and *Back to the Future,* among many others. Television sets you'll recognize include those from "Murder, She Wrote," "Dr. Quinn, Medicine Woman," "Leave It To Beaver," "McHale's Navy," and "Sliders."

The World of Cinemagic provides insights into special effects used in *Back to the Future* and *Psycho.* Several audience members can participate in the demonstrations. One show teaches how sounds and voices are dubbed into an already-shot film through Foley and ADR (automated dubbing replacement technique).

Cost: Backlot tram tour price is included in the general admission charge for Universal Studios; 2-day tour passes are also available.

Freebies: No

Videos Shown: Many attractions include videos.

Reservations Needed: No, except for groups of 20 or more people.

Days and Hours: Mon–Sun 9:00 AM–7:00 PM. Open later during peak days and in the summer. Box office opens ½-hour prior to park. Closed Thanksgiving and Christmas.

Plan to Stay: All day at Universal Studios. The Backlot tour is 45 minutes.

Minimum Age: None

Disabled Access: Yes

Group Requirements: Groups of 20 or more people should call Group Sales (818-622-3771) 3–4 days in advance or write Universal Studios (at the above address) to reserve tickets. Groups receive 10 percent discount off box-office prices.

Special Information: A booth at the studio offers free tickets to TV show productions; however, some of these shows are not filmed at Universal. In addition to the Backlot tram tour, other Universal Studios' movie-related attractions include "Jurassic Park—The Ride," "Waterworld—A Live Sea War Spectacular," "Back to the Future—The Ride," "The E. T. Adventure," "Backdraft," and "The Wild, Wild, Wild West Stunt Show"; a new attraction is added each year.

Gift Shop: Many gift shops sell posters, videos, clothes, jewelry, mugs, and toys, with logos.

Directions: Located between Hollywood and the San Fernando Valley just off the Hollywood (101) Frwy., Universal Studios is accessible from either the Universal Center Dr. or Lankershim Blvd. exits. Follow "Universal Studios" signs and marquee to park.

Nearby Attractions: Paramount Pictures, NBC Studios, and Warner Bros. Studios tours (see pages 31, 29, and 35); Audiences Unlimited offers free tickets for taped TV shows (call 818-506-0067).

Warner Bros. Studios   *movies and television shows*

4000 Warner Boulevard
Burbank, CA 91522
(818) 954-1744

By some estimates, entertainment is the United States' second-largest export and pumps $50 billion into the U.S. economy. Begun in 1918, when films were silent, today Warner Bros. displays the latest technological advances in filmmaking.

The Warner Bros. tour is different from any other studio tour in California. Here, you will take an exclusive VIP tour designed for small groups seriously interested in the inner workings of a major studio. Because this is a VIP tour, production schedules are checked every morning to ensure that visitors see the most action possible. Some of the biggest stars, both human and animated, have worked at Warner Bros.—since this is a busy studio, don't be surprised if you see one of them walk by!

You will travel by electric cart to a variety of television and movie sets. Since these sets change with each new film, you may find yourself under a blazing sun in the Sahara, in romantic moonlight on Paris' Left Bank, or on an exotic, narrow avenue in crowded old Shanghai, all while actual movies or TV shows are being filmed.

Your guide may take you into the extensive Prop Shop and explain, "No, it's not a garage sale or fire sale, it's the Prop Shop." Or you may visit the impressive Wardrobe Department (with one of the world's largest costume collections) or the Mill (where sets are created). You may explore exterior sets like Laramie Street, used in a number of Warner Bros. Westerns, and French Street, where many scenes from *Casablanca* were filmed. Discover that these exterior sets are basically shells with open backs. At the Sound Facilities, you may catch a symphony orchestra recording a movie's theme song, actors redoing dialogue that couldn't be properly recorded on the set, or technicians creating sound effects.

Opened in 1996, the Warner Bros. Museum features costumes, props, animation cels, and film clips. See the black-and-white hats from *My Fair Lady*, original

correspondence about Humphrey Bogart, and candid shots of Errol Flynn. Stand between Bugs Bunny and Daffy Duck in a human-scale animation cel to see how you would look in cartoons.

Cost: $29 per person ($2 AAA discount).
Freebies: A VIP tour brochure
Video Shown: 10-minute video shows highlights from Warner Bros. films since the first talking film, *The Jazz Singer,* in 1927.
Reservations Needed: No, but recommended
Days and Hours: Mon–Fri 9:00 AM–3:00 PM, every ½ hour. Tour schedule can vary. During summer, some holiday tours can be specially arranged.
Plan to Stay: 2¼ hours for video, museum, and tour, plus time for gift shop.
Minimum Age: 10
Disabled Access: Yes
Group Requirements: Electric cart capacity is 12 people. Groups larger than 12 take walking tour of 110-acre lot. Call in advance for reservations. $7 discount per person for groups larger than 20 people.
Special Information: Wear comfortable walking shoes. Limited photography.
Gift Shop: Sells T-shirts, pins, and hats with W.B. logo. Open Mon–Fri 9:30 AM–4:00 PM.
Directions: From San Fernando Valley, take 101/134 Frwy. (Ventura Frwy.) East to Pass Ave exit. Turn right onto Pass Ave. Turn left onto Riverside Dr. Turn right onto Hollywood Way; the Hollywood Way gate (Gate 4) is 1 block down the street. From Hollywood, take 101 Frwy. (Hollywood Frwy.) North. Take the Barham Blvd. exit. Turn right onto Barham Blvd., and when you cross the Los Angeles River, Barham becomes Olive Ave. The studio is on your right. Stay on Olive Ave. as it curves around the studio, until you reach Hollywood Way. Turn right into the studio and park at VIP tour center.
Nearby Attractions: NBC Studios, Paramount Pictures, and Universal Studios tours (see pages 29, 31, and 34).

Celestial Seasonings   ～ *tea*
4600 Sleepytime Drive
Boulder, CO 80301-3292
(303) 581-1202

At the corner of Sleepytime Drive and Zinger Street, named after their two best-selling teas, lies the home of Celestial Seasonings. Since it began in 1969 with Mo's 36, president Mo Siegel's own herbal tea blend, Celestial Seasonings has become the largest U.S. herbal tea manufacturer—1.2 billion cups of tea per year. This tour offers much more than a standard factory floor tour. You also learn about the company's marketing approach and get your sinuses cleared while visiting the Peppermint Room.

After an enthusiastic introduction by your guide in the countrified welcoming area (be sure to hug the cuddly, 6-foot Sleepytime Bear), you may participate in a consumer test. Next to the lobby is a gallery showing the original paintings for the tea box designs. The tour then continues to the marketing area.

The storage and production areas are a maze of pallets stacked with burlap bags of herbs. In a mini botany lesson, learn that black tea comes from the *camelia sinensis* tea plant and herbal "tea," from a variety of plants and herbs. To prevent its absorbing other flavors, the black teas are isolated in their own rooms, in wooden crates stenciled with their country of origin. As the tour guide raises the metal door allowing you to enter the world of mint, you will be bombarded with intense peppermint and spearmint aromas.

On the main production floor, rock 'n' roll music plays over the roar of the machines. Here you'll see how tea gets into those little bags and brightly printed boxes. Package-forming machines simultaneously fold recycled cardboard and insert liners. Look for the big machines in the center of the production floor with wheels of porous, coffee filter–like paper and a hopper on top. As the continuous stream of tea drops between the merging top and bottom paper layers, the paper is heat-sealed to form the bags. Groups of 24 bags are then inserted into boxes. When the open boxes roll past you on the conveyor belt, take a peek in at your freshly formed favorite flavors.

Cost: Free
Freebies: Samples of any or all flavors in the Tea Shop & Emporium.
Video Shown: No
Reservations Needed: No, except for groups of 8 or more people.
Days and Hours: Hourly tours Mon–Sat 10:00 AM–3:00 PM and Sun 11:00 AM–3:00 PM. Closed holidays.
Plan to Stay: 45 minutes for tour, plus time in Tea Shop & Emporium, Celestial Café, and herb garden.
Minimum Age: 5, for factory floor.
Disabled Access: Yes
Group Requirements: Groups of 8 or more people should call (303-581-1317) 1 month in advance for reservations. Groups larger than 20 will be divided into smaller groups.
Special Information: No photography. Flat shoes recommended. For busy summer tour season, arrive well in advance of desired tour time. Breakfast and lunch available at the Celestial Café.
Gift Shop: Tea Shop & Emporium sells all Celestial Seasonings teas and many logoed items, including mugs and magnets with tea-box designs, Sleepytime Teddy Bear T-shirts, hats, and aprons. Available items range from inexpensive sample tea packets to more expensive sweatshirts and teapots. Bargain boxes of teas. Catalog available from (800) 2000-TEA. Open Mon–Fri 9:00 AM–6:00 PM, Sat 9:00 AM–5:00 PM, Sun 11:00 AM–4:00 PM. Closed holidays.
Directions: From Denver, take I-25 North to U.S. 36 West. Take Hwy. 157 (Foothills Pkwy.) North, which becomes Hwy. 119 heading northeast. Turn right onto Jay Rd. Turn left onto Spine Rd., then turn left onto Sleepytime Dr. From Boulder, travel northeast on Hwy. 119 (Longmont Diagonal) and follow directions above.
Nearby Attractions: Leanin' Tree Museum of Western Art; Boulder's attractions, including Pearl Street outdoor mall and hiking in the Rockies, are about 15 minutes away.

Coors ⟷ *beer*

12th and Ford Streets
Golden, CO 80401
(303) 277-BEER

The world's largest single-site brewery sits at the base of the Colorado Rockies between two "tabletop" mountains. In addition to the distinctly nonindustrial setting, the brewery tour has other memorable sights. The "Coors Copper Kitchen" brewhouse observation area is bordered on two sides by 50 handmade copper kettles, each the size of an above-ground swimming pool. Each kettle's sides are white ceramic tile, while its top is a dome of shiny copper with a long, narrow, copper neck. The kettles have assigned roles in the brewing process, which your guide will gladly explain.

Founded in 1873, Coors claims it is the only brewer in the U.S. to do most of its malting on-site. Before barley can be used in the brewing process, its starch must be converted into malt. The barley steeps in two-story-deep stainless-steel tanks, which prepares it for growth. Next, the barley is spread out on long screens called "germination beds." After the seeds sprout, the barley is roasted for 14 hours in immense kilns, then aged and milled.

The stillness of the malting process contrasts with the speedy aluminum-can packaging machine area. Thousands of cans converge here every minute and then roll by in six-, 12-, and 24-pack cartons.

Cost: Free

Freebies: 3 beer samples in Coor's hospitality lounge for visitors age 21 or older, with picture ID. Serves most Coors brands and assorted soft drinks.

Videos Shown: Peter Coors' welcome message, shown at tour entrance area. Another video shows can and bottle manufacturing, filling, packaging, shipping, and distributing.

Reservations Needed: No, except for groups of 20 or more people.

Days and Hours: Mon–Sat 10:00 AM–4:00 PM. Closed holidays. Call for schedule around holidays.

Plan to Stay: 30 minutes for brewery tour, plus time for beer sampling, gift shop, and

shuttle-bus tour from Coors parking lot through Historic Golden. Coors grounds also have interesting features, including a 16-foot-high, 13-foot-wide original copper brew kettle used in the 1880s. (It stands at the main entrance.) A veterans' memorial salutes the "Defenders of Freedom."

Minimum Age: Under 18 must be accompanied by adult.

Disabled Access: Yes, an alternative route is available.

Group Requirements: Groups of more than 20 people should make reservations 1 week in advance (call 303-277-2552). Coors facilities are available for special events and meetings call 303-277-3709.

Special Information: For sign-language tours call (303) 277-6363. Foreign language, TTY, and special needs tours are available (call 303-277-2552). Tours also offered at Coors' Memphis, TN, brewery (call 901-368-BEER).

Gift Shop: Coors & Co. sells a wide range of logoed clothes and beer paraphernalia, including mugs, glasses, and tap handles. Look for the popular blinking bottlecap buttons and a variety of Coors pins. Open Mon–Sat 10:00 AM–5:00 PM. Closed holidays.

Directions: From Denver, take I-70 West to Hwy. 58 West to Golden. Exit at Washington Ave. and turn left on Washington, then left onto 13th St. to Ford St. for visitors' parking. You're in Golden when you see the archway over the main street ("Howdy, Folks! WELCOME TO GOLDEN—Where the West Lives!") and smell the malted barley. Parking-lot shuttle takes you on brief tour around Golden and then to brewery.

Nearby Attractions: Hakushika Sake tour (call 303-279-7253); Colorado Railroad Museum; Foothills Art Center; Buffalo Bill Memorial Museum and Grave; Rocky Mountain Quilt Museum; Golden Pioneer Museum; Heritage Square Village.

Current ➝ *cards, wrapping paper, and catalog*

1005 East Woodmen Road
Colorado Springs, CO 80920
(719) 531-2535

Current, much like a card shop in a catalog, started in 1950 as a way to sell Post-A-Notes to churches by mail. Now Current's catalog line now includes greeting cards, stationery, gift wrap and gift items, calendars, cookbooks, and home accessories. The largest direct-mail marketer of value-priced quality "social expression" paper and gift products in the U.S., Current produces 55 percent of its 2,500 items in-house.

You'll get a thorough tour of Current's main complex, which houses the corporate offices, art department, manufacturing, and shipping and distribution center. With the Rocky Mountains in the background, you'll see keyers opening mail-order envelopes and speedily keying in as many as 30,000 orders per day. In cubicles, merchandisers plan and develop new products. Boards in the technical design area show the steps that transform original artwork into final production samples, including original illustrations redrawn and color-separated on computer.

More movement takes place in the production area. Watch a massive roll of gift wrap, equivalent to 42,000 individual rolls, unwrap itself and roll around individual cardboard tubes. Wound with the brightly colored wrap, the tubes receive a shrink-wrapped outer layer before rolling down a conveyor belt into a shipping box. In the personalized area, workers hand-paint names on mugs, lunch boxes, Christmas ornaments, rulers, and refrigerator magnets. As you walk around the cavernous production floor, you can't help but notice the maze of conveyor belts and overhead pipes.

In the packing area, the case erector quickly folds flat cardboard into boxes, which move along the 3-mile-long "pick lines" that loop around this section of the warehouse. Workers called "pickers" reach into the bins of their three-tiered stations and pick merchandise to fill customer orders. Once orders are packed, they proceed to the center conveyor for quality control inspection. They pass under a huge royal-blue funnel from which padding fills the boxes for safe shipping.

Cost: Free

Freebies: Small gift bag and Current catalog.

Video Shown: 15-minute video covering design to printing to shipping of gift wrap and greeting cards.

Reservations Needed: Preferred for individuals, required for groups over 4 people.

Days and Hours: Tue and Thur 10:00 AM and 2:00 PM. Closed holidays. Manufacturing and order fulfillment are busiest from September to February. During the summer, these areas may not be working.

Plan to Stay: Usually 45 minutes–1 hour, plus time in catalog store.

Minimum Age: Under 18 with signed consent.

Disabled Access: Yes

Group Requirements: Groups over 4 people should call 1 day in advance to make reservations. No minimum group size. Groups over 8 people will be split into smaller groups.

Special Information: No photography. You'll see more production during 10:00 AM tour. Wear comfortable shoes for the 2 to 3 miles of walking.

Catalog Store: Sells "social expression" products such as gifts, gift wrap and ribbon, and greeting and note cards. Carries all first-quality items featured in Current's most recent catalog at the lowest catalog prices. Bargain box includes discount cards. Open Mon–Sat 9:30 AM–5:00 PM. Closed holidays. Catalog available at (800) 525-7170. Factory outlet nearby.

Directions: From Denver, take I-25 South. Pass North Academy Blvd. Take Woodmen Rd. exit. Make left onto Woodmen Rd. Current is on your right.

Nearby Attractions: Van Briggle Art Pottery tour (see page 43); Simpich doll factory tour (see page 40); Pike's Peak; Garden of the Gods; White House Ranch; The Broadmoor; Air Force Academy; Manitou Springs.

Michael Ricker Pewter ～ *pewter sculptures*

2050 Big Thompson
Highway 34 East
Estes Park, CO 80517
(970) 586-2030 / (800) 373-9837

What do former President Gerald Ford, golf great Arnold Palmer, and basketball star Magic Johnson have in common? All have been featured in pewter sculptures by Michael Ricker. Ricker has not only created sculptures of people but also designed elaborate chess sets, animals, and even corporate gifts (including a trash can for a waste-management company!).

Notice his grand pewter projects, such as America's Moments 1950's Drive-In and Park City. Your tour guide will point out the incredible details, from squirrels in the trees to a working carousel. The size is also astounding: Park City, the world's largest pewter sculpture, covers about 300 square feet. Ricker likes to think of them as three-dimensional history books, capturing a sense of American life in an earlier era.

Visitors who have made earlier reservations can tour the casting studio. After donning protective glasses, you'll leave the quiet serenity of the gift shop and walk downstairs to the controlled chaos of the studio floor. The process begins when liquid rubber is poured around an original Michael Ricker wax sculpture to form a mold. The mold is cast repeatedly using a pewter alloy brought to liquid form at 500°. These multiple castings are then used to form vulcanized rubber molds which, when spun in a centrifugal casting machine, will create up to 20 castings with each pour of molten pewter. Upon cooling, these castings are forced from the mold and separated. An artisan removes flashing (the jagged edges) and applies graphite patina and clear sealer. Some designs require welding, sanding, and adornment before being mounted on bases, packed, and shipped to galleries across the country.

Most of the sculptures are produced in limited editions, and many of the editions are sold out before production even begins. Michael Ricker tends to be a "night owl" and does most of his artistic work late into the night. However, he is often in the gift shop in the afternoons, meeting customers.

Cost: Free

Freebies: Small pewter snowflakes

Video Shown: 10-minute video about Michael and his commissioned pieces.

Reservations Needed: No, for the museum tour. Yes, for VIP tour of casting studio.

Days and Hours: Museum: Summer (Memorial Day through Labor Day): Mon–Fri 9:00 AM–9:00 PM, Sat 9:00 AM–6:00 PM, Sun 10:00 AM–6:00 PM. Winter: Mon–Sat 9:00 AM–5:00 PM, Sun 11:00 AM–5:00 PM. Closed Thanksgiving, Christmas, and New Year's. VIP Factory Tour: Mon–Fri 9:00 AM–3:00 PM. Closed Thanksgiving, New Year's, and last 2 weeks in December.

Plan to Stay: 30 minutes for the tour of the museum, plus time in gallery. VIP tour lasts 20 minutes.

Minimum Age: None for museum; 6 for VIP tour.

Disabled Access: Yes

Group Requirements: For VIP factory tour, groups should call 1 week in advance. Groups over 6 people will be split into smaller groups.

Special Information: A kiosk keeps a database of 35 galleries, the active market for Ricker sculptures. Many collectors also belong to the Michael Ricker Collector's Society, which publishes a quarterly magazine featuring Michael's newest sculptures and the latest secondary market reports.

Gallery: Carries a large assortment of Ricker's work, from large, rare figures to small gift pieces. Open same days and hours as museum.

Directions: Take I-25 to Hwy. 34 West. Travel through Loveland and up Thompson Canyon into Estes Park. Michael Ricker Pewter is the grey building on left after mouth of the canyon.

Nearby Attractions: Celestial Seasonings tea tour (see page 36); the Stanley Hotel; Rocky Mountain National Park; Estes Park.

Simpich ⟶ *dolls*
2413 West Colorado Avenue
Colorado Springs, CO 80904
(719) 636-3272

Simpich Character Dolls

The Simpich Dolls story begins like a fairy-tale: Once upon a time (that's 1952), two newlyweds on a limited budget made dolls for family Christmas gifts. Today, although they no longer work out of their home, Bob and Jan Simpich still design all Simpich character dolls themselves. Bob specializes in elves, Santas, and historic figures, while Jan prefers cloud babies, angels, and children's storybook figures.

Ideas for character dolls come from everywhere—history, religion, and even their own children and grandchildren. Bob and Jan create the originals out of a clay-like, plastic "supersculpy," which is oven-baked and sent to the casting department for an original, or "mother," mold. It may take several tries to create the perfect mother mold that captures all the facial feature details.

The "factory" thrives behind a Tudor facade and above its retail doll shop in the Old Colorado Historic District. The self-guided tour of this "Santa's workshop" takes you through the painting, sewing, and finishing steps. Astonishing attention to detail is required to paint the cheeks, mouths, eyes, and beards of these intricate miniature heads. Racks of dangling painted heads wait to join their bodies. Labeled racks, including Santas, angels, and elves, fill a long wall in the sewing room. Home workers handle many intermediary steps, such as base-wrapping each body's wire skeleton with raw cotton batting, piece-sewing petticoats and other outfit parts, and partial assembly.

The pieces magically come together in the sewing and finishing rooms. As many as a dozen outfit parts are hand-sewn onto each doll, and some even get individually designed bouquets and hats to match their costumes. In the finishing room, dolls are attached to bases and receive final accessories. You will leave with affection for the dolls and an appreciation of the four-month process from mother mold to completed doll.

Cost: Free

Freebies: Catalog and newsletter

Video Shown: No. Future video or display on casting process planned.

Reservations Needed: Only for guided group tour.

Days and Hours: Mon–Sat 10:00 AM–5:00 PM. You'll see the most production Mon–Fri. Closed holidays and Christmas through the week following New Year's.

Plan to Stay: 20–30 minutes for self-guided tour, plus time in retail store.

Minimum Age: None

Disabled Access: Doll shop, finishing, and originals are on street level. Workshop is upstairs.

Group Requirements: Groups larger than 20 people will be divided into smaller groups. Call 1 day in advance to arrange for a tour guide.

Special Information: Casting department is not on the tour.

Retail Store: Doll shop sells all Simpich character dolls, including storybook, historical, and Christmas dolls, in creative displays. Look for the glass case showing a small selection of Simpich dolls created since 1952 and newspaper articles documenting the company's growth. Open Mon–Sat 10:00 AM–5:00 PM. Closed holidays and the week following New Year's. Simpich catalog and information about the David Simpich marionettes available at above number.

Directions: From Denver, take I-25 South to Garden of the Gods exit. Turn right onto Garden of the Gods Rd. Turn left onto 30th St. Turn left onto Colorado Ave. Simpich is on your right at 24th St.

Nearby Attractions: Van Briggle Art Pottery tour (see page 43); Current Catalog Company tour (see page 38); Patsy's Candies tour (call 719-633-6777); Old Colorado Historic District shops and restaurants; Michael Garman Gallery; The Broadmoor; Cave of the Winds; Pike's Peak; Garden of the Gods.

Stephany's Chocolates

6770 West 52nd Avenue
Arvada, CO 80002
(800) 888-1522

*chocolates
and toffee*

Colorado's high altitude and low humidity are important ingredients in Stephany's award-winning Colorado Almond Toffee. Of course, butter, almonds, and sugar help, too. On this candy-maker tour, you will be allured by sweet smells, warmed by the care given each chocolate, and tempted to stick your fingers into the chocolate or toffee bowls for tastes. This is truly chocolate-lovers' heaven.

A rich toffee smell permeates the toffee area. Melted with sugar and almonds, 68-pound blocks of butter swirl around a copper fire kettle. Two workers grab the fire kettle and pour the luscious mixture onto a cooling table. One worker uses a trowel to spread the toffee to the uniform thickness marked by metal strips at the edge of the table. The worker rolls a bladed metal rolling pin over the length and width of the table, cutting the slab into small sections. The toffee solidifies quickly. Workers then break it into individual bars, which await a chocolate shower and a chopped-almond bath.

You smell the peppermint long before you reach the Denver Mint room. Here, chocolate and mint layers are poured and spread onto a wooden former bowling lane, now a table covered with brown paper. A worker pushes a bladed rolling pin to cut 1-inch squares. A roller on tracks moves beneath the brown paper to break the mints apart. From one end of the table, a worker pulls out the brown paper, and the mints fall like dominoes onto a holding tray.

Walk between the two candy enrobing machines. Notice that each and every nut or filling is individually placed by hand on the conveyor belt. After each piece receives a chocolate coating, a thin chocolate stream flows through a stringer to put a design on top. Then it's off through the refrigerated tunnel for cooling. In the chilly packing room, workers grab different chocolates from the shelves and place them into brown paper-cup liners and gift boxes. A few

strokes with the badger brush shines the chocolates and readies the gift box for shrink-wrapping or ribbons and holiday ornaments.

Cost: Free

Freebies: Taste of raspberry cream and small piece of toffee. Also, a paper hat to wear on the tour.

Video Shown: No

Reservations Needed: Yes. Families and individuals need to join scheduled group tours.

Days and Hours: Mon–Thur at 10:00 AM. Closed holidays.

Plan to Stay: 45 minutes for tour, plus time in retail store.

Minimum Age: 12, although exceptions made when with parents.

Disabled Access: Yes. While there are several steps at main entrance, the tour is on one level.

Group Requirements: Minimum group is 6 people. Groups larger than 15 people are split into smaller groups. Call at least 3 days in advance.

Special Information: Wear rubber-soled shoes—the floor can be slippery.

Retail Store: Sells various size boxes and gift baskets of Colorado Almond Toffee, Denver Mints, and assorted chocolates; also, individual candies, discounted seconds, and solid chocolate sculptures such as dinosaurs, Ferraris, and teddy bears. Open Mon–Fri 9:00 AM–5:00 PM. Catalog available at above number. Other Stephany's retail stores throughout Colorado.

Directions: From Denver Airport, take I-70 West to Wadsworth Ave. North to 52nd Ave. Turn right and proceed 3 blocks. Stephany's Chocolates is on the right.

Nearby Attractions: U.S. Mint tour (see page 42); Mile High Stadium, Coors Field, and other Denver attractions, including Denver Art Museum, Confluence Park, and Larimer Square, about 20 minutes away.

U.S. Mint   ~~~ *coins*

320 West Colfax Avenue
Denver, CO 80204
(303) 844-3582

The Denver U.S. Mint produces over 8 billion coins per year. From a glass-enclosed observation area you'll see many of the production steps. The Mint starts with pre-shaped blanks for pennies and 8,000-pound metal coils for other coins. These coils first pass through presses that punch out blanks, which are slightly larger than the finished coins. Blanks are very hard, so they are softened in a 1,400° annealing furnace.

In the coin press room, shiny blanks are converted into their familiar identities. Watch workers dump crates of blanks into the top of the machine. The coin presses are sheltered in blue huts for noise abatement. The large blue Bliss press can produce about 250 coins per minute. Its smaller, longer counterpart, the Schuler press, can produce over 700 coins per minute, with each die stamp lasting about one million strikes.

In the counting and bagging area, the enormity of the production process becomes clear. Overhead hoists dump gondolas filled with shimmering coins into vibrating hoppers on top of the counting machines. Workers standing in front of the machines use hand-held sewing machines to seal each bag once it is filled with the proper number of coins. As the tour ends, you walk through richly decorated, marble-floored hallways of the original mint building, complete with nine grand turn-of-the-century chandeliers. You will also see a machine gun nest by the stairs, the foremost means of disuading robbers in the 1930s.

Cost: Free
Freebies: Brochures in English and 4 foreign languages on the Mint's history and how coins are made.
Video Shown: No
Reservations Needed: No
Days and Hours: Mon–Fri 8:00 AM–2:45 PM, except for 9:00 AM start on Wednesdays. Tours begin at 20–30-minute intervals on a first-come, first-served basis. Call the above number for recorded information. Closed government holidays and 2 weeks at the end of September.
Plan to Stay: 40 minutes for exhibits, videos, and tour, plus time for numismatic sales room and tour waiting lines.
Minimum Age: Children under 14 must be accompanied by an adult.
Disabled Access: Yes
Group Requirements: Bus groups should make advance reservations by letter addressed to the Public Affairs Division. Summer bus tours should be booked by May.
Special Information: No photography. Expect lines to enter the building during summer, so arrive early in the day to ensure a tour. Tours available at U.S. Mint in Philadelphia, PA (see page 275).
Sales Room: Sells proof and commemorative sets, medals produced by U.S. Mint, and other numismatic items. Has an authentic 1946 press for visitors to stamp their own Denver Mint Souvenir Medals. Store is on Delaware Street, just south of Colfax. Open same hours as tour. Closed government holidays. Catalog information at (202) 283-2646.
Directions: Located in downtown Denver, between Delaware and Cherokee Sts. From I-25, take exit for downtown Denver and follow signs to Denver Mint. Look for the building with Gothic Renaissance architecture. Park on the street or in a downtown lot.
Nearby Attractions: Stephany's Chocolates tour (see page 41); downtown Denver attractions, including the Denver Art Museum, Colorado History Museum, and State Capitol.

Van Briggle ～ *pottery*

600 South 21st Street
Colorado Springs, CO 80904
(719) 633-7729

The original designs for Van Briggle Art Pottery date back to 1899. Van Briggle's "Despondency," a vase with a figure of a despondent man molded around the rim, was first exhibited in Paris in 1900, where it won first place. A reproduction can be viewed in the Van Briggle masterpiece reproduction area. In addition to winning many awards, Artus Van Briggle reproduced a creamy, dull glaze known as "dead" matte glaze, which had been used by fourteenth-century Chinese. A tour of the company gives you a sense of the man and of his wife's continuation of his legacy, and an understanding of the process of making art pottery.

At the beginning of the guided portion of your tour, a potter demonstrates throwing pottery on an original early-1900s Van Briggle kick wheel. Next you move into the casting department, where rows of white chalky plaster molds are used to duplicate sculptured and wheel-thrown pieces. Liquid clay, or "slip," is poured into these molds. As the slip conforms to the exact design of the mold, the mold absorbs moisture from the slip. The longer the slip stays in the mold, the thicker the piece becomes. Excess slip is poured from the mold, leaving a hollow clay piece that is removed by hand.

The balance of your tour is self-guided, allowing you to spend as much time as you want viewing different processes and reviewing the explanatory displays, tape, and historical photographs. In the etching department, watch workers use damp sponges, carving instruments, and small turntables to smooth and refine the patterns of the unfired clay pieces called "greenware." Pottery stacked on shelves awaits one of the two kiln firings required to finish a piece. Between the first (or "bisque") firing and the second, glaze is applied to add color. In front of the kilns, displays show the piece's progression from a mold to the finished work.

Follow the curved shape of the building, past one of the largest wheel-thrown vases,

to the historical photographs of Artus Van Briggle and early studios. Additional photographs show the transformation of the 1899 Colorado Midland Railroad roundhouse, where trains once chugged under the building's archways, to the current home of Van Briggle Art Pottery.

Cost: Free
Freebies: No
Video Shown: No
Reservations Needed: No, except for groups larger than 20 people.
Days and Hours: Mon–Sat 8:00 AM–4:30 PM (opens at 8:30 on Saturdays). Limited production on Saturday. Closed Thanksgiving, Christmas, and New Year's.
Plan to Stay: 20 minutes for partially self-guided tour, plus time in showroom.
Minimum Age: None
Disabled Access: Yes
Group Requirements: Groups larger than 20 people should call 1 day in advance.
Showroom: Sells Art Nouveau decorative pottery and lamps with pottery bases and shades decorated with genuine butterfly wings, grasses, and flowers. Also sells Van Briggle pottery collectors' books. Open Mon–Sat 8:00 AM–5:00 PM (8:30 AM on Saturdays) and Sun 1:00 PM–5:00 PM (year round but best to call ahead). Catalog available from (800) 847-6341.
Directions: From Denver, take I-25 South to Exit 141. Follow U.S. 24 West to 21st St. You're there when you see the curved shape and large tan bricks of this former railroad roundhouse building, now on the National Registry of Historic Places. From Pueblo, take I-25 North to Exit 141. Follow the directions above.
Nearby Attractions: Current Catalog Company and Simpich Character Dolls tours (see pages 38 and 40); Patsy's Candies tour (call 719-633-6777); Pioneer's Museum; Ghost Town; The Broadmoor; Cave of the Winds; Pike's Peak; Garden of the Gods; Old Colorado City.

Mystic Color Lab *film developing*

Mason's Island Road
Mystic, CT 06355-9987
(800) 367-6061

More than 90 percent of U.S. households own cameras, accounting for over 847 million rolls of film per year. Mystic Color Lab, started in 1969, first contracted out its film processing before moving into the mail-order end of the business. Mystic Color Lab processes three million rolls of film per year, making it the third-largest mail-order film processor in the U.S.

Rolls of film wake up at 5:00 AM, as they are delivered in big canvas pouches from the post office. Because of Mystic's guarantee to return customers' prints within 24 hours of receipt, a given day's workload depends on the weight of these canvas pouches. Each pouch holds up to 500 rolls of film. The number of rolls received each morning determines how long production will take that day. As you might expect, film developing is tied to the travel industry and holiday seasons, with peak demand coming immediately after Christmas and during the summer.

The rolls are manually sorted by film size, desired picture size, and requested finish (matte or glossy). A machine opens individual mailer bags, scans in customer information such as account number and address (a keypuncher assigns this information for new customers), and processes payment. Another machine cracks open and flattens the metal case surrounding each roll of film. The roll is assigned a computer number, which follows it through the entire process, and then is spliced together with 59 other rolls to form a large reel of film.

Once negatives are developed in the darkroom, new state-of-the-art Agfa machines develop up to 18,000 prints per hour. Each of the rapid ticking sounds represents an exposure being made onto paper. The machines record the number of photos printed per customer, for invoicing purposes. Another machine prints the customer order number and picture number on the back of the photo, to facilitate reprint ordering.

You will be amazed to see streams of photos emerge from the automatic printing room. Inspectors, with eyes that are not only trained but also fast, place stickers on flawed photos as they speed by. Negatives are mated with their prints, invoice, and reorder mailer, and manually stuffed into an envelope, which is hand-sorted by zip code and returned to the post office for a good night's rest before its journey back to the customer.

Cost: Free
Freebies: No
Video Shown: No
Reservations Needed: Helpful but not necessary for individuals. Groups, see below.
Days and Hours: Mon–Fri 11:00 AM–3:00 PM. Closed holidays.
Plan to Stay: 30 minutes
Minimum Age: None
Disabled Access: Yes
Group Requirements: Maximum group size is 30 people. Call at least 1 day in advance for reservations.
Special Information: Can arrange custom tours to your interest. No photography.
Factory Store: Sells film, cameras, photo albums, and frames. Offers drop-off and pickup service. Open Mon–Fri 9:30 AM–5:30 PM. Closed holidays. Catalog available.
Directions: Take I-95 to Mystic Seaport exit. Turn right onto Rt. 27 and left onto Rt. 1. Turn right on Mason's Island Rd. and right onto Harry Austin Dr.
Nearby Attractions: Hood Ice Cream tour for groups of 10 or more in Suffield (call 860-623-4435); ESPN tour in New Britain, space very limited (call 860-585-2000); Branford Craft Village at Bittersweet Farm, watch artists at work (call 203-488-4689); New England Carousel Museum, watch carousel carving and restoration in Bristol (call 860-585-5411); Warren Wool mill tour 1 hour away in Stafford Springs (call 860-684-2766); Comstock, Ferre Seeds tour in Westerfield (call 860-571-6590); Mystic Seaport; Mystic Aquarium; U.S.S. *Nautilus*; Mashantucket Pequot Indian Casino; Stonington Vineyards; Barnun Museum about 1½ hours away in Bridgeport.

Nanticoke Homes ⟿ *manufactured housing*

Route 13 South
Greenwood, DE 19950
(302) 349-4561 / (800) 777-4561

While everyone has seen houses slowly being constructed outdoors for months, this company does it on an assembly line in, basically, six days. Since 1971, Nanticoke has been an industry leader in building homes off-site and indoors in a controlled environment. The custom-designed houses, which can be as big as mansions, are transported from the factory in modules to the homesite and carefully positioned on the foundation, then the roof is raised.

This tour shows you what happens on each of those six days, with each station on the production line equaling one day. All the tools, sounds, and smells of a standard construction site are there: air guns, drills, saws, hammers, paints, and glues. With houses in different stages of construction, you can usually see all the days' work in your one-hour visit. On the first day, the stick-built construction begins. The frame is constructed, windows are inserted, and the exterior and interior walls, which are stapled and glued, come together. At day two, which is only a few yards away, workers install the basic piping and electrical wiring and start building the roof and putting in the insulation.

Day three shows the drywall installation, with workers spackling the nails and seams, and roof-shingling. On day four, the inside of the house is painted and wallpapered, and the vinyl flooring installed. The sinks and toilets, lighting, molding, and cabinets go in on day five. On the final day the house's trim is painted or varnished, the building is boarded up, and all systems are tested.

Now the house, which is 85 percent complete when it comes off the assembly line, needs a homesite. To help transport the house, the roof is built with a hinged system that allows the two sides of the roof to be lowered and raised like a matchbook cover. Notice how one minute the roof is on an angle, and the next it is flat. Specially designed house-carriers with custom hydraulic systems carefully load the sections

for delivery. If you could follow the trucks to the homesite, you'd see that cranes take about four hours to set a typical house on its foundation.

Cost: Free

Freebies: Refrigerator magnets, brochures

Video Shown: 6-minute video, "Built with Pride by People Who Care."

Reservations Needed: No, except for groups over 10 people.

Days and Hours: Mon–Fri 8:00–11:00 AM and 1:00–3:00 PM, on the hour. Tour at 4:00 PM for buyers of homes currently in production. Sat 9:00 AM–2:00 PM, but no production.

Plan to Stay: 1 hour for tour and video.

Minimum Age: 5

Disabled Access: Yes

Group Requirements: Groups over 10 people should call 1 week in advance. No maximum group size.

Special Information: No photography allowed of the machines used or production process, but photos of finished houses and exteriors are OK. Optional tour of cabinet and molding shop (time permitting).

Gift Shop: No

Directions: From Wilmington, take U.S. 13 South. When 23 miles south of Dover, look for big gold sign with the blue Nanticoke lettering. From Baltimore/Washington, D.C., area, cross Bay Bridge to U.S. 50 East. Turn left onto U.S. 404 East. Take U.S. 404 to MD 16 East to DE 16 East. Turn left on U.S. 13 North in Greenwood. When you see sign, turn left at highway crossover in front of gate (about 1 mile).

Nearby Attractions: Delaware's Rehoboth and Lewes beaches and outlets about 35 minutes away. Cape May–Lewes Ferry is 45 minutes away.

Bureau of Engraving and Printing ~ *money*

14th and C Streets, S.W.
Washington, D.C. 20228
(202) 874-3188

After entering the mammoth gray federal building that houses this bureau, you'll be showered with a wealth of information in display cases and videos about our nation's paper currency and other items, such as U.S. postage stamps. From a narrow, glass-walled, overhead walkway, the guided tour allows you to watch several steps in paper currency production. In the first step, not included on the tour, engravers hand-cut the currency design into soft steel. This engraving, used to create the master die and plate, begins the unique "intaglio" printing process that deters counterfeiting.

The printing itself is mesmerizing. Sheets of money, each with 32 bills in a four-by-eight pattern, rhythmically spin off the press at 8,000 sheets per hour. Stacks of money, called "skids," are everywhere. You'll wonder how the workers appear to treat their jobs with such detached calm. After inspections, overprinting of the serial number and Treasury seal, and cutting, the final product is a "brick" of 4,000 notes sent to the Federal Reserve Districts for local distribution.

The Bureau opened tours of the stamp production area in late 1994, which was also the 100th year that the Bureau has been producing U.S. postage stamps. Here you will see the web-fed process of making U.S. postage stamps.

Cost: Free
Freebies: Unfortunately, no money! "Visitors Guide" and informational brochures from the gallery and the Visitors Center.
Videos Shown: A short video, "The Buck Starts Here," explains the history of paper currency in the U.S. While you wait in line, a 20-minute overhead video quiz challenges your trivia knowledge of currency and stamps.
Reservations Needed: No
Days and Hours: During peak season (April–September): Mon–Fri 9:00 AM–2:00 PM. June through August: evening tours also, Mon–Fri 5:00 PM–7:30 PM. Tours every 10 minutes. Tickets marked with a designated time

must be obtained at the booth on Raoul Wallenberg Place (formerly 15th St.). Tickets may be gone by 11:00 AM, so get in line early (booth opens at 8:00 AM). Also can obtain tickets for tours later in same week. Booth opens at 3:30 PM for evening tours. During non-peak season (October–March): Mon–Fri 9:00 AM–2:00 PM. Line forms on the 14th St. side of the building for the tour. Congressional VIP tours Mon–Fri. 8:00 AM only. Peak season (June–August) also offers evening congressional VIP tour at 4:00 PM. Ask your congressperson about tickets for this tour. Closed federal holidays and week between Christmas and New Year's.
Plan to Stay: 45 minutes, including displays, videos, and tour, plus time for the visitors center gift shop, and waiting time.
Minimum Age: None
Disabled Access: Yes. Upon request, accommodations for the hearing-, sight-, and physically impaired.
Group Requirements: Maximum group size is 60 people.
Special Information: Upon request, group tours in French, German, Japanese, Spanish, and Hebrew.
Gift Shop: Sells a variety of items relating to paper money, including uncut sheets of new money and bags of shredded currency. There are videos on engraving, stamp production, and the identification of mutilated currency. Open Mon–Fri 8:30 AM–3:30 PM. Located on the opposite side of the building from the tour entrance.
Directions: Located immediately southwest of the Washington Monument grounds and west of Jefferson Memorial. Parking is nearly impossible to find in this area. Take the Metro (subway) blue line/orange line to the Smithsonian stop and walk out the Independence Ave. exit. Turn left on 14th St. or Raoul Wallenberg Pl., depending on where you need to obtain tickets.
Nearby Attractions: United States Holocaust Memorial Museum; Washington Monument; Jefferson Memorial; Smithsonian Institute.

Correct Craft   *Ski Nautiques water-ski boats*

6100 South Orange Avenue
Orlando, FL 32809
(407) 855-4141

After seeing the water-ski extravaganza at nearby Sea World in Orlando, you may wonder how Ski Nautiques, their official ski towboats, are made. A tour of Ski Nautique manufacturer Correct Craft shows you in one hour the two-week process of building the premier inboard water-ski towboat. Correct Craft, started in 1925 by W. C. Meloon, is now a third-generation family business.

A short van ride from the corporate offices brings you to the open-air factory. Starting with a mold, fiberglass boats are actually built from the outside in. To create the shiny, colorful stripes of the hull's exterior, the interior surface of the mold is sprayed in sections with gelcoat. Then workers wearing floor-length aprons and safety gear use spray guns resembling oversized dentist-drill arms to apply the initial "skin coat" of fiberglass. A mixture of fiberglass and epoxy resin shoots out of the gun, looking like cotton candy when it hits the mold. Next, the entire inside of the mold is coated with cloth-like fiberglass sheets to form a solid unit. Workers use hand-rollers to smooth the hull's surface and inhibit the development of air pockets.

In another area, you can touch a smooth hull or deck just hoisted out of its mold. To reduce vibration and noise, ISODAMP CN (used by the Navy), is put on the inside of the hull's walls and the floor. In the engine area, a carousel-like crane swings around to lower an engine onto its frame. After the engine is bolted into place, workers install the dashboard, carpeting, interior trim, and seating. Each boat is tested under actual running conditions for at least 30 minutes in a nearby lake before decorative decals and graphics are applied. The water-skiers who go on this tour will immediately want to take one of the boats out for a pull.

Cost: Free
Freebies: Choice of small item such as logoed water bottle or lapel pin.
Video Shown: Upon request, a detailed 15-minute video on company history and

production process is shown in the waiting area.
Reservations Needed: Yes
Days and Hours: Mon–Fri 10:00 AM and 2:00 PM. Closed 2 weeks around Christmas and 2 weeks in July. Call for specific dates of shutdowns.
Plan to Stay: 1 hour
Minimum Age: 10
Disabled Access: Yes
Group Requirements: Groups should call ahead. Large groups will be split into groups of 10–15 people.
Special Information: You'll see more production on the morning tour. Even though it's an open-air facility, you'll get a strong resin smell in the area where the fiberglass is applied. Watch out for forklifts moving through the maze of hulls and decks in various stages of production. Look for a 1934 wooden replica of a Correct Craft displayed in the waiting area.
Gift Shop: Fashion Nautique carries a wide array of Correct Craft clothing and accessories. Open Mon–Fri 9:00 AM–4:00 PM.
Directions: From I-4 West, turn left onto Michigan, right onto Orange Ave. Company offices are on right. From I-4 East, take Kaley exit, head east, then turn right onto Orange.
Nearby Attractions: Magic of Disney Animation Studios and Nickelodeon Studios tours (see pages 51 and 52); Regal Marine (call 800-US-REGAL); Sea World; Wet 'n' Wild. In Sarasota, on Florida's west coast, Wellcraft boat manufacturer gives tours (call 941-753-7811).

E-One ⟶ *fire trucks*
1601 S.W. 37th Avenue
Ocala, FL 34478
(352) 861-3524

Whether you've wanted to be a firefighter since childhood or you've just watched the trucks careen around street corners, this will give you a new appreciation for fire trucks. In less than 20 years, Emergency-One has become one of the world's leading manufacturers of emergency vehicles, building fire trucks, airport crash and fire rescue vehicles, and ambulances.

They make custom fire trucks according to the customer's specific requirements, such as community water sources and building heights. Two- to four-person teams work on the trucks in various stages of production. As you proceed through the factory floor tour, notice the different fire truck varieties (aerial and pumper), and the many cab, body, and chassis designs.

In the body plant, power shears resemble guillotines as they chop diamond-patterned aluminum sheets. See sparks fly as a face-shielded worker welds the body frame together. Once the body is structurally sound, sanders and grinders transform it into a bright, shiny fire engine. In the paint shop you'll notice that there is no one official "fire-engine red" color. We've heard there are 1,200 different shades of fire-engine red! (Be sure to ask your tour guide why fire engines are red and for additional anecdotes.)

In the assembly area, two rows of black chassis patiently await their bodies and other accessories, such as pumps and electrical wiring. At the end of the line, a crane lowers a freshly painted custom cab onto its chassis. Check the shipper ID label on the dashboard window or cab—some fire-fighting vehicles are headed for Small Town, U.S.A., others to some exotic South Pacific island. In the final rigging area, you'll want to climb up into a fire-engine cab, sit in the thickly padded seats, touch the sophisticated control panel, and turn the steering wheel, pretending you're a firefighter.

Cost: Adults, $6; seniors, $4; children 12 and under, free. Firefighters and their immediate families, free.
Freebies: Logoed hat
Video Shown: No
Reservations Needed: No, except for groups larger than 10 people.
Days and Hours: Mon–Fri 8:00 AM–3:00 PM. Closed holidays and week between Christmas and New Year's.
Plan to Stay: 1 hour, plus time for the gift shop.
Minimum Age: 6. Children under 6 receive a 20-minute abbreviated tour of the vehicle delivery center.
Disabled Access: Yes, call ahead.
Group Requirements: Group size limited to 25 people per tour guide. Call at least 1 week in advance.
Special Information: See more production before 2:00 PM. Since tours are handled on a drop-in basis, you may have to wait until the guide returns to begin your tour. If there are 5 or fewer people on the tour, you'll ride around in a golf cart. Otherwise, you'll walk the tour route, so wear comfortable shoes. Occasionally, you may hear the sound of a fire-truck siren. Don't worry, it's just a test.
Gift Shop: The Fire Locker Shop sells T-shirts, clothes, hats, mugs, bags, and even ceramic Dalmatians, Christmas ornaments, and scale models of fire trucks, all with the E-One logo. Open Mon–Fri 8:00 AM–5:00 PM. Catalog available from (800) 788-3726 or (352) 237-1122.
Directions: From the Florida Tpk., take I-75 North to Exit 69 (the second Ocala exit). You can see the plant on the right from I-75. Go right at exit. Turn right at S.W. 33rd Ave., then right at S.W. 7th. Follow service road that cuts back to left. The Welcome Center is the first building on the left.
Nearby Attractions: Silver Springs Attractions; Wild Waters; Don Garlits' Drag Racing Museum.

Hoffman's ~ *chocolates*

5190 Lake Worth Road
Greenacres City, FL 33463
(561) 967-2213 / (888) 281-8800

Begun in 1975, when Paul Hoffman and Theresa Hoffman Daly paid $1,400 at an auction for an existing candy shop, this family-operated company now makes 200,000 pounds of candy per year. In this Tudor-style chocoholics' heaven, viewing windows at the right side of the store overlook the kitchen.

Directly in front of the observation window, the enrobing machine coats candy centers with an avalanche of chocolate. You may be lucky enough to watch peanut brittle or "jitterbugs" being made. Two workers pour a 300° mixture of butter, sugar, and almonds from a copper kettle onto a marble slab. They spread the mixture with metal spatulas, cut it in half with a pizza cutter, and flip it over. Then, with a comb-like spatula, they spread out the edges to "stretch" the peanut brittle.

Further back in the kitchen, butter cream centers proceed on a wire belt to another enrober. A worker waits for the chocolates to emerge, then hand-marks the type of center (for example, "R" for raspberry). After watching these candies being made, you'll be ready to sample some, especially their famous chocolate-covered pretzels.

You can walk off these extra calories in Hoffman's ¾-acre botanical gardens. Stroll among exotic and rare plants, a rainforest area, a miniature cacao plantation, and a fruit-salad section with pineapple, banana, and orange trees.

Every holiday season the garden is transformed into Hoffman's Holiday Wonderland, sparkling with more than 100,000 lights. It includes a giant gingerbread house, animated carolers, a custom-made Menorah, a 15-foot Christmas tree, a life-size Nativity Scene, and Santa's North Pole Village.

Another garden highlight is the Candyland Railroad, a G-scale model community with more than 500 feet of track. Railcars make stops at Coconut Cream Cottage, Rocky Candy Mine, and Pecan Truffle Pond. The formal garden features topiaries shaped like a golfer, unicorn, and reindeer.

Cost: Free

Freebies: Sample chocolates

Video Shown: 13-minute video about chocolate-making, the botanical gardens, and Candyland Railroad.

Reservations Needed: No, except for groups larger than 15 people.

Days and Hours: Mon–Fri 9:00 AM–4:00 PM. Closed Thanksgiving, Christmas, New Year's, and Easter.

Plan to Stay: 25 minutes for self-guided viewing through observation window and video, plus time for gardens, trains, and Chocolate Shoppe.

Minimum Age: None

Disabled Access: Yes

Group Requirements: Groups larger than 15 people should call 1 week in advance to arrange a customized presentation. Groups over 40 people will be split into smaller groups. No maximum group size.

Special Information: Best time to see production is from August 15 to Easter. During summer, call ahead for production schedule.

Retail Store: Chocolate Shoppe sells Hoffman's 80 varieties of chocolates. Open Mon–Sat 9:00 AM–6:00 PM, Sun 12:00 PM–6:00 PM, and daily 9:00 AM–9:00 PM, the Saturday before Thanksgiving to December 31. Closed Thanksgiving, Christmas, New Year's, and Easter. Catalog available from (888) 281-8800.

Directions: From I-95, exit at 6th Ave. South in Lake Worth. Head west approximately 2 miles to Military Trail. Turn right onto Military Trail. Turn left onto Lake Worth Rd. Hoffman's is down the road on left. From Florida Tpk., take Exit 93 (Lake Worth Rd.). Turn left and travel about 3 miles. Hoffman's is on right.

Nearby Attractions: Palm Beach and Knollwood Orange Grove tours (see pages 53 and 50); International Museum of Cartoons; Kravis Center; Lion Country Safari; Palm Beach Community College Museum of Art; Morikami Museum and Japanese Gardens; Lake Worth Beach.

Knollwood Groves ✎ *citrus fruit*

8053 Lawrence Road
Boynton Beach, FL 33436
(561) 734-4800 / (800) 222-9696

Knollwood Groves

If citrus fruits are what you crave, and you want some time away from the beaches and malls, Knollwood Groves offers a relaxing experience. It's one of Palm Beach County's oldest citrus groves, first farmed with grapefruit trees in 1930 by partners in the famous "Amos and Andy" radio show. Your tour on the tram (the Orange Blossom Special) meanders through the grove's 30 acres.

You'll learn more than just the citrus-farming business, as the narrator talks about Florida history, native American Indians, and alligator-handling. After you pass the turtle and alligator pond, perhaps with snowy white egrets within view, you'll spend most of the time viewing the variety of trees. The grove has 20 kinds of citrus trees, which are pruned to between 6 and 10 feet to allow easy picking, along with larger water oak, banyan, avocado, fig, cypress, sapodilla (source of chewing gum), and Florida cherry trees. The gumbo-limbo tree is a favorite, as its bark color and texture has led locals to rename it the "sunburned tourist tree." The area where the trees are densest, which is particularly cool on hot days, is called a jungle "hammock" by the Indians—a higher ground of trees that forms a natural roof overhead.

The sites on the covered-tram ride include some eclectic places that give the tour a very homegrown, natural feel. You stop briefly to explore an authentically recreated Hallpatee Seminole Indian Village, with a live-alligator pit nearby. When Martin Two-Feather leads his longer tour, he provides extra doses of Florida Indian history and demonstrates alligator-handling. Plus, you can't miss waving to Pork Chop, the grove's cute pet boar. At the end of the peaceful, tractor-pulled tram ride, you enter the busy processing area, where the fruit is automatically washed and sorted, and then hand-packed.

Cost: Standard tour, $1; special alligator-handling tour, $3–$5; children under 3, free.
Freebies: Samples of fresh juice and fruit.
Video Shown: No. (Developing video.)

Reservations Needed: No, except for groups over 20 people.
Days and Hours: November through May, Mon–Sun 10:00 AM–4:00 PM (tours on the hour). April through October (off-season, call for exact dates), Mon–Sat, usually 12:00 PM and 2:00 PM. Closed holidays. Special alligator-handling tour with Martin Two-Feather: Sat 2:00 PM and during weeks around Christmas and Easter, Mon–Sun 2:00 PM.
Plan to Stay: 30 minutes for standard tour, plus time for gift shop and fruit store, snack bar, and picnic area. Longer tour with Martin Two-Feather, which features demonstrations at the Indian Village and alligator handling, lasts about 1½ hours.
Minimum Age: None
Disabled Access: Advance notice appreciated for lifting wheelchairs into tram.
Group Requirements: Minimum group size is 20 people, with 2 days' advance notice. Special tour times can be arranged for motorcoach tours. School-group tours in morning. Maya miniature theater shows held Thur and Sat at 3:00 PM or by arrangement.
Special Information: Can watch juicing machines at small building near restrooms.
Gift Shop and Fruit Store: Sells variety of fresh fruit, vegetables, and juices, orange jams and jellies, citrus candy, local gourmet products, fudge, and Native American crafts. Snack bar with sandwiches and spiral-cut, open-face apple pie. Mail-order department in gift shop for shipping fruit and gift baskets. Open same days as tours, 8:30 AM–5:30 PM. Catalog available at above number.
Directions: Take I-95 to Gateway exit. Head west on Gateway Blvd. to Lawrence Rd. Turn right; company is ahead on left.
Nearby Attractions: Palm Beach Groves and Hoffman's Chocolate tours (see pages 53 and 49); Loxahatchee Game Preserve; Lion Country Safari; and the beach.

Magic of Disney Animation Studios ⟶ *animated features*

Disney-MGM Studios
Walt Disney World Resort
Lake Buena Vista, FL 32830-0040
(407) 824-4321

The Walt Disney Company, with its giant theme parks, real estate holdings, and Oscar-winning movies, started as an animation studio in 1923. Whether you wonder how cartoon characters (like the ubiquitous Mickey Mouse) are drawn or what the newest Disney animated film will be, the answer is found on the Magic of Disney Animation tour at Disney-MGM Studios. The lobby displays of Disney Studios' Oscars and of animation cels from current movies, the entertaining videos throughout the tour, and the busy animators all combine to bring this creative art to life.

Through glass walls surrounding the animation studio, you oversee the production of animated shorts and movies. Animators have assigned roles, much like the characters they draw. Some animators sketch the character only at its furthest points of movement, while other artists add the in-between positions, redraw the series to refine the detail, or create special effects and the "sets" on which the animated characters perform.

Although computers have crept into the process, the Disney family remains committed to the art of hand-drawn animation. The animators, whose cubicles display interesting collections of personal knickknacks and posters, sketch a few lines and flip back to other drawings on their light boards to see if the current etching follows sequence, often erasing and resketching. Other parts of the self-guided tour show you what's involved in transferring the paper drawings to plastic cels, in mixing the paints and inking the cels to create the colors needed for every character and scene, and in photographing the cels to create the illusion of life.

Cost: Included in admission charge to the theme park at Walt Disney World Resort.
Freebies: No
Videos Shown: At the beginning of the tour you watch a collection of Disney cartoons. During the self-guided tour, overhead videos explain each department. At the end

of the tour a brief video shows what it's like to be an animator and presents clips from classic Disney animated films.
Reservations Needed: No
Days and Hours: Mon–Sun 9:00 AM–7:00 PM. Most activity during Mon-Fri 9:00 AM–5:00 PM. Hours change depending on theme park hours and season. Open 365 days a year.
Plan to Stay: All day at Disney-MGM Studios. The Magic of Disney Animation tour lasts 35 minutes, plus the wait time before the tour.
Minimum Age: None
Disabled Access: Yes
Group Requirements: Groups larger than 10 people can call (407) 824-6750 in advance to order tickets to the theme park.
Special Information: Take this tour in the morning to avoid the longest lines and try to go during animators' standard business hours. Tour is available during weekends and holidays, and you'll sometimes see an animator hard at work on a project. Other animation tours for student groups available through Youth Education Series. Call (800) 833-9806 for more information.
Gift Shop: The Animation Gallery (follow the Roger Rabbit footsteps at the end of tour) sells figurines and cels of your favorite animation characters, along with books, videos, and other Disney cartoon character items. Open same hours as theme park.
Directions: From Orlando, take Exit 26 off I-4 and follow the signs. From Kissimmee, stay on U.S. 192 and enter at the main Disney entrance.
Nearby Attractions: All rides and shows at the Disney-MGM Studios. The Special Effects and Production tour and the Backstage Studio tour teach you about moviemaking and television production, and provide glimpses of current Disney projects in production.

Nickelodeon Studios   ～   *television shows*

Universal Studios Florida
3000 Universal Studios Plaza
Orlando, FL 32819
(407) 363-8500

On this tour you'll learn about sophisticated television technology. You may also taste Gak or get green-slimed with edible green goo. Sound contradictory? It won't, once you visit the world's first television network designed especially for kids. Nickelodeon's production complex at the Universal Studios Florida theme park is a combined state-of-the-art television studio and backstage tour facility. On days that shows are taped, your kids can sometimes join the live studio audience.

Look down through glass windows at the cobweb of lighting-grid hoists that hover over the ultra-modern sound stages. Each stage is big enough to park a 747 jet. See the sets for Nick shows. You'll appreciate the magic of television when you notice the difference between how sets for "Kenan & Kel" or "Allegra's Window" look in person, compared to on television. Glass walls also expose the audio and video working control rooms. The 50 monitors in the video control room resemble a giant jigsaw puzzle, with the director picking the best shots for the program.

You'll also see the wardrobe room, the hair/make-up room, and the open-walled "kitchen" where they "cook" green slime, Gak, and other recipes unique to Nick programs (there's actually a Gak-meister who concocts messes). After viewing the behind-the-scenes stuff, kids and their families can engage in some favorite Nick games and help create new ones. In the Nickelodeon Game Lab, you feel like you're on a real game show, as you participate in "Double Dare" stunts—with luck, you may get green-slimed! You leave with a new pop-culture vocabulary and an appreciation for what's involved in producing kids' TV.

Cost: Included in the general admission charge for Universal Studios Florida.
Freebies: Sometimes
Videos Shown: Throughout the tour, brief videos describe the production process. The videos add to the tour, especially if shows are not in rehearsal during your visit.

Reservations Needed: No
Days and Hours: Mon–Sun 10:00 AM–5:00 PM. Universal Studios Florida open later during peak days and in summer. Last tour 1 hour before Universal Studios closes. Open 365 days a year.
Plan to Stay: All day at Universal Studios. Nickelodeon tour is 40 minutes, plus any wait in line before the tour.
Minimum Age: None
Disabled Access: Yes
Group Requirements: For group ticket information to Universal Studios Florida, call (407) 363-8210.
Special Information: Tour lines are shorter in the morning. As you wait in line, kids will be entertained by Sega video games and the Green Slime Geyser, a 17-foot high green fountain made of pipes, tubes, and other odd-looking machines, that rumbles, hisses, and periodically erupts slime. It's a landmark at the Nick studio entrance. Call (407) 363-8586 two or more weeks in advance to find out what shows will be in production or whether a live audience is needed. Families should check with Guest Services lobby on day of visit.
Gift Shop: A cart on the corner sells Nick T-shirts and sweatshirts, Ren & Stimpy dolls, and other Nick paraphernalia.
Directions: Take I-4 to Exit 29 or Exit 30B. Follow the signs for Universal Studios.
Nearby Attractions: Over 40 rides, shows, and attractions at Universal Studios Florida, including the Production Tram tour, "Hitchcock's 3-D Theatre," "ET Adventure," "King Kong Kongfrontation," and "Back To The Future . . . The Ride."

Palm Beach Groves ~ *citrus fruit*

7149 Lawrence Road
Lantana, FL 33462-4808
(561) 965-6699

More citrus fruit grows in Florida than almost anyplace else in the world. Unfortunately, none of the large commercial groves and processing plants offers public tours. However, at Palm Beach Groves you can tour a small working grove, visit the processing and packing area, wander through tropical gardens, and go home with plenty of fresh fruit and juice from their abundantly stocked retail store.

You'll see and learn about a wide variety of citrus fruits during your ride through the grove in a tractor-pulled covered cart. Each type of orange, such as navel, temple, and honeybell (a hybrid between grapefruit and tangerine), has a four- to 15-week season. Surrounded by orange trees, you'll enjoy the peaceful, fragrant journey—a real contrast to the noisy South Florida malls. After the tram ride, walk through the areas where the fruit is washed, sorted, and packed, the intermediate steps between the tree and your table. Nearby you can look through glass windows at machines that squeeze oranges and grapefruits for juice.

On the washing line the oranges wiggle and roll around through a shallow water-bath and rinse, then travel to the sponge and hot-air dryers. Notice the simple but effective method of mechanically sorting the oranges by size. The grading machine resembles a pinball machine. The fruit rolls down a ramp, leaning against an opening that gradually increases in size. The smaller fruits fall through the narrowest opening at the beginning and the biggest, most expensive ones fit through the largest opening toward the end. The oranges drop into hammocks, which cushion their fall into wooden crates. Try to guess which orange will fall into which size crate.

Cost: Free
Freebies: Tastes of refreshing citrus fruits; samples of juice and other foods.
Video Shown: No
Reservations Needed: No

Days and Hours: Mid-October (call for date) through April only: Mon–Sun 10:00 AM–4:00 PM on the hour for orange grove tours. Tour of the packing and processing area is self-guided. Call ahead to see when they will be packing and processing the fruit (busiest November–March).
Plan to Stay: 20 minutes for tour, plus time for Marketplace, gift shops and gardens.
Minimum Age: None
Disabled Access: Yes; a few steps up to tram.
Group Requirements: Can handle any size group. Suggest 1 day's advance notice.
Special Information: A small nature walk through the grove's tropical gardens features colorful wandering peacocks and a unique sausage tree. Make sure you try some of the seasonal oranges, such as the juicy honeybells (available only in January).
Marketplace and Gift Shop: Marketplace sells a variety of tasty items, including a wide selection of fresh citrus fruit, Florida-made products such as jellies and gourmet sauces, homemade fudge, and fresh soups and sandwiches. Also sells native foliage and plants. For special deals, go to the Juice Fruit Room, where you pack your own fruit that's irregularly shaped, sized, or slightly overripe. Gift shop sells Florida-related items such as citrus perfumes, shells, and T-shirts. Visit or call mail-order department for shipments of fresh fruit and gift baskets. Open mid-October through April only, Mon–Sun 9:00 AM–5:30 PM. Catalog available from 800 number above.
Directions: Take I-95 to Hypoluxo Rd. exit, then go west to Lawrence Rd. Turn left and go about ¼ mile. Look for signs on right.
Nearby Attractions: Knollwood Groves and Hoffman's Chocolate tours (see pages 50 and 49); Loxahatchee Game Preserve; Lion Country Safari; the beach.

Whetstone Chocolates   *chocolates*

Two Coke Road
St. Augustine, FL 32086
(904) 825-1700

The small ice-cream and candy shop founded by Henry and Esther Whetstone in 1967 is now a 53,300-square-foot chocolate candy factory that produces 500 chocolates per minute. This self-guided tour provides a view of the major steps in making Whetstone's specialty chocolates. Although much of the production is now automated, workers still make the animal and shell-shaped candies by depositing liquid chocolate into small molds.

In the molding room, the chocolate begins its 35-minute journey from liquid to finished product. Approximately 350 molds, each containing as many as 24 cavities, wait patiently to be filled with chocolate from a 10,000-pound melter. The melter, which resembles a double boiler, maintains the chocolate at a temperature of 115°. The chocolate is pumped from the melter into a tempering machine, which cools it to 85° by moving it through a series of cooling chambers, giving the chocolate a shiny appearance. The tempered chocolate is then sent through heated pipes to the depositors, which funnel it into the molds. If the product requires a filling (such as a nut, caramel, or truffle center), the molds are sent to another filling station. After filling, more chocolate is added to finish the piece.

As you walk along the factory's elevated, glass-enclosed walkway, signs above the machines give a brief description of the processes below. The chocolates move into the packing room, where stacks of boxes await filling. Here, the pieces are inspected for flaws (unacceptable chocolates are recycled) and then hand-packed. Some varieties of Whetstone chocolates are individually adorned with printed foil wrap by the wrapping machine before being packaged.

The specialty room is used to make novelty candies. You might see chocolate pumped from a melter into dolphin, bunny, or alligator molds. Chocolate bars and truffles are also produced here, as well as Whetstone's famous chocolate shells. Look for the "enrober" machine, where nuts, toffee crunch, or caramel squares on a conveyor pass under a chocolate stream. In this room, Whetstone also researches and tests new flavors and shapes of chocolate.

Cost: Free

Freebies: Shell-shaped chocolate sample

Video Shown: 15-minute video in theatre shows the history and technology of chocolate making.

Reservations Needed: No, except for groups larger than 15 people.

Days and Hours: Mon–Sat 10:00 AM–5:30 PM. Best time to view production is Mon–Fri 10:00 AM–2:30 PM. Limited production on Saturdays. Closed holidays and the week between Christmas and New Year's. Since factory production schedules frequently change, call ahead to find out when factory is in operation. Call (904) 825-1700, ext. 25, for 24-hour recorded message.

Plan to Stay: 30 minutes for self-guided tour and video, plus time for the Chocolate Shop.

Minimum Age: None

Disabled Access: Yes

Group Requirements: Groups larger than 15 people can request a special guided tour by calling (904) 825-1700, ext. 24, in advance. Large groups will be split into groups of 25 people. Bus groups welcome.

Outlet Store: The Chocolate Shop sells entire selection of Whetstone chocolates and candies (such as Caramel Pecan Monkeys and Florida Sea Shells), souvenirs, and gift items. Catalog available at (800) 849-7933. Cocoa Café features a chocolate dessert bar and refreshment area with a West African theme. Open Mon–Sat 10:00 AM–5:30 PM.

Directions: From I-95, take SR 207 North to SR 312 East. Whetstone is located at the intersection of SR 312 and Coke Rd.

Nearby Attractions: St. Augustine's Historic District includes the Nation's Oldest House, Castillo de San Marco Spanish fort, Spanish Quarter Museum, Lighthouse Museum and Lighthouse; coastal beaches.

A worker at Whetstone Chocolates in St. Augustine, Florida, prepares chocolate shells for the foil wrap machine.

Chocolate shells receive their shiny jackets in the foil wrap machine.

CNN ⌇ *television news*

One CNN Center
Atlanta, GA 30348-5366
(404) 827-2300

CNN Center's naturally lit atrium greets you at the global headquarters of Turner Broadcasting System. Your tour begins as you ride one of the world's largest free-span escalators (eight stories) to an area exhibiting the TBS Collection. A wall of interactive monitors lets you view any of 12 Turner television networks. Other featured exhibits include MGM film memorabilia, such as an Oscar won by *Gone with the Wind* and popular cartoons from Hanna-Barbera and the Cartoon Network, as well as Atlanta sports paraphernalia.

Follow your tour guide into the CNN Special Efx Studio. Examine the TelePromTer. It is like those used in newsrooms around the world. Watch your guide on a monitor point to various graphics just as your favorite newscaster points to a weather map. You may be surprised to discover they are actually pointing to a blank blue wall. This high-tech Chroma Key system allows maps and other graphics to be superimposed onto the blank wall by the camera. But beware, if the newscasters are also wearing blue, they'll disappear!

Peer through glass walls high above the main newsroom floor and observe the researching, gathering, and reporting of news. The tour guide explains how producers, writers, and anchors work together on the complex news-gathering process, which continues 24 hours a day, seven days a week. It takes two to three hours to put together a news segment, but late-breaking stories can be broadcast immediately. Everywhere you look on the news floor, dozens of neatly dressed people seem to be staring intently, either up at the news monitors, ahead at their computer screens, or down at their keyboards and notes while talking on phones. Satellites feed the news from around the world into hundreds of computer terminals.

Cost: Adults, $7; seniors 65 and older, $5; children 12 and under, $4.50; VIP, $24.50.
Freebies: CNN "Press Pass"

Video Shown: Short video in the CNN Control Room Theater highlights the history of TBS and CNN.
Reservations Needed: No, but advance reservations recommended. Same-day reservations not available. Yes, for VIP tours.
Days and Hours: Mon–Sun 9:00 AM–6:00 PM, except holidays. Each day's tour tickets go on sale at 8:30 AM.
Plan to Stay: 45 minutes including video and tour, plus time for the Turner Store.
Minimum Age: 7
Disabled Access: Yes, with 1 day's notice.
Group Requirements: Groups of 35 or more people should call 2 months in advance for reservations and can receive discounts on tours Mon–Fri.
Special Information: No photography. VIP tours limited to 10 people. These tours visit areas not accessible to general public and ascend to three newsroom floors. These 1½-hour-tours require reservations.
Gift Shop: The Turner Store, on the retail level of CNN Plaza, sells logoed merchandise including CNN, TBS, TNT, the Cartoon Network, and Sport South Network. Open Mon–Sun 10:00 AM–6:30 PM. Closed holidays. Call (404) 827-2100.
Directions: By train, take MARTA to Stop W1, "Omni, World Congress Center, Georgia Dome." By car, take I-75/85 North to Exit 96 (International Blvd.). Follow signs to the Georgia World Congress Center. From I-75/85 South, take Exit 99 (Williams St./Downtown). Again, follow signs to the Georgia World Congress Center. CNN Center is on the corner of Techwood Dr. and Marietta St. in downtown Atlanta, across the street from the Georgia World Congress Center and next door to the Omni.
Nearby Attractions: Downtown Atlanta's attractions, including World of Coca-Cola Atlanta (see page 58), World Congress Center, and Underground Atlanta.

See color photos, page 173

Gulfstream Aerospace ~ *corporate jets*

500 Gulfstream Road
Savannah, GA 31408
(912) 965-3407

In 1959, then part of Grumman Corporation, Gulfstream Aerospace built the Gulfstream I, the first small jet designed specifically for business use. Since it became an independent company in 1978, Gulfstream has become a major manufacturer of corporate-business and government jets. The highly acclaimed Gulfstream IV broke not only sales records, but also two around-the-world flight records, piloted by then-president Allen Paulson. The company's newest jet under design, the Gulfstream V, has a flying range of 6,300 nautical miles, which allows it to fly nonstop from New York to Tokyo. Even if you're not a corporate executive or high-ranking government official, Gulfstream lets you tour this plant—as long as you make reservations and fax in the names of all accompanying visitors.

Gulfstream builds approximately 30 jets per year, so the production moves at a pace that is easy to grasp. It's like assembling a jigsaw puzzle: lots of small pieces come together to form the complete picture. After you walk through the Quality Hall of Fame (which recognizes employees who make substantial contributions), your guide takes you out to the main manufacturing area used for assembly, installation, and testing. Here you'll see the big pieces of the aircraft, such as the fuselage (the framework of the body that holds passengers and cargo), and how they come together. When all sections of the fuselage are joined together and spliced, the resulting unit is affectionately known as the "cigar" because that's what it looks like. It takes about four days to splice the cigar together, but workers spend 12 days stuffing the cigar with its electrical wiring.

After the electrical, hydraulic, air conditioning, controls, and avionics are installed in the cigar, an overhead crane picks it up and places it on top of a set of wings (wings are made by an outside vendor). This step is performed early in the morning, primarily for safety reasons, but also because it is fairly spectacular and would draw a crowd of workers if done during the day shift. In the completion center hangar, workers install the custom interior of the aircraft, which can seat up to 20 passengers. Even if you don't know much about aerospace technology, you'll appreciate the company's care and enjoy a close-up look at what's involved in building the jets.

Cost: Free

Freebies: Photographs of all Gulfstream jets and product literature.

Video Shown: No

Reservations Needed: Yes. For security reasons, once you make reservations by phone, you must fax in the names of all persons who will be taking tour. Send fax to (912) 965-4183.

Days and Hours: Tue 10:00 AM. Closed holidays and week between Christmas and New Year's.

Plan to Stay: 45 minutes for tour, plus time for gift shop.

Minimum Age: 12

Disabled Access: Yes

Group Requirements: Groups larger than 12 people should call at least 1 week ahead. No maximum group size.

Special Information: No photography.

Gift Shop: Sells logoed items, such as cups, T-shirts, pins, and scale-model planes. Open Mon–Fri 11:00 AM–1:30 PM. Closed holidays.

Directions: Located near the Savannah International Airport. From I-95, exit at Hwy. 21. Take Hwy. 21 South and turn right onto Gulfstream Rd. Plant is on the left.

Nearby Attractions: Savannah's beaches and historic sites, including Cathedral of St. John the Baptist, Savannah Historical Museum, Ft. McAllister Historic Site, and River Street.

World of Coca-Cola Atlanta   ~~~ *soda*

55 Martin Luther King, Jr. Drive SW
Atlanta, GA 30303-3505
(404) 676-5151

A mammoth neon logo and colorful flags from 200 Coca-Cola-enjoying nations welcome you to this Coca-Cola museum. At this three-story, multimedia celebration of Coke, you will learn about the savvy marketing that catapulted what originally started as a headache remedy into the world's number-one soft drink. In fact, if all the Coca-Cola ever produced were placed in 6½-ounce bottles and laid end-to-end, the line would stretch to the moon and back 1,045 times. (This and other impressive facts are continuously flashed on an electronic billboard.)

View the "Bottling Fantasy," a whimsical sculpture that turns the bottling process into art. Then take a nostalgic journey through 100-plus years of history, past display cases showing early bottling equipment and advertisements, billboards, and trinkets featuring 1920s vaudeville stars. For more interactive time travel, step into giant Coca-Cola cans called "Take 5 Units" and touch the video screens inside. Five-year sips of world events and lifestyles from 1886 to the present are combined with Coca-Cola history. Sit in a replica 1930s soda fountain, while a soda jerk flicks the fountain handle one way for fizz and the other way for flavored syrup.

The Coca-Cola Great Radio Hits kiosk blares with music stars singing Coke radio jingles from the 1960s to the present. (Even the Moody Blues sang "Things Go Better with Coke"!) View Coke's classic television commercials.

In Club Coca-Cola, aerial liquid jets deliver your free soft drink. Once you place your cup under the fountain, an infrared sensor triggers overhead spotlights that illuminate your cup. The glass tubing and neon around you begin to pulsate, and soda arches 20 feet from a hidden high-pressure nozzle, scoring a hole-in-one into your cup. After leaving this futuristic soda fountain, be sure to watch the international Coca-Cola commercials and sample exotic flavors (like Fanta Peach from Botswana).

Cost: Adults, $6; seniors 55+, $4; children 6–12, $3; under 6 (with adult), free.

Freebies: Large variety of Coca-Cola products, plus 18 exotic flavors not available in the U.S.

Videos Shown: Optional 10-minute presentation called "Every Day of Your Life," shown in large-screen, high-definition cinema. Other videos shown throughout the exhibits. All videos close-captioned for the hearing impaired.

Reservations Needed: No. Recommended for groups over 20 people.

Days and Hours: Mon–Sat 10:00 AM–9:30 PM; Sun 12:00 PM–6:00 PM. Last admission 1 hour before closing. Expect long waits during holiday periods and special Atlanta-area events. Closed some holidays.

Plan to Stay: 1½ hours for displays, plus time for gift shop and waiting period.

Minimum Age: None

Disabled Access: Yes

Group Requirements: Groups larger than 20 people can make reservations in advance to receive a 50¢-per-person discount. Call (404) 676-6074 Mon–Fri 9:00 AM–5:00 PM.

Special Information: Foreign language overviews. Arrive earlier in day to avoid longest wait. World of Coca-Cola Las Vegas retail and entertainment facility planned.

Retail Store: "Everything Coca-Cola" features logoed clothing, gifts, and collectibles. Open same hours as museum. Catalog available from (800) 872-6531.

Directions: From I-75/85 North, take Exit 91 (Central Ave. exit). Follow Central Ave. as it goes over expressway to Martin Luther King, Jr. Dr. Museum is at intersection. From I-75/85 South, take Exit 93 (State Capitol/MLK Dr.). Go straight on Martin Luther King, Jr. Dr. 3 blocks to intersection with Central Ave.

Nearby Attractions: Downtown Atlanta's attractions, including CNN tour (see page 56); Underground Atlanta; State Capitol; Georgia World Congress Center; Atlanta Heritage Row (history museum).

Website: www.cocacola.com/museum

The dramatic entrance welcomes you to the World of Coca-Cola Atlanta.

Club Coca-Cola features free exotic sodas from around the world.

Big Island Candies

chocolate-covered
macadamia nuts
and cookies

500 Kalanianaole Avenue
Hilo, HI 96720
(808) 935-8890 / (800) 935-5510

You may be surprised at how far Big Island Candies will go to in order to keep its customers entertained. Priding itself on its uniqueness, the company tries dipping almost anything in chocolate, and some of its successful (albeit unusual) experiments have produced chocolate-covered animal crackers, fortune cookies, and even chocolate-covered *ika* (cuttlefish). Its more conventional products include original and chocolate-dipped shortbread and local favorites such as macadamia ("mac") nuts. Big Island Candies has been producing high-quality chocolates since 1977, when owner Allan Ikawa sold everything, including his boat and his house, to open the company.

On a self-guided tour, you may be tempted to dive through the factory's big glass windows into one of the cylindrical white melters that melt up to 1,000 pounds of chocolate into liquid form. The stainless-steel melters also temper (stir) the chocolate, thus ensuring that it will have a glossy finish. As you move to the next window, smell the shortbread cookies baking in the factory's six ovens. Big Island Candies is one of the few facilities of this size that still do hand-dipping, making chocolates the old-fashioned way. Dippers clad in red shirts and black aprons walk over to the melters to fill their bowls with the sweet brown liquid.

Returning to their station, the dippers pour mac nuts into the chocolate-filled bowl. Skillfully grabbing a nut (or a cuttlefish, cookie, or animal cracker) with one hand, they smother it with more chocolate with the other hand and pop it into the cavity of a candy tray that stands on a scale in front of them. The scale ensures that each tray of candy has the proper weight. You may be amazed by the swiftness with which some of the dippers cover items with chocolate, deftly filling their trays at top speed and with incredible dexterity.

Knowing that many visitors come to Big Island Candies in search of *omiyage* (gifts bought for friends and family, following an Asian tradition), the company creates distinctive packaging for its candies. You leave Big Island Candies knowing that the gourmet candies and chocolates inside those beautiful boxes are made with skill and care.

Cost: Free
Freebies: Chocolate, cookie, and Kona coffee samples.
Video Shown: No
Reservations Needed: No, except for groups larger than 25 people.
Days and Hours: Mon–Sun 8:30 AM–5:00 PM, with the best time to see production Mon–Fri before 3:30 PM. Limited production on weekends and holidays.
Plan to Stay: 30 minutes for the self-guided tour, plus time in gift shop.
Minimum Age: None
Disabled Access: Yes
Group Requirements: Groups of over 25 people should call at least 1 day in advance.
Special Information: Japanese-speaking sales representatives are available.
Gift Shop: Sells all of the company's products, including chocolate-covered mac nuts, rocky road (mac nuts, marshmallows, and chocolate), crunchies (mac nuts, potato chips, and chocolate), crunch (mac nuts, crisp rice, and chocolate), and chocolate-dipped shortbread cookies, fortune cookies, animal crackers, and *ika*. Open Mon–Sun 8:30 AM–5:00 PM. Open every day of the year. Gift guide available from above number.
Directions: From Hilo airport, turn right onto Kanoelehua Ave. (Hwy. 11) and right onto Kamehameha Ave. Stay on the left side, drive about ½ mile, and Big Island Candies will be on your right. From Hamakua coast, stay on Kamehameha Ave. It will eventually become Kalanianaole Ave. Big Island Candies will be on right.
Nearby Attractions: Mauna Loa Macadamia Nuts and Holualoa Kona Coffee tours (see pages 63 and 61); Hilo Bay; Hawaii Volcano National Park (with its live volcano).

Holualoa Kona Coffee ～ *Kona coffee*

77-6261 Mamalahoa Highway
Holualoa, HI 96725
(808) 322-9937 / (800) 334-0348

When you sit down to drink your morning coffee, do you know whether you're drinking peaberry, extra fancy, or triple X? Did you know that it takes 100 pounds of picked coffee to produce just 15 pounds of roasted coffee? Become an informed coffee consumer and watch coffee being processed and roasted at Holualoa Kona Coffee Company, located in the heart of Kona coffee country, a 50- to 60-mile region on the Western side of the Big Island. Hawaii is the only state in the U.S. that produces coffee, and only coffee grown in this region may carry the Kona label.

At Holualoa, your guide describes the life of the coffee bean from the moment it's picked from the tree as a red "cherry," until it's dried to become the beige bean called "parchment." Then you see the hulling process, where parchment beans are dumped into a tall, thin elevator. The elevator pours the parchment into the huller, which removes the parchment skin from the beans to reveal green coffee beans, which are then dropped by another elevator into the grader. The grader comprises a series of screens with different-size holes stacked one atop another. The screens shake, causing the coffee beans to fall through the appropriately sized holes. The largest (and best) beans, including grades like peaberry, extra fancy, and fancy, are separated from the smaller, lower grades such as number one, prime, and triple X. Peaberry, the most valuable bean, has a distinct flavor and shape. A gravity table further separates the coffee, this time by density.

In the next building you'll watch the coffee whirling around in the 40-pound roaster, which resembles a large oven. During roasting, air from a blower tosses the coffee beans around to prevent burning. The person who does the roasting explains how to take care of your coffee and how to distinguish good beans from low-quality ones. You'll learn that medium-roast coffee has more caffeine than dark roast because the longer coffee is roasted, the more caffeine is roasted out. By the end of this tour, you'll have a good understanding of what it takes to get the coffee from the tree to your cup.

Cost: Free
Freebies: Cup of iced Kona-mocha and, in the morning, fresh-brewed coffee.
Video Shown: No
Reservations Needed: No, except for groups larger than 10 people.
Days and Hours: Mon–Fri 7:30 AM–3:30 PM, with the best time to see production from 9:00 AM–2:00 PM. Closed holidays and the Friday before Easter.
Plan to Stay: 30 minutes, plus time in gift area and working farm.
Minimum Age: None
Disabled Access: Yes
Group Requirements: Groups of over 10 people should call 1 day in advance. Groups of over 30 people will be divided into smaller groups.
Gift Area: Holualoa T-shirts and coffee are sold in the packaging room, where the tour ends. Open Mon–Fri 7:30 AM–3:30 PM. Brochure available from above number.
Directions: From Keahole Airport, take Hwy. 11 South. Turn left at the sign for Holualoa. Go all the way to the top of the mountain and turn right onto Mamalahoa Hwy. Turn left at the sign for Maika'i Ranch. Drive up to the big white barn-like building, where the tour begins. From the south, take Hwy. 11 North. Turn right at sign for Holualoa/Keauhou. Turn left onto Mamalahoa Hwy. Turn right at sign for Maika'i Ranch, just past the mile 2 marker.
Nearby Attractions: Big Island Candies and Mauna Loa Macadamia Nuts tours (see pages 60 and 63); Kona Coffee Country driving tour map available from Kona-Kohala Chamber of Commerce (call 808-329-1758); November Kona Coffee Cultural Festival; Kailua-Kona, a resort town with sports fishing, snorkeling, surfing, and beaches.

Maui Divers of Hawaii   ～   *jewelry*

The Maui Divers Jewelry Design Center
1520 Liona Street
Honolulu, HI 96814
(808) 943-8383

MAUI DIVERS
OF HAWAII

Since its days of filling scuba tanks, back in 1958, Maui Divers has become the world's largest precious coral jewelry manufacturer. The company's founders initially experimented, making jewelry with rare black coral from the deep waters off Lahaina, then branched out into pink and gold coral. The video and tour show how they currently make their unique jewelry, which combines coral with gold, diamonds, pearls, rubies, or other precious gems.

You can watch most of the detailed process. Designers make sketches for the goldsmiths, who then turn the drawings into three-dimensional jewelry carved from gold. The lost-wax casting process involves wax patterns of the jewelry being assembled into what looks like a small tree. Plaster molds are formed around this tree and heated in an oven to melt away the wax patterns, hence the name "lost wax." Once shattered, the molds reveal an exact gold replica of the wax tree. Gold rings and pendants are cut from the tree, then sanded and polished.

Notice the vacuum hoods behind many of the machines in the finishing areas. These draw the gold mist into a central water bath, which is then refined. This gold recovery process amounts to over $500,000 per year.

The tour guide escorts you through other areas, where skillful workers carefully cut, solder, polish, and inspect the gold pieces, or set precious gems into them. Notice the "Million Dollar Wall" in the coordinating area. Here, diamonds, pearls (some from the South Seas), emeralds, and sapphires are sorted and sized.

Cost: Free
Freebies: No
Video Shown: 9-minute video on deep-sea coral mining and jewelry production. Available in major foreign languages.
Reservations Needed: No, except for groups larger than 50 people.
Days and Hours: Mon–Sun 8:00 AM–8:00 PM. No production Sat, Sun, and holidays,

although tours show video and see manufacturing area and display cases on production steps.
Plan to Stay: 30 minutes for video and tour, plus time for gift stores.
Minimum Age: None
Disabled Access: Yes
Group Requirements: 2 hours advance notice requested for groups larger than 50 people. No maximum group size. Light refreshments for groups on request.
Special Information: No photography
Showroom: Sells the world's largest selection of original fine coral jewelry designs, including black, red, and pink coral rings, earrings, cufflinks, and pendants in 14-karat gold settings; pearl and South Sea pearl earrings and necklaces; and gold dolphins, pineapples, and whales. Open same hours as tour. Second-floor stores have costume jewelry, gift items, and a selection of designer line items.
Directions: Free shuttle bus available from many hotels. Within walking distance of Ala Moana Shopping Center. If driving, take Alawai Blvd. Turn right onto Kalakaua Ave. Turn left at Beretania St., left at Keeaumoku St., and left at Liona St. Maui Divers is on your left.
Nearby Attractions: Royal Hawaiian Mint tour (see page 64); Waikiki Beach; Ala Moana Shopping Center; Academy of Art Museum; Capitol Building; Iolani Palace.

See color photos, page 183

Mauna Loa *macadamia nuts and candy*
Macadamia Road
Hilo, HI 96720
(808) 966-8612

Few factory tours offer the sweet smells of roasting nuts and melting chocolate along with a nature trail to walk off the free samples and goodies available at the gift store. Although almost all the macadamia nuts (or "mac nuts") sold worldwide are produced in Hawaii, the nut is actually native to Australia and wasn't grown in Hawaii until 1921. When C. Brewer, the oldest U.S. corporation west of the Rocky Mountains, began marketing mac nuts under the Mauna Loa brand in 1976, their popularity mushroomed. This tour of the world's largest mac nut company provides a look through gallery windows at mac nut processing and packaging and at chocolate production.

Fresh from the 40-foot-high macadamia tree, the mac nut kernel sits inside a leathery brown, extremely hard shell. After shelling (burnt shells and husks fuel the entire plant), the nuts enter the main processing factory. Electric eyes automatically grade and sort the nuts, allowing only light, uniformly colored specimens to continue along to the roaster. Blue-hatted workers stand over the conveyor belt, also searching the stream of nuts for rejects.

The nuts are dry-roasted in large rectangular ovens, traveling slowly through the ovens on conveyor belts for 15 minutes. When roasting ends, the nuts are sorted again, and some are salted, candy-glazed, or made into mac nut brittle. Watch the packaging machine shoot them into fast-moving open metal tins, which then move down the line for vacuum-sealing.

The smell of chocolate replaces the aroma of mac nuts in the candy factory, where chocolate waits in big steel melters. The nuts drop onto chocolate pads, then travel through the enrobing machine that covers them in a wave of chocolate. Rows of white-gloved, blue-smocked workers neatly hand-pack the chocolates in boxes after they leave the long cooling tunnels.

Cost: Free
Freebies: Samples of nuts and candy.
Video Shown: 7-minute video on mac nut farming, harvesting, and production. Shows continuously on the lanai near the gift store. Available in Japanese.
Reservations Needed: No, except for groups larger than 50 people that want a guided tour.
Days and Hours: Mon–Sun 8:30 AM–5:00 PM. Limited production 11:00 AM–noon. Guided tours about every 30–45 minutes, starting at 9:30 AM. Self-guided tour with overhead signs all other times. Even though no production on holidays and on weekends from late February through July, can still walk through tour route.
Plan to Stay: 15 minutes for tour, plus time for video, nature walk, and gift store.
Minimum Age: None
Disabled Access: Yes, for candy factory; 20 stairs in the mac nut processing factory.
Group Requirements: Groups larger than 50 people should call 5 days ahead to schedule guided tour. No maximum group size.
Special Information: September–February is busiest production schedule. Call for production schedule during other months.
Gift Shop: Sells all Mauna Loa mac nuts and candies, mac nut ice cream, mac nut popcorn, and logoed items including shirts, hats, and key chains. Open same hours as tour. Catalog available from (800) 832-9993.
Directions: Take Hwy. 11 to Macadamia Rd. Turn left if coming from Hilo and right if coming from Hawaii Volcanoes National Park. Drive through the Keaau Orchards to the yellow-and-blue Mauna Loa Macadamia Nut Visitor Center on left.
Nearby Attractions: Big Island Candies and Holualoa Kona Coffee tours (see pages 60 and 61); Hawaii Volcanoes National Park; Mauna Loa Village and Marketplace about 2½ hours away.

Royal Hawaiian Mint

commemorative
gold coins

1427 Kalakaua Avenue
Honolulu, HI 96826
(800) 808-6468

Royal Hawaiian Mint is the only private mint in the world that's open to the public, and it prides itself on its personal approach to teaching visitors about coin manufacturing and Hawaiian history. The 4,000-square-foot building was designed by mint co-founder and trained architect Bernard von NotHaus.

The "Gold in All Its Forms" exhibit in the Gallery of Masters area contains around $100,000 worth of natural ore, nuggets (some collected by von NotHaus and his sons on expeditions to Alaska), dust, and gold bars. At the "Gold Window," an elaborate antique teller's window, you enjoy one of the benefits of the mint's personal approach (and high security) when your guide drops a $40,000 gold bar in your hand.

Von NotHaus compares coin manufacturing with Chinese cooking: lots of prep work and very little cooking. And since production at the mint is unscheduled, you may see some "prep work," including rolling, weighing, and melting, or you may see only the "cooking"—the minting itself. You may see a bar of gold being melted into smaller ingots; a rolling machine flattening the gold or silver into sheets, which are then made into blanks; or the polishing process.

Stand only 7 feet away from the 600-ton hydraulic press, a machine that resembles one table atop another and is capable of exerting the same amount of pressure as 200 Cadillacs stacked on top of each other. Watch the mintmaster insert a raw disc of gold or silver, called a "planchet," between two steel dies, which come together with so much pressure that the metal transforms into a liquid. The liquid gold or silver then flows into the cavities of the coin's design. When the press stops—at precisely the right moment—the mintmaster removes a coin. What was a blank disc moments ago is now the finished coin, with a dignified profile of King Kamehameha, the first king of Hawaii, or perhaps the Pearl Harbor Memorial. You leave with images of Hawaii's history imprinted in your memory and perhaps a coin or two in your pocket to commemorate your visit to Hawaii's own mint.

Cost: Free

Freebies: Free coin with purchase of another coin. Visitors who arrive on the Waikiki Trolley can make and keep their own coin.

Video Shown: A video depicting both the process and a historical perspective of coin minting shown upon request.

Reservations Needed: No, except for groups over 30 people.

Days and Hours: Mon–Fri 10:00 AM–5:00 PM, Sat 10:00 AM–2:00 PM. Closed holidays, including June 11 (Kamehameha Day).

Plan to Stay: 10–20 minutes to see minting, Gallery of Masters, and sales display cases.

Minimum Age: None

Disabled Access: Yes

Group Requirements: Groups over 30 people should call 1 week in advance. Maximum group size is 35.

Special Information: Production is unscheduled, though something is usually being minted. New Waikiki branch of mint offers demonstrations and video.

Sales Displays: Sells gold, silver, bronze, platinum, and palladium Hawaiian coins as well as coin jewelry—earrings, pendants, and money clips. Pay at the "Gold Window." Items are repriced daily. A newsletter/catalog is available from above number. Open same hours as mint.

Directions: Located ½-mile from Waikiki. Walk or take bus #2 west on Kalakaua Ave. past the Convention Center to the Royal Corner (the intersection of Kalakaua Ave. and King St.). From the downtown/Iolani Palace area, take Bus #1 on King St. for about 1 mile to the Royal Corner. Validated parking is available at the Cinerama Theater. Also can take Waikiki Trolley, which originates at Royal Hawaiian Shopping Center in Waikiki.

Nearby Attractions: Maui Divers of Hawaii jewelry tour (see page 62); Kamehameha statue; Iolani Palace; Waikiki Beach; Ala Moana Shopping Center.

Website: www.rhmint.com

Photo: Jerry Stanfield/Video Flair Productions, and Small Business Hawaii

Got it in the bag! Bernard von NotHaus and assistant Talena Presley have cornered the Hawaiian market with the successful Royal Hawaiian Mint.

Photo: John Titchen

Mintmaster Bernard von NotHaus carefully checks a finished coin at the Royal Hawaiian Mint in Honolulu, Hawaii.

Potlatch   *lumber, paperboard, and tissue*
805 Mill Road
Lewiston, ID 83501
(208) 799-1795

Potlatch

While most plants just have a lumber or paper mill, Potlatch's Lewiston complex is an integrated sawmill, pulp and paper mill, and tissue mill. The tour lets you see the transformation of wood into lumber, paperboard, and tissue products, all at one site. Wood waste from the lumber mill is used by the pulp mill and is also converted into energy for the entire complex.

The sawmill produces approximately 120 million board feet of lumber annually, enough to build about 8,000 average-size homes. The mill's saws are computer-assisted and use laser scanners to determine the best combination of cuts. The buzz of saws and the clatter of chains and conveyors moving the logs through the process of debarking, squaring, edging, and trimming make the mill a very noisy place.

Large piles of woodchips and sawdust wait near the digesters that cook them into pulp. The digesters (not on the tour) break down the natural glue, called "lignin," that holds the wood fibers together. The pulp goes to the fiber line, which removes additional lignin and purifies and whitens the pulp. The seemingly endless paper machines produce the paperboard used in milk and juice cartons, paper cups, and other food packages. The extruders laminate polyethylene to the paperboard to make liquid-tight containers.

The tissue machines produce paper towels, toilet paper, napkins, and facial tissue (at a rate of one mile per minute), which is sold under private label by major supermarket chains. The mixture of pulp and water is formed on a screen that drains water from the sheet. Additional water is squeezed from the sheet before it circulates around a large, steam-heated "Yankee" dryer. A thin blade then peels the dried tissue sheet from the Yankee, and the tissue sheet is wound onto what looks like the world's largest paper-towel roll. For some products, such as bathroom and facial tissue, parent rolls are combined to make multiple-ply tissues.

It's no surprise that they manufacture enough single rolls of toilet paper each year to supply the equivalent of at least one roll to every American.

Your tour ends in the calm of the greenhouse. Row upon row of young pine, fir, and cedar seedlings, each under one foot tall, illustrate how much wood is used in the production of lumber and paper products. The greenhouse produces over 2.5 million seedlings per year for reforesting the company's lands.

Cost: Free
Freebies: Pencils and brochure about the company and its product manufacturing.
Video Shown: 12-minute video overviews the tour, with kids interviewing their parents and grandparents who work at the plant.
Reservations Needed: Yes
Days and Hours: Tue–Thur 9:00 AM and 1:30 PM, but subject to change. Closed holidays and during week-long maintenance shutdowns.
Plan to Stay: 3 hours
Minimum Age: 10, accompanied by adult.
Disabled Access: Stairs throughout tour route. Can do drive-through tour if prior arrangements are made.
Group Requirements: Groups larger than 15 people should make reservations at least 1 week in advance.
Special Information: No flash photography. Some areas are very noisy and can be hot during the summer. Wear comfortable shoes for at least 1 mile of walking. Certain areas may not be open due to construction.
Gift Shop: No
Directions: In Lewiston, follow Main St. East to Mill Rd. You will see signs for Potlatch. Enter complex at the main gate. Guard will direct you to parking.
Nearby Attractions: Luna House Museum; Nez Perce National Historical Park; Appaloosa Horse Club Museum; Hell's Canyon Recreational Area.

Chicago Tribune ⟿ *newspaper*

Freedom Center
777 West Chicago Avenue
Chicago, IL 60610
(312) 222-2116

The *Tribune* printed 400 copies of its first issue on June 10, 1847. It now prints that many papers in less than one second on ten massive offset presses that produce up to 70,000 newspapers per hour and more than one million every Sunday. This tour gives you a firsthand look at how the *Tribune* is printed, inserted, bundled, and delivered by one of the world's largest and most technologically advanced newspaper printing facilities.

If you look into the mammoth newsprint warehouse area, about the size of two football fields, the amount of paper used to print this popular newspaper seems overwhelming. Looking straight up you'll see newspaper rolls the size of small cows. The *Tribune* uses 5,000 one-ton paper rolls every week. Fortunately, the newsprint produced by the *Tribune*'s major supplier is made from 60 percent recycled paper. Train tracks run alongside the warehouse to accommodate the 18 railroad cars full of paper it receives five days per week.

From the observation deck you'll see the tower presses move so fast that the newspaper looks like a gray checkerboard blanket rolling up and down along the plates and cylindrical drums. Each press is a series of ten units. The *Tribune* is proud of its increased color-printing capacity, which is the tenth unit. The color tower units contain four vertically stacked printing machines, one each for blue, red, yellow, and black ink. Each press also cuts and folds the paper into sections.

From an overhead walkway in the busy packaging area, you'll see how the advertising sections are automatically bundled for insertion into the completed paper. Machines stack the papers, bundle them together with a brown paper wrap stamped with an ink code, and send them on their way in bright yellow carts. The tour guide, taped messages from a speaker system, and display cases help explain the production process over the roar of the presses and packaging equipment.

Cost: Free

Freebies: Special section of famous *Tribune* front pages, ranging from the Bulls' first NBA title to Abraham Lincoln's election as president, and a button.

Video Shown: 9-minute video reviews the *Tribune*'s history and the process of writing, printing, and selling the newspaper.

Reservations Needed: Yes

Days and Hours: Tue–Fri 9:30 AM, 10:30 AM, 11:30 AM, and 1:30 PM.

Plan to Stay: 1 hour

Minimum Age: 10

Disabled Access: Yes. One attendant needed for each individual using a wheelchair.

Group Requirements: Maximum group size is 50 people, with 1 adult required for every 10 children. Make reservations as far ahead of tour date as possible.

Special Information: Cannot always predict whether presses will be running during your visit. Most local newspapers give tours; contact your local paper for tour information.

Gift Shop: Not in Freedom Center. Store in the Tribune Tower at 435 N. Michigan Ave. sells *Chicago Tribune* merchandise (books, clothing, etc.). Open Mon–Fri 8:00 AM–5:00 PM. Call (312) 222-3080.

Directions: From I-90/94, take the Ohio St. exit. Turn left onto Orleans St. and left onto Chicago Ave. The guard in the security booth will direct you to visitors' parking.

Nearby Attractions: Chicago Board of Trade and Chicago Mercantile Exchange tours (see page 68); U.S. Post Office tour (see page 77); *Chicago Sun Times* tour (call 312-321-3000). Chicago's attractions include Sears Tower, Shedd Aquarium, Adler Planetarium, Lincoln Park Zoo, and the Museum of Science and Industry.

Chicago Board of Trade   *grain and financial futures and options*

141 West Jackson Boulevard
Chicago, IL 60604
(312) 435-3590

 Chicago Board of Trade

Chicago Mercantile Exchange   *livestock and financial futures*

30 South Wacker Drive
Chicago, IL 60606
(312) 930-8249

CHICAGO MERCANTILE EXCHANGE°

Major futures markets at work combine Super Bowl competitiveness, Rose Bowl Parade colors, and Mardi Gras pandemonium. Unless you're a serious investor or financial professional, the viewing experiences at the Chicago Board of Trade (CBOT) and the Chicago Mercantile Exchange (Merc) are basically the same. From large, glass-walled observation galleries above the trading floors, you'll see throngs of traders feverishly shouting, waving their arms, using hand signals, and throwing pieces of paper. The CBOT also has a new trading floor for financial instruments that is accessed from the agricultural gallery.

The trading floors themselves are bigger than the combined playing fields of the Chicago Cubs and the White Sox. At the tops of the side and far walls are boards with numbers that show futures prices. Overhead monitors and computers around the trading floor don't block your view as they do at the New York Stock Exchange (see page 220).

In the various "pits," traders use a variation of the centuries-old auction system—appropriately called the "open outcry method"—for buying and selling. With all the skill of a third-base coach, they also use hand signals to cut through the noise. The sea of colors comes from ID badges and lightweight jackets worn by floor personnel. After examining the mechanics of floor trading, you'll be even more intrigued by the process.

Cost: Free

Freebies: CBOT: brochure and a card illustrating hand signals; Merc: brochure and postcard of the trading floor.

Videos Shown: CBOT: included in presentation. Merc: visitors' gallery has interactive videos that explain the trading process and Merc history.

Reservations Needed: No, except for groups over 10 people at both CBOT and Merc.

Days and Hours: CBOT: Mon–Fri 8:15 AM–1:15 PM, with presentations and video at 9:15 AM, 10:00 AM, then every ½-hour until 12:30 PM. Merc: Mon–Fri 7:15 AM–3:15 PM (hours vary by trading floor), with presentations between 8:00 AM–12:00 PM. CBOT and Merc closed national holidays.

Plan to Stay: 30 minutes each, plus time for videos and displays.

Minimum Age: No, except for groups.

Disabled Access: Yes

Group Requirements: Both CBOT and Merc require reservations at least 2 weeks in advance for groups of 10 or more, with customized presentations available. Minimum age for groups is 8th grade for Merc and 16 years for CBOT.

Gift Shop: CBOT and Merc visitors' galleries both have gift counters that sell logoed items, including pens, caps, T-shirts, mugs, golf tees, and teddy bears. CBOT catalog available at number above.

Directions: CBOT and Merc are within a few blocks of each other in downtown Chicago. The landmark art deco CBOT building, topped by a 31-foot statue of Ceres (Roman goddess of grain and harvest), is at the intersection of LaSalle and Jackson. Merc is at Wacker and Monroe, 1 block from Sears Tower.

Nearby Attractions: Chicago Post Office tour (see page 77); *Chicago Tribune* tour (see page 67); Chicago Stock Exchange Visitors Gallery (call 312-663-2222); Chicago Board Option Exchange Observation Gallery (call 312-786-5600); Federal Reserve Bank Visitors Center and tour (call 312-322-5111); Quaker Oats Lobby Exhibit (call 312-222-6887).

Website: www.cbot.com

Throngs of traders work on the floor of the Chicago Board of Trade.

The clock and sculpture above the base of the landmark art deco Chicago Board of Trade building in downtown Chicago, Illinois.

Haeger Potteries ⟋ *artwork pottery*

7 Maiden Lane
East Dundee, IL 60118
(847) 426-3033 / (847) 426-3441

Founded by David Haeger in 1871, Haeger Potteries today is directed by Alexandra Haeger Estes—the fourth generation of the Haeger family to be involved with the company. Started as a brickyard that helped rebuild Chicago after its Great Fire, Haeger Potteries is now one of the world's largest art pottery factories.

After an introductory talk about the production process, your tour begins downstairs in the "closet" where extra molds are stored. Watch the automatic casting machines fill plaster molds with "slip"—liquid clay. Notice the hanging "trolley" system that slowly travels its 4-mile course with dried pottery ("greenware") perched on wooden shelves that look like birdcage swings.

Workers carefully pry the molds open, then give each artwork a hand sponge bath before drying. The block-long kiln and the round kiln are located in the Great Kiln room, where you'll feel the heat. The brown brick kilns are 220° at the entrance and 2,000° in the center. Workers neatly stack the greenware pieces—close to each other but not touching—onto railcars headed for a 12-hour trip through the kiln.

After its first kiln baking, the "bisque" is hand-dipped into a water-based glaze. The glaze, absorbed into the dry, porous bisque, dries almost immediately. A worker then takes the piece from a lazy-Susan table and showers it with glaze in a spray booth. These alternative glazing methods give the pottery its vibrant colors when it's fired again in the kiln.

Upstairs is a museum that includes a vase determined by the *Guinness Book of World Records* to be one of the world's largest. Made in 1976 by Haeger's master potter, it took three months and 650 pounds of clay to complete. Among other Haeger items, the display cases show discontinued ceramic animal designs, a Harley-Davidson hog bank, a sculptured bust of Carl Sandburg, and a large

Hummel figure (Hummel and Haeger exchanged artworks on Haeger's 100th anniversary). The tour ends in the 25,000-square-foot, seven-showroom outlet store that sells most of Haeger's 800 different items.

Cost: Free
Freebies: No
Video Shown: No
Reservations Needed: No, except for groups of 10 people or more.
Days and Hours: Mon 10:00 AM and 12:30 PM, and sometimes Thursdays at the same times. No tours during holidays, July tent sale, and 2-week summer shutdown.
Plan to Stay: 30 minutes for tour, plus time for museum and outlet store.
Minimum Age: 4, when accompanied by responsible adult; 5, for school groups.
Disabled Access: No, in factory; outlet store and museum are accessible.
Group Requirements: Groups of 10 people or more need to make reservations. Other times can be scheduled. Groups larger than 20 will be split into smaller groups. Call (847) 426-3033 for more information.
Special Information: Temperature can be very warm because of heat from kilns. Some tours begin with a demonstration by the master potter in the back of the outlet store.
Outlet Store: Sells pottery lamps, vases, bowls, sculptures, the best-selling *Rendezvous* (lovers back-to-back), dried and silk floral arrangements, housewares, factory seconds, overruns, and one-of-a-kind and discontinued pieces. Open Mon, Thur, and Fri 10:00 AM–6:00 PM. Open Sat, Sun, and most holidays 11:00 AM–5:00 PM.
Directions: From Chicago, take I-90 West to Rt. 25 North. Turn left onto Rt. 72. Turn left onto Van Buren St. Haeger Potteries is on your right.
Nearby Attractions: Spring Hill Mall; Santa's Village Theme Park and Racing Rapids Action Park; Fox River Recreational Trail; the Milk Pail Village.

John Deere   ~   *harvesters*

Harvester Works
1100 13th Avenue
East Moline, IL 61244
(309) 765-4847

The harvester, or "combine" as it's called in the trade, is one of the machines that revolutionized farming and made possible America's tremendous production of grain and corn. For example, a combine with a claw-like "header" attachment can harvest as many as 12 corn rows at a time, picking and shelling the ears along the way. At John Deere, the world's largest producer of agricultural equipment, you'll see many steps involved in making its Maximizer combines.

The techniques definitely differ from those used by pioneer blacksmith John Deere when he started the company in 1837. Along with the hissing and thumping machines heard at most factories, you'll also see robots welding, lasers cutting steel, and electrical charges applying paint in this 260-acre, world-class manufacturing plant. Considering this factory's size, don't be surprised to see workers scurrying around on bicycles. Your John Deere–retiree tour guide will hand you a piece of metal. Feel the smooth cut on it, made by the combination laser-and-punch machine. Sparks fly as hooded welders apply their skills on smaller pieces, while robotic arms on the automated welding systems seal frames and grain-tank cells.

Watch a combine body slowly emerge and then hover on its hoist after being dipped into an electrically charged bath of green paint. The electric charge bonds the paint to all exposed surfaces on the submerged combine, even in joints and hidden crevices. After seeing several subassembly stations, you'll watch combines come to life on the main production line. Assemblers carefully position completed parts, such as the power shaft, cab, feeder house, and engine. You will sense the pride of the worker who smoothly applies the finishing touch: the John Deere decal.

Cost: Free
Freebies: Brochure with description and pictures of the manufacturing process.
Video Shown: No
Reservations Needed: Yes, ask for map.

Days and Hours: Mon–Fri 10:00 AM. Closed major holidays, the week between Christmas and New Year's, and 2 weeks in the summer (usually end of July and beginning of August).
Plan to Stay: 1½ hours
Minimum Age: 12
Disabled Access: Yes. You ride through the factory in a tram pulled by a small John Deere tractor.
Group Requirements: Make reservations at least 1 month in advance. Maximum size is 80 people.
Special Information: No video cameras allowed. For write-up on Waterloo, IA, tractor plant, see page 91. For information on other John Deere factory tours, call above number.
Gift Shop: Adjacent to the new John Deere Pavilion at the John Deere Commons. Sells a variety of John Deere memorabilia, replica toys, and logoed clothing.
Directions: When you make reservations, ask the Visitor Services Department for a map, since many area highways have multiple designations—almost guaranteeing confusion. From Chicago, take I-88 to the exit for Hwy. 5. Turn right at 70th St., which becomes 7th St. Turn right on 13th Ave. Look for the big green John Deere Maximizer combine parked on the factory's front lawn. From Iowa, take I-80 to I-74 East. Get off at the John Deere Rd. East exit. Turn left at 70th St. and follow the above directions.
Nearby Attractions: Open in 1997, John Deere Pavilion in Moline features interactive displays about agriculture, plus modern and vintage farm equipment. Deere & Co. Administration Center, with display of current and historical John Deere products, Girard Mural (includes more than 2,000 farming-related historical items dated 1837 to 1918), and video tour of this architecturally famous world headquarters. (Directions available from tour guide.) John Deere factories in Moline and Davenport, IA (call above number for information on all company tours); John Deere Historic Site.

Kathryn Beich

chocolates, caramels, and candies

Nestlé Fundraising Company
2501 Beich Road
Bloomington, IL 61701
(309) 829-1031

Kathryn Beich, Inc., is one of the oldest continuous candy-makers in the country, founded by Paul F. Beich in 1854. It's well known for its flavorful Laffy Taffy caramels and its fundraising candies such as Katydids and Golden Crumbles. With its 1984 purchase by Nestlé, it also became the home of Bit-O-Honey. This factory provides one of the few opportunities in the U.S.A. to watch a major candy manufacturer making its sweet stuff.

An elevated, glass-enclosed walkway leads you through a main part of the factory. On your left, retail products Bit-O-Honey and Laffy Taffy are made. A narrow stream of gooey mixture travels from the "kitchen" area through machines that cut, wrap, and box the bars and bite-size pieces.

It's a real treat to watch the Katydid and Golden Crumbles lines on your right. Katydids begin with thousands of pecans moving down the assembly line. Rich dollops of caramel plop on top, followed by a chocolate cascade. When candies emerge from the cooling tunnel, workers hand-pack the Katydids at such a fast rate that they have avoided replacement by robots. The Golden Crumbles, crunchy puffs of freshly ground peanut butter, have been made almost the same way for over 70 years. See the light outer-shell mixture cooking in copper kettles, the grinding of nuts for the peanut-butter center, and the handwork that combines them into small "golden pillows."

Cost: Free

Freebies: Candy bar, although depends on what's in stock.

Video Shown: 20-minute video entitled "The World in a Wrapper" gives the history of chocolate, the Nestlé company, and chocolate manufacturing. Shows parts of the process not seen on the tour, such as the making of chocolate bars.

Reservations Needed: Yes, but will take a limited number of walk-ins if the tour group has not reached its 60-person maximum.

Days and Hours: Mon–Fri 9:00 AM, 10:00 AM, 11:00 AM, 1:00 PM, and 2:00 PM. Closed holidays, last 2 weeks of June, and week between Christmas and New Year's.

Plan to Stay: 45 minutes for the tour and video, plus time for gift shop.

Minimum Age: None

Disabled Access: Limited; a flight of 20 stairs leads to the video room and glass walkway overlooking the factory floor.

Group Requirements: Advance notice required for large groups; longer notice necessary for the spring tours. Maximum group size is 60 people. 1 adult for every 10 children.

Special Information: No photography. Assembly lines for retail candies run almost year-round. Fund-raising candy lines are busiest September through February.

Gift Shop: Sells bags, boxes, and tins of all the candies made here, including Krunch Bars, Katydids, Golden Crumbles, Imps, Truffles, and chocolate-covered pretzels and cookies. Specials on factory seconds and overruns. Open Mon–Fri 9:30 AM–5:00 PM and Sat 9:30 AM–2:00 PM. Open during plant shutdown periods but not holidays.

Directions: From the north, take I-55/I-74 to the Veteran's Pkwy. exit. Take first left off Veteran's Pkwy. at Cabintown Rd., make immediate right onto service road (Springfield Rd.) that parallels Veteran's Pkwy. Turn left onto Beich Rd. and follow the signs. (You will cross over I-55/I-74 just before turning left onto the plant service road.) From the south, either take I-74 and follow the directions above, or take I-55 to the Shirley exit (154) and turn right onto the Beich service road.

Nearby Attractions: Mitsubishi car tour (see page 74); Beer Nuts Factory Outlet (has video of how Beer Nuts are made, call 309-827-8580); Miller Park Zoo; Dave Davis Mansion; McLean County Historical Society; Constitution Trail; Prairie Aviation Museum; ISU Planetarium.

McDonald's Museum ⟿ *fast food*

400 North Lee Street
Des Plaines, IL 60016
(847) 297-5022

If you're a hungry traveler, the sign advertising 15-cent hamburgers may beckon you like a desert mirage. But after parking next to a vintage Chevrolet Bel Air coupe and walking up to this retro-restaurant's counter you'll realize that what you've discovered is not the cheapest burger this side of 1960, but the McDonald's Museum.

This museum is an exact replica of the first McDonald's franchise on its original site. Four clean-cut mannequins tend the restaurant. The menu is simple: burgers, cheeseburgers, fries, shakes, milk, coffee, and soda. Nothing of the compact, clean operation is hidden from customers. Outside on the original sign, Speedee, a winking little logo-man with a hamburger head, advertises "speedee" service and 15-cent burgers.

It was restaurants like this that launched the McDonald's empire, which now includes more than 18,000 restaurants in close to 100 countries. In 1955 milkshake multimixer salesman Ray Kroc, intrigued by an order for eight of his products, flew out to California to observe the restaurant operation of brothers Dick and Maurice McDonald. Kroc left California as the brothers' franchise agent. He had a vision that the future was fast food, and opened his first franchise on April 15, 1955.

The museum was built according to the original blueprints for that first franchise. In the customer service and food preparation areas, you'll see the authentic equipment used in those days. Hamburgers and cheeseburgers were grilled; fresh potatoes were sliced, blanched, and fried; while milkshakes were whipped up, of course, on multimixers. Although these techniques may not strike you as antiquated, the prices will. The most expensive item on the menu was a 20-cent milkshake. A museum host will happily answer any questions and serve up McDonald's trivia. Downstairs, in the small exhibit area, you can examine memorabilia such as a training manual, old advertisements, and Ray Kroc's ledger book.

Cost: Free
Freebies: Postcard of museum
Video Shown: 3-minute video on McDonald's history.
Reservations Needed: No, except recommended for groups larger than 10 people.
Days and Hours: June through August: Thur–Sat 12:00 PM–4:00 PM, but call to confirm since entire schedule changes every year. Closed balance of the year.
Plan to Stay: 20 minutes
Minimum Age: None
Disabled Access: Restricted to upper floor
Group Requirements: Groups larger than 10 people, call at least 15 days in advance. Maximum group size is 25 people inside at one time.
Special Information: The high-tech Ray Kroc Museum, located in McDonald's Oak Brook corporate headquarters, is open to visitors by invitation only. Multimedia presentations feature Ray Kroc from his beginnings as a salesman to his success as a business legend.
Gift Shop: No, but if you're hungry, a real McDonald's is across the street.
Directions: Located in vicinity of O'Hare Airport. From the south, take I-294 (Tri-State Tollway) North to Dempster West exit. Go west on Dempster (U.S. 14) to Lee St. Turn right onto Lee and go about 2 blocks. Just before Lee converges with Rand Rd., you'll see the Museum on your left. From the north, take I-294 to Golf Rd. West exit. Go west on Golf Rd. (Rt. 58) to Mannheim Rd./River Rd. (U.S. 45). Turn left on U.S. 45 and proceed south. Just after you cross Rand Rd., you'll see the Museum on your right.
Nearby Attractions: Revell-Monogram tour (see page 76); Botanical Gardens; Des Plaines Historical Museum; Chicago's attractions, including the Sears Tower, are about 30 minutes away.

Mitsubishi ⟶ *cars*

100 North Mitsubishi Motorway
Normal, IL 61761-8099
(309) 888-8203

Mitsubishi started building this new plant in 1986 and begin producing its first cars here in 1988, originally in a joint venture with Chrysler under the name "Diamond-Star Motors." The plant, which occupies more than 2 million square feet—the equivalent of about 44 football fields—was designed to make several different models intermixed on one assembly line. With close to 4,000 employees, the factory makes such popular models as the Mitsubishi Eclipse, Eclipse Spyder convertible, Mitsubishi Galant, Eagle Talon, Dodge Avenger, and Chrysler Sebring. The catwalk tour shows you the advanced robotics and just-in-time inventory management that have made the facility one of the most technologically advanced auto assembly plants in the world.

The plant produces far more car parts than is typical of other assembly plants, which usually have most parts shipped to them from other facilities. Out of your view, the body parts are stamped on five massive presses, and the bumper (fascias) is formed in nine injection molding machines. You can't miss the automated guided vehicles (AGV) that transport parts and equipment between areas of the plant. Without any apparent human intervention, the AGVs follow bumps and wires on the floor to deliver racks of stamping to waiting workers. These AGVs remind you of a well-trained dog that fetches the morning newspaper.

The plant has more than 550 robots that perform the monotonous, cumbersome, more dangerous tasks. The body shop is 90 percent automated, with robots installing doors, hoods, tailgates, and welds according to a highly synchronized order. With color-ful sparks flying, the robots, which look and move like metallic and wire-filled praying mantises, precisely fit and weld the body parts together.

More robots assist workers on the trim and final assembly line, installing seats, windshields, and instrument panels. The way the robotic arms pick up glass and put it in place may remind you of Michael Jordan palming a basketball and then smoothly heading over the top to stuff it in the basket. If you find all the noise, sparks, and technology unnerving, just listen to the Beethoven and Mozart music that plays throughout the plant. It signifies the stopping and starting of the line.

Cost: Free
Freebies: No
Video Shown: 10-minute video that provides background on factory and shows all stages of production, including those not on tour.
Reservations Needed: Yes
Days and Hours: Thur and Fri 9:00 AM and 1:30 PM. Closed holidays. Closed for a week at the end of June or beginning of July and between Christmas and New Year's.
Plan to Stay: 1½ hours for video, discussion, and tour.
Minimum Age: 10
Disabled Access: Yes
Group Requirements: Large groups need to make reservations 2–3 months in advance.
Special Information: No photography
Gift Shop: No
Directions: From Rockford or Chicago, once on I-55/74, exit at the I-74 West exit 163 (Peoria). Off I-74, exit at Rt. 150 East (this is also called Mitsubishi Motorway, or exit 125). Mitsubishi Motor Manufacturing will be on left (you can't miss this massive plant). Follow the signs to visitor parking, located by the 5 flagpoles. From Decatur, St. Louis, or Champaign, once on I-55/74, take exit 160B (Pekin). Follow around until on Rt. 9. Turn right at the traffic light onto Rt. 150. Factory will be on right.
Nearby Attractions: Kathryn Beich candy factory tour (see page 72); Beer Nuts Factory Outlet, with video of Beer Nuts being made (call 309-827-8580); Bloomington's other attractions, including, Prairie Aviation Museum, Illinois State University Planetarium, are about 20 minutes away.

Motorola ⟶ *electronics*

Museum of Electronics
1297 East Algonquin Road
Schaumburg, IL 60196
(847) 576-6400

 **MOTOROLA**

After touring this museum, you will not doubt U.S. companies' technological prowess or their ability to innovate. From the mezzanine, look over the airy museum. Notice the 1930s Oldsmobile, the 1950s TV sets, the 35-foot radio antenna tower, and the robots used to manufacture circuit boards

After watching the introductory video, view the historical displays that frame the exhibition hall. Then explore the center section, devoted to electronics technology. Learn about Motorola's pioneering work in radio, including the first car radios, its famous WWII Handie-Talkie two-way portable radio, its television designs, and its early development of integrated circuits. Follow Motorola's advancement into microchips, its redirection toward such sophisticated commercial electronic products as pagers and portable phones, and its flexible manufacturing.

The museum is filled with hands-on exhibits. You can sit in the 1930s-style living room to hear broadcasts from the Golden Age of Radio. To learn about high-tech manufacturing and Motorola's "smart factories," you can use real industrial robots to make a souvenir plastic circuit board.

The exhibits appeal to all levels of knowledge. At the microelectronics display you can read about silicon wafer design, manufacturing, testing, and packaging; look at a full size clean room where computer chips are made; and play binary bingo. Another favorite multimedia exhibit lets you become a radio dispatcher to learn about the use and design of communication systems. You must respond to a simulated 911 emergency call by selecting the proper police, fire, and ambulance crews. You can also design the best radio communication system for cowboys or taxicab drivers. Interactive exhibits let you experience the electronics technology revolution, and learn about the intertwined evolution of Motorola and the electronics industry.

Cost: Free

Freebies: Postcard, plastic circuit board

Videos Shown: "In One Lifetime" provides an overview of Motorola's history and the museum exhibits. Throughout the museum, videos explain the displays.

Reservations Needed: Yes, except family days

Days and Hours: Mon–Fri 9:00 AM–4:30 PM. Will assign a tour guide if available; otherwise, audio-tape tours available in English and other languages. Closed holidays observed by Motorola and the first 2 weeks in January.

Plan to Stay: At least 1½ hours, depending on your interests in the displays, selected videos, and interactive exhibits.

Minimum Age: None for families; 6th grade for school and camp groups.

Disabled Access: Yes

Group Requirements: Does not encourage traditional bus-group tours. Museum geared to educational groups from 6th grade up, with maximum size of 60. Special tours and programs for students from schools and camps, grades 6 through 12. For information, call the above number.

Special Information: Dress appropriately— the museum is in the corporate education complex. Displays change for new products and developments.

Gift Shop: No

Directions: From Chicago, take I-90 West to the Rt. 53 North (Rolling Meadows) exit. Remain in the right lane, and immediately exit at Rt. 53 to Rt. 62 (Algonquin Rd.). Follow the exit ramp around to the traffic light and turn right onto Algonquin Rd. Motorola Center is past the intersection of Algonquin and Meacham Rds. Enter the Motorola visitors' entrance gate. Can also take I-290, exiting onto Rt. 53 as described above.

Nearby Attractions: Historic Long Grove; Cuneo Museum and Gardens; Chicago's attractions, including the *Tribune*, Board of Trade, and Post Office tours (see pages 67, 68, 77), are approximately 25 miles away.

Revell-Monogram — *plastic model kits*

8601 Waukegan Road
Morton Grove, IL 60053-2295
(847) 966-3500

This plant makes more tires than Goodyear, more cars than General Motors, and more airplanes than Boeing. The big difference is that here, the product is made of plastic and is a fraction of the original's size. This factory floor tour gives you a close-up view of the steps involved in designing, manufacturing, and packaging plastic scale-model kits.

In the design area, artists draw schematics for models. They then turn these drawings into wooden models. Notice the details on the wooden cars and airplanes—you might think you're in the studio of a skilled whittler instead of a plastic model factory.

Revell-Monogram boasts that its kits have a "healthy glow." The plastic in its models start as small pellets, no larger than confetti, which the tour guide lets you feel. In addition to using various colored pellets, the company adds clear polystyrene. This mixture of colored and clear pellets gives their models a special shine, as a clear-coat does for a real automobile.

The automatically blended combination of different color pellets is piped to the injection molding machines that occupy most of the factory. These machines resemble cannons. At the heart of each one is a metal mold that forms all the model's pieces together on a frame. The machine electronically heats and injects the plastic pellets into the mold. The mold then closes. About 20 seconds and thousands of pounds of pressure later, the warm parts tumble out in one connected piece. Workers carefully inspect the parts as they drop out of the injection molding machine.

After the pieces cool, they are bagged almost as quickly as they are made. On the packaging lines, the plastic parts are assembled into finished kit boxes to be shipped to stores. You leave amazed at how little time it takes to produce and package the plastic model pieces that you spend many happy hours snapping or gluing together.

Cost: Free

Freebies: Plastic model or toy, depending on availability and tour group age.

Video Shown: No

Reservations Needed: Yes. Individuals and families need to join a scheduled group tour.

Days and Hours: Usually September through May only. Mon 12:00 PM–2:30 PM, Tue–Thur 9:00 AM–2:00 PM., although subject to yearly changes. Closed holidays.

Plan to Stay: 40 minutes

Minimum Age: 4. Children must be able to wear safety goggles, which company provides.

Disabled Access: Yes

Group Requirements: Tours should be scheduled at least 2 weeks ahead. Maximum group size is 25 people. Does not want standard bus-group tours; prefers children.

Special Information: No photography. This is a factory floor tour, so for safety reasons, children must be reminded not to touch anything. Tour guide is the injection molding manager, so limited tour spaces available. Company now owned by Binney & Smith, makers of Crayola crayons, so tour route and policy may change.

Gift Shop: No

Directions: Take I-294 North and exit at Dempster St. (Rt. 14 East). Stay on Dempster St. for about 3 miles. Turn right at Waukegan Rd. Revell-Monogram is on the left near traffic light.

Nearby Attractions: McDonald's Museum (see page 73); Chicago's attractions, including Sears Tower, are about 30 minutes away.

U.S. Post Office   *mail*

433 West Harrison Street
Chicago, IL 60607
(312) 983-7550

There are few things we take more for granted than the delivery of our mail. This is one of the newest, most technologically advanced mail-distribution centers in the world. It replaces the post office building next door that was once the world's largest post office. After the tour you'll no longer wonder what happens to your letter between the time you drop it in the mailbox and the time it's delivered. You'll discover the steps involved in processing the mail, from initial cancellation of postage stamps to final sorting by carrier route.

Automation plays a big role. In the old, massive, warehouse-like building, the post office simultaneously used different generations of technology, so the tour presented a living museum on the evolution of automation equipment. Mail sorting in the new building relies on high-tech equipment that moves at lightning speed, using bar code technology and optical character readers (OCRs) to sort the mail. The OCR scans the address and sprays a bar code on the bottom of each letter at a rate of 11 pieces of mail per second. The OCR does a rough sort by region, with other machines reading the bar codes to sort by delivery route. The mail moves so quickly through these machines that it looks like one continuous stream of paper. The mail races through the bar code readers and parks itself in the proper zip code slot.

Machines in other areas cancel the stamps, weed out oversized pieces, or handle bundles and large flat pieces. Computers then automatically direct the sorted mail to the proper transportation route. The next time you open your mail, you'll appreciate what that envelope has been through.

Cost: Free
Freebies: No
Video Shown: No
Reservations Needed: Yes. Keep trying—it can sometimes be hard to get an answer at the above number.

Days and Hours: Mon–Fri 10:30 AM and 12:30 PM. Closed national holidays.
Plan to Stay: 1–2 hours depending on what areas you visit.
Minimum Age: 10
Disabled Access: Yes
Group Requirements: Can handle groups of up to 100 people with at least 1 week's advance notice. Lunch available in cafeteria with advance notice.
Special Information: Substantial walking involved. Guides can individualize tour to special interests, which is why tour length varies. Many post offices like to give tours, so contact your local P.O. for information.
Gift Shop: Philatelic store in building lobby. Sells a large collection of commemorative stamps and books. Open Mon–Fri 8:00 AM–9:00 PM, Sat 8:00 AM–5:00 PM.
Directions: From I-90/94, take the exit for Congress Pkwy. East. Take the Canal St. exit and turn left. Post office is located on corner of Harrison and Canal. Customer parking lot on Harrison. From I-290, take the Canal St. exit.
Nearby Attractions: Chicago's attractions include Chicago Board of Trade and Chicago Mercantile Exchange tours (see page 68), *Chicago Tribune* tour (see page 67), Quaker Oats Lobby Exhibit (call 312-222-6887), Sears Tower, Shedd Aquarium, Adler Planetarium, Lincoln Park Zoo, Art Institute, and the Museum of Science and Industry.

Amish Heritage Furniture ⌒ *furniture*

52886-A State Road 13
Middlebury, IN 46540
(219) 825-1185 / (800) 870-2524

Company founder R. Gene Beachy's great-grandfather was an Amish farmer in northern Indiana who built furniture in his spare time. Out of respect for this elder, the tour begins in front of an elegant, popular piece of furniture the company calls "Grandpa's Secretary," a desk-and-cabinet reproduction that dates back to 1892. While the company's construction methods make use of electric saws, planers, drills, and sanders, reminding you of a modern woodshop, you'll also see carpentry techniques that would make great-grandfather proud.

The company's workforce is almost entirely Amish. The scarcity of farming jobs has led the Amish to work in factories such as this one. If your only experience with the Amish is watching them in horse-drawn buggies, you may be surprised to see men and women skillfully handling power tools. Except for the sneakers, the men wear the typical Amish plain pants and hats, and the women wear solid-colored dresses and bonnets—very different than the T-shirt and jeans worn by many American factory workers.

The furniture's solid-lumber construction begins with piles of pine, oak, or cherry boards cut to the required length in the mill area. To make the wood panels used to build the furniture, the boards interlock by tongue-and-groove cutouts and are placed on what looks like a steamboat's paddle wheel. Glue is placed between each pair of boards and the pressure applied produces an almost-seamless wood panel.

Each piece is then individually bench-built, so you can watch a craftsperson use panels or wood spindles to construct a desk, table, chair, or dresser. Workers sand the wood, spray stains, and hand-rub oil finishes. Hovered over a dresser, for example, you may see a worker hammering nails, fitting a mortise-and-tenon joint, or showing their pride in the furniture's quality by signing and dating the piece.

Cost: Free

Freebies: No

Video Shown: 10-minute video on furniture-making runs in showroom area.

Reservations Needed: Yes, for guided tour. No, to watch production from observation window in back of showroom.

Days and Hours: Mon–Fri 1:30 PM and 3:00 PM for guided tour. Can watch production through window Mon–Fri 9:15 AM–12:00 PM and 12:30 PM–4:00 PM. Closed holidays.

Plan to Stay: 20 minutes for tour, plus time for showroom.

Minimum Age: 6, for guided factory floor tour; none, to observe from window.

Disabled Access: Yes

Group Requirements: No maximum size. Larger groups will be split into 12 people per tour. Prefers 2 days' advance notice.

Special Information: No photography, since the Amish do not want photographs taken of themselves. Tour loop for area furniture-makers planned (for information contact Elkhart Convention and Visitors Bureau, 800-262-8161).

Showroom: Sells all furniture made at factory, including dining-room tables, chairs, desks, dressers, and bed frames. Occasional discounts available. Open Mon–Fri 9:00 AM–5:00 PM and Sat 10:00 AM–5:00 PM. Usually open until 8:00 PM on Tue, except in winter months. Closed holidays.

Directions: From I-80/90 (Indiana Toll Rd.), take Exit 107. Turn right onto SR 13 South. Company is ahead on left.

Nearby Attractions: RV tours, including Coachmen, Jayco, and Holiday Rambler (see pages 80, 84, and 82); Walter Piano's tour (see page 89); Deutsch Kase Haus cheese factory, with observation windows in back of gift shop (call 219-825-9511 about production schedule); Shipshewana Flea Market and Auction, the Midwest's most popular outdoor flea market; Swartzendruber Hardwood Creations, located in the restored Old Bag Factory in Goshen, has an observation deck (call 219-534-2502).

Berne Furniture ⟶ *furniture*
150 Berne Street
Berne, IN 46711
(219) 589-2173

Step into an Old World oasis in the middle of Indiana. Settled by Mennonite immigrants from Canton Bern in Switzerland, Berne, Indiana, is known for its Amish village, quaint Swiss chalets, flower boxes, and congenial atmosphere. In the midst of it all, you'll find Berne Furniture, established in 1925 by Swiss settlers. Today Berne Furniture is still highly dedicated to the quality and excellence of Swiss custom upholstery.

Wood from nearby lumber mills is brought directly to Berne Furniture. Inhale the fresh smell of cut wood and brace yourself against the whir of the saw blades. Watch a craftsman guide a wood block against the jigsaw to achieve the perfect curve for a chair back. After the pieces are cut, holes are bored into the wood so the pieces can be connected, without nails, by inserting dowels.

After the frame is complete, steel springs are attached by hand. The worker tacks down the rows of springs along the seat of the frame, a mass of coils bobbing and swaying slightly like an exhibit of modern art. Each spring is then hand-tied with twine in eight directions for stability, so the base looks like a spider's web. Each end of the twine has to be nailed to the base. Hold your breath as the craftsman holds the nails in his mouth! With a magnetic hammer he grabs a nail from his mouth and swiftly pounds it into the frame.

In the cutting room, 1,000 different fabrics of every color and texture line the wall. Cutting tables 13 yards long fill the room, making it look like a giant banquet hall. Cutters use heavy cardboard patterns to determine the piece shapes. Each cutter pays special attention so that the design on the fabric will match from one piece to another. They cut meticulously straight edges with heavy, 13-inch-long shears.

You will be surrounded by the whirring and clicking of 30 sewing machines as you walk right through the middle of the sewing room. On your right, seamstresses nimbly maneuver fabric for cushions and throw pillows. On your left, they work on the pieces that will upholster the arms, backs, and bases. Not quite like your grandmother's sewing machine, these computerized electronic machines help the seamstresses be efficient and precise.

The upholsterers wrestle the fabric into exactly the right position before tacking it to the frame with an air-powered staple gun. When the master upholsterer is finished, another person will apply a hand-tailored skirt or artfully carved legs. Finally, all the loose threads are cut, stray padding is brushed away, and the Berne label is applied to every cushion.

Cost: Free
Freebies: Brochure detailing the company's history, products, and process.
Video Shown: No
Reservations Needed: Yes, 1 day in advance.
Days and Hours: Mon–Thur 9:30 AM, 10:30 AM, and 1:00 PM. Other times can be arranged. Closed holidays and July 4th week and between Christmas and New Year's.
Plan to Stay: 1 hour
Minimum Age: 12, although younger children may attend if well supervised.
Disabled Access: Yes
Group Requirements: Maximum group size 25–30 people. Larger groups can be split.
Special Information: Visitors are required to wear safety glasses.
Gift Shop: No. Will provide directions to local dealers.
Directions: From Fort Wayne, take Hwy. 27 South to Rt. 218 East (Main St.). Turn left on Behring St. Berne Furniture is on the corner of Berne and Behring Sts.
Nearby Attractions: Hitzer Stove Factory tour (call 219-589-8536); Swiss Heritage Village; Amishville USA; July Swiss Days Festival.

Coachmen   *recreational vehicles*

423 North Main Street
Middlebury, IN 46540
(219) 825-5821

The RV industry has many start-up stories as colorful as Bill Gates' at Microsoft and Steven Jobs' at Apple Computer. The Corson brothers (Tom, Keith, and Claude) founded the company back in 1964, naming it after an inn Tom spotted along the Ohio Turnpike. From a meager start in capital, Coachmen now has record sales growth and revenues exceeding $500 million.

At this sprawling industrial complex, you'll get picked up for your tour at the Coachmen Caravan Visitors Center in a modern bus or a new motor home like those coming off the line. On the way to the tour site, the guide (who is also a sales representative) points out the buildings where the cabinets are made, and where the floors, walls, and ceilings are formed and laminated in the vacubond process. Across from the chassis prep/frame shop/body shop building sits what looks like a football field's worth of Ford and Chevy chassis.

Walking through the travel trailer and fifth-wheel building you can see these RVs come to life. At each station along the line, a different feature is added, whether it be the flooring, walls, or the familiar Coachmen Dalmatian logo. Saws buzz, overhead cranes lift front and rear fiberglass RV cabs and walls, and workers nimbly insert wiring and plumbing.

The Class A motor home tours usually occur after production ends at that plant for the day. Therefore, it offers a quieter industrial experience that gives you time to explore the RV innards. At different points along the inverted L-shaped assembly line, these big, bus-size motor homes sit in various stages of their evolution. At one point the RV just has its floors, then the next RV also has its side walls, and the next has its appliances, and so on. Near the end of the line is a big "rain booth" that exposes the finished RV to storm conditions for up to one hour, revealing any leaks.

Cost: Free

Freebies: A small item at Visitors Center.

Video Shown: No, but can request video in Visitors Center.

Reservations Needed: No, except for groups over 25 people.

Days and Hours: May 1 through October 31: travel trailers and fifth-wheels, Mon–Fri 12:20 PM; class A motor homes, Mon–Fri 3:00 PM. November 1 through April 30: travel trailers and fifth-wheels, Mon, Wed, Fri 12:20 PM; class A motor homes, Tue and Thur 11:50 AM. Closed holidays.

Plan to Stay: 1 hour for tour, plus time for gift area in Visitors Center.

Minimum Age: None

Disabled Access: Yes, but must be careful of tools and wires on plant floor.

Group Requirements: Requests that groups larger than 25 people call 1 day in advance. No maximum group size.

Special Information: Travel trailer and fifth-wheel tours available at their Fitzgerald, GA, plant (call 912-423-5471). Also can see travel trailer production at Grants Pass, OR, plant (call 541-471-6461).

Gift Area: Coachmen Caravan Visitors Center sells Dalmatian-logoed items including T-shirts, jackets, key chains, and potholders. Open Mon–Fri 8:00 AM–5:00 PM. Closed holidays. Price list available at above number.

Directions: From I-80/90 (Indiana Toll Rd.), take Exit 107. Turn right onto SR 13 South, which becomes Middlebury's Main St. At the north end of Middlebury, you'll see a friendly billboard at entrance to company complex. Tour begins at Caravan Visitors Center.

Nearby Attractions: RV tours, including Jayco and Holiday Rambler (see pages 84 and 82); Elkhart County is the RV manufacturing capital of the world. Local Convention & Visitors Bureau lists companies that give tours (call 800-262-8161). RV/MH Heritage Foundation Museum (call 219-293-2344); Amish Heritage Furniture tour (see page 78); Deutsch Kase Haus cheese factory, with observation windows in back of retail store.

Coca-Cola Bottling ～ *soda*

2305 North Davis Road
Kokomo, IN 46903
(317) 457-4421 / (800) 382-8888 (within Indiana)

When pharmacist Dr. John Pemberton invented Coca-Cola in 1886, he could not have imagined that it would be manufactured by thousands of bottling plants throughout the world. Very few of these Coca-Cola bottling plants are independently owned, and even fewer give tours open to the general public. The Severns family purchased the Coca-Cola franchise for the Kokomo area in 1936 and is very proud of what it gives to the community, including welcoming tour visitors. With the third generation of Severns active in the business, a sense of the family's influence pervades the company.

Standing next to the bottling line you may see different sizes ranging from 8-ounce to 2-liter Classic Coke plastic bottles being filled (aluminum cans are not filled at this factory). Try to follow one bottle's journey through the filler and capper machines. Pre-labeled bottles are rinsed and move single-file along a conveyer belt to the circular filling machine. The bottles ride up and down like a merry-go-round. At the top of its ride, each bottle is automatically attached to a filler head. Hear rhythmic bursts of carbon dioxide gas shoot into each bottle, giving the soda its fizz. The 2-liter bottles are gravity-filled with syrup and water at the rate of 98 bottles per minute, with 20-ounce bottles speeding up to 230 per minute.

At the capping machine, red plastic caps slide down a chute and screw onto each spinning bottle. This happens in less than one second, to prevent any bubbles from escaping. Then the bottles march single file to the packaging area. The packing machine grabs eight 2-liter bottles and drops them into red plastic logoed trays. These cases waddle up the conveyor belt and overhead to the warehouse.

In the syrup room, white 5,000-gallon tanks contain liquid sugar, corn syrup, or the top-secret-recipe Classic Coke syrup. Silver tanks hold syrup for individually mixed drinks, such as Sprite. Your guide explains that one gallon of syrup concentrate yields 178 cases of soda—enough soda for a person's lifetime.

Cost: Free
Freebies: Refreshment during tour and souvenir key chain or magnet.
Video Shown: No
Reservations Needed: Yes
Days and Hours: Tue and Thur at 10:00 AM or 1:15 PM. Other times possible. Closed holidays.
Plan to Stay: 30 minutes
Minimum Age: None
Disabled Access: Yes
Group Requirements: Groups over 10 people should call 2 weeks in advance. Call further in advance for June, September, and October tours.
Special Information: Chlorine smell in water treatment room. If plant is making artificially sweetened drinks such as Diet Coke or Diet Sprite, you can taste the NutraSweet in the air, even though you can't see it. Watch for puddles of soapy water used to lubricate the machines. Coca-Cola fans will also want to visit World of Coca-Cola Atlanta in Atlanta GA (see page 58), and Coca-Cola Bottling plant in Elizabethtown, KY (see page 97).
Gift Counter: Small lobby area sells logoed Coca-Cola clothing and Christmas ornaments. Open Mon–Fri 9:00 AM–4:00 PM. Closed holidays.
Directions: From Indianapolis, take U.S. 31 North through Kokomo. Turn left onto Morgan St. Turn right onto Davis Rd. The plant will be on your left. From Ft. Wayne, take U.S. 24 West to U.S. 31 South. Turn right onto Morgan St. Turn right onto Davis Rd. The plant will be on your left.
Nearby Attractions: Kokomo Opalescent Glass tour (see page 83); Seiberling Mansion; Elwood Haynes Museum (invented first successful gasoline-powered car); Circus Hall of Fame located about 20 miles away in Peru.

Holiday Rambler  *recreational vehicles*
1028 East Waterford Street
Wakarusa, IN 46573
(219) 862-7211

Holiday Rambler began in 1953, when Richard Klingler and his father built a boxy little 13-foot trailer in their garage. It might not have been much to look at, but it had all the necessary furnishings for a family getaway: bunk beds, dinette, hot plate, icebox, and heater. Klingler and the company he founded, however, were not satisfied with bare necessities. Today, 45 years later, Holiday Rambler, now a division of Monaco Coach Corporation, continues their trademark style and technological innovations, such as their Alumaframe construction and exclusive kitchen suite slide-outs.

After your guide tells you about the company's history and the production of premium recreational vehicles, you'll visit the factory floor to watch the construction of motorized and towable RVs. Over 800 employees work on the RVs as they move down the line. HR is especially proud of its Alumaframe construction; all Holiday Ramblers are built with this durable, lightweight frame. Workers carefully interlock C-channel aluminum studs at the joints, then double-weld each joint together.

Notice how employees fit two layers of insulation and a moisture barrier into the frame before adding aluminum skin on the outside and paneling on the inside. Equal care is taken with the roof. Workers busily rivet and seal the roof together and onto the frame to prevent leakage.

All cabinets are made on the premises. Peek inside at the wooden cabinets and interiors—you'll be reminded more of a luxury hotel than wilderness. Enjoying the great outdoors does not have to include "roughing it"!

Cost: Free
Freebies: Holiday Rambler pen and product literature.
Video Shown: No
Reservations Needed: No
Days and Hours: Mon–Fri 10:00 AM and 1:30 PM; Winter months (November–April),
1:30 PM only. Closed holidays, week between Christmas and New Year's, and first 2 weeks in July.
Plan to Stay: 2 hours
Minimum Age: No small children
Disabled Access: Yes
Group Requirements: None
Special Information: New corporate headquarters for Holiday Rambler and Monaco Coach will be completed in the fall of 1997. Tours will include this new state-of-the-art motorhome production facility. Information available about the Holiday Rambler RV Club, the oldest company-sponsored enthusiast organization in the industry.
Gift Shop: No
Directions: From the west, take Tollroad 80/90 East to the first South Bend exit. Take Hwy. 20 Bypass East to SR 19 South, then go south 7 miles to Wakarusa. Take a left at light at intersection of SR 19 and County Road 40 (Waterford St.). First driveway to the left is Plant 39, and tour originates from the service department on the east side of the building. From the east, take Tollroad 80/90 West to Elkhart exit. Take SR 19 South. Proceed as above.
Nearby Attractions: RV tours, including Coachmen and Jayco (see pages 80 and 84). Elkhart County is the RV manufacturing capital of the world. Local Convention & Visitors Bureau lists companies that give tours (call 800-262-8161). The RV/MH Heritage Foundation (call 219-293-2344) features museum, library, exhibition hall, and Hall of Fame dedicated to recreational vehicle and manufactured housing industries.

Kokomo Opalescent Glass ⟶ *opalescent and cathedral glass*

1310 South Market Street
Kokomo, IN 46902
(317) 457-1829

Spiritual stained-glass church windows, drooping floral-patterned Tiffany lampshades, and whimsical suncatchers are some of the most common uses of Kokomo opalescent glass. Founded in 1888, the company prides itself on creating its sheet glass the same way for over 100 years. The company, now run by the great-grandsons of the founders, is the oldest maker of opalescent glass in the world. It originated the cat's-paw texture for Tiffany & Co.

As soon as you walk into the factory, you feel the heat wafting from the 2,600° circular furnace. Each of the 12 fiery-orange glowing portholes of the furnace contains a cherry clay pot that holds 1,000 pounds of molten glass.

Once the table man rings a bell, each ladler scoops up to 70 pounds of molten glass out of the furnace and skips along the concrete floor, bouncing the ladle to keep the glass from hardening. Their stride resembles a Native American ceremonial dance. Since up to five colors can be cast per sheet of glass, five men follow each other in rapid succession, repeating this dance. Using a long-handled two-prong pitchfork, the table man blends the glass, swirls it around, stretches it, tosses it like pizza dough, and almost effortlessly eases this 50-pound glob of molten glass onto the rollers. The rollers swallow up the glass and flatten it, with the bottom roller controlling the texture.

The ⅛-inch-thick glass sheet travels through the 140-foot-long annealer for its one-hour cooling. As the glass hardens, its colors and patterns reveal themselves. Using T-squares and glass cutters, workers trim off the excess glass to create 32-by-80-inch sheets. Room 4, the stockroom, houses sheets of glass in narrow, wooden, two-tiered racks. Since Kokomo makes approximately 540 colors and color combinations of sheet glass, this room contains a paintbox of color and texture. Next time you go to your church or synagogue, you'll admire the stained-glass windows, wondering whether

they were newly created or restored with Kokomo Opalescent Glass.

Cost: Free
Freebies: No
Video Shown: No
Reservations Needed: No, except for groups over 4 people or if alternative tour day desired.
Days and Hours: Wed and Fri 10:00 AM. Closed holidays. No tours in December and 4th of July week. Call first, since company shuts down occasionally for repairs.
Plan to Stay: 1 hour, plus time in Op Shop.
Minimum Age: None, but must be extremely careful since you are near people carrying hot molten glass, and broken glass is on floor.
Disabled Access: Yes
Group Requirements: Groups larger than 4 people should call 2 weeks in advance. Maximum group size is 20 people.
Special Information: The extreme heat, especially in summer, can cause heat exhaustion for older visitors. No photography.
Gift Shop: Op Shop sells paperweights, perfume bottles, vases, and suncatchers utilizing Kokomo opalescent glass. Hobbyists can buy sheets of rolled art glass by the pound. Custom design work is also available upon request. Open Mon–Fri 9:00 AM–5:00 PM, with seasonal Saturday hours.
Directions: From Indianapolis, take U.S. 31 North. Turn left onto Markland Ave. in Kokomo. Turn left onto Home Ave. Turn right onto State St. Cross railroad tracks. Kokomo Opalescent Glass is at the corner of State and Market Sts.
Nearby Attractions: Coca-Cola Bottling Plant tour (see page 81); other glass-related attractions, including Seiberling Mansion, utilize Kokomo glass; Greentown Glass Museum; several companies 30 miles away in Elwood give tours, including the House of Glass, which makes paperweights and bottles (call 317-552-6841); Elwood Haynes Museum (invented first successful gasoline-powered car).

Jayco ≈ *recreational vehicles*
58075 State Road 13 South
Middlebury, IN 46540
(219) 825-5861

Since the mid-1960s, when Jayco founder Lloyd Bontrager first built his "pop-up camper" prototypes in a converted chicken coop, family members and friends have been an integral part of Jayco's success. Watching the construction of fifth-wheel travel trailers, the RVs that fit into the back of a pickup truck, you still sense that family feeling, even though Jayco is now one of the five largest RV manufacturers in the country. About 75 percent of Jayco's 1,200 workers are Amish, and their dedication to quality is evident as you travel through the factory.

Every Jayco trailer begins as a tubular steel frame built by a firm that specializes in RV frames. Workers lay an insulated tongue-and-groove plywood floor with fiberglass fabric on the bottom. Following these steps, you'll see the entire trailer flipped upside-down, like an immense turtle on its back. Workers attach axles and wheels to the underbelly and install a fresh-water tank. The unit is turned back over and placed on dollies that run down a track to various workstations in the plant.

Workers attach white-pine sidewalls, cover the wood with glue, and install the inside paneling. Next, they lay the carpeting and linoleum. Look up and you'll see the cabinet shops above the plant floor. Wood from the mill room is assembled into cabinets. Each line of Jayco trailers—the economy Eagle, the lightweight Eagle SF, and the top-of-the-line Designer series—has its own cabinet shop. Carpenters slide the finished cabinets down a ramp to the production area.

Toward the end of the trailer's construction, workers attach the roof. They screw on tapered two-by-fours for the rafters, then stretch a rubber or aluminum roof over them. The area resounds with whining drills. The trailer's "skin" of .024-gauge aluminum (fiberglass on the Designer series) is drilled into position. Once the trailer's body is complete, appliances, drawer and cabinet fronts, windows and custom-made upholstery are added. Afterwards, at your leisure, you can view completed trailers displayed in a campground setting.

Cost: Free

Freebies: Product brochures. A follow-up letter includes a Jayco key chain.

Video Shown: 15-minute video on the company's history and production methods.

Reservations Needed: No, except for groups larger than 10 people.

Days and Hours: Tour Mon–Fri at 1:30 PM; June through August also 9:30 AM tour. Display area and Visitors' Center open Mon–Fri 8:00 AM–5:00 PM. Closed holidays. No production 4th of July week, and week between Christmas and New Year's.

Plan to Stay: 1½ hours for video and tour, plus time for gift area, display area, and Visitors' Center.

Minimum Age: None

Disabled Access: Yes, although must be careful of tools and wires on factory tour.

Group Requirements: Groups larger than 10 people need to make reservations 10 days in advance. Maximum group size is 50.

Special Information: No video cameras allowed. Upon request, tours available of the mini–motor home and fold-down production buildings. Visitors' Center displays Jayco memorabilia, including brochures from 1968.

Gift Area: Sells logoed items, including mugs, clothing, and license plates. Open same hours as Visitors' Center. Closed holidays.

Directions: From I-80/90 (Indiana Toll Rd.), take Exit 107 for SR 13 South to Middlebury. Located on right, just south of the intersection with U.S. Rt. 20.

Nearby Attractions: Holiday Rambler and Coachmen tours (see pages 82 and 80). Elkhart County is the RV manufacturing capital of the world. For a list of tours, call 800-262-8161. The RV/MH Heritage Foundation (call 219-293-2344) features museum, library, exhibition hall, and Hall of Fame dedicated to recreational vehicle and manufactured housing industries.

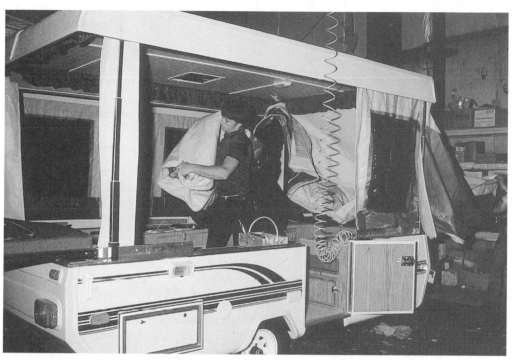

Watch the construction of RVs that fit in the back of a pickup truck at Jayco.

When you visit Jayco in Middlebury, Indiana, you'll see a predominantly Amish workforce building RVs.

Perfection Bakeries   ∼ *bread*

350 Pearl Street
Fort Wayne, IN 46802
(219) 424-8245 / (800) 347-7373 (ext. 289)

Food manufacturing is highly automated in big bakeries with lopsided ratios of workers-to-units-produced. Perfection Bakeries has about 30 production people who make 180,000 loaves per day of such well-known breads as Sunbeam, Aunt Millie's, Country Hearth, and Holsum. This tour shows you high-speed bread-making at its most mechanized, with techniques very different from those used in 1901, when the company started baking wafers.

As you would do at home, Perfection combines ingredients in the mixer, bakes dough in the oven, and slices the bread before eating. But there the comparison ends, since Perfection's process is much bigger, faster, and more intensely aromatic. About every ten minutes, a trough filled with 2,000 pounds of dough rises above a "J" divider and drops a mushy blob of dough into a machine, which separates it into softball-size portions. A "rounder" machine then rounds and flours the dough before it heads for the "proofer."

Once the dough comes out of the overhead proofer, it moves through a "sheeter," which rolls it flat to remove gases and air bubbles. Then it falls into pans on five-across trays. Even the ovens seem to be in constant motion, welcoming and expelling loaves after an 18-minute baking. The depanners magically lift the hot bread from the pans using small suction cups. The baked loaves cool on a 1-mile overhead conveyor-belt cooling system. While cooling, the bread is inspected for foreign objects; occasionally you'll see a loaf almost mysteriously flying off the line.

Slicing and packaging must be done quickly, while the bread is still warm; otherwise, the slices lose moisture that keeps the loaf fresh. The tour guide explains some nuances of slicing bread, such as why pumpernickel is sliced thinnest. The bagging process is like inflating a balloon, except that the loaf follows the air into a bag that is then automatically tied. After watching state-of-the-art mass bread production, you'll never again take for granted that bread in your local supermarket.

Cost: Free
Freebies: Samples of warm bread with jam and margarine; gift bag of promotional items.
Video Shown: 12-minute video on bread production.
Reservations Needed: Yes. Individuals and families need to join scheduled group tours or form a group of at least 7 people.
Days and Hours: Mon, Wed, and Thur 9:00 AM. Closed holidays.
Plan to Stay: 1½ hours for talk on nutrition and company history, video, tour, and sampling.
Minimum Age: 10
Disabled Access: Yes
Group Requirements: Minimum group size is 7, maximum is 35. Book 2 weeks in advance.
Special Information: No photography. Warm during summer tours.
Thrift Store: Located on the west side of building. Sells 2-day-old breads at discount. Open Mon–Fri 9:00 AM–5:30 PM and Sat 8:30 AM–4:00 PM. Closed holidays.
Directions: Atop the bakery is a unique billboard of bread slices continuously spilling from a bag of Sunbeam bread. More than 750 million slices have "fallen" from the yellow wrapper. Find this billboard and bakery from I-69 by taking Exit 102 to the east (Hwy. 24 W). This becomes Jefferson Blvd. Follow Jefferson Blvd. into the city. Turn left (north) onto Ewing St., right onto Main St., and immediate left into the Light & Breuning parking lot.
Nearby Attractions: Seyfert's snack food and Sechler's pickles tours (see page 88 and 87); Fort Wayne Newspapers (call 219-461-8274); Botanical Gardens.

Sechler's ～ *pickles*
5686 State Route 1
St. Joe, IN 46785
(219) 337-5461

Like all pickles, Sechler's start out as cucumbers, salt, and water. Now in its third generation, Sechler's started making pickles in 1921. The first packing was done in the basement of Ralph Sechler's home, now the plant's office.

Trucks full of fresh cucumbers are unloaded into zigzagging grading machines. From a 20-foot elevation, the cucumbers fall into slats; smaller cukes roll through the first slats, and larger ones fall through slats at the end. Once sorted into seven sizes, the cukes are weighed in 20-bushel (1,000-pound) boxes. Farmers are paid by the number of pounds of each size cucumber, midgets (or "gherkins") are the most expensive.

In the tank yard, 120 10-foot-high wooden pickle vats stand in neat rows. Each holds up to 750 bushels (or 37,000 pounds) of pickles. The cucumbers are placed in these tanks by size, salt brine is added, and the tanks are closed with wooden lids. The pickles are usually in these tanks for at least ten weeks, but may stay as long as 1½ years, depending on demand and the cycle relative to next year's crop.

In the processing room, pickles cook in 110° to 140° water for 24 hours to remove some of the salt. Cutting machines slice, dice, chip, grind, and chop the inspected pickles into numerous shapes and sizes. The pickles marinate for one to two days in dill brine, or seven to ten days in vinegar and spices for sweet flavoring. Smells of hot peppers, raisins, or oranges fill the air, depending on the variety in production.

Workers stand at a stainless-steel table hand-packing spears and peppers. Machines pack whole pickles, relishes, and hamburger chips. Jars move along the conveyor belt single-file, filling with pickles. The excess pickles roll into a cylinder below and recirculate back to the top of the machine. Down the line, the "juicer" overflows the jars with juice or brine. As the cap is put on, a burst of steam shoots across it, cooling, condensing, and pulling down the center of the lid to form a pressure seal. The "dud" detector measures the jar's resulting vacuum level by measuring the recess in the lid. If the center isn't pulled down enough, the machine rejects the jar and sends it back through the line.

Cost: Free

Freebies: Paper hat and samples of all varieties in the showroom.

Video Shown: Sechler's 75th anniversary video, with historic and product footage. Request to see video in showroom.

Reservations Needed: No, except for groups over 6 people.

Days and Hours: Tours only April 1 through October 31. Mon–Fri 9:00 AM–11:00 AM and 12:30 PM–3:00 PM, every ½-hour. Closed holidays.

Plan to Stay: 30 minutes for tour and tasting, plus time in showroom.

Minimum Age: None

Disabled Access: Yes

Group Requirements: Groups larger than 6 people should call 2 days in advance. No maximum group size.

Special Information: Wear comfortable shoes. Be alert for wet floors and forklift.

Showroom: Sells over 30 varieties of pickles, such as orange-flavored spears and candied raisin crispies. Display cases show company history. Open year-round Mon–Fri 8:30 AM–4:30 PM, Sat 8:30 AM–12:00 PM. Closed major holidays. Mail-order form available from (800) 332-5461.

Directions: From Fort Wayne, take I-69 North to Dupont exit. Turn right on Dupont. Go straight through traffic light onto SR 1 North. Sechler's is 20 miles ahead (through farm country) on your left. From Auburn, take SR 8 East. Turn right onto SR 1 South. Sechler's is on your right.

Nearby Attractions: Auburn Cord-Duesenberg Museum; National Automotive and Truck Museum; Fort Wayne's attractions, including Perfection Bakeries and Seyfert's snack food tours (see pages 86 and 88), are 20 miles away.

Seyfert's   *potato chips and pretzels*

1001 Paramount Road
Fort Wayne, IN 46808
(219) 483-9521

When Charles Seyfert left his Pennsylvania farm for the Chicago World's Fair, he hoped to earn his fortune from selling pretzels. His dreams ended rather quickly, however, when only a handful of fairgoers dared to try his snacks. Discouraged, he headed back to Pennsylvania, stopping only in Fort Wayne for one more try. The pretzels failed again, but his potato chips were a hit, especially in bars and saloons. Seyfert stayed in Fort Wayne and opened Seyfert Foods in 1934. Today Seyfert's produces snack foods at a 3-acre plant not far from the original site.

Charles Seyfert once said he would retire only when his business reached a production level of 500 pounds of chips a week. Today the business produces 9,000 pounds of chips *an hour.* The pretzel machines, which finally began production in 1976, turn out almost 100,000 pretzels each hour.

You will first be greeted by your tour guide, usually Myrtle Young, who has been on several talk shows displaying her famous potato-chip collection. One of the industry's foremost experts on potato-chip lore, Myrtle shows you each step involved in making chips and pretzels. She encourages questions and loves to discuss her unique collection before you head out to watch production from a long, narrow, windowed corridor.

In the pretzel-making area, the newest part of the factory, watch the ingredients being mixed and sent through machines that twist and spurt out pretzels at unbelievable speeds. Pretzel sticks are produced at even faster speeds before joining their three-ring cousins for the next step. They all travel by conveyor belt to the cookers and salters, then head for packaging. Pretzels dive into bags and boxes and are stored in the warehouse before shipping out to stores.

In the potato-chip section, spuds arrive in tractor-trailers driven onto hydraulic lifts. As the lifts tip the trucks back, hordes of potatoes come barreling down into the factory, where bins catch them and take them to the washers. Here you can first view the potatoes as they are scrubbed, inspected, and mechanically peeled and sliced. For every pound of potatoes that enters the washer and peelers, only about 3.2 ounces leave. The rest is discarded in the form of skin, starch, and water. Potato slivers travel by conveyor to the cookers and salters. After inspection for imperfections, the chips travel a maze of conveyor highways to be machine-packed for shipping.

Cost: Free

Freebies: Sample bags of pretzels and potato chips.

Video Shown: No

Reservations Needed: Yes. Individuals and families will usually be combined into larger groups.

Days and Hours: Mon–Thur 9:00 AM–3:00 PM. Closed holidays.

Plan to Stay: 45 minutes

Minimum Age: None, although the 400 feet of walking may not be suitable for very young children.

Disabled Access: Yes, but let reservations operator know ahead of time so appropriate accommodations can be made.

Group Requirements: Maximum group size is 30 people. Groups should make reservations at least 1 day in advance. Groups with more than 15 people will be divided into smaller groups.

Special Information: No photography

Gift Shop: No

Directions: Take I-69 to Exit 111A. Seyfert's is straight ahead in the industrial park.

Nearby Attractions: Perfection Bakeries and Sechler's Pickles tours (see pages 86 and 87); Fort Wayne Newspapers tour (call 219-461-8274); Botanical Gardens; Lincoln Museum; Franke Park Zoo; Diehm Museum; Cord-Duesenberg Museum 20 miles away in Auburn.

Walter Piano *pianos*
25416 County Road 6
Elkhart, IN 46514
(219) 266-0615 / (219) 674-0467

Elkhart, Indiana is probably the musical instrument manufacturing capital of the U.S., with major saxophone, clarinet, flute, and other companies located in this area. The most accessible general-public tours are at Walter Piano, one of the only six piano manufacturers left in the U.S. A family-owned company, Walter Piano, which started making high-end consoles and upright pianos in 1970, is as much cabinetmaker as pianomaker.

It takes four to five weeks to make one complete piano. You'll first feel like you've walked into a large cabinet shop. Workers hand-sand, saw, and drill cherry, oak, or mahogany cabinet parts. The cabinet parts for four pianos travel together on each cart. In spray booths, workers spray various stains, sealers, and lacquers.

In another area, a worker attaches the cast-iron piano plate to a wooden soundboard/frame assembly. Over 400 bridge pins are hammered by hand at an angle into the treble and bass bridge. With an air hammer, the worker punches in about 250 shiny nickel-plated tuning pins, then slides the frame assembly over to the next station. Pulling wire from coils overhead, the stringer hand-threads the wire through the hole in each tuning pin, snips it, and wraps the wire around the pin three times with a special tool. The stringer weaves the wire around the bridge pins and back through and around the next tuning pin for all 250 pins. It takes an experienced stringer one hour to do it all, while a new stringer takes eight hours.

After the cabinet and strung back are mated, soundboards travel through the factory to receive actions, hammers, and keys. (Since actions and keys are no longer made in the U.S., they are the only non-U.S.–made parts.) Pianos are tuned, weighted, and adjusted at each stage before final tuning and regulation.

The company recently started making grand pianos, so you may be lucky enough

to catch them bending the rim for one. This may be the only time you'll see a grand piano standing vertically, 6 feet tall. Strips of veneer, 16 feet long, are first glued together. A small crane raises the center of the glued strips, allowing the veneer to droop around the inside rim bending form, called an "inner cull." The outer cull is then lowered, and workers clamp the two culls together to compress and mold the layers of veneer.

Cost: Free
Freebies: Felt-covered piano hammers
Video Shown: No
Reservations Needed: Yes
Days and Hours: Mon–Fri 8:00 AM–4:00 PM. Best times to see production are 10:30 AM, 1:00 PM, and 2:30 PM. Closed holidays, first 2 full weeks of July, and week between Christmas and New Year's.
Plan to Stay: 45 minutes for tour plus time in the showroom.
Minimum Age: None
Disabled Access: Yes
Group Requirements: Minimum group size is 12 people; maximum group size is 30. Call at least 2 days in advance.
Special Information: While there are strong lacquer fumes in the finishing room, it is possible to bypass this room. No photography.
Showroom: Wide variety of console and grand pianos made by Walter Piano as well as other manufacturers. Also sells grandfather clocks. Open Mon–Fri 10:00 AM–5:00 PM with extended hours Mon and Thur until 7:00 PM, Sat 10:00 AM–4:00 PM.
Directions: From I-80/90, take Elkhart Exit 92. Turn left onto Cassopolis St. At second traffic light, turn left onto CR 6. Walter Piano is about 1 mile ahead on your right.
Nearby Attractions: Other musical instrument manufacturers give tours on a limited basis. Contact the Elkhart Convention and Visitors Bureau for a list (call 800-862-2161); Amish Heritage Furniture, Jayco RV, and Coachmen RV tours in Middlebury (see pages 78, 84, and 80); Amish Acres.

Ertl ~ *farm toys and die-cast vehicles*
Highways 136 and 20
Dyersville, IA 52040-0500
(319) 875-5699

Dyersville, Iowa, home to three of the premiere farm-toy manufacturers, prides itself on being the "Farm Toy Capital of the World." Started in 1945 by Fred Ertl Sr. in his Dubuque, Iowa, basement, Ertl (part of U.S. Industries) is now the largest of the three and the only one to offer regular public tours. With thousands of die-cast trucks, cars, and tractors coming off its production lines daily, Ertl makes more tractors than any tractor manufacturer and more trucks than the largest truck manufacturer. This factory-floor tour shows what's involved in making and packaging their large-scale die-cast replica toy tractors, as well as replica cars, trucks, and banks.

It takes more steps than you imagine to produce a scale tractor, truck, or car from start to finish. The metal parts come from the nearby foundry building (not on the standard tour). The production of the die-cast parts is tricky, as the temperature and timing have to be perfect or the mold and/or part will be destroyed. The heated metal is shot into the mold, cooled with water, and then ejected. The paint department uses over 120 different colors and over 32,000 gallons of paint per year.

Everywhere you look in the final assembly and model packaging areas, it seems that miniature parts are moving along conveyor belts. Quick hands apply tires, seats, mufflers, fenders, steering wheels, and decals. When the last parts are attached, tractors are stamped with a date code before being packed in individual boxes and then in shipping cartons. The cartons travel by overhead conveyor belt to the case sealer and then to the warehouse. If you've toured factories that make real tractors, cars, and, trucks, you'll appreciate Ertl's efforts to produce toys that are "Just Like the Real Thing, Only Smaller."

Cost: Free

Freebies: Ertl commemorative coin good for collecting or using as a $1 discount at the nearby outlet store. Brochure includes information and statistics you see on the poster-size boards throughout tour.

Videos Shown: 25–minute video in lobby may detail company history or spotlight various farm toy collectors. Short videos along the tour route show manufacturing steps not seen on tour.

Reservations Needed: Recommended; however, can take a few walk-ins if space allows.

Days and Hours: Mon–Fri 9:00 AM, 10:00 AM, 11:00 AM, 1:00 PM, 2:00 PM, and 3:00 PM. Call for schedule changes. Closed holidays.

Plan to Stay: 45 minutes

Minimum Age: Small children should be in strollers, which Ertl can supply if available.

Disabled Access: Yes

Group Requirements: With 3 days' advance notice, can handle all group sizes. Special times available for groups of 30 or more people.

Special Information: No photography. Be alert for forklift trucks.

Outlet Store: Located ¼-mile away on Hwy. 136. Sells entire Ertl line of die-cast replicas, plastic model kits, miniature action figures, and items produced at other Ertl plants worldwide. Many specials and some factory seconds are red-tagged. Open Mon–Sat 9:00 AM–5:00 PM. Longer hours in summer.

Directions: From Dubuque, take Hwy. 20 West. Take the exit for Hwy. 136 in Dyersville. Turn left onto Hwy. 136. The factory is on your left. For outlet store, turn right on Hwy. 136.

Nearby Attractions: *Field of Dreams* movie site; National Farm Toy Museum; Basilica of St. Francis Xavier; Becker Wood Carver Museum; Heritage Trail; Dyer/Botsford Doll Museum.

John Deere   *tractors*

Waterloo Works
3500 East Donald Street
Waterloo, IA 50701
(319) 292-7801 / (if no answer, call 309-765-4235)

Deere began building tractors in downtown Waterloo in 1918 and moved to the current location in 1981. Many of the old two-cylinder John Deere tractors, manufactured from 1918 to 1960 and affectionately known as "Johnny Poppers," are still in active use. The tour shows you manufacturing techniques that produce the tractors that *Fortune* magazine called one of the "100 Products That America Makes Best."

A company retiree leads your tour through the tractor assembly building (48 acres under one roof). The air is filled with the scent of machine oil and the sound of presses and conveyors. Tractor-building requires many subassembly steps, such as constructing the cab, before the main assembly lines put it all together. A computer system guides the tractors through assembly, keeping tabs on parts drawn from some 40,000 storage bins. Hydraulic presses, with a force of nearly 2,000 tons, form pre-sized sheet steel blanks into tractor frames, fenders, and other parts. Lasers cut out plates for the sides of fuel tanks. Robotic welders join parts with impressive consistency and rainbows of sparks.

An overhead conveyor carries completed parts on a 2-mile journey through paint operations. Three chassis lines and three final assembly lines move at a measured pace. In about two hours the tractor frames become complete machines. Notice how carefully the cab and other parts are lowered from an overhead conveyor hoist and mounted on the tractor frame. Near the end of the line, after fluids are added, workers test wheel-less tractors for such features as engine start-up, speed and power levels, and brake and park/lock security.

Unlike row-crop tractors, the heavy-duty four-wheel-drive tractors are assembled using a modular, team concept. The production area is arranged in process groups called "cells," with each cell's operators responsible for assembling a related family of parts. Once a cell's work is completed and checked, the tractor moves to the next cell.

Cost: Free

Freebies: Brochure on tractor production

Video Shown: 18-minute video overviews the entire John Deere Waterloo Works.

Reservations Needed: Preferred for individuals and families. Required for groups larger than 10 people.

Days and Hours: Mon–Fri 9:00 AM and 1:00 PM. Closed major holidays and week between Christmas and New Year's. Summer shutdown last week of July through first week of August. (Call about more extended summer shutdown.)

Plan to Stay: 2½ hours

Minimum Age: 12

Disabled Access: Yes

Group Requirements: Groups larger than 20 people should make reservations 10 days in advance.

Special Information: No photography. For information on John Deere factory tours nationwide (including Davenport, Dubuque, Des Moines, and Ottumwa, IA), call Visitors' Services at Corporate Headquarters in Moline, IL (309-765-4235). East Moline, IL, plant produces harvesters (see page 71).

Gift Shop: Sells wide variety of logoed items, including T-shirts, hats, belt buckles. Open to tour visitors. Call (319) 292-7564 about other hours.

Directions: From Dubuque, take Hwy. 20 West to Exit 68 North in Waterloo. Follow exit road north. Turn left onto Gilbertville Rd. Turn right onto North Elk Run Rd. Turn left onto East Donald St., which leads directly to John Deere's Waterloo Tractor Assembly Division. From Des Moines, take I-80 East to Hwy. 63 North. Exit at Hwy. 20 East to Waterloo Exit 68 North. Follow the directions above.

Nearby Attractions: Other John Deere tours in Waterloo available at the Foundry, Component, and Engine Works (call 319-292-7801 for information); Wonder Bread bakery tour (call 319-234-4447); Groute Museum of History and Science; Waterloo Recreation and Arts Center; George Wyth Memorial Park.

Krauss Furniture Shop ⟋ *furniture*

2783 Highway 6 Trail
South Amana, IA 52334
(319) 622-3223

Krauss Furniture is located in Iowa's Amana Colonies, which were founded in 1855 by German immigrants escaping religious persecution. The Amana Colonies offer an abundance of family activities, including many craftswork tours. The moment you walk in the company's door, the smell of walnut, cherry, and oak woods mixed with the odor of fresh varnish will tell you this is a furniture factory. As you saunter between the yellow lines on this self-guided tour, you watch as many as 15 craftsmen building custom-made tables, chairs, cupboards, bedroom sets, rockers, and clock cabinets. Krauss completes up to 1,000 pieces per year.

You'll see many different types of woodworking tools, some brand new and others over 80 years old. In the cutting area, workers dry, machine, glue, and rough sand all the lumber used. A lathe-worker, covered head-to-toe with sawdust and chips, turns spindles to make the furniture legs. Planers reduce the boards to equal thickness. They are then glued into panels, rough sanded, and cut into rough lengths.

Krauss does not use an assembly line to make furniture. Each craftsman has his own workbench and builds the furniture, one piece at a time, from start to finish. The method is the old-time hand-fitted, dovetailed or mortise-and-tenon joinery. Wood-worker hobbyists will covet these craftsmen's tools, time, and skill in building furniture. In the finishing area, the workers sand and finish the pieces. The finish, Krauss Furniture's pride, is painstakingly sprayed and brushed on (as many as seven coats) and sanded off until it is completely smooth. When the oil is finally applied for a hand-rubbed finish, workers show the same affection as parents brushing their children's hair.

Cost: Free
Freebies: Product brochure
Video Shown: No
Reservations Needed: No, except for motorcoach tours.

Days and Hours: Mon–Fri 8:00 AM–4:00 PM, Sat 9:00 AM–4:00 PM. Not always in full production on Saturday, so call ahead. Closed major holidays.
Plan to Stay: 15 minutes for the self-guided tour, plus time for the showroom.
Minimum Age: None
Disabled Access: Yes
Group Requirements: Bus tour groups can get guided tour. Call 1 week in advance.
Special Information: Sawdusty setting.
Showroom: Sells all Krauss wood pieces, from large furniture to smaller gift items. Most smaller wooden items, such as magazine racks and picture frames, are made by local retired people. Picture albums show custom-designed furniture that can be built to order. Open Mon–Fri 8:00 AM–5:00 PM, Sat 9:00 AM–5:00 PM, and May through December also Sun 1:00 PM–4:00 PM. Catalog available.
Directions: From I-80, take Exit 225 for Hwy. 151 North. At the T-intersection with Hwy. 6 Trail, go left 2 miles. Krauss Furniture is on the north side of Hwy. 6 Trail (large clock outside building). From Hwy. 6 Trail West, Krauss is about 1 mile east of South Amana.
Nearby Attractions: The Amana Colonies have a number of attractions and a worldwide tradition of craftsmanship. Some other local businesses that offer tours or work-area viewings include Amana Woolen Mill (call 319-622-3432), Schanz Furniture and Refinishing (call 319-622-3529), Amana Furniture and Clock Shop (call 319-622-3291), and Ehrle Brothers Winery (call 319-622-3241).

Winnebago ~ *motor homes*

1316 South 4th Street
Forest City, IA 50436
(515) 582-6936

Winnebago Industries was born in 1958, when a group of local businesses, worried about Iowa's depressed farm economy, persuaded Modernistic Industries of California to build a travel-trailer factory in Forest City. Local businessmen soon bought the factory and, in 1960, named it Winnebago Industries, after the county in which it is located. Since 1966, when the company started making motor homes, the name Winnebago has become synonymous with "motor home."

You will not doubt Winnebago's self-proclaimed position as an industry leader after touring the world's largest RV production plant. The company prides itself on its interlocking joint construction and on the fact that it produces almost everything in-house, including fabric covers for its seats and sofas. The 200-acre factory includes the main assembly areas (which you'll see on the tour), metal stamping division, plastics facility, sawmill and cabinet shop, and sewing and design departments.

In the chassis prep building (not on tour), parts of the all-steel frame are stamped out on the "Dinosaur." Sparks fly as workers weld floor joints and storage compartment to the chassis. The completed RV (including windshield wipers and doors) will be set into this steel frame. The front end drops from a mezzanine onto the chassis and is aligned by laser beams.

The motor-home production lines are in a building employees affectionately call "Big Bertha." From your vantage point on the catwalk, you'll see the developing motor homes creep down three 1,032-foot-long assembly lines at 21 inches per minute. First, workers install a heat-resistant laminated floor. Next they screw the Thermal-Panel sidewalls (made of block foam embedded with an aluminum frame and steel supports), interior paneling, and an exterior fiberglass skin onto steel outriggers extending from the floor of the motor home. Further down the line, furniture and cabi-

nets are installed. Finally the entire unit receives a one-piece, fiberglass-covered, laminated roof. The completed motor home is rigorously inspected in the test chambers, where it "travels" through rainstorms and over potholes—while standing still.

Cost: Free
Freebies: Winnebago brochures
Video Shown: 22-minute "Winnebago Factory Tour" video takes you through a detailed view of the world's largest motor-home factory. When no factory tours, visitors can watch this video as well as informative videos on individual Winnebago, Itasca, Vectra, Rialta, and Luxor motor homes.
Reservations Needed: No, except for groups larger than 6 people.
Days and Hours: April through October Mon–Fri 9:00 AM and 1:00 PM; November through mid-December Mon–Fri 1:00 PM. No tours mid-December through March 31. Closed holidays and 1 week in July.
Plan to Stay: 1¼ hours for video and tour, plus time for Visitors Center motor-home exhibits and wall displays.
Minimum Age: No, but small children must be accompanied by an adult.
Disabled Access: Yes, for Visitors Center. Factory tour includes 3 staircases.
Group Requirements: Groups larger than 6 people should make reservations 2 weeks in advance.
Special Information: Photography allowed in Visitors Center but not in plant.
Gift Shop: Winnebago-Itasca Travelers Club gift shop sells logoed items, including jackets, shirts, and caps. Open 8:30 AM–4:00 PM year-round. Closed holidays.
Directions: From I-35, exit at Hwy. 9 West. At junction of Hwy. 9 and Hwy. 69, take Hwy. 69 South. Turn right on 4th St. in Forest City. Visitors Center is on right.
Nearby Attractions: Pammel RV Park; Pilot Knob State Park; Mansion Museum; Waldorf College; Holtan Farm Museum; Timberland Museum.

See color photos, page 188

Country Critters   *plush toys and puppets*

217 Neosho
Burlington, KS 66839
(316) 364-8623 / (800) 369-8623

In 1977 self-described "country boys" Lawrence "Bud" and Jim Strawder acquired some Korean puppets from a bankrupt company to sell in their S&S Bargain Center. The puppets sold well when the Strawders "wore" them and made them come alive. But they would sell better, the Strawders reasoned, if they were more realistic, better quality, and—most importantly—made in the U.S.A. Today, though Country Critters is one of the world's largest puppet manufacturers, you may still find Bud demonstrating a three-week-old baby pig–puppet himself. You'll wonder if the pig really is alive as Bud remarks, "I've been feeding him out of a bottle, but I sure would like to teach him to drink out of a glass."

Acrylic fabric used in quality imitation-fur coats is specially designed for these lifelike puppets: pink for tongues and insides of ears; shiny black for skunks, baby pigs, bears, puppies, and kittens; and striped for raccoon tails. In the cutting room, four people cut, clean, and sort parts fast enough to keep 75 people sewing. The 30-ton computer-controlled hydraulic press cuts up to six rolls of material at once. Many machines have been adapted or converted from other uses. Look for the "cleaner" Bud made from an old piano, plywood, microwave, furnace, and wire screen. It cleans the excess fuzz off freshly cut plush pieces.

Sewing machines designed for fur-coat production stitch a more secure seam. Parts are turned inside out, and a converted button machine secures eyes into place. A converted farm grinder fluffs up the animal stuffing. Arriving in big bales, the polyester fibers are torn apart to make them softer, then pumped through a pipe to stuff each animal. Sewers hand- or machine-sew the final hole closed.

Then the animal puppets head for the beauty shop for brushing and grooming—even for haircuts and decoration with ribbons. To ensure that their new owners give the puppets continued loving care, workers include hang tags explaining what to feed the animals and how to care for them. Puppets are then shipped from this 3,000-person town all over the U.S. and even overseas.

Cost: Free
Freebies: No
Video Shown: No
Reservations Needed: Yes
Days and Hours: Mon, Wed, and Fri 9:30 AM, 12:00 PM, and 2:00 PM. Other times by appointment. Closed major holidays.
Plan to Stay: 1½ hours, plus time for showroom; allow 2 hours for large groups, since Bud often leads these anecdote-filled tours himself.
Minimum Age: None
Disabled Access: Yes
Group Requirements: Groups larger than 20 people should make reservations 1 week in advance. Reserved tours of 10 or more people receive a 25 percent discount in the showroom. Maximum group size is 40.
Showroom: Sells all Country Critter plush toys and puppets. Look for the entire bear family, from 8-inch Tipsy to 66-inch Grandpa bear. The assortment ranges from the popular raccoon, pig, and skunk hand puppets to ride-on giant plush horses and cows. Also sells pocket-size stuffed toys called "Cottage Critters," made by home sewers. Bargain area sells imperfect or discounted items. Open Mon–Fri 7:30 AM–4:00 PM; from Thanksgiving to Christmas, usually open Saturdays with varying hours. Catalog available from nearby Made In Kansas store (call 800-728-1332).
Directions: From Kansas City, take I-35 South to Beto Junction. Take U.S. 75 South to Burlington. Turn left onto Neosho St. Country Critters is on your right.
Nearby Attractions: Coffey County Museum; Craft Barn Mall.

Reuter ⤳ *pipe organs*

612 New Hampshire Street
Lawrence, KS 66044
(913) 843-2622

Since 1917 Reuter Organ Company has produced custom-built organs for churches, universities, and homes. Housed in an 1880 building (originally a shirt factory), 40 organ-builders and craftsmen assemble six to 12 pipe organs per year. Construction of each organ takes two to four months, so you'll see several in progress during your tour.

Each organ's size depends on its site, so engineers draw individualized musical and architectural plans. Musical plans incorporate the setting's size and other aspects that affect acoustics. Architectural plans specify arrangement of the parts and perhaps a rendering of the finished and installed organ. Guided by these plans, workers cut raw lumber, metal for pipes, and electrical cables.

In the pipe department, workers cut sheets of zinc, copper, and spotted metal (a tin-lead alloy) to each pipe's size and shape. Metal is rolled on mandrels to form the pipes, then pipes are hand-soldered or tig-welded. Pipes range from 32 feet to pencil size, and actually look more like missiles than organ pipes. The number of pipes varies from four or five ranks, each with 61 pipes, to 100 ranks—over 6,000 pipes! Each rank is analogous to an orchestral instrument. "Voicers" allow these new organ pipes to "sing," then refine their sound so each rank's pipes sound identical.

As you tour this four-story factory building, notice the skilled woodworkers and metalsmiths meticulously hand-fashioning organ parts. As you smell the raw wood and hear the drills and saws, appreciate the more easygoing pace that handwork allows over machinery. The console mechanism of switches, keys, combination action, and expression controls is installed into the console case. The wood used for the console case, organist's bench, pedal keys, and decorative case matches the purchaser's decor.

Everything comes together in the assembly room. Here, workers assemble the wind chest and build the framework that supports the organ. They test the organ musically, in the same arrangement as its final destination. Now you hear the full "color of sounds" that the different organ ranks create. Once you see the fully assembled organ, you'll understand why some larger organs require two 45-foot-long trucks to transport them to their final destinations.

Cost: Free
Freebies: Brochures and postcards
Videos Shown: Short videos of manufacturing process
Reservations Needed: Preferred for individuals. Required for groups (see below).
Days and Hours: Mon–Fri 9:00 AM–2:00 PM, break from 12:00 PM–1:00 PM. Closed holidays and Christmas through New Year's week.
Plan to Stay: 1 hour
Minimum Age: No, for families; age 12, for groups.
Disabled Access: Yes, via freight elevator.
Group Requirements: Groups larger than 15 people will be divided into smaller groups, each with its own guide. Call 2 weeks in advance for reservations. Maximum group size is 25–30 people.
Special Information: Recommends walking shoes. Finished organs are not tested on every tour because an organ is completed every 1–2 months. Call ahead to arrange your tour accordingly.
Gift Shop: No, but can purchase concert recital CDs from the office.
Directions: From Kansas City, take I-70 West to East Lawrence exit. Go left onto North Second St. Cross Kansas River, and turn left immediately after bridge onto 6th St. As you go around curve, factory is on the left. From Topeka, take I-70 East to East Lawrence exit, and follow above directions.
Nearby Attractions: Riverfront Mall; Kansas University; Haskell Indian Nations University; Kansas City's attractions, including the Hallmark Visitors Center (see page 195), are about 45 minutes away.

American Printing House for the Blind

1839 Frankfort Avenue   *Braille and large-type*
Louisville, KY 40206   *publications and audio books*
(502) 895-2405

American Printing House for the Blind (APH) is the world's oldest (founded in 1858) and largest nonprofit company devoted to making products for visually impaired people. The company likes to say that the tour through this multi-media company teaches visitors about a "world they never saw before."

Your journey begins in the display room surrounded by the range of APH products, including a McDonald's menu in Braille. Turning a print book into Braille is not a simple process in which workers magically scan in a print page and out pops a perfect Braille version. It begins with computers and software that help workers with the first step in translating the written text into Braille.

Proofing this computer-generated output is the key to the Braille publications' accuracy. A blind person reads an entire book aloud from the Braille proof pages, while a sighted person follows along in the print copy, marking errors and corrections. The corrections are made on the computer disk, and the disk output is sent straight to a machine that punches the raised dots of the Braille alphabet onto printing plates. You can walk next to the modified rotary and clamshell presses as they spin out Braille pages from these plates.

APH has ten recording studios for turning print books into talking versions. Peek in at the professional narrator and technicians at work. In the audio tape duplication areas, 40 duplicators spin simultaneously to make copies from the master. Either before or after your tour, visit the interactive museum that chronicles the international history of the education of blind people.

Cost: Free
Freebies: A Braille copy of the special Edition of *My Weekly Reader*, a grade school–age magazine in Braille, and a Braille alphabet card.
Video Shown: No
Reservations Needed: No, except for groups of 10 or more people.
Days and Hours: Plant tour: Mon–Fri 10:00 AM and 2:00 PM. Museum: Mon–Fri 8:30 AM–4:30 PM. Closed holidays.
Plan to Stay: 1 hour, plus time for museum and gift counter.
Minimum Age: No required minimum for museum or plant tour for small groups, but recommend 2nd grade and up. Approximately 10 percent of the 300-person workforce is disabled. Watching blind people and others with disabilities at work in productive jobs provides children with a lasting lesson.
Disabled Access: Yes
Group Requirements: Groups over 10 people can receive guided tour of the plant and/or museum by calling 1 week in advance. Maximum size is usually about 45 people (one busload), although larger groups may be accommodated with 4 weeks' advance notice. Minimum age for school groups for plant tour is 4th grade. School groups of 1st- to 3rd-graders will have hands-on museum tour and partial plant tour.
Special Information: No photography in plant. National Braille Press in Boston, MA, also offers public tours (see page 135).
Gift Counter: Sells T-shirts with Braille alphabet, Braille key chains, and note and holiday cards. Usually open just during tour hours, but you can ask to purchase items at other times. Catalog available for all APH products by calling (800) 223-1839.
Directions: From I-64 East, take Exit 7, Story Ave. Then immediately turn left at Spring St. Turn left at Mellwood Ave. After you go under highway, turn right on Frankfort Ave. APH is at top of hill on left. From I-64 West, take Exit 7 for Mellwood Ave. Turn right onto Frankfort Ave. and follow directions above. Company can fax you directions from different locations.
Nearby Attractions: Louisville area attractions, including Colonel Harland Sanders (KFC) Museum, Ford trucks, Ford sport-utility vehicles, Louisville Stoneware, and Hillerich & Bradsby (Louisville Slugger) tours (see pages 100, 103, 102, 106, and 104).

Coca-Cola Bottling ⟋ *soda*

Schmidt's Coca-Cola Museum
1201 North Dixie Highway
Elizabethtown, KY 42701
(502) 737-4000

Visiting this bottling plant and adjoining Coca-Cola museum takes you from the present to the past, from the lightning speed and clamoring action of the bottling line to the serenity of the extensive memorabilia collection. Fountains grace the bottling plant entrance. A colorful stained-glass mural reflects in the lobby's Japanese carp (koi) pool. Hidden Coca-Cola bottle and can shapes create a fascinating optical illusion in this mural.

On a self-guided tour, watch the filing line from an observation gallery. The filler shoots 12 ounces of soda into 1,500 aluminum cans per minute. Once the cans have left this roaring carousel, they twirl single-file along the line so fast that the writing on their labels blurs. This noisy, busy freeway has no honking or bottlenecks. Instead, cans and bottles simply squeeze their way from four lanes to one.

After the fast-moving machines, you'll appreciate the museum's calm. The world's largest privately owned collection of Coke memorabilia begins with a mirror dated 1885, one year older than Coca-Cola itself, and continues to 1969. Beautiful "Coca-Cola Girl" calendars identify the dates of the memorabilia below them. It's fun to see what was fashionable in the year you were born. You'll find yourself exclaiming, "I wore that!" or "That's my first car!"

The Schmidts, now in their third and fourth generations of bottling Coca-Cola in Kentucky, have filled the floors with old vending machines, coolers, and street signs. There's even a full-scale 1890s soda fountain. Painstaking care over the years has preserved the picturesque paper festoons that used to hang in soda fountains.

In tracing Coca-Cola's history, the museum also illustrates the history of advertising in the U.S. The red script Coca-Cola trademark appears on many familiar, everyday objects, such as beverage glasses, playing cards, trays, and dishes. The logo was placed nearly anywhere it would fit—even on ax handles!

Cost: Plant: free; Museum: adults, $2; seniors and tour groups, $1.50; students, 50¢; preschoolers, free.

Freebies: A cup of Coke, Sprite, or Diet Coke in the lobby area.

Video Shown: No

Reservations Needed: No, except for bus groups.

Days and Hours: Museum: Mon–Fri 9:00 AM–4:00 PM. Plant: 8:00 AM–5:00 PM. Closed holidays.

Plan to Stay: 1 hour for self-guided tour and museum.

Minimum Age: None

Disabled Access: Flight of stairs into building lobby and up to production-area balcony and museum. Part of the bottling and canning visible from the lobby area.

Group Requirements: Bus groups should call in advance. Group discount on museum admission. Groups of 15 people or more can get guided tours if booked a few days in advance.

Special Information: Frequently no canning or bottling on winter Fridays. A new handicapped-accessible, 3-story museum, showcasing the Schmidts' extensive Coca-Cola memorabilia collection, is due to open 5 miles away in 1998.

Gift Counter: A small counter in the museum sells Coca-Cola paraphernalia, from the standard (postcards, key rings, T-shirts) to the unusual and collectible (clocks, trays, breakdancing Coke can), and also *Schmidt's Museum Collection Book*. Call the above number for mail orders.

Directions: From the north, follow I-65 South to Exit 94. Take U.S. 62 to Ring Rd. to U.S. 31W. Go south 1 mile to Coca-Cola plant. From the south, take I-65 North to Exit 91, and take Western Kentucky Pkwy. to U.S. 31W Bypass. This goes directly to the plant. Look for fountains in front.

Nearby Attractions: Freeman Lake Park; Patton Museum at Fort Knox; Abraham Lincoln Birthplace.

Churchill Weavers ⟶ *blankets, throws, and scarves*

100 Churchill Drive
Lorraine Court
Berea, KY 40403
(606) 986-3127

It takes hard work and heritage to hand-weave a beautiful Churchill Weavers blanket or throw. Churchill Weavers, nestled in a small college town where Kentucky's Bluegrass meets its Cumberland Mountains, encompasses history, pride and craftsmanship. MIT graduate and industrial engineer Carroll Churchill and his wife, Eleanor, an English schoolteacher, returned from missionary work in India to found Churchill Weavers in 1922. Eleanor chose Lila and Richard Belando to continue the Churchill legacy. In 1996 Crown Crafts, a leader in home fashion textiles, acquired Churchill Weavers. Today Lila and Richard still carry on the leadership of this unique company.

Your self-guided tour includes the historic loomhouse, residence to almost 50 looms. Notice that the weathered brown of the looms matches the building's ceilings, walls, and wooden plank floors. In the loomhouse is the waterwheel-like "warper." Threads are wrapped around it according to a written pattern, then wound onto a warp drum that fits into the back of a loom.

The highlight of the tour is watching wooden looms in action, as women weave baby blankets, throws, table linens, scarves, and fabric for decorative pillows. Watch an agile weaver alternate between pulling the beater forward with her left hand and "throwing" the shuttle with her right. At the same time, as if playing an organ, she steps on foot pedals to create a pattern. The rhythm of the weavers at their looms sounds like the hoofbeats of galloping horses. The rhythm breaks only when a weaver stops to replace a yarn-filled bobbin in the shuttle, then it begins again.

Menders check newly woven cloth on light boards and repair flaws. From warping to weaving to tying the fringes, you will observe this timeless, hands-on process of "constructing" fabrics. These beautiful "high-touch" items, made by loving hands, help balance the "high-tech," fast-paced world in which we live.

Cost: Free

Freebies: No

Video Shown: 4-minute optional video in gift shop shows the company's history and its weaving process.

Reservations Needed: No, for self-guided tour. Yes, if groups want tour guide.

Days and Hours: Mon–Fri 9:00 AM–12:00 PM, 1:00 PM–4:00 PM. Loomhouse hours vary seasonally. Closed Christmas and New Year's.

Plan to Stay: 20 minutes for tour, plus time for video and gift shop.

Minimum Age: None

Disabled Access: Yes

Group Requirements: Maximum group is 40 people. Tour guide can be arranged if booked 3–4 days in advance.

Special Information: Due to the intense concentration required by the weaving process, please do not disturb the weavers at work.

Retail Store: Sells baby blankets, scarves, stoles, throws, and decorative pillows made by Churchill Weavers, and pottery, candles, baskets, and woodcrafts from all over the U.S.A. The outlet room sells woven seconds and overruns by well-known craftspeople. Open Mon–Sat 9:00 AM–6:00 PM, Sun 12:00 PM–6:00 PM. Catalog available from the above number.

Directions: From Lexington, take I-75 South to Exit 77. Follow Walnut Meadow Rd. past 4-way stop light to traffic light at Berea College campus. Turn left onto Rt. 25 North and pass Berea Hospital. Bear right onto Hwy. 1016. Follow the signs to Churchill Weavers. From the south, take I-75 North to Exit 76. Stay on Rt. 25 North through town, past Berea Hospital. Continue with above directions.

Nearby Attractions: Berea is the folk arts and crafts capital of Kentucky. You can purchase the works of local craftspeople while observing them in their studios scattered throughout the town. At Berea College you can watch students produce a variety of crafts.

Website: www.churchill-weavers.com

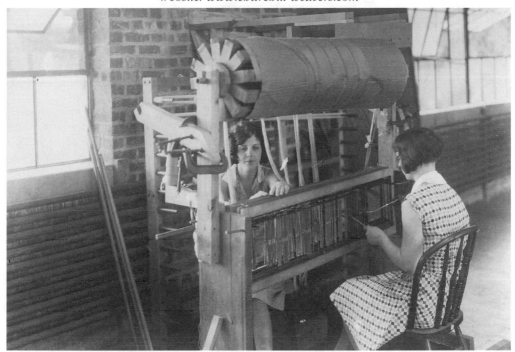

In this 1930s photograph, employees wrap a warp before placing it on a loom at Churchill Weavers in Berea, Kentucky.

A silent loomhouse awaits the "click-click-click" sounds of production at Churchill Weavers.

Colonel Harland Sanders Museum   *fast food*

KFC International Headquarters
1441 Gardiner Lane
Louisville, KY 40213
(502) 456-8300 / (502) 456-8353

In Japan, Colonel Sanders is *Ohji-san*, or "Grandfather," and his statue stands near every one of the restaurants he inspired. A life-size statue also graces the entrance to this small museum, which honors the man who above all else demonstrated that the little guy can succeed in America.

An old-style black-and-white movie called *Portrait of a Legend* shows how Harland Sanders, born in 1890, held many jobs to support his family—streetcar conductor, cook, justice of the peace, and automobile mechanic.

Some of the rare photos around the room show Sanders' Court Restaurant. About 1930, Sanders began cooking chicken for customers at his auto service station (later a restaurant) along busy U.S. 25. At Sanders' Court he perfected his famous secret blend of 11 herbs and spices, and developed the innovation of frying chicken in a pressure cooker. You'll see the original cooker and learn why it made such a difference. In 1935 Governor Ruby Laffon made Sanders an honorary Kentucky colonel for his contribution to the state's cuisine.

Unfortunately, a highway bypass closed the restaurant in the early 1950s. After paying his bills, Sanders had nothing to live on except his social security check. With his wife Claudia, he hit the road, making samples of his chicken and offering franchise deals to restaurant owners. The idea was so successful that, in 1964, he sold his interest in Kentucky Fried Chicken and became the company's spokesman, wearing his now-famous white suit (one is displayed at the museum).

The pictures on the wall show that the Colonel traveled extensively around the world, met many dignitaries and celebrities, and gave millions of dollars to charities. Watch classic U.S. and foreign television commercials and clips of the Colonel's other television appearances. You'll also see the Colonel's favorite award, a wire chicken presented to him by the National Restaurant Association. KFC is the world's second-largest restaurant chain—9,600-plus restaurants in 70-plus countries. But after touring this compact museum, you'll forever associate KFC with the 66-year-old man who began an empire with a $105 social security check.

Cost: Free
Freebies: No
Videos Shown: An optional 25-minute film about Sanders and history of KFC; 8-minute video of commercials and interviews.
Reservations Needed: No, except for groups larger than 15 people.
Days and Hours: Mon–Thur 8:00 AM–5:00 PM, Fri 8:00 AM–1:00 PM. Closed standard holidays.
Plan to Stay: 40 minutes
Minimum Age: 8
Disabled Access: Yes
Group Requirements: Groups of 15 people or more should call at least 2 weeks in advance. Maximum group size is 40.
Special Information: Museum is in the lobby of the KFC corporate headquarters, so dress appropriately. The café and motel in Harland, Kentucky, where the Colonel concocted his secret recipe, has been restored to its mid-1940s glory (call 606-528-2163).
Gift Shop: No, but the closest KFC is on Bardstown Rd.
Directions: Take I-264 to Newburg Rd. exit. Go south and turn right onto Bishop Ln. Turn right onto Gardiner Rd. Museum is in KFC corporate headquarters, which has an antebellum plantation facade.
Nearby Attractions: Ford Truck, Ford Explorer, American Printing House for the Blind, and Louisville Stoneware tours and Louisville Slugger Museum (see pages 103, 102, 96, 106, and 104); Hadley Pottery tour (call 502-584-2171); Louisville's attractions include J.B. Speed Art Museum, Churchill Downs/Kentucky Derby Museum, and Kentucky Art and Craft Center.

Corvette 〜 *sports cars*
Corvette Drive
Bowling Green, KY 42101
(502) 745-8419 / (502) 781-7973

Since it was first built in 1953, General Motors' Corvette has become an American automotive icon, representing muscle, fantasy, and youth. The television series "Route 66," about two bachelors who traveled American highways in their 'Vette, increased the car's popularity. In 1981 GM moved Corvette assembly to a Bowling Green complex the size of 22 football fields.

You know this tour is going to be fun when you look up and see half of a 1983 Corvette above the tour entrance door. Led by a guide who points out the car's special features, you'll walk on the plant floor to witness the major steps in the sports car's production. See the frame and body take shape, the engine and drive train go together, the windshields attached, and the joining of the chassis and body.

Computerized robots weld the steel frame together before the Corvette receives its signature fiberglass body panels. Once the panels are painted, they return to the main assembly floor, where workers install them along with other parts such as seats, wheels, and removable roof. While the car's body is being assembled in the trim area, the engine and drive train are assembled in another area. When the two come together it's called "body marriage," with workers scampering underneath the car to connect the chassis and body.

Almost everywhere you look, Corvettes in some stage of assembly move past on a multi-level network of conveyors that cover about 6 miles. A worker sits in the car and starts the engine. Like a baby's first cry, the engine makes its initial roar. It may take a couple of seconds for the car to start but, once running, it idles for some time while workers make various checks throughout the car. Only when the car is fully built do all four wheels touch the ground for the first time. Even if you didn't arrive as a diehard Corvette enthusiast, you'll leave as one.

Cost: Free

Freebies: No

Video Shown: 15-minute video on the car's proud history and production, including steps not on the tour, such as body painting.

Reservations Needed: No, except for groups of 10 people or more.

Days and Hours: Mon–Fri 9:00 AM and 1:00 PM. Closed holidays, week between Christmas and New Year's, 2 weeks in summer (usually starting early July), and for model changes and production shutdowns. Always call ahead.

Plan to Stay: 1¼ hours for tour and video, plus time in gift shop.

Minimum Age: None, but children under 6 may be intimidated by the noise.

Disabled Access: Yes

Group Requirements: For groups larger than 10 people, call (502) 745-8287 for reservations 1 week in advance. Maximum group size is 50 people, and other times can be scheduled.

Special Information: No photography on tour. 1 mile of walking.

Gift Shop: Sells Corvette memorabilia including T-shirts, hats, and key chains. Open during tour hours.

Directions: From I-65 take Exit 28. For plant, turn right at Corvette Dr., then right after entering the gate. Follow signs to tour parking. For museum, turn left at Corvette Dr.

Nearby Attractions: National Corvette Museum across the street from the plant (call 502-781-7973); Beech Bend Raceway Park; Mammoth Cave National Park.

Ford   *sport-utility vehicles and pickup trucks*
Fern Valley Road at Grade Lane
Louisville, KY 40213
(502) 364-3728

Since 1913 Ford has had operations in Louisville, KY, which now includes both the Louisville Assembly Plant and its massive heavy-truck plant (see page 103). Ford made 12 Model Ts a day back in 1913. Now the home of the popular Explorer, Ranger, and Mercury Mountaineer, this plant has substantially quickened its pace to 87 vehicles per hour (the auto industry norm is 60, making this plant possibly the fastest in the world). You get to see almost all the production steps, although not in the order of assembly, as all the vehicles are built on one long line.

The body area is always one of the most exciting places to visit at an automobile plant. It's the scene most often shown of car factories on TV: skeleton car bodies and robots marching together in perfect unison, with colorful sparks flying. Here you can watch the real thing. With the help of over 140 robots, the stamped sheet metal that comes from other Ford plants is precision-fitted and welded to exact specifications. The robots help transfer parts, spot-weld, and apply sealer. The body then heads to the paint area, which is usually not on the tour.

In the trim area most of the vehicles' insides are added, filling up the painted shell. It's truly an industrial symphony of sounds from the machines and tools that buzz, crunch, and hiss. With robots' assistance, workers bend, twist, and reach to install various interior and exterior parts, such as wiring, door glass, windshields, door handles, instrument panels, and horns.

The chassis is built in another area. Notice how the frame is actually upside down when workers install the fuel and brake lines, body mounts, and wiring. The frame is then flipped over before the bumpers are added, along with the engine, transmission, and driveshaft. Another favorite site is the "body drop." The body, hanging from a part of the 20-plus miles of conveyors in the factory, is lowered and secured to the frame. After more parts are added, including the all-important tires and

seats, the vehicle is started and heads off for final inspection. The inspectors act like the pickiest buyers, checking even the tiniest mechanical and visual details.

Cost: Free
Freebies: Brochures about the history of Ford in Louisville and the assembly process
Video Shown: 10-minute video of material similar to that covered in the brochure.
Reservations Needed: Yes
Days and Hours: Mon at 9:30 AM (moved to Tue if Mon is holiday), although special tours occasionally arranged. Usually only 1 tour per month in the summer. Closed 2 weeks in July and week between Christmas and New Year's.
Plan to Stay: 2 hours for talk, video, and tour.
Minimum Age: None, but young children could be intimidated by the noises.
Disabled Access: Yes
Group Requirements: The total number of visitors is limited to 150 each session. Groups need to schedule months in advance to assure space availability.
Special Information: Will walk approximately 1½ miles during tour. In 1995 Ford's St. Louis Assembly Plant became the second plant to build the Explorer; limited tours offered (call 314-731-6365).
Gift Shop: No
Directions: From I-65, exit at Fern Valley Rd. Plant is visible from exit regardless of which direction you travel. Drive to plant entrance and park in administrative lot.
Nearby Attractions: Ford truck plant (see page 103); UPS Louisville air tour (call 502-359-8727); Louisville's attractions, including Louisville Stoneware and American Printing House for the Blind tours and Louisville Slugger and Colonel Harland Sanders (KFC) Museums (see pages 106, 96, 104 and 100), and Churchill Downs/Kentucky Derby Museum, are about 30 minutes away.

Ford ⟷ *trucks*
3001 Chamberlain Lane
Louisville, KY 40232
(502) 429-2146

In a site larger than 400 football fields, Ford manufactures medium- and heavy-duty trucks along 9½ miles of conveyor belts. (Ford has sold its extra heavy–duty truck business to Freightliner, so this plan no longer makes big trucks). With a recent expansion, they now also build commercial light trucks, making this one of the lartest truck assembly plants in the Western World.

For most of the standard tour, you'll walk next to the final chassis assembly lines, where the truck's pieces all come together. Since the major components attached to a frame are so heavy, the frame is built upside down, and everything is laid on top of it for mounting. After turning right-side-up, the frame travels by overhead conveyor through a robotic frame-paint booth and paint-baking oven. The chassis frame "touches down" from an overhead sloping conveyer at the start of the final chassis, line. The cabs reach the chassis lines in job sequence from the four-level automated cab-stackers. Overhead hoists lower the cabs onto the chassis, and they are bolted down in a process called "cab decking." The hood assemblies, front ends, and engines are also decked into place, with the trucks soon ready to drive off the assembly line.

Notice how the engines travel around the plant on their own magic carpets, the computer-controlled automatic guided vehicles (AGVs). From the receiving sections to engine build-up and final assembly lines, the yellow AGVs transport the engines along a guide path in the plant's floor, using sonar to direct their journey. In the tire/wheel mounting area, a rotary mounting machine has automated the difficult process of putting tubeless truck tires around metal rims and then inflating them.

The assembly line moves at a slow enough speed that you can study the making and installing of up to 27,000 truck parts. Workers are very friendly; many have been assembling Ford trucks for over 20 years. Truck owners like to shake hands with the people who actually produce their rigs, so the workers are used to talking with visitors. If something interests you, take a closer look (safety permitting) and ask questions. Don't be surprised if next time you see trucks on the highway, you find yourself looking for the medallion logos of the company that built them.

Cost: Free

Freebies: Brochure describing the plant and its main production areas.

Video Shown: No

Reservations Needed: Yes

Days and Hours: *Ford sporadically gives public tours but focuses on customer tours; at time book was printed the public tours were on hold.* Closed the week between Christmas and New Year's and usually the first 2–3 weeks of July.

Plan to Stay: 1 hour

Minimum Age: 10

Disabled Access: Yes

Group Requirements: 2 weeks' advance notice. Call tour coordinator for size limits.

Special Information: No photography. Tour involves at least 1 mile of walking. Standard tour can be modified to meet special interests. Plant is hot during the summer.

Gift Shop: No

Directions: Take I-71 North to I-265 South. Get off at West Port Rd./Chamberlain Ln. exit. Head in the direction of Chamberlain Ln. Enter plant through Gate 3.

Nearby Attractions: Louisville's attractions include Ford Explorer and Louisville Stoneware tours and Louisville Slugger and Colonel Harland Sanders (KFC) Museums (see page 102, 106, 104, and 106), and Churchill Downs/Kentucky Derby Museum.

Hillerich & Bradsby ✐ *Louisville Slugger baseball bats*

Louisville Slugger Museum
800 West Main Street
Louisville, KY 40202
(502) 588-7228

Louisville Slugger®

The Louisville Slugger bat, first created by Bud Hillerich in 1884, has been called "one of the greatest original American products ever made." In 1996 Hillerich & Bradsby moved their plant from Jeffersonville, Indiana, to their signature product's namesake town, Louisville, Kentucky. They also opened the Louisville Slugger Museum, a tribute to baseball's greatest hits and hitters. You'll see actual bats swung by such legendary sluggers as Ty Cobb, Lou Gehrig, and Joe DiMaggio, plus the bat Babe Ruth used during his 1927 record-setting 60-home-run season. Listen to Hall of Fame broadcasters call baseball's greatest moments. Take the field in a replica of Orioles Park. Choose a famous pitcher to throw the ball in your direction at 90 miles per hour.

After walking through the museum and a replica of a Northern white ash forest, take a guided tour of the plant. With the ever-present smell of wood in the air, H&B uses three techniques to turn the Northern white ash billets into bats. Most of the bats are made on automatic lathes that carve out the most popular models, about one every 15 seconds.

It takes about 40 seconds to make a bat on the tracer lathes. Workers use a metal pattern of the exact bat shape and guide the machine to trace this pattern, a process similar to copying a key at the hardware store. Only about 5 percent of their professional bats are hand-turned, a technique used only for unusual models.

With sizzle and smoke, the famous oval trademark, bat model number, and the player's autograph are seared into the "flat of the grain." Behind the branders are large green cabinets holding over 8,500 professional baseball players' autograph brands. The bats go through more production steps, but it's the thrill of watching the branding that you'll remember the best. You'll leave the museum and tour having witnessed a part of true Americana.

Cost: Adults, $4; seniors 60+, $3.50; children 6–12, $3; children 5 and under, free.

Freebies: 16-inch miniature wood bat.

Video Shown: 13-minute film, "Heart of the Game," relives some of the greatest hits in baseball.

Reservations Needed: No, except for groups larger than 15 people.

Days and Hours: Mon–Sat 9:00 AM–5:00 PM (Eastern Standard Time in winter, Eastern Daylight Time in summer). Last factory tour is at 3:45 PM. Closed holidays. Call regarding schedule for week between Christmas and New Year's.

Plan to Stay: 1½ hours for tour and museum, plus time for gift shop.

Minimum Age: Discourages children under the age of 5.

Disabled Access: Yes

Group Requirements: Reservations needed for groups over 15 people. Groups larger than 75 people will be split. At least 1-month advance notice suggested for summer tours. Call (502) 588-7227.

Special Information: No photography in plant.

Gift Shop: Sells Louisville Slugger, PowerBilt, and Louisville Hockey logoed items, including T-shirts, hats, towels, gym bags, and pen bats. Catalog available. Open Mon–Sat 9:00 AM–5:00 PM. Closed holidays.

Directions: From Indianapolis, take I-65 South to I-64 West. Exit on 3rd St. Turn right onto River Rd. Turn left onto 8th St. You can't miss the Louisville Slugger Museum—just look for the world's tallest bat. From Cincinnati, take I-71 South to I-64 West and follow above directions.

Nearby Attractions: Colonel Harland Sanders (KFC) Museum, Ford Truck, Ford Explorer, Louisville Stoneware, and American Printing House for the Blind tours (see pages 100, 103, 102, 106, and 96); Louisville Science Center (across the street from the Louisville Slugger Museum); Kentucky Derby Museum; Churchill Downs.

Maker's Mark ～ *bourbon*
3350 Burks Spring Road
Loretto, KY 40037
(502) 865-2099

An illustration of the Maker's Mark distillery appears on its bottles; the label invites you to visit "any time you're in the neighborhood," so you know the place must be special. Just as Bill Samuels Sr. wanted to create his own distinctive bourbon by using gentle winter wheat instead of rye, he wanted to restore a historic distillery complex into the home of Maker's Mark.

Your tour of this National Historic Land-Mark distillery begins near the stone-walled creek that runs through the peaceful, land-scaped grounds, where you'll hear a brief history of the distillery. Its black buildings feature bright red shutters with a Maker's Mark bottle cut-out. Unlike larger distilleries' 600-barrel-per-day production, Maker's Mark crafts about 40 per day.

In the still house you'll smell corn, wheat, and malted barley cooking. The bubbling yellow mash ferments in century-old cypress vats. Vaporization of the mash in the shiny copper still separates out the whiskey, which is placed in charred oak casks for aging. When you enter the aging warehouse's ground floor, the aromas alone tell you what's in the barrels. Barrels reach maturity only after completing a rotation system in which the newest barrels are placed on the warehouse's hot upper floors and are gradually moved to the cooler lower levels.

Only in the bottling house does the production pace quicken. Near the end of the line, two women dip each bottle's glass neck into red sealing wax and then twist the bottle out to allow the excess to drip off and run down the neck. Notice each worker's distinctive dipping and twisting technique.

Cost: Free
Freebies: Iced tea and lemonade; bottle labels; great smells.
Video Shown: No
Reservations Needed: No, except for groups larger than 25 people.
Days and Hours: Mon–Sat 10:30 AM, 11:30 AM, 12:30 PM, 1:30 PM, 2:30 PM, and 3:30 PM, Sun

1:30 PM, 2:30 PM, and 3:30 PM. No production from mid-August to mid-September, but tour still runs. Limited weekend production. Closed Thanksgiving, Christmas Eve, Christmas, and New Year's.
Plan to Stay: 40 minutes for the tour, plus time for visitors center, Quart House, and Gift Gallery. Once a pre–Civil War distiller's home, the visitors center has pieces from the Samuels' collection of early-1800s furniture, a set of old cooper's tools, and other historical and crafts items. The Quart House is a restored pre-Prohibition retail package store.
Minimum Age: Recommends that children under 10 be accompanied by an adult.
Disabled Access: Visitors center fully accessible. Bottling house and aging warehouse have a few steps. Distillery building has a flight of stairs. Gravel walking paths between buildings.
Group Requirements: Requests at least 2 weeks' notice for groups of 25 people or more. Maximum group size is 50, but can handle larger groups in special situations.
Special Information: Wax dipping of bottles does not occur every day, but tour guide will demonstrate.
Gift Shop: The Gift Gallery in the visitor center sells logoed and craft items, including shirts, sweaters, jackets, key chains, and shot glasses. Also, gourmet sauces and candies made with Maker's Mark. Open Mon–Sat 10:00 AM–4:30 PM, Sun 1:00 PM–4:30 PM. Call number above for mail-order product list.
Directions: From Bardstown, take KY 49 South and follow signs to distillery. You're there when you see the sign that says "You've Just Found the Home of Maker's Mark."
Nearby Bourbon-Related Attractions: Heaven Hill Distillery tour (call 502-348-3921); Oscar Getz Museum of Whiskey History (call 502-348-2999); Jim Beam's American Outpost (call 502-543-9877); Annual Bardstown September Bourbon Festival.

Louisville Stoneware ~ *pottery*

731 Brent Street
Louisville, KY 40204
(502) 582-1900

Raw clay, mined from Western Indiana, forms a small hill against the back wall of the clay-making room. Since 1905 this has been the main ingredient for the artistic, durable, authentic American pottery made by Louisville Stoneware. The guided tour includes the clay-making room, where clay dirt is vigorously mixed with water to make a clay "soup." Under high pressure, a press pushes liquid clay through filters with water dripping out the bottom. In the pug mill, the resulting firm "cakes" of fine clay are chopped into stiff or soft mud or turned into liquid "slip" clay. In a process called "slip casting," this fluid slip is poured into angular, geometric-shaped plaster molds to form items such as bird feeders and birdhouses.

The self-guided tour shows you the "jiggering," handle-pulling, glazing, hand-painting, and kiln-loading. Jiggering, another process of romancing the clay, is used for more concentric shapes. Leaning over a spinning pottery wheel, a potter places clay onto a concave plaster mold (shaped like the inside of a bowl) and then lowers the jigger handle to form the plate or bowl. The potter uses a water-drenched sponge to smooth the clay's surface. Each plate hardens on its individual plaster mold. Throughout the factory, you will see earthenware drying on 6- to 10-foot-high storage conveyors, whose shelves can be rotated or advanced when full.

You can stand next to the artists as they hand-paint traditional patterns directly onto the dried clay piece. At first appearing pastel, the final underglaze colors reveal themselves only after a white translucent glaze is applied and the piece is fired at a high temperature. You'll feel the heat emerging from the three kilns, which hold 1,000 pieces each. The whole firing process takes almost a full day—ten hours to reach 2,350°, and then 12 hours to cool.

Cost: Free
Freebies: No
Video Shown: No

Reservations Needed: No, except for groups larger than 8 people.
Days and Hours: Self-guided tour Mon–Fri 8:30 AM–5:00 PM. Guided tour Mon–Fri 10:30 AM and 2:30 PM. Closed holidays. Additional guided tours possible if a leader is available.
Plan to Stay: 15–25 minutes for the tour and video, depending on whether you see the clay-making process, plus time for outlet store.
Minimum Age: None
Disabled Access: Yes
Group Requirements: Groups larger than 8 people should call 1 day in advance for desired time. Large groups will be split.
Special Information: Since there are 3 firing kilns, the factory can be hot.
Outlet Store: Sells factory seconds at 30–40 percent off regular prices, and firsts of Kentucky-related items (mugs with horse designs, etc.). Product line includes colorful dinnerware, outdoor products (birdhouses, etc.), and stoneware. Look for the big "Night Before Christmas" soup tureen with the entire poem written on its outside. Open Mon–Sat 8:00 AM–5:00 PM. At the annual tent sale, in July, seconds sell at additional savings. Catalog available from (800) 626-1800.
Directions: From Lexington, take Rt. 64 West to 3rd St. South (one way). Turn left onto Broadway, then right onto Brent St. Located 2½ blocks ahead on left. From the Louisville area, take Rt. 65 North to Broadway exit. Turn right onto Broadway, then right onto Brent St.
Nearby Attractions: Louisville Slugger and Colonel Harland Sanders (KFC) Museums and Ford Truck and American Printing House for the Blind tours (see pages 104, 100, 103, and 96); Hadley Pottery tour (call 502-584-2171); J.B. Speed Art Museum; Churchill Downs/Kentucky Derby Museum; Kentucky Art and Craft Center.

See color photos, page 181

A potter "jiggers" soft clay to form a bowl at Louisville Stoneware in Louisville, Kentucky.

Old Kentucky Candies　～　*chocolates*

450 Southland Drive
Lexington, KY 40503
(800) 786-0579

Bourbon Chocolates, Bourbon Cherries, Chocolate Thoroughbreds, and Kentucky Derby Mints—the names alone are enough to attract you to this candy-factory tour. Combine the tour with plentiful free samples before, after, and even right off the assembly line, and you have the makings of a tasty experience.

The chocolate in these famous Kentucky candies starts as 10-pound bars of Guittard Chocolate. In the molding area, melted chocolate sits in a mixer while a rotating blade slowly turns it into a creamy paste. While the tour guide is pointing to overhead photographs and explaining how cocoa beans are harvested and the chocolate is made, you'll be tempted to sneak your finger into the mixer for a taste. Nearby are stacks of Old Kentucky's popular molds, including a 75-pound Easter bunny, dentures, and a horse's behind.

As you stroll through the candy "kitchen," you often see 8-by-3-foot slabs of fudge and candy centers cooling before they are cut with a ridged rolling pin. In the production room, glass jars of maraschino cherries may be marinating in 101-proof Jim Beam bourbon. Stand next to the conveyor belt while the candies receive a bottom chocolate base, then go through a "chocolate car wash" that coats them in chocolate. Looped chains drop down to caress the tops of the candies, creating a swirl design. After the candies exit the cooling tunnel, workers carefully hand-pack the chocolates—a job that must require great willpower to prevent nibbling.

Cost: Free
Freebies: Plentiful candy samples, including a candy directly off the assembly line.
Video Shown: No
Reservations Needed: Yes. Individuals and families must join a group tour.
Days and Hours: Mon–Fri 10:30 AM–3:30 PM, with Saturday tours and other times available upon request. Closed holidays.

Plan to Stay: 20 minutes for tour, plus time for gift shop.
Minimum Age: None
Disabled Access: Yes
Group Requirements: 1 day's advance notice for groups. No maximum size. Large groups split into groups of 25 people.
Special Information: If interested in seeing specific candies made, ask when you book the tour.
Retail Store: Sells all of the company's different kinds and shapes of candies. Look for gift baskets shaped like horse heads, horseshoes, and Kentucky maps. Glass showcases filled with truffles sit next to canisters of various free samples. On the store's front table, notice the upside-down mushroom-shaped jar filled with cherries aging in bourbon. (Unfortunately, once the cherries are aged, Kentucky liquor laws do not allow the sale of this cherry-flavored bourbon.) Open Mon–Fri 9:00 AM–6:00 PM, Sat 9:30 AM–5:30 PM, Sun 1:00 PM–5:00 PM. Catalog available from above number.
Directions: From Cincinnati, take I-75 South to Exit 115 for Newtown Pike. Go west on Circle 4 (New Circle Rd.). Take exit for Harrodsburg Rd. toward Lexington. Turn right onto Lane Allen Rd., which becomes Rosemont Garden. Turn right onto Southland Dr. Old Kentucky is on the right. Factory is in the back of its retail store, in a shopping center. From Louisville, take Rt. 64 West to I-75 South. Continue with above directions.
Nearby Attractions: Toyota tour (see page 112); Three Chimneys horse farm tour (see page 109); Kentucky Horse Park; Boonesborough State Park; Fort Harrod State Park.

Three Chimneys 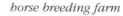 *horse breeding farm*

Route 1, Old Frankfort Pike
Versailles, KY 40383
(606) 873-7053

Although a tour of a horse-breeding farm is a slight diversion from the other companies in this book, we decided to include Three Chimneys because the thoroughbred industry is the third-largest industry and the number-one tourist attraction in the state of Kentucky. In fact, Kentucky-bred horses are a majority among winners of the world-famous Kentucky Derby.

As you leave the city of Lexington and drive along the Old Frankfort Pike, you will be calmed by the gently rolling hills, and the black or white ribbons of fencing that zigzag across green pastures dotted with sleek brown horses. Enjoy this scenic drive past other horse farms while watching for the low, forest-green sign that identifies Three Chimneys.

Walk along the red brick walkway to the office, poshly decorated with colonial furniture and Oriental rugs. Further down the red-brick path, past the great oaks, is the limestone stallion barn. This five-star equine hotel, lined with oak panels, trimmed with palladium windows and topped with a skylight in a cupola ceiling, is home to champion racehorses, now studs worth millions of dollars. Each 16-foot-square stall has black bars with black-and-gold engraved nameplates. Grooms attend to the stallions' every need.

These knowledgeable grooms are available to answer all your questions and list each of their charges' accomplishments; for example, Seattle Slew won the Triple Crown in 1977 and has sired six champion racehorses and stakes winners. His foals have won millions of dollars in purse money. Seattle Slew's son Slew O' Gold, who lives two stalls away, has produced four Grade One winners in his first foal crop.

Every day, the stallions graze and stretch their legs in their individual 1- to 2-acre paddocks. They are also ridden or walked daily for exercise. Breeding sessions are twice daily, February through July. To ensure the safety of mares and stallions, the round

walls of the breeding shed are lined with foam-rubber-padded vinyl, and the floor is covered with woodchips and a raised cocoa mat. Five grooms assist with the breeding—a brief act, but one that can be worth $100,000 to Seattle Slew's owners.

Cost: Free. Tips to grooms are appreciated.
Freebies: No
Video Shown: No
Reservations Needed: Yes. For tours in April, July, and September through November call 2–3 months in advance; other times of the year, call 2 weeks ahead of time.
Days and Hours: Mon–Sun 10:00 AM and 1:00 PM. No tours the week before the Kentucky Derby (first Saturday in May). Closed holidays.
Plan to Stay: 1 hour
Minimum Age: None
Disabled Access: Yes
Group Requirements: Standard bus tours are discouraged.
Special Information: Please respect the grounds and horses. This is neither a zoo nor a public riding stable.
Gift Shop: No
Directions: From Lexington, take Rt. 4 (New Circle Rd.) to Old Frankfort Pike. Drive west for 8 miles, passing a red brick church on your right. The farm is ½-mile ahead on your left. From Cincinnati, take I-75 South to I-64 West to Midway exit. Follow signs on Rt. 62 West through Midway to a 4-way stop. Turn left onto Old Frankfort Pike. Farm is 2 miles ahead on your right.
Nearby Attractions: Toyota tour (see page 112); Kentucky Horse Park; Keeneland Racecourse; Calumet Farm tour (organized through Historical Tours at 606-268-2906).

Rebecca-Ruth Candies

chocolates and Bourbon Balls

112 East 2nd Street
Frankfort, KY 40601
(502) 223-7475 / (800) 444-3766

Kentucky's famous 100-proof bourbon whiskey—and a lot of local pride—are key ingredients in this family-owned company's world-renowned chocolates. These chocolates are as rich as the history surrounding the Rebecca-Ruth name itself. Founded in 1919 by two uncommonly courageous schoolteachers, Rebecca Gooch and Ruth Booe, the company's popularity grew as a result of the women's highly acclaimed chocolates and was aided by their creative sales techniques—which included loudly plugging their products on streetcorners. Ruth Booe originated the "Bourbon Ball." Made with real Kentucky bourbon and crowned with a Southern pecan, this confection has become the treat of the South.

The brightly striped awning shading this small, house-like store and factory creates an unpretentious atmosphere. The ten to 15 employees (some of whom have been here for over 30 years) make about 100,000 pounds of confections a year.

In the cream-candy room are articles about Rebecca-Ruth from national magazines such as *Southern Living* and *Gourmet.* Workers pull candy cream on a hook by hand and then use a taffy-pull machine. When it's "just right," the rope of candy is cut into pieces and left to sit. It becomes very creamy, rich, and flaky. Pecan brittle and pecan butter are also made in this room.

In the kitchen, the cast-iron candy furnace and copper kettles emit the sweet scent of hand-stirred, melting sugars. In the production area, large mixers prepare rich fillings for their assembly-line journey down the enrobing line. First the candy dough is extruded onto a belt, and then it goes through a "chocolate waterfall." Two workers personally apply the finishing touches: a luscious southern pecan, sprinkles, or a swirled flourish on top.

The real treat of any tour is meeting Edna Robbins, who has been with the company for close to 70 years. Although she is semi-retired and now "makes candy as she feels up to it," she crafts her handmade delicacies on the same marble table used by Rebecca and Ruth. (Ruth bought "Edna's table" for $10 in 1917.)

Cost: Free

Freebies: Samples of the original Bourbon Balls and other chocolates (children receive nonalcoholic samples only).

Video Shown: No

Reservations Needed: No, except for bus groups.

Days and Hours: January through October: Mon–Thur 9:00 AM–4:30 PM. Closed holidays. Tours given on a limited basis 3 days before Valentine's Day, Easter, and Mother's Day.

Plan to Stay: 10–15 minutes, plus time in retail store.

Minimum Age: Young children should be accompanied by an adult.

Disabled Access: No

Group Requirements: Bus operators should call (800) 444-3766 to make reservations or obtain additional information.

Special Information: Video cameras not allowed. Production more likely in mornings, before candy holidays, and in September and October.

Retail Store: Sells a wide variety of liquor-cream chocolates (including Bourbon Balls, Kentucky Irish Coffees, and Kentucky Mint Juleps), nut clusters, butter creams, and Kentucky Creamed Pull Candy. Open year-round Mon–Sat 8:30 AM–5:30 PM. Closed Christmas, New Year's, and July 4th. Catalog available from 800 number above.

Directions: From Lexington, take I-64 West to Frankfort Exit 58, then take U.S. 60 West. Turn left onto Second St. Rebecca Ruth is ½ block ahead on left. From Louisville, take I-64 East to Frankfort Exit 53. Take Rt. 127 North to U.S. 60 East, which becomes Second St. Stay on Second St. Cross over Capital Ave. Rebecca-Ruth is ½ block ahead on left

Nearby Attractions: Three Chimneys horse farm and Toyota tours (see pages 108, 109, and 112); Ancient Age Distillery tour (call 502-223-7641).

Delicious bourbon balls crowned with Southern pecans overflow from this Rebecca Ruth Candy ceramic gift mug.

The house-like headquarters of Rebecca Ruth Candy Factory are located in Frankfort, Kentucky.

Toyota ⟿ *cars*

1001 Cherry Blossom Way
Georgetown, KY 40324
(502) 868-3027 / (800) 866-4485

In 1988 Toyota began building its popular Camry in this small Kentucky town. Since then, the plant has been through two major model changes and now also produces the Avalon and the Sienna minivan. As the largest Toyota automobile manufacturing plant outside of Japan, the plant employs 7,000 "team members" (Toyota's name for its employees) who produce more than 1,600 vehicles a day. The tour shows the process and pride of Toyota Motor Manufacturing (TMMK), Kentucky and its uniformed team members.

The Camry and the Avalon begin in the Stamping area as gleaming coils of steel. The steel is cleaned, straightened, and stamped into sheet-metal components that make up the vehicle bodies. With loud thumps and hundreds of tons of pressure, automated presses shape metal, bend edges, pierce holes, and trim excesses.

The sheet-metal components move to the Body Weld area, where robotic and human arms hold the equipment that welds together a body shell. Watch sparks fly, as computer-controlled robots perform thousands of welds in synchronized unison. The new vehicle bodies travel by overhead conveyors to the Paint Shop and then down the trim, chassis, and final assembly lines.

As you tour the plant, your guide points out specialties of the Toyota Production System, including examples of *kaizen* (continuous improvement), "just-in-time" parts delivery, and the Andon system (any team member can stop the line at any time to address quality concerns or problems. One example of *kaizen* is the mechanical arm that now automatically installs the spare tire in the trunk, once a difficult manual process. Just-in-time delivery is vividly demonstrated by the different color car bodies, each corresponding to an order, moving down the assembly line. The seat manufacturer delivers the correct color seats as the corresponding body shells emerge from the Paint Shop.

In addition to tours of the manufacturing plant, there is a Visitor Center, where guests can spend time looking at Toyota products, participating in interactive video displays, and learning about the Toyota Production System and Toyota operations around the world.

Cost: Free

Freebies: Key chain and brochure on TMMK and Toyota manufacturing.

Video Shown: 10-minute video gives a brief plant overview, some production steps not on the tour, and interviews with team members about TMMK's impact in Kentucky.

Reservations Needed: Yes, for tour; no, for Visitor Center.

Days and Hours: Tours: Tue and Thur; hours vary. Call to get public tour times. Schedule may vary depending on school tours. *Toyota reserves the right to cancel or reschedule tours if production needs demand changes.* Visitor Center: Mon, Wed, Fri 10:00 AM–4:00 PM, Tue and Thur 8:00 AM–7:00 PM. Closed holidays, July 4th week, and 2 weeks at Christmas.

Plan to Stay: 1½ hours, including tour, video and Visitor Center.

Minimum Age: 8 for tour; none for Visitor Center.

Disabled Access: Yes

Group Requirements: Maximum group size is 65–70 people. Best to call several months in advance for large groups.

Special Information: No photography.

Gift Shop: Sells logoed items including golf shirts, T-shirts, and caps. Open same hours as Visitor Center.

Directions: From Lexington, take I-75 North (toward Cincinnati) to Exit 126 (Georgetown/Cynthiana). Turn right on U.S. 62 (Cherry Blossom Way). Visitor Entrance is about 3 miles from the exit. (You'll pass several Toyota entrances before you reach the Visitor Entrance.)

Nearby Attractions: Three Chimneys horse farm, Rebecca-Ruth Candies, and Old Kentucky Candies tours (see pages 108, 109, and 110); Factory Stores of America Outlet Center; Georgetown College.

Website: www.toyota.com

Seventy-four robots perform thousands of welds on the main framing body line to form a Camry or Avalon body shell.

Seat installation is a good example of the just-in-time process Toyota employs.

Wild Turkey — *bourbon*

1525 Tyrone Road
Lawrenceburg, KY 40342
(502) 839-4544

Wild Turkey Distillery sits on a hill next to the Kentucky River. Water from this naturally filtered limestone riverbed and corn from nearby farmers are the main ingredients in bourbon, a uniquely American whiskey. This tour shows almost all steps in crafting the bourbon named after founder Thomas McCarthy's private stock taken on a wild turkey hunt.

The first surprise is the metal-barred windows on the big, gray, square warehouses throughout the grounds. What could be mistaken for jailhouses are actually rack houses where the bourbon ages. The tax-hungry government once required installation of the bars to prevent any barrels from leaving without proper fees being paid.

The initial step in producing bourbon is mixing corn, rye, and water. The mix is cooked and cooled, then malted barley is added. With special yeast added, this sour mash ferments in cypress-wood or stainless-steel tanks. Watch the slow, gentle swirl of the thick yellow mash in the vats; carbon-dioxide bubbles rise to the surface as the yeast changes sugar to alcohol, called "distiller's beer." Stand next to the 40-foot-high copper still, where the alcohol is separated in a vaporization process.

Charred white-oak barrels then become the colorless whiskey's home. The tour guide explains that the burnt layers of wood inside the barrel give bourbon its distinctive flavor and color (whiskey must be aged in new, charred-oak barrels for two years to be legally called "bourbon"). Inside a cool warehouse amid racks of barrels on wood planks, you'll enjoy the sweet bourbon smell. Wild Turkey calls this the "angels' share" because one-third of each barrel's contents evaporates over the bourbon's eight years of aging. It's not until you walk through the quality control lab and the bottling area that the process seems any different from what it must have been 100 years ago.

Cost: Free
Freebies: Food made with Wild Turkey, such as a bourbon brownie; a barrel bung; lemonade; coffee; and recipes that use Wild Turkey; smells.
Video Shown: No
Reservations Needed: No, except for groups of 20 or more people.
Days and Hours: Mon–Fri 9:00 AM, 10:30 AM, 12:30 PM, and 2:30 PM. Closed holidays.
Plan to Stay: 45 minutes for tour, plus time for snacks and visitors center. The visitors center is in a restored building with a small display of ceramic Wild Turkey decanters, historical mementos, a scale model of the bourbon production process, and a gift shop.
Minimum Age: No
Disabled Access: Visitors center is fully accessible. Remainder of the facility has gravel paths and flights of stairs to some areas.
Group Requirements: Advance notice requested for groups of 20 or more. No maximum size.
Special Information: Wear comfortable walking shoes. Tour runs all year, but not all areas are in production during certain weeks in July and August.
Gift Shop: Sells hats and clothes, including T-shirts and shorts with the Wild Turkey logo and popular "Too Good To Gobble" slogan (Bruce gave this to his mom!), other logoed items, and barbecue sauce. Open Mon–Fri 8:30 AM–4:00 PM. Catalog available from (800) BUY-TRKY.
Directions: From Louisville, take I-64 East to Rt. 151 South to Rt. 127 South. Turn left on Rt. 44, which turns into U.S. 62 East. Bear right onto Tyrone Rd. (Rt. 1510) to distillery. From Lexington, take U.S. 60 West (take Business Route at split) to Versailles to U.S. 62 West to distillery. You're almost there when you see billboards announcing "Bird Sanctuary Ahead" and "Home of Wild Turkey."
Nearby Attractions: Beaver Lake and Taylorville Lake; Ripplewood Estate.

See color photos, page 174

Blaine Kern's Mardi Gras World

233 Newton Street *parade floats and props*
New Orleans, LA 70114
(504) 361-7821

You know this tour is going to be fun as soon as you arrive. Colorful Mardi Gras props—such as a gigantic jester, alligators, and Marilyn Monroe—perch in front of this fantasy factory. Blaine Kern, known locally as "Mr. Mardi Gras," is the world's largest float builder. His family-run company, begun in 1947, creates 75 percent of Mardi Gras– parade floats. The Kern Companies also build props for casinos and amusement parks, plus floats for up to 60 parades nationwide annually.

After a guide and a video explain the history of Mardi Gras and the company, you can dress up in authentic Carnival costumes. Don sequined headdresses, gowns, and regal coats of armor and imagine yourself as a noble king or queen of the ball! During the self-guided portion of your tour, you'll enter a maze of amazing props. In one area, heaps of props await repair. A 15-foot torso of Cleopatra stands nearby.

Follow the yellow arrows to the next "den" (float artists' warehouse). It's a big carpentry and paint shop, where workers build sensational floats for each "krewe" (club). Artists, painters, and sculptors decorate each float with brightly colored themed scenes. Gold and silver foil on the sides of the floats glisten and flutter in the breeze. The floats are as colorful and animated as Saturday morning cartoons, and strings of lights trace their outlines at night.

In den 7, also used as a unique function room for parties, gigantic King and Queen Kong figures flank the performance stage. Completed tractor-trailer-sized floats constructed of wood, papier mâché, fiberglass, and Styrofoam rest here waiting to be set free along their parade routes. Notice the famed "Bacchasaurus" float, with stairs under its belly to assist the krewe members in climbing onto the float. It's the Trojan Horse meets *Jurassic Park*!

The Mardi Gras floats come alive when krewe members dance, sing, throw kisses, wave their arms, and toss beads, doubloons, stuffed animals, and cups from their floats.

Cost: Adults, $6.50; seniors, $5.50; children under 12, $3.75; under 3, free.

Freebies: Mardi Gras gift pack, on request.

Video Shown: 11-minute video covering Mardi Gras and company history.

Reservations Needed: No, except for groups over 25 people.

Days and Hours: Mon–Sun 9:30 AM–4:30 PM. Closed Mardi Gras, Easter Sunday, Thanksgiving, and Christmas. Depending on the season, time, and day, you will see differing amounts of float-building activity.

Plan to Stay: 1 hour for introductory talk, video, costume try-on, and self-guided tour, plus time for the gift shop.

Minimum Age: None

Disabled Access: Yes

Group Requirements: During Carnival Season (January 6 to the day before Ash Wednesday), groups of 25 or more people should call 2 weeks in advance. Otherwise, 1 day is sufficient. Group discounts available. King Cake available for $2 per person (the King Cake tradition is that whoever eats the piece containing a baby figure must host the next party).

Special Information: Excellent site for parties, complete with miniature parades and lit floats. Call (800) 362-8213.

Gift Shop: Sells Carnival paraphernalia including beads, cups, and doubloons, plus T-shirts, books, and posters. Ships King Cakes. Open same hours as tour.

Directions: From New Orleans, cross Crescent City Connection to Westbank. Take General De Gaulle Dr. East exit. Turn left onto Shirley Dr. Follow signs to Mardi Gras World. From Downtown/French Quarter, take free Canal St. ferry and then free shuttle bus. Future plans for paddle-wheel steamboat directly to Mardi Gras World dock.

Nearby Mardi Gras–Related Attractions: New Orleans Mint, Arnaud's Restaurant, and Musee Conti—the Wax Museum of Louisiana Legends.

See color photos, page 172

Bruce Foods ⟶ *pepper sauces and Cajun foods*

1653 Old Spanish Trail
St. Martinville, LA 70582
(318) 365-8101 (ext. 261)

BRUCE FOODS CORPORATION

Bruce Foods, discreetly headquartered on a country highway between Lafayette and New Iberia, is the quiet, family-owned giant of food companies in the South. The company that began in 1928 with one product, a pepper sauce, today has more than 300 products marketed to 100 countries around the world—Bruce Foods is one of the top exporters in the U.S. As the product display case in the reception area shows, the company now produces everything from Cajun seasonings to Mexican mixes, in addition to its well-known pepper sauces ("Original" Louisiana brand).

Although the tour is not set up to handle large volumes of visitors, it takes you onto the production floor. In part of the packaging area, clinking, empty bottles ride around a carousel where they're filled with colorful red pepper sauce. You can walk down the lines as the bottles are labeled, capped, and boxed. On the lines that package "wet" and "dry" products, notice the computerized packaging machines with electronic switches and sensors.

In another area, the pungent smell of several varieties of cured peppers fills the air as the peppers are mashed to make different sauces. The vinegar is added, and the microcut machines apply thousands of cuts per second to the filtered coarse pepper mash. The residue, or "chaff," from the peppers looks like wet, red sand. It's so combustible it can ignite on its own if dried and left in the sun. The chaff is sold to restaurants for pepper seasoning in crab boil.

The factory also has an open-air production area where trucks drop off the peppers fresh from the field. You'll see a gargantuan colander that rinses freshly cut pepper slices. You'll also stare at rows of pickling vats the size of kiddie pools and a field's worth of sky-high, 23,650-gallon tanks—88 in all—that look like they could hold oil or gas reserves. Actually, they store concentrated pepper mash that will age like fine wine for one to two years to ferment before heading inside the factory for final processing. All this concentrated mash is needed to make the famous hot sauces that will fill everything from Bruce's 2-ounce bottles to its tanker trucks.

Cost: Free

Freebies: Product brochures

Video Shown: No

Reservations Needed: Yes. Individuals and families need to join scheduled group tours.

Days and Hours: Mon–Fri 8:00 AM–5:00 PM, although tours are limited. Closed holidays and the week between Christmas and New Year's.

Plan to Stay: 30–45 minutes

Minimum Age: 6

Disabled Access: Cramped quarters make access difficult for wheelchairs.

Group Requirements: Maximum group size is 10 people. Groups should call 1 week in advance.

Special Information: Production is busiest August through November during pepper harvest season. The company recently started giving public tours, so requirements and tour route are still evolving. No photography. Factory floor busy with forklifts and may be wet, so wear sneakers. Tours at other Bruce Food factories available upon request: Lozes, LA (canned yams and other southern vegetables); El Paso, TX (Mexican food products); and Wilson, SC.

Gift Shop: No. Catalog available for full line of food products and Chef John Folse's cookbooks and black iron pots (call 800-299-9082). Catalog may soon be available for logoed clothing line.

Directions: From New Orleans, take I-10 West. Exit at 103A. Follow U.S. 90 through Lafayette to Cade/St. Martinville exit. Turn left off exit onto LA 182 (Old Spanish Trail). Factory is several miles down on left.

Nearby Attractions: Konriko tour and McIlhenny tour (see pages 118 and 120).

Kliebert's Turtle and Alligator Tours

41067 West Yellow Water Road   *turtle and alligator farm*
Hammond, LA 70403
(504) 345-3617 / (800) 854-9164

Harvey Kliebert knows a good business opportunity. After raising turtles for 35 years and alligators for 25 years, in 1984 he decided to turn the farm into a tourist attraction. This example of agri-tourism has not only added to his income but also turned the colorful Harvey and his farm into celebrities. While you're there, you can check out the airboat used in the Burt Reynolds' movie *Gator*. Harvey himself appears occasionally in MTV interviews.

It's still an authentic turtle and alligator farm, dotted with duckweed and clove-covered ponds that the breeding turtles and alligators call home. Over 17,000 laying turtles produce over 1 million eggs per year. Once the turtles lay their eggs, which they do up to three times between April and August, Harvey and his crew dig up the eggs from the dirt nests on the pond banks. They then dip the eggs in a pressure machine that removes salmonella. All of the hatchlings are sold outside the U.S. for aquariums, children's pets, or food.

The gator breeding pond provides the most excitement for visitors, with gators lounging at the water's edge. Egrets and herons nest in trees overhead. Harvey has about 250 breeder alligators, all born in 1957. The big ones grow to 14 feet long and 1,200 pounds. If you watch the workers throw the gators dead chicken, fish parts, or ground nutria, you can happily assume that they're not too hungry during your visit.

Around June 1 of every year, the female gators start building their nests, piling dirt and grass in mounds 2 feet high. They then lay eggs just once per year, sometime between June 15 and July 1. As the tour guides/alligator farm workers glibly explain, the female will attack any animal or person that comes around the nest. Fortunately, Harvey and his crew have developed methods of chasing the female away so they can grab her eggs. After incubation, the gators live in pens until they are sold for their meat and hides, or sold to breeders in Florida.

Cost: Adults, $4; children, $2; children under 2, free.
Freebies: Recipe sheets
Video Shown: No
Reservations Needed: No, but recommended for groups over 20 people.
Days and Hours: Open year-round, weather permitting, Mon–Sun noon until dark. The farm is open only during the afternoon so visitors don't scare nesting turtles. No tours during extreme cold or storms. Closed holidays.
Plan to Stay: 45 minutes for tour, plus time for gift shop.
Minimum Age: None
Disabled Access: Yes
Group Requirements: Groups over 20 people should call 1 week in advance. No maximum group size. Group discount of 25 percent off for 10 or more people. School groups receive 50 percent discount.
Special Information: Turtles lay eggs April through July; alligators lay eggs June 15–July 1. Annual Alligator Day the third Saturday of August, although may be moved up 1 month. Company plans to expand tour, with larger welcome center and gift shop.
Gift Shop: Sells alligator heads, fingers, teeth, jewelry, turtle-foot back-scratchers, and just about any gift or food you can imagine that can be made and sold out of alligator or turtle parts. Open Mon–Sun from 11:00 AM until dark. Closed holidays. List of products available from above number.
Directions: From New Orleans, take I-10 West to I-55 North to the Springfield exit. Take LA 22 West, which crosses over I-55. Turn right onto the frontage road that runs parallel I-55. Turn left onto Hoffman Rd. Turn right on Yellow Water Rd. and follow signs. From Baton Rouge, take I-12 East to I-55 South. Take Springfield exit. Take LA 22 West and follow directions above.
Nearby Attractions: Abita Brewing Company tour in Abita Springs (call 504-893-3143); Global Wildlife Center in Folsom.

Konriko   ⌒   *rice and Cajun seasonings*

309 Ann Street
New Iberia, LA 70560
(800) 551-3245

The best place to start a tour of the Konriko Rice Mill is in the Konriko Company Store, a replica of an old plantation company store located adjacent to the mill. While you wait for a tour to begin, the friendly Cajun staff offers you a cup of strong, flavorful South Louisiana–style coffee. Something is always cooking for visitors in the store, too: one day it might be Konriko red beans and rice; another day, Konriko's jambalaya mix with rice. Once you've sampled some good Cajun coffee and cooking, the tour officially begins.

After watching an informative slide presentation, you move next door to America's oldest rice mill. Konriko's mill was built by founder Philip Conrad in 1912, and has been in continuous operation ever since. Made of wood and corrugated tin, the mill is loud and rickety when in operation. But it has great character and is on the National Register of Historic Places.

Before entering the mill, you'll see the outdoor scale and dryer that weighs and dries the unmilled rough rice local farmers deliver. An average truckload of rice is about 30,000 pounds. Next to the dryer is a bin that stores the rice before it is processed. When full, the bin holds 1 million pounds of rice—about $100,000 worth. And don't overlook Konriko, the company's "guard" dog, sometimes sleeping in the sun.

Inside, your guide uses a scale model of a mill as a visual aid to explain how different varieties of rice are milled. Walk on the wooden floors between boxes of rice, piles of cardboard containers, burlap bags, and packaging machines. You'll enter several aromatic rooms where workers mix and package Konriko rice and seasonings. Peek into the rice-cake production room. If you're lucky, your tour guide will give you a hot rice cake fresh from the oven to top off the tour.

Cost: Adults, $2.75; seniors 62 and over, $2.25; children under 12, $1.25.
Freebies: Fresh, hot coffee; cooked Konriko products; and recipes.

Video Shown: 20-minute "historically correct" slide presentation on Cajun culture and Konriko's development.
Reservations Needed: No, except for groups over 15 people.
Days and Hours: Mon–Sat 10:00 AM, 11:00 AM, 1:00 PM, 2:00 PM, and 3:00 PM. No production on Saturdays, holidays, and during factory repairs, but tours usually run.
Plan to Stay: Approximately 40 minutes for video and tour, plus time for gift shop.
Minimum Age: None
Disabled Access: Full access to Konriko Company Store. Four steps lead to mill.
Group Requirements: Groups over 15 people should call 2 weeks in advance. Maximum group size is 50. Group rates available for 40 or more. Special tour times can be arranged.
Special Information: Mill can be loud. Hot in the summer.
Gift Shop: Konriko Company Store sells local foods and crafts, complete assortment of Konriko rice cakes, brown rice crackers, famous Wild Pecan Rice, mixes, T-shirts, novelty items, even Cajun dance video and music tapes. Open Mon–Sat 9:00 AM–5:00 PM. Closed Thanksgiving, Christmas, New Year's, and July 4th. Catalog available at above number.
Directions: From I-10, take Lafayette/U.S. Hwy. 90 exit (Exit 103), and follow U.S. 90 through Lafayette toward New Iberia. At LA 14 (Center St.) in New Iberia, exit and turn left. Turn right on St. Peter St., then right on Ann St. Rice mill is on left.
Nearby Attractions: McIlhenny and Bruce Foods tours (see pages 120 and 116); Shadows-On-The-Teche; Live Oak Gardens on Jefferson Island; Rice Museum in Crowley; Delcambre Shrimp Boat Landing; Vermilionville, Acadian Village, and Jean Lafitte National Historical Park/Acadiana Cultural Center in Lafayette.

Visit America's oldest rice mill; it has been in continuous operation since 1912.

Learn how brown rice is made into white rice! A "pearler" takes off the bran at Konriko in New Iberia, Louisiana.

McIlhenny Company 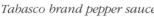 *Tabasco brand pepper sauce*

Avery Island, LA 70513
(318) 365-8173

This concentrated hot-pepper sauce, first created after the Civil War on the McIlhenny family's exotic 2,300-acre island in the South Louisiana bayou country, has such a lively flavor that it is now sold in more than 100 countries around the world and its labels are printed in 15 foreign languages. McIlhenny Company grows the *Capsicum frutescens* peppers (tabasco peppers) in several countries to insure a good harvest. But there is only one Tabasco sauce factory, and you'll recognize this modern red-brick building as soon as you open your car door and whiff the piquant pepper aroma.

A film explains that McIlhenny planted hot peppers seeds a friend brought from Mexico. He created his sauce (brand-named Tabasco, a Central-American Indian word) by mashing the peppers with Avery Island salt, aging the mash in wooden barrels, adding vinegar, and then straining the mixture.

Along a corridor in the modern factory, observe four lines of Tabasco sauce bottling from behind a long glass wall. The smell here isn't nearly as strong as it must be inside the packaging room. Some lines produce over 300 bottles of Tabasco sauce a minute, helping the factory produce over 400,000 bottles a day.

After the bottles are spun around in the carousel and injected with the hot red-pepper sauce, they journey naked down the assembly line. Machines automatically clothe the bottles with the familiar bright red octagonal caps, green foil neckbands, and diamond-shaped labels. The dressed bottles are then mechanically packed in boxes, ready to travel. Their final destination will be dining tables from Pennsylvania to Peking, where their red caps will be removed and they will "drop in" to spice up a meal.

Cost: Free
Freebies: Miniature Tabasco sauce bottle, recipes, and other McIlhenny products.
Video Shown: 8-minute overview of McIlhenny's history and operations, as well as

Tabasco brand pepper sauce origins and the full processing, including harvesting of peppers, mashing, aging, mixing with vinegar, and bottling.
Reservations Needed: No, except for groups over 20 people.
Days and Hours: Mon–Fri 9:00 AM–4:00 PM, Sat 9:00 AM–12:00 PM. Last tour ½-hour before closing. May not see production on Saturdays. Closed holidays and long weekends.
Plan to Stay: 25 minutes for video and tour, plus time for gift shop and grounds.
Minimum Age: None
Disabled Access: Yes
Group Requirements: Groups larger than 20 people should make advance reservations; 1 week's notice appreciated.
Special Information: Some production-process details are in photos and captions above the viewing window.
Gift Shop: Tabasco Country Store sells a wide variety of Tabasco brand specialty foods and novelty items, from pepper earrings to lithographs, toys, cookware, ties, cookbooks, and spices. Open same hours as tour. Gift shop at Jungle Gardens entrance open until 5:30 PM (sells similar items). Catalog available at (800) 634-9599.
Directions: From New Orleans, take I-10 West to Exit 103A. Follow U.S. 90 through Lafayette toward New Iberia. Exit at LA 14 and turn left. At LA 329 junction, turn right. Stay on LA 329 approximately 6 miles. The road dead-ends at Avery Island, where the toll road has a nominal charge per vehicle. Signs will direct you to factory.
Nearby Attractions: Konriko and Bruce Foods tours (see pages 118 and 116); Jungle Gardens and Bird City on Avery Island; Live Oak Gardens on Jefferson Island. Hot-sauce lovers may also want to tour smaller companies such as All Cajun Food Company in Breaux Bridge (call 318-332-3613).

See color photo, page 192

Motivatit Seafoods ⟿ *oysters, blue crab, and crawfish*
412 Palm Street
Houma, LA 70361
(504) 868-7191

Louisiana is known for its tasty seafood, and few factories process more of it than Motivatit. The Voisin family, owners of the company, have been involved in the seafood industry since their ancestors arrived in Louisiana from France in 1770. The oyster plant shucks 400 to 500 burlap sacks (40,000 to 50,000 pounds) of oysters daily. The nearby blue crab and crawfish plant processes 25,000 to 30,000 pounds of blue crabs daily, in addition to 5,000 to 6,000 pounds of crawfish between February and June.

Most food-processing plants you visit seem highly automated. Workers appear to spend their hours monitoring or assisting the computerized, fast-moving machines. But this is not so at seafood-processing plants. The removal of the shells and the meats from oysters, crabs, and crawfish is too gentle and dexterous a motion for machines to handle. Sure, you'll see half-shelled oysters move down an assembly line; modern refrigeration units; big, steaming vats for crabs; and what looks like a giant kaleidoscope of metal rods to sort crab leg sizes; but human hands do the real work of getting the meat from the shell.

You enter what looks like the world's largest raw-oyster bar. If you close your eyes, you can easily imagine that you're next to the ocean listening to carpenters build a house. Rows of rubber-aproned workers stand in front of metal tables piled with fresh, salty-smelling oysters. These professional shuckers, working on one oyster at a time, use hammers to crack the hinge holding the shells together. They pry open the oyster, scoop out the meat with a small knife, and toss the meat and shells into separate buckets. The best shuckers can repeat this rhythmic hammering, prying, and tossing at a rate of almost 500 oysters per hour.

At the crab and crawfish plant, the tour often begins in front of big colanders filled with reddish-colored steamed crabs. In an adjoining room, thousands of cooked crabs are piled high on a table, with the workers grabbing them to pull off the backs and claws. Once the crabs are debacked, it's much easier to get at the lump meat. In the picking rooms, the workers' speedy, careful hands manipulate small paring knives to pluck out all the meat from the crab (or crawfish, in season). It reminds you of an old-time sewing bee. Nothing seems to go to waste at this plant, as even the crab shells are decorated for re-use as Christmas-tree ornaments.

Cost: $5 per person
Freebies: Occasionally, a dirty-colored Louisiana oyster.
Video Shown: No
Reservations Needed: Yes. Individuals need to either join a scheduled group tour or form a group.
Days and Hours: Mon–Fri 8:00 AM–5:00 PM. Before 11:00 AM is best time to see production. Closed holidays.
Plan to Stay: 30–45 minutes for tour of each plant. Visitors pick one factory to tour.
Minimum Age: None, but children must be supervised.
Disabled Access: Yes
Group Requirements: 1 week's advance notice; longer during peak travel seasons.
Special Information: Floors are wet. Oyster production busiest, as the locals say, the "months with the Rs" (September–April). Crab and crawfish processing is busiest during spring and summer.
Gift Shop: No
Directions: From New Orleans, take Hwy. 90 West to Houma. Turn left at Gum St. Oyster plant and corporate headquarters are at the corner of Gum and Palm Sts. Directions to crab and crawfish plant available upon request.
Nearby Attractions: Southdown Plantation Home/Terrebonne Museum; swamp tours; Louisiana Universities Marine Consortium (LUMCON)-Marine Research Facility tour in Chauvin (call 504-851-2800). Annual Breaux Bridge Crawfish Festival (first full weekend in May) 2 hours away.

Tony Chachere's 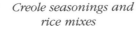 *Creole seasonings and rice mixes*

533 North Lombard Street
Opelousas, LA 70570
(800) 551-9066

We love stories about people who start new businesses at the age most people focus on retirement. The late Tony Chachere started his third career at the age of 67. Having retired from successful stints in pharmacy and insurance, he decided to fulfill a lifelong desire to write and publish a cookbook. While a member of Cooks Unlimited, a men's cooking club, he had developed a "secret" spicy seasoning mix that he used in many of the book's recipes. The popularity of the seasoning recipe in his cookbook encouraged Tony to start manufacturing the blend for consumers. Today the seasoning is the number-one-selling spice mix in the Cajun/Creole category.

After a brief talk about Tony's and the company's histories, your tour guide leads you into the refrigerated ingredients room. It's piled high with boxes and burlap bags filled with spices. Smell the pungent aromas emanating from the boxes of ground red pepper, cloves, cinnamon, and oregano. The company uses 6 million pounds of spices and 3 million pounds of salt each year—and it all begins here.

Because of the overwhelming smell on the second floor, you can't observe the actual mixing together of the spices. Even on the first floor, you'll notice workers wear portable air units that filter the pungent air around them. Next, your guided factory-floor tour takes you into the packaging area. The spices drop down through overhead pipes to several different fast-moving assembly lines. Each day, the auger processor fills 2,000 cases of 8-ounce "little green cans" with the seasoning mix. On another line, gumbo and jambalaya mixes are automatically sealed between two sheets of foil (creating bags) and inserted into boxes.

During the current tour, you walk through the warehouse. Here, finished products of all types and sizes wait in large brown boxes for shipment to stores and distribution points worldwide. As you pass by the food scientists' kitchen, you may smell

the product being tested. In the UPS shipment area, used for smaller orders, you'll be surprised to see a popcorn popper. The company uses popcorn as a more environmentally conscious packing material than Styrofoam, plus it has the added benefit of enhancing the flavor of your package. A true indicator of where you live may not be the zip code on your UPS package, but rather the size of the can of Tony Chachere's Creole Seasoning you order—locals always keep 17-ounce cans on their kitchen tables.

Cost: Free
Freebies: Bag of souvenir items, including catalog, pamphlet cookbook, and available product samples.
Video Shown: No, in planning stages
Reservations Needed: No, except for groups larger than 10 people.
Days and Hours: Mon–Fri 9:30–11:00 AM and 1:30–3:00 PM. Closed limited holidays.
Plan to Stay: 30 minutes for tour
Minimum Age: 7
Disabled Access: Yes
Group Requirements: Groups over 10 people should call 2 weeks in advance. Special times can be arranged. No maximum group size.
Special Information: No photography
Gift Shop: No, in planning stages. However, can purchase all of their seasoning and rice mixes, some of which are not even in stores. Also available for purchase is Tony's last cookbook, *Tony Chachere's Second Helping*. These memoirs contains more than 300 mouth-watering recipes accumulated through a lifetime steeped in Cajun culture and Southern hospitality. Catalog available at number above.
Directions: From I-10, take I-49 North to U.S. 190 West. Turn right onto Lombard St. Factory is 5 blocks ahead on left.
Nearby Attractions: Savoie Sausage Kitchen occasional tour (call 318-942-7241); Opelousas Museum and Interpretive Center; Chretien Point Plantation.

Mead Paper ~ *paper*

35 Hartford Street
Rumford, ME 04276
(207) 369-2727

Deep in the heart of Maine's Western Mountains you'll find Mead's papermaking complex (previously owned by Boise Cascade), where production began in 1901. Some of the mill still works much as it did over 95 years ago, with the No. 4 Paper Machine (PM) in operation since 1904. Many workers today follow in the footsteps of their great-grandparents in the long and proud tradition of papermaking.

Papermaking begins with woodchips that are cooked in digesters (large cooking vats) to make pulp. The pulp, resembling Cream of Wheat, is blended with additives to make the stock. The stock, 99.5 percent water, jets from the headbox of the paper machine onto a mesh screen called a "wire." Here, water drains and is suctioned off. Look down at the wire of the No. 4 PM, then climb upstairs to see the wire of the enormous No. 15 PM—it's four times the size of the No. 4 PM and as long as a football field.

The stock, now called a "paper web," moves to the press section of the machine. The web rumbles through, over, and under a series of rollers. Try to follow the actual course of the speeding paper. The heavy rollers press even more water out of the paper web. A granite roller on the No. 15 PM weighs over 4 tons. After going through the presses, the web is much smoother but still contains 60 percent of its water.

The dryer section looks similar to the press section, but here the rollers are hollow cans heated with steam. The intense heat evaporates almost all of the remaining water. The paper can be uncoated, coated on one side (like a Campbell's soup label), or coated on both sides (like the pages of a *National Geographic* magazine). A series of rollers transfers the coating—made of clay, latex, and starches—onto the paper. The paper then rolls across a very sharp blade that removes the excess coating.

At this point the paper, although coated, does not look glossy. It moves to the super-calender, a vertical alignment of steel and cotton rolls. At the "nip point," where the rolls meet, the paper is subject to such intense heat and pressure that the coating melts and is pressed flat for a high gloss.

At the lighting lab see some of the Oxford Specialty Papers. Here, on a light table or under an ultraviolet light, you may examine the watermarks on security papers used for checks and stock certificates, or study the delicate pale blue and pink papers used to package spoonfuls of sweeteners.

Cost: Free

Freebies: Brochure detailing how paper is made, coloring book, and paper samples; regional recreation map with campsites and hiking trails.

Video Shown: 20-minute video explains papermaking process and safety rules.

Reservations Needed: Yes, 4 working days in advance for individuals.

Days and Hours: End of June through end of September only: Tue and Thur, 10:00 AM. Special group times can be arranged.

Plan to Stay: 2½ hours

Minimum Age: 9

Disabled Access: Yes

Group Requirements: Groups should call 2 weeks in advance to reserve space. Maximum group size is 13 people. Larger groups can be split.

Special Information: No photography in mill. All-day forestry tours and special combined mill and forestry tours can be arranged by calling above number.

Gift Shop: No

Directions: From Portland, take I-95 (Maine Tpke.) North. Take Exit 12 for Rt. 4 North. Turn left on Rt. 108 North. Turn right on Canal St. Mill Administration Building is directly ahead at end of road.

Nearby Attractions: Sunday River Ski Resort; Western Mountains; Rangeley Lake Tour Region, 1 hour away; Portland 1½ hours away.

See color photos, page 176

Tom's of Maine   *natural toothpaste*

Railroad Avenue
Kennebunk, ME 04043
(207) 985-2944

Over 25 years ago, Kate and Tom Chappell moved to Maine to live a simpler life and to create a company committed to developing all-natural personal hygiene products, such as toothpaste, mouthwash, soap, and deodorant. While we don't know if they found a simpler life, they have created a successful, socially conscious, environmentally committed company. In fact, their tasty toothpaste—made without artificial preservatives, sweeteners, or coloring—is the top-selling brand in many major stores.

All Tom's of Maine products are made in a restored railroad station, a very different setting from most successful companies' plants. On the first floor, toothpaste ingredients are mixed in a 3,000-pound vat. Ingredients for liquid products such as mouthwash or shampoo have a second mixing area.

As you walk upstairs to the second floor, you'll know what products the toothpaste and liquid lines are packaging. If you smell cinnamon, they're packaging that flavor toothpaste or mouthwash. An intense coriander smell usually means deodorant. You cannot miss the machine that pumps the still-warm toothpaste into recyclable tubes and clamps the backs closed. Notice how the company tries to reduce the amount of product packaging. For the mouthwash, the outer paper carton has been replaced with a thin leaflet that folds into the back of the recyclable plastic container.

What's most interesting about this tour isn't so much the production process, but the sense that the workers enjoy their jobs and take seriously their responsibility for quality control. The smiles you see aren't just to show off good teeth. Every hour, most workers on the packaging line switch positions. A worker who just put the tubes into the filler machine now boxes toothpaste. While you may be bored brushing your teeth, the people who make your toothpaste aren't!

Cost: Free

Freebies: Product sample

Video Shown: 12-minute video, "Common Good: The Story of Tom's of Maine," covers company history and production. Also, special video for kids. Videos also shown in the outlet store.

Reservations Needed: Yes

Days and Hours: Call for hours since the tour dates and times may vary. Closed holidays. When tours not available, you can watch video of production in the nearby outlet store.

Plan to Stay: 1 hour for the tour and a talk about the company and its philosophy, plus time for video and outlet store.

Minimum Age: 5

Disabled Access: Flight of stairs leads to factory. Can view video in fully accessible outlet store.

Group Requirements: Groups larger than 10 people should call 1 month ahead. Groups larger than 15 people may be split into smaller ones (some groups go to the outlet store before the tour).

Special Information: No photography.

Outlet Store:. Located about 1 mile away on Storer St. (call 207-985-3874). Sells all Tom's natural personal-hygiene products, including discounted factory seconds. Open Mon–Sat 9:30 AM–5:00 PM. Closed holidays and the week of July 4th.

Directions: Tours meet at the Tom's of Maine Outlet store. From I-95, take Exit 3. Turn left onto Rt. 35. At fork just past school, bear right. The outlet store is in the Lafayette Center (a renovated brick factory along the Mousam River) approximately ½ -mile ahead on right.

Nearby Attractions: Kennebunkport Brewing Co. tour (call 207-967-4311; larger plant gives tours in Portland, call 207-761-0807); Wedding Cake House; Brick Store Museum; Kennebunkport resort area, beaches, and former President Bush's residence.

Bartley Collection

65 Engerman Avenue
Denton, MD 21629
(800) 787-2800

wooden furniture reproductions

Have you ever yearned for a magnificent Queen Anne sideboard or an 18th-century Chippendale night stand? If you are at all handy with woodworking, you can use Bartley antique reproduction kits to make your own highboys, four-poster beds, dining tables, chairside tables, jewelry boxes, and more. With the plant manager as your guide, you can tour the one-acre factory where these antique reproductions are designed, created, and packed.

Pass the hardware department, where you may see a worker assemble each kit's perfectly reproduced brass fittings. When Bartley designers find desirable antiques to reproduce, they make rubberized castings of the original hardware and intricate moldings. These castings become the foundations for brass pourings and guide workers in reconfiguring their machines.

As you enter the rough mill, the scent of lumber and sound of ripsaws prevail. Bundles of 8- to 16-foot-long rough-cut boards crowd the aisle. Workers plane the rough-cut lumber, revealing the grain and color. Different saws cut the boards to the proper dimensions. Despite a dust collection system, a faint film of sawdust clings to everything in the plant, an unavoidable mark of the woodworker's craft.

The wide sections of wood are matched by grain and color; edges are aligned (or recut) and glued. Notice the radio-frequency gluer: it sends energy through the wood, activating a catalyst in the glue that cures it. The wide belt sander's five sanding heads, with progressively finer grades of sandpaper, then smooth the surfaces.

Amid conventional routers, bandsaws, drill presses, and shapers are two computerized routers. A vacuum sucks air through holes in the tabletop, holding the board in place. The router's patterns are programmed by a designer in the main office, and it runs automatically, without a worker's intervention. The table moves forward and back as the six router heads spin. Before seeing the showroom, watch the cabinetmakers in the sample shop create prototypes, following the designers' sketches and building reproductions from scratch.

Cost: Free
Freebies: No
Video Shown: No
Reservations Needed: Yes, since tours not often given.
Days and Hours: Mon–Thur 9:00 AM–4:00 PM. Closed holidays, Christmas week, and certain floating holidays.
Plan to Stay: 20 minutes for tour, plus additional time in showroom.
Minimum Age: 12
Disabled Access: Limited aisle space and sawdust on floors makes it unsuitable for wheelchairs and walkers.
Group Requirements: Groups should call 1 week in advance. No more than 6 people can be accommodated at a time.
Special Information: Wear sneakers and clothing that will not be harmed by sawdust. Parts of plant can be noisy.
Showroom: Most reproductions are on display. Kits can be purchased or ordered. Open Mon–Fri 9:00 AM–5:00 PM, Sat 10:00 AM–3:00 PM. Catalog available from above number.
Directions: From Annapolis, MD, and points west, cross the Bay Bridge and take Rt. 50 South to Easton. Turn left on Rt. 404 East. In Denton, turn left into the Denton Indutrial Park. The Bartley Collection is the second factory on the left. From Norfolk, VA, take Rt. 13 North toward Salisbury. Continue on Rt. 13 to Bridgeville, DE. In Bridgeville, take Rt. 404 West toward Denton. Turn right into industrial park.
Nearby Attractions: St. Michaels and Oxford, old ship-building towns with antique shops, restored buildings, and boat-builders; Black Water Wildlife Refuge, Wild Goose Brewery tour (call 410-221-1121), and Brooks Barrel Company tour (410-228-0790) in Cambridge, 20 minutes away; Atlantic Ocean beaches 1 hour away.

Moore's Candies ~ *chocolates*

3004 Pinewood Avenue
Baltimore, MD 21214
(410) 426-2705

How often have you been on a tour where the company owner accompanies you, introduces you to the employees (many of whom are immediate family members), and lets you make your own candy? Here's the place! Don't look for a factory or industrial park—this plant is in the 1,500-square-foot basement of the family residence. The company has produced treats from this same space since 1929. In fact, one employee has been dipping Moore's chocolates since the 1920s.

Owner Jim Heyl grew up in the house's upper level. When young Jim needed to raise money for his Cub Scout pack, his parents worked for and eventually bought Moore's Candies, known for helping groups with fund-raising. These fund-raising sales are still important to Moore's Candies' business. Recently Jim's son, Dana, came into the business to take it into the third generation.

The tour is an informal look at this small, hands-on candy-making operation. Tour guide Jim enthusiastically describes the chocolate "waterfall," the home nut-roaster, and the fillings prepared by all of the candymakers. Rich aromas draw you from one table to the next, where caramel or vanilla butter cream fillings are prepared for their chocolate bath, or special-order chocolate swans are filled with home-dry-roasted cashews.

Watch one worker hand-dip chocolates while another uses a wooden paddle to stir bubbling caramel in a copper cauldron. Cherries roll around in rotating kettles, getting a sugar coating before their journey through the enrober, which workers call the "I Love Lucy" machine, for a chocolate cover. This chocolate coating seals in the cherries, whose natural citrus acid reacts with the coating to form the liquid inside a chocolate-coated cherry. Before you leave, be sure to run your own pretzel through the enrobing machine and eat the rewards of your efforts.

Cost: Adults $2; Children $1.

Freebies: Sample chocolate right off the packing line; Official Candymaker Certificate.

Video Shown: No

Reservations Needed: Suggested for individuals. Required for groups over 10 people. Call ahead to see if in production.

Days and Hours: Tue and Thur 10:00 AM and 1:00 PM. Closed holidays, 1 week in July, and between Christmas and New Year's. No tours 4 weeks before major candy holidays.

Plan to Stay: 20 minutes, plus time in gift area.

Minimum Age: 10

Disabled Access: Yes

Group Requirements: Minimum group size is 10; maximum is 40; 3–5 days' notice required. Special tours may be arranged. For groups larger than 15, with 5 days' advance request, 10-minute slide presentation covers origins of the cocoa bean, harvesting, roasting, and how chocolate is made.

Special Information: Most production in fall through early spring. No photography.

Gift Area: Assorted candies include Maryland chocolate and confection specialties (Crabs by the Bushel, Crab Pop, Chesapeake Chocolates, and Maryland honey caramel). Open Mon–Fri 9:00 AM–4:00 PM and Sat 10:00 AM–3:00 PM. Closed holidays and Saturdays in August. Mail-order price list available.

Directions: From Baltimore Beltway (Rt. 695), take Exit 31A. Take Rt. 147 South for 2 miles. Turn left onto Pinewood Ave. Factory is the first building on the left, a brick house that looks like a residence. Park in rear and use building's rear entrance.

Nearby Attractions: Pompeian Olive Oil tour (see page 127); Seagram's tour (call 410-247-6019); GM Minivan tour (call 410-631-2111); White Marsh Shopping Mall; Fire Museum; Baltimore's attractions include Museum of Industry (call 410-727-4808, museum also organizes tour of area companies), Fort McHenry, Inner Harbor Area, Lexington Market, and National Aquarium.

Pompeian Olive Oil
4201 Pulaski Highway
Baltimore, MD 21224
(410) 276-6900 / (800) 638-1224

olive oil and
red wine vinegar

Did you know that it takes 2,000 olives to make 1 quart of olive oil? Or that olive oil was one of the earliest products traded internationally? Do you know the differences between types of olive oil, the recommended way to toss a salad, or the uses of olive oil (even in desserts)? Discover these and other interesting historical, gastronomical, and international business facts on a tour of Pompeian, headquartered in East Baltimore since 1906. The company is America's oldest and largest importer, bottler, and distributor of olive oil and red wine vinegar.

Pompeian prides itself on tailoring its educational tour to each group's specific interests. Though there is no "typical tour," the basic tour includes the historic mill, tank storage system, quality control, and bottling process. The 200-year-old, 22-ton granite mill in front of the plant was found in pieces in Spain, restored, and shipped to Baltimore for permanent display at Pompeian. Although earlier mills were human-powered, this mill was originally steam-operated to produce olive oil, a natural fruit juice. Notice the four cone-shaped grinding stones on a 15-foot-wide base. This mill is the only one of its kind in America.

The tour highlight is going underground to see the extensive storage tank system, which covers the length of a football field. The 18 tanks hold 1.5 million gallons of extra-virgin olive oil. The underground temperature naturally maintains itself around 64°. In Spain, the oil is pressed from olive fruit within 72 hours after picking; it's then shipped to Baltimore for storage in these tanks. In the quality control area, learn about the different types of tests performed, the chemical composition of olive oil, and the fundamentals of general nutrition. In the bottling areas, you may see oil pouring into 4-ounce bottles or gallon jugs. From another bottling line, smell the pungent aroma of red wine vinegar aged in casks in Spain for 15 years. The tour ends with a culinary treat, ranging from light snacks to an olive-oil tasting.

Cost: Free

Freebies: Nutrition literature and recipes, light snacks.

Video Shown: 17-minute video, "Olive Oil: From Tree To Table," sent out to groups in advance. Provides overview of olive oil production in Spain and at Baltimore plant.

Reservations Needed: Yes. Provides group tours only (individuals and families join scheduled group tours).

Days and Hours: Mon, Wed, Thur 10:00 AM and 1:00 PM. Closed holidays. No tours in December.

Plan To Stay: 1½ hours for tour and snacks.

Minimum Age: 8. Because of the high level of tour's educational content, company's recommended minimum age is 12.

Disabled Access: Yes

Group Requirements: Minimum group is 10 people; maximum is 30. Groups should call 2 weeks in advance for reservations.

Special Information: Vinegar aroma can be strong. For a tour of an olive processing company, see the feature on Graber Olive House, Ontario, CA (page 21).

Gift Shop: No, but can purchase cases of 16-ounce bottles at a discount.

Directions: From I-695 (Beltway), take Rt. 40 toward Baltimore (Rt. 40 is Pulaski Hwy.). Pompeian is on the left at their billboard.

Nearby Attractions: Moore's Candies tour (see page 126); GM Minivan tour (call 410-631-2111); Seagram's tour (call 410-247-6019); Fells Point; Inner Harbor Area; Baltimore Museum of Industry (call 410-727-4808, museum also organizes tours of nearby companies); Fort McHenry; National Aquarium; Camden Yards.

Salisbury Pewter

2611 North Salisbury Boulevard
Salisbury, MD 21804
(410) 546-1188 / (800) 824-4708

pewter tableware,
ornaments, and gifts

Although Salisbury Pewter was founded in 1979, its craftspeople follow the same production process used 200 years ago. Pewter-spinning is one of the oldest crafts in American history. During your guided tour of Salisbury Pewter, you'll learn the components of their lead-free, nontarnishing pewter and the history of pewter (did you know that during the Civil War, pewter tableware was melted down for bullets?), and observe pewter-smithing from behind Plexiglas walls.

In the spinning department, watch an apprentice or master spinner, trained for up to ten years, clamp a flat disk (or "blank") onto a lathe. As the disk spins on the lathe, the craftsman sways back and forth. Using a steel rod—which each spinner designs personally—the spinner gently urges the pewter into shape around the brass mold (or "chuck") to form a bowl, coffeepot, or serving tray. During detailing (or "kurling"), a worker uses a tool resembling an architect's compass to add lips and curved bases. The pewter shavings flying into the air are later remelted to avoid waste.

As you walk down the hall, notice raw materials, tools, and pewter cups in various stages of production. In the back, craftspeople wearing white gloves sit in front of rapidly spinning polishing wheels. To polish a large serving tray, a worker must always keep it moving against the cotton-compound spinning wheel. With the tray on their knees, they rock their bodies from side to side and swings their arms back and forth—it's quite a rigorous workout. During the three-step polishing process, different grades of compound polish the pewter to high-bright or satin finishes. A worker proudly stamps the trademark on the bottom of the finished piece.

Cost: Free
Freebies: No
Video Shown: 8-minute optional video covers the history of pewter and Salisbury Pewter's production process.

Reservations Needed: No, except for groups over 45 people.
Days and Hours: Mon–Fri 9:00 AM–4:00 PM. No production week between Christmas and New Year's, and July 4th week, but can watch video and view equipment and display cases. Closed holidays.
Plan to Stay: 15 minutes for tour, plus time for the video and outlet.
Minimum Age: None
Disabled Access: Yes
Group Requirements: Groups over 45 people should call 1 day in advance.
Special Information: This new Salisbury location was built with tours in mind. Other outlet store in Easton has limited tour opportunities (call 410-820-5202).
Showroom: This 3,000-square-foot store sells Salisbury Pewter's 300 items, including jewelry and jewelry boxes, wedding and decorative gifts, picture frames, and such Maryland souvenirs as thimbles with Maryland flags, crab figurines, and Bay Cups. First-quality items sold at outlet prices (20 percent off) and factory seconds discounted up to 75 percent. Open Mon–Fri 9:00 AM–5:30 PM and Sat 10:00 AM–5:00 PM. Between Thanksgiving and Christmas, also open Sun 12:00 PM–5:00 PM. Closed holidays. Catalog available from above number.
Directions: From Ocean City, take Rt. 50 West. Take Rt. 13 North. Salisbury Pewter will be on your right in approximately ½ mile. You'll be greeted by the "Watch Our Craftsmen Work" sign. From Washington/Baltimore area, take Rt. 50 East. Take Rt. 13 North. Follow directions above. (Alternatively, from Rt. 50 East, turn left onto Naylor Mill Rd. Turn left onto Rt. 13 North. Salisbury Pewter will be immediately on your right).
Nearby Attractions: Bartley Furniture Collection tour (see page 125); Maryland Crab Meat Co. in Crisfield (call 410-968-2481/0532); Salisbury Zoo; Ward Museum of Wildfowl Art; Ocean City beaches 30 miles away; Chincoteague and Assateague Islands, VA, are 1 hour away.

Boston Beer ~ *Samuel Adams beer*

30 Germania Street
Boston, MA 02130
(617) 368-5080

In 1984 founder Jim Koch revived his great-great-grandfather's beer recipe and launched the Boston Beer Company. Almost immediately, the company's full-bodied Samuel Adams beers started winning awards. To ensure freshness, Samuel Adams brews most of its beer at other breweries that are located nearer to retailers nationwide. It develops its new beers in a part of this urban development park that once housed the Haffenreffer Brewery. Lining the walls of the beer museum are lithographs tracing the history of this urban brewery site, plaques describing the history of beer, and other beer memorabilia.

The tour guide, often a brewer, begins by handing out tastes of barley malt and hops. As you chew on barley malt, which tastes like Grape Nuts cereal, your guide explains that the use of only these ingredients (plus yeast and water) makes Samuel Adams one of the few beers to pass Germany's purity laws; thus, it can be sold and brewed in Germany.

All the shiny tubs, vats, and kettles of the brewhouse are viewed in one small area, providing a good introduction to the steps involved in brewing beer. Each vessel is labeled so you can identify the mash tub, copper brew kettle, or glass-lined stainless-steel aging tank. The custom-made "Jules Verne Tank" resembles a submarine standing on end, complete with portholes and interior lights. If fermentation is beginning, you can see the sudsy froth from the top porthole. Although Samuel Adams makes only a small percentage of its output at this Boston site, you'll leave with the full story of the company and its beer.

Cost: $1, which is donated to the Boys and Girls Club of Greater Boston.

Freebies: 7-oz. logoed tasting glass. Free postage for Samuel Adams postcard to friends or family. In the tap room, glasses of beer and perhaps a taste of seasonal ale brewed only at this location.

Video Shown: In the tasting room, a short video tells why Jim Koch, a sixth-generation brewer, started the company and how it operates.

Reservations Needed: No, except for groups larger than 25 people.

Days and Hours: Thur–Sat 2:00 PM; Sat also 12:00 PM and 1:00 PM. Call above number for schedule changes. No beer production during Saturday tours. Closed holidays.

Plan to Stay: 1 hour for tour and tasting, plus time for gift shop and beer museum.

Minimum Age: None. Children are welcome. Root beer is available for minors.

Disabled Access: Yes

Group Requirements: Groups larger than 25 people should call 2 weeks in advance for reservations (call 617-497-3209).

Special Information: For safety reasons, you will not see bottling line in operation.

Gift Shop: Sells logoed half-yard and yard glasses, hats, T-shirts, and baseball jackets. Open during tour time periods.

Directions: Take I-93 just south of downtown Boston to Exit 18 (Massachusetts Ave.). Bear left off the ramp onto Melnea Cass Blvd. Continue straight on Melnea Cass Blvd. to the eighth traffic light. Then take a left onto Tremont St. (note: Tremont St. eventually becomes Columbus Ave.). Continue straight on Tremont to the 11th traffic light, then turn right onto Washington St. Take your 4th right onto Boylston St. Continue straight on Boylston St. for 2 blocks, then turn left onto Bismark St. Watch for the "Samuel Adams" signs.

Nearby Attractions: National Braille Press and Wm. S. Haynes flutes tours (see pages 135 and 137); Mass Bay Brewing Co. tour (call 617-574-9551); Doyle's restaurant, a nearby pub full of Irish family history, has all Samuel Adams beers fresh on tap; *Boston Globe* newspaper tour (call 617-929-2653); Phillips Candy House tour (call 617-282-2090); Franklin Park Zoo; Arnold Arboretum.

Cape Cod Potato Chips ⌒ *potato chips*

100 Breeds Hill Road
Hyannis, MA 02601
(508) 775-3206 / (508) 775-7253 (recording)

Cape Cod Potato Chips still follows the company's original intent—"to make the best potato chip possible." Just as when Steve Bernard founded it in 1980, the company still kettle-cooks its potato chips one batch at a time. Cape Cod's production, which started in 1980 at 200 bags per day, is now 150,000 to 200,000 bags a day, using 28 million pounds of potatoes each year.

From the plaques in the entranceway, you'll learn that 4 pounds of potatoes yield 1 pound of potato chips and that, depending on the month, the potatoes come from different eastern seaboard states. Each truckload of 45,000 to 50,000 pounds of potatoes is unloaded into its own silo, since the potatoes must be inspected for solid mass (or "gravity"), external defects, size, and color before farmers receive payment. Different rollers and brushes, depending on the skins' thickness, wash and peel the inspected spuds, which then tumble down to the trim table for further inspection and halving of large potatoes.

Through glass windows you watch sliced potatoes feed into one of the three production lines, each with six gas-fired cooking kettles. Raw potatoes sizzle in hot oil, creating clouds of steam. In the midst of this steam, workers rake the potatoes back and forth in the 8-by-3-foot vats with stainless-steel rakes. The steam subsides as the cooking cycle ends. A worker tilts a scoop into the kettle for the cooked batch of potato chips. Oil drips back into the kettle through the scoop's screen bottom. The worker tilts the scoop back to its original position, allowing the potato chips to slide into a white basket with holes. This centrifuge spins for four minutes, allowing excess oil to drain through the holes. Other workers pour the drained chips onto a long cooling conveyor belt.

As you walk along the production line, read the plaques that describe potato-chip making. Along the opposite wall of the corridor, a schematic diagram explains how popcorn is produced. Further down the corridor, workers inspect the cooled chips along a vibrating table that moves them forward without breaking them. The chips pass under the salter box and are transported by "bucket elevator" to the next room for packaging. On each packaging line a carousel of 14 hoppers weighs and releases the correct amount of chips into the bagging machine. Workers hand-pack bags into cardboard boxes, which are shrink-wrapped for shipment or storage in the warehouse.

Cost: Free
Freebies: Sample bag of potato chips.
Video Shown: No.
Reservations Needed: No, except for groups over 25 people.
Days and Hours: Mon–Fri 9:00 AM–5:00 PM. July and August also Sat 10:00 AM–4:00 PM. Closed holidays.
Plan to Stay: 15 minutes for self-guided tour, plus time in gift shop.
Minimum Age: None, except difficult for small children to see activity beyond cooling chip conveyor.
Disabled Access: Yes
Group Requirements: Groups over 25 people should call 2 weeks in advance.
Special Information: No photography. On rainy summer days, allow for waiting time to enter the tour.
Gift Shop: Sells all Cape Cod potato chips, popcorn, logoed caps, golf balls, handmade chip and dip bowls, and T-shirts. Open same hours as tours. Closed holidays.
Directions: From Rt. 6, take Exit 6 for Rt. 132 South. At fourth traffic light, turn left into Independence Park. Factory is on the right after the airport.
Nearby Attractions: Pairpoint Crystal tour (see page 136); Cape Cod Mall; JFK Museum; Hyannis waterfront and beaches; Thornton Burgess Museum.

Cranberry World

Ocean Spray Cranberries, Inc.
225 Water Street
Plymouth, MA 02360
(508) 747-2350

cranberry juice and related products

Cranberries were named because the plant's blossom resembles a crane's head—a "craneberry," which eventually became "cranberry." This native North American fruit is grown primarily in Massachusetts, Wisconsin, New Jersey, Oregon, Washington, and parts of Canada. Cranberry World offers these and other "berry" unusual facts, along with exhibits and interactive audio-visual displays tracing cranberry cultivation from pre-Pilgrim times to the present. You'll also sample Ocean Spray juice drinks and taste cranberry treats fresh from the demonstration kitchen.

Along the short boardwalk to the entrance, notice the two small cranberry bogs and the flags of the states in the cranberry and citrus farmers' cooperative known as Ocean Spray Cranberries, Inc. Once inside, look for the "rocker" scoop, a wooden cranberry-harvesting implement used from the late 1800s to 1950s. On hands and knees, a grower-harvester put the scoop into the cranberry vines. The scoop's long wooden teeth gently tugged the berries off the vine, then the farmer rocked the scoop and the berries rolled back. At best, the scoop method yielded an average of 400 pounds per day; today's mechanical picking machines average 5,800 pounds daily.

Other highlights include the wooden one-third-scale model of the "bounce machine," a quality control device that tests "bounceability." Ask a guide to put wooden beads into this machine to simulate cranberries. Good berries bounce and are sold as fresh fruit; bad berries are discarded.

Downstairs, a display shows Ocean Spray packaging designs for various products from 1912 to the present. Push buttons activate brief videos on cranberry sauce and cranberry juice production, and television commercials dating back to 1955. Learn tricks of the trade (like freezing cranberries makes them easier to slice) and watch a cook whip up a cranberry delicacy in the demonstration kitchen.

Cost: Free

Freebies: Tastes of Ocean Spray juice drinks, treats prepared in kitchen; recipe leaflet.

Videos Shown: Brief videos throughout the museum: history of immigrants' role in cranberry industry; old commercials; videos on harvesting and on sauce and juice production.

Reservations Needed: Only for guided tours for groups of 10 or more people.

Days and Hours: Open May 1—November 30 only. Mon–Sun 9:30 AM–5:00 PM. Demonstration kitchen open 9:30 AM–4:30 PM.

Plan to Stay: 45 minutes–1 hour for museum, videos, and kitchen, plus time for the gift counter.

Minimum Age: None

Disabled Access: Yes

Group Requirements: Groups of 10 or more must call in advance to arrange guided tour.

Special Information: View juice-making process through glass windows at Cranberry World West, their Henderson, NV, plant and visitors center (see page 202).

Gift Counter: Sells cranberry-related items (such as cranberry honey, cranberry wine vinegar, and cranberry-colored glass); also, Ocean Spray products. Open same hours as visitors center.

Directions: From Boston, take I-93 South to Rt. 3 South to Rt. 44 East. Continue to waterfront. Turn left around rotary onto Water St. Cranberry World is on the right. From Cape Cod, take Rt. 6. Cross Sagamore Bridge. Take Rt. 3 North to Rt. 44 East. Follow the above directions.

Nearby Attractions: The Massachusetts Cranberry Harvest Festival held Columbus Day Weekend features operation of harvesting equipment, historical displays, and cranberry-related cooking and crafts demonstrations; Plymouth Rock; *Mayflower II*; Whale-Watch Cruises; Plymouth National Wax Museum; Plymouth Plantation; beaches.

See color photos, page 168

Crane ~~~ *paper*

Crane Museum
Routes 8 and 9
Dalton, MA 01226
(413) 684-2600

Crane's fine papers are used by the White House for stationery and by the Bureau of Engraving and Printing for currency (see page 46). Since 1801 Crane has produced 100 percent cotton paper that offers strength, durability, and surface texture unsurpassed by paper made from wood. The company has even started using denim scraps from Levi Strauss jeans and worn dollar bills to make recycled paper. This family-owned company's mills are in Dalton, in western Massachusetts. The Crane Museum, housed in the company's Old Stone Mill (built in 1844), has welcomed visitors since 1930.

The museum sits on the banks of the Housatonic River, which supplied water to wash the rags and drive the machines of the early Crane paper mills. This ivy-covered stone building has a completely different feel from the modern, multimedia-filled company museums built recently. The museum's interior resembles the Old Ship Church in Hingham, Massachusetts with rough-hewn oak beams, colonial chandeliers, many-paned windows, and wide oak floorboards. The ceiling looks like an upside-down ship's hull, possibly because the structure was built by shipbuilders instead of carpenters.

After you watch the video on Crane's modern paper-production techniques, walk through exhibits on the history of the company and of papermaking since the Revolutionary War. A scale model of the vat house in the original Crane mill shows the laborious process of hand-making paper one sheet at a time. This process, used by company founder Zenas Crane, contrasts with the modern method of making long continuous rolls of paper.

Among the many different kinds of paper displayed in glass cases are those used for currency, American Express checks, stock certificates, and the stationery of presidents and movie stars. One exhibit of corporate innovation features Crane's paper collars, which the company made after the Civil War. Although they are rarely seen today, at the time these disposable collars were fashionable and very profitable.

Cost: Free

Freebies: Package of Crane stationery papers.

Video Shown: 20-minute video on company's history and papermaking methods.

Reservations Needed: No, except for groups larger than 10 people.

Days and Hours: Open June through mid-October only. Mon–Fri 2:00 PM–5:00 PM. Closed major holidays.

Plan to Stay: 30 minutes for exhibits, plus time for video.

Minimum Age: None

Disabled Access: Museum is all on one ground-level floor. However, there are a couple of steps to reach it.

Group Requirements: With 1 week's notice, Crane can handle groups up to 50 people.

Special Information: Can visit museum before 2:00 PM if call a few days ahead. Company retirees run museum; they answer questions and offer interesting anecdotes.

Gift Shop: No

Directions: From I-90 (Mass Pike), take the Lee Exit. Follow Rts. 7 and 20 North through Pittsfield. Take Rts. 8 and 9 East about 5 miles. Turn right onto Housatonic St. At bottom is Pioneer Mill. Museum is on the right at the end of Mill.

Nearby Attractions: Berkshire attractions include Clark Art Museum, Mt. Greylock, Berkshire Museum, and Tanglewood.

Harbor Sweets   ⁓   *chocolates*

Palmer Cove
85 Leavitt Street
Salem, MA 01970
(978) 745-7648 / (800) 234-4860

While Salem is known for its witches' potions, Harbor Sweets brews only the sweet variety. The company's key players are its 150 part-time/flex-time employees (many disabled, elderly, or foreign-born) and its innovative founder, Ben Strohecker, the former Schrafft's Candy marketing director, who launched Harbor Sweets in 1975.

While the company has expanded into three connected brick buildings, visitors see only the first room. From the slightly raised gift-shop platform, you can observe the labor-intensive production of Sweet Sloops, one of their most popular nautical New England theme candies; you can also see molded candies at the far end. Even though you don't enter the production areas, workers will gladly answer your questions. The air smells of caramel, toffee, and chocolate.

Notice the home-style, four-burner gas stove in the back. Leaning over copper cauldrons, workers stir batches of almond butter crunch and caramel with wooden paddles. The butter crunch is poured onto a cooling table and then smoothed. With a bladed metal rolling pin, a worker scores the crunch into squares and then triangles. A helper breaks the triangles apart. The triangles proceed through the enrober for a coating of white chocolate. With a long metal ice-cream spoon, a worker draws lines representing the mast and jib. After the cooling tunnel, workers hand-dip the Sweet Sloops into melted chocolate and chopped pecans, often a tough job—they must eat their mistakes.

All other candies are molded. Depending on the candies being made, melters contain milk or dark chocolate, some with crushed orange or peppermint crunch. A worker holds a 16-cavity plastic mold, while the "depositor" drops a specially timed amount of chocolate into each cavity. Another worker inserts dollops of raspberry/cranberry ganache and white chocolate from a hand-held funnel. After they have been chilled, the candies are individually foil-wrapped before being beautifully gift-boxed.

Cost: Free

Freebies: Chocolate sample from a silver serving platter.

Video Shown: No

Reservations Needed: No, except for groups over 6 people.

Days and Hours: Mon–Fri 8:30 AM–4:30 PM. Call about Saturday hours preceding candy-giving holidays. Closed holidays and 2 weeks in July. Limited production May through August.

Plan to Stay: 10–15 minutes for self-guided viewing, plus time in gift shop.

Minimum Age: None

Disabled Access: Yes

Group Requirements: Groups larger than 6 people should call 1 week in advance to arrange a tour guide. Groups over 12 will be split into smaller groups. No maximum group size.

Special Information: Best time to see production is September 1 to Easter.

Gift Shop: Sells Harbor Sweets' 6 varieties of nautical New England–theme candies in a variety of gift box–sizes. Open Mon–Fri 8:30 AM–4:30 PM, Sat 9:00 AM–3:00 PM, with extended hours before holidays and shorter hours in summer. Catalog available from (800) 243-2115.

Directions: From Rt. 128, take Rt. 114 East to Salem. Turn left onto Leavitt St. Harbor Sweets is the last building on the left. From 1A North (follow Rt. 1A as it meanders to Salem), turn right onto Leavitt St.

Nearby Attractions: Saugus Iron Works, first integrated ironworks in North America, with reconstructed blast furnace, 17th century iron mill, and working waterwheel (call 781-233-0050); Salem's attractions include Pickering Wharf, Salem Witch Museum, House of Seven Gables, and Peabody/Essex Maritime Museum.

Other Eastern Massachusetts Candy Tours: Stowaway Sweets candy tour in Marblehead (call 800-432-0304); Phillips Candy House tour (call 617-929-2653).

Interstate Brands   *Wonder Bread and Hostess Cakes*

330 Speen Street
Natick, MA 01760
(508) 655-2150

Did you ever wonder how the sweet cream gets into the Hostess Twinkies (invented in 1930) or the seven-loop cupcakes (invented in 1919)? You can witness the sweet cream in action, as Interstate Brands fills thousands per minute! Over 1 million giant Wonder Bread loaves (sliced bread was invented in 1924) per week flow out of its ovens and into the colorful balloon-pictured plastic bags.

As you stroll through this 6-acre bakery, leaving footprints on the lightly floured floor, you follow the making of bread and cakes. They start as ingredients in 50- to 100-pound bags and end as finished goods in a maze of hundreds of 7-foot, 14-shelf-high shipping racks. Surprisingly, the aroma isn't much more intense than at your local bakery, except that the whiff hits you a half-mile down the road and lingers in your nostrils for a few hours after the tour.

Wherever you look, future baked goods in some stage of production roll by on conveyors. Dough sits in big troughs waiting to be dropped into bread pans. Giant ovens swallow 2,700 loaves in five-pan rows for their 22-minute transformation from dough to bread. Suction cups gently pull the hot baked loaves from their pans for an overhead cooling-off journey above and across the factory floor four times, until ready for slicing at 110°. Quality control workers grab rejects from the line and toss them into bins headed for the pig farm. At mind-boggling speed, loaves are sliced and packaged into plastic bags. On the cake side of the factory, injection machines shoot sweet cream into the behinds of newborn Twinkies and cupcakes.

Cost: Free
Freebies: Samples of the freshest Wonder Bread and Hostess Cakes you've ever eaten.
Video Shown: No
Reservations Needed: Yes. Since production schedules change, call at beginning of month to schedule tours for that month. Individuals and families need to join a scheduled group tour.

Days and Hours: Mon, Wed, Fri 9:00 AM–4:00 PM. Because of the heat from the ovens, no tours from May through the beginning of September. Closed holidays. *Tours have been temporarily suspended because of increased demand and scheduling difficulties.*
Plan to Stay: Approximately 1 hour, depending on what is in production.
Minimum Age: 5, with 1 adult required for every 4 children.
Disabled Access: Yes. Advance notice required for people with wheelchairs.
Group Requirements: Groups must call at beginning of month to schedule tours for that month. No maximum group size.
Special Information: Wear sneakers or rubber-soled shoes, as floor can be slippery. For sanitation and noise reasons, the bakery provides hair nets and earplugs that must be used.
Thrift Store: Sells Hostess cupcakes, Twinkies, and Wonder Bread at discounted prices. Open Mon–Fri 9:00 AM–8:00 PM, Sat 9:00 AM–7:00 PM, and Sun 10:00 AM–5:00 PM.
Directions: From I-90 (Mass Pike), take Exit 13. Take Rt. 30 East. Turn right on Speen St. Follow your nose and park in the Wonder Bread Thrift Store parking lot.
Nearby Attractions: Garden in the Woods; Lake Cochituate; Shoppers World; Natick Mall. Boston's attractions, including Boston Beer Co. (Samuel Adams beer) and Wm. S. Haynes (flutes) tours (see pages 129 and 137), Back Bay, and Fanueil Hall, are about 15 miles away.

National Braille Press ~ *Braille publications*

88 Saint Stephen Street
Boston, MA 02115
(617) 266-6160

National Braille Press

National Braille Press, founded in 1927, is one of only five companies in the U.S. that mass-produce Braille materials, and the only one that publishes original self-help books for the blind. The company prides itself on its leading-edge position in computer-assisted production of Braille publications and on hiring people with disabilities (almost half of its 35-person in-house staff).

The company produces approximately 23 million Braille pages per year from this four-story converted piano factory on a tree-lined street in the Northeastern University area. Specialized translation software helps workers transcribe the written word into Braille pages. To find any errors in the transcription, blind proofreaders listen to an audio-tape of what should be written while following the Braille version with their hands. The proofreading room chatters with the sound of the Braille typewriters that proofreaders use to note mistakes.

Once the pages are corrected, a software version of the publication to be printed directs the computerized plate-embossing machines, which punch the raised dots of the Braille alphabet onto zinc printing plates. For any new errors, a small hammer knocks dots out or in on the zinc plates. In the cluttered printing area, you'll watch and hear reconditioned Heidelberg cylinder presses spin out up to 8,000 Braille pages per hour. Workers then hand-collate Braille versions of well-known magazines such as *Parenting* or *Book World*, computer manuals for Microsoft, or popular children's books, before stitch-binding completes the production process.

Cost: Free, but donation requested.
Freebies: Samples of Braille materials
Video Shown: No
Reservations Needed: Yes
Days and Hours: Mon–Fri 10:30 AM. Closed holidays.
Plan to Stay: 1 hour

Minimum Age: While there is no official minimum age, children should be at least 6 years old to appreciate the tour. The company tries to make the tour more interactive for children. Watching blind people and those with disabilities working at productive jobs provides kids with a lasting impression.
Disabled Access: Yes; enter from bottom floor.
Group Requirements: Can handle groups up to 12 people with 5 days' advance notice.
Special Information: Carefully supervise children around the printing presses. Tours also available at the American Printing House for the Blind in Louisville, KY, the largest and oldest (1859) publishing house for the blind (see page 96).
Gift Shop: No
Directions: By subway, take the "E" train on the Green Line to the Northeastern University stop on Huntington Ave. Cross Huntington onto Opera Pl. and turn right onto St. Stephen St. The building is 1 block ahead on your right. By car, take the Massachusetts Ave. exit on I-93 (Southeast Expwy.). Turn right on Massachusetts Ave. and go straight until you cross Huntington Ave. At Symphony Hall (on your left), turn left on St. Stephen St. National Braille Press is ahead on your left.
Nearby Attractions: Wm. S. Haynes flute tour (see page 137); Boston Beer (Samuel Adams) tour (see page 129); *Boston Globe* newspaper tour (call 617-929-2653); Phillips Candy House tour (call 617-282-2090); Symphony Hall; Christian Science Center; Northeastern University; Boston's museums and attraction, include the Museum of Science and the Back Bay.

Pairpoint Crystal ⟨⟨⟨ *glass*

851 Sandwich Road
Sagamore, MA 02561
(508) 888-2344 / (800) 899-0953

Since Pairpoint's philosophy is "made in America the old-fashioned way," it utilizes the same hand tools and processes as when Deming Jarves founded the company in 1837. Pairpoint makes cup plates (many are collectors' items), limited editions, and other fine pieces for such museums as New York City's Metropolitan Museum of Art and Boston's Museum of Fine Arts.

Though the observation window shields you from the furnaces' 2,500° heat, you know the factory below is hot—the artisans wear shorts year-round. Watch a "gaffer," the most experienced glassblower on the five-person team, fill his cheeks with air and blow into the blowpipe. Once the glass at the other end of the pipe reaches the desired size, he twirls the rod like a baton to elongate the glass.

Using another rod, a team member gathers glass from the furnaces and brings it to the gaffer, who attaches it to the original piece, snips it with shears, then shapes the piece with wooden and metal hand tools. Eventually the piece is transferred to the "pontil" rod and cracked off from its original blowpipe. The gaffer inserts the work, perhaps a vase or a flask, into a reheating furnace called a "glory hole" and then shapes its opening.

Cup plates, widely used in the mid-1800s as plates for handle-less cups of hot tea, have increased in popularity since Pairpoint started pressing them in the early 1970s. A "gob" of 34-percent lead crystal glass is placed in a mold, and an artisan pulls on a lever to exert just the right amount of pressure. While the standard patterns on these 2-inch-diameter cup plates include endangered species, birds, and geometric shapes, you will also want to see the gift-shop display of collector's cup plates commissioned by companies, clubs, and towns.

Cost: Free

Freebies: Product brochures

Video Shown: 20-minute continuously running video covers company history and the glassmaking process. Shown in gift shop.

Reservations Needed: No, unless guided factory-floor tour desired.

Days and Hours: May through December: Mon–Fri 9:00 AM–12:00 PM and 1:00 PM–4:30 PM. February through April: Mon-Fri 10:00 AM–5:00 PM with limited production. Closed January and holidays.

Plan to Stay: 20 minutes for self-guided tour, plus time for video and gift shop.

Minimum Age: None, for gallery; 6, for floor tour.

Disabled Access: Yes, for galley; steps down to factory floor.

Group Requirements: Maximum group size for factory-floor tour is 10. Call 1 week in advance for reservations.

Special Information: Call to find out about production January through April. Although factory-floor tours can get quite hot, you are closer to the action and also see inspecting and packing areas.

Retail Store: Sells works by the artists, including museum reproductions, vases, candlesticks, and cup plates. Open May through December, Mon–Sat 9:00 AM–6:00 PM and Sun 10:00 AM–6:00 PM. Open January through April, Mon–Sat 10:00 AM–5:00 PM and Sun 11:00 AM–5:00 PM. Closed holidays. Catalog available from (800) 899-0953.

Directions: From Boston, take I-93 South to Rt. 3 South to Sagamore Bridge. After bridge, take first exit onto Rt. 6A. Pairpoint is on your left. From Hyannis, take Rt. 6 West. Take last exit before bridge. Turn left onto Adams St. and left onto 6A. Pairpoint is on your right.

Nearby Attractions: Sandwich Glass Museum; Thornton Burgess Museum; Sandwich Boardwalk (look for nearby plaque designating site of original Boston and Sandwich Glass Co., also founded by Jarves); Yesteryears Museum; Old Grist Mill.

Wm. S. Haynes   ⟿   *flutes and piccolos*

12 Piedmont Street
Boston, MA 02116
(617) 482-7456

THE HAYNES FLUTE
MFD BY
WM. S. HAYNES CO
BOSTON, MASS

Flutists from all over the world travel to Boston just to visit this famous flute factory. Since 1888, when William S. Haynes opened his flute-making shop in the heart of downtown Boston, legendary artists like Jean-Pierre Rampal have refused to play anything but Haynes flutes.

After viewing the dozens of autographed photos of famous musicians in the front office, you will be guided to the first floor of the factory. Every part of a Haynes flute is made by hand on the premises, except for the hollow silver tube body, purchased prefabricated from a precious-metal supplier. If the diameter of this tube is off by more than $1/1000$th of an inch (less than the thickness of a human hair) it is returned.

The first stages of flute-making begin in this downstairs workshop, where artisans learn the basics of their craft in what looks more like a machine shop than the birthplace of these beautiful instruments. Drill machines line the walls in a corner where your guide explains Haynes' method of "drop forging," which is more precise and laborious than the casting process used by other flute-makers. The craftsmen hunch over their tables, laboring on the precise placement of the "tone holes" on the body.

The upstairs workshop resembles a jewelry shop, where trained artisans work with tiny silver keys. Each craftsman serves a five-year apprenticeship next to a 20-year veteran in order to learn precisely the craft of hand-finishing the keys. Behind a glass window, watch an artisan polish the flutes to their shiny final appearance with the delicacy and accuracy of a surgeon. You understand why artists around the world proudly send the company records and CDs on which they play their beloved Haynes instruments.

Cost: Free

Freebies: Catalog, price list, and literature.

Video Shown: No. However, "The Haynes Story," a brief video on flute-making and Haynes' history, is for sale.

Reservations Needed: No, except for groups of 6 or more people.

Days and Hours: Mon–Fri 9:00 AM–3:00 PM. Closed holidays.

Plan to Stay: 30 minutes. Flutists should allow extra time at the end of the tour to try out the gold flutes.

Minimum Age: No minimum age, but to best appreciate the tour, a child should be of high-school age or play the flute.

Disabled Access: Yes

Group Requirements: Groups of 6 or more should call 1 week in advance.

Special Information: Best time to tour is Tue or Thur 11:00 AM–2:00 PM, when the tester plays the flutes to check their quality. Parts of the tour can be loud.

Gift Area: Videos, posters, and Haynes logo T-shirts available in the front office. Open 8:00 AM–4:00 PM.

Directions: By subway, travel to Arlington Stop on the Green Line. Walk in the direction of traffic down Arlington St. Piedmont St. is the third street on the left. By car from the west, take I-90 (Mass Pike) East to Prudential Center exit. Go towards Copley Square. Follow ramp onto Stuart St. Turn right onto Arlington St. and left onto Piedmont St.

Nearby Attractions: National Braille Press (see page 135); Boston Beer (Samuel Adams) tour (see page 129); *Boston Globe* newspaper tour (call 617-929-2653); Phillips Candy House tour (call 617-282-2090); Downtown Boston's attractions include Boston Symphony Hall, Carl Fisher Music Store, Berklee School of Music, Fanueil Hall, Boston Common, Public Garden, and the Back Bay.

Yankee Candle ⌒ *candles*

Route 5
South Deerfield, MA 01373
(413) 665-8306

Yankee Candle Company

If you've ever made candles by melting wax and crayons, you have something in common with Mike Kittredge, founder of Yankee Candle. While you can no longer tour the factory, you can take a self-guided tour of the 2,500-square-foot company history area (which includes videos of production) and see demonstrations in the candlemaking museum.

Start where it all began, at the antique Queen Atlantic gas stove Mike used to melt wax in his parents' cellar at age 17 in 1969. The walls display a pictorial history of the company's development from his parents' house to a renovated paper mill in 1974 to the current 80,000-square-foot Yankee Candle Complex.

Through a series of videos, you'll see almost all the steps performed at the nearby factory to make taper, jar, pillar, and sampler candles. Yankee Candle's workers describe the factory, which has piped-in music, as a huge craft studio that smells like a spice rack. The automatic taper-candle-dipping machine, resembling a chandelier with wicks instead of light bulbs, dips up to 2 miles of wicks per day. To create the standard 7/8-inch taper candle, the machine dips braided cotton wicks into liquid wax as many as 30 times, alternating with dips into a cooling water bath. Workers then hand-dip the final, harder wax layers to create smooth, dripless candles.

Textured pillar candles start as colorful solid-wax cylinders. Workers place four smooth pillar candles on pedestals to begin their transformation. The candles, pushed up through 300° grooved rings, emerge from the top of the press as ionic (vertically grooved) or twist (spirally grooved) pillars. The making of jar candles will remind you of Jell-O molding: a machine fills eight glass containers at a time with hot, colorful, fragrant wax.

Adjacent to the history area is the Candlemaking Museum, set up as an 1810 chandler's workshop. Workers dressed in period garb give continuous live demonstrations, hand-dipping bayberry, beeswax and tallow candles. After you watch the candlemaking, you'll want to dip your own candles and test-sniff some of the 250 samplers in the Candle Emporium. Fragrances include the traditional (cranberry), the unexpected (Bavarian cake), the delicious (vanilla), and the inspirational (fresh lilac).

Cost: Free
Freebies: No
Video Shown: Continuously running videos provide close-up shots of the production processes.
Reservations Needed: No
Days and Hours: Mon–Sun 9:30 AM–6:00 PM. Extended hours around the holidays. Closed Thanksgiving and Christmas.
Plan to Stay: 30 minutes for self-guided tour, videos, and Candlemaking Museum, plus time for retail stores and any special events on the grounds.
Minimum Age: None
Disabled Access: Yes
Group Requirements: None
Retail Store: Sells Country Kitchen and Housewarmer jar candles, aromatic samplers, and scented and unscented tapers. Upstairs, Seconds Room has overruns and flawed candles at marked-down prices. Open Mon–Sun 9:30 AM–6:00 PM; longer hours during Christmas season. Catalog available from (800) 243-1776. Entire 80,000-square-foot complex includes Post and Beam Candle Shop, Bavarian Christmas Village, Kringle Market, and Candle Emporium.
Directions: Take I-90 (Mass Pike) to I-91 North to Exit 24. Turn right on Rtes. 5 and 10. Yankee Candle is on your left.
Nearby Attractions: Yankee Candle Car Museum; Mt. Sugarloaf State Reservation; Historic Deerfield; Mohawk Trail Autoroad.

Amon Orchards ~ *cherries and cherry products*

8066 U.S. 31
Acme, MI 49610
(800) 937-1644

Northern Michigan is the self-proclaimed cherry capital of the world. The roads in and around Traverse City are lined with bright red cherry trees during the summer. Stands selling the juiciest, freshest cherries you've ever tasted appear along most roads.

David Amon accurately predicted a sharp drop in the price of cherries and added tourism and specialty products to Amon Orchard's agriculture business. The company also branched out to other types of fruit production and now enjoys taking visitors through the fields to see and learn about it all.

Relax as you ride in a shaded, canvas-topped, open-sided trolley that meanders through rows of 8- to 10-foot-tall trees on this 200-acre, family-run orchard. Your driver (perhaps David himself) spouts interesting facts you probably never knew about cherries. You learn that the "fresh" cherries with stems in your supermarket were hand-picked in Oregon or Washington long before they were tree-ripened.

The driver stops the trolley to let you pull a ripe fruit from a tree; perhaps one of the three different apricot or nectarine varieties or seven different types of peaches they grow. From the trolley you can also reach some red tart, light, or dark sweet cherries. The juice from these fresh, ripe fruits will squirt into your mouth, and if you're not careful, onto your shoes!

One of Amon's missions through the tour is to teach people about the changes in agriculture, such as integrated pest management systems that use "good" bugs to eat "bad" bugs, thus requiring less pesticide. Another proudly pushed theme is that cherries aren't just for dessert anymore. Creative uses of cherries include many of the specialty products you'll want to sample in the retail store before or after the tour.

Cost: $1 donation for trolley ride.
Freebies: Ripe fruit from trees, cherry juice, gourmet product samples, recipe brochure.
Video Shown: No

Reservations Needed: No, during National Cherry Festival (first or second week in July). Recommended for individuals and families for other weeks of summer. Advance notice required for motorcoaches.
Days and Hours: Mid-June through October only. Mon–Sat 10:00 AM–4:00 PM. Arrangements can be made for motorcoach groups year-round.
Plan to Stay: 1 hour for trolley tour, petting farm, u-pick (call for the Ripe and Ready Report and map, telling you what months the different fruits are best for picking), and retail store. In October wander around the maze carved through 8-foot-tall cornstalks.
Minimum Age: None
Disabled Access: Yes
Group Requirements: Call at least a few days in advance for motorcoach group tours year-round. Call for group tour rates.
Special Information: Orchard is particularly scenic during spring blossom season, with special tours available. Family Fall Festival on October weekends features u-pick pumpkins.
Retail Store: Grandma Amon's Country Market and gift shop sells fresh-picked fruit from orchard, jams, gourmet cherry products including "Fudgie" sauce, cherry hot-pepper jelly, cherry Mexican salsa, dried cherries, and baked goods. Daily in-store specials. Mid-June through October, Mon–Sun 10:00 AM–6:00 PM. November through December, Tue–Sat 10:00 AM–5:00 PM. Catalog available from above number.
Directions: From Traverse City, take U.S. 31 North. Orchard is about 8 miles ahead on your right. From Mackinaw City, take I-75 South to U.S. 31 South. Orchard is on your left 10 miles south of Elk Rapids.
Nearby Attractions: National Cherry Festival week (first or second week in July) events include cherry pie–eating contests, Cherry Royale Parade, and Taste of Cherries. Kilwin's chocolates tour (see page 148); Good Harbor Vineyards tour (call 616-256-7165); the Music House; Grand Traverse Bay.

See color photos, page 162

Amway ⌇ *household and personal care products*

7575 East Fulton Street East
Ada, MI 49355
(616) 787-6701

Amway believes hard work and diligence give individuals the power to control their own destinies by owning their own businesses. A new Visitor Center completed in fall of 1997 in the headquarters lobby has a 16-foot bronze sculpture, *Building Together The American Way*, showing how the Amway direct-selling system works. Near the sculpture and other displays are statues of Amway's founders, Rich De Vos and Jay Van Andel. The 3.5-million-square-foot manufacturing and distribution center supplies merchandise and support that make individual distributors' dreams of owning their own businesses a reality.

Although you can no longer tour the facility, a video shows you product development, R&D, manufacturing, printing, and distribution. In the Michigan Regional Distribution Center, a conveyor maze carries merchandise from the warehouse shelves to the staging area, where it is packed and shipped to supply much of the state. As you would expect, the whole operation is computerized, and each box is labeled with the recipient's name and address before being loaded into the appropriate semi-trailer.

Still within the confines of the city-like Amway complex (which even has its own fire department) is one of the largest in-house commercial printing operations in the Midwest. With rivers of multicolored paper running up, down, and around at a mind-boggling rate, these gargantuan printing presses produce much of Amway's letterhead, catalogs, and promotional materials. They print some 2,300 different pieces in all and use 500 to 800 rolls of paper per day.

After watching the video, explore the different displays surrounding the theater. See the evolution of a product from concept to delivery to customers. At a CD-ROM terminal, you can pull up information about any international Amway affiliate; international visitors can find data in their native language telling where Amway is based and what products it sells in their country. Sit in a small booth to hear famous speeches given by the company founders. You leave understanding more about the attitude that built Amway into a successful, worldwide, direct-selling business.

Cost: Free

Freebies: Travel-size bottles of body lotion and shampoo.

Videos Shown: 12-minute video introduces the company and details some processes used in manufacturing soap powder and other household products. 3-minute video on cosmetic production available upon request.

Reservations Needed: No, except for groups of 10 or more people.

Days and Hours: Mon–Fri 9:00 AM, 11:00 AM, 1:00 PM, and 3:00 PM. Closed for long holiday weekends and 1 week in June for annual convention.

Plan to Stay: 45 minutes

Minimum Age: None, although children under 16 must be accompanied by an adult.

Disabled Access: Yes

Group Requirements: Maximum group size is 50 people.

Gift Shop: No. Catalog available from distributors by calling (800) 544-7167.

Directions: From Grand Rapids, take I-196 East, which becomes I-96 just east of Grand Rapids, to Exit 39 for M-21. The exit road becomes Fulton Rd. In about 5 miles, turn left into the Amway World Headquarters Building. Look for the row of international flags in front.

Nearby Attractions: Public Museum of Grand Rapids; Grand Rapids Art Museum; Gerald R. Ford Museum; Grand Rapids Symphony Orchestra.

Brooks Beverages

7-Up, Canada Dry, and other sodas

777 Brooks Avenue
Holland, MI 49423
(616) 396-1281

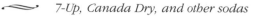

Gleaming stainless-steel tanks holding the essence of some of your favorite refreshments—Canada Dry, Squirt, Hires, 7-Up, Hawaiian Punch, Tahitian Treat—fill the syrup room, an early sight on one of the few soda-bottling plant tours you can take without reservations. Phillips Brooks founded the company in 1934, producing 7-Up in his basement. The company has remained 100-percent family-owned, and is now run by Phil's grandson. A handout explains the processes you'll see through windows on the plant's observation deck since machines and windows are not labeled.

Each unit of the highly concentrated extract in the syrup room produces 400 cases of soda! NutraSweet or corn sweetener combines with the extract to form syrup, which fills even larger tanks (some hold enough syrup for 20,000 cases). In the filling room, a larger area crammed with oversized equipment and speeding conveyor belts, the blender machines mix syrup into fresh, purified, charcoal-filtered water before the mixture is cooled to 35°. Injecting the mixture with carbon dioxide completes the recipe, and the "pop" is ready for bottling.

Plastic containers and cans race at dizzying speeds along three filling lines. On the front lines, bottles are filled and joined with caps on a continuous carousel. You may be surprised to see that the cans are not filled through the holes from which you drink. Rather, machines rinse the topless cans, fill them from the top, seal on the flip-top lid, then flip the cans over to heat them and check for leaks. The white foam all over the floor isn't "escaped" soda pop—it's a soap lubricant that keeps the conveyors whirling at high speed without overheating and jamming. The can line fills almost 1,200 cans per minute, nearly 27,000 cases per eight-hour shift.

Follow the bottles' conveyor-belt passage through the wall into and out of the filling room. At times, steam clouds hover over warmers, which bring the filled cans and bottles up to room temperature to avoid condensation damage to the cartons. Every month, Brooks produces over 1 million cases of soda. During your tour alone, 25,000 containers will finish the bottling journey.

Cost: Free

Freebies: Soda cans from cooler near window overlooking the syrup tanks.

Video Shown: No

Reservations Needed: No, except for groups larger than 10 people who want a guided tour.

Days and Hours: Open Mon–Thur 8:00 AM–5:00 PM. Call ahead, since production shuts down once every few weeks for a short inventory. Closed holidays.

Plan to Stay: 15 minutes for self-guided tour.

Minimum Age: None

Disabled Access: A few steps to get into building, and observation deck is up 1 flight of stairs.

Group Requirements: Groups larger than 10 people can request guided tour by calling 1 week in advance.

Special Information: No photography. Production is heaviest in the summer and before holidays. Avoid starting your tour in late afternoon, when the bottling lines may be closing down. A small display on the company's history is at the top of the stairs.

Gift Shop: No

Directions: From Grand Rapids, take I-196 West to Exit 52 (16th St. exit). Turn right onto 16th St., left onto Waverly Rd., and right onto 32nd St. Plant is ahead on left, at corner of 32nd St. and Brooks Ave.

Nearby Attractions: Original Wooden Shoe Factory tour (see page 150); DeKlomp/Veldheer tour (see page 143); Annual Tulip Time Festival (in May); Downtown Holland's art galleries; Holland State Park Beach.

Chelsea Milling ⟿ *"JIFFY" baking mixes*
201 West North Street
Chelsea, MI 48118
(313) 475-1361

JIFFY *mixes*

You recognize JIFFY mixes by their little blue-and-white boxes and low prices, not by any supermarket coupons or fancy advertising campaigns. Chelsea Milling Company, founded in 1887, prides itself on this and has been producing its all-purpose JIFFY baking mix since 1930 in a low-key fashion. Grandma Mabel Holmes named the famous biscuit mix (archrival of General Mills' Bisquick) after hearing her father's housekeeper say, "The muffins will be ready in a jiffy." Howdy Holmes, ex-racecar driver, is now at the helm of this family-run business.

The family feeling extends to the tour program, as well. The head tour guide has been conducting tours for over 20 years—following in the footsteps of her mother, who also led tours for nearly 20 years. After watching the slide show, you walk upstairs into the factory to watch the packaging process.

The dark blue, heavy, well-oiled, vintage 1950s and '60s machinery hisses as it works hard 24 hours a day. As you walk next to the circular box-making machine, a stack of flat boxes (or "shells") feeds into the machine. Simultaneously, a roll of waxed paper threads through and is cut and shaped around a metal block. The cardboard boxes form around the waxed paper.

As you walk to the filling area, notice the floor vibrating under your feet. For corn muffin mix, the number-one prepared food mix in the U.S., maize-colored powder funnels down from the second floor to fill each box, one at a time. Along each of the 16 different small-box lines, funnels fill the boxes in a two-step process. The boxes march single file along a conveyor belt over a scale and to the boxtop-sealer. At this circular machine, each station along the wheel performs one step toward sealing the waxed paper and then the box.

Workers hand-pack 24 small boxes into each carton, and two cartons of like product are glued together to form a piggyback carton. These piggyback cartons travel along a roller-coaster conveyor belt to the warehouse. And if the boxes are not dizzy enough already, a driver will release two double-stacked pallets onto the Lanwrapper, which spins the cartons around while they are covered with heavy-duty shrink-wrap.

Cost: Free
Freebies: Recipe booklet; small box of JIFFY mix (2 boxes for people 13 years old or older).
Video Shown: 15-minute slide show covers company history, flour-milling process, and packaging.
Reservations Needed: Yes
Days and Hours: Mon–Fri 8:30 AM–1:30 PM. Closed holidays. Closed between Christmas and New Year's.
Plan to Stay: 1½–2 hours
Minimum Age: Prefers 1 adult for every child under 6.
Disabled Access: Some accessibility. Call for more information.
Group Requirements: Groups should call at least 1 week in advance for reservations. Regular group maximum is 45 people; however, special arrangements can be made for larger groups.
Special Information: No photography inside factory.
Gift Area: Guests can purchase 24-pack variety tour case containing an assortment of mixes and a recipe booklet. Also, individual products can be purchased by the case.
Directions: From I-94, take M-52 North. As you roll into Chelsea's Main Street, go through four traffic lights. As you cross the railroad tracks, notice white "Jiffyville" and 120-foot-high white silo with blue lettering to your left. Their white shipping trucks with the familiar JIFFY logo wait next to the railroad tracks. Take first left onto North St. and park on right.
Nearby Attractions: Jeff Daniels' Purple Rose Theater; Stagecoach Stop U.S.A.; Ann Arbor's attractions, including University of Michigan, are 20 minutes away.

DeKlomp/Veldheer
wooden shoes and delftware

12755 Quincy Street off U.S. 31
Holland, MI 49424
(616) 399-1803

Holland, Michigan, is full of Dutch recreations, at least one of which you'll feel enticed to visit. The Tulip Time Festival (usually the second or third week of May) will pleasantly overwhelm you with the dazzling colors of millions of tulips in full bloom. At DeKlomp, the only delftware factory in the U.S., watch delftware and wooden shoes being made through windows in the back of the large retail store. Also enjoy Veldheer's tulip farm and show garden.

Delftware originated with pottery brought to the Netherlands from the Orient in the thirteenth century. In 1310 Dutch artists in the village of Delft adapted the Oriental patterns, giving birth to the familiar blue-and-white hand-painted floral designs and Dutch scenery. Much of what passes for delftware in this country is actually mass-produced and stencil-decorated. However, DeKlomp's small staff of artisans paint each individual piece with the blue-and-white designs.

Dressed in traditional Dutch costume during Tulip Time, the artisans happily discuss each step of the production process, from molding the clay to decorating the final product. All materials—clay, molds, and machinery—are imported from the Netherlands. Walk by the paint room, where pottery is hand-painted and signed on the bottom.

At the next window, notice the unique machines used to create wooden shoes; ask to see them in action. Using a "dual-action" shaper machine and a pattern, a worker makes the left and right shoes simultaneously. By rotating a block counterclockwise, the machine traces a mirror image, thus producing a matched pair. The narrow shelves along the wall contain wooden shoe patterns. A worker places one of these patterns on the center rod of the dual-action carving machine. The right rod carves the right shoe, and the left rod, the left shoe. You will also see the only automated wooden shoe carving machine in the U.S. and a shaper machine that makes souvenir 3½- to 12½-cm. shoes—sometimes as many as five in a row, resembling a totem pole.

Cost: Production viewing: free. Gardens: adults, $2.50.

Freebies: No

Video Shown: No

Reservations Needed: No, except for groups over 20 people.

Days and Hours: June through December: Mon–Fri 8:00 AM–6:00 PM, Sat and Sun 9:00 AM–5:00 PM. January through April: Mon–Fri 9:00 AM–5:00 PM. Tulip Time Festival (10 days in May, starting the week before Mother's Day): Mon–Sun 8:00 AM–dusk. Closed Thanksgiving, Christmas, and New Year's. Wooden shoes not carved January through March. Painting and shoes sometimes not in production at other times during the year.

Plan to Stay: 10 minutes for self-guided tour of production through windows in the back of the retail store, plus time for gift shop and Veldheer's Tulip Gardens.

Minimum Age: None

Disabled Access: Yes

Group Requirements: Groups over 20 should call in advance to arrange a guided tour. No maximum group size.

Retail Store: Large gift shop carries all of the shoes and delftware made in the factory, including delft canister sets and Christmas ornaments, miniature wooden-shoe souvenirs, and a wide variety of Dutch gifts and foods. A separate store sells tulip bulbs. Open same hours as tour. Price list available from above number.

Directions: From Grand Rapids, take I-196 West to Exit 55 (Business Rt. 196 West). Then exit at U.S. 31 North and follow it to Quincy St. The factory is at the corner of Quincy St. and U.S. 31.

Nearby Attractions: Original Wooden Shoe Factory and Brooks Beverages tours (see pages 150 and 141); Downtown Holland's art galleries; Dutch Village; Holland State Park Beach; Windmill Island; Saugatuck, an artists' colony.

General Motors   ⟶   *Buick cars*

Buick City
902 East Hamilton Avenue
Flint, MI 48550
(810) 236-5000 / (810) 236-4494

From the outside, Buick City looks just as you would expect any other 1905-vintage factory to look—big and brown, with lots of smokestacks. This early-1900s exterior, however, conceals one of General Motor's most sophisticated automobile assembly facilities. Starting in 1982, GM and UAW Local 599 worked together to turn this old factory into a competitive modern plant. The tour allows you to see many of the major steps in manufacturing a Buick. While workers are important to most of the assembly steps, it's the extensive use of robotics you'll remember most.

After body parts—the side frames, underbody, roof, and other steel parts—have been stamped, the car begins to come together in the Robogate Station, where computerized body-welding robots move with surgical precision. A throng of the long-necked, reptilian robots simultaneously dances in and out of each vehicle. They weld each section of the body frame, producing a brilliant fountain of sparks with each weld. On another part of the seemingly endless assembly line, robots automatically install and seal windshields and rear windows. A robot arm picks up the glass with vacuum suction cups and sets it precisely into place. Other robots apply adhesive and primer and even clean the glass.

The seat installation process shows the latest in just-in-time manufacturing. At the loading docks, a line of trucks brings the prefabricated seats into Buick City. There is never more than a one-hour supply of seats in the plant at any time. As each truck pulls up, a robot reaches into the trailer, pulls out the correct color seat, and delivers it directly to the appropriate place on the assembly line, where it is installed by a worker. The engine, which travels by trailer from the adjoining engine plant, is attached to drivetrain components such as the transaxle and exhaust system. Automatic Guided Vehicles (AGVs) place the assembled drivetrain beneath the car body, and workers bolt drivetrain and body together. When you see workers do a detailed quality check of the car, you appreciate how robots have become the autoworker's best helper.

Cost: Free

Freebies: Safety glasses provided at the start of the tour; brochure on Buick City and production process.

Video Shown: No

Reservations Needed: Yes

Days and Hours: Normally Thur 9:30 AM and 12:00 PM. Closed holidays and 2 weeks in July, usually at end of month. *Because of the addition of a third assembly line to manufacture the Buick Park Avenue, the tour is on hold. Its fate is uncertain. See nearby attractions below for other GM Michigan tours.*

Plan to Stay: 1½–2 hours for tour and Q&A.

Minimum Age: 6

Disabled Access: Yes

Group Requirements: Maximum group size is 40. Make reservations at least 1 month in advance for summer tours.

Special Information: No photography. Tour does not include paint department.

Gift Shop: No

Directions: From Detroit, take I-75 North to I-475 North (at Flint) to Exit 8B (Stevers-Broadway). From the exit you can drive only 1 way on Stevers until Broadway. Turn left on Broadway. At the river, Broadway becomes Hamilton. Continue on Hamilton to North St. and turn right. Enter the plant grounds at the second entrance gate.

Nearby Attractions: GM Truck and Bus tour (call 810-236-4978 or 810-236-0893); GM car assembly plant tour in Lansing (call 517-885-9676); Alfred B. Sloan Museum; Crossroads Village/Huckleberry Railroad; Flint Institute of Arts; Children's Museum; For-Mar Nature Preserve and Arboretum; Frankenmuth's (known as "Michigan's Little Bavaria") attractions are about 20 miles away.

Henry Ford Museum and
Greenfield Village ~ *U.S.A. manufacturing and cars*

20900 Oakwood Boulevard
Dearborn, MI 48121
(313) 271-1620 / (800) 835-5237

It's getting difficult to take a car-factory tour in Michigan. Fortunately, Michigan has a good substitute with the constantly improving Henry Ford Museum (not affiliated with the Ford Motor Company or the Ford Foundation). The "Made in America" exhibit inside this sprawling, high-ceilinged museum should be a favorite of factory-tour lovers.

You'll be attracted to the entrance of the football field–size exhibit area by the clanking machine that assembles electrical switches and by the swinging robotic arm that sprays paint on a farm-tractor chassis. Encircling the exhibit area is a constantly moving, overhead conveyor belt with chairs, propellers, wheels, bike frames, sinks, and more hanging from it. Full-size displays, along with videos (many with historic footage), photographs, talks, and hands-on activities, offer a creative look at U.S. manufacturing history and processes.

While you'll be fascinated by the machines, such as the one that made light bulbs from ribbons of molten glass, take time to read the text descriptions and watch the videos scattered throughout. Displays explain the workers' roles and the positive and negative impact of machines on them. For example, the display of the "clean room" used in fabricating computer chips tells how workers in this controlled environment suffer stress-related injuries.

"Made in America" has a few historical displays on car manufacturing, such as the area devoted to Ford's Highland Park plant of the 1920s that revolutionized mass production with its moving assembly line. Car buffs will want to visit another area of the museum for the exhibit on "The Automobile in American Life." It's filled with big, intriguing, and a seemingly overwhelming number of artifacts. These include the actual 1961 Lincoln in which President Kennedy was assassinated and the experimental automobile (quadricycle) that Henry Ford invented in 1896.

Greenfield Village features the original buildings and homes of famous American inventors and industrialists, such as Thomas Edison, the Wright brothers, and Henry Heinz.

Cost: Adults, $12.50; senior citizens 62 and over, $11.50; children 5–12, $6.25; children under 5, free. Museum and Village admission is separate. Combination tickets (visit both sites for 2 days): Adults, $22; children 5–12, $11.

Freebies: Drawings made by rubbing crayons over brass etchings.

Videos Shown: In the museum video clips and features appear everywhere.

Reservations Needed: No, except for groups of 15 or more people.

Days and Hours: Museum and Village open Mon–Sun 9:00 AM–5:00 PM. Call for extended summer hours. Closed Thanksgiving and Christmas. Village building interiors closed January though March.

Plan to Stay: Full day for both Museum and Village.

Minimum Age: None

Disabled Access: Yes

Group Requirements: Groups of 15 or more people should call 2 weeks in advance for reservations and group discounts. Educational programs for school groups: calling 2 weeks in advance.

Special Information: Special events throughout the year; call the above number for schedule. Partially air-conditioned museum gets hot.

Gift Shops: 5 stores offer gets books, souvenirs, crafts, toys, and logoed items related to exhibit themes. At least 4 cafés and cafeterias. Open same hours as museum.

Directions: From I-94, exit northbound on Oakwood Blvd. (Exit 206), then follow signs. From I-75, exit Southfield (M-39) north, drive 8 miles; then exit northbound on Oakwood Blvd. (Exit 4) and follow signs. From I-96, exit Southfield (M-39) south, drive 11 miles; exit northbound on Oakwood Blvd. (Exit 4) and follow signs.

Nearby Car-Related Attraction: Henry Ford Estate-Fair Lane tour (call 313-593-5590).

Hoegh Industries   *pet caskets*

317 Delta Avenue
Gladstone, MI 49837
(906) 428-2151

Hoegh Industries is the world's largest manufacturer of pet caskets, cremation urns, and memorial plaques. Dennis Hoegh began the business in 1966, after meeting a dog owner who could not find a casket worthy of his beloved sled dog. The company now produces over 30,000 caskets annually in eight sizes and 22 styles, ranging from a hamster-sized 10-inch case to a 52-inch box fit for the grandest Great Dane. Molded of high-impact styrene plastic and equipped with a padded cloth interior, the caskets are made by a crew of eight workers.

Your tour starts near the computerized ovens; each one heats and softens four pieces of plastic simultaneously. Plastic sheets in different sizes—some pink, some blue, most buff—line the corridor awaiting their turn in the ovens. Entering the oven as a rigid sheet clamped into a metal frame, the plastic undergoes a startling transformation. The rigid sheets become flexible, cloth-like membranes, vibrating and jiggling as they're pulled out of the oven. As a plastic sheet hovers in the air, a mold rises up to meet it. Vacuum pumps suck all the air from the space between plastic and mold, and a pet casket forms.

Once cool, molded bottoms are lifted out of the frame so a worker can cut off the flashing and scrape the edges. One worker collects this excess plastic and feeds it into a waist-high grinder, creating tiny plastic pebbles. Beyond the grinder machine you can see where the polyurethane foam is added. The casket bottom sits in a wooden support, while a worker sprays a thin stream of superheated chemicals along the bottom inside edge. The worker must quickly insert, brace, and clamp down the interior wall, since the chemicals immediately begin to expand like exploding meringue. Confined by the interior and exterior casket walls, the foam expands within the cavity into a sturdy insulation, creating a double-walled eternal vessel. Home workers sew the cloth interiors for the caskets.

Step outside to admire the model pet cemetery. Most intriguing is a wall of remembrance plaques. A pet's photograph can be engraved onto a durable metal plaque, along with a name, dates, and a brief comment. Look for the plaques for Chuck the lizard, Fruit Loops the toucan, and the pet turkey who would walk on a leash, who died at age 13.

Cost: Free

Freebies: Postcards, brochures, rulers, pencils, pens, occasionally calendars.

Video Shown: Optional 17-minute video highlights the production process and shows a model pet cemetery. Video usually shown in winter or bad weather; also can be sent to groups, upon request.

Reservations Needed: No, however preferred for groups larger than 10 people. Individuals and families may want to call ahead (same day) to give the factory notice.

Days and Hours: Open Mon–Fri 8:00 AM–4:00 PM. Lunch break from 12:00 PM–12:30 PM. Closed holidays.

Plan to Stay: 30-45 minutes

Minimum Age: No minimum if accompanied by a parent. Children in groups should be 10 years old.

Disabled Access: Yes

Group Requirements: Groups larger than 10 people should call at least 1 day in advance.

Special Information: Umbrella tables are available for picnicking in the outdoor area.

Gift Shop: No

Directions: Take I-75 North. At the Mackinaw Bridge, follow U.S. 2 West. When you reach Gladstone, turn left on Delta Ave. The factory is on the right.

Nearby Attractions: Iverson Snowshoes tour (call 906-452-6370); DeLoughary's Sugar Bush maple syrup and cream tour (call 906-466-2305); Fayette State Park; Seney National Wildlife Refuge; Hiawatha National Forest.

Kellogg's Cereal City USA ~ *breakfast cereal*
171 West Michigan Avenue
Battle Creek, MI 49017
(616) 962-6230

Twelve years after Kellogg's discontinued their popular plant tours in 1986, Heritage Center Foundation will open Kellogg's Cereal City USA in the summer of 1998. This 45,000-square-foot extravaganza will include factory simulation, museum, corporate heritage gallery, and family entertainment center.

The "Cereal Production Line" simulates a Kellogg's Corn Flakes production line using some actual equipment. At the flavoring preparation and storage station, walk through an old copper mixing tank. In the stylized representation of Kellogg's cooking room, every few minutes an overhead car full of kernels of corn and flavoring travels the rail and stops to release its contents into the cooking tank. While this tank is being filled, another cooking tank slowly revolves and empties its contents onto a conveyor belt.

Walk by and feel the warmth from the drying oven. See the corn pass through on metal screens as it dries. Learn that tempering equalizes the moisture in the grain and is therefore the single most important step in the process. A large, loud re-creation of a separator divides the tempered corn into single kernels before the pressing units roll them into flakes. Walk past the oven that bakes the flakes golden brown.

The decade-by-decade timeline area starts with W.K. Kellogg's fateful discovery of flaked cereal in 1894 and the "Great Cereal Gold Rush," when more than 100 cereal companies had Battle Creek addresses (only three remain). In the 1920s section, see early sketches of Rice Krispies elves Snap, Crackle, and Pop. The Depression and the 1930s brought about boxtop premiums. The timeline takes you into the present.

Cereal City is the heart of the facility. A fountain features Tony the Tiger and an interactive exhibit teaches about health and nutrition. At the cereal lab, learn why cereals sink or swim, and why some cereals crunch more than others. You will definitely leave Kellogg's Cereal City USA saying, "It's GR-R-REAT!"

Cost: Adults, $5. Senior and child discounts. Yearly family passes available.

Freebies: No

Videos Shown: The main theater shows a 15–20-minute video overview of the cereal industry, Kellogg brothers, and Kellogg characters. You feel as though you've been shrunk to the size of a salt shaker and relocated onto the breakfast table of a classic Michigan farmhouse. Videos at each station along the production line contrast old and new production methods. Other videos in the advertising and historical theaters.

Reservations Needed: No, except groups over 25 people.

Days and Hours: Mon–Sun 10:00 AM–6:00 PM. Open Memorial Day through Labor Day until 8:00 PM. Closed holidays.

Plan to Stay: 3 hours, plus time in gift shop and restaurant.

Minimum Age: None

Disabled Access: Yes

Group Requirements: Groups over 25 people should call 2 weeks in advance. Group discounts and educational group tours available.

Special Information: Battle Creek festivals include June Cereal Festival Parade and World's Largest Breakfast Table (call 616-962-8400), June International Balloon Festival (call 616-962-0592), and December International Festival of Lights (call 800-397-2240).

Gift Shop: Assortment includes Tony the Tiger housewares, apparel, Toucan Sam stuffed toys, boxtop premium reproductions, and cereal treats. Purchase your image on a cereal-box cover. Themed restaurant. Open same hours as Visitor Center.

Directions: From I-94, take Exit 98B for I-194 North/M-66 North. Turn left onto West Michigan Ave. Kellogg's Cereal City USA is about 2 miles ahead on your left.

Nearby Attractions: Binder Park Zoo; Kalamazoo Air Museum; Kalamazoo Valley Public Museum; Kingman Museum.

Kilwin's Chocolates *fudge, chocolates, and ice cream*

355 North Division Road
Petoskey, MI 49770
(616) 347-3800

Among its popular tourist attractions, Northern Michigan and Mackinac Island have an abundance of candy and fudge shops, with few more respected than Kilwin's. At most of its 30-plus retail stories in Michigan and Florida, you can watch them make creamy fudge. All of the store's chocolate candies and brittle are made and shipped from this small factory on the outskirts of Petoskey, the resort town where Don and Katy Kilwin opened their first shop in 1947 as a sideline to their bakery business.

What we like about tours of small to mid-sized candy companies is how close you get to the action. In the production area you may see candies boxed, cream centers mixed, peanut brittle poured, chocolate blocks warmed in melters, liquid chocolate funneled into molds, or pecans marching through the enrobing machine. Making peanut brittle is at least a two-person operation that requires more muscle than you might expect. Two workers pick up a copper kettle and pour its dense, hot mixture of mostly peanuts, sugar, and butter onto a cold steel table. Once the brittle is partially cool, the rubber-gloved workers slice the 9-foot slabs into three pieces. They then hover over the pieces, flipping and stretching out each part so it's not too thick with peanuts.

To make the solid milk chocolate tool kits and ice-cream-cone suckers, liquid milk chocolate is poured into molds, which cool on metal trays in a nearby room. A worker then adds the "decorations" to create the ice-cream effect. Watch a worker gently dip the top part of the sucker into white chocolate. It's a real skill to get just the right amount of white chocolate onto the candy so that the cone-looking part stays dry. Sprinkling "jimmies" (tiny bits of candy) on top completes this production feat.

Cost: Free

Freebies: Sample of one of their popular chocolates, such as the tuttle (caramel, pecans, and chocolate).

Video Shown: No

Reservations Needed: No, during summer season, except for groups over 10 people. Yes, for remainder of year.

Days and Hours: June, July, August, (sometimes September) only. Mon–Thur 10:30 AM, 11:00 AM, 2:00 PM, and 2:30 PM. Tours only by special request other months of year. Closed holidays and unscheduled plant shutdowns.

Plan to Stay: 20 minutes for tour, plus time in retail store.

Minimum Age: None

Disabled Access: Yes

Group Requirements: Motorcoach tours can visit all year with 1 week's advance notice. Call (616) 347-4831.

Special Information: Production changes daily, so call ahead if you have favorites. Limited ice-cream production on tour. Plans to remodel factory building into a traditional European chocolate-factory design.

Retail Store: Sells full line of 300 confectionery products, including fudge, tuttles, truffles, and sugar-free chocolate. Open year-round Mon–Fri 9:00 AM–4:30 PM. Closed holidays. Catalog and franchise information available at above number.

Directions: From the south, take I-75 North to Gaylord Exit 282. Turn left on Rt. 32 West to Rt. 131 North. Turn right to Petoskey. Turn left onto Division Rd. Kilwin's is immediately on left. From the Upper Peninsula, take I-75 South and exit at the Indian River Exit 310. Turn right onto Rt. 68 West. Take Rt. 31 South to Petoskey. Turn left onto Division Rd. Kilwin's is on the right at top of hill. Park where sign reads "Chocolate Lovers Parking—All Others Will Be Towed."

Nearby Attractions: Amon Orchards tour (see page 139), Boyer Glassworks (call 616-526-6359); Petoskey's Gas Light District; Lake Michigan's beaches; Mackinac Island (self-proclaimed fudge capital of world), 35 miles away.

Lionel — *model trains and accessories*

26750 Twenty-Three Mile Road
Chesterfield, MI 48051-2493
(810) 949-4100, ext. 1211

Just about every American over 35 recognizes the Lionel brand name. Back in 1949, people of all ages used to stop by the company's showroom on East 26th Street in New York City to see the famous miniature railroad display. Store buyers and collectors would come to watch as small locomotives pulled freight cars through pretend towns and over imitation mountains. In 1964 the showroom closed its doors. But today, thanks to the hard work, dedication, and volunteer efforts of the employees at Lionel's Michigan headquarters, you can once again enjoy seeing Lionel trains in action and learning the story behind the company that started in 1900.

Your visit begins with a video about Lionel, its heritage, and its manufacturing. Then you enter the showroom. Lights rise slowly over the 14-by-40-foot railroad display, illuminating a fascinating arrangement of trains, tracks, and scenery that will remind kids (and kids at heart) why they love collecting model trains.

This classic display features multiple levels of tracks with four different rail lines. Buttons around the display allow visitors to operate accessories themselves, including trains on a smaller layout just for young kids.

The design of the main display's bottom level includes elements from the original 1949 layout, such as the underground passenger platform and the yard and roundhouse area. The next level reveals more modern-era trains, including more freight cars and diesel-powered engines. The top, overhead level uses the American Flyer line, which, although different in size from the other model trains, fits in perfectly with the rest of the display.

While watching the chugging, rumbling trains, don't forget to enjoy the impressive scenery of a small, semi-real city. The workers who created this extraordinary display thought of every detail, right down to the park statues, railyard workers, and store signs. Also notice the company timeline on the wall, illustrating over nine decades of model train history. It includes rare and unique prototype train models, artifacts, historic ads, and photos.

Cost: Free
Freebies: Souvenir pin and product catalog.
Video Shown: 10-minute video on company history and manufacturing process, narrated by Lionel Chairman and CEO Richard Kughn.
Reservations Needed: Yes
Days and Hours: Wed and Thur 10:00 AM, 3:00 PM, and 4:00 PM; Fri 10:00 AM, 1:30 PM, and 2:30 PM; Sat 9:00 AM, 10:00 AM, 11:00 AM, and 12:00 PM. Times change seasonally, so call for recording. Closed holidays.
Plan to Stay: 1 hour for video and tour of visitors center, plus time for gift shop.
Minimum Age: None
Disabled Access: Yes
Group Requirements: For groups of 20 or more people, additional visitors center tour times may be available. Maximum group size is 60 people.
Special Information: Information available about Railroader Club membership.
Gift Shop: Sells the Visitors Center Boxcar (available only at this store), other trains, starter sets, train accessories, and logoed items including T-shirts, signs, and clocks. Discount for Railroader Club members. Open Tue–Fri 1:30 PM–4:30 PM, Sat 10:00 AM–12:30 PM. (Call ext. 1443 for seasonal hours.)
Directions: From I-94, take Exit 243 (Twenty-Three Mile Rd./New Baltimore exit). Veer left at exit if coming from Detroit and stay on Twenty-Three Mile Rd. Turn left at second light onto Russell Schmidt Rd. (You'll see "Lionel" sign.) Turn right into visitor parking.
Nearby Attractions: Morley Candy factory tour (groups only, call 810-468-4300); Yates Cider Mill; Anchor Bay Aquarium; Military Air Museum; Detroit's attractions, about 30 minutes away.

Original Wooden Shoe Factory

447 U.S. 31 at 16th Street   *wooden shoes*
Holland, MI 49423
(616) 396-6513

No trip to this quaint Dutch village near Lake Michigan is complete without a visit to a wooden-shoe factory. Opened in 1926, Original Wooden Shoe is the oldest such factory in North America, and the only factory still using early 1900s, European-made wooden-shoe-making machines which turn out the shoes one at a time.

As you walk from the large gift shop into the small shoe factory, you smell the poplar and aspen wood and hear the sounds of the old machines at work. Stand behind a protective screen. A pile of logs is first sawed into lengths determined by shoe size and then quartered according to the width of the shoe. The "roughing" machine, dated 1908, strips off the logs' bark and imperfections. A worker clamps wood onto the "shaping" machine as you would put a chicken on a rotisserie spit. This machine gives shoes their basic outside shape.

A few steps further down the line a worker strains with the "boring" machine. This contraption, made in France in 1914, uses a pattern shoe to bore out the inside of the new shoe to the desired specifications, just as the hardware store's key-cutting machine uses your old key as a guide to create an exact duplicate. Certain days you see a worker, using his drawknife fastened to a ring at the end of his cutting log, skillfully hand-carve and trim the outside of the shoe and smooth the edges. Finally, artists personalize the finished product by painting or wood-burning traditional Dutch decorations and your name onto each shoe. Whether you call their wooden shoes *klompen* (Dutch) or *sabots* (French), you can leave with a pair fitted just for you.

Cost: 25 cents per person
Freebies: No
Video Shown: No
Reservations Needed: No, but best to call ahead to ensure production in off-season (December through March).

Days and Hours: Mon–Sat 8:00 AM–4:30 PM. Tulip Time Festival (10 days in May, starting the week before Mother's Day): Mon–Sun 8:00 AM–6:00 PM. Limited tours in off-season (December through March). Closed Thanksgiving, Christmas, and New Year's.
Plan to Stay: 10 minutes for self-guided tour, plus time for gift shop. The production steps are well labeled.
Minimum Age: None
Disabled Access: Yes
Group Requirements: Groups larger than 25 people are asked to call 1 or 2 hours in advance of arrival. No maximum group size. No admission charge for bus tours.
Special Information: In addition to the early 1900s machines that are the major attraction, the factory also operates relatively modern "dual-action" machines that make both shoes at the same time. In addition, hand-carving demonstrations are conducted frequently during Tulip Time Festival and by appointment the rest of the year.
Gift Shop: Sells a wide variety of Dutch food and gifts, including wooden shoes (produced on-site or mass-produced in Europe) and hardwood salad bowls (made on-site in a nonpublic factory). Souvenirs include T-shirts, baskets, and knickknacks. Open Mon–Sun 8:00 AM–6:00 PM. Tulip Time Festival and July 4th–Labor Day: Mon–Sun 8:00 AM–8:00 PM. Price list available from above number.
Directions: From Grand Rapids, take I-196 West to Exit 52 (16th St. Exit). Turn right onto 16th St. Factory/retail store entrance is 2 miles ahead on left at intersection with U.S. 31.
Nearby Attractions: During Tulip Time Festival in May, the entire town is alive with color and activities. DeKlomp/Veldheer wooden shoes, delftware, and gardens (see page 143); Brooks Beverages tour (see page 141); downtown Holland's art galleries; Holland State Park Beach; Dutch Village; Windmill Island; Saugatuck artists' colony, 8 miles away.

Wolverine World Wide

Hush Puppies shoes and Wolverine work boots

465 Wolverine Street
Rockford, MI 49341
(616) 866-5514

HUSH PUPPIES®

Few American shoe brands are better known than Hush Puppies. With foreign competition accounting for 80 percent of the men's and women's shoes sold in the U.S., it's a good feeling to visit Wolverine World Wide, which supplies millions of pairs of shoes annually from 11 domestic factories. The company was founded in 1883, but Hush Puppies weren't introduced until 1957. They were named after hush puppies fried corn-dough balls used by farmers to quiet their barking dogs. Extremely popular in the 1950s and '60s, these casual suede shoes were recently revamped and revitalized in Day-Glo shades of green, purple, and pink.

One of the best aspects of this tour is that you walk right onto the busy factory floor, close to all the action. You hear the stammering and hissing of the different machines, and smell the glue used in cement construction. Shoes in progress chug along the line like sitting ducks in a shooting gallery. At each station, a worker takes them off the line and performs the next step in the process of building a pair of shoes.

Trays with two pairs of upside-down ivory-colored lasts (the plastic molds around which the shoes are constructed) move down the four-row production line. An insole is tacked onto each last. The flange machine heats a counter (thermoplastic insert that reinforces the heel) to 450° to soften it before it is shaped around an ice-cold mold. When the worker steps on the foot pedal of the toe-laster machine, pinchers stretch the pigskin leather upper around the toe.

One worker places the sides and heels into the automatic machine that seals and flips them over into the heat-set oven. Another worker oversees the machine that automatically applies cement to the bottom of the shoe. While these steps may not appear very automated, they replace the previous elbow, wrist, and paintbrush system of applying the glue. Further down the assembly line, a worker matches already-sewn uppers with soles, places them upside down in the sole-lay machine, and clamps it shut under 550 pounds of pressure. Once the shoes are cleaned, several workers pop out the lasts, insert shoelaces, and inspect and box the shoes to be shipped to 80 countries worldwide.

Cost: Free
Freebies: No
Video Shown: No
Reservations Needed: Yes, 1 week in advance.
Days and Hours: Mon, Tue, Thur, Fri 9:30 AM–11:00 AM and 12:30 PM–1:30 PM. Closed holidays, 1–2 weeks around Christmas and New Year's, and usually first 2 weeks of July.
Plan to Stay: 30 minutes for a tour of either the Hush Puppies or Wolverine work boot plants, plus time in the nearby outlet store.
Minimum Age: 5
Disabled Access: Yes
Group Requirements: Groups should call 2 weeks in advance. Maximum group size is 50 people.
Special Information: High noise level; can be hot; strong smells.
Outlet Store: Nearby retail outlet sells discounted first- and second-quality shoes, small stuffed Hush Puppies animals, and apparel with company logos. Small historical display shows antique miniature shoes, oversized Hush Puppies statue, and early company photographs. Open Mon–Fri 9:00 AM–8:00 PM, Sat 9:00 AM–6:00 PM, and Sun 12:00 PM–5:00 PM. Closed holidays.
Directions: From Grand Rapids, take I-131 North to 10 Mile Rd. exit. Turn right onto 10 Mile Rd. Turn left onto Main St. In ¾ mile, turn left onto Wolverine St. Plant is 1 block ahead on left.
Nearby Attractions: Amway household and personal-care products visitor center (see page 140); Squire Street Square; Rockford Area Historical Museum (open May–October, limited hours); Grand Rapids attractions, including Gerald R. Ford Museum, about 15 miles away.

Arctco

600 Brooks Avenue South
Thief River Falls, MN 56701
(218) 681-8558 / (800) 279-0179

*Arctic Cat snowmobiles,
personal watercraft, and
all-terrain vehicles*

The Arctic Cat snowmobile has often set the standards for the North American snowmobile industry. In 1962 the Arctic Cat was the first front-engine snowmobile ever produced in this country; in the early 1970s it was the top selling snowmobile. Tough times for the industry and the U.S. economy in the late 1970s halted production. During the early 1980s the "Boys from Thief River" restructured the company; now, once again, it manufactures award-winning racing and touring snowmobiles (one-millionth model built in July 1993). The company also produces Tigershark-brand personal watercraft and the Arctic Cat ATVs.

Depending on the month, your tour shows what's involved in making the Arctic Cat, Tigershark, or ATVs (although not in sequential assembly order) and numerous subassembly steps. The first thing you see is a line hanging with parts that have been through the powder paint shed, on their way to an oven that bakes the paint into the metal parts. Throughout the tour, you often see parts on conveyors moving in and out of cleaning, priming, and painting booths.

Robots and workers weld together the chassis. Workers put the parts in the "jig," a frame that holds them together during assembly. With sparks flying, a robotic arm moves from spot to spot welding the chassis. Down the line, workers bolt some parts and robotic arms weld others to the chassis, including the skis. As your guide explains in the Tigershark production area, the fiberglass bodies are made from the outside in, with chopped-up fiberglass and resin shot into molds.

The foam cushion seats start as liquid chemicals, with the mix determining the desired plushness. This mixture is squirted into preheated molds and, within a few minutes, out pops a cushion. After the vinyl is stretched around it, the seat is ready for the silk-screened logo. In the main assembly area, each chassis moves down the line with a parts cage that contains all its pieces;

workers pull out parts as needed. When they test the engine, you think about the fun of riding the machine on the nearby Thief River.

Cost: Free
Freebies: Balloons, bumper stickers, decals, product literature.
Video Shown: No
Reservations Needed: No, except for groups larger than 25 people.
Days and Hours: Mon–Fri 1:00 PM. Closed holidays and usually the week of July 4th. Special arrangements possible for other tour times. Occasional shutdowns when waiting for parts, so call ahead about the day you want to visit.
Plan to Stay: 45 minutes for tour, plus time for gift counter.
Minimum Age: None
Disabled Access: Yes
Group Requirements: 1 week's advance notice for groups larger than 25 people so that additional tour guides will be available.
Special Information: No photography. Other than during spring months, snowmobiles and personal watercraft are not in production simultaneously.
Gift Shop: Sells logoed items, including T-shirts, caps, mugs, and scale-model Arctic Cats and trucks. Open Mon–Fri 1:00 PM–5:00 PM or after tour, if earlier. Catalog with full line of clothes and accessories available at above number. Information about Cat's Pride, the world's largest organized snowmobile owners club, available from (800) 279-8558 (800-461-1987 in Canada).
Directions: From Hwy. 2, take Hwy. 59 North through center of Thief River Falls. Turn left onto Brooks Ave. (Bowling Center on the corner). Arctco is on your right. From Hwy. 32, turn left at Brooks Ave.
Nearby Attractions: Christian Brothers hockey stick factory tour in Warroad (see page 154); Polaris snowmobile tour (see page 158) in Roseau; Red Lake River; Pioneer Park; Agassiz Wildlife Reserve.

Blandin Paper   ～ *paper*

115 S.W. 1st Street
Grand Rapids, MN 55744
(218) 327-6682

BLANDIN PAPER

Since pioneer days, northern Minnesota has depended on the forest products industry. Today sophisticated machinery replaces late 1800s logging camps. Blandin Paper specializes in making coated paper for such magazines as *Time*, *Forbes*, and *Sports Illustrated*, and Spiegel and Eddie Bauer catalogs.

The huge, new No. 6 paper machine—375 feet long, 35 feet wide, and 60 feet high—fills your view as the guided tour begins. It produces 4,000 feet of paper per minute (45 mph) with only a few people driving it. The pulp, 99.3 percent water, flows in at the machine's "wet end." Paper is initially formed on a wire screen; the water content is decreased by suction, gravity, and presses. The paper then enters the dryer, where it takes a roller-coaster ride through 40 heated cylinders that reduce the moisture content to less than 3 percent. Look for the electronic hole-detectors that find flaws in the paper as it runs around the cylinders. The machine marks the edge of the web with blue dye where it senses holes, which are patched when the paper is rewound.

The 20-ton rolls (45 miles of paper) then go through the coater machine for a thin layer of coating formula, consisting mostly of clay. The running web is immersed in a coating bath, and excess is scraped off with blades. Air foils, steam-heated dryer cans, and gas-fired infrared burners dry the coating on one side, then the other side goes through the same processes.

Next, the roll goes through the "supercalenders" to receive its glossy shine. The paper spins rapidly between vertical stacks of fiber and metal rolls to polish the coated surface. The space between the rollers determines the amount of gloss. Winder machines cut the jumbo rolls and rewind them into smaller-diameter rolls, though each still averages the size of two men. This process produces up to 1,370 tons per day.

Cost: Free

Freebies: Brochure illustrating the paper-making process.

Video Shown: 8-minute video about the company, its commitment to quality, the foresting of trees, and the mill.

Reservations Needed: No, except for groups larger than 12 people.

Days and Hours: Tours from the first Monday in June through the Friday before Labor Day. Mon, Wed, Fri 9:00 AM–4:00 PM. Closed July 4th. Call (218) 327-6226 about tours at other times of the year.

Plan to Stay: 45 minutes for video and tour.

Minimum Age: 10. Children ages 10–14 must be accompanied by an adult.

Disabled Access: Mostly accessible, although a few steps lead to the control room and tour involves a lot of walking.

Group Requirements: Groups larger than 12 people need 1 week's advance notice; call (218) 327-6226.

Special Information: No photography. Will be 10–15° warmer than outside temperature. Machines are very loud. The chemically-produced kraft pulp needed for paper production is not manufactured at the mill, so there's none of the sour odor that bothers some people at paper mills.

Gift Shop: No

Directions: From the intersection of Hwy. 169 and Hwy. 2 (at Central School), go 1 block south on Pokegama Ave. Turn right at 3rd St. N.W. Tour information center is 1½ blocks ahead on the left.

Nearby Attractions: Blandin Forest 9-mile self-guided tour of tree plantations and logging operations (call above number for map); Blandin Tree Nursery tour; Forest History Center; Gunn Park; Judy Garland Museum. Other Minnesota paper industry tours include Lake Superior Paper Industries in Duluth (call 218-628-5100) and Boise Cascade in International Falls (call 218-285-5011).

Christian Brothers   *hockey sticks*

Highway 11
Warroad, MN 56763
(800) 346-5055

Who is better equipped to make hockey sticks than a former hockey star and Olympic Gold medalist, or two? Brothers Roger and Billy Christian combined their hockey acumen—honed during the 1960 (U.S.A.'s first Olympic gold in hockey) and 1964 Winter Olympics—and their carpentry skills to found Christian Brothers in 1964 with Hal Bakke. Today the company is one of the world's best-known hockey-stick manufacturers, only two of which are in the U.S.A. Your tour guide explains some of the company history.

Particularly during winter, you can follow along as workers create sticks for National Hockey League (NHL) professional hockey players and silk-screen the famous players' names onto the shafts. Whether the sticks are for a schoolyard team or the NHL, they start as ash and elm blanks, cut to the general length and width of a handle. A grader, using a specially designed bending machine, tests the wood for strength and integrity. (In fact, all of the factory's machines were custom-designed for the Christians; several are one-of-a-kind inventions.) Workers then add a block of wood to the handles, slice the block, and glue the blade form together. A carousel-like machine heats the sticks two by two, setting the glue and bonding blade and handle together. Each time the machine turns, workers add two more sticks.

After going through a sander machine so powerful that its operation literally shakes the ground around it, the sticks enter the steamer for softening. Workers hand-press the curve into the blades. Each NHL pro who uses a Christian stick has sent the factory a sample stick with a blade curve that lies on the ice just the way he likes. New sticks are made with the exact dimensions of this template.

Christian Brothers' best playmaker is a machine that forces a fiberglass-like tube over the blade and cuts it off, edge-free, with air scissors. After another hand-smoothing and an epoxy bath, 1,200 sticks per hour pass through the silk-screener, which affixes the company's name (and, for custom orders, the player's name) to three sides of each handle.

Cost: Free
Freebies: Posters, brochures, sometimes miniature hockey sticks (drink stirrers).
Video Shown: No
Reservations Needed: No, except for groups over 40 people.
Days and Hours: Mon–Fri 10:30 AM and 3:00 PM. Closed holidays, week between Christmas and New Year's.
Plan to Stay: 20 minutes
Minimum Age: None
Disabled Access: Yes. A few aisles may be too narrow for wheelchairs.
Group Requirements: Groups larger than 40 people should call 1 week ahead. Large groups will be split into groups of 15.
Special Information: No photography. Factory filled with sawdust. Winter visits are the best time for seeing NHL pros' custom orders. Plant busiest with retail stock orders April through June. Company also manufactures protective equipment for hockey and in-line skating but at other plants.
Gift Shop: Christian Brothers hockey sticks and athletic wear are available at retail stores in Warroad.
Directions: From the east, take Hwy. 11 West to Warroad, which lies 6 miles south of the U.S./Canada border. Christian Brothers sits prominently on your left. From I-29, take Hwy. 11 East to Warroad.
Nearby Attractions: Polaris snowmobile tour (see page 158) in Roseau; Arctic Cat snowmobile tour in Thief River Falls (see page 152); Marvin Windows tour (call 218-386-1430); Warroad Library & Heritage Center; Lake of the Woods Recreational Area.

Faribo   *wool blankets and throws*

1819 N.W. Second Avenue
Faribault, MN 55021
(507) 334-1644

Faribo

Long ago, 800 central-U.S. mills made woolen blankets. Today only three carry on, the largest being Faribo Woolens. Faribo produces more than half the wool blankets made in the United States. It is one of the few "fully vertical" mills left (a soup-to-nuts mill, starting with raw wool and ending with a finished blanket). Although automated machines help with the weaving, the process is still labor-intensive. Workers handle fibers, comb batting, spin yarn, and finish and bind woven pieces—human touches that machines cannot replicate.

In the wool stock area, huge bales of raw wool await your inspection. You may catch the scent of wet wool. Touch Faribo blankets' three component fibers: domestic wool, merino wool, and acrylic. Each fiber feels softer than the next. Scouring and blending operations clean the wool stock before the dyeing vats color it. In carding, the fibers are combed into huge fluffy sheets of batting. Workers slice the batting into strips of roving, which will then be spun into yarn. Your tour guide may let you feel how soft and weak the roving is, easily torn by the gentlest tug. Then try tearing the spun yarn apart—you'll hurt your hand before you succeed!

In the weaving room, elephantine computerized looms transform the yarns into blankets. Shuttles fly from side to side on the looms so rapidly that the human eye cannot follow. Horizontal "packing bars" move back and forth to pack in the just-woven yarns. Faribo's 26 automated looms can create over 2,000 items a day. Watch the careful inspectors at the burling station, where each woven piece is backlit and inspected, inch by inch, for snags, flaws, and finished quality, then measured and sized.

The final stop is the finishing area. Massive presses pull the blankets and throws, squaring them, truing the edges, and preparing them for the sewers. Using yarn as thread, the sewers add silken tapes to bind blankets' edges or overstitch the edges with sergers. These laborious personal touches continue as the final products are carefully prepared for shipment worldwide.

Cost: Free
Freebies: Logoed souvenir item
Video Shown: 15-minute video runs continuously in the retail store. Features a mother sheep describing the blanket-making process to her lamb.
Reservations Needed: No, except for groups over 10 people.
Days and Hours: Mon–Fri 10:00 AM and 2:00 PM. Closed New Year's, Easter, Thanksgiving weekend, last week in June, and the first 2 weeks in July, and 2 weeks around Christmas. Plan to arrive 15 minutes before tour.
Plan to Stay: 40 minutes for tour, plus time for retail store.
Minimum Age: None, for families; 12, for groups.
Disabled Access: Only to the first floor of the factory (can see everything except the first and last production steps).
Group Requirements: Groups larger than 10 people should make reservations at least 1 or 2 weeks in advance. Large groups will be split into groups of 12–14.
Special Information: Automated looms in the weaving area are loud, and portions of the tour can be hot during summer.
Retail Store: Sells Faribo first-quality blankets and throws as well as discontinued lines and irregulars, various manufacturers' all-season clothing for men, women, and children, and one-of-a-kind antique bobbins. Open Mon–Sat 9:00 AM–5:30 PM, Sun 12:00 PM–4:00 PM (until 5:00 PM in summer). Closed holidays. Catalog available from (800) 448-WOOL.
Directions: From Minneapolis, take Rt. 35 South to Faribault. Then follow billboards directing you to factory and store.
Nearby Attractions: Rice County Historical Museum; Alexander Faribault Park; Cannon River Dam.

Hormel First Century Museum/
SPAMTOWN USA   *meat processing*

1301 N.W. 18th Avenue
Austin, MN 55912
(507) 437-5100

While we chose not to include meat processors in this book, we couldn't resist an American icon such as SPAM luncheon meat. When George Hormel opened his meat-processing factory in 1891, he probably didn't realize that his company would be living high on the hog these days from his son's 1937 invention of SPAM. The tinned meat, made of spiced ham and pork shoulder, earned its name through a contest held by the company.

This multi-display-case museum explains how SPAM, Dinty Moore beef stew, and other Hormel favorites were conceived. You also view an array of paraphernalia and historical items depicting the company's colorful past, including original court documentation of company employee Cy Thompson's embezzlement of over $1 million in 1921—a scandal that almost broke the company.

In the "Office" section of the octagonal-shaped museum, ledgers and invoices spread out on Hormel's original desk chronicle his activity as the company grew and illustrate a typical early-1900s workday. Follow the growth and modernization of the packing house in "Operations," where the huge processing engine purchased in 1889 sits surrounded by mesh gloves, knives, and other tools of the meat-packing trade.

The 3-by-4-foot can of SPAM luncheon meat dominates the next display case and certainly alerts visitors to the museum's central attraction. Caps, lanterns, lunch boxes, and even a sponsored NASCAR racer bear the familiar round yellow lettering. Many old SPAM labels from the past, engraved coins, aprons, and printing tools comprise the "Publications" display, documenting Hormel's "self-contained" approach to company advertising and promotion with the establishment of his print shop in 1930.

The food line even achieved celebrity status, as seen in the "Marketing" area, where products endorsed by George Burns and Gracie Allen sit amid posters created during the post-WWII era. The unusual and entertaining trivia found throughout the museum may not explain why the canned "spiced ham" continually experiences enormous sales spurts, but its appeal both as a food item and a souvenir-generator just might last as long as the product's shelf life!

Cost: Free
Freebies: No
Videos Shown: Film topics which vary by day, include the plant's beginnings, a 1960s film about George Hormel's autobiography, production, talk-show footage, and a 1950 film documenting Hormel's invention of the first resealable luncheon-meat bag.
Reservations Needed: No
Days and Hours: Mon–Sun 7:00 AM–9:00 PM. Closed Christmas.
Plan to Stay: 30–45 minutes
Minimum Age: None
Disabled Access: Yes
Group Requirements: Guided group tours can sometimes be arranged through the Austin Convention and Visitors Bureau (800-444-5713, ext. 300).
Special Information: This small museum is not usually staffed and can be crowded. There are tentative plans to move the museum to a larger site, so call the Hormel Foods Archive and Gift Center (507-437-5100) before you visit.
Gift Shop: The Games People Play shop, down the street, features a large selection of SPAM and Hormel souvenirs. Hormel Foods' 36-page "SPAMtastic" gift catalog is available by calling (800) 686-SPAM.
Directions: From I-90, take 14th St. NW exit. Enter the Oak Park Mall at the NW entrance. The museum is right inside the NW entrance.
Nearby SPAM/Hormel Foods Attractions: Jay C. Hormel Nature Center (hiking, canoe rentals, skiing); Hormel Foods Archives/SPAM Merchandise Shop (open to bus groups only); George A. Hormel Home; annual SPAM Jamboree (Saturday of July 4th weekend).

Kuempel Chime Clock Works

21195 Minnetonka Boulevard   ⚊ *grandfather clocks*
Excelsior, MN 55331
(612) 474-6177 / (800) 328-6445

Kuempel Chime
Clock Works and Studio

When Reuben Kuempel needed a staff for the clock shop he founded in 1916, he hired the only people with time to spare. He put his retiree customers to work crafting the fine grandfather clocks that are still made by a second-career work force. In fact, virtually all the grandfather clockmakers are grandfathers, with an average age of 67, and it is their camaraderie that keeps the workshop ticking as consistently as the fine clocks themselves.

Surrounded by the rhythm of clocks chiming in unison every quarter-hour in the display showroom, your guide explains the fascinating history of the company, sharing anecdotes about its founder's gift for gab and the company's unusual atmosphere, where age is irrelevant when everyone works together effectively. A tour through the gadget- and machinery-filled workroom enables visitors to watch various stages of production, from the planing and sanding of boards to the final wind of the pendulum on a finished clock.

In the cabinet shop, bandsaws hum as workers cut panels of cherry, red oak, and black walnut wood. Grabbing a soft cloth, a worker brushes away the sawdust, revealing a smooth edge ready to be fitted to another panel of the frame. Another worker punches the winding arbor holes in a clock face with a treadle-operated metal punch. Later the face will be coupled with a moon wheel, the little disk at the top of the clock that rotates slowly in measured increments.

Because they are custom-designed, the face and case designs of the clocks vary. One clock wheel may feature a pet goat, while another displays an antique wrench. Still others include landscapes of the hemisphere. Workers place beveled or etched glass windows into the case to show off the tubular bells and shiny pendulum keeping time. A worker explains that tubular bells—often the most popular—provide the best ringing sound, while the mellow sounds of rods are better for smaller homes.

The grandfather craftsmen pack 90 to 120 parts into each clock. Kuempel Clocks turns out about 300 clocks per year. The pride and skill with which they make the clocks lends an extra-special touch to the finished product.

Cost: Free
Freebies: Homemade cookies and coffee.
Video Shown: 17-minute video of news stories featuring Kuempel Clocks plays in showroom upon request.
Reservations Needed: No, except for groups of 10 or more people.
Days and Hours: Mon–Fri 9:00 AM–2:30 PM. Closed major holidays.
Plan to Stay: 45 minutes for tour, plus time in showroom.
Minimum Age: None. Children should be supervised.
Disabled Access: Yes
Group Requirements: Groups of 10 or more people should call at least 1 week in advance.
Special Information: Best days to see production are Monday through Wednesday. The company offers clock-making workshops which require ordering clock kits 1 month in advance. Call the number above for schedules and information.
Showroom: Displays variety of clocks that can be custom ordered. Sells cuckoo clocks, jewelry, and desk clocks. Open Mon–Fri 8:30 AM–4:30 PM, Sat 9:00 AM–12:00 PM. Also open by appointment. Closed holidays. Catalog available by calling the number above.
Directions: From I-494, take Hwy. 7 West for 5½ miles. When you approach the intersection of Hwy. 7 and Christmas Lake Rd. (CLR), get in the right lane. ¼ mile beyond CLR, turn right on Division St. Go 100 yards to Old Excelsior Blvd. Turn left and go 100 yards to Minnetonka Blvd. Turn right. Kuempel Clocks is about 1 mile ahead on right.
Nearby Attractions: Lake Minnetonka; Mall of America; Minneapolis attractions include Guthrie Theater, Minnesota Orchestra, Minnesota Vikings, and Steamboats on Mississippi are 20–25 minutes away.

Polaris

snowmobiles, all-terrain vehicles, and personal watercraft

301 5th Avenue, S.W.
Roseau, MN 56751
(218) 463-2312

Polaris is the world's largest manufacturer of snowmobiles (40-percent market share) and also a major producer of all-terrain vehicles (ATVs) and personal watercraft. Its resurgence is somewhat similar to that of Harley-Davidson (see page 261), which regained competitiveness after its management buyout from AMF. Polaris' was a division of Textron, a multi-national conglomerate, before its own management buyout in 1981. At that low point in Polaris' history, the company had about 100 employees and the Roseau plant was shut down. Now it has more than 2,500 workers and over $1 billion in annual sales.

Even with the company's big investment in labor-saving technology and robotics, this huge plant in rural northwestern Minnesota, 10 miles from the Canadian border, has become one of the biggest employers in the region. The tour lets you see firsthand how Polaris assembles snowmobiles and ATVs (all the parts are made in other Polaris plants in Osceola, Wisconsin; Spirit Lake, Iowa; and a Hudson, Wisconsin, engine plant jointly owned with Fuji Heavy Industries). You can walk between the two snowmobile and two ATV lines, observing the subassembly, preassembly, final assembly, and testing areas of the line.

In the snowmobile subassembly area, workers and robots put the parts together and prepare the skis and frame. Most of the metal parts are E-coated for corrosion resistance, then sprayed with a powder-coat finish. Preassembly adds the chain case, suspension, and tracks. Heading over to the final assembly area, notice the finished hoods hanging from the monorail on their way from the plastics area. A visitor favorite is watching the motor being hoisted, lowered, and quickly fastened into place.

After all the final parts, tubes, and wires are connected, finishing touches such as the reflector tape and Polaris nameplate are added. Finally, the snowmobile or ATV travels to the test shacks that sit near the ends of each line. The workers give them a little gas,

start the engines, and test all the parts and critical features.

Cost: Free

Freebies: Small packet with decals, stickers, and pin.

Video Shown: No

Reservations Needed: No, except for groups over 15 people.

Days and Hours: Mon–Fri 2:00 PM. Closed holidays and week between Christmas and New Year's. Special tours can be arranged at other times.

Plan to Stay: 45 minutes

Minimum Age: None, but quite noisy for young children.

Disabled Access: Yes

Group Requirements: Headphones available only to groups smaller than 10 people. Large groups should call at least 2 days in advance. No maximum group size, but ratio is 10 people per guide.

Special Information: Noisy; groups receive headphones or earplugs depending on number of people on tour. No photography. Tours available of the Polaris Spirit Lake, IA, plant that manufactures personal watercraft (call 712-336-6702).

Gift Shop: A dealer's store that sells snowmobiles, logoed clothing, and other accessories is a few blocks away on Hwy. 11.

Directions: From the west, take Hwy. 11 East. At the first traffic light in Roseau, turn right at Hwy. 89 (also 5th Ave., SW). Polaris will be on your right. From the east, take Hwy. 11 West and turn left at Hwy. 89 in Roseau. Polaris will be on your right. From the north, take Hwy. 310, which becomes Hwy. 89 in Roseau; plant is a few blocks ahead on right.

Nearby Attractions: Christian Brothers hockey stick and Arctic Cat snowmobile tours (see pages 154 and 152); Marvin Windows tour (call 218-386-1430); Roseau River Wildlife Area; Lake of the Woods; Roseau City Park and Museum.

Peavey Electronics

music amplifiers and electric guitars

Peavey Visitors Center and Museum
4886 Peavey Drive
Meridian, MS 39302
(601) 486-1460

Hartley Peavey, founder of the world's largest music and sound equipment manufacturer, grew up in this eastern Mississippi railroad town. As a teenager in 1965, he constructed his first guitar "amp" in his parents' basement. Today his company employs 2,000 workers in Mississippi, Alabama, and England, and markets amplifiers, guitars, keyboards, and sound systems in 103 countries. Every form of music—from punk to polka, from country to classical—has been touched by Hartley Peavey's products.

Though its factories are not open for tours, the company celebrates its history— R&D and manufacturing—at the Visitors Center. In its first life, the building was a U.S. Department of Agriculture research facility, specializing in sugar-producing crops. Peavey lovingly restored the exterior to its original Federalist style. But the interior is now strongly post-modern, with splashes of chrome, teal, yellow, and black—colors found on many Peavey's products.

Called the Peavey World Tour, the center presents exhibits and video programs and has become a mecca for musicians of all types who trust their stylings only to equipment bearing the Peavey logo. The first-floor galleries provide a personal view of the company's founder. Look for a 1901 photograph of Hartley Peavey's grandfather and the original lightning-bolt logo drawn on notebook paper. One room recreates the basement where Hartley made his first amplifier, complete with tools and old issues of *Popular Mechanics* and *Popular Science*. Upstairs galleries chronicle the company's growth from this basement workshop to 19 facilities.

Follow the yellow banister downstairs to today's "world of Peavey" and make your own music on some of the world's most sophisticated and coveted sound systems. Test the full Peavey line, including electric guitars, electronic keyboards, amplifiers, and complex studio mixing equipment. Peavey Electronics designed this hands-on space for visitors of all ages. Several guitars are mount-ed on the floor, giving toddlers a chance to pluck away at the taut steel strings.

Cost: Free

Freebies: Copy of *Monitor*, the company magazine.

Videos Shown: 18-minute video details company history and goals; 35-minute optional video covers history until the 1992 Peavey family's acceptance of the Literacy Award at the White House.

Reservations Needed: No, except for groups of 50 or more.

Days and Hours: Open Mon–Wed and Fri 10:00 AM–4:00 PM, Sat–Sun 1:00 PM–4:00 PM. Closed holidays.

Plan to Stay: 1 hour for museum and playing instruments, plus time in gift shop.

Minimum Age: None

Disabled Access: 5 steps to first-floor historical exhibits. Staircase down to video theater and hands-on equipment display.

Group Requirements: Groups of 50 or more need reservations; call (601) 484-1460.

Special Information: Set up for self-guided tours, but guided visits can be arranged.

Gift Shop: Axcess shop sells Peavey-related items, from $2 key chains to $100-plus satin "tour" jackets. Open center hours. Catalog available from (800) 752-7896.

Directions: From Jackson, take I-20 East through Meridian as it changes to I-20/59. Take Exit 157B for Hwy. 45 North. Take the first exit (for Sonny Montgomery Industrial Park). At bottom of ramp, turn right onto Marion Russel Rd. After you cross railroad track (about 1 mile), turn right into the center's parking lot.

Nearby Attractions: The Jimmie Rodgers Museum (Meridian is the birthplace of Jimmie Rodgers, the father of country music); Annual Jimmie Rodgers Country Music Festival; Grand Opera House of Mississippi (tours of "The Lady" are available; call 601-693-LADY); Merrehope Mansion; Dunn's Falls Water Park; the Dentzel Carousel.

Viking Range ~ *cooking equipment*

111 Front Street
Greenwood, MS 38930
(601) 455-1200

VIKING RANGE CORPORATION

What might you find in the homes of many rich and famous, on the set of "Friends," or in the White House? A Viking Range, manufactured in the heart of the Mississippi Delta. On the tour, it's hard to determine which is more surprising—the vast array of products, colors, and sizes available or the fact that such a big company manufactures the majority of its parts right at this local, small-town plant. In 1983 founder Fred E. Carl Jr. developed the first commercial-type range for home use when he wanted a heavy-duty range for his new house. The cooktops, ovens, ventilation products, dishwashers, and waste disposers the company added to its line in recent years can be found in the homes of celebrities and professional cooks alike.

In the receiving area, forklifts heave large quantities of raw materials such as sheet steel and wiring into the factory. The Vipros turret punch press, one of the company's newest, most powerful, and most impressive machines, loads the sheet metal mechanically onto the press table. Silver shavings drop soundlessly to the floor as the machine's sharp prongs drill screw holes. Intricate software allows the Vipros to seem as if it runs on its own. Once the Vipros makes enough of one part, it automatically makes the required number of another part. Hydraulics keep this giant press running more quietly than you would expect.

After the drilling stage, other machines fold the shiny metal with ease. You'll recognize the oven bases as the shaped pieces move down the assembly line. Because they're built from the bottom up, each oven part fits into the next: the sides into the base, the windows into the front door panel, the cut-outs for the burners and knobs into the stove top.

The expertise required by the workers themselves, who wire the ovens for their features, is as impressive as the machines. Reaching into the cavity of a nearly completed oven, the workers intricately connect wires of different shapes and sizes. With the insides in place, workers add the exteriors. Since they are custom-made, the assembled appliances vary from one to the next. In vibrant shades such as plum, green, and blue, as well as stainless steel, the ovens resemble sculptured works of art inspiring enough to make you want to fire up the burner and cook something!

Cost: Free
Freebies: No
Video Shown: No
Reservations Needed: Yes. Call 1 day in advance.
Days and Hours: Mon–Fri 8:30 AM–3:30 PM. Closed holidays. No production during the weeks of Thanksgiving, Christmas, and July 4th.
Plan to Stay: 45 minutes
Minimum Age: 12
Disabled Access: Yes
Group Requirements: Groups over 10 people should call 2 weeks in advance. No maximum group size.
Special Information: No photography
Gift Shop: No
Directions: From Memphis, take I-55 South to Grenada. Take Hwy. 7 South to Greenwood, and turn right on Hwy. 82. Take Main St. exit. Bear right onto Main St. and turn right on Market St. Bear left at traffic light onto Medart Rd. Factory is on left in about 1 mile. From Jackson, take I-55 North to Winona. Take Hwy. 82 West to Greenwood, and take Main St. exit. Bear right onto Main St. Turn right on Market St. and bear left at traffic light onto Medart Rd. Factory is on your left in about 1 mile.
Nearby Attractions: Historic Cotton Row District of Greenwood; Mississippi Delta; Cottonlandia Museum; Florewood Plantation State Park.

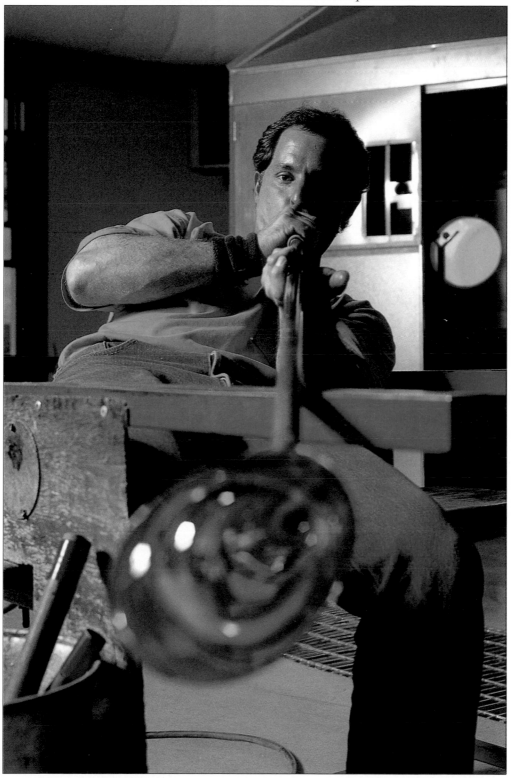

At the Windsor, Vermont, facility, a Simon Pearce craftsman blows glass through a blowpipe.

See description on page 310

During your Amon Orchards tour, sample the juiciest, freshest cherries you've ever tasted.

Visitors enjoy the wide selection of fresh fruit, baked goods, and gourmet cherry products at Amon Orchards in Traverse City, Michigan.

See description on page 139

Boehms Chocolates, Washington

Phone: (425) 392-6652 • Website: www.forsuccess.com/chocolate/boehms

Photo:©Journal American

Candymakers show off the sweet stuff at Boehms Chocolates in Issaquah, Washington.

See description on page 318

Tillamook Cheese, Oregon

Phone: (503) 842-4481

Using three lines, Tillamook Cheese in Tillamook, Oregon, packages 120,000 pounds of cheese every day.

See description on page 255

Bacardi Corporation, Puerto Rico

Phone: (787) 788-1500 • Website: www.bacardi.com

A sculpture commemorating the 50th anniversary of Bacardi stands in front of the distillery building in Cataño, Puerto Rico.

Wide oak barrels are used for the aging of Bacardi rum.

See description on page 279

A 2½-acre cactus garden adds color to the Henderson, Nevada, home of Ethel M Chocolates.

Above, candies move through a chocolate enrober for the delicious chocolate coating.

See description on page 203

BMW, South Carolina

Discover BMW's tradition through a unique display of a championship motorcycle and Formula I, II, and M3 race cars.

Learn about BMW through its heritage, environmental initiatives, and state-of-the-art technology displays at the BMW Zentrum in Greer, South Carolina.

See description on page 282

Phone: (888) TOUR-BMW • Website: www.bmwzentrum.com

Self-directed work teams create and adapt products in BMW's Assembly Department in Greer, South Carolina.

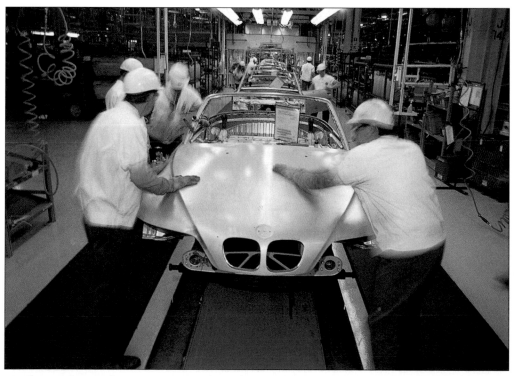

Craftsmanship and communication heavily outweigh automation at the BMW Body Shop.

See description on page 282

Cranberry World, Massachussets

Phone: (508) 747-2350 • *Website: www.oceanspray.com*

Photo: © David C. Bitters

Taste cranberry treats in the demonstration kitchen at Cranberry World Visitors Center.

Photo: © Ocean Spray Cranberries, Inc.

You can view cranberry harvesting by video at Cranberry World Visitors Center in Plymouth, Massachussetts, or in person at the annual Cranberry Harvest Festival.

See description on page 131

Phone: (702) 566-7160 • Website: www.lasvegasnv.com/cranworldwest

Different flavors of warm fruit juice flow before your eyes through a maze of pipes at Cranberry World West.

Carina the Cran-Cran girl greets you at Cranberry World West in Henderson, Nevada.

See description on page 202

Phone: (800) 765-1055 • Website: www.budweiser.com

The historic Brew House offers tour guests a nostalgic look at turn-of-the-century elegance.

See description on page 193

Learn about Anheuser-Busch's Beechwood aging process in the Lager Cellar.

A worker inspects bottles on a high-speed packaging line that fills thousands of cans and bottles every minute.

See descriptions on pages 193 and 206

Heads of props await repair as a 15-foot torso of Cleopatra stands nearby at Mardi Gras World float factory in New Orleans, Louisiana.

Alice In Wonderland's rabbit gets the finishing touches from a Mardi Gras World artist in the Prop Shop.

See description on page 115

Phone: (404) 827-2300 • Website: www.cnn.com/StudioTour

CNN's newsroom floor is bustling with activity as reporters and researchers constantly receive reports of world events.

A guide demonstrates how "blue screens" are used in weather reporting on CNN's tour in Atlanta, Georgia.

See description on page 56

Bourbon ages in white oak barrels for at least eight years at the Wild Turkey Distillery.

Master Distiller Jimmy Russell samples a batch of bourbon at the Wild Turkey Distillery in Lawrenceburg, Kentucky.

See description on page 114

A polisher puts the finishing touches on a Custom Shop D-45 with pickguard and bridge inlays at Martin Guitar in Nazareth, Pennsylvania.

See description on page 266

In autumn, the Mead mill is surrounded by brilliant New England foliage.

The No. 15 Paper Machine at Mead in Rumford, Maine, produces over 500 tons of paper per day and is as long as a football field!

See description on page 123

At Vermont Teddy Bear's whimsical factory, bears come to life before your eyes.

Fill your hungry teddy bear with special ingredients at Vermont Teddy Bear's "Make A Friend For Life" fun factory in Shelburne, Vermont.

See description on page 312

Movie posters in the atrium gallery in Port Washington, Wisconsin, show some of the famous feet cushioned by Allen-Edmonds' shoes.

Pulling the upper over the last is one of the 212 steps involved in making an Allen-Edmonds shoe.

See description on page 335

Phone: (205) 507-3300 • Website: www.mercedes-benz.com

The Mercedes-Benz Visitors Center in Vance, Alabama, houses entertaining exhibits on the company's history, products, technology, and commitment to safety.

The final product of the M-Class plant is this sporty yet comfortable four-wheel-drive Mercedes-Benz M-Class All-Activity Vehicle.

See description on page 4

Each conch machine's granite rollers mix cocoa butter, sugar, milk, and liquid chocolate to make 10,000 pounds of chocolate paste at the Hershey's factory in Oakdale, California.

A Hershey's Kiss is one of the world's most recognizable shapes.

See description on page 23

Phone: (502) 582-1900

A potter pulls a handle and attaches it to a mug at Louisville Stoneware in Louisville, Kentucky.

Clay pitchers are painted by hand before being fired in kilns at high temperatures.

See description on page 106

Phone: (707) 428-2838 • Website: www.jellybelly.com

Herman Goelitz Rowland, a fourth-generation member of the Goelitz candy-making family, stands in front of acres of Jelly Belly jelly beans.

Kids get a hands-on tour of Jelly Belly's factory in Fairfield, California.

See description on page 22

Phone: (808) 943-8383 • Website: www.mauidivers.com

A designer carefully finishes the detailing on a black coral pendant at Maui Divers in Honolulu, Hawaii.

Precious black coral, diamond, and 14-carat gold make up this Yin and Yang ring.

See description on page 62

Basic Brown Bear Factory, California
Phone: (415) 626-0781 • *Website: www.basicbrownbear.com*

Merilee Woods, owner, stands with her furry friends at Basic Brown Bear.

You can stuff your own bear on a tour at Basic Brown Bear in San Francisco, Calfornia.

See description on page 14

Phone: (816) 274-5672 • Website: www.hallmark.com

Photo: ©Hallmark Cards, Inc.

A press operator demonstrates the process of foil stamping on greeting cards.

Photo: ©Hallmark Cards, Inc.

You can push a button to make your own bow at the Hallmark Visitors Center in Kansas City, Missouri.

See description on page 195

Freshly peeled potatoes become tasty potato chips, which are packed on this line at Herr's in Nottingham, Pennsylvania.

Visitors can see pretzels shaped and then baked to a golden brown at Herr's.

See description on page 262

Castle Springs, New Hampshire

Phone: (800) 729-2468 • Website: www.castlesprings.com

Castle in the Clouds in Moultonborough, New Hampshire, is nestled in the Ossipee Mountains above Lake Winnipesauke.

See description on page 208

Mack Trucks, Pennsylvania

Phone: (610) 709-3566 • Website: www.macktrucks.com

A Mack dump truck hits the road.

See description on page 264

An RV comes off the final assembly line at Winnebago's 200-acre factory in Forest City, Iowa.

The Luxor hits the open road headed for a factory tour.

See description on page 93

Phone: (503) 648-4181 • *Website: www.rodgerscorp.com*

Rodgers Instrument Corporation is known for its classic church organs, theater organs, and instruments for the studio and home.

Rodgers employees build traditional organs and contemporary keyboards in Hillsboro, Oregon.

See description on page 254

Miller Brewing, Wisconsin

Phone: (414) 931-BEER • Website: www.mgdtaproom.com

Huge, gleaming brew kettles are one of the tour sights at Miller Brewing in Milwaukee, Wisconsin.

See description on page 341

Rowena's, Virginia

Phone: (800) 980-CAKE • Website: www.infi.net/rowenas

Almond Pound Cake and Lemon Curd are made by Rowena's in Norfolk, Virginia.

See description on page 315

Phone: (607) 974-8271 • Website: ww2.corning.com/cgc

Demonstrations are held seven days a week at the new Steuben demonstration area at Corning Glass Center in Corning, New York.

Corning Glass Center houses a world-famous collection of more than 26,000 glass objects.

See description on page 215

The bottling line at McIlhenny Company's Tabasco Brand Pepper Sauce factory is a colorful sight, along with Jungle Gardens and Bird City on Avery Island.

See description on page 120

Anheuser-Busch

Budweiser beer

12th and Lynch Streets
St. Louis, MO 63118
(314) 577-2626

This tour of Anheuser-Busch's headquarters and birthplace (founded 1852) puts a face on the world's largest brewer. The facility offers historical and architectural delights that nicely complement the beer-making. As the tour guide leads you from the tour center to the Budweiser Clydesdale stables to the lager cellar Brew House and Bevo Packaging Plant, a sense of history and the smell of hops surround you. Three of the red-brick buildings are on the National Historic Register.

As part of the second fermentation, Budweiser uses the beechwood-aging process, which distinguishes it from other major brewers. In the lager cellar, stainless steel lager tanks have layers of beechwood chips spread on the bottoms. The chips provide more surface area for the action of the yeast, which settles on the chips and continues to work until the beer is completely fermented. Each of these tanks holds enough beer to fill 200,000 six-packs.

The historic 6-story Brew House, with its elaborate trim and dominant clock tower, is a tour favorite. Built in 1891, complete with gleaming copper kettles, ornate wrought-iron railings, and hop vine chandeliers from the 1904 World's Fair, the Brew House maintains a nostalgic feel even after a multimillion-dollar renovation. Enjoy a multimedia presentation on the brewing process before viewing the mash tanks, brew kettles, straining tanks, and control room, all essential tools in brewing fine beer.

It's the 10-foot-tall, whimsical fox sculptures perched on each corner of the Bevo Packaging Plant that really amuse you. The foxes are munching on chicken legs and drinking mugs of Bevo, a nonalcoholic cereal beverage manufactured between 1916 and 1929. The Bevo Packaging Plant's 27 acres of floor space made it the world's largest bottling facility under one roof when it was built in 1917. It can produce 16 million 12-ounce beers per day. Inside the building, watch the bottles and cans speed through the machines that rinse, fill, cap, label, and package them.

Cost: Free

Freebies: Beer, soda, and snacks.

Video Shown: 2 6-minute videos on brewing process and packaging.

Reservations Needed: No, except for groups of 15 or more.

Days and Hours: January through May and September through December, Mon–Sat 9:00 AM–4:00 PM; June through August, Mon–Sat 9:00 AM–5:00 PM. Closed select holidays.

Plan to Stay: 2 hours for tour, video, and sampling, plus time for shopping and Tour Center (look for the display of beautiful beer steins).

Minimum Age: Under age 18 must be accompanied by adult.

Disabled Access: Yes

Group Requirements: Groups larger than 15 should call 1 week ahead. No maximum group size.

Special Information: Anheuser-Busch also gives tours in Columbus, OH; Merrimack, NH; Williamsburg, VA; Jacksonville, FL; Fort Collins, CO; and Fairfield, CA. For general information on all tours, call (800) 765-1055. See page 206 for feature on Merrimack, NH, tour.

Gift Shop: BUDWORLD sells logoed items and beer memorabilia, including T-shirts, mirrors, dart boards, beer steins, and a Bud can–shaped cooler. Open Mon–Sat 9:00 AM –5:30 PM. June through August open 9:00 AM –6:30 PM. Closed select holidays.

Directions: Take I-55 to Arsenal St. exit. Follow signs to Tour Center (on 12th and Lynch Sts.).

Nearby Attractions: St. Louis area attractions include McDonnell Douglas Museum (see page 200), Grant's Farm, St. Louis Zoo, Gateway Arch, Union Station, Botanical Gardens, St. Louis Science Center, and National Bowling Hall of Fame and Museum. Tour Center front desk has information sheet with directions and hours for nearby attractions.

See color photos, pages 170–171

Chrysler *minivans and pickup trucks*

1050 Dodge Drive
Fenton, MO 63026
(314) 343-2418

Since Chrysler introduced the minivan to the market in 1984, its minivans have earned many awards and the number-one position in sales. The Dodge Caravan was *Motor Trend* magazine's 1996 "Car of the Year." Since 1987, Chrysler's St. Louis Assembly Plant II has built the long-wheelbase minivan. In 1992 this factory became the first North American assembly plant to successfully initiate a three-shift schedule, operating three seven-hour production shifts five days a week and two nine-hour shifts on Saturday. (Plant I builds the Dodge Ram pickup truck.)

Building the skeleton frame in the metal shop starts the production process. Parts arrive by train and truck from the stamping plant. Fenders, doors, and roofs are attached on the assembly line to create the gray frame. Chrysler is proud of its extensive use of robotics. The plant underwent a $578-million renovation to launch a new generation of minivans in January 1995 and increased the number of robots to over 400. Look for the robotic arm that uses large suction cups to pick up the roof panel and, with workers' guidance, place it precisely. The minivan then heads through a tunnel that automatically welds the roof joints.

Sparks fly when the entire frame heads down a row of robots, each with an assigned place to spot-weld the body frame. Once the frame is assembled and its dimensions tested, it receives a primer-coat bath. The entire frame is immersed in 73,600 gallons of paint (resembling a whale as it's lowered into the vat), then moved through the rinsers. By negatively charging the body and positively charging the paint, the primer bakes into the frame's smallest corners.

From the paint area, the shiny frame travels through the assembly lines that bring the minivans to life. Some lines install the interior electric systems; others, the engine and axles, and ergonomic robot arms help with steps such as seat and windshield installation. Ask the tour guide to explain the Joint UAW/Chrysler Product Quality Improvement Partnership and point out worker suggestions that have been successfully implemented. Notice the overhead signs at different assembly stations that say "Critical Buzz, Squeak, and Rattle Operation." At the tour's end, peek into the test booth where the minivan "travels" (on rollers) up to 65 miles per hour, while a worker analyzes the electrical systems, transmission, and engine.

Cost: Free

Freebies: Brochure with production pictures and statistics.

Video Shown: No

Reservations Needed: Yes. Company prefers that individuals and families join a scheduled group tour.

Days and Hours: Mon–Fri based on tour guides' schedules. Closed holidays, Christmas week, and one week in summer, usually at the end of July.

Plan to Stay: 1½–2 hours for tour.

Minimum Age: 13

Disabled Access: Wheelchairs and walkers not allowed on factory floor. Special arrangements can be made for physically challenged if a cart is available.

Group Requirements: Groups of 10 or more get a plant retiree as a tour guide. No maximum group size with 1 week's advance notice.

Special Information: You'll walk at least 1 mile on tour. No photography.

Gift Shop: No

Directions: From I-44 West, take Exit 275 onto North Highway Dr., which runs parallel to I-44. Turn right before overpass onto Marez Ln. Plant entrance is last driveway on left. You must drive a UAW-made car to park in the visitors' lot.

Nearby Attractions: St. Louis attractions, including Anheuser-Busch (Budweiser) brewery tour (see page 193), about 25 minutes away. Limited tours at Ford plant in Hazelwood (call 314-731-6365).

Hallmark Visitors Center ~ *greeting cards*

Crown Center Complex
25th and Grand Avenue
Kansas City, MO 64141
(816) 274-5672

Hallmark's slogan, "When You Care Enough to Send the Very Best," applies to its visitors center. You're surrounded by the world of Hallmark (founded by Joyce Hall in 1910) as you walk through 14 exhibits that tell the story of the world's largest greeting-card company. Your activities vary: See a 40-foot historical timeline with memorabilia from Hallmark's history intertwined with world events; view classic commercials or clips from Hallmark Hall of Fame television dramas; watch a Hallmark technician create dies for die-cutting or embossing cards; and even make your own star-bow on the automatic bow-making machine.

One of the most popular exhibits expresses the creativity involved in developing new cards. Step through a giant keyhole into a room filled with six-foot pencils, markers, brushes, paint tubes, and jars, all on a floor that resembles an artist's drawing board. You'll think you're on the movie set from *Honey, I Shrunk the Kids*. Sit on oversized paint jars and view a video on how Hallmark artists draw, letter, paint, sculpt, and stitch designs.

The color separation display explains how Hallmark turns the original artwork into a product. Hallmark plant employees operate two presses that produce greeting cards: one applies colored foil, and the other cuts unusual card shapes.

Exhibits also show other Hallmark products, including gift wrap, art supplies, Christmas ornaments, personal expression software, collectibles, and Crayola crayons. Hallmark employees' affection for company founder Hall shows in a display of Christmas trees that employees gave Hall from 1966 to 1982. Each tree's decorations reflect a theme of importance to the company during that year. To experience Hallmark's international appeal (cards sell in more than 100 countries), rub Snoopy's nose on one of the cards to hear birthday greetings in 12 languages.

Cost: Free

Freebies: Postcard and a bow

Video Shown: 13-minute film, "Coming from the Heart," follows Hallmark artists and photographers during a week-long creativity retreat on a picturesque rural-Missouri farm. Shown on the hour. Throughout the visitors center are other short videos on topics related to the exhibits.

Reservations Needed: No, except for groups of 10 or more.

Days and Hours: Mon–Fri 9:00 AM–5:00 PM and Sat 9:30 AM–4:30 PM. Closed Thanksgiving, Christmas, and New Year's. Also usually closed the first 2 weeks in January for yearly renovations.

Plan to Stay: 1 hour for exhibits, plus time for videos.

Minimum Age: None

Disabled Access: Yes

Group Requirements: Escorted tours available for groups of 10 or more people. Groups should make reservations 2 to 4 weeks in advance. School/ youth groups need 1 adult for every 7 children. Call (816) 274-3613.

Special Information: Braille available on all major exhibits. Some Hallmark Production Centers conduct tours by advance reservation; check with visitors center.

Gift Shop: Not in visitors center. The closest of the 21,000 independently owned Hallmark stores is in Crown Center.

Directions: Located in Crown Center Complex, about 1 mile south of downtown Kansas City. Take Grand Ave. to 25th St. and park in the Crown Center Parking Garage. Proceed to third level of Crown Center shops. The visitors center is located outside Halls department store.

Nearby Attractions: Hoechst Marion Roussel Visitor Center (see page 196); Ford tour (call 816-459-1356); Kaleidoscope children's interactive exhibit (reservations only, call 816-274-8301); Arabia Steamboat Museum; Toy and Miniature Museum.

See color photos, page 185

Hoechst Marion Roussel ◁∿▷ *pharmaceuticals*

Visitors Center
10245 Marion Park Drive
Kansas City, MO 64137
(816) 966-7333 / (816) 966-4253

This company museum captures the spirit of Ewing Marion Kauffman, founder of Marion Laboratories, and the success of the company (Mr. K's company merged with Merrell Dow Pharmaceuticals in 1989, which was acquired by Hoescht). Colorful, interactive displays show how this company began and grew and how pharmaceutical companies develop and manufacture new drugs. Like many newer corporate visitors centers, this one extensively uses clever videos and larger-than-life displays to explain complex topics.

In the spacious wood and slate-tiled entranceway, spend a few minutes looking at the company's products and history. Unless you're a doctor or pharmacist, you may not be aware of the company's range of products. In the room on manufacturing, you'll almost think you're in a factory. A mannequin stands inside the entranceway and floor-to-ceiling pictures show machines and workers making, packaging, and distributing the company's drugs. To discover more about each of these processes, such as tablet and capsule production, you simply push a button to see a video.

The drug research and development room depicts the stages through which a compound moves to become a new drug. The product lifeline begins with displays about drug sources, such as plants. The lifeline continues to scenes of post-FDA-approval activities. In a unique exhibit called the "Product Experience," you discover how an antihistamine works to control allergies. The exhibit combines animation with sound-and-surround visual techniques.

Another portion of the Visitors Center is devoted to Mr. K. This airy, windowed gallery overlooks a small lake and landscaped grounds. You can "interview" Mr. K by selecting from a menu of questions and viewing his refreshing responses on video. Additional displays highlight specific Kauffman Foundation projects, including Project Choice, Project Star, and Project Early. As you look at the display of his actu-

al office, with the pipe on his desk, the private phone line for baseball business, and the frayed black chairs, you understand a little more of this company's roots.

Cost: Free
Freebies: Postcards
Video Shown: At start of visit, 8-minute video on company and its products. Other videos on a different topics throughout the museum.
Reservations Needed: Yes
Days and Hours: Tue and Thur 8:00 AM–4:30 PM. Other days available. Closed holidays and week between Christmas and New Year's.
Plan to Stay: 1 hour
Minimum Age: None, but company suggests 5th grade and some interest in science.
Disabled Access: Yes
Group Requirements: 1 week's advance notice required for groups larger than 25. No maximum group size.
Special Information: Ask the Visitors Center director for materials on Ewing Marion Kauffman Foundation.
Gift Shop: No
Directions: Take I-435 to exit for Hickman Mills Rd. Turn left at exit. Turn left on 103rd St. and left again onto Marion Park Dr. After the guard station, the Visitors Center is on your immediate right (follow the lake). Can also take Wornall Rd. to Bannister Rd., which is 95th St. Turn left onto Bannister to Hickman Mills Rd. Turn right on Hickman Mills Rd. and follow above directions.
Nearby Attractions: NCAA Visitors Center (call 913-339-0000); Country Club Plaza; Kansas City Board of Trade (816-753-7500); Ford Motor Plant tour (816-459-1356); Kansas City's downtown area attractions, including Hallmark Visitors Center (see page 195), about 20 miles away.

McCormick Distilling

One McCormick Lane   *bourbon, whiskey, and*
Weston, MO 64098   *other alcoholic beverages*
(816) 640-2276 / (888) 640-4041

As the oldest continually active distillery in the U.S.A. and the only distillery west of the Mississippi, McCormick's history runs deep—so deep that you'll enter the cave where founder Ben Holladay (1856) stored his whiskey. Meriwether Lewis and William Clark charted the property's limestone springs, a crucial ingredient in fine whiskey, during their 1804 expedition. The springs and distillery are on the National Historic Register.

In 1985 McCormick stopped distilling here and focused the facility's activities on bottling, aging, and distribution. The tour visits the now-quiet fermentation and still rooms, with their 17,000-gallon fermentation tanks and 46-foot worn copper still, while your guide describes whiskey-making. You can imagine what it was like when mash bubbled in the fermenters and alcohol vapors rose in the still condenser.

It's a peaceful walk up to three silver-painted aging warehouses, set on a small hill to capture cool breezes. In the entrance, the sweet whiskey aroma hits you. Whiskey ages in rows of white-oak barrels on the rack house's six floors. Changes in weather make the liquid expand and contract into the barrels' charcoal linings, flavoring and coloring the whiskey while it's aging.

In the bottling house McCormick packages all of its products, including whiskey, bourbon, gin, brandy, rum, vodka, and tequila. With up to three lines in operation it's often a noisy place. From a small raised platform, watch the synchronized bottling process. Bottles travel single-file to the filling unit, where they are injected with liquor and spun around to the capping machine. A suction device affixes brand labels. The rattling sound comes from the case-packing machine, which operates and sounds like a pin-setter in a bowling alley, lifting filled bottles from the conveyer belt and mechanically guiding them into even rows in cardboard cartons.

Cost: Free

Freebies: Samples (10¢) for visitors who have aged at least 21 years.

Video Shown: 10-minute slide show on distillery's history and company's products.

Reservations Needed: Yes

Days and Hours: *While company welcomed visitors during our research and personal visit for the first edition, it is expanding and has needed to put tours on hold.* Call about current status. Production video shown at Country Store.

Plan to Stay: 45 minutes for tour and slide show, plus time for pavilion, picnic area, and Country Store.

Minimum Age: None

Disabled Access: The cave and first level of fermentation and still house are accessible. Small flight of stairs into the bottling house and warehouse.

Group Requirements: Groups larger than 15 should call at least 3 days in advance. No maximum group size.

Special Information: Best time to see production is Mon–Fri before 3:00 PM, during bottling house operation.

Gift Shop: Country Store in downtown Weston on Main Street (call 816-640-3149) sells memorabilia and logoed items, including key chains, T-shirts, jackets, long johns and shot glasses, and all McCormick Distilling products. Open year-round Tue–Sat 11:00 AM–6:00 PM, Sun 12:00 PM–5:00 PM.

Directions: From Kansas City, take I-29 North to Platte City exit (Exit 20). Go west on Hwy. 92 to Hwy. 273 West. Follow signs to Weston. When Hwy. 273, Hwy. 45, and Rt. JJ join at stop sign and blinking light, continue straight and you'll be on Rt. JJ West. Distillery is ahead on the left.

Nearby Attractions: Pirtle's Winery (call 816-386-5728); Weston's historic attractions include Weston Historical Museum and restored 1840s downtown area.

Purina Farms   *pet food*

Ralston Purina Company
Route 2
Gray Summit, MO 63039
(314) 982-3232

From its 1894 beginnings as a horse- and mule-feed store to its position today as the world's largest producer of pet food, Ralston Purina Company remains focused on animal care and nutrition. Located on the grounds of the oldest and largest animal nutrition center in the world, Purina Farms wants visitors to gain a greater appreciation and understanding of their pets. While the Visitor Center has a few displays about Ralston Purina and its products, the complex resembles a family-oriented petting zoo more than a promotion-laden company museum.

Since the company celebrated its 100-year anniversary in 1994, Purina Farms has been adding new exhibits. A new timeline will trace the company's history and product development. Another will play classic Ralston Purina commercials for products such as Dog Chow, the nation's leading dry dog food. An exhibit installed in 1996 lets you experience the sights and sounds of a pet food factory. Interactive displays teach the basics of pet nutrition and the remarkable sensory and physical abilities of domestic animals. Scent boxes help you experience how a dog smells things, while other displays show the differences between your vision and that of dogs and cats.

The Farm Animal Barn contains sheep, cows, horses, hogs, rabbits, and turkeys. Roll up your sleeves here to romp in the hayloft, pull a rope to determine your "horsepower," pet piglets, or milk a cow. Inside the Pet Center, home for different breeds of dogs, cats, puppies, and kittens, you'll see cats lounging and climbing on a five-story Victorian mansion, complete with special windowsills, stairways, and mantelpieces. Petting windows and outdoor areas for dogs let you cuddle and play with them. The Pet Center also features videos and newsletters with tips on pet care. You leave having learned more about your favorite pets and about Ralston Purina's efforts to keep them well-fed.

Cost: Free, except for some special events.

Freebies: Brochures on pet care and the company's products are available by request from front desk.

Videos Shown: 2 videos shown in a converted 48-foot grain barn: 1 provides a brief history of Ralston Purina; the second captures the special role animals play in human lives. Other short videos shown at selected exhibits.

Reservations Needed: Yes, although they can usually accommodate a large number of visitors.

Days and Hours: Open mid-March to mid-November only. Spring and Fall: Wed–Fri 9:30 AM–1:00 PM, Sat–Sun 9:30 AM–3:00 PM. Summer: Tue–Sun 9:30 AM–3:30 PM. Closed holidays.

Plan to Stay: 2 hours for displays in main building, videos, Farm Animal Barn, animal demonstrations, and Pet Center, plus additional time for fish ponds, children's play areas, picnic area, and gift shop.

Minimum Age: None

Disabled Access: Yes

Group Requirements: No maximum group size. Requests 1 week's advance notice for large groups.

Special Information: Special events scheduled throughout the year include Kids' Catfish Derby, St. Louis City Police Canine Training, and the very popular Haunted Hayloft. Call for schedule.

Gift Shop: Sells animal-decorated items including mugs, cards, pencils, and banks; also logoed clothes and hats. Open same hours as visitors center.

Directions: From St. Louis, take I-44 West. Pass Six Flags Over Mid-America. Take the Gray Summit exit and turn right onto Hwy. 100. Turn left on Country Road MM. Follow signs to Purina Farms.

Nearby Attractions: Shaws Arboretum; Six Flags Over Mid-America.

Website: www.ralston.com/farm.html

Play with dogs and cats at Purina Farms' Pet Center in Gray Summit, Missouri.

Purina Farms includes the Farm Animal Barn, Pet Center, theater, and exhibits.

McDonnell Douglas   ⟿ *airplanes, missiles, and spacecraft*

Prologue Room
McDonnell Boulevard and Airport Road
St. Louis, MO 63134
(314) 232-5421

McDonnell Douglas Corporation (MDC) calls its company museum the Prologue Room, after William Shakespeare's comment that "what is past is prologue." To MDC, its past achievements are not history but the beginning of each new technical advancement. As you stand on the steps overlooking the museum room, you'll realize MDC's part in aviation's past, present, and future. Models of commercial planes, missiles, spacecraft, and fighter jets of all sizes and colors seem to be everywhere.

MDC aircraft downed every enemy fighter shot down during Operation Desert Storm. With this track record, the display of military planes will pique your curiosity. A wide, oval glass case shows the evolution of MDC military planes from aviation's golden age in the 1930s to the most current technology. In the center of the oval are 1/7th scale models of the F/A-18 Hornet, F-15 Eagle, and AV-8B Harrier combat fighters, and the AH-64 Apache helicopter. A glass oval in the front of the museum has a similar display for the generations of the company's commercial aircraft, from the DC-1 (the first successful commercial passenger plane) to the MD-11.

Although the museum does not show how MDC builds its products, displays do provide a complete history of its aviation products. Aviation buffs can study aircraft and fighter plane lineage charts and display cases depicting MDC's numerous firsts, such as building the first planes to land at the North and South Poles. The center of the museum contains full-size engineering mock-ups of the Mercury and Gemini spacecraft that carried America's early astronauts into space. In the era before computer-aided design, engineers had to build these full-scale models to test the practicality of their hand-drawn designs.

Notice the aviation-art gallery, which features oil paintings by several artists whose work is also displayed in the National Air and Space Museum in Washington, D.C.

You leave understanding how since 1920 MDC products have affected wars' outcomes, made worldwide travel possible, and helped explore the universe.

Cost: Free
Freebies: No
Video Shown: Optional video in gallery area runs for 2 hours. Consists of shorter videos, presenting company history, building of jet fighters, and MDC planes in flight accompanied by music. Can watch 5 minutes of it or the entire video.
Reservations Needed: No, except for groups larger than 20 people.
Days and Hours: June through August only, except for school programs. Tue–Sat 9:00 AM–4:00 PM. Closed July 4th.
Plan to Stay: 45 minutes for museum, plus time for video.
Minimum Age: None, but 6 years old recommended to appreciate displays.
Disabled Access: Yes
Group Requirements: Groups larger than 20 should call ahead to arrange a guided tour. During school year, programs available for 4th, 5th, and 6th graders, with maximum group size of 40.
Special Information: The merger with Boeing may cause changes. Call ahead.
Retail Store: Located 5 minutes away at 5900 N. Lindbergh Blvd. (314-895-7019), corner of Lindbergh and McDonnell Blvd. Sells aviation posters, photos, and models, plus MDC-logoed items including T-shirts, caps, jackets, mugs, and key chains. Open Tue–Fri 10:00 AM –6:00 PM and Sat 10:00 AM–3:00 PM year-round.
Directions: From downtown St. Louis, take I-70 West to I-170 North. Turn left onto Airport Rd. Enter through MDC World Headquarters gate 2 blocks ahead on the left. Look for large black glass building.
Nearby Attractions: St. Louis' downtown attractions, including Anheuser-Busch (Budweiser) Brewery tour (see page 193), are 20 minutes away.

Weaver's ⟶ *snack food*

1600 Center Park Road
Lincoln, NE 68512
(402) 423-6625

Since 1932 Weaver's Potato Chips has used home-grown potatoes to produce some of the most popular potato chips in its area of the Midwest. It started on Mr. Ed Weaver Sr.'s stove with a scrub brush, knife, and kettle. Over 90 percent of Weaver's potato-chip ingredients come straight from Nebraska. Every day 100,000 pounds of these potatoes are trucked into the factory, where they are dumped into large bins and sent on a short trip through the plant, then a longer trip to stores in 14 states as potato chips.

Unlike most snack-food companies, Weaver's currently allows you to view the process up close, sometimes only five feet away from the machines, instead of seeing it from an observation deck or overhead walkway. You can watch as the whole, uncooked potatoes jump into the washers for a hot bath and scrub-down (they always scrub, rather than peel, the potatoes to retain the vitamins). The clean potatoes are then sent to the slicers, where razor-sharp blades quickly slice the potatoes into pieces 1/100th of an inch thin. A spiked roller pierces little holes in the chips to prevent blistering while they cook. The slices move to the 35-foot fryer and cook until crispy. You and the cooked chips then move ahead to the packaging room.

The potato chips enter a very modern, high-tech piece of chip-making machinery: an optic sorter. Although you will not be able to see this particular process up-close, your tour guide will explain it to you. The optic sorter takes photographs of the chips as they move past the camera's lens. Dark brown, green, and other imperfect potato chips are actually blown off the conveyor by air jets. The rest of the chips move on to the packaging room. Chips are gently conveyed to the sophisticated packaging equipment that automatically weighs, fills, and seals bags. Workers inspect the bags and then hand-pack them into cardboard boxes for storage in the warehouse. Delivery trucks pick them up and deliver them to stores all across the Midwest. Be sure to taste your free sample on the way out.

Cost: Free
Freebies: Half-ounce bag of potato chips.
Video Shown: No, although company plans to include video displays in the future.
Reservations Needed: Yes
Days and Hours: Mon–Thur 9:00 AM–11:00 AM and 12:00 PM–1:30 PM. Closed holidays.
Plan to Stay: 30–40 minutes
Minimum Age: None
Disabled Access: Yes
Group Requirements: Groups larger than 20 people should call 5 days in advance. Groups larger than 20 people will be split into smaller groups.
Special Information: Wear comfortable shoes, since there is a lot of standing and walking on the factory floor. Weaver's plans to expand tour to other production areas, including popcorn, cheese puffs, and Puffins, and possibly to add a visitors center.
Gift Shop: No
Directions: From I-80, exit at Hwy. 2 in Lincoln. Follow Hwy. 2 West to Rt. 77 South. Take second left into the industrial park. Plant is red, white, and blue building on the left.
Nearby Attractions: Sugar Plum Candies tour (call 402-420-1900); Christian Record Services Braille Printer tour (call 402-488-0981); Pendelton Woolen Mills tour 1 hour away in Fremont (call 402-721-6393); State Capitol; University of Nebraska; Chet Ager Nature Walk; Star City Shores; Pioneer Park; Folsom Children's Zoo; Children's Museum.

Cranberry World West

cranberry juice and related products

1301 American Pacific Drive
Henderson, NV 89014
(702) 566-7160

As proponents of factory tours, we love it when companies build new facilities with tours in mind. In 1994 Ocean Spray opened this new $50 million juice-processing and distribution plant with a 10,000-square-foot visitors center and glass observation deck along the bottling line. Your visit combines history, education, a speedy bottling line, and tasty cranberry treats.

The "History of Harvesting" display includes artifacts and antique harvesting equipment. At the wet-harvesting simulation, you can push a button to turn a steel paddle wheel, which would churn up berries in a flooded bog. A 5-foot-tall cut-out berry teaches the fruit's anatomy. One museum highlight is guessing the original years of various Ocean Spray television commercials.

Walk along the 50-foot-long observation window to see the single-serve production line, where 11½-ounce cans or 16-ounce glass bottles are filled. The labeler dresses empty glass bottles with the recognizable blue Ocean Spray logo. Different flavors of warm fruit juice flow through the maze of overhead pipes to the filler machine. On the single-serve line, bottles are filled at the rate of 600 per minute.

Once capped, the bottles twirl their way over the conveyor's rollers through the 30-foot-long cooling machine, which sprays them with a water mist to cool them off. At the end of the line, they're boxed into 24-unit cases and then head up the ramp and out of your sight to be shrink-wrapped. Five wooden kiosks show videos of production steps you can't see, such as the trains delivering fruit juice concentrate or the juice-blending in the blend deck.

Everyone eagerly waits for the last part of the tour—the demonstration kitchen. Most mornings a cook will whip up a cranberry delicacy, such as cranberry chocolate-chip bars or cranberry coffeecake. You'll leave with a mind full of "berry" interesting facts and a stomach full of cranberry treats.

Cost: Free

Freebies: 10 different juice flavors, craisins, baked goods with cranberries, Wellfleet Farms gourmet items and recipe brochure.

Video Shown: 7-minute video, hosted by mascot Carina, covers company history and production. Shown in 100-seat theater.

Reservations Needed: No, except for groups over 10 people that want a tour guide.

Days and Hours: Mon–Sun 9:00 AM–5:00 PM. Demonstration kitchen open same hours, with demonstrations most mornings between 9:30 and 11:00 AM. Plant closed holidays and few days around July 4th and Christmas.

Plan to Stay: 35 minutes for self-guided tour, plus time in gift shop.

Minimum Age: None

Disabled Access: Yes

Group Requirements: Groups over 10 people should call 24 hours in advance for a tour guide.

Special Information: October Cranberry Festival features harvesting and cooking demonstrations, plus a parade. Ocean Spray also has a visitor center in Plymouth, MA (see page 131).

Gift Shop: Large gift store sells cranberry baked goods, Wellfleet Farms gourmet items, logoed clothing, cranberry glass, and cranberry novelties such as cranberry rock candy or cranberry bubble bath. The demonstration kitchen takes advance orders for their baked goods. Mail-order list available for Wellfleet Farms items. Open same hours as visitors center.

Directions: From Las Vegas, take I-95 South to Sunset Rd. exit. Turn right onto Sunset Rd., left onto Stephanie St., and left onto American Pacific Dr. Visitors center and plant will be on your right.

Nearby Attractions: Henderson Factory Four includes Cranberry World West, Ethel M Chocolates, Favorite Brands International, and Ron Lee's World of Clowns (see pages 203, 204, and 205); Sunset Station Casino.

See color photos, page 169

Ethel M Chocolates ~~~~• *chocolates*

Two Cactus Garden Drive
Henderson, NV 89014
(702) 433-2500

Only in Las Vegas would a candy factory identify its product lines with flashing red neon signs. Thousands of people come here daily as a diversion from Las Vegas' casinos. Ethel M began in 1981 with one shop and now has around 20 in six states. A tour of the facility not only shows you how premium chocolates are made, but also offers you relaxation in their cactus garden.

Stroll along pathways that meander through the Ethel M cactus garden's 350 varieties of shrubs, succulents, and cacti. Species collected from South Africa, the Red Sea, South America, and Japan are up to 60 years old. The garden blossoms with red, orange, and purple flowers from late March to May, but the stone benches soothe visitors year-round.

Start your self-guided factory tour at the kitchen. From a corridor, observe the chocolate-making through glass windows. Depending on when you visit, you'll see different production steps. Batches of toffee bubble in copper kettles, then workers pour this Almond Butter Krisp onto cooling tables. Butter creams (maybe raspberry or chocolate) or liqueur creams (perhaps Amaretto) swirl slowly in shallow, round mixers. Metal blades stir these candy "centers" until they're smooth.

Further along the corridor, notice the two massive pale-yellow machines. An overhead video explains the processes occuring inside the machines. Empty plastic coin-shaped molds, patterned after a U.S. 1904 Series, methodically move along the conveyor belt through the long machine. Liquid milk or dark chocolate pours through spigots to fill the molds. Some even get mint cream centers. The molds are vibrated to shake out air bubbles, conveyed through a cooling tunnel, and then flipped over to release the chocolate coins. You exit into the retail store, where you are greeted with a sample chocolate of the day.

Cost: Free

Freebies: Sample chocolate of the day.

Videos Shown: Short overhead videos explain chocolate-making.

Reservations Needed: No

Days and Hours: Mon–Sun 8:30 AM–7:00 PM. Closed Christmas. No production for 1 week in July, but can visit cactus garden and view videos.

Plan to Stay: 15 minutes for self-guided tour and videos, plus cactus garden and shops.

Minimum Age: None

Disabled Access: Yes

Group Requirements: Can accommodate very large groups; those larger than 200 people need to call (702) 435-2641 in advance for special tour times.

Special Information: Best times to see production are Mon–Sun 9:00 AM–2:00 PM. Guided cactus garden tours for groups of 10 or more with 1 day's advance notice to (702) 435-2641. Special Christmas season cactus garden display.

Gift Shops: Chocolate Shoppe sells entire Ethel M line—over 60 varieties of chocolates. Offers 1-pound assortment gift boxes, the popular 29-ounce "Taste of Las Vegas" assortment, with a photograph of Las Vegas's neon lights on the cover, and silver "Las Vegas slot machines" filled with chocolate coins. Open same hours as tour. Closed Christmas and shorter hours on Thanksgiving. Catalog available from (800) 4-ETHELM. Cactus Shoppe offers cactus plants, books, and T-shirts.

Directions: From Las Vegas strip, drive east on Tropicana. Turn right onto Mountain Vista. Turn left onto Sunset Way (Green Valley Business Park) and follow signs. From Hoover Dam, take Boulder Hwy. to Sunset Rd. Turn left onto Sunset Rd. Turn right onto Sunset Way. Follow above directions.

Nearby Attractions: Henderson Factory Four includes Ethel M chocolates, Cranberry World West, Favorite Brands International, and Ron Lee's World of Clowns (see pages 202, 204, and 205); Sunset Station Casino.

See color photos, page 165

Favorite Brands International

1180 Marshmallow Lane   ⟶   *marshmallows*
Henderson, NV 89015
(702) 564-3878 / (800) 234-2383

Welcome to the magical world of marshmallows, including Marshall, a stuffed 5-foot talking marshmallow, more white than a hospital room or a six-inch snowstorm. Are you surprised that the factory is located on Marshmallow Lane?

In 1895 Kidd & Co. began in a small Chicago store where Albert Kidd produced lemon drops and roasted peanuts. Because of sugar rationing during WWII, the company produced marshmallow creme as a sugar substitute. The company continued to manufacture marshmallow creme until 1978, when it started efficiently making marshmallows, predominantly for private-label brands. In 1996, this fourth-generation, family-owned company was bought by Favorite Brands International, the fourth largest confections company in the U.S. and the largest manufacturer of non-chocolate candies. Favorite Brands International consists of Farley's, Sathers, Kidd & Co., Dae Julie, and the confections division of Kraft Foods, Inc.

Overhead signs briefly explain the process as you take your self-guided tour. In the kitchen, corn syrup and sugar cook in big stainless-steel kettles. A mixture of gelatin and water meet the corn syrup and sugar in another enclosed metal vat, where vanilla flavoring is added. Air is injected to puff up the mixture—marshmallows consist of 80 percent air.

Walk along the corridor, looking through the glass windows, and follow the marshmallows' journey. The marshmallow mixture is forced through the "extruder," which contains a pipe with a series of holes in it. The resulting ropes of marshmallows slowly flow along the conveyor belt under a snowfall of cornstarch. A blade chops the ropes into uniform lengths, producing bite-size marshmallows. Once cut, the marshmallows drop into a rotating cylindrical tunnel and bounce around to absorb more cornstarch, which prevents sticking and gives them a smooth skin. The conveyor belts and revolving cylindrical drums provide the only silver color in this otherwise entirely white room.

The marshmallows eventually move to the next room for bagging into more than 200 private-label brands. After being heat-sealed for freshness, the plastic bags are hand-packed into boxes and shipped to customers. Whatever the season, you'll leave longing for campfires with roasted marshmallows and s'mores or hot chocolate with mini-marshmallows.

Cost: Free

Freebies: 1½-ounce bag of marshmallows.

Video Shown: No

Reservations Needed: No, except for groups that want guided tour.

Days and Hours: Mon–Sun 9:00 AM–4:30 PM. Closed Thanksgiving, Christmas Eve, Christmas, New Year's, and Easter.

Plan to Stay: 20 minutes for self-guided tour, plus time for gift shop.

Minimum Age: None

Disabled Access: Yes; wheelchair available upon request.

Group Requirements: Groups should call 1 day in advance for guided tour. No maximum group size. However, groups larger than 20 will be split.

Gift Shop: Sells marshmallows and logoed items such as T-shirts, sweatshirts, mugs, and baby clothes. Open same hours as tour.

Directions: From Las Vegas, take I-95 South to Sunset exit. Turn left on Sunset and right on Gibson Rd. Turn right onto Mary Crest Rd. and continue onto Marshmallow Ln. Look for building with copper roof. From Hoover Dam/Boulder City, take Boulder Hwy. to Lake Mead Blvd. Turn left onto Lake Mead and right on Gibson Rd. Turn left onto Mary Crest Rd. Follow above directions.

Nearby Attractions: Henderson Factory Four includes Favorite Brands International, Cranberry World West, Ethel M Chocolates, and Ron Lee's World of Clowns (see pages 202, 203, and 205); Sunset Station Casino; Wholesale Clothing Outlet; Clark County Heritage Museum; Hoover Dam; Lake Mead.

Ron Lee's World of Clowns

330 Carousel Parkway   *clown and*
Henderson, NV 89014   *animation figurines*
(702) 434-1700 / (800) 829-3928

Ron Lee has come a long way since 1976, when he started sculpting animal figures in his garage and playing accordion in a band to support his family. The designer of "Hobo Joe" and other clowns now creates 1¼-inch to 18-inch pewter sculptures of Bugs Bunny, Popeye, Superman, the Flintstones, and other popular animated characters.

When you enter the 30,000-square-foot building, you can take a ride on the beautiful hand-painted 30-foot Chance Carousel that stands inside a glass pavilion in the lobby. Display cases feature 600 goose eggs dressed up as faces of famous Clown Hall of Fame–inductee clowns, such as Emmett Kelly Sr. Notice the 5-by-11-foot miniature amusement park sculpted by Ron Lee.

On the self-guided tour, look through glass windows at nine stations to see the making of figurines by hand. Even though the windows are not presented in the chronological order of the process, videos help you understand the steps. In the hand-painting department, 20 artisans apply colorful acrylic paints to tiny clowns, Looney Tunes characters, and Flintstones. At another window, a worker deburrs the metal casting with a tool that resembles a jeweler's grinding bit on a drill. This process removes the imperfections in the casting.

Walk further down the hallway to see the casting of the pewter sculptures. Watch as two workers pour molten metal into the opening of a spinning, round blue machine that contains the mold for a sculpture. The force of the spinning packs the metal more tightly into the mold. A craftsman hand-cuts molds out of rubber and cooks them in a Vulcanizer at yet another window, while in the spray-booth room, a worker applies a high-gloss clear finish to the figures with a spray gun. In the finishing room, you may see Betty Boop, Snow White, and Bugs Bunny lined up, waiting to be mounted on onyx or to be shipped or numbered. End your tour in the Gallery,

where on most days Ron Lee himself greets visitors and signs autographs amid his numerous colorful creations.

Cost: Museum and tour: free. Carousel ride: $1.
Freebies: None
Videos Shown: Videos explain the process taking place behind each window.
Reservations Needed: No, for self-guided tours. Yes, for guided tours and groups.
Days and Hours: Mon–Fri 8:00 AM–5:00 PM, Sat 9:00 AM–5:00 PM, Sun 11:00 AM–5:00 PM. Usually no production on weekends, but visitors can watch videos. Closed holidays.
Plan to Stay: 20 minutes for tour, plus time for Gallery and Carousel Café.
Minimum Age: None
Disabled Access: Yes
Group Requirements: Groups of 5 or more people can request a tour given by Lara, the resident clown. No maximum group size. Groups of 20 or more should call 1 day in advance.
Special Information: Members of the Ron Lee Collectors Club receive discounts and enjoy the 3-day Ron Lee Convention.
Gallery: Sells Ron Lee figurines as well as items available exclusively at the gallery, such as T-shirts, mugs, and some sculptures. Call (702) 434-3920 or (800) 829-3934 for information. For Carousel Café, call (702) 434-1847. Both open same hours as tour.
Directions: From Las Vegas, take Las Vegas Blvd. south. Turn left onto Warm Springs Rd. and take it into Henderson. Turn right onto Carousel Pkwy. The factory is at the end of the road. From I-95 North, turn left onto Lake Mead Dr. Turn right onto Gibson St. and left onto Warm Springs Rd. Then turn left onto Carousel Pkwy.
Nearby Attractions: Henderson Factory Four includes Ron Lee's World of Clowns, Cranberry World West, Ethel M Chocolates, and Favorite Brands International factory tours (see pages 203, 202, and 204); Las Vegas; Lake Mead.

Anheuser-Busch   *Budweiser beer*

221 Daniel Webster Highway
Merrimack, NH 03054
(603) 595-1202

One of every two beers consumed in America is made by Anheuser-Busch, with this brewery serving all of New England. Of Anheuser-Busch's 12 U.S. breweries, this brewery is in the prettiest setting, located in the picturesque Merrimack Valley. It can package 8 million 12-ounce servings in 24 hours.

Your tour guide will lead you to the brewery, built in 1970, past a life-size replica of a Clydesdale horse. In the brewhouse, a mixture of water and rice or corn fills three stainless-steel mash tanks. Malt enzymes break the starch in the corn or rice into fermentable sugars. Once strained, the remaining liquid ("wort") is boiled and hops are added. After cooling, the liquid is pumped into 45° fermentation cellars. On the ground floor of this four-story cellar, you may see a worker place a layer of beechwood chips in the stainless-steel tanks. These chips provide a surface area on which yeast settles during secondary fermentation.

On your way to the packaging area, notice the 8-foot carved mahogany mural of the Anheuser-Busch corporate trademark. Through glass windows, watch the tightly woven maze of filling lines. Once rinsed, bottles proceed to the rotating bottle-filler. They then speed through capping and labeling to packaging. After the brewery tour, don't miss the Old World–style Clydesdale Hamlet, modeled after an eighteenth-century German Bauernhof. This stable and courtyard are home base for the traveling East Coast Clydesdale eight-horse show hitch. This close-up look at the Budweiser Clydesdales (special photo opportunities first Saturday of each month) is a highlight of the tour.

Cost: Free
Freebies: Beer, soda, and snacks.
Video Shown: If packaging line isn't operating, 2 6-minute films show packaging and brewing processes. Also, 3-minute video about responsible drinking on "Know When to Say When" display.

Reservations Needed: No, except for groups larger than 15.
Days and Hours: November through April: Thur–Mon 10:00 AM–4:00 PM; May, September, October: Mon–Sun 10:00 AM–4:00 PM; June through August: Mon–Sun 9:30 AM–5:00 PM. Call to see if bottling on weekends or holidays. Generally closed day before and day of Thanksgiving, Christmas, and New Year's.
Plan to Stay: 1¼ hours for tour, hospitality room, and Clydesdale Hamlet, plus time for shopping and tour assembly room displays.
Minimum Age: Under age 18 must be accompanied by adult.
Disabled Access: Yes
Group Requirements: Groups larger than 15 should call 1 day in advance. Groups of more than 35 people will be split into smaller groups. No maximum group size.
Special Information: No photography inside brewery. First Saturday of each month is Budweiser Clydesdale Camera Day (1:00 PM–3:00 PM), when you can pose with one of the Clydesdale horses. Tour includes indoor and outdoor walking, and some stairs. See page 193 for St. Louis feature and information about other Anheuser-Busch brewery tours.
Tour Center Store: Sells logoed items, including T-shirts, bathing suits, steins, neon signs, and jackets. Closes 1 hour later than tours.
Directions: From Boston, take I-93 North to I-495 South to Rt. 3 North. In New Hampshire, Rt. 3 becomes Everett Tpk. Get off at Exit 10. At end of ramp, go right. At the next set of lights, turn left onto Daniel Webster Hwy. At the next traffic light, turn right into the brewery. Park in second lot on right. From Rt. 101, take Everett Tpk. South to Exit 10 in Merrimack. At end of ramp, turn left. At the second set of lights, turn left onto Daniel Webster Hwy. Follow to next traffic light and turn right into brewery.
Nearby Attractions: Stonyfield Farm Yogurt and Top of the Tree baking company tours (see pages 210 and 211).

See color photos, page 171

Hampshire Pewter

pewter tableware, ornaments, and gifts

43 Mill Street
Wolfeboro, NH 03894
(603) 569-4944

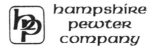

Wolfeboro is the oldest summer resort in the U.S., making it a fitting home for Hampshire Pewter. In fact, current owners Jenine and Bob Steele left their computer-industry jobs for this distinctly small-town setting. Using skilled craftspeople and modern machines, the company has revived the craft of colonial pewter-making. As high-tech manufacturers strive to develop lighter, stronger, and more durable metals, it's good to know that pewter is still valued.

On your guided tour, watch through glass windows as craftspeople mix pure tin with other fine metals to create Queens Metal Pewter. Hampshire Pewter is the only U.S. company to use this special alloy, which consists mostly of tin. Unless you remember your high-school chemistry, you probably don't think of metal as a liquid. But to combine the metals, a worker liquefies them at over 1,900° in a big pot in the back of the small foundry, "cools" the mixture to 600°, then carefully pours it into specially designed, heavy bronze molds to form shapes.

When the temperature cools to 450°, the liquid becomes a solid. The crafter carefully judges when the pewter has solidified enough to be carefully knocked from the mold. The different castings that make up an item, such as the stem and bowl of a goblet, must be soldered together quickly—otherwise the flame's heat may melt or scorch the joined pieces.

In the workshop area, craftspeople called "finishers" then "turn" the pewter piece on a lathe, using chisels to chip away all the rough, gray metal. As a piece spins, the finishers artfully and gently carve the fine details of traditional designs. Delicately holding the pewter pieces, a crafter buffs them on cotton wheels to obtain the soft pewter luster. When you see workers finish the process by stamping each piece with the distinctive "touchmark" that identifies a Hampshire Pewter original, you know that the trademark is well deserved.

Cost: Free

Freebies: No

Video Shown: 8-minute video on history of pewter and close-up views of the Hampshire Pewter production process.

Reservations Needed: No reservations needed June through mid-October, except for groups of 15 or more people. Reservations are needed mid-October through May.

Days and Hours: Memorial Day to Columbus Day: Mon–Fri 10:00 AM, 11:00 AM, 1:00 PM, 2:00 PM, and 3:00 PM. Labor Day to Columbus Day: same schedule except no 1:00 PM tour. Call for hours and reservations mid-October through May. Closed holidays.

Plan to Stay: 20 minutes for tour and video, plus time for gift shop.

Minimum Age: None, but viewing windows start 4 feet up from the ground.

Disabled Access: Yes

Group Requirements: 10 days' advance notice for groups of 15 or more people.

Special Information: No photography

Retail Store: Tabletop Shop sells full selection of 200 different hand-cast pewter items, ranging from teddy bear birthday-candle holders to flower vases and classic goblets. Personal engraving available. Open Mon–Sat 9:00 AM–5:00 PM. Closed Memorial Day, Thanksgiving, Christmas, and New Year's. Downtown store nearby on Main St. has longer hours and is open Sun and holidays. Catalog available from (800) 639-7704.

Directions: From Boston and Southern New Hampshire, take I-95 North. Exit at Rt. 16 North. From Rt. 16, exit at Rt. 11 North. At the traffic circle, take Rt. 28 North. Stay on this road into Wolfeboro. Soon after the center of town, turn right on Mill St. Hampshire Pewter is in a red barn-like building on your right.

Nearby Attractions: Castle Springs bottling plant and castle tour (see page 208); Pepi Herrman Crystal tour (call 603-528-1020); Annalee Dolls Museum (call 800-43-DOLLS); Lake Winnipesaukee; Libby Museum.

Castle Springs

bottled spring water and beer

Route 171
Moultonborough, NH 03254
(603) 476-2352 / (800) 729-2468

You know this isn't your typical factory tour when you drive into the main entrance of this 5,200-acre estate and the road winds you near the "Falls of Song" 50-foot cascading waterfall. When retired RJR Nabisco chairman and CEO J. Paul Sticht bought the property in 1992, he sensed a good tourism and manufacturing opportunity. The company is proud of its 100 percent environmental control and for being selected to produce commemorative bottles with a papal label for the 1995 U.S. visit of Pope John Paul II.

From the visitors center, a short tram ride takes you to the Castle in the Clouds (the one on the label really exists!) nestled in the Ossipee Mountains above Lake Winnipesaukee. Built in 1913 as a retirement home for Thomas Plant, a former shoe-factory owner, the castle was a wedding present for his second wife. Enjoy the self-guided tour of the castle's interior and back patio. Notice that the kitchen's hard rubber floor tiles adhere together like a jigsaw puzzle.

Ride through the woods to one of the natural spring sites. A green roof shades a 2-foot deep, swimming pool-sized spring enclosed with arched Plexiglas. Water is gravity-fed 1 mile away from the source through an underground pipe to the bottling plant 220 feet below the spring.

Another scenic ride takes you to the bottling plant for a quick peek through glass windows at the shiny new filling line. A circular machine rotates clockwise, turning empty bottles upside down and rinsing them. For sparkling water, carbon dioxide is added first. Natural spring water fills 325 small bottles or 175 large bottles per minute. The bottles then pass through the blue capping machine. Caps appear to be magically airlifted and placed onto each bottle.

In 1996 the company opened a microbrewery in a new bottling plant that adjoins the water bottling facilities. Handcrafted premium beers are bottled under the brand name "Lucknow," which was Plant's original name for his castle.

Cost: Brewery and bottling plant tours: free. Combined general admission to grounds, castle tour, and bottling plants: adults, $10; seniors, $9; students, $7; children 10 and under, free. Horseback riding additional.

Freebies: 12-oz. bottle natural spring water, 10-oz. bottle sparkling water at the plant, and two 8-oz. glasses of Lucknow beers.

Video Shown: Short video shows bottling processes and advertising clips.

Reservations Needed: No, except off-season.

Days and Hours: Mid-May through mid-June: Sat and Sun 9:00 AM–5:00 PM. Mid-June through Labor Day: Mon–Sun 9:00 AM–5:00 PM. Labor Day through mid-October: Mon–Sun 9:00 AM–4:00 PM. Mid-October through mid-May: castle and grounds closed; bottling plant and brewery tours available by appointment. Closed holidays and Christmas week.

Plan to Stay: 30 minutes for bottling plant tours; 2–3 hours (or all day) for waterfall, castle, bottling plant and spring site, snack bar and carriage house, gift shop, and hiking trails, trout pond, and picnic areas.

Minimum Age: None

Disabled Access: Yes

Group Requirements: Groups of 15 people or more should call at least 1 day in advance. No maximum group size. Group rates available. Private function room available for luncheons, receptions, and banquets.

Special Information: Grounds are particularly scenic during foliage and lilac seasons.

Gift Shop: Sells logoed T-shirts, mugs, and hats, plus novelties such as soda-bottle bird feeders. Snack bar. Open same days and hours as above.

Directions: From I-93, take Rt. 104 East to Meredith. Take Rt. 25 East to Moultonborough. Take Rt. 109 South to Rt. 171 South. Bottling plant is ½ mile ahead on left. Main entrance is 2 miles ahead on left, which is where you should start unless visiting only the bottling plant.

Nearby Attractions: Hampshire Pewter tour (see page 207); Science Center; Washington Cruise Ship.

See color photo, page 187

Natural spring water fills 324 small bottles or 175 large bottles per minute at the Castle Springs bottling facility in Moultonborough, New Hampshire.

Castle Springs also microbrews its own premium beer, "Lucknow."

Stonyfield Farm ⟿ *yogurt*
10 Burton Drive
Londonderry, NH 03053
(603) 437-4040

As the name suggests, Stonyfield Farm Yogurt began on a farm. But meteoric growth forced this award-winning company to its present location in Londonderry. Developed in 1983 by two environmentalists, the all-natural yogurt can now be found in grocery stores nationwide. Their original mission hasn't changed—to demonstrate that a company can do good in the world and still be profitable. The tour shows you how they work their "magic" and live their corporate mission.

Follow your enthusiastic tour guide down the hall lined with laminated "love letters" from consumers. In the Yogurt Works area, watch the pasteurization of milk as it travels through a network of pipes to a tank where Stonyfield's secret concoction of healthy yogurt bacteria (or "culture") is added. The milk moves through a big funnel and a tangle of yellow tubes to fill plastic cups containing a predetermined amount of fruit. Next, the safety sealer machine, acting like a cookie cutter, punches out circles from clear plastic sheets to form the cups' safety seals. Once filled and packaged, the containers may appear ready to ship to the stores, but they are actually still filled with warm milk.

Next, you walk inside to "experience" the warm incubator. While it may appear calm, there is plenty of activity. Inside each yogurt cup, the yogurt cultures are multiplying, digesting the milk and turning it into yogurt. Once the yogurt reaches the correct pH level, it is moved into the "chill cells"—the most popular spot on the tour. After the hot incubator, the Arctic wind inside each cell will cool you right off. Then return to the visitors center to sample some frozen yogurt.

Cost: $1; under 5, free. Half of all admission collected donated to family farmers or farm organizations.
Freebies: Frozen yogurt sample, grocery coupons, and Moos-letter.
Video Shown: 12-minute video covers company history and close-up views of production process.

Reservations Needed: No, except for groups larger than 6 people.
Days and Hours: February through November: Tue–Sat 10:00 AM–4:00 PM on the hour. Closed December except for the week between Christmas and New Year's. Closed holidays and special Stonyfield days. Call 603-437-4040, ext. 243, for current schedule.
Plan To Stay: 45 minutes for tour, video, and sampling, plus time in gift shop.
Minimum Age: Recommended minimum age is 4; however, strollers welcome.
Disabled Access: Yes
Group Requirements: Groups with more than 6 people should call in advance. No reservations accepted for July and August. Maximum group size is 50 people, with groups over 20 split. $1 per person regardless of age.
Special Information: In the summer there is often production on Saturdays. No photography. Stonyfield is developing a demonstration farm.
Gift Shop: Logoed and cow-motif products such as bibs, mugs, and MOO-LA-LA T-shirts and sweatshirts. Refrigerated case stocks discounted yogurts. Sells *Stonyfield Farm Yogurt Cookbook* and pancake mix. Moochandise cowtalogue available from above number. Open Tue–Sat 9:30 AM–5:00 PM. Closed holidays and special Stonyfield days.
Directions: From Boston, take I-93 North to Exit 5. Turn left onto Rt. 28 North. After 2 miles, turn left onto Page Rd. Take second left onto Webster Rd. Turn left at stop sign and go 1 mile. Turn right onto Burton Dr. From Everett Tpk. take Rt. 101 East to S. Willow St. Turn right onto Rt. 28 South. At fork, bear right onto Harvey Rd. (follow as it turns right in 1 mile). Turn right onto Burton Dr.
Nearby Attractions: Top of the Tree and Anheuser-Busch (Budweiser) Brewery tours (see pages 211 and 206); Redhook Brewery tour in Portsmouth (call 603-430-8600); Currier Gallery of Art; Canobie Lake Park; The Met Children's Museum.

Top of the Tree ~ *apple pie*
4 Delta Pieway
Londonderry, NH 03053
(603) 434-2743

Finally you can watch that which is truly all-American: the making of the apple pie. A new company has sprouted in New Hampshire. Gordon Weinberger (a.k.a. Pieberger) founded the company after winning Londonderry's Old Home Day baking contest two years in a row with his great-grandmother's apple pie recipe. Slowly spreading its marketing base across the country, Top of the Tree hopes to follow in the footsteps of such employee-friendly and socially responsible companies as Ben & Jerry's.

After examining the spray-painted touring bus with Gordon on one side and Great-Grandma on the other, enter the pie factory and inhale the delicious aroma of baking pies. You'll encounter perhaps the only company directory written in "pie language." Your guide, dressed in tennis shoes and blue jeans, was probably once a top executive in corporate America.

After hearing the company story, walk into the bakery. Dough is made fresh every day in a huge old Hobart mixer. Pallets of flour and sugar sit nearby. The baker (none of the employees had any previous commercial baking experience) weighs the mixed dough on a scale to ensure the right proportions. The dough is laid in a pan and placed under Duchess, a machine whose blades lower to divide the dough into cubes. Each piece of dough will become either a top or bottom crust.

Those destined to be bottom crusts are placed in a pan. A heated, form-fitting press spreads the dough to fill the pan exactly, with no waste. The tops are taken to a sheeter, a mechanical rolling pin.

At the far end of the room, a worker takes an apple from one of the 15-bushel bins and places it in a cup on the apple-peeling machine, affectionately named Dudley. The cup spins the apple next to a blade, which peels the apple in just seconds. Then the apple goes through the corer. (The local pigs love the cores and peels.) A worker inspects each apple before dropping it onto a spindle that slices it. On a shaker table, the slices are shaken so that little pieces of core pod and seeds fall through the screen.

After the apple is inspected, a human mixer gets the honor of combining the spices with the apples by hand. The filling is carefully weighed according to the type of pie so the exact amount can be put into each pie shell. The pies roll over to the topping station, where the tops are sealed on the pies. Finally the pies are cooked, cooled, wrapped, and if you're lucky, available in a store near you!

Cost: Free

Freebies: Children in groups may each receive an apple.

Video Shown: No

Reservations Needed: Recommended for individuals; necessary, for groups.

Days and Hours: Since the printing of the second edition, the company moved its baking facilities out of the area.

Plan to Stay: 20 minutes

Minimum Age: None

Disabled Access: Yes

Group Requirements: Maximum group size 15–20 people. Larger groups can be split. Young children can play at a dough table while they wait.

Gift Area: Sells T-shirts and "impiefect" pies.

Directions: From Rt. 93, take Exit 5 for North Londonderry. Take Rt. 28 North toward Manchester. Turn left on Page Rd., left on Webster Rd., and left on Harvey Rd. Factory in ¼ mile on left at corner of Harvey and Delta Rds. Turn left on Delta Pieway and park in rear of building.

Nearby Attractions: Stonyfield Farm and Anheuser-Busch (Budweiser) tours (see pages 210 and 206); mid-August Old Home Day festival; Mack's Apples orchard (call 603-432-3456); Redhook Brewery tour in Portsmouth (call 603-430-8600); Currier Gallery of Art; Canobie Lake Park; The Met Children's Museum.

Ford ⟶ *Ranger pickup trucks*

Edison Assembly Plant
939 U.S. Highway 1
Edison, NJ 08818
(732) 632-5930, ext. 5306

The Big Three auto companies owe part of their resurgence to the mushrooming popularity of non-car cars: pickups, minivans, and sport-utility vehicles. Classified as "trucks" for purposes of energy and safety regulations, this is one of the few vehicle segments that Japanese manufacturers were slow to exploit. The Ford Ranger compact pickups made at this plant are ranked as one of the most popular vehicles sold in the U.S.A., along with the Ford full-size pickup, the Chevrolet full-size pickup, and the Ford Taurus.

As Ford's second-smallest assembly plant, the Edison facility produced only cars from the 1947 Lincoln up to the Ford Escort in the late 1980s. In 1990 Ford switched the plant to making pickups, extensively retooling the factory and retraining the workers. Production went from 85-percent manual to about 85-percent robotic, so here you'll see the latest in automation and robotics. The tour begins on the final trim lines, where workers install small pieces like the mirrors, instrument panel, and back windshield as the pickups move by on the ubiquitous conveyors.

Robots do over 90 percent of the body welding. No people seem to be nearby as the steel body shell moves down the line in a synchronized pattern, allowing the robotic welding arms to do their jobs hundreds of times the exact same way every day. If you're not too startled or amazed by the waterfall of sparks generated by each weld, study the different role each robot plays in building the body.

Another part of the plant constructs the frame that supports the engine, cab, and other truck parts. Watch how the engine is "decked" to the frame and, later, how the frame (at this point resembling a giant go-cart more than a pickup) is decked with the body cab. "Pit" workers test the pickup's features such as brake- and gas lines. More robots help with the front windshield and seat installation. Giant praying mantis–like arms pick up the glass and slap it into place. With all the advanced technology you'll encounter during the tour, you'll enjoy debating your fellow visitors about what was the coolest thing you saw.

Cost: Free

Freebies: Pins or pens, when available.

Video Shown: No

Reservations Needed: Yes. Individuals and families are either joined with a scheduled group tour or formed into a group.

Days and Hours: Mon 10:00 AM and sometimes Fri 10:00 AM. Closed holidays, 2 weeks around Christmas, and month of July. Because of limited tour times, it is difficult to book a tour.

Plan to Stay: 1¼ hours

Minimum Age: 15

Disabled Access: Yes

Group Requirements: Minimum group size is 15 people; maximum, 35. Call 4–6 weeks in advance to schedule tour.

Special Information: No photography. Tour does not visit paint department, although tour guide explains the process. About every year or so the plant has an open house that offers tours all day, a look at new pickup models, and food.

Gift Shop: No

Directions: From the New Jersey Tpk., take Exit 10. Take 287 North to Hwy. 1 South. Plant is on right.

Nearby Attractions: Edison National Historic Site in West Orange, featuring Thomas Edison's house, laboratory complex, and exhibits on his inventions and life (call 973-736-0550); American Labor Museum in Haledon tells the story of American workers, their unions, and their diverse ethnic heritage (call 973-595-7953); Delaware and Raritan Canal State Park.

Wheaton Village ⟿ *glass and other crafts*

1501 Glasstown Road
Millville, NJ 08332-1566
(609) 825-6800 / (800) 99-VILLAGE

In 1888 Dr. T.C. Wheaton, interested in making medicine bottles, purchased a Millville glass factory, which burned down in 1889. A working replica of this original factory is the centerpiece of Wheaton Village. Established in 1968, Wheaton Village focuses on the art and heritage of American glassmaking, regional craft, and folklife.

At set times, workers demonstrate traditional glassblowing. One worker narrates as another gathers molten glass onto a long rod (a "punty"). To make a paperweight, the "gaffer" inverts the "gob" of glass onto a mold, perhaps flower-shaped. The gob absorbs colored powdered glass from inside the mold. At other times, you can also observe these workers without narration.

Sharing the floor are glassworkers on fellowship from all over the world, making contemporary sculptures. While casting, workers wear protective outfits and face protection. With a saucepan-size ladle, a worker pours 30 to 50 pounds of molten glass into a sand-casting (made in sand) mold.

The Museum of American Glass houses the largest collection of entirely American-made glass. Its 7,500-plus objects include paperweights, chandeliers, prisms, and the nearly-9-foot-tall, 193-gallon *Guinness Book of World Records'* largest bottle. The museum covers the glass industry from the first factory (1739), through the 1800s, when South Jersey was a major glassmaking center, to today. The glass whimsy exhibit contains objects such as walking canes that workers made from leftover glass.

The Crafts and Trades Row building contains several studios and historical exhibits. Two potters transform clay into pots as pottery wheels spin. Over a torch, a lampworker manipulates glass rods of various colors and diameters to create marbles. Each colored swirl requires a separate rod. You may see a worker forming miniature animals or people at a tiny tea table. Afterwards, enjoy the peaceful, 60-plus-acre grounds' picnic tables, shrubs, shady pine trees, scampering squirrels, and flocks of birds and Canada geese—or browse the unique museum shops.

Cost: Adults, $6.50; seniors, $5.50; students, $3.50; under 5, free.

Freebies: No

Video Shown: No

Reservations Needed: No. Groups, see below.

Days and Hours: Village hours: January through March Wed–Sun 10:00 AM–5:00 PM (Crafts and Trade Row closed); April through December Mon–Sun 10:00 AM–5:00 PM. Glass demonstrations: 11:30 AM, 1:30 PM, and 3:30 PM, when village is open. Closed Easter, Thanksgiving, and Christmas.

Plan to Stay: 2½ hours, plus time in shops.

Minimum Age: None

Disabled Access: Yes

Group Requirements: Groups of more than 25 adults or 10 schoolchildren need reservations 1 month in advance. Craft Sampler Days (provide hands-on crafts participation for school groups) must be arranged 4–6 months in advance.

Special Information: Make Your Own Paperweight Program available to individuals and groups over age 21 with 1 week's advance notice. Call (800) 998-4552 for special events calendar or more information.

Gift Shops: Shops sell works made at Wheaton Village and those by other American glassmakers; also, crafts, books, and even penny candy. Open same hours as Village.

Directions: From Philadelphia, take Walt Whitman Bridge (follow signs to Atlantic City) to Rt. 42 South. Take Rt. 55 South to Exit 26. Signs lead to main entrance. From Atlantic City, take Atlantic City Expwy. West to Exit 12. Take Rt. 40 West. Turn left onto Rt. 552 West. At first traffic light in Millville, turn right onto Wade Blvd. Follow the signs.

Nearby Attractions: Parvin State Park; Atlantic City's beaches and casinos, 35 miles away; Cape May's beaches and Victorian homes, 40 miles away.

Heart of the Desert 〜 *pistachios*

Eagle Ranch
7288 Highway 54/70
Alamogordo, NM 88310
(505) 434-0035

According to ancient Turkish legend, young lovers walked through moonlit pistachio groves to test their love. If they heard pistachios splitting open on the trees, they knew their love was indeed true. Centuries later, in another desert thousands of miles away, the Schweers family may have had this romantic legend in mind when they chose Heart of the Desert Pistachios as their trademark. As owners and operators of Eagle Ranch Groves, New Mexico's first and largest pistachio farm, the Schweers have put years of love and hard work into producing these delicious nuts.

Tours are offered year-round, but if you visit Eagle Ranch in September, you can watch the mechanical shaking machines harvest the pistachios. The shakers clasp and vibrate the trees, releasing showers of nuts that are then transported into bins by conveyor belt. The pistachios move past a group of "gals" who remove blemished or deformed nuts. The good pistachios enter a needle sorter, a 6-foot-diameter barrel open at both ends. The needles that line the inside of the barrel hook into the split nuts' green meat, leaving the unsplit pistachios to roll out the bottom. The unsplit nuts are shelled, and these nut meats are flavored, roasted, and packaged.

The split nuts, meanwhile, flow across a sloped, vibrating sizing machine comprised of flat plates with various-size holes. As the pistachios jump along the vibrating plates, the smaller nuts fall through the tiniest holes into bins underneath. The remaining nuts continue along the machine, dropping into openings of increasing size until each bin along the way holds larger-sized pistachios.

In another process, pistachios move downhill on a hopper that feeds into a seemingly benign color-sorting machine. Suddenly you may hear a machine gun-like blast as nuts shoot out of the color sorter. A jet of air kicks out on a trajectory those nuts whose hue does not match the machine's prescribed color standards. The remaining pistachios are either sprayed with chile fla-

vors or salted, then roasted in a huge oven. Workers insert and remove 40-pound trays of nuts from the 10-foot-tall roaster in a non-stop workout. Meanwhile you can take a relaxed stroll into the gift shop, where you can sample and "go nuts" over Heart of the Desert pistachios.

Cost: Free

Freebies: Pistachio samples

Video Shown: No

Reservations Needed: No, unless groups larger than 10 people want different tour times.

Days and Hours: Memorial Day through Labor Day: Mon–Fri 10:00 AM and 1:30 PM. Labor Day through Memorial Day: Mon–Fri 1:30 PM. Closed Thanksgiving and Christmas.

Plan to Stay: 45 minutes for tour, plus time for gift shop, visitors center, and art gallery.

Minimum Age: None

Disabled Access: Yes

Group Requirements: Groups larger than 10 people should call 1 week in advance for alternative tour times. No maximum group size.

Special Information: Adjacent to gift shop is a visitors center with background information on the farm and pistachios, and an art gallery.

Retail Store: Sells pistachios, Southwestern Indian jewelry, gourmet items, gift baskets, pottery, and T-shirts with Southwestern themes. Open Mon–Sun 9:00 AM–6:00 PM. Mail order brochure available from (800) 432-0999.

Directions: From I-25 or I-10, take Hwy. 70 North. Eagle Ranch is 4 miles north of Alamogordo on Hwys. 54/70.

Nearby Attractions: Apache Trail attractions include White Sands National Monument, Space Hall of Fame, Ruidoso Downs Race Track, Lincoln National Forest, Museum of the Horse, Valley of Fires State Recreation Park, and Lincoln Historical District (Billy the Kid Museum and Lincoln Heritage Center).

Corning Glass Center   ~ *glass*

151 Centerway
Corning, NY 14831
(607) 974-8271

CORNING
GLASS
CENTER

Like a glass prism, a visit to the Corning Glass Center is multifaceted. The complete experience of the Corning Museum of Glass, the Hall of Science and Industry, and the Steuben Factory illuminates the history of glass, optical-fiber communications, and glassmaking. The Museum's world-famous collection of more than 26,000 glass objects traces 35 centuries of human experience with glass, starting in ancient Egypt's 18th Dynasty, when the search for perfectly clear crystal glass began. The 11-foot-high Tiffany window, now in the museum's permanent collection, was originally part of a private residence destined for destruction.

Learn how light transmits information through optical fibers in "Master of Light," one of the Hall's interactive educational exhibits. Also notice the 200-inch mirror disk, one of the most massive glass pourings ever, planned for the Mt. Palomar telescope. In the Hall, watch a craftsman melt rods of glass tubing over a single gas-flamed jet and form tiny glass animals.

The real fascination is watching the production of world-renowned Steuben glass. During a self-guided tour, you sit on wide, carpet-covered steps in front of a glass wall to watch master glassworkers perform their art. Gaffers collect gobs of red-hot glass from a central tank. Glassblowers' cheeks resemble Louis Armstrong's when he's playing the trumpet as they blow into the long blowpipes. They shape each piece with wooden and metal hand tools.

Along a walkway you see the engraving process that makes Steuben glass so unique and valuable. The engraver first coats the glass with protective shellac, then transfers an image onto its surface with India ink. To cut the design, the engraver presses the glass upward against as many as 50 different fine copper wheels on a rotating lathe. Intricate designs may take 300 hours to engrave. You will leave with respect and admiration for the Steuben glassmakers' skills and the technological advances of glass in science.

Cost: Adults, $7; senior citizens, $6; ages 6–17, $5; children under 6, free. Families with children 6–17 years old are charged $16 family rate regardless of number of children in family.

Freebies: No

Videos Shown: Overhead videos during self-guided tour of Steuben factory explain glassblowing. Overhead videos in museum illustrate glassmaking methods.

Reservations Needed: No, except for groups larger than 20 people.

Days and Hours: Open Mon–Sun 9:00 AM–5:00 PM; July and August, Mon–Sun 9:00 AM–8:00 PM. Closed Thanksgiving, Christmas Eve and Day, and New Year's. Best time to see Steuben factory production is Mon–Fri 9:00 AM–5:00 PM. Demonstrations 7 days a week.

Plan to Stay: 2 hours

Minimum Age: None

Disabled Access: Yes

Group Requirements: Groups of 20 or more should call 2 weeks in advance for special group rates and reservations (call 607-974-2000). No maximum group size.

Special Information: No photography in Steuben factory visitor's gallery.

Gift Shop: Glass Center features 5 shops selling Steuben and other glass objects, glass-related books, souvenirs, and Corning table-top and cookware products. Open same hours as Center. July and August "Just Uncrated" sale offers discounted Corning products, "how to use Corningware" presentations, ongoing food demonstrations, and recipes from local restaurants.

Directions: From New York City, take Rt. 17 West. Take Corning exit and follow signs. From Rochester, take I-390 South to Rt. 17 East. Follow above directions.

Nearby Attractions: At Historic Market Street shopping district, watch live demonstrations at glass studios; Rockwell Museum; Taylor Winery Visitor Center (call 607-569-6111); Benjamin Patterson Inn; Glenn Curtiss National Soaring Museum.

See color photos, page 191

George Eastman House   ⟋ *photography*
900 East Avenue
Rochester, NY 14607
(716) 271-3361

In the 1980s Eastman-Kodak stopped giving public plant tours. While we wouldn't normally include a company founder's home, the extensive $1.7-million restoration, completed in 1990, and the exhibits and videos on George Eastman and Kodak provide a personal look at the company's roots. America's great companies begin and grow with individuals, and Kodak owes its existence to this hardworking inventor and businessman. (He probably would also have loved this book.)

George Eastman lived in this house from 1905 to 1932. The 50-room mansion and grounds have been authentically restored. Your guide's amusing gossip and anecdotes give you a sense of this great American entrepreneur, inventor, and marketer. In the conservatory, stand under a huge replica of an elephant's head and tusks while you listen to the story about why Eastman stood his ground to take a photo of an onrushing rhino. It provides a lesson on how he built his successful business.

Colorful displays in two second-floor rooms capture his personality, lifestyle, philanthropy, management techniques, and marketing strategy. Kodak's early history is intertwined with George Eastman's life, so the displays also show the company's development. You'll learn many tidbits, including why Eastman named his company "Kodak," why he gave away 500,000 "Brownie" cameras—one to every child who turned 12 in 1930—and see early Kodak advertising campaigns featuring themes still used today. You'll leave with a taste of how Eastman turned new scientific inventions into enormously popular products—a trait American companies have relearned.

Cost: Adults, $6.50; seniors and students, $5; children 5–12, $2.50; children under 5, free.
Freebies: No
Videos Shown: A second-floor room continuously screens videos about George Eastman and Kodak. The Kodak video shows manufacturing process and overviews company's new products and direction.
Reservations Needed: No, except for groups larger than 30 people.
Days and Hours: Museum: Tue–Sat 10:00 AM–4:30 PM, Sun 1:30 PM–4:30 PM. Closed holidays. During May (Lilac Festival in Rochester), open Mon-Sun 10:00 AM–4:30 PM. Tours: Tue–Sat 10:30 AM and 2:00 PM, Sun at 2:00 PM.
Plan to Stay: 2 hours for house and gardens tour (which can be self-guided), watching most of both videos, visiting second-floor exhibits. You'll even have time for the excellent International Museum of Photography and Film attached to the house (one of the world's greatest collections of photography, film, technology, and literature). All are included in the admission fee above.
Minimum Age: None
Disabled Access: Yes
Group Requirements: Groups larger than 30 people must schedule tours in advance by calling (716) 271-3361, ext. 238. Group rates available.
Gift Shop: Books, posters, collectors' items and other photography-related gifts available in museum's gift shop. Open same hours as museum.
Special Information: Devices available to assist hearing-impaired.
Directions: Take New York State Thrwy. to Exit 45 and go north on Rt. 490 toward Rochester. At Exit 19, go north on Culver Rd., then left on East Ave. The museum is on the right.
Nearby Attractions: Memorial Art Gallery; Strong Museum; Rochester Museum and Science Center; Highland Park (annual May Lilac Festival); Seneca Park Zoo; Susan B. Anthony House.

Website: www.it.rit.edu/~gehouse

The dining room of the George Eastman House in Rochester, New York, has been restored to its early 20th-century grandeur.

Photo: Barbara Puorro Galasso

George Eastman, founder of Kodak, lived in this house from 1905 to 1932.

Maidenform Museum   *intimate apparel*

200 Madison Avenue
New York, NY 10016
(212) 856-8900

Don't come here expecting cheap, kinky thrills. The curator of this one-room museum took painstaking effort in developing this detailed, historical retrospective of the largest privately held intimate apparel company in the U.S. There are no live models or even robust mannequins. Instead, decade-by-decade display cases parallel the evolution of the Maidenform bra with popular culture and fashion trends.

In the 1920s, when the flat-chested, "boyish look" was popular, the Maiden Form bra gave women a more natural look. The bras were sewn directly into dresses until women began requesting them as separate garments. This led to the 1927 patent for the seamed uplift brassiere designed by Maiden Form's President and Chief Designer William Rosenthal.

The 1930s to 1940s display cases show a photo of the all-male sales force. A re-creation of a specialty store window from the 1930s displays a miniature mannequin wearing a tiny satin and lace bra, which retailed for the popular price of $1. During WWII bedsheets, curtains, and tablecloths were used to make limited quantities of plaid and other unusually patterned bras.

The year 1949 was a big one for the company. The Dream Campaign featured women wearing Maidenform bras in public places, living out fantasies of independence, romance, and adventure. The display cases show some of these ads—"I Dreamed I was Being Followed in My Maidenform Bra." One display case features spoofs of this campaign, including one from the *Harvard Lampoon*: "I Dreamed I was Arrested for Indecent Exposure in My Maiden Firm Bra."

That same year, 1949, also brought the introduction of their most popular bra, Chansonette. Its popularity spanned the years 1949 to 1978, when almost 90 million units were sold. The display case shows one of the modified Singer sewing machines used to make Chansonette's concentric circles that accentuated and rounded out the bust.

Decade by decade display cases take you to the present.

Cost: Free

Freebies: Brochure detailing the company's history

Video Shown: 13-minute video chronicles nearly 70 years of arts, current events, and Maidenform radio and TV advertising campaigns from the 1930s to 1990s.

Reservations Needed: Yes. Individuals often added to planned group tours. *Unfortunately, just as we went to press we learned this museum will probably be closing.*

Days and Hours: Mon–Fri 9:00 AM–5:00 PM.

Plan to Stay: 45 minutes–1 hour for video and guided tour of museum.

Minimum Age: None

Disabled Access: Yes

Group Requirements: Groups should call at least 2 weeks in advance. Maximum group size is 15 people.

Special Information: Photography allowed for personal use only. Written permission required for photographic reproduction.

Gift Shop: No

Directions: Take Lexington Ave. subway 6 to 33rd St. and Park Ave. Walk west 1 block to Madison Ave. and turn right. Museum is between 35th and 36th Sts.

Nearby Attractions: NBC Studio and Radio City Studio tours (see pages 219 and 224); J. Pierpoint Morgan Library; Empire State Building; Macy's; New York Public Library.

NBC Studios ⌁ *television programs*
30 Rockefeller Plaza
New York, NY 10112
(212) 664-4000

NBC prides itself on being the first radio network (1926), the first coast-to-coast television network (1951), and the first to broadcast a series in color (1953, "Kukla, Fran & Ollie"). This tour of the network headquarters (NBC employees call it "30 Rock") reflects that spirit. After seeing the behind-the-scenes hardware that helps edit, select, and broadcast shows to millions of homes, you appreciate what's involved when you flick on your TV.

While you will see neat technical TV hardware, the tour's highlight is visiting the sets of well-known shows or possibly meeting a TV star in hallways lined with NBC promotional posters and interactive exhibits. With your guide you may explore the versatile Studio 3K, used for several NBC sports and entertainment programs. Examine the imitation wood, plants, and other background materials that look so realistic on television.

Up to 12 different sets appear simultaneously in "Saturday Night Live" ("SNL" in TV jargon) Studio 8H, with the band and monologue sets the only two "permanents." During the show, actors jump between stages, and workers move walls and props preparing for upcoming skits. If you're here the week a new "SNL" is taped, you can briefly watch a rehearsal through glass walls, with the casually clothed director, guest host, camera operators, and production assistants going over segments. But don't let the relaxed dress fool you. As employees walk briskly by, you can feel the pressures and deadlines of live television. You'll also have a hands-on experience with the news and weather in the mini-studio at the end of the tour.

Cost: $10
Freebies: Small "NBC Studio Tour" sticker and the possibility of meeting a TV star.
Video Shown: 10-minute video explains NBC history and the television production process. During the introductory time period, you can also participate in an old-time radio show.
Reservations Needed: No, except for groups larger than 10 people.

Days and Hours: Mon–Sun 9:15 AM–4:30 PM, every 15 minutes. Call about extended hours during busy December and summer seasons. Closed Thanksgiving, Christmas, New Year's, Easter, and Labor Day. Purchase tickets early in the day; they can sell out by mid-morning.
Plan to Stay: 1 hour for video and tour, plus time for NBC Studio Store.
Minimum Age: 6
Disabled Access: Yes
Group Requirements: Groups larger than 10 people need at least 1 week's advance reservations (call 212-664-7174). Maximum group size is 80. Group rates available.
Special Information: No photography. The tour varies with fast-breaking news or broadcast schedule changes. For show tickets, write NBC Tickets at the address above. At corner of 49th Street and Rockefeller Plaza, you can look through the glass walls at the street-level "Today Show" studio. NBC Burbank, CA (see page 29) also gives tours.
NBC Page Program: Tour guides are part of the NBC Page Program that gives people an opportunity to break into broadcasting. For more information, contact NBC Page Program, Employee Relations at above address.
NBC Studio Store: Sells T-shirts, caps, mugs and other novelty items, many with logos of your favorite shows and NBC Sports. Open Mon–Fri 9:00 AM–7:00 PM, Sat 9:00 AM–11:00 PM (closes at 5:00 PM in summer), and usually Sundays when tours run. Catalog available at (800) NBC-8760.
Directions: Located in GE Building on 50th St. between 5th and 6th Aves. Subway stops below building, so take B, D, or F subway. Get off at the 47–50th St./Rockefeller Plaza station, then walk up a few flights to building lobby.
Nearby Attractions: Radio City Music Hall tour and Maidenform Museum (see pages 224 and 218); IBM Gallery of Science and Art (call 212-745-5214); Madison Square Garden tour (call 212-465-5800); Museum of Television and Radio.

New York Stock Exchange *stocks and bonds*

20 Broad Street
New York, NY 10005
(212) 656-5165

While the New York Stock Exchange (NYSE) isn't a factory, it is the place many companies in this book rely on to raise money. Over 400 million shares are traded on an average day at the world's leading equities marketplace. Even if you have no background in finance, the video, architecture, and action on the trading floor give you an enlightened view of our economic system.

At your first look through the visitor gallery's glass windows, there seems to be nothing but confusion on the trading floor below. But once you concentrate on the activities at the individual trading posts, listen to the continuously playing audiotaped explanation, and look at the diagrams, the activities begin to make sense.

The 37,000-square-foot trading floor covers four rooms. From the newly renovated Visitor Center Gallery, you see the largest, the Main Room. Approximately 200 listed issues trade at each of the 17 trading posts on the trading floor. Overhead high-definition flat panel color screens flash the most current trading data for the stocks traded at that location.

The brokers and specialists (NYSE-assigned dealers) buy and sell stock in a continuous auction process. Orders to buy and sell originating from anywhere in the world are fully executed in 22 seconds, on average. The brokers operate from the communication booths located around the perimeter of the trading floor. Before you leave the gallery, examine the room's beautiful architecture, with its ornate gilded ceiling, marble walls, and famous wall of windows.

Displays describe the NYSE's function, workings, and development since it was founded in 1792 to trade New York banks' stocks and bonds that covered revolutionary war debts. The exhibits teach financial neophytes about stock and bond trading and answer common questions. Other displays show more experienced investors how to retrieve computerized information on stocks, bonds, futures, and options. The newspaper's stock price tables will have new meaning after your visit.

Cost: Free

Freebies: NYSE literature at information desk.

Video Shown: 10-minute video in the Presentation Theater, "A View From the Floor," features some historical footage and close-ups that take you onto today's trading floor.

Reservations Needed: No, except for groups of 10 or more people.

Days and Hours: Mon–Fri 9:15 AM–4:00 PM. Outside the building, tickets are distributed daily starting at 9:00 AM and often run out by mid-morning. Open the day after Thanksgiving (this is the most popular day of the year for visitors) and Christmas Eve only until 1:00 PM. Closed official NYSE holidays.

Plan to Stay: 40 minutes for trading-floor viewing gallery, video, and displays, plus time for gift counter.

Minimum Age: None

Disabled Access: Yes

Group Requirements: Groups of 10 or more people need reservations at least 1 month in advance. Maximum group size is 25 people. Call (212) 656-5165.

Special Information: No photography. Tight security. Taped explanation in viewing gallery available in major foreign languages.

Gift Shop: Marketplace Gift Shop sells NYSE publications and logoed items, including caps, T-shirts, mugs, and key rings. Catalog available from (212) 656-5166.

Directions: Take the No. 2, 3, 4, or 5 subway to Wall St. stop. Look for the six-Corinthian-column facade of building's Broad St. entrance.

Nearby Financial Attractions: Museum of American Financial History (call 212-908-4110); Commodities Exchange Visitors Gallery (call 212-748-1000); New York Federal Reserve Bank tour (call 212-720-6130). South Street Seaport also nearby.

The Original American Kazoo Company

8703 South Main Street   ⟨—⟩   *kazoos*
Eden, NY 14057
(716) 992-3960

"If you can hum . . . you can play the kazoo" is the motto of the Original American Kazoo Company, the only metal-kazoo factory in the world. The kazoo is truly an American instrument, invented in the U.S. in the 1840s. Since kazoos are made the same way today as when the company started in 1916, we can say some things never change.

Pass through the toy and gift shop into the museum and factory. Wander around the small museum area looking at exhibits of kazoo trivia, history, and memorabilia. Learn that "Kazoo" was once a brand name for underwear and that the navy ship U.S.S. *Kalamazoo* was nicknamed "the Kazoo"— its sailors owned kazoos printed with the ship's real name. Display cases show a variety of creative kazoos. Look for the liquor bottle–shaped kazoo (made in 1934 to "Kazelebrate" the end of Prohibition) and even a Woody Woodpecker model.

An 18-step process transforms sheets of metal into the classic submarine-shaped kazoo, without soldering, welding, or gluing. Pieces are joined by shaping and crimping metal. From behind a railing, you watch as workers operate individual presses (built in 1907) that flange edges, curve bottoms and tops, and stamp out the air hole. Parts are "seamed" together over a sword-shaped mold, then workers hand-insert the resonator and screw on the cap. Notice the single ten-horsepower motor that drives all of the presses, as you listen to the rhythmic thump of the metal blanks being transformed into kazoos.

Don't blow off this place because the manufacturing steps sound confusing— posters describe how the company makes kazoos to the tune of about 35,000 per week. In fact, you'll probably leave playing your favorite song on a kazoo.

Cost: Free
Freebies: No
Video Shown: 10-minute video in the museum shows news clips about the company.

Reservations Needed: No, except for groups larger than 12 people.

Days and Hours: Mon–Sat 10:00 AM–5:00 PM, Sun 12:00 PM–5:00 PM. Production takes place Mon–Fri until 2:30 PM. Closed holidays, week between Christmas and New Year's, and inventory days.

Plan to Stay: 20 minutes for self-guided tour, video, and the museum displays, plus time for gift shop.

Minimum Age: None, for families; 6, for school groups.

Disabled Access: Yes

Groups Requirements: Reservations required 2 days in advance for group tours given Mon–Fri 10:15 AM–2:30 PM. Minimum group size is 12. Groups larger than 20 people are split into shifts. Minimum age is 6 for school groups. Groups receive a discount on one kazoo per customer.

Special Information: The tour does not take you onto factory floor. As you stand behind the viewing area railing, a worker describes the manufacturing process and answers questions.

Gift Store: Sells kazoos of all kinds, toys, wind chimes, cards, hand-crafted instruments, and children's books. Also sells jewelry, glassware, and other gift items. Open Mon–Sat 10:00 AM–5:00 PM; Sun 12:00 PM–5:00 PM. Closed holidays.

Directions: Take New York State Thrwy. to Exit 57A. Turn left onto Eden-Evans Center Rd. When you reach the first traffic light, turn right onto Main St. (Rt. 62). The company is 2 blocks ahead on the left.

Nearby Attractions: Leon, NY, an Amish community, is 20 minutes away. Perry's Ice Cream (see page 222) and Buffalo's attractions, including QRS Music tour (see page 223), are about 45 minutes away.

Perry's Ice Cream ~ *ice cream*

One Ice Cream Plaza
Akron, NY 14001
(716) 542-5492 / (800) 8-PERRYS

When H. Morton Perry started his business in 1918, he bottled milk for dairy farmers in the Akron area. Every so often he made small batches of ice cream for his family and friends—to rave reviews. By 1932 he began selling his ice cream to the public, and Perry's Ice Cream Company was born. H. Morton's grandchildren now run the business. You'll see that modern freezers have taken the place of ice-cooled storerooms, and a fleet of trucks has replaced horse-drawn wagons. You'll view an impressive manufacturing facility that makes millions of gallons of ice cream and related frozen treats every year.

After watching a video that covers Perry's proud history and the production of its quality ice cream, you'll walk up to a mezzanine area and peer through glass walls that survey the production floor. To your right are vats that hold the base mixes for ice cream and yogurt. In the center are the ever-moving machines that make ice cream and "novelty items," what they call treats like ice-cream sandwiches and cones. In this area, up to eight movable production lines may be in action. To the left are freezers for the finished products. While you're taking in the view, you'll munch on a free novelty item.

The various ice-cream flavors start as base mixes and then journey through enclosed machines and pipes that add goodies like pecan halves, caramel sauce, chocolate chips, or strawberries. Look for the line that makes ice-cream sandwiches. The vanilla ice cream is piped in and squirted between two traveling chocolate wafers. The ice cream and wafers come together in a continuous stream that makes and packages 120 sandwiches per minute.

Perry's can make cones a lot faster than your local ice-cream parlor. The cones are loaded into one end of the production line. Ice cream is shot inside, then chocolate sauce and nuts drop on top. Quicker then you can say "another scoop, please," the cones are packaged and off to the massive freezer.

Cost: Free
Freebies: Ice-cream novelty item of your choice.
Video Shown: 10-minute video on Perry's history and production process.
Reservations Needed: Yes
Days and Hours: Mon–Fri 9:00 AM–12:30 PM. Hours vary seasonally. Closed holidays.
Plan to Stay: 30 minutes for video and tour.
Minimum Age: No
Disabled Access: Stairs lead to production viewing area.
Group Requirements: Maximum group size is 40 people. Should call 1 month in advance.
Special Information: No photography of production floor.
Gift Counter: Sells logoed T-shirts, mugs, and key chains from a cabinet in the room where you watch the video. Open after tour.
Directions: From the east, take I-90 West to Exit 48A (Pembroke). Take Rt. 77 South. Turn right onto Rt. 5 West, then right onto Rt. 93 North. Follow Rt. 93 as it turns and curves through Akron. Turn right at Ice Cream Plaza. From the west, take I-90 East to Exit 49 (Depew). Turn left on Rt. 78, then right on Rt. 5 East. Turn left on Rt. 93 North to Ice Cream Plaza.
Nearby Attractions: The Original American Kazoo Company tour (see page 221); Eric County Park; Octagon House; Niagara Falls is 35 miles away.

QRS Music ⌒ *player-piano rolls*

1026 Niagara Street
Buffalo, NY 14213-2099
(716) 885-4600

At the world's oldest and largest mass manufacturer of player-piano rolls, you see how computer technology now makes a product whose prime was in the Roaring Twenties. You've gotta love a tour that begins by letting a nostalgic visitor play a popular tune on a player piano. Next to this old-fashioned roll-playing piano sits a baby grand equipped with Pianomation, a contemporary piano-playing system run from CDs.

Enter the memorabilia-filled waiting area, where old ads and letters from Jackie Gleason and Princess Grace of Monaco adorn the walls. In the corner sits a 1912 QRS "marking piano," which produces master rolls by recording an actual performer. The modified piano keys are pneumatically connected to a stylus that makes small markings on a roll of paper in the recorder.

Upstairs, look through glass windows at the predecessor of today's high-tech recording studio. To make the master roll, the "arranger" played a song beat-by-beat on a "recording piano" that put holes directly on a master sheet. With this time-consuming process (eight hours to make a three-minute song) the roll could not be played back until the recording was finished. Now, a computerized process produces the master roll. Watch the arranger enter keystrokes on the computer and instantly play them back for accuracy. The floppy disk, not holes in paper, creates the master.

In the manufacturing area, a worker feeds the disk into a perforator machine that cuts a pattern on sheets of paper according to computer code. Nearby, another worker handles the printer that puts song lyrics and other information onto the rolls. Look for the device that slurps up the sheets into finished piano rolls. As the tour ends, you're happy that our world of CD players and digital audio tapes still has room for player-piano music.

Cost: Adults, $2; children over 6, $1.
Freebies: No
Video Shown: 12-minute historical slide show on company history and how player-piano music is created. Tour guide explains more recent developments.
Reservations Needed: No, except for groups larger than 8 people.
Days and Hours: Mon–Fri 10:00 AM and 2:00 PM (2 tours daily). Closed holidays.
Plan to Stay: 1 hour for slide show and tour, plus time to look at items in waiting area and seconds area.
Minimum Age: 7
Disabled Access: Small flight of stairs to the exhibits in the waiting area. However, most of tour is not wheelchair accessible.
Group Requirements: Groups larger than 8 people should call 2 weeks in advance. Maximum group size is 20.
Special Information: The tour is a mecca for people with player pianos and will be most interesting for those with some player-piano experience. For a comparison to the production of CDs, the most modern form of recorded music, see the feature on Cinram/Disc Manufacturing, Huntsville, AL, page 2.
Sales Desk: Sells 3,500 QRS rolls in stock, including children's music, Broadway and movie musicals, country and western hits, and rock 'n' roll hits. Seconds are half-price, but you must sift through individual boxed and unboxed rolls for the song titles. Also sells audiocassettes and CDs of player piano music. Tour admission is redeemable toward purchase. Open Mon–Fri 8:00 AM–4:00 PM. Catalog available from above number.
Directions: From Rt. 33, take Rt. 198 West to Rt. 266. Turn left on Rt. 266, which is Niagara St. QRS 1 mile ahead on the right.
Nearby Attractions: The Original American Kazoo Company (see page 221); Rich Products History Exhibit in Rich Renaissance Niagara building (call 716-878-8422); Buffalo area attractions include Buffalo Museum of Science and Albright Gallery. Niagara Falls is about 20 miles away.

Radio City Music Hall   *live entertainment*

1260 Avenue of the Americas
Rockefeller Center
New York, NY 10020
(212) 632-4041

No, this isn't a factory. But they do create the Radio City Rockettes here and produce some of America's best-loved entertainment, such as the Radio City Christmas Spectacular. This behind-the-scenes tour of a New York landmark, built in 1932, combines architecture with a glimpse of what it takes to put together a U.S.-made show that's famous worldwide.

While standing in the art deco Grand Foyer, your theatrical tour guide expounds on the history of Radio City Music Hall, which gained National Historic Landmark status in 1978. Many of its original features have been restored, including the 24-carat goldleaf ceiling, which rises 60 feet over the Grand Foyer. In the Grand Auditorium, sit in the ocean of nearly 6,000 red velvet seats. Inspired by an ocean sunrise, rays of yellow, red, and orange theatrical lights can shine down from the coves between the Grand Auditorium's 60-foot-high arches. Four 70-foot-wide hydraulic elevators divide the stage's floor into sections that allow for many special effects. For example, the front "pit" elevator can descend 27 feet for loading an ice-skating rink.

Peek into the costume shop to see a variety of unique costumes and the original sewing machines and tables. Walk through the private apartment used by Roxy, Radio City's famed impresario. Visit one of the two rehearsal studios. The worn wooden floors resemble an old high-school gymnasium floor. Instead of basketball court markings, painted lines designate the stage elevators. Even numbers along a line denote where the Radio City Rockettes stand.

While you may not see a Radio City Rockette practice her legendary "eye high" kicks, you will meet a member of the world's most famous precision dance troupe. Wearing a custom costume, she talks about the history of the Rockettes.

Cost: Adults, $13.75; children under 13, $9.

Freebies: Grand Tour button, opportunity to take a photo with a Radio City Rockette.

Video Shown: 4-minute video of TV clips of recent news stories about Radio City.

Reservations Needed: No, however tickets sold on first-come, first-served basis in the Radio City Avenue Store. Tour content and prices may change. Groups, see below.

Days and Hours: Mon–Sat 10:00 AM–5:00 PM, Sun 11:00 AM–5:00 PM. Open 365 days a year. Tours depart approximately every 30 minutes from the Grand Foyer.

Plan to Stay: 1–1¼ hour for tour, plus time in Radio City Avenue Store.

Minimum Age: None

Disabled Access: Yes. Call (212) 632-3954 2 weeks prior to tour to arrange for elevator escort to all tour areas except rehearsal halls and costume shop.

Group Requirements: Groups of 25 or more people should call (212) 632-3555 for reservations and discount information. Call at least 2 months in advance for Christmas and spring season.

Special Information: Photography allowed, except during rehearsals. Most likely to see some type of rehearsal or part of a show in progress from mid-October to Christmas and 2 weeks before Spring Spectacular.

Gift Shop: Radio City Avenue Store sells the popular Radio City Rockette doll, coffee mugs, postcards, and magnets featuring the colorful Radio City marquee and other New York scenes. Open Sun–Thur 11:00 AM–6:00 PM; Fri and Sat 11:00 AM–9:00 PM.

Directions: Accessible by 5th and 6th Ave. bus lines. Subway stops below building, so take B, D, Q, or F subway to 47–50th St./Rockefeller Plaza station. When you walk upstairs, you'll see the bright marquee lights. Buy tickets at the Radio City Avenue Store.

Nearby Attractions: NBC Studios tour (see page 219); Maidenform Museum (see page 218); Madison Square Garden tour (call 212-465-5800); IBM Gallery of Science and Art (call 212-745-5214).

Steinway & Sons ~ *pianos*

1 Steinway Place
Long Island City, NY 11105
(718) 721-2600

STEINWAY & SONS

A piano mecca exists inside a four-story building in urban Queens, New York. Part lumberyard, woodshop, fine-cabinet studio, music-playing room, and back-office operation, Steinway & Sons is a world microcosm, with 33 different nationalities of workers. Over 300 craftspeople, trained by apprenticeship, handbuild 2,500 pianos each year. Since it takes one year and approximately 12,000 parts to make a Steinway piano, you will be amazed by the number of pianos in progress.

One tour highlight is the rim bending. Six men carry a laminated, rock-maple board (often with 18 layers) to one of the piano-shaped presses, the same ones invented 100 years ago by the founder's son. They wrestle the wood, bending it around the press, then hammer, screw, and clamp the wood into place. Each rim stays one day on the press. Once removed, rims rest calmly for at least six weeks in a sauna-hot, dark room. Here you appreciate the range of piano sizes, as the rims stand from 5 to 9 feet tall.

The belly department is rumored to be named after the original beer-drinking workers whose bellies hung over the pianos as they worked here. Soundboards are custom-fit into each piano. Workers hammer in the bridge to which strings will be attached. Saws hiss and the floors vibrate with the rhythmic banging and drilling. Cast-iron plates suspended in air wait for installation into rims. In the stringing department, you'll watch with fascination as a worker attaches each metal string to the plate (or "harp"), loops it tightly around the bridge, and then clamps it around the tuning pin. This process is skillfully repeated until all strings are installed.

The final stage is tuning. Master voicers in soundproof rooms regulate the "action," which is how piano-makers refer to the key/hammer mechanism. To ensure that all hammers rise to the same height, voicers hit each key and watch the corresponding hammer bob like a woodpecker's head. Once the action is regulated, the voicer inserts it into the front of the piano and tests its musical quality, adjusting its tuning and brightness before the piano's first performance in Carnegie Hall, or your living room.

Cost: Free
Freebies: Catalog and refreshments at end of tour.
Video Shown: No, but can purchase 15-minute video that alternates between factory and pianists' performances.
Reservations Needed: Yes
Days and Hours: Most Fri (possibly Thur) 9:00 AM. No tours July and August. Closed holidays and week between Christmas and New Year's.
Plan to Stay: 2½ hours
Minimum Age: 16
Disabled Access: Yes, via freight elevators.
Group Requirements: Maximum group size is 25 people. Call several weeks in advance for reservations.
Gift Area: Can order books, videos, posters, and logoed items including mugs, T-shirts, and pens, with delivery in 7–10 days. Product listing available at above number.
Special Information: Since factory covers 450,000 square feet and 4 floors that may be sawdusty, wear comfortable walking shoes.
Directions: From LaGuardia airport, take Grand Central Pkwy. West. Take first exit and turn right onto Steinway St. to 19th Ave. Steinway & Sons is on your left. From Manhattan, take Triboro Bridge toward Queens. Take first exit in Queens. Stay in right lane to get onto Astoria Blvd. Turn left onto Steinway St. Follow above directions. Call for subway directions. (N train to Ditmars Blvd.)
Nearby Attractions: Radio City Music Hall tour (see page 224); Shea Stadium; Manhattan's music attractions include Lincoln Center, Carnegie Hall, nearby Steinway Hall (company's piano showroom and museum —call 212-246-1100).

Fieldcrest Cannon   *sheets and textiles*

Cannon Village Visitors Center
200 West Avenue
Kannapolis, NC 28081
(704) 938-3200

You cannot help noticing the tall, red brick smokestack, bearing the Fieldcrest Cannon name, that towers against the background as you drive into Kannapolis. (Appropriately, the town's name combines two Greek words meaning "City of Looms.") You'll pass some of the 1,600 "mill houses" constructed for employees in the early 1900s. Here, on land that was once a 600-acre cotton plantation, farming and textiles are interwoven with the history of the land. The museum, with its old wooden looms and textile artifacts, is located in the Cannon Village Visitor's Center and provides an introduction to the textile industry. The museum includes photographic history of the plant, early to modern towels made by Fieldcrest Cannon, other displays, and a video about the process of producing towels and sheets.

You will learn that when bales of fresh cotton are received, the dirty cotton is cleaned to remove lumps and alien fibers. Enormous barrels of spun, coiled cotton ropes wait to be processed. In the card room, large, noisy card machines align webs of soft cotton side by side.

To make the famous cotton/poly 50/50 blend, a drawing machine processes four barrels each of cotton and polyester. Over 550 looms in the nearby plant weave threads into muslin and percale sheeting; another plant bleaches, prints, and dyes it. At a Concord, North Carolina, facility the sheet is cut, hemmed, labeled and packaged.

Cost: Free
Freebies: Coupon booklet for discounts at various Cannon Village shops, including a coupon for a complimentary item from the Fieldcrest Cannon outlet store.
Video Shown: 20-minute video covers history of the town and company. Shows towel-manufacturing process.
Reservations Needed: No
Days and Hours: Mon–Sat 10:00 AM–5:00 PM, Sun 1:00 PM–6:00 PM. Closed Thanksgiving, Christmas, and Easter.

Plan to Stay: 1 hour for museum, plus time for Cannon Village shops.
Minimum Age: None
Disabled Access: Yes
Group Requirements: None
Special Information: For insurance reasons, plant tour was discontinued.
Outlet Store: Fieldcrest Cannon Bed & Bath is in Cannon Village (call 704-939-2869). Open Mon–Sat 9:00 AM–7:00 PM, Sun 1:00 PM–6:00 PM, with extended hours around Christmas. Closed Christmas.
Directions: From I-85 North, take Exit 58 for Kannapolis. Take Hwys. 29 & 601 North. Travel under bridge. Take first right, onto 1st St. and into Village. Go to Cannon Village Visitor's Center. From I-85 South, take Exit 63. Follow Lane St. into Kannapolis.
Nearby Attractions: Cannon Village has many specialty shops, factory outlet stores, and restaurants; Charlotte Motor Speedway.

Furniture Discovery Center 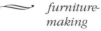 *furniture-making*

101 West Green Drive
High Point, NC 27260
(910) 887-3876

While High Point's famous furniture factories no longer give public tours, you'll experience the furniture manufacturing process from A to Z at this unique interactive museum. The displays in the main exhibit area, set up to simulate the "flow of production" in an ideal furniture factory, offer a comprehensive look at the detailed production involved in crafting dressers, china cabinets, highboys, and upholstered chairs.

Approach a designer's studio desk, where manufacturing always starts, and pick up the drafting tools and wood samples. Mascots "Joe" and "Josephine"—life-size blueprints detailing the measurements of an average-size man and woman—stand upright as a reminder of the human dimensions of furniture design.

Visit Harvey Hardwood, a 500-pound solid red oak that gives a two-minute lesson about forestry and the use of hardwood. His animated face and motion-triggered presentation entertain children and adults alike.

A giant blueprint of a Queen Anne highboy greets you in the casegoods section, where your "factory tour" officially begins. Displayed (although not running) are the machines used to shape, carve, sand, and assemble. You can grip the handles of band saws, lathes, and drills. The multi-spindle carver is fascinating; follow the contours of a model and see how spinning blades produce 16 identical matches.

Grab an air-powered nail gun in the upholstery section and begin simulating the assembly of a frame for a loveseat. A large blueprint outlines the furniture's design. Touch more than 15 samples of fabric and then select your favorite on the interactive computer, which allows you to design your own sofa by picking a style and watching it come together frame by frame on the screen. Sit on an upholstered chair and you'll appreciate the sturdy craftsmanship and design.

In the special exhibit area, the Serta Miniature Bedroom Collection contains reproductions of famous bedrooms, such as King Tut's and Kublai Khan's (whose round, moon-shaped, carved bed is a favorite among visitors). Crafting large or small furniture requires precise measurements, a steady hand, and an eye for detail—all of which are comprehensively explained in the heart of High Point, the furniture-making capital of the world.

Cost: Adults, $5; seniors, students, and children over 15, $4; children 6–15, $2; under 6, free.

Freebies: No

Video Shown: No

Reservations Needed: No, except for groups of 15 or more people.

Days and Hours: Mon–Sat 10:00 AM–5:00 PM, Sun 1:00–5:00 PM. Closed holidays and Mondays November through March. Call for extended hours during April and October International Home Furnishings Market.

Plan to Stay: 1 hour, plus time for gift shop.

Minimum Age: None

Disabled Access: Yes

Group Requirements: Groups of 15 or more people should make reservations 2 weeks in advance for a guided tour. Discounts available for groups over 15 people.

Gift Shop: Sells a wide selection of furniture books, furniture-shaped chocolate, jewelry, logoed T-shirts, and bookmarks. Open same hours as museum.

Directions: From I-85, take downtown High Point exit. Head 2 miles north. Turn left on West Green Dr. Discovery Center is ½ block on left in the back of the Convention and Visitors' Bureau. From Hwy. 68, turn left on Hwy. 311. Head south and turn right on West Green Dr. Discovery Center is ½ block on left.

Nearby Attractions: Young/Spangle furniture factory tour (see page 230); Angela Peterson Doll and Miniature Museum; High Point Museum and Historical Park.

Replacements

1089 Knox Road
Greensboro, NC 27420
(910) 697-3000 / (800) REPLACE (800-737-5223)

china, crystal, flatware, and collectibles

REPLACEMENTS, LTD.

For a special dinner party, you carefully set the table with the fragile bone china Aunt Millie willed you. But a guest accidentally dropped a precious teacup while helping clear the table. Once you see Replacements, Ltd.'s rows of shelves (62,000, to be exact!) stacked 16 feet high with 65,000 different patterns of china and crystal, you will feel confident about matching Aunt Millie's teacup. Replacements, the world's largest supplier of obsolete, active, and inactive china, crystal, and flatware, receives 15,000 pattern requests every month.

In the research department, "detectives" identify discontinued china, crystal, and flatware patterns for desperate customers, who send pictures, photocopies, or pencil rubbings of their treasures. The researchers use old catalogs (one prize possession is a 1936 Fostoria Catalog) and pictures to identify patterns. Antique dealers and a 2,000-buyer network receive Replacements' 600-page bimonthly "wish list" of customer requests. Buyers scour auctions, estate sales, and flea markets worldwide in search for specific patterns.

Wearing goggles that protect their eyes, skilled restoration-area workers carefully smooth out small (less than ⅛-inch) chips in crystal. Besides restoring crystal to its original beauty, workers reglaze and fire certain china pieces to remove scratches. Paintbrushes in hand, these artists expertly dab special paint onto the gold and platinum trim on ornate, elegant porcelain.

One tour highlight comes when your guide leads you down an aisle of the 3.2-million-piece warehouse. Looking without touching is difficult—but required—as you peer at towering shelves and spot anything from the elegant stem of a Baccarat crystal to a Limoges dessert plate. Equally impressive is the flatware department. Here you see gleaming silver serving spoons and shiny butter-knives being inspected, identified, and inventoried. Workers polish precious pieces on high-speed buffing machines,

then seal them in their own plastic bags to retard tarnishing. You leave with a true appreciation of the effort and dedication involved in researching, restoring, and replacing the "irreplaceable."

Cost: Free
Freebies: Logoed key chains and calendars.
Video Shown: No
Reservations Needed: No, except for groups larger than 25 people.
Days and Hours: Mon–Sun 8:30 AM–8:00 PM, every 30 minutes. Closed Thanksgiving and Christmas.
Plan to Stay: 20–30 minutes, plus time in showroom and museum.
Minimum Age: None
Disabled Access: Yes
Group Requirements: Groups larger than 25 should call 2 days ahead; will be split into smaller groups.
Special Information: Wear comfortable shoes. Museum adjacent to showroom focuses on Ohio River Valley's early 20th-century glass industry.
Retail Store: 10,000-square-foot showroom displays porcelain, crystal, and metal collectibles in antique mahogany, oak, and walnut showcases (some dating back to the 1800s, and many with their original glass!). Also, Masons' lamps (Wedgwood), crystal perfume bottles, and jewelry. Open Mon–Sun 8:00 AM–9:00 PM.
Directions: Take I-85/40 and exit at Exit 132. Go north (left if coming from Greensboro, right from Burlington) on Mt. Hope Church Rd. and turn left on Knox Rd. Replacements is on left.
Nearby Attractions: Seagrove area potteries tours about 40 miles away (see page 229); Thomas Built Buses gives limited tours (call 910-889-4871); Greensboro's attractions include Colonial Heritage Center, Greensboro Arboretum, Greensboro Cultural Center at Festival Park; Burlington Factory Outlets; Winston-Salem's attractions are 25 miles away.

Seagrove Area Potteries   ~~~ *pottery*

Friends of the North Carolina Pottery Center
124 Main Street
Seagrove, NC 27341
(910) 873-7887 / (910) 873-7425

More than 75 pottery studios scattered across the countryside make up the Seagrove pottery community. Within a 20-mile radius of the tiny, rural town of Seagrove (population approximately 357), the potteries are located along Route 705, Potters' Row, and its snaking secondary roads. Hand-painted 12-foot wooden signs point up different roads toward clusters of studios. At the Friends of the North Carolina Pottery Center, you can obtain a map marking all the locations, find help focusing your exploration, and view a sampling of the pottery styles made in the area.

Starting in the 1750s, English potters migrated to the Seagrove area for its good clay and its location on a major commercial road. Despite the influx of twentieth-century mass production, several potteries have persevered; some are now in their eighth and ninth generations. Now the largest community of potters in the U.S., Seagrove maintains the feeling that its people have been making pots for a long time.

In this laid-back, Old World–style community, many of the potteries are small family operations. Some are in backyards; some have dirt, brick, or concrete floors, all covered with clay dirt. Many use North Carolina "native" clay, which fires up to a light orange/brown terra-cotta color.

In a low-ceilinged log building with an earthen floor, Vernon Owens, owner of Jugtown Pottery, and his wife make salt-glazed crocks, milk churns, molasses jugs, and other traditional pieces. They throw salt onto the pots during the firing inside the 2,300° wood-burning kiln. The salt melts, bonds with the silica in the clay, and leaves a clear, bumpy, orange-peel texture. At Holly Hill Pottery, one of the area's larger potteries, you'll see up to four potters transforming mounds of clay into tea glasses or dinner plates. Another potter may be loading the 1,000-cubic-foot gas-fired kiln. As you visit many potteries, you'll recognize their distinctive characteristics. In fact, by looking at the shapes and silhouettes of each potter's antique-like pitchers, experienced eyes can classify them not only as North Carolina pots, but specifically as Seagrove pots.

Cost: Free
Freebies: Potteries of the Seagrove Area map available at Friends of the North Carolina Pottery Center and at all the potteries.
Video Shown: No
Reservations Needed: No, unless motor-coach groups want a guide (see below).
Days and Hours: Generally Mon–Sat 9:00 AM –5:00 PM. Call the above numbers regarding schedules.
Plan to Stay: 1–2 days, although it's impossible to visit every pottery shop.
Minimum Age: None
Disabled Access: Yes, for most studios.
Group Requirements: Call 1 week in advance (910-873-7425) to arrange for a motor-coach step-on guide.
Special Information: Kilns are especially hot in the summer. The Seagrove Pottery Festival, held the Sunday before Thanksgiving, features pottery demonstrations and sales.
Friends of the North Carolina Pottery Center: Sells annual Seagrove Area Pottery Shop Guide. Open Mon–Fri 10:00 AM–2:00 PM, Sat 9:00 am–3:00 PM. Reduced winter hours. New museum planned.
Showrooms: Sell each studio's wares, including face jugs, grape pitchers, Seagrove traditional and functional stoneware, and contemporary stoneware with pastel designs. Open generally Mon–Sat 9:00 AM–5:00 PM. Closed holidays.
Directions: From Greensboro intersection of I-85 and I-40, take I-73/I-74 South (old Rt. 220). After sign for area potteries, take Seagrove Exit 45. Turn left onto Rt. 705. Friends of the North Carolina Pottery Center is in an old brick building on right.
Nearby Attractions: North Carolina Zoological Park; Southern Pines and Pinehurst golf communities.

Young/Spangle ⟿ *furniture*

1150 Tryon Road
High Point, NC 27260
(910) 884-4535 / (800) 962-3694

North Carolina is known for furniture-making, and High Point is the furniture capital of the world. The large factories do not give public tours. However, Young/Spangle, a small family-owned and -operated business that has been manufacturing custom furniture since 1941, graciously opens its doors to visitors. Instead of the hustle-bustle and noisy atmosphere of many manufacturers, you hear the steady hum of sewing machines and intermittent hammering and stapling. Roll upon roll of different colored and patterned fabric catches your eye.

Seated at sewing machines, several women stitch together hand-cut pieces of upholstery fabric. The common work area is one large open space that has a folksy, informal feeling. In one spot a worker staples or hammers fabric to a wooden frame, carefully matching the fabric to make sure all the petals of a flower, for example, align correctly. In another space a worker fills a cushion with fiberfill, feathers, or down.

Since the company specializes in custom pieces (they can even reproduce something from a magazine photograph!), you will see different types of furniture. The introductory video and your tour guide, one of the company owners, explain processes that you may not see. Furniture pieces, such as overstuffed mauve chairsleepers, receive final touches before being shipped. For the company's regular line of leather furniture, workers cut hides according to certain patterns and sew cushions and other upholstery parts.

The guide turns over a chair and explains the quality craftsmanship that goes into making each piece. She points out the double-dowel and corner block joint frame construction, which is sturdier than stapling. "Eight-way hand tying," a manual process of tying string in eight different directions around the furniture's springs and frame, makes furniture more durable and prevents sagging springs. In addition to manufacturing comfortable and sturdy made-to-order furniture that can be passed down and reupholstered through generations, the company restores original furniture. Upon personally testing one of their chairs, you will agree that Young/Spangle deserves its reputation.

Cost: Free

Freebies: No

Video Shown: 14-minute video on how company makes furniture.

Plan to Stay: 30 minutes

Reservations Needed: Yes. Individuals can call for same-day reservations. Groups, see below.

Days and Hours: Mon–Fri 9:00 AM–2:30 PM. Closed holidays and week between Christmas and New Year's.

Minimum Age: None

Disabled Access: Yes

Group Requirements: Groups larger than 20 people should call 1 week in advance; will be split into smaller groups.

Special Information: Groups larger than 15 people can arrange tours of other furniture factories and showrooms by calling High Point Convention & Visitors Bureau 1 month in advance (910-884-5255).

Retail Store: No, but can place catalog or custom orders. Open for ordering Mon–Fri 9:00 AM–3:30 PM.

Directions: From I-85, look for High Point sign and take Business I-85. Take West Green Dr. Turn left onto Tryon Ave. Look for brick building on the right at the end of street. From I-40, take Hwy. 68 South. Turn left onto Ward St. Turn left onto Prospect St. and right onto Courtesy Rd. Young/Spangle is at corner of Courtesy Rd. and Tryon Ave.

Nearby Attractions: Furniture Discovery Center (see page 227); Atrium Furniture Mall.

Pipestem Creek

7060 Highway 9
Carrington, ND 58421
(701) 652-2623

*sunflower
bird-feeders and wreaths*

Named for the beautiful, pristine stream that flows through the nearby prairie, Pipestem Creek makes an unusual natural product. Ann Hoffert, a former nurse-practitioner, established Pipestem Creek in 1991 at her dad's 7,500-acre farm. Her wreaths and bird-feeders are made of home-grown sunflowers, millet, barley, ornamental corn, burgundy amaranths, and everlasting flowers. The plants are carefully dried, preserved, and hand-fashioned into large and small edible wreaths, suitable for bird-feeders or home decorations. The wreaths, called SunFeeders, and the home decorations, called SunFlorals, sell through national mail-order catalogs as well as in specialty shops and direct orders.

The drive to Pipestem Creek takes you past acres of planted fields, towering grain elevators, and rumbling tractor/combines, which service the feed business run by Ann Hoffert's father and her husband on the family farm. Several red, wooden, old-fashioned granary buildings and a train depot house Pipestem Creek's drying, shipping, and gift-shop facilities. In the white production building, bedecked with vines in the summer and surrounded by flowering beds, workers at large tables carefully assemble the sweet-smelling sunflower heads, corn husks, amaranths, and sheaths of millet or green barley. It can take a worker up to an hour to create one of the largest wreaths.

The head gardener comes and goes with armfuls of dried materials, distributing fragrant supplies to the workers. Some assemblers are neighborhood farmwives, who take home raw materials and return later with finished components. One wall is covered with pictures and informational materials spelling out Pipestem Creek's history and illustrating its varied marketing methods.

If you visit during summer, your tour guide (probably Ann herself, perhaps accompanied by one of her daughters) will walk you past a big farmhouse and through the maintained private gardens to admire the 1,500 feet of rainbow-colored beds planted in everlastings. One of the tall, red, wooden granary buildings houses edible crops while they're drying. Cast your gaze upward at the ceiling—a cornucopia of sunflower heads, each one bound with wire and hung separately to dry, head-down, free from destructive mold and hungry critters. Other edible grains, along with sparkling burgundy amaranths and colorful heads of Indian corn, fill every blank space.

Cost: $2.50; free for children.
Freebies: No
Video Shown: No
Reservations Needed: No, except for groups over 10 people.
Days and Hours: Mon–Fri 8:30 AM–4:30 PM, weekends by appointment or chance.
Plan to Stay: 1 hour, plus time for gift shop.
Minimum Age: None. Youngsters who are bored watching the production can play with the four Hoffert girls, feed the farm horses, or pet the kittens and bunnies.
Disabled Access: Grounds and gift shop accessible. Stairs in production areas.
Group Requirements: Groups larger than 10 people should call 1 week in advance. No maximum group size.
Special Information: August is the best month for viewing sunflower fields. To also see the everlasting flower fields, specialty crops, and gardens tour from May to October.
Gift Shop: Features sunflower-based products, SunFeeders, SunFlorals, and dried flower arrangements. Housed in a 10-sided wooden granary. Open same hours as tour. Catalog available at above address for $3.
Directions: From I-94, take Hwy. 281 North. Turn right onto Hwy. 9 East. Pipestem Creek is about 1 mile ahead on the right.
Nearby Attractions: Dakota Growers Pasta tour (call 701-652-2855); Arrowwood National Wildlife Refuge; Foster County Museum; Hawksnest Ridge; McHenry Railroad Loop.

Airstream   ⟋ *recreational vehicles*

419 West Pike Street
Jackson Center, OH 45334
(937) 596-6111

AIRSTREAM

Wally Byam invented the Airstream back in 1932 because his wife refused to go camping unless she could take her kitchen. He decided to build a trailer with built-in comforts that copied the sleek, bullet-shaped design of an airliner, which could travel the roads like a "stream of air." Little could he have imagined that it would become the Rolls Royce of RVs, one of the finest examples of American industrial design, and be used as television and movie stars' offices and dressing rooms on studio backlots.

The tour at this Thor Industries subsidiary (Thor is the second-largest RV manufacturer in the U.S.) shows you what makes these trailers and motor homes so unique: aircraft-type manufacturing. To build the shiny aluminum shell, the individual sheets of aluminum are laid up and measured for the curved roof and side walls, drilled, and then riveted together and connected to the end cap and interior metal ribs. Approximately 4,000 rivets are used. Spaces for the doors and windows are cut out of this aluminum shell.

In another area the chassis rails are laid down. A high-grade aluminum skin seals the underbelly from beneath. Fiberglass insulation is inserted before workers put down the tongue-and-groove plywood floor that seals the chassis, from above. Hoists lift the aluminum shell and place it gently on the chassis, which sits on special leveling jacks. Workers then bolt the chassis and shell together.

Once the exterior shell is sealed and married to the chassis, it's thoroughly checked for water leaks. In the water check, huge pumps spray hundreds of gallons of heavy water on the top and sides of the RV body. Meanwhile, workers inside the RV use flashlights to help search for any leaks at the seams and rivet holes. Any needed additional caulking and weather-sealing is done from the inside.

With the outside and chassis completed, the workers turn to the RV's inside. The toilets are always the first interior objects installed. Although the interiors can be highly adjustable, the toilet has to go over the septic-tank hole, and everything else goes in around it. Workers then rivet on the interior skin. Electrical wiring, carpeting, plumbing, and furniture are installed. All cabinets and furniture, built at the plant, are anchored to the interior metal frame. When complete, the RVs go to the mechanics building, where mechanics inspect one of the "99 things that Americans make best."

Cost: Free

Freebies: No

Video Shown: No

Reservations Needed: No, except for groups over 20 people.

Days and Hours: Mon–Fri 2:00 PM. Closed holidays, weeks around Christmas and New Year's, and usually at beginning of July.

Plan to Stay: 1 hour for tour and gift shop.

Minimum Age: None, but supervision needed for school-age children. Noise could startle young children.

Disabled Access: Yes

Group Requirements: Groups over 20 people should call 2 days in advance. No maximum group size. Special tour times can be arranged.

Special Information: No photography. Wally Byam Caravan Club International headquarters in town (call 937-596-5211 about Homecoming Rally of Airstream owners).

Gift Shop: The Wally Byam Store at the Factory Service Center sells full collection of logoed items and accessories, including T-shirts, caps, and scale-model RVs. Open Mon–Fri 8:15 AM–4:45 PM. Closed holidays, but not during factory shutdown periods.

Directions: From I-75, take the Indian Lake/Jackson Center Exit 102. Take SR 274 East and head into Jackson Center. Plant is on left.

Nearby Attractions: Wally Byam Memorial Park; Dayton's attractions, including Wright-Patterson Air Force Base and Neil Armstrong Space Museum, 50 miles away.

American Whistle ~ *whistles*

6540 Huntley Road
Columbus, OH 43229
(614) 846-2918

"How does that little ball get into the whistle?" is the question asked by most curious children (and adults) who tour the American Whistle Corporation. The answer is, "The corking machine does it." The little solid-cork ball is squeezed and then shot by air compression through a clear plastic tube into each already-assembled whistle.

The corking machine is just one of the many whistle-making steps you'll see at the only metal-whistle manufacturer in the U.S.A. As you journey through the factory's work stations, with the din of the press in the background, you'll be amazed to learn from your tour guide that over 1 million whistles are manufactured each year in this neat, compact facility. Watch whistles being cut, stamped, soldered, baked, bathed, polished, and packaged.

The press is your first stop, after an initial briefing by your tour guide. Here, in rapid succession, a large, overhanging piece of machinery fitted with a die (a piece similar to a cookie cutter) stamps down on each small brass square with 78,000 pounds of compressed air pressure. One after another, brass cut-outs resembling miniature sets of Mickey Mouse ears are punched out. In a later process, the ears fold upward to become the sides of the whistle.

During another part of the tour, you are privileged to view the whistles in their own private bathing area—a tiny room off the main factory floor. Here, in a large, open, circular trough called a vibratory, the whistles take a stone bath. The stones resemble rough jade pieces and are placed in with the whistles and a tiny bit of liquid. Then the vibratory actually vibrates for seven hours to smooth any rough edges off them. The finished, bright, shiny whistles, lined side-by-side for inspection and packaging, are the same whistles you see being tooted by policemen at busy traffic intersections or by referees at the Super Bowl.

Cost: $3 per person
Freebies: New "American Spirit" chrome whistle.
Video Shown: No
Reservations Needed: Yes. Individuals and families must join scheduled group tour.
Days and Hours: Mon–Fri 10:00 AM–4:00 PM. Closed holidays.
Plan to Stay: 1 hour for tour
Minimum Age: None
Disabled Access: Yes
Group Requirements: Minimum group size of 15 people, or $45. Call at least 1 week in advance. Maximum 45 people per group.
Special Information: Photography restricted in parts of the factory.
Gift Counter: Display case is located in the factory at the end of the tour. Whistles (metal, plastic, and even 24-karat gold), lanyards, and mouthpiece covers available in many colors. Catalog available from above number.
Directions: From I-71, exit for Rt. 161 (Dublin-Granville Rd.). Go west on Rt. 161 to Huntley Rd. Turn right onto Huntley Rd. Factory is on the right in about 1 mile—roughly halfway between Rt. 161 and Schrock Rd.
Nearby Attractions: Anheuser-Busch (Budweiser) Brewery tour (call 614-888-6644); Krema Peanut Butter tour (call 614-299-4131); Anthony Thomas Candy tour (group tours only, call 614-272-9221); other Columbus attractions include State House (recently had $120 million renovation), Columbus Zoo, and Center of Science and Industry.

Ballreich's  *potato chips*

186 Ohio Avenue
Tiffin, OH 44883
(419) 447-1814 / (800) 323-CHIP

When Fred Ballreich was working as a baker in the Army during WWI, he never expected to make a career out of it. Unable to find a job to support himself and his wife, Ethel, he opened his own potato-chip business in an unfinished garage. While Fred fried potatoes in a copper kettle, Ethel packaged the finished chips. On a good day, they produced 14 pounds of chips. Before the evening ended, Fred loaded his truck with the day's supply of chips and sold them to anyone who wanted them. That was in 1920.

Ballreich Brothers has come a long way since then. Today the modern factory produces about 2,000 pounds of chips every hour, sending bags, boxes, and cans to stores across the United States, and even the world. The company's marcelled chips, with big, wavy ridges, have fans everywhere. It takes only 18 minutes for a raw potato to become a potato chip. And with machines taking Ethel's place in the packing room, 80 1⅛-ounce bags, or 22 11-ounce bags, are filled in one minute.

Your Ballreich tour takes you onto the factory floor, past almost every part of the chip-making process. Potatoes arrive on the second floor from an enormous bin at ground level. An automatic abrasive peeler washes and peels the spuds before workers remove spots and eyes. Conveyors carry potatoes to the slicers, where razor-sharp blades rapidly chop them. The slices are washed and dumped into a long rectangular fryer, which begins the day with 2,000 pounds of soybean shortening and receives 1,250 pounds more every hour. Paddles move the slices through the shortening.

Potato slices exit the fryer by conveyor and head for the salter, drying out during the trip. The chips leave the salter and fall into buckets, which carry them to the packaging room. Bags of chips are automatically filled, measured, and sealed before being chuted to the shipping area. From here they are trucked to warehouses all over Ohio, and they reach the stores by the next day.

Cost: Free
Freebies: Sample bag of potato chips.
Video Shown: No
Reservations Needed: Preferred, especially for groups larger than 10 people.
Days and Hours: *For insurance reasons, this tour was discontinued at press time.* Mon, Tue, Thur, and Fri 8:00 AM–10:00 AM. Closed holidays.
Plan to Stay: 45 minutes for the tour, plus time for gift counter.
Minimum Age: None
Disabled Access: Yes
Group Requirements: Groups larger than 10 should call 1 week ahead to schedule a tour. No maximum group size.
Special Information: No photography. Floor can be slippery.
Gift Counter: Sells all varieties of chips in different size bags and boxes. Open Mon–Fri 8:00 AM–4:00 PM. Price list available from above number.
Directions: From I-20, take SR 53 South into Tiffin. Turn left on Huss St. Bear right after bridge onto Ohio Ave. Plant is ahead on the left. From I-75, take Rt. 224 to the intersection of State Rtes. 224 and 18. Follow SR 18 through town. After Heidelburg College, go straight on SR 101. Turn left onto Dwight St. and then right onto Ohio Ave.
Nearby Attractions: Maxwell Crystal tour (call 419-448-4286); Seneca County Museum.

Creegan ⟶

510 Washington Street
Steubenville, OH 43952
(614) 283-3708

*animated figures and
costume characters*

The coal- and steel-industry problems in this tri-state area of West Virginia, Pennsylvania, and Ohio may have left a void in Steubenville. However, few places have more vigor than the family-owned and -operated Creegan Company, the nation's largest manufacturer of animated and costume characters. You may recognize Beary Bear, Plentiful Penguin, or Strawberry Bunny from your local retail store windows and seasonal mall displays. Creegan also designs characters for Sea World, Hershey's Chocolate World, and Disney World. Inside the former Montgomery Ward department store, Creegan employees bring an array of characters to life.

Your guide leads you into a virtual craft heaven containing what must be thousands of spools of ribbon of every color, pattern, and texture. Puppet heads, scenery, and props lurk behind silk flowers and craft paraphernalia. A large, lifelike white gorilla stands beside three rosy-cheeked elves. During some tours, an employee dressed as Beary Bear wanders around. Up a wide staircase is the art shop, where workers make costumes and paint faces on molded plastic heads. On the main floor, a huge vacuum-form machine presses out the puppets' faces. Here you may see sheets of stark white plastic being pressed over molds into various facial configurations.

Downstairs in the sculpting area, one woman sculpts all of the character-head molds. Shelves contain hundreds of plaster molds shaped like heads, feet, hands, and animals. Further along is the mechanics/electronics department, full of workbenches laden with toolboxes, hand saws, lathes, vises, and drill presses. Peek inside some headless mechanized bodies to discover some figures' detailed electronic insides and to see how the parts unite to produce a character's body movements. After a tour of the Creegan Company, you will agree with their motto: "We make things move."

Cost: Free

Freebies: Cake, candy, or cookie samples from Fancy Food section of the store.

Video Shown: No, however some are for sale, including "Strawberry Bunny Visits the Creegan Company."

Reservations Needed: Preferred

Days and Hours: Mon–Fri 10:00 AM–4:00 PM, Sat 10:00 AM–2:00 PM (tours by request on Saturdays during summer). Call for extended tour hours November 1 through December 31. Closed Easter, Christmas, and New Year's.

Plan to Stay: 30 minutes, plus time for shops.

Minimum Age: None

Disabled Access: Yes

Group Requirements: 1 day's advance notice is requested for groups larger than 10 people. Inquire about group discounts on store merchandise.

Special Information: Individuals not part of a group may walk through the factory on their own, or may join a group led by one of the entertaining tour guides.

Retail Stores: Showroom displays and sells Creegan's most recent animated figures and scenery. Year-round Christmas shop offers ornaments, gifts, and novelties. Retail store carries a variety of items, including cake-decorating and candy-making supplies and seasonal decor items. Open Mon–Fri 10:00 AM –5:00 PM, Sat 10:00 AM–2:00 PM, Sun by appointment; November 1 through December 31, Mon–Thur 9:00 AM–6:00 PM; Fri–Sun 10:00 AM–5:00 PM. Catalog available.

Directions: From I-70, take SR 7 North to Steubenville. Turn left on Washington St., then left on Fifth St. Creegan's is on the corner of Washington and Fifth Sts.

Nearby Attractions: Hall China, Homer Laughlin China, and Brooke Glass tours (see pages 237, 331, and 330); Weirton Steel Mill tour (call 304-797-8597); Welsh Jaguar Classic Car Museum. Steubenville is the "City of Murals," with 21 beautifully painted historic murals throughout the city.

Goodyear World of Rubber

tires and rubber

Goodyear Tire & Rubber Company
1144 East Market Street
Akron, OH 44316
(330) 796-7117

Akron, Ohio, is so closely identified with the beginnings and growth of the rubber industry that it is acknowledged as the rubber capital of the world. Most of the rubber and tire factories have moved out of Akron, however, so the closest you can get is to visit the Goodyear World of Rubber. This traditional company museum's exhibits trace the history of the company and of the rubber industry.

Enter the museum through a small grove of rubber trees that gives you the ambiance of a rubber plantation. When you look up at the lush tree leaves and down at the rubber trunk, you'll imagine yourself in a tropical setting. Now that you have gained respect for nature's role in rubber production, bounce through the other exhibits, which describe synthetic rubber, the evolution of tires, the history of the blimp (with models), rubber-making and tire-building processes, and the interstate trucking industry. Short, informative videos accompany many exhibits.

The museum includes a replica of Charles Goodyear's workshop, where he discovered a process for vulcanizing rubber to give it elasticity. The workshop looks like a kitchen because it really was one. Legend has it that Goodyear accidentally discovered his rubber-curing process when he stuck the rubber recipe in the oven to hide it from his wife. The Goodyear Memorial Collection features paintings and many personal mementos acquired from heirs of this famous inventor. You'll also be surprised to learn that the Goodyear Tire & Rubber Company is connected to Charles Goodyear in name only. The company was founded in 1898 by Frank A. Seiberling, 38 years after Charles Goodyear's death.

The museum displays many Goodyear products, including the intriguing artificial heart and moon-tire displays. Finally, two Indianapolis 500 racecars with Goodyear tires illustrate the company's strength: making world-class, high-quality tires.

Cost: Free

Freebies: No

Videos Shown: Optional 25-minute video on tire production process shown in theater. If not playing, ask museum staff to start it. Other short videos throughout museum complement the displays.

Reservations Needed: No, except for groups of 20 or more people.

Days and Hours: Mon–Fri 9:00 AM–4:30 PM. Closed holidays.

Plan to Stay: 1 hour for museum and main video.

Minimum Age: None, but children should be at least 6 to appreciate the displays.

Disabled Access: Yes

Group Requirements: Groups of 20 or more need to call for reservations; special guided tours available by calling 1 month in advance.

Special Information: No photography

Gift Shop: Gift Center sells Goodyear-logoed items, including miniature blimps, jewelry, and clothing. Open same hours as museum.

Directions: Expressway is being reconfigured, so call to confirm directions and exits. From I-76 West, take Martha Ave./Goodyear Tech Center exit and turn right (north). From Martha Ave., go north, and turn left on East Market. Visitors' parking lot is on the right before you reach the red brick building, Goodyear Hall. From I-76 East, take Martha Ave. exit going south, turn around at the Tech Center, and proceed north on Martha. Follow above directions.

Nearby Attractions: Stan Hywet Hall; Hale Farm and Village; Akron Art Museum; John Brown Home; Quaker Square.

Hall China   ∼   *china*

Anna Avenue
East Liverpool, OH 43920
(330) 385-2900

What seems to be a small cluster of red brick buildings on the outskirts of East Liverpool is actually 11 acres of production, retail, and office space for Hall China, founded in 1903. Since its early years, Hall has been recognized as an industry leader in hotel and restaurant china production. Hall produced the first lead-free glazed chinaware, which requires only one firing at 2,400°.

Walk up the steps into the 1940s-style foyer, and the receptionist will point you in the direction of yellow arrows that lead you into the factory and on your way through the self-guided tour. Immediately you see stacks of bowls and pitchers as you hear the clinking of china being hand-packed. Next you're surrounded by tall, freestanding, wheeled racks loaded with unfinished gray clay pottery pieces ranging from pasta bowls to mugs, waiting to be glazed and fired.

The facility's ambiance is friendly and easygoing. When asked questions, workers eagerly explain the pottery-making process. Some workers sit at potter's wheels, while others, bent over wooden work benches, hand-sponge and trim away seams to smooth the just-formed mugs and bowls.

Glance over into the plant's interior to see workers making bowls out of hunks of raw clay. A long, stout log of gray clay is mechanically sliced into thick rounds. A worker places each slice into a bowl-shaped mold. Two new automatic casting machines dry these molds continuously.

The jiggering machines mechanically spin and shape each hunk of raw clay into a bowl. The inverted wet clay bowls are placed on conveyors fitted with 149 horizontal shelves, which rotate upward into a dryer for 1¼ hours. A new massive computerized jigger machine transforms logs of clay into dried ware without human touch.

As you near the tour's end, you smell the wax and glaze mixtures that will coat the clay pieces. You may see a woman stirring a large cauldron of glaze with a long wooden paddle. Before each piece is glazed, a work-

er air-sprays it to remove any dust or particles. Watch as a worker places both hands inside two crocks to lift them, then simultaneously dips them into the pot of glaze. Slowly and carefully, she twists her wrists to uniformly cover each piece with glaze. The two crocks are then set upon a grate to dry. Kiln firing at 2,400° fuses the clay with the glaze and gives each piece its shiny color.

Cost: Free

Freebies: No

Video Shown: No

Reservations Needed: No, except for groups larger than 10 people.

Days and Hours: Mon–Fri 9:15 AM–2:00 PM. Lunch break 12:00 PM–12:30 PM. Closed holidays. Minimal production week between Christmas and New Year's.

Plan to Stay: 20 minutes for self-guided tour, plus time in Hall Closet.

Minimum Age: None. Children must be accompanied by adult.

Disabled Access: Yes

Group Requirements: Call at least 3 weeks ahead to reserve guided tour for groups of 10 or more people.

Special Information: Wear comfortable shoes and lightweight clothing, since factory is warm.

Gift Shop: Hall Closet offers overruns of first-quality Hall China products, such as cookware and bowls, at slightly discounted prices. Open Mon–Sat 9:00 AM–5:00 PM.

Directions: Take Rt. 7 North, which becomes SR 39. Follow it east until it takes a sharp, 90-degree turn. Immediately after the turn, look for Boyce Church sign and make a left onto Anna Ave. At the cluster of red brick buildings, turn right into parking lot.

Nearby Attractions: Homer Laughlin China and Creegan Animation tours (see pages 331 and 235); Sterling China tour (call 330-532-4907) in Welsville, OH; East Liverpool Museum of Ceramics; Beaver Creek State Park; Thompson Park.

Harry London Candies   ~   *chocolates*

5353 Lauby Road
North Canton, OH 44720
(330) 494-0833 / (800) 321-0444

A triangular glass portico entrance, a classy maroon awning, and the meticulously landscaped grounds (the flower beds are mulched with cacao shells) welcome you to Harry London Candies. Before the tour, a friendly white-smocked candy-maker offers you a mocha meltaway or chocolate peanut-butter "buckeye," and your taste buds come alive!

Stroll through the Chocolate Hall of Fame. Old photographs and memorabilia show how Harry London first started manufacturing his quality chocolates out of his Ohio home in 1922. Gleaming white tanks and large vats swirl, mix, and heat up to 80,000 pounds of the rich, smooth brown confection a day. Foot upon foot of tubing starts here and transports the warm, liquid "food of the gods" (from the Latin meaning of "cacao") to the state-of-the-art candy-making processes you witness along the rest of your tour.

Floor-to-ceiling glass walls separate you from the fast-paced and efficient world of mass-producing quality chocolate. Look down on four 80-foot-long enrobing lines. Workers hand-place cookies, marshmallows, cherry cordials, or cream centers at the beginning of the line. Once the centers are coated with chocolate, workers hand- decorate them. Using a pastry bag, workers draw Zs with hot liquid dark chocolate onto "zebras," named for their chocolate cream centers with white chocolate on top.

The candies proceed through the cooling tunnel and then on to packaging. Videos and signs explain as you watch employees operate the wrapping machine (it wraps 72 to 100 pieces per minute) and the centrifugal-force table, where chocolate is spun into every conceivable shape. After this spellbinding trip through the world of Harry London candy-making, you'll agree that "any sane person loves chocolate."

Cost: Adults, $2; children 6–18, $1; children under 6, free.
Freebies: Chocolate samples on arrival and at end of tour. Fudge and caramel pecan popcorn samples while they are being made in the store.
Videos Shown: 7-minute video covers history of Harry London Candies and of chocolate manufacturing, plus 1-minute videos along tour path describing various candy-making procedures.
Reservations Needed: Yes
Days and Hours: Mon–Sat 9:00 AM–4:00 PM, Sun 12:00 PM–3:30 PM. Tours run every ½-hour. Closed major holidays. Call for seasonal hours.
Plan to Stay: 1 hour for tour, plus time for retail store.
Minimum Age: None
Disabled Access: Yes
Group Requirements: Groups should call at least 1 month in advance for reservations. No maximum group size. Call for special tours to be given to groups with a specific interest (such as marketing students or small children).
Special Information: No photography
Directions: Take I-77 to Exit 113 for Akron-Canton Airport. Turn right onto Lauby Rd. Turn right at the second entrance and "Harry London Candies" sign.
Retail Store: The 2,400-square-foot retail store features over 500 varieties of chocolate and gourmet candy, including pretzel joys, Weird Cedric's Butterscotch, and Hawaiian Gold. The store is designed with a lot of natural light, a large brick fireplace, and an authentic candy kitchen for making fudge and caramel corn as you watch. Catalog is available to order directly. Open Mon–Sat 9:00 AM–6:00 PM, Sun 12:00 PM–5:00 PM.
Nearby Attractions: Goodyear World of Rubber museum (see page 236); I-77 is known as the "Hall of Fame Highway," including Rock and Roll Hall of Fame, Inventors Hall of Fame, and NFL Football Hall of Fame.

Honda ⟶ *cars and motorcycles*
Honda Parkway
Marysville, OH 43040
(513) 642-5000

HONDA

Honda is the first Japanese automaker to build cars (1982), motorcycles (1979), lawn mowers (1984), and engines (1985) in the U.S.A. It's also the first to export its U.S.A.-made cars to overseas markets Taiwan (1987) and Japan (1988). Its five U.S. plants (Accord and motorcycles in Marysville, OH; Civic in East Liberty, OH; engines in Anna, OH; power equipment in Swepsonville, NC) employ over 12,000 workers, or "associates." For many years, Accord has been the best-selling American-made car. Honda plans North American production of all Accord and Civic automobiles sold in the U.S.A.

Honda offers no regular factory tours, but does have a visitors center ("Welcome Center") in the lobby of its Associate Development Center. Honda motorcycle enthusiasts will find more to explore than fans of its cars will. Behind the glass entrance are five motorcycles, dating back to Honda's first U.S.-built bikes.

The exhibit featuring the Gold Wing motorcycle, Honda's luxury touring bike made only in the U.S. and exported worldwide, is the Welcome Center highlight. The Gold Wing sits on a pedestal, bathed in spotlights. On another pedestal sits a cutaway of the powerful Gold Wing engine, giving you a look into its inner workings.

A monitor plays a selection of videos geared to your interest. Tell the Welcome Center host that you're interested in engineering or auto racing, and you'll soon watch a video on the topic. You'll have fun playing with an interactive CD-ROM system that can take you on a virtual tour of Honda's U.S. plants. In another area, a shiny Accord and Civic wait peacefully. Under the large "Honda of America Manufacturing" sign are pictures of associates involved in manufacturing and the products or parts they built. Notice the photos on Honda's international auto- and motorcycle-racing championships. Honda uses racing as a training ground for its engineers. While the center does not hold the excitement of a factory tour, it provides some insight into Honda's history, production process, and commitment to manufacturing in the U.S.A.

Cost: Free
Freebies: Company brochures
Video Shown: Different videos and CD-ROMs available, ranging from history to basics of car manufacturing. Tell the Welcome Center associate what you want to see.
Reservations Needed: No, for Welcome Center. No public plant tour currently available.
Days and Hours: Mon–Fri 8:30 AM–4:30 PM. Closed holidays, week between Christmas and New Year's, and week of July 4th.
Plan to Stay: 30 minutes for displays, videos, and interactive CD-ROM.
Minimum Age: None
Disabled Access: Yes
Group Requirements: No maximum group size, although advance notice appreciated for large groups.
Special Information: Factory tours available on special request, but not open to regular public tours. Information on auto and motorcycle plant tours available from Corporate Communications Department at above address, or call (513) 642-5000. Annual Honda motorcycle homecoming last Thur–Sat in July (includes tours of plant).
Gift Shop: No
Directions: From Rt. 33 East, take second Honda Pkwy. exit. Turn left, drive over Rt. 33 and enter through first gate (East). From Columbus, take Rt. 33 West past Marysville. Exit at first Honda Pkwy. exit and turn right. Plant is on right.
Nearby Attractions: Navistar International truck plant tour (see page 244); Mad River Mountain; Piatt Castles; Ohio Caverns; Columbus attractions, including American Motorcycle Association Heritage Museum, about 30 miles away.

Lee Middleton Original Dolls   *baby dolls*

1301 Washington Boulevard
Belpre, OH 45714
(614) 423-1481 / (800) 233-7479

Lee Middleton began creating dolls at her kitchen table in 1978, using her children as the first models. While the kitchen table may have given way to a 37,000-square-foot "doll-house" factory (hidden behind a pastel-colored Victorian gingerbread facade), the same detailed, labor-intensive production process continues. The tour, led by guides dressed like Lee's most popular dolls, shows the intricacy involved in making her vinyl and porcelain collectible baby dolls and clothing.

All dolls start with molds for heads, fore-arms, and lower legs. A measured amount of liquid vinyl fills metal mold trays. The vinyl "cures" to a solid state in rotational molding ovens. After the molds cool, workers pull a small plug from each one. Then they use pliers to magically yank warm, hollow vinyl parts from each mold's tiny opening. For porcelain doll heads, arms, and legs, liquid porcelain ("slip") is poured into plaster molds to produce soft "greenware." After it dries, workers delicately hand-sand the surface to remove all seams and bumps. Kilns then fire the pieces at 2,300°, changing the consistency from white chalk to flesh-colored, silky porcelain.

Stencils based on Lee's prototypes are used in painting vinyl doll faces. One head may require different stencils for eyebrows, lips, and teeth, while blush on the cheeks is done freehand. Air is pumped into the head, temporarily expanding it like a balloon and enlarging the eye sockets. Workers then insert eyes into the openings and focus them, before delicately applying eyelash strips. Even more painstaking steps are involved in creating porcelain doll faces. Eyelashes, for example, must be inserted individually, in groups of four or five hairs at a time. When the heads, arms, and legs are attached to polyfill-stuffed bodies to complete the dolls, you appreciate the "labor" involved in their birth. Lee includes a Bible with each of her "babies" because she wants to thank God for giving her the talents that make her collectible dolls so special.

Cost: Free

Freebies: No

Video Shown: No

Reservations Needed: No, except for groups.

Days and Hours: Mon–Fri 9:00 AM, 10:15 AM, 11:00 AM, 12:30 PM, 1:15 PM, 2:15 PM, 3:00 PM (less production). Will try to accommodate tours at other times until 3:00 PM. Closed holidays and week between Christmas and New Year's.

Plan to Stay: 20 minutes for tour, plus time for gift shop.

Minimum Age: None

Disabled Access: Yes

Group Requirements: Large groups should call in advance. No maximum group size.

Special Information: No photography. May not always see porcelain-doll production.

Gift Shop: Sells "less than perfect" Lee Middleton Original Dolls, limited-edition "first quality" dolls, designer doll accessories (including clothing and nursery furnishings), and other gift and souvenir items. Open Mon–Sat 9:00 AM–5:00 PM. Catalog available from above number.

Directions: From I-77, take Parkersburg, WV, exit for Rt. 50. Head west across Ohio River. Once over the bridge, road becomes Washington Blvd./Rt. 618. Look for large building with gingerbread front, ¾ mile ahead on left. From the east, take Rtes. 7 & 50. Turn right on Farson Ave. and left on Washington Blvd. Signs guide you to factory (on the right).

Nearby Attractions: Fenton Art Glass tour (see page 332); Stahl's Christmas Shop; Children's Toy and Doll museum; Doll Showcase store; Historic Marietta, OH; Blennerhassett Island and Museum.

Longaberger ～ *baskets*

5563 Raider Road (State Route 16)
Dresden, OH 43821-0073
(614) 754-6330

Tree-lined streets and beautifully restored Victorian houses create historic charm in Dresden, Ohio, also home to Longaberger Baskets. A short drive from Dresden's center is the world's largest basket-making plant—6½ acres under one roof! Upon entering Building A, you are struck with the beauty of all the product displays in the Gallery. Here you can see nearly all of the products Longaberger has offered over the years and watch a video explaining the history of the company, the manufacturing process, and the Hartville plant.

After leaving the Gallery, look down to a view of hundreds of weavers from a ¼-mile mezzanine. Guides along the way explain the different processes. The maple logs used to make the baskets are first "cooked" for eight hours, then cut and metered into the proper length wood strips for each style of basket. Weavers' fingers nimbly maneuver the moist, flexible maple strips to create the mosaic of the weave. The basket gradually takes shape as the craftsperson weaves, then taps the weave with a hammer to ensure a secure, tight, durable result.

Near the end of the process, the basket receives a "haircut" to trim away excess up-splints (the basket's vertical strips of wood). The weaver wraps the last band of wood around the circumference of the basket, hand-tacks it into place, then dates and signs the completed artwork.

Take a shuttle bus to Building B to see the staining, quality assurance, and packing and shipping areas. One of the few automated processes you'll see at Longaberger occurs in the staining chamber. Here, baskets are hooked onto circular overhead racks called "spinners." As the spinners rotate them, the baskets move down a conveyor belt through the chamber where they are doused with stain. You leave with the image of row upon row of wooden baskets waiting to be filled with strawberries, fresh-baked bread, just-picked daisies, or even today's newspaper.

Cost: Free

Freebies: No

Video Shown: 18-minute optional video gives company history, describes the basket-making process, and discusses the Hartville plant. Shown in the Gallery.

Reservations Needed: No, except for groups larger than 15 people.

Days and Hours: Mon–Sat 8:00 AM–4:00 PM. April through October: also Sun 1:00 PM–7:30 PM. November through March: also Sun 1:00 PM–6:00 PM. To see weaving, tour the plant Mon–Fri before 1:00 PM. No weaving on Sat or Sun. Weaving demonstration in the Gallery 7 days a week. Closed holidays.

Plan to Stay: 2 hours for Gallery, Building A, Building B, and Just For Fun shop.

Minimum Age: None

Disabled Access: Yes

Group Requirements: Groups larger than 15 people should call 1 day in advance to arrange tour. No maximum group size.

Special Information: On-site shuttle bus provides transportation to and from parking and in between buildings.

Gift Shop: Just For Fun Shop, at the end of the tour in Building A, sells Dresden Tour Baskets I and II—the only style baskets available without contacting a Longaberger Independent Sales Associate. Logoed T-shirts, gifts, and basket accessories are available. Open the same hours as tour. "Wish List" catalog with entire Longaberger basket and pottery line is available from an Independent Sales Associate at (800) 966-0374.

Directions: Take I-70 to Zanesville, then SR 60 North. Turn left onto SR 16. Plant is ahead 2.8 miles on your right. Stop at gatehouse for directions.

Nearby Attractions: The World's Largest Basket; Triple Locks and Side-Cut Canal; the Longaberger Make a Basket Shop; the Longaberger Restaurant, where baskets are everywhere!

Malley's Chocolates ⌐ *chocolates*

13400 Brookpark Road
Cleveland, OH 44135
(216) 362-8700

You cannot miss the enormous ice-cream sundae that adorns the top of Malley's Chocolates' 60,000-square-foot building. This landmark commemorates Malley's first ice-cream and chocolate shop, opened in 1935. Like the best candy-factory tours, this one begins with a sample, great chocolate smells, and a brief introduction to chocolate-making. To put you in the right mood, they pipe in sounds of the tropical rainforest. The immediate landscape is festooned with banana and cocoa trees hand-painted in lively pastels. Temporarily you return to the very origins of chocolate—to the tropics where cocoa beans grow.

As you gaze out over the expansive, modern candy kitchen, your tour guide describes chocolate's journey from its birth in the cocoa plantations to the creamy liquid that you see swirling and churning in the 500-pound chocolate melter. This is Malley's secret chocolate recipe, which is kept under lock and key. Meanwhile, in the center's kitchen, anything from strawberry to caramel centers may be bubbling away in copper kettles on gas stoves. Amid all this modern equipment, look for the antique gas stove dating back to the company's inception.

Your attention is drawn to the center of the room, where the automated kettle-lift pours 60 pounds of chewy, gooey hot caramel onto one of several cooling tables. Like a construction worker hurrying to smooth out a layer of concrete before it hardens, a chocolatier uses a huge spatula to quickly spread and smooth the thick caramel. A large rolling-and-cutting instrument is used to cut the still-soft caramel into pieces.

In another area, you see the enrober automatically coating the candy centers with chocolate. Before your tour concludes, you pass by the design center to glimpse some of Malley's specialty items.

Cost: $2 per adult; $1 per child.
Freebies: Samples at beginning and end of tour, and a take-home treat.

Video Shown: 3-minute video describes hand-packing process.
Reservations Needed: Yes. Individuals and families must join scheduled group tour.
Days and Hours: Mon–Fri 10:00 AM, 11:00 AM, and 1:30 PM, with more tours added seasonally. Closed holidays. Plant shutdowns are unusual and unpredictable.
Plan to Stay: 1 hour for tour, plus time in retail store.
Minimum Age: None
Disabled Access: Yes
Group Requirements: Minimum group size is 15 people; maximum is 45. Reservations needed 2 weeks in advance (4 weeks during holiday seasons).
Special Information: No photography. Best days to see production are before major holidays.
Retail Store: Sells full selection of Malley's chocolates including assorted chocolate creams, molded chocolate dinosaurs, and, of course, Grandpa Malley's Favorite Almond Crunch. Look in rear of store for Sweet Slips, bags of chocolates discounted due to minor flaws. Hand-painted walls and floral prints add to the flavor of a real sweet shop. Open Mon–Sat 10:00 AM–6:00 PM. Catalog available from (800) ASK-MALL.
Directions: From the east, take I-480 West to West 130th St. exit. Turn left onto West 130th. Turn right on Brookpark Rd. Malley's is on the right. From the west, take I-480 East to West 130th St. exit. Turn left at end of exit ramp. Malley's is on the left.
Nearby Attractions: *Cleveland Plain Dealer* newspaper tour (call 216-999-5665); Great Lakes Brewing Company tour (call 216-771-4404); NASA-Lewis Research Center (call 216-433-2000); Cleveland's attractions include Cleveland Zoo, Tower City, The Flats, Rock and Roll Hall of Fame, Great Lakes Science Center, and Cleveland Museum of Art.

Mosser Glass ~ *glass*

State Route 22 East
Cambridge, OH 43725
(614) 439-1827

A beautiful country landscape is the backdrop for the little red farm cottage located conveniently just off the road. The front porch framed in white columns beckons you in. As you enter Mosser's "Little Red House" showroom, the sparkle of glass from every corner catches your eye. In this glass menagerie you see glass of all colors and shapes. Walls are decorated with everything from miniature punchbowls to figurines of clowns and frogs—samples of what you will see made in the factory downstairs.

The first part of the tour takes you through the shipping area. After viewing hand-packing, your guide points out a display case of colored particles. These are the various chemicals used in Mosser's recipes for coloring glass. What really catches your eye, however, is stacks of over 200 intricately designed cast-iron molds, used in creating all of the hand-pressed glass shapes.

As you move past the batch room, you see machines that resemble inverted cement mixers forming an initial mixture of silica sand and soda ash. Large furnaces that heat the mixture to about 2,500° then come into view as you enter the open, high-ceilinged, cement block factory. From this point on, the pressing of each piece of glass is done by a four-person human assembly line. While you watch glass being made, you are facing a furnace and its four-person team; beyond is an enormous factory window fitted with huge exhaust fans. The window is wide open to a panoramic view of the Ohio countryside.

Watch the glassmaking team in action as the glowing molten mixture is removed from the furnace by the "gatherer." Another person cuts and then presses the hot material into the mold. A third worker removes the hot piece of glass from the mold and puts it onto the fire polisher, which smooths any rough edges or mold marks left from pressing. Finally, the last worker places the glass piece onto a slow conveyor belt for the "lehr," or cooling oven, where it undergoes a gradual, 3½-hour cooling process.

As your tour ends at the lehr, you see the warm finished shapes being removed from the conveyor belt. Along one wall you observe glass figures receiving an acid rinse in a large tub to produce the soft, brushed effect of frosted glassware.

Cost: Free
Freebies: No
Video Shown: No
Reservations Needed: No, except for groups larger than 15 people.
Days and Hours: Mon–Fri 8:00 AM–3:00 PM. Lunch break from 11:00 AM–11:45 AM. Closed holidays, 2 weeks in July, and last week of December.
Plan to Stay: 15 minutes for tour, plus time to browse Little Red House showroom.
Minimum Age: None
Disabled Access: Yes, for factory; 4 steps into showroom.
Group Requirements: Groups larger than 15 should call a few days in advance for reservations. No maximum group size, since large groups will be split into groups of 8.
Special Information: No sandals or open-toed shoes. Factory can get quite warm in the summer.
Gift Shop: Little Red House showroom offers everything from glass candlesticks, paperweights, and miniatures, to antique reproductions. Open Mon–Fri 8:00 AM–4:00 PM. Closed holidays.
Directions: From I-77, take Exit 47. Take SR 22 West. Mosser Glass is ½-mile ahead on the right.
Nearby Attractions: Boyd's Glass tour (call 614-439-2077); Degenhart Paperweight & Glass Museum (call 614-432-2626); Salt Fork State Park and Lodge; Cambridge's antique shops and glass museums.

Navistar International 〜 *trucks*

6125 Urbana Road
Springfield, OH 45501
(513) 390-5848

This facility is the highest-volume producer of medium and heavy trucks and school-bus chassis in the world. Navistar vehicles are seen every day on U.S. highways, delivering farm produce to market, transporting school children to classes, and moving freight cross-country. A company retiree happily leads your tour through the assembly plant. The nearby body plant produces sheet-metal stamping and subassemblies from the doors to the truck cabs.

At the assembly plant, you'll walk along the two final assembly lines, each a half-mile long and fed by miles of conveyer systems carrying parts to workers stationed along the lines. While many components are received on a just-in-time delivery basis, others are stored in the plant's high-rise warehouse. In the subassembly area, look for the robots that use waterjet cutters to slice floor mats.

The trucks, each one custom-built for the buyer, begin as two steel frame rails placed on moving conveyors in the frame room. The frame rails are the part on which the truck body, whether it be school bus or cargo trailer, is installed. After holes are pierced in the frames by computer-controlled presses, steel crossmembers lock the rails squarely together; the front and rear axles are then added. The engine is dropped into place, chassis paint is applied, tires are mounted, and fuel tanks and fuel lines are installed. The cab, which you see painted by robots in the new, state-of-the-art paint facility, arrives through a second-floor hatch and a hoist lowers it into position.

While you observe workers mounting more parts, such as the hood, seats, and bumper, the real thrill is sitting in the completed truck during its "road test" in the dynamometer chamber. The truck moves nowhere at 65 mph (on roll bars), while a worker tests all aspects of its performance. Since workers enjoy talking with visitors, they gladly explain the inspection steps—they may even let you try the horn!

Cost: Free

Freebies: Brochures about the plant and International trucks, available upon request.

Video Shown: No

Reservations Needed: Yes. Prefers that individuals and groups of less than 5 people join scheduled group tour.

Days and Hours: Tue and Thur 8:00 AM–3:30 PM. Closed holidays, week between Christmas and New Year's, and first 2 weeks of July. Possible additional summer shutdown.

Plan to Stay: 1½ hours (minimum) to tour assembly plant; additional hour for body plant or paint facility.

Minimum Age: 14 or high-school freshman for children with their families.

Disabled Access: Yes

Group Requirements: Groups need reservations at least 1 week in advance. Maximum group size is 65.

Special Information: No photography or open-toed shoes. Can be hot in summer and noisy any time. While Navistar likes to give public tours, customer-related tours receive scheduling priority. Body plant and paint facility tours available upon special request.

Gift Shop: Eagle's Nest sells logoed T-shirts, sweatshirts, pens, and model trucks. Open Mon–Fri at hours based on shift changes (call 513-390-4118).

Directions: Take I-70 to Rt. 68 North; freeway will end. Exit at Rt. 334 East and take second exit to continue on Rt. 68 North, Urbana Rd. Turn left into plant at the big "Navistar" sign. From the north, take Business Rt. 68 (which becomes Urbana Rd.) and turn right into plant.

Nearby Attractions: Honda Welcome Center, Marysville (see page 239); Dayton's attractions, including Wright Memorial Air Force Museum, 15 miles away.

Robinson Ransbottom Pottery

Ransbottom Road   *stoneware pottery*
Roseville, OH 43777
(614) 697-7355

There is something heart-warming, appealing, and even patriotic about being in the deep Midwestern interior of Ohio, winding your way through beautiful expanses of countryside and heavily vegetated landscape, and finally encountering a business that blends so inextricably with its surroundings that you do not realize you've reached a manufacturing facility. The country you have just driven through is the earth from which Robinson Ransbottom mines the clay for its timeless stoneware. The raw materials used in the pottery are all obtained within a 5- to 10-mile radius of this rustic plant.

As you embark on your self-guided tour, you enter one of a series of warehouses and production facilities. A dark earthiness surrounds you, as arrows direct you to various stops. At Stop One you may view any of a variety of glazing and hand-decorating techniques, such as pottery being hand-dipped (the procedure is called "slipping"), rolled, or mechanically spray-glazed.

One of the plant's most interesting areas is the "beehive" kilns. These two kilns were built in the mid-1800s, and they literally look like enormous beehives. You may see the kilns being loaded ("set") or unloaded. Each kiln holds about 30 tons, or 20,000 pieces, of pottery, and reaches a temperature between 2,300° and 2,400°.

As you exit the plant through the stock area, pass stack upon stack of stoneware birdbaths, vases, urns, and crockery. Robinson Ransbottom Pottery is such a down-to-earth operation that it's hard to believe the company processes about 700 tons of clay per month. Since it was founded in 1900, Robinson Ransbottom boasts that its products are "Old as yesterday, modern as tomorrow."

Cost: Free
Freebies: No
Video Shown: 10-minute video on pottery-making process, shown at Pot Shop.
Reservations Needed: No, except for groups larger than 25 people.

Days and Hours: Mon–Fri 9:00 AM–2:15 PM. Closed holidays and for 2 weeks around the beginning of July.
Plan to Stay: 20 minutes for self-guided tour, plus time for video and Pot Shop.
Minimum Age: None
Disabled Access: Yes
Group Requirements: Groups larger than 25 should call 1 week in advance for guided tour. No maximum group size.
Special Information: No photography. At Stop Two, safety laws prohibit any conversation with employees. You are asked to be silent while watching at this stop so as not to distract the workers.
Gift Shop: Pot Shop offers housewares, gardenware, and novelties. Seconds shop located at back of store. Open Mon–Sun 9:00 AM–5:00 PM. May be closed weekends January–March.
Directions: From I-70, take SR 22 South to Rt. 93 South. After crossing railroad tracks, turn left on Zanesville Rd. Turn left at traffic light onto Elm St. Take Elm St. to end and turn left on Ransbottom Rd. Robinson Ransbottom Pottery is 1 mile ahead on the left.
Nearby Attractions: Roseville-Crooksville pottery-communities attractions include Alpine Pottery tour (call 614-697-0075), Beaumont Bros. Pottery tour (call 614-982-0055), Ohio Ceramic Center (Crooksville), Cope Gallery, and July pottery festival featuring tours of other pottery factories; Zanesville's attractions, including Zane Landing Park, Zanesville Art Center, Historic Freight Station, and Shultz Mansion, are within a 10-mile radius.

Velvet Ice Cream   〜 *ice cream*

State Route 13
Utica, OH 43080
(614) 892-3921

A picturesque farm-country landscape welcomes you to Velvet Ice Cream's 20-acre site. The scene is complete with a mill stream, pond, ducks, and an 18-foot antique water-powered grist mill, taking you back in time to another century. Ye Olde Mill, whose original hand-cut stone foundation dates back to 1817, is featured on the company's ice-cream cartons. It's hard to imagine that adjacent to it is Velvet Ice Cream's modern, state-of-the-art ice cream factory, capable of producing over 2,000 gallons of ice-cream products each hour!

The company has been owned and run by the Dager family since 1914. A stroll through their ice-cream museum reveals some of the antique ice cream–making equipment used throughout history—and lots of fun facts about America's favorite dessert. You can just picture the workers slowly and laboriously turning cranks by hand in what must have been a tedious, painstaking process. The museum also tells the history of milling, the world's oldest industry.

After the museum, visit the factory viewing gallery. A sign near the viewing windows proudly boasts: "Welcome to Ohio's Ice Cream Capital." Your attention is drawn to hundreds of feet of stainless-steel tubing, which seems to outline every corner and angle of the factory. The cold mixture of cream, milk, and sugar is pumped through this labyrinth of tubing to the processing machinery.

You might see juicy red strawberries being dumped into the mix at the flavor vats. The filling operation follows, as the ice cream is pumped into carton after carton. A maze of conveyor belts transports the filled containers as they are lidded and wrapped in polyethylene for shipping. They finally disappear into freezer storage where, within a few hours, they are frozen. Look for the novelty machines making ice cream–sandwiches, pushups, or the 1817 gourmet ice cream–bar—vanilla and peanut-butter ice cream coated in chocolate—yum!

Cost: Free

Freebies: No

Video Shown: 2-minute video shows ice cream–making process.

Reservations Needed: No, except for groups larger than 5 people that want a guide.

Days and Hours: Mon–Fri 8:00 AM–5:00 PM for the viewing gallery. Lunch break from 11:30 AM–1:00 PM. See Gift Shop section below for museum days and hours. Closed holidays.

Plan to Stay: 1 hour for self-guided viewing gallery and museum, plus time for Ye Olde Ice Cream Parlor and scenic grounds.

Minimum Age: None

Disabled Access: Yes

Group Requirements: Groups larger than 5 people that want a guided tour should call 1 week in advance. School groups receive ice-cream sample.

Special Information: Arrive before 4:00 PM to see production. No photography allowed in viewing gallery. Annual Memorial Day Weekend Ice Cream Festival, Buckeye Tree Festival (second Sunday in September), and other special events throughout the summer.

Gift Shop: Ye Olde Mill contains a replica of an old-fashioned early-1800s ice-cream parlor, restaurant, and gift shop. Restaurant offers homemade food and, of course, ice cream. Gift shop sells nostalgic gifts, Ohio-made handcrafted items, Ohio food products, and Olde Mill souvenir items. Hours for museum, restaurant, ice-cream parlor, and gift shop are May 1 through October 31, Mon–Sun 11:00 AM–9:00 PM (after September 1, closing time is 8:00 PM).

Directions: Take SR 62 to Utica. Turn onto Rt. 13 South and go 1 mile. You're there when you see Ye Olde Mill.

Nearby Attractions: Dawes Arboretum; Mound Builders Park (Indian burial grounds).

Frankoma Pottery   〜 *pottery*

2400 Frankoma Road
Sapulpa, OK 74067
(918) 224-5511

The name "Frankoma" combines founder John Frank's name with that of Oklahoma, a source of rich clay deposits. In 1927 Frank left Chicago to teach art and pottery at the University of Oklahoma. Five years later, equipped with one small kiln, a butter churn for mixing clay, a fruit jar for grinding glazes, and a few other crude tools, he started his own pottery studio. Several fires, expansions, and a generation later, Frankoma Pottery has grown to 70,000 square feet.

As your guide leads you through this facility, you will observe Frankoma's two methods of forming pottery. In the casting department, "slip" (liquid clay) is poured into plaster molds. The molds absorb water from the slip, leaving harder clay against the mold's walls. Excess slip is poured out. After four hours of drying, the piece is removed from the mold and allowed to dry overnight. The second, more interesting method is pressing, which is used for plates and flat pieces. A 50-ton hydraulic press slams down on a solid slab of clay to form each object. It smashes the clay around a mold, pushing excess clay out the sides. Regardless of how it is formed, each piece is taken to the trim line, where rough edges are hand-trimmed with a paring knife and smoothed with a wet sponge.

After the pottery is fired, it is ready for glazing. A hand-held air gun sprays glaze on flat pieces. Deep pieces are "dipped" in glaze to coat the inside and then sprayed on the outside. The brushing department "dry-foots," or removes the glaze from the pieces' bottoms, so they do not stick to the kiln.

Look through the continuously firing tunnel kiln, which is open on both ends. Long, pottery-filled kiln cars enter one end. Each kiln car reaches a maximum temperature of 2,000° at the center, allowing the clay to solidify and the glaze to melt and change color. The car emerges from the other end at 350°. You will leave with a new appreciation for the hands-on nature and collectibility of Frankoma pottery.

Cost: Free
Freebies: No
Video Shown: No
Reservations Needed: No, except for groups larger than 10 people.
Days and Hours: Mon–Fri 9:30 AM–3:00 PM. Lunch break from 12:00 PM–1:00 PM. Call to check for Friday and holiday schedules and for week-long plant vacations around July 4th and Christmas.
Plan to Stay: 30 minutes, plus time in gift shop.
Minimum Age: None
Disabled Access: Yes
Group Requirements: Advance reservations preferred for groups of 10 people or more. Groups larger than 25 will be split into smaller groups. School groups get free clay to take back to their schools.
Special Information: Since kilns fire constantly, it can get hot in the summer.
Gift Shop: Sells full line of microwavable, oven-proof, and dishwasher-safe Frankoma dinnerware and accessories. Look for baking pans, relish dishes, and bean pots shaped like Oklahoma, Texas, Louisiana, and Arkansas. Seconds sold at discount. Open Mon-Sat 9:00 AM–5:00 PM, Sun 1:00 PM–5:00 PM. Closed holidays. Catalog available from above number.
Directions: Take Turner Tpk. to Exit 215 (Sapulpa exit). Turn left on Hwy. 97, then right onto Hwy. 166 East to Old Hwy. 66 (Frankoma Rd.). Turn left; Frankoma is on your right.
Nearby Attractions: Keepsake Candles tour (see page 248); Mr. Indian store; Tulsa's attractions, including Philbrook and Gilcrease Museums, are about 20 minutes away.

Keepsake Candles ~ *decorative candles*

Route 3
Bartlesville, OK 74003
(918) 336-0351

Keepsake Candles®

It's known as the "church fund-raising project that got out of hand." In 1969 Ed Ririe agreed to make candles molded in the shape of his mother's antique glassware for the church Christmas Bazaar. The color for the candles came, despite protest, from his daughters' crayons. Now Ed's wife, Alice Ririe, manages the company, and the candles are sold in all 50 states and around the world. Built in the 1950s by the government as part of a radar station, the factory was once a half-court gymnasium. You'll find other equipment of unique origin on your tour, such as work tables made from hospital gurneys, a melting vat that was once a dairy tank, and a storage cabinet that was formerly an analog computer.

Enter this unique structure and you're confronted with a huge stack of wax slabs. The slabs are melted in a vat that can hold 1,400 pounds of liquid wax. The wax for the candles' outside shell is mixed with other substances in order to raise the melting point so the shell holds its shape as the candle burns down.

A shellmaker takes a bucketful of melted wax and adds a wax-based dye. The shellmaker then carefully pours some colored wax into a pliable silicon rubber mold. The worker hand-twists the mold to make sure all sides have an even coating of wax. After about four layers, the shell will be thick enough to stand on its own. Similar to a process the Romans used to make lead pipes 2,000 years ago, this is called slush molding.

A worker splits apart the flexible mold to reveal a brightly colored shell that resembles a piece of antique pattern glass. Touch the still-warm mold and the hard shell. The shell is polished using pantyhose, the same way you would use sandpaper on wood.

The worker uses an old coffeepot to pour the clear, scented, liquid wax into the shells. Depending on the day, peppermint, strawberry, or cinnamon may permeate the air around you. After it cools, each candle is tagged with its color, scent, date, pattern, and style.

Cost: Free
Freebies: No
Video Shown: 4-minute video covers manufacturing, shown in retail store.
Reservations Needed: No, except for groups over 10 people.
Days and Hours: Mon–Fri 10:00 AM–3:00 PM. Closed most holidays.
Plan to Stay: 15 minutes for tour, plus time in the Country Store.
Minimum Age: None
Disabled Access: Yes
Group Requirements: Groups should call 1–2 weeks in advance. Maximum group size 45 people. Large groups will be split into groups of 10–12 people.
Special Information: Factory is not air-conditioned; it can be very hot in summer. Grounds have antiques, including farm equipment and buggy. Railroad cars and caboose in front of store.
Country Store: Shop has 5 rooms, each with its own theme. Candles are displayed on antique stoves, cupboards, and sewing machines. Seconds sold at discount. Also sells baskets, gourmet foods, candleholders, and seasonal items. Open Mon–Fri 9:00 AM–5:30 PM, Sat 10:00 AM–5:00 PM, and Sun 1:00 PM–5:00 PM. From Thanksgiving to Christmas, hours extended until 6:00 PM daily. Closed most holidays. Catalog available from above number.
Directions: From U.S. Hwy. 75, take U.S. Hwy. 60 West through Bartlesville; 2 miles past Phillips Research Center, turn right onto CR 3235. Keepsake Candles is at the top of Radar Hill.
Nearby Attractions: Frankoma Pottery tour (see page 247); Phillips' Mansion; Wild Horse Refuge; Woolaroc Museum and Game Refuge; Tallgrass Prairie; Frank Lloyd Wright's Price Tower; June Oklahoma Mozart Festival.

Franz Family Bakery

breads, buns, and donuts

340 N.E. 11th Avenue
Portland, OR 97232
(503) 232-2191, ext. 365

Since its 1906 beginnings in a simple two-story frame home, Franz Bakery has fed millions of people in the Pacific Northwest. Franz's plant now covers six city blocks and turns out over 85 million pounds of baked goods each year. Your tour guide provides many impressive statistics, such as the company's daily production of 75,000 loaves, 684,300 buns, and 45,000 donuts from 250,000 pounds of flour. Yet, until you see the dough marching in and out of the ovens, it sounds impossible.

To create baked goods in these huge quantities, the process is highly automated, with constant movement of dough and bread everywhere you look. Even with machines 100 times bigger than those you use at home, it takes 17 steps to make Franz bread, from the sifting of the flour to the loading it on delivery trucks. You'll stare at dough being kneaded in mixers that work it into 1,200-pound pieces. The divider and rounder machines turn this hunk of dough into softball-size pieces that relax in the overhead proofer before being molded into loaf shapes and dropped into pans.

After the proof box, which allows the dough to rise to its proper size, the pans enter 100-foot-long ovens. Bread stays inside for 19 to 21 minutes, while buns only need a seven- to nine-minute experience. You'll enjoy the heat from these ovens on chilly, rainy Portland days. Once the pans move out of the oven, vacuum-suction cups gently lift the bread from the pans and place the hot bread onto a 4,000-foot-long cooling rack. After one hour and 18 minutes of cooling, the bread moves through machines that slice it, slip it into plastic bags, tie the ends, and code the packages. In the time it takes you to eat one slice of bread, 75 to 100 loaves are packaged.

Cost: Free

Freebies: Donuts, coffee, milk, and take-home Franz sack with bread miniloaf, goodies, and pencil.

Video Shown: 15-minute video on company's history and products.

Reservations Needed: Yes. Individuals and families need to join group tour. Call (503) 232-2191, ext. 365. Company prefers to give tours to people in its distribution area.

Days and Hours: Mon–Fri 9:00 AM–4:00 PM. Closed holidays, and July and August.

Plan to Stay: 1 hour for tour and tasting, plus time in thrift store.

Minimum Age: 7

Disabled Access: Yes, for most of tour.

Group Requirements: Minimum group size is 5 people; maximum is 60. Tours scheduled 4–6 weeks in advance.

Special Information: No photography. Sneakers or walking shoes required. The intense smells may bother some people. Snyder's Bakery in Spokane, WA, another United States Bakery subsidiary, also gives tours (call 509-535-7726).

Outlet Store: Thrift store sells excess breads, buns, pastry, and muffins at discount. Open Mon–Fri 9:00 AM–5:30 PM. Sat 9:00 AM–5:00 PM. Closed holidays.

Directions: Company requests that you call above number for directions.

Nearby Attractions: Blitz-Weinhard Brewery tour (call 503-222-4351); Oregon Convention Center; Lloyd Center; Holladay Park; Portland's downtown attractions, including Rose Test Gardens and Japanese Gardens, are about 15 minutes away.

Harry and David

1314 Center Drive
South Gateway Center
Medford, OR 97501
(541) 776-2277 / (800) 547-3033

*Royal Riviera pears
and gift baskets*

Since brothers Harry and David Holmes began mailing succulent Royal Riviera pears around the country in the 1930s, their company has grown into a mail-order business whose gift baskets are an institution at holiday time. From an overhead balcony, watch workers hand-pack these beautiful baskets. Each packer receives a wooden box containing all of the components that go into the basket (which may include fruit, preserves, nuts, and candies), the basket itself, and a Styrofoam form that resembles a cowboy hat. After the packer fills the basket, it is transported by conveyor belt to workers who cover it with cellophane and send it to the shrink-wrap machine.

Around Christmas, you see the packing and wrapping of the Towers of Treats—five boxes, each containing a different product such as fruit, cookies, or cheese, stacked in a tower and wrapped with a ribbon. Each worker fills a box and passes it to the next person, who covers the box with a lid and adds another box on top. Once all five boxes are stacked, one member of a two-person team holds the ribbon, while the other wraps the ribbon around the tower and adds a pre-made bow and baubles on top. You see the ribbons flying as each team assembles up to 1,500 towers a day.

In the bakery, watch as pies, cookies, and cakes are prepared by hand and placed into and removed from the ovens. Enter the candy kitchen, where the smell of chocolate wafts from vats that stir the brown liquid with rotating blades. Here you'll see the chocolate poured into molds and put through the enrober, the cooling chamber, and the cool room before being packed and frozen for later use in gift boxes.

Cost: Free
Freebies: Chocolate samples
Video Shown: No
Reservations Needed: Recommended for individuals, required for more than 10 people.

Days and Hours: Mon–Fri 9:30 AM, 10:30 AM, 12:30 PM, and 1:45 PM. January through March may be fewer tours. Closed holidays and July 4th week.

Plan to Stay: 1 hour for tour, plus time for Harry and David Country Village and Jackson & Perkins Rose Garden.

Minimum Age: 7

Disabled Access: Limited access for tour due to 3 flights of stairs; Harry and David Country Village stores accessible.

Group Requirements: Groups over 10 people should call 1–2 months in advance. Maximum group size is 60.

Special Information: October through mid-December is the best time to see production. While the candy kitchen and bakery operate year-round, during the spring and summer you'll see less packing of gift boxes and more packing of roses and perennials for Jackson & Perkins, the division that sells mail-order roses and bulbs.

Gift Shop: Harry and David's Country Village comprises a gift shop, pantry, fruit stand, and deli. It carries factory seconds of fruit and baked goods as well as candies, local food products, clothing, and gift baskets. Open Mon–Sun 9:00 AM–7:00 PM. Closed holidays. Catalog and Fruit-of-the-Month Club information available from 800 number.

Directions: From Portland, take I-5 South. Take Medford Exit 27 onto Barnett Rd. Turn left at second light onto Center Dr. Store is on right. From San Francisco or Sacramento, take I-5 North to Medford Exit 27. Turn left after exiting and go over freeway. Turn left onto Stewart Ave., then left onto Center Dr. Store is on right. You will be transported to the plant, 1 mile away, by van.

Nearby Attractions: Peter Britt Summer Music Festival in Jacksonville; the Oregon Shakespearean Festival in Ashland.

Luhr-Jensen *fishing lures*

400 Portway Avenue
Hood River, OR 97031
(541) 386-3811 / (800) 366-3811

Established in 1932 in an unused chicken coop on a Depression-ridden fruit ranch, Luhr-Jensen has become the largest manufacturer of fishing lures in the United States, and possibly the world. The family-owned company manufactures each lure, from raw metal to a jewelry-finished product ready for the dealer's tackle department. The plant is located in one of the country's best fishing areas—about 50 feet away from the Columbia River that separates Oregon from Washington.

A guided tour through the plant reveals all of the steps involved in creating Luhr-Jensen fishing lures, from stamping out the basic metal blade to plating, painting, assembling, and final packaging. Even before entering the punch-press area, you can hear these big machines stamping lure blades from long ribbons of brass. Literally millions of varying sizes, shapes, and thickness are punched out each year. One day you may see the popular Krocodile lures stamped out, while another day it may be spinner blades for the Willy Wobbler. The nearby plating room is a bustle of activity as chromium, nickel, copper, and even 24-karat gold and pure silver are coated onto the brass lure blades.

Nearby, in the paint room, watch workers with airbrushes carefully applying red, chartreuse, green, and other brightly colored fish-attracting patterns to the metal blades. In the main assembly area, hear the sounds of pneumatic wire-twisting machines and the rattle of blades, beads, clevises, and metal bodies. Spinners, lake trolls, and other wire-shafted lures are assembled by hand. In an adjacent area, the steady hum of printing presses signals preparation of the packaging material for the final step in preparing the lures for shipment to dealers throughout the world. You'll want to head directly for the nearby Columbia River and use your free lure to land steelhead and salmon.

Cost: Free

Freebies: Fishing lure

Video Shown: Short video that shows production process and fishing.

Reservations Needed: No, except for groups larger than 15 people.

Days and Hours: Mon–Fri 11:00 AM and 1:30 PM. Closed holidays.

Plan to Stay: 45 minutes for tour and video, plus additional time for store.

Minimum Age: None

Disabled Access: Yes

Group Requirements: Groups larger than 15 should make reservations at least 1 week ahead. No maximum group size.

Special Information: No photography

Company Store: Sells lures, fishing accessories, closeout items, hats, T-shirts. Usually open Tue–Fri 8:00 AM–5:00 PM, Sat 9:00 AM –1:00 PM. Catalog of fishing tackle and accessories available from (800) 535-1711.

Directions: From Portland, take I-84 East to Exit 63. Turn left, back over freeway, and follow frontage road (Portway Ave.) toward river. Luhr-Jensen is on the riverfront, adjacent to a large boardsailing-event parking area. From I-84 West, take Exit 63, turn right and follow frontage road toward river.

Nearby Attractions: Catch the Wind Kites tour (call 541-994-7500); Mt. Hood; river rafting, fishing, boardsailing, mountain biking, hiking, and enjoying Hood River area scenery. Hood River is the "Boardsailing Capital of the World." Companies such as Da Kine Hawaii, makers of windsurfing and other sports accessories, offer limited tours (call 800-827-7466).

Oregon Connection/ House of Myrtlewood

1125 South 1st Street
Coos Bay, OR 97420
(541) 267-7804

wooden tableware and golf putters

The myrtle tree is a broadleaf evergreen found in a small area of the Pacific Coast. The wood looks yellow and brown when finished, and its fine grain makes it more durable than well-known redwood. At House of Myrtlewood, videos and guided tours reveal all the mysteries of this beautiful hardwood and how it's turned into everything from salad bowls to patented golf putters.

If you like the smell of freshly cut wood, you'll enjoy walking through the small sawmill area where logs are sliced into 6- to 8-foot sections of varying thicknesses. Watch the workers use disks of various sizes as patterns to draw circles on the wood slabs, trying to avoid knotholes or other flaws. They cut out these circles, called "blanks," and drill holes in the center to prepare them for the initial "rough out" on the lathe. Large, wet woodchips fly off the lathe during the rough-out turning. Next the pieces go to the drying room, where it takes about nine weeks to dry the wood down from about 50 percent moisture to a 6.5 percent moisture content.

On the main factory floor, watch the "finish turning" of the dried rough-out. Turners do not use a pattern to shape bowls and trays. Instead, each piece is individually turned; no two pieces are exactly alike. Look up at the humming overhead drive line (whose design dates back to the 1850s and the Industrial Revolution), which powers the lathes. The pieces are then sanded and receive either a gloss or oil finish. When workers burn in the company name, you appreciate the effort that went into that finished piece.

Cost: Free
Freebies: Homemade fudge samples in gift shop; coffee or tea.
Video Shown: Three short videos throughout tour describe myrtle tree, sawmill, and processing of myrtlewood products. Videos provide good close-ups of processes you see from behind glass windows.

Reservations Needed: No, except for groups larger than 40 people.
Days and Hours: May through September, Mon–Sun 8:30 AM–5:30 PM, October through April, Mon–Sat 9:00 AM–5:00 PM, Sun 10:00 AM–4:00 PM. Factory operates Mon–Thur, but tours run every day. Closed Christmas, New Year's, and Thanksgiving.
Plan to Stay: 20 minutes, plus time for gift shop.
Minimum Age: None
Disabled Access: Yes
Group Requirements: Groups larger than 40 people should call a day ahead.
Special Information: Limits on flash photography, for safety reasons. You may not see all 15 steps involved in making products.
Gift Shop: Carries full range of myrtlewood wares, from bowls, trays, cutting boards, and candleholders to Wooden Touch golf putters. (Putting green available for testing patented, hand-crafted putter.) Also sells other gift items, homemade fudge, Northwest wines, and Oregon gourmet foods. In the hobby room, craftspeople will find myrtlewood for turning and carving. Open same hours as tour. Catalog available from (800) 255-5318.
Directions: From Portland, take I-5 South to Hwy. 38 West. Then go south on Hwy. 101. Company is just off Hwy. 101 in South Coos Bay, in a wood building with large myrtle tree–shaped sign and American flag on top. From California, take I-5 North to Dillard-Winston exit and go west. Follow directions to Hwy. 42 West. Then go north on Hwy. 101. In approximately 5 miles, billboard will direct where to turn.
Nearby Attractions: The Real Oregon Gift myrtlewood factory tour (call 541-756-2582); Tillamook Cheese factory tour, about 4 hours up the Oregon coast (see page 255); Oregon Coast beaches; Shoreacres State Park.

Pendleton Woolen Mills

wool processing and weaving

Blanket Mill
1307 S.E. Court Place
Pendleton, OR 97801
(541) 276-6911

Beginning with Indian blankets in 1909, Pendleton Woolen Mills has grown to include 13 plants producing men's and women's sportswear, blankets, and fabrics. The company operates on the "vertical" system of manufacturing, which means that it performs all the steps in processing raw wool into finished products. In Pendleton, Oregon, you can tour the original Pendleton plant, which began as an Indian trading post. Pendleton does 95 percent of its manufacturing in the U.S., in contrast to 30 percent for others in the apparel industry.

Once the wool is graded and washed in the Portland, Oregon scouring plant and dyed in the Washougal, Washington mill, it's shipped to this facility as big bales. Upstairs, the carding machines transform the loose wool into thin, straight, round strands called "roving." The spinning machines convert the roving to yarn by drawing out and twisting the fiber strands. The twisting gives the yarn its strength.

The first floor vibrates under your feet as you walk into the weaving room. The 8- to 10-foot-wide electronic looms pound as their harnesses move up and down. The 19 Jacquard looms produce complex patterns, such as Indian designs. A tape that carries a pattern of punched holes (similar to that of a player-piano roll) controls the sequence in which the yarns are raised and lowered. Depending upon the warp that was wound onto a loom (could weigh over 1,000 pounds), it may require more than a month of weaving time.

Once completed, blankets and fabric are inspected before shipment to the Washougal Mill for finishing. Finished blankets are ready for distribution. The fabric may be shipped to the Milwaukee, Oregon plant to be made into men's Pendleton "damn good wool shirts," icons of the Northwest lifestyle.

Cost: Free

Freebies: No

Video Shown: "From Fleece to Fashion" shows the process from sheep in the fields to finished blankets or clothing. Continuously shown in Sales Room.

Reservations Needed: No, except for groups larger than 8 people.

Days and Hours: Mon–Fri 9:00 AM, 11:00 AM, 1:30 PM, and 3:00 PM. Closed holidays, 2 weeks in summer (usually August), and week between Christmas and New Year's.

Plan to Stay: 20–25 minutes, plus time for video and Sales Room.

Minimum Age: None, except difficult to keep ear protection on young children.

Disabled Access: Yes, for first floor. No, for second floor carding and spinning.

Group Requirements: Groups larger than 8 people should call 1 week in advance.

Special Information: Company most interested in giving tours for local community. No photography. Pendleton's Washougal (WA) Weaving Mill (in Portland area) gives tours of the dyeing and fabric- and blanket-finishing process (call 360-835-1118). Near the Washougal mill is a seconds store open Mon–Sat 8:00 AM–4:00 PM. In Portland, OR, watch spinning then weaving of wool at the Foundation plant (call 503-273-2788).

Sales Room: Carries full line of Pendleton menswear, fabric, plus Indian bed and baby blankets, shawls, and robes. Offers seconds and discontinued items. Sells logoed T-shirts and sweatshirts. Open Mon–Sat 8:00 AM–5:00 PM. Closed holidays. The Murphy House, 1½ blocks away, carries Pendleton women's wear. Call (800) 447-6359.

Directions: From Portland, take I-84 East to Exit 210. Turn left under Frwy. Turn left at stop sign at bottom of hill. Turn right under bridge (viaduct). Turn right at "Yield" sign onto S.E. Court Place. Pendleton will be on your left in ½ block.

Nearby Attractions: Pendleton Underground Tours; Umatilla County Historical Society Museum; Wildhorse Gaming Resort.

Rodgers Instrument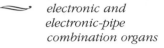
1300 N.E. 25th Avenue
Hillsboro, OR 97124
(503) 648-4181

*electronic and
electronic-pipe
combination organs*

Next time you're in New York's Carnegie Hall or Philadelphia's Academy of Music, listen for beautiful music from an organ made by this leading builder of classic electronic and pipe organs. Rodgers prides itself on technical innovation in organ-building, whether by making the first transistorized organ amplifier (1958) or by introducing Parallel Digital Imaging technology (1991) to create warmer, more authentic pipe-organ sounds. The technology and craft of organ-building resonate throughout the manufacturing area.

This guided tour shows all the steps involved in organ-making. Regardless of your interests—woodworking, electronics, or music—you'll find the process appealing. Don't expect huge machines or speeding assembly lines here; it takes weeks to make an organ. Instead you'll see skilled workers painstakingly laboring over each piece. Be sure to look for the Shoda machines in the cabinet shop area, where all the organ's wood parts begin their journey. The Shoda drills, saws, and shapes the wood according to a computerized program, while a vacuum seal holds the wood to the cutting table. This vacuum is so strong that a dollar bill placed on the work table cannot be pulled across the surface!

Cut parts from such woods as Sitka spruce, American black walnut, oak, and mahogany are assembled in the case-up area. Here, sides, feet, key deck, back rails, and other support pieces are glued and clamped together, insuring a dimensionally correct case. A "white sanding" process utilizes fine-grit sandpaper to give the wood a white flour-like surface. In the finishing department, instrument cases, benches, and pedalboard frames are stained, lightly sanded, and given a lacquer "top coat." Notice that, despite all the sanding, the area is dust-free: air curtains outside the white-sanding room and finishing area prevent the dust from migrating.

It's often the multiple ranks of 61 pipes each that give organs their powerful presence. Look for pictures of the largest organ Rodgers ever designed and built—the 194-rank (11,000 pipe) organ at Houston's Second Baptist Church, which took 1½ years to build. Throughout the tour you'll see and hear the roles that traditional external pipes and internal electronics (now mostly computer circuit boards) play in organ music. This contrast of technology and traditional craftsmanship makes the tour diverse: in one room an artisan hand-sands wood cases, while a computer technician next door tests circuit boards.

Cost: Free

Freebies: Tour guide booklet

Video Shown: 12-minute video covering company history, organ construction, and sound technology, shown upon request.

Reservations Needed: Yes

Days and Hours: Mon–Thur 9:00 AM–4:00 PM, Fri 9:00 AM–12:00 PM. No production Friday afternoons. Closed for 1 week in August.

Plan to Stay: 45 minutes–1 hour

Minimum Age: No, but children must be able to wear safety glasses. Kids will enjoy the tour more if they're interested in music.

Disabled Access: Yes

Group Requirements: Groups must call 10 days in advance to make reservations. Maximum group size is 100 people.

Special Information: No photography. Tours can be customized to your interests.

Gift Shop: No

Directions: From Portland, take I-5 South to Rt. 26 West. Get off at Cornelius Pass Rd. exit and turn right. Turn right onto Cornell Rd. Immediately after Hillsboro airport, turn right onto 25th Ave. Rodgers is on the right.

Nearby Attractions: Shute Park; Fairgrounds' events; Trolley Car Museum in Forest Grove. Portland's attractions, including Washington Park Zoo, Rose Test Gardens, and Japanese Gardens, are about 20 miles away.

See color photos, page 189

Tillamook Cheese   ～ *cheese*

4175 Highway 101 North
Tillamook, OR 97141
(503) 842-4481

Tillamook may be the largest and most auto-mated cheese-maker in the Northwest, but its tour begins by showing respect for the raw material that underlies its success: a plastic life-size cow with attached milking machine. The 176-member Tillamook Coun-ty Creamery Association turns one of the finest milk supplies in the U.S. into 50 mil-lion pounds of cheese yearly. A self-guided tour and accompanying videos show you what's involved in making and packing its famous Tillamook Cheddars.

On the cheese-making side of the plant, peer through glass windows at the shiny enclosed cooking vats, each the size of an oval swimming pool. Notice the electronic control panels that direct the heating, thick-ening, and stirring of each vat's 25,000 quarts of milk. When the cooking is com-plete, the curds and whey are pumped to the Cheddarmaster machine, which looks like the side of a silver ocean liner with its screen-covered portholes. Inside this ma-chine, the curd is drained of the whey, mat-ted together, turned and tested for proper body, milled by cutting into finger-sized pieces, salted, and stirred.

Then the curd travels to the pressing tow-ers, where pressure and vacuum remove any remaining whey. Watch the 40-pound cheese blocks eject from the tower into clear, vacuum-sealed bags for their stay in the aging room. About four months of aging or curing at 40° is required for medium-flavored cheese, and nine months for sharp.

While most of the cheese-making happens inside the machines, you see more action on the packaging side of the plant. The properly aged 40-pound blocks are transformed into 5-pound loaf, 2-pound baby loaf, 9-ounce random cut, and snack-bar sizes. The spin-ning assembly-line machines, with help from paper-hatted workers, do all the cutting, weighing, wrapping, sealing, and packaging at a mesmerizing pace. The colorful Tilla-mook label moves past too quickly for read-ing, but you know there's tasty cheese inside.

Cost: Free

Freebies: Tillamook Cheese samples. Try the cheese curds that squeak in your mouth!

Videos Shown: Throughout self-guided tour, continuously running videos cover Creamery's history, dairy workings, and an inside view of cheese-making machines.

Reservations Needed: No, unless group wants a guide or plans to eat lunch at deli.

Days and Hours: Summer, Mon–Sun 8:00 AM –8:00 PM; September through Memorial Day, 8:00 AM–6:00 PM. Closed Thanksgiving and Christmas. Not always in full production on weekends and holidays.

Plan to Stay: 30 minutes for self-guided tour and historical and dairy displays, plus time for gift shop.

Minimum Age: None

Disabled Access: Yes

Group Requirements: Bus groups and groups larger than 20 people should call 1 week in advance to reserve a tour guide, who gives brief historical sketch of Tillamook County and explains cheese-making facility and process.

Gift Shop: Sells all varieties of Tillamook Cheese, logoed shirts, hats, other cow-emblazoned items, and Oregon specialty foods. Special sales offer cheeses at 99¢ per pound. Open same hours as tour. Call (800) 542-7290 for catalog. Deli and ice-cream counter offer about 30 different flavors of Tillamook Ice Cream.

Directions: From Portland, take Rt. 6 West and go north on Hwy. 101. Factory is on your right about 2 miles north of Tillamook town.

Nearby Attractions: Oregon Connection/ House of Myrtlewood tour, down the coast about 4 hours (see page 252); Pioneer Museum; Blimp Hanger Museum; Three Capes Scenic Driving Loop; Oregon Coast.

See color photo, page 163

Weyerhaeuser ~ *paper*
785 North 42nd Street
Springfield, OR 97478
(541) 741-5478

Weyerhaeuser

We make paper in many forms in the U.S., with much of it coming from the abundant forests of the Pacific Northwest. This Weyerhaeuser mill makes the ubiquitous brown paper that forms the smooth inside and outside layers of corrugated boxes. As in most paper mills, this one surrounds you with new sights, sounds, and smells.

To produce "linerboard," as it's called in the paper industry, Weyerhaeuser starts with a combination of woodchips from local sawmills and recycled paper. Before the plant opened in 1949, sawmills incinerated the chips as waste. Today these chips are a precious resource. In addition, recycled paper has become an important source of fiber. Weyerhaeuser uses more than 450 tons of recycled paper per day, producing linerboard with up to 40 percent recycled content. You'll notice hills of woodchips surrounding the mill buildings, with whole trucks being lifted skyward to unload more chips. The woodchips' density makes them look like a desert of light brown sand.

On your tour, you'll see stacks of huge bales of recyclable paper—corrugated boxes, office paper, and more. The bales are dropped into a massive blender that whirls the fiber into a slurry. Nonpaper materials, such as adhesives, plastic liners and dirt, are removed through a sophisticated screening process.

In the pulp mill, the chips are cooked to separate out the pulp (for safety reasons you do not see that process). Once cooked, the fibers are washed, refined, and blended with the recycled paper slurry. The mixture then enters 500-foot-long machines that turn the pulp into paper at speeds of up to 2,250 feet per minute. Make sure you feel the pulp that the tour guide takes from the front of the machine. To some, it feels like thick applesauce.

Follow the pulp's path through the noisy machine, as it is transformed from a slurry (99.5 percent water) to a finished sheet (8 percent water). It travels over and under

rows of rollers, which press and dry out the water to make the paper that is then wound onto 30-ton reels. A new reel is produced about every 30 minutes. The reels, each holding 15 miles of linerboard, are cut into 1- to 2-ton rolls, banded, and shipped to Weyerhaeuser box-manufacturing plants via waiting trucks and boxcars.

Cost: Free
Freebies: No
Video Shown: No
Reservations Needed: No, except for groups.
Days and Hours: Mon and Fri 9:00 AM. Other times may be available. Closed holidays and week between Christmas and New Year's. Semi-annual closings for maintenance during selected days in April and October.
Plan to Stay: 1½ hours
Minimum Age: Children must be able to walk and wear earplugs. No strollers.
Disabled Access: Stair-climbing and extensive walking inside and outside the mill.
Group Requirements: Groups should call 1 week ahead. No maximum group size.
Special Information: As with all paper mills in the Northwest, this one can be hot, humid, and noisy, while outdoor weather may be cold and damp. Dress appropriately and wear sturdy shoes. No open-toed footwear.
Gift Shop: No
Directions: From I-5, take I-105 East to 42nd St. exit. Go south on 42nd St. Mill complex is about 1 mile ahead. Turn left at third traffic light. Visitors must check in at main gate.
Nearby Attractions: James River paper products tours (call 541-369-2293); Willamalane Park and Swim Center; Lively Park Wave Pool; Springfield Museum; Dorris Ranch; University of Oregon.

Website: www.weyerhaeuser.com

The third largest recycler in the U.S., Weyerhaeuser recycles more than 2 million tons of paper per year.

A roll of paper waits to be cut at the end of the paper machine.

Anderson Bakery 〰 *pretzels*

2060 Old Philadelphia Pike
Lancaster, PA 17602
(717) 299-2321

Although you may not have heard of Anderson pretzels, chances are you've eaten them. Besides their own brand of pretzels, Anderson makes most of the generic and store-brand pretzels in the U.S. For more than 100 years, Anderson has been baking pretzels in almost every flavor, shape and size imaginable, including pizza-flavored, cheese-flavored, unsalted ("baldies"), and their newest recipe, peanut-butter-filled pretzels.

This self-guided tour begins with a walk past a photo display of the company's impressive history, from its beginnings in 1888 in Lancaster, in the heart of Pennsylvania Amish country, to its latest building and warehouse expansion. The pictures also illustrate the history of pretzel-making in the U.S. In 1946, for example, a one-day shift produced 500 pounds of pretzels, compared to the 80,000 pounds each Anderson shift turns out today.

Farther down the observation walkway is a glass-enclosed corridor, where you can watch Anderson's employees and the huge pretzel-making machines. The pretzels' ingredients wait patiently in several huge storage tanks before being piped directly into four large mixers. Batches of pretzel dough are mixed, weighed, and sent to the production line, where machines with small mechanical "fingers" twist slices of dough into thick "Bavarian Dutch" pretzels (at the astonishing rate of 50,000 pretzels an hour).

The dough pretzels move to the ovens by way of the "proof belt." Here, intense heat forces the pretzels' yeast to rise, or proof. The longer the proof belt, the thicker the pretzel; thick Bavarian Twists travel up to 140 feet on these belts. The proofed pretzels are sent to the "cooker," which bakes them brown, and then the "salter," where salt rains down on the still-moist dough.

In another area, watch "extruders" force fresh dough slabs through openings in a die plate and slice the strands with moving knife blades. Suddenly, thousands of long, thin pretzel sticks are born. You can see high-ways of pretzel twists, gems, rods, logs and "minis" travel by conveyor to the cooker and the baking room, where enormous ovens bake them crispy brown. Their final destination is the packaging room where the pretzels, each shape on its own route, dive into boxes, cartons, tins and bags for their journeys to stores all over North America.

Cost: Free

Freebies: Bavarian Dutch pretzel sample

Video Shown: No

Reservations Needed: No, except for groups larger than 40 people.

Days and Hours: Mon–Fri 8:30 AM–4:00 PM. Closed most major holidays.

Plan to Stay: 30 minutes for tour, plus time in factory outlet.

Minimum Age: None

Disabled Access: Yes (there is an elevator to the second floor).

Group Requirements: Groups larger than 40 should call in advance for reservations.

Special Information: The soft-pretzel shop offers a pretzel sample fresh from the oven and a cold drink, April through October.

Factory Outlet: All Anderson products available, plus T-shirts, hats, and other company souvenirs. Special deals on large cartons of broken pretzels. Catalog available from above number. Open year-round, Mon–Fri 8:30 AM –5:00 PM, April through December, also Sat 8:30 AM–3:30 PM.

Directions: From Pennsylvania Tpk., take Exit 21 (Reading/Lancaster) to Rt. 222 South. When highway ends, take Rt. 30 East to Rt. 340 East exit. Turn right onto Rt. 340 and drive through 1 traffic light. Anderson is on the right.

Nearby Attractions: Sturgis Pretzel tour (see page 274); Jam and Relish Kitchen viewing window in Kitchen Kettle Village (call 800-732-3538); Pennsylvania Amish attractions; Dutch Wonderland Amusement Park; dozens of factory outlet stores; James Buchanan House.

Benzel's ⟨⁓⟩ *pretzels*

5200 6th Avenue
Altoona, PA 16602
(814) 942-5062 / (800) 344-4438

Whether you love trains, pretzels, or big, fast machines, you'll enjoy this factory tour. In 1911 Adolf Benzel stepped off a boxcar at the Altoona, Pennsylvania, train station with his family and all his worldly belongings and started the Benzel tradition. Railroad buffs will enjoy the caboose parked on the grounds and the massive train mural along the Outlet Store's back wall. The mural depicts the railroad's influence on the Altoona area, including an unusual look at the Horseshoe Curve.

Benzel's is one of the few companies in the U.S.A. that still produces pretzels from the flour-malt-yeast-and-salt concoction first used by Catholic monks, except that now machines do it at the rate of 50 million pretzels a day. Through glass partitions you'll see the entire process, from dough being mixed to bags being boxed. Overhead signs on this self-guided tour help you understand what's involved in mixing the dough, shaping it into pretzel form in the extruder, salting the pretzels, then baking and bagging them.

At a rapid rate, pretzels are fed in long rows out of the extruder onto conveyer belts. As they travel down the proofing belt, the pretzels rise, get steamed, and are salted. The belts constantly roll with pretzels marching in and out of the 100-foot oven. Benzel's special slow-bake process bakes out the moisture, producing a lighter, crispier pretzel.

Since you watch the process at ground level, you see what happens inside the machinery. Notice the salt rhythmically falling on each row of pretzels like confetti and the intense flames that bake the pretzels in minutes. While Grandpa Benzel didn't make his "bretzels" the same way in 1911, his grandson's products and factory still continue the family's traditions and basic recipe.

Cost: Free
Freebies: Fresh pretzels hot off the line and 1-ounce sample bag.
Video Shown: Short video explains Benzel family's pretzel-making history and process.

Reservations Needed: No, except for groups larger than 40 people.
Days and Hours: Mon–Fri 9:00 AM–5:00 PM, Sat 9:00 AM–1:00 PM. Usually no production on Saturdays, but you can view video and look at machines. Closed holidays, second full week in August, and Christmas week.
Plan to Stay: 25 minutes for video and self-guided tour, plus time in outlet store.
Minimum Age: None
Disabled Access: Yes
Group Requirements: Groups larger than 40 should call a few days ahead. Guide will be provided upon request. No maximum group size.
Special Information: Benzel's has special seasonal activities and promotional give-aways throughout the year.
Outlet Store: Sells all Benzel's products, including oat bran pretzel nuggets, various decorated tins, logoed T-shirts, bibs, and canvas totes. Also sells other snack foods and candies in bulk. Open same hours as tour. Catalog available from 800 number above.
Directions: From Pennsylvania Tpk., exit at Rt. 220 North. Follow Rt. 220 North to Altoona, then take Rt. 764 North. Benzel's is ¼-mile past 58th St., on the left across from 52nd St. Look for old train caboose in front. From I-80, exit at Milesburg. Follow Rt. 220 South to Altoona, then to 17th St. bypass in Altoona. Turn right onto 17th St. Turn left onto 7th Ave., which joins 6th Ave. Continue on 6th Ave. Benzel's is on the right across from 52nd St.—1 block past traffic light at the corner of 51st St.
Nearby Attractions: Horseshoe Curve National Historic Landmark; Altoona Railroaders Memorial Museum; Mishler Theatre; Baker Mansion; Boyer's Candy Outlet; Lakemont Park.

Crayola Factory

Two Rivers Landing
30 Centre Square
Easton, PA 18042-7744
(610) 515-8000

*Crayola crayons
and markers*

You can't help feeling like a kid again when you visit the Crayola Factory at Two Rivers Landing, the discovery center built in 1996 by Binney & Smith, makers of Crayola products. In fact, don't be surprised if the experience raises many childhood memories. You may remember when the now-classic 64-crayon box with built-in sharpener was introduced in 1958; or you may remember your tenth birthday, by which time you, like the average American child, had probably worn down 730 crayons.

The "Factory Floor" level of the discovery center features crayon manufacturing and marker assembly, using machinery transferred from the nearby production plant. Behind a glass wall is the flatbed molder that makes a small percentage of the company's crayons. Watch a worker pour a mixture containing melted paraffin wax and powdered pigment from a bucket onto a long table with thousands of small holes. Bright yellow wax seeps into the holes. After four to seven minutes of cooling, 1,200 crayons magically appear as they are pushed up and out of the molds! The worker also demonstrates and explains the labeling and packaging machines.

In the marker assembly area, the marker machine has actually been slowed down so you can follow the process of mating the barrels, cylinders, and marker caps. At normal speed, this machine can make 42,000 markers in one eight-hour shift.

Follow the ramp down to the "Creative Studio," which begins the playful, interactive portion of your visit. Draw on clear glass walls with special glass-writer markers. Step into "Cool Moves," where a computer captures your image on a huge video screen.

In the "Easton Press and Bindery," you can lay out the front page of a newspaper. In the "Light Zone," mix up different colored rays of light or lie on your back daydreaming under the "Dreamscapes" exhibit. At the end of your colorful experience, add some of your own personal touches to the continuously designed "Super Sculptures."

Cost: Adults and children, $7; seniors 65+, $6.50; under 3, free.

Freebies: Box of 4 crayons and a marker from the assembly lines, front page of newspaper and other art projects you create while there.

Videos Shown: 10-minute video covers products made by the company, including Silly Putty, chalk, paint, and crayon production. Another video shows TV clips.

Reservations Needed: No, with walk-ins accommodated on a first-come, first-served basis until day is sold out. Groups over 10 people, see below.

Days and Hours: Tue–Sat 9:30 AM–5:00 PM, Sun 12:00 PM–5:00 PM. Closed Mondays, except Federal holidays. Closed Easter, Thanksgiving, Christmas, and New Year's.

Plan to Stay: 1½–2½ hours, plus time in gift shops.

Minimum Age: None

Disabled Access: Yes

Group Requirements: Groups over 10 people should call 2 weeks in advance. Groups over 70 people will be split.

Gift Shops: General Store sells logoed clothing, candy, and toys. Open same hours as Crayola Factory. The 7,200-square-foot Crayola Store, next door, sells a range of Binney & Smith products, from mini to large boxes of crayons and posters waiting to be colored to teddy bears wearing logoed sweatshirts. Open Mon–Sat 9:00 AM–6:00 PM, Sun 12:00 PM–6:00 PM. Closed holidays.

Directions: From Philadelphia, take Northeast Extension of Pennsylvania Tpk. to Allentown Exit onto Rt. 22 East. Get off at the 4th St. exit (last exit in PA). At traffic light, turn left on Buskill St. Turn right onto N. 3rd St. Follow signs to "The Crayola Factory."

Nearby Attractions: National Canal Museum located in same building; Martin Guitar and Mack Trucks tours (see pages 264 and 266); Allen Organ Company tour (call 610-966-2202); canal boat ride and walking tour of Easton; Lehigh Valley attractions, including Dorney Park and Wildwater Kingdom.

Harley-Davidson   ⌁   *motorcycles*
1425 Eden Road
York, PA 17402
(717) 848-1177

The company that Bill Harley and the Davidson brothers started in 1903, when they motorized a bicycle to drive through Milwaukee, now produces one of the U.S.A.'s most recognized and respected products. After this antique motorcycle museum and final assembly plant tour, you'll know what it takes to make one of their stylish motorcycles.

Your journey with fellow Harley enthusiasts begins at the Rodney C. Gott Motorcycle Museum, for a fascinating look back through the impressive Harley-Davidson annals. Tour guides glory in telling about Harley's resurgence after the management buyout from AMF. The museum displays 90 years of actual Harleys, along with motorcycle club memorabilia and pictures of famous Harley owners with their bikes. Stare at the spectacular examples of sleek limited- and commemorative-edition cycles, including one of the Harleys donated by Malcolm Forbes' estate from his extensive collection.

The factory tour takes you around the shop floor, past many stages of motorcycle assembly. Except for the robots that weld parts of the frame, workers and machines labor together to build the cycles. See how presses transform sheets of metal into fenders, teardrop gas tanks, and tailpipes. Once the frame is assembled, it journeys by conveyor to different assembly stations where workers drill, screw, and attach parts. Notice, however, that three-member work teams follow one ultramodern XLH Sportster bike through all assembly stages.

When it's almost complete, the cycle cruises into the testing station, where it is placed on rollers and "driven" at speeds up to 75 miles per hour. While the engine rumbles, the stationary rider checks every electrical component, plugging in different devices to test the bike's performance. Although you can't buy one at tour's end, you do get to "test sit" the newest models.

Cost: Free

Freebies: Copy of *The Enthusiast*, Harley owners' and fans' magazine; product catalog.

Video Shown: Continuously running short video in waiting area shows production steps not on tour, such as paint shop.

Reservations Needed: No, except for groups of 10 or more. Recommend calling, since plant tour times may change.

Days and Hours: Plant and museum tour: Mon–Fri 10:00 AM and 1:30 PM. Museum-only tour: Mon–Fri 12:30 PM and Sat 10:00 AM, 11:00 AM, 1:00 PM, and 2:00 PM. *Harley-Davidson recommends calling in advance;* taped message explains hours and special "no tour" days. Museum-only tour (on Saturday schedule) is given in July and when no plant tours. Closed major holidays.

Plan to Stay: 1½ hours for museum and factory tour (30 minutes for museum-only tour), plus time for video and gift shop.

Minimum Age: 12 for factory tour.

Disabled Access: Yes

Group Requirements: Groups of 10 or more must be scheduled in advance.

Special Information: Photography allowed only in museum. Harley Owners' Group (HOG) has annual 3-day open house at factory end of September. Tours of Wisconsin engine and transmission plant available (call 414-535-3666). Status of tours at new plant in Kansas City, MO, (scheduled for 1998 completion) uncertain at press time.

Gift Shop: Small gift shop in plant lobby sells T-shirts, hats, souvenir books, and cigarette lighters. Open around tour hours.

Directions: From I-83, take Exit 9E (Arsenal Rd.–Rt. 30 East). Turn onto Eden Rd. at "Harley-Davidson" sign. Visitors' parking is in first lot on left. From Rt. 30, take Eden Rd., then follow above directions.

Nearby Attractions: Pfaltzgraff Pottery tour (see page 269); Wolfgang Candy Company tour (call 717-843-5536); York County Historical Museum; Gates House and Plough Tavern; outlet stores and antique shops; Gettysburg, Hershey, and Lancaster nearby.

Herr's ⚬ *snack food*

Visitors Center
Herr Drive and Route 272
Nottingham, PA 19362
(800) 63-SNACK

Herr's snack food production has come a long way from when the company used a small, old-fashioned cooker in a barn. It now has an advanced and highly automated plant that makes tens of thousands of potato chips, corn chips, tortilla chips, popcorn batches, cheese curls, and pretzels every day. The comfortable, specially designed visitors center and snack bar, creative video, and extensive guided tour provide a tasty education in how Herr's makes its products.

While watching the action through glass walls, you'll "ooh" and "aah" at the panoramic views. In the pretzel area, gaze at a 100-yard stretch of pretzel twists, in rows of 20 to 24 across, marching to massive ovens. In the corn chip, cheese curl, potato chip, and popcorn production sections, your vista overlooks the entire process. Follow the raw ingredients—either corn or potatoes—as they tumble in by the truckload at the beginning of the production line; travel along a conveyor belt through a series of machines that wash, slice, cook, or season them; then head out on bucket lifts to a sorting and bagging area. Other memorable images include machines and workers bagging and boxing together in almost symphonic unison, and the cavernous warehouse filled with snack-food boxes.

Except for boxing of bags, machines do most of the work. Notice how only a few people oversee production in most areas. Smart machines can even sense discolored potato chips and use air shoots to blow these rebels off the line. The guides salt and pepper the tour with interesting facts and figures about the company, including Herr's recycling efforts. But the best thing the guides do is grab samples of warm potato chips directly from the quickly moving conveyer belt. Bagged chips will never again taste the same!

Cost: Free
Freebies: Warm potato chips during the tour; basket of Herr's other products in Visitors Center; small bag of corn or tortilla chips as a souvenir.

Videos Shown: 25-minute award-winning video, entitled "The Magical World of Herr's." Chipper the Chipmunk takes 2 kids on a Herr's factory tour, providing background information on company and close-up views of production through the ChipperCam. Great for young children.

Reservations Needed: Yes, but can take walk-ins if space permits.

Days and Hours: Mon–Thur 9:00 AM–3:00 PM on the hour, Fri 9:00 AM, 10:00 AM, and 11:00 AM. Closed holidays.

Plan to Stay: 1½ hours, including video, tour, gift shop, and snack bar.

Minimum Age: None

Disabled Access: Yes

Group Requirements: With advance notice, can handle any size group, which will split into smaller ones for tour. Video shown in 140-seat auditorium.

Special Information: If you are interested in particular products, such as tortilla chips or cheese curls, call ahead for production schedule on day of your visit.

Gift Shop: Sells Herr's food products, logoed clothing items, Nottingham, PA T-shirts, scale model of Herr's delivery truck, and Chipper the Chipmunk doll. Open Mon–Thur 8:00 AM–5:00 PM, Fri 8:00 AM–4:00 PM. Call for extended holiday hours. Catalog available from above number.

Directions: From Philadelphia, take I-95 South to Rt. 322 West exit. From Rt. 322, turn left onto Rt. 1 South. Turn left onto Rt. 272 South and right onto Herr Dr. Factory and Visitors Center at end of road. From Baltimore, take I-95 North to Exit 100. Take Rt. 272 North. Turn left onto Herr Dr.

Nearby Attractions: Longwood Gardens; Plumpton Park Zoo; Franklin Mint Museum; Brandywine River Museum; Lancaster County attractions about 30 miles away.

See color photos, page 186

Hershey's Chocolate World

Visitors Center   *chocolate*
Park Boulevard
Hershey, PA 17033
(717) 534-4900

This visitors center dedicated to chocolate features a wall display of the Hershey's chocolate story and a 12-minute journey through a simulated chocolate factory. The entire chocolate-making process, from harvesting the bean to packaging the bar, will be revealed to you with true-to-life machines, overhead speakers, and videos. You will find new respect for "The Great American Chocolate Bar."

As you stand in line for the ride, take some time to read the company history displayed on the wall; watch the video describing how cocoa beans are cultivated and harvested in South America and Africa before their trek to Hershey, Pennsylvania. Enjoy the indoor tropical garden at the center of Chocolate World. The exotic plants and palm trees displayed here come from regions of the world where cocoa beans are harvested.

Riding inside a cocoa-bean-shaped cart, you pass scenes depicting the chocolate-making process. Glance at the initial process of cleaning and sorting the beans. You'll understand the true cocoa-bean experience as you enter the roaster and feel the air temperature suddenly rise. Ride past the extractor, which removes the center "nibs" from the bean. Smell the luscious aroma of liquid chocolate as it flows by to be mixed with milk and sugar. Toward the end of your ride, an impressive display of Hershey's products will confront you, as recorded children sing "It's a Hershey's Chocolate World!" You'll see how Hershey distributes its product worldwide and know why, at Chocolate World, they say, "Wherever you go, no matter how far, you'll always be near a Hershey bar."

Cost: Free
Freebies: Samples of Hershey's Miniatures, Hershey's Kisses, or other chocolate products.
Videos Shown: Continuously running video in waiting area explains cocoa-bean harvesting and initial processing. Videos throughout ride provide close-up view of the real production process.

Reservations Needed: No
Days and Hours: Mon–Sun 9:00 AM–5:00 PM; some extended hours in summer and some holidays, so it's best to call in advance. Closed Easter, Thanksgiving, Christmas, and New Year's.
Plan to Stay: 12-minute ride, plus time for displays, gift shops, and restaurants.
Minimum Age: None
Disabled Access: Yes
Group Requirements: None
Special Information: Expect long lines during summertime, although they tend to move quickly. During the 1970s, the company had to close well-known tour of Hershey plant because of overwhelming crowds and safety concerns. Hershey's specially designed factory in Oakdale, CA, is the only U.S. Hershey plant that gives public tours (see page 23).
Gift Shops: Gift shops and food court sell Hershey's products, ranging from T-shirts and mugs to the more unusual Hershey's Kisses–shaped cap with silver foil and pull string, and a hollow Kisses-shaped piñata that can hold up to 10 pounds of Kisses. Open same hours as ride. Catalog available from (800) 544-1347.
Directions: From the west, take I-83 to Rt. 322 East. Exit at Rt. 39 West to Hersheypark Dr. Chocolate World is the first "Hershey Attraction" on the right. From the east, take Pennsylvania Tpk. to Exit 20. Follow Rt. 72 North to Rt. 322 West, then follow above directions. From Lancaster, take Rt. 283 West to Rt. 743 North and follow signs to Hershey. Call (800) HERSHEY for recorded directions.
Nearby Attractions: Hersheypark entertainment complex (87-acre amusement park); ZooAmerica North American Wildlife Park; Hershey Gardens; Hershey Museum; The Hotel Hershey; Hersheypark Arena, with concerts, sports, and special events year-round.

Mack Trucks   *trucks*

Macungie Assembly Operations
7000 Alburtis Road
Macungie, PA 18062
(610) 709-3566

Many Americans use the term "Mack truck" to mean any big truck on the highway. But it's actually the brand name for one of the U.S. largest producers of trucks, founded by the Mack brothers in 1900. This plant makes all but four of the company's heavy-duty truck models. The tour shows you the production steps needed to build a truck that is a world-wide symbol for strength and endurance.

The cavernous plant (1 million square feet) is filled with all the sights, sounds, and smells that make factory tours fascinating. The tour guide, often a Mack retiree, enjoys explaining how the manufacturing process is constantly going through extensive quality improvements. Everything you see, from workers bolting on side-view mirrors to their guiding an 80-pound fuel tank into place, has been videotaped and studied with the scrutiny given to an Olympic athlete.

From the cab assembly line, you stroll through the warehouse and the chassis prep area, walk down the final assembly lines, and peek into the painting booths. Everywhere you look it seems that air hoses and drills hang from the rafters. Different things may catch your attention. It could be the huge steel-frame rails that form the chassis of each truck, the moving platforms that workers stand beside to build the cab, the massive engines, or the process used to lower and bolt the engine or the cab onto the chassis.

The dynamometer is every visitor's favorite when it is in operation. To simulate road conditions, the trucks are placed on rollers that spin around at 65 miles per hour. A worker sitting in this moving-but-stationary truck tests the drive train, gauges, and electrical systems. Meanwhile, workers at another station inspect the truck's brakes, lights, and other systems.

The process for putting the tires on the rims demonstrates how truck-building has changed. Previously workers used a sledge hammer and basically beat the tire onto the rim. Now a worker guides the tire while a machine lifts, stretches, and rolls it snugly onto the rim. When you walk through the Mack Trucks Museum (now in its new location) you can imagine how hard it must have been to build all those now-vintage trucks (remember to ask how Mack earned its "Bulldog" nickname).

Cost: Free
Freebies: No
Video Shown: No
Reservations Needed: Yes. Need to form or join a group of at least 5 people. Make Museum reservations separately.
Days and Hours: Tours: Mon–Fri 8:00 AM –1:00 PM. Museum: Mon, Wed, Fri 10:00 AM –4:00 PM. Closed holidays, last week of July, first week of August, week after Thanksgiving, and 2-week period including Christmas and New Year's.
Plan to Stay: Tour: 1½ hours; Museum (exhibit of Mack truck models from 1907 to 1973, along with memorabilia): 15 minutes to 2 hours, depending on interest.
Minimum Age: Specific ratios of adults to children based on age of children.
Disabled Access: Tight spaces on factory floor and in museum.
Group Requirements: 5-person minimum, with no maximum. Appreciates 3 weeks' advance notice for large groups.
Special Information: Plant can be warm during summer months.
Gift Shop: Macungie Mack Shop sells hats, toy trucks, T-shirts, belts, pins, and more, all with the famous Mack Bulldog logo (stuffed bulldogs, too). Open Tue and Fri 9:00 AM– 3:00 PM. Usually also open after tour. Mack Shop also in company's headquarters in Allentown; open Mon–Fri 10:00 AM–4:00 PM. Call (610) 709-3459 for more information.
Directions: From I-78, take Rt. 100 South. After Laidlaw school-bus parking facility on right, turn right at next street, which is Alburtis Rd. (unmarked). Factory is ahead on left.
Nearby Attractions: Allen Organ Company tour, almost next door (call 610-966-2202); Martin Guitar tour and Crayola Factory Visitor Center (see pages 266 and 260).

See color photo, page 187

Website: www.macktrucks.com

The Mack Trucks final assembly line is part of their 1-million-square-foot plant.

Martin Guitar   *guitars*

510 Sycamore Street
Nazareth, PA 18064
(610) 759-2837 / (800) 345-3103

Ever since C.F. Martin Sr. started making guitars in 1833, Martins have been widely recognized as one of the top U.S.-made products. The company has received highest accolades from the Buy America and Made in the USA foundations. Many popular musicians use Martins, including Paul McCartney, Willie Nelson, and Eric Clapton. The craftsmanship you'll see on this tour demonstrates why these famous musicians are among over 500,000 satisfied Martin owners.

The guitar-making area resembles a large woodshop. Only recently have power tools and machines appeared, although most of the approximately 300 separate steps that go into making a Martin are done by hand. With so many things to see (including string-making), the guided tour moves quickly.

Stand beside workers as they diligently bend, trim, shape, cut, glue, fit, drill, finish, sand, stain, lacquer, buff, and inspect the different woods that will become Martins. Look for the station where a craftsman uses ordinary clothespins as clamps. These distinctly low-tech devices help secure for drying a glued, serrated strip of wood along the interior edge of the guitar's curvaceous sides. This lining provides additional surface area for attaching the front and back of the body.

Craftsmen use a variety of files, carving knives, and rasps to shape, finish, and attach the neck. Notice how the dovetail neck joint is meticulously trimmed and then checked to ensure a proper fit with the body. When you view a historic Martin or play a modern one in the museum after the tour, you'll really appreciate the three to six months of craftsmanship required to convert rough lumber into a Martin acoustic guitar—a true American classic.

Cost: Free. Group tours, $2 per person.
Freebies: Sound-hole cut-outs; product literature.
Videos Shown: Optional videos show production process, including interviews with C.F. (Chris) Martin IV, the sixth-generation

family member who oversees the company. Request showing in Martin Museum.
Reservations Needed: No, except for groups.
Days and Hours: Mon–Fri 1:15 PM. Closed holidays, week between Christmas and New Year's, and week of July 4th. Small lobby-area museum is open Mon–Fri 8:00 AM–5:00 PM.
Plan to Stay: 1½–2 hours, including tour, video, gift shop, and museum.
Minimum Age: None for families; 12, for groups.
Disabled Access: Yes
Group Requirements: Group tours must be arranged in advance. Will split larger groups into groups of 10.
Special Information: Photography permitted without flash. No video cameras.
Gift Shops: 1833 Shop sells Martin guitars, antique and used Martins on consignment, strings, supplies, books, clothing, and other memorabilia. Nearby in the old Martin factory (10 W. North St.) is Guitar-maker's Connection, which sells acoustic guitar tonewoods, kits, parts, instrument-making supplies, strings, and construction/repair books. Both open Mon–Fri 8:30 AM–5:00 PM. Combined catalog available from (800) 247-6931.
Directions: We suggest contacting Martin Guitar for directions from New York City and other points and their detailed map, "Navigating Nazareth." From Northeast Extension of Pennsylvania Tpk., take Exit 33. Take Rt. 22 East to intersection with Rt. 191 North. In Nazareth, Rt. 191 turns left onto Broad St. Stay on Broad St. even though Rt. 191 turns right. Pass the Nazareth Boro Park, turn right onto Beil Ave., then right onto Sycamore St.
Nearby Attractions: Crayola Factory and Mack Trucks tour (see pages 260 and 264); Old Martin Homestead (call 610-759-9174); Allen Organ Company tour (call 610-966-2202); Lehigh Valley's attractions include Bushkill Falls, Dorney Park, and Wildwater Kingdom.

See color photo, page 175

Martin Guitar Company has been producing award-winning guitars since 1833.

Hand finishing and shaping of a guitar neck is part of the fine craftsmanship practiced at Martin Guitar Company in Nazareth, Pennsylvania.

Pennsylvania Dutch Candies   ∼ *chocolates*

408 North Baltimore Street
Mt. Holly Springs, PA 17065
(800) 233-7082

As the company name suggests, Pennsylvania Dutch Candies specializes in candy with a regional touch. From the Amish horse and buggy parked outside the factory to the small mementos for sale inside the store, some inscribed with Pennsylvania Dutch sayings, you will be surrounded by this uniquely American culture. When in production, the overpowering aroma of chocolate will catch your nose and entice the rest of you to follow.

Before you enter the factory's production rooms, look at the antique bicycles in the small museum at the rear of the store. Here, bikes date back to the late 1800s, including some that look odd by today's standards. Picture yourself trying to ride the bike with a giant front wheel and tiny back wheel. Displayed on the wall is bicycle race memorabilia, from races all over the East Coast. In the back of the museum, you can see old tools and utensils used by Pennsylvania Dutch cooks who made chocolate and candy years ago.

Once in the production room, you will see how this small factory makes chocolate "the old-fashioned way." Don't expect the huge and intimidating processing machines you may see in larger factories. Here, blocks of milk or dark chocolate become liquid in the melter. The fluid chocolate is poured into molds and formed into one of the many shapes Pennsylvania Dutch sells. Your temptation to grab a piece of chocolate off the conveyor belt will be satisfied when your guide gives you a sample.

In the next room, chocolate is packaged. Piles of boxes patiently wait to be stuffed with chocolate before being loaded onto trucks. This room is also a packing room for candies such as candy corn, gummy worms, mints, and "buttons," which are often brought in from other factories in the area. Measured amounts of hard candies are fed into a machine resembling a giant funnel, which pours the candy into waiting bags. Like the chocolate boxes, these bags are loaded onto trucks and sent to stores across the country.

Cost: Free
Freebies: Chocolate from production line
Video Shown: No
Reservations Needed: Preferred. If guide available, can ask for tour in retail store.
Days and Hours: Mon–Fri 9:00 AM–12:00 PM and 1:30 PM–3:30 PM. Closed holidays and last 2 weeks of December. Museum open same hours as retail store.
Plan to Stay: 30 minutes, plus time for bicycle museum and retail store.
Minimum Age: None
Disabled Access: Yes
Group Requirements: No maximum group size. Will split large groups into smaller groups of 10–15. Should call 1 week in advance.
Special Information: Call to make sure production line is operating.
Retail Store: Sells entire Pennsylvania Dutch Candies line, including chocolate drops, bars, butter mints, peanut brittle, cashew crunch; also, other local and imported candy. During holiday seasons, specialty candy is available (candy eggs are an Easter favorite). Don't leave without checking the Pennsylvania Dutch knickknacks and souvenirs—this part of the store is almost a museum itself. Open Mon–Sat 9:00 AM–5:00 PM, Sun 12:00 PM–5:00 PM. Closed limited holidays. Product list available.
Directions: From Rt. 81, take Exit 14. Follow Rt. 34 South about 5 miles to Mt. Holly Springs. Go through light; factory and store are in big yellow building on left, with Amish horse and buggy parked out front.
Nearby Attractions: Historic Carlisle; Allenburry Playhouse; Gettysburg's attractions about 45 minutes away. Hershey's Chocolate World Visitors Center (see page 263), about 1 hour away.

Pfaltzgraff *pottery*
Bowman Road
Thomasville, PA 17364
(717) 792-3544

PFALTZGRAFF

The Pfaltzgraff family name has been connected to pottery for centuries. George Pfaltzgraff began creating fire-glazed crocks and jugs in rural York County, Pennsylvania, in the early 1800s. Your guided tour takes you through the modern pottery-making process, from the preparation of the clay to the firing, decorating, and glazing of each piece of pottery.

At the cup-forming machines, "pugged" (solid) clay is placed on a pedestal and spun rapidly to form a cup or mug. The new piece journeys through a dryer before being "sponge-bathed" to remove small particles of excess clay. After handles are attached with "slip" (liquid clay), workers methodically and laboriously hand-paint cups or mugs using a sponge-rubber stamp and small brush to create one of Pfaltzgraff's dozens of different designs.

Odd-shaped pottery pieces, squares or ovals, are made in a special station. Instead of molds, ram presses form each piece. Two plaster dies (called "male" and "female") exert 2,200 pounds of pressure on a piece of clay, squeezing out excess water. Suddenly, what was a lump of clay becomes a piece of pottery. The piece joins others like it on shelves waiting for the carousel glaze machines or hand-applied decorations.

As you walk past the enormous kiln, you will feel its heat. The temperature near the entrance is "only" about 500°, rising to 2,200° in the center of the kiln! This allows the glaze to achieve its glassy appearance as the clay hardens. Each piece spends about 12 hours in the kiln, until it "cools down" to 400°. Pieces are then shelved for inspection later.

Since Pfaltzgraff pottery comes in many styles and shapes, including special holiday and seasonal lines, different decorating methods are used. Some pieces are hand-decorated with decals which, when soaked in water, come off the paper and stick to the clay. The pieces are glazed and kiln-baked one more time, sometimes for up to eight hours, to ensure that the decals adhere.

While a plate made on a plate roller is handled by workers an average of 32 times before completion, only one person handles items made in the dry-press facility, from forming through firing and sorting. Even the transporting process, which removes and shelves the plates, is mechanical.

Cost: Free
Freebies: Small pottery piece
Video Shown: No
Reservations Needed: Yes, at least 2 days in advance.
Days and Hours: Mon–Fri 10:00 AM. Closed holidays, week of July 4th, and Christmas week.
Plan to Stay: 1½ hours
Minimum Age: 6
Disabled Access: Yes
Group Requirements: Maximum group is 8 people.
Special Information: No photography. Floor can be slippery from clay. Machine noise can make it hard to hear the retiree tour guides.
Outlet Store: Pfaltzgraff factory outlet in Village at Meadowbrook (2900 Whiteford Road, York, 717-757-2200) sells all Pfaltzgraff stoneware, including holiday collections, factory seconds, and discontinued lines. Map to outlet store available at factory.
Directions: From York, take Rt. 30 (Lincoln Hwy.) West to Thomasville. Turn right onto Bowman Rd. at Pfaltzgraff sign. Park in visitors lot at left.
Nearby Attractions: Harley-Davidson factory tour and museum (see page 261); Utz Quality Foods potato chip tour (see page 278); Hershey's Chocolate World Visitors Center (see page 263); Wolfgang Candy Company tour (call 717-843-5536); Martin's Potato Chips tour (call 717-792-3565); York County Historical Museum.

QVC ⤳ *electronic retailing*
Studio Park
West Chester, PA 19380-4250
(800) 600-9900

While QVC (Quality, Value, Convenience) manufactures no products, QVC is all about products—in fact, it sells them via live television, 24 hours a day, seven days a week, including some products made by companies featured in this book. The largest electronic retailer in the world, QVC recently moved into its new headquarters at Studio Park, a state-of-the-art broadcast facility on 80 wooded acres.

Through a special entrance, you'll enter a lobby that includes a gift shop and ticket window. Before watching the company video a Studio Guide will give you a brief history of QVC, including the fact that this $1.8 billion company was founded in 1986 by Joseph Segal, also founder of The Franklin Mint. QVC is really two businesses: QVC the merchandiser that searches for, tests, and prepares thousands of different products each year for QVC the Network, a round-the-clock live television production.

Follow your QVC Studio Guide on a route above and around the new studio. Half the size of a football field, the studio houses living-room and kitchen sets so products can be displayed and demonstrated in their natural habitats. Studio Park includes over a dozen stages, backdrops for an almost limitless variety of sets. Along the way the Guide will tell you about the three-dimensional and often humorous displays: a replica of The QVC Local, their big orange mobile studio, crashing through the wall; a product Hall of Fame that includes some best-sellers and company favorites; trash cans outside the Quality Assurance Lab containing "rejected" products. The climax is the Observation Deck that juts out into the studio. Here you can watch the live show in progress and check out some up-to-the-second statistics on incoming calls and product sales. QVC averages two customers per second!

By the end of the tour, you'll understand how the whole thing works, from product selection and testing to on-the-air sales, order processing, and shipping. Millions of calls come in, and millions of products are shipped out each year. In fact, QVC reaches over 61 million homes across the U.S. and 75 million homes worldwide. You learn about shopping on the Internet via iQVC and about the company's ventures around the world, including Germany and the U.K. You might even spot one of QVC's many hosts or guests, such as Joan Rivers, or have a chance to be part of a studio audience.

Cost: Adults, $7.50 (members) or $10 (non-members); children under 12, $5.
Freebies: To be determined
Video Shown: 5-minute video covers "a day in the life" at QVC.
Reservations Needed: Yes, for tour and studio audience.
Days and Hours: Wed–Sun 9:30 AM–6:00 PM. Last tour begins at 4:00 PM. Group tours available Tue–Sun. Days and hours subject to change. Call above number for information.
Plan to Stay: 1¼ hours
Minimum Age: Not recommended for children under 6.
Disabled Access: Yes
Group Requirements: Groups of 10 or more people should call for discounts.
Special Information: At press time, QVC planned to have their tour up and running by October 1997; call ahead for more information.
Gift Shop: Sells T-shirts, pens, postcards, mugs, and unique gifts. Located in the Studio Tour lobby. Call for hours of operation.
Directions: From Philadelphia, take I-76 West to Rt. 202 South. Exit at Boot Rd. Turn left at light onto Boot Rd. At the second light, turn right onto Wilson Dr. At the stop sign, cross Airport Rd. and follow the signs to the QVC Studio Tour entrance.
Nearby Attractions: Anderson Bakery and Sturgis Pretzel tours (see pages 258 and 274); Longwood Gardens; Franklin Mint Museum; Winterthur Museum; Brandywine River Museum; Lancaster County attractions are about 20 miles away.

Website: www.qvc.com

Program host Bob Bowersox, here on QVC's kitchen set, is just one of the people you might see on the QVC Studio Tour in West Chester, Pennsylvania.

Sherm Edwards ⟿ *chocolates*

509 Cavitt Avenue
Trafford, PA 15085-1060
(412) 372-4331 / (800) 436-5424

"Good Chocolate is Not Cheap. Cheap Chocolate is Not Good." The sign greets you as you embark on your tour of this 50-plus-year-old, family-owned candy manufacturer. The inescapable aroma of rich chocolate fills your nostrils as you witness Sherm Edwards' very own special blend of chocolate being mixed in 500-pound melters on the factory floor. Dark, light, and white chocolate blends are then pumped into molds of everything from gourmet chocolate spoons (that really enhance a cup of coffee!) to 3-foot tall Easter bunnies.

As you progress through the 3,600-square-foot plant thats walls are stacked high with huge bars of raw chocolate, you notice workers, hands awash in chocolate, coating the bottoms of fruit-and-nut eggs. Conveyer belts then transport the eggs through enrobers, where chocolate cascades envelop each egg before it travels into the cooling tunnel to solidify the coating.

Another corner of the factory is the candy kitchen, packed with equipment such as 80-quart mixers, enormous copper pots for caramel-making, and marble slabs for cooling fudge and jellies. Award-winning Sherm Edwards' Pecan Crisp is created here, with lots of real butter and pecans and just enough crunchy-sweet brittle to hold all the pecans together. You'll discover just how they make chocolate-covered cherries and strawberries. The liquid filling around the fruit of these cordials is produced in the panner, a machine resembling a miniature cement mixer, which spins the fruit to coat it with sugar. The fruit is then dipped in chocolate and the sugar coating liquefies, producing the syrup inside the chocolate cordials.

Cost: Free
Freebies: Various candy samples
Video Shown: No
Reservations Needed: Yes. Prefers that individuals and families join group tours.
Days and Hours: Mon–Sat 9:00 AM–3:00 PM. Limited production on Saturdays. Closed major holidays. Easter through mid-September, production slows to 1 or 2 days per week.
Plan to Stay: 30 minutes for tour, plus time for retail outlet store.
Minimum Age: None
Disabled Access: Retail store is accessible. Stairs lead from retail store down to factory floor.
Group Requirements: Can handle groups from 10–45 people with 1 day's advance notice. Local Radisson and Conley Hotels arrange bus tours for groups staying at hotels. Group discounts on purchases.
Special Information: Candy production depends on holidays; for example, chocolate hearts produced before Valentine's Day and molded chocolate bunnies and eggs before Easter.
Retail Store: Sells chocolates, fudges, and nut brittles made on the premises, over 300 varieties of molded chocolate novelties, and hard candies and jellybeans. Slightly imperfect factory seconds available. Open Mon–Sat 9:00 AM–5:00 PM. Call about holiday hours. Price list available.
Directions: Take I-376 East to Exit 16A. Take Rt. 48 South to Rt. 130 South to Trafford. Cross over bridge into Trafford. Take first left, then immediate right, then another right onto Cavitt Ave. Sherm Edwards Candies is on the right. From Pennsylvania Tpk., take Exit 6 to Business Rt. 22 West to Rt. 48 South, then follow above directions.
Nearby Atractions: Westinghouse Airbrake Museum (call 412-825-3009); Pittsburgh's attractions about 30 minutes away.

Snyder's of Hanover   *pretzels and potato chips*
1350 York Street
Hanover, PA 17331
(717) 632-4477

Pennsylvania is the snack-food capital of the U.S. Small family businesses that hand-twist pretzels and mega-companies that churn out over 400,000 pounds of pretzels and potato chips a day cover the state, particularly in the area surrounding York and Lancaster Counties.

Now best known for its Sourdough Hard Pretzel, Snyder's of Hanover actually began as a potato-chip company in 1921, when the Snyder family started chipping potatoes in their home. It wasn't until 1970 that Snyder's produced a full range of pretzel items, and now it can produce 420,000 pounds of pretzels each day.

When you tour Snyder's state-of-the-art facility, your retiree tour guide gives a brief introduction full of interesting facts—but can't divulge top-secret baking times, oven speeds, and formulas. Since this is a reverse-chronology tour, first follow your guide down the corridor overlooking the shipping warehouse. At the palletizer, pretzel boxes travel down the conveyor single file and line up to make rows of three boxes, with four of these rows (12 boxes) filling each case.

Further down the corridor, look through windows at what is probably the most automated packaging system in the snack-food industry. Machines build boxes from flat cardboard cut-outs; machines fill the bags, and more machines close the boxes. Notice the two new auto case-packers in the far corner. These machines perform all the packaging steps, except for sealing the cartons.

To your left, pretzels shake along conveyor belts on their way to the form- and fill-machines. To your right, potato chips vibrate along a conveyor highway to their own set of form- and fill-machines. These stainless-steel, circular machines each consist of 14 buckets that weigh and release the appropriate amount into bags that are just being formed below.

The most impressive sight on the tour is the oven room, with seven of the largest ovens in the world. As you keep walking down the hall, it seems like you'll never reach the end of these 150-foot-long, massive gray ovens. Silver exhaust stacks rise through the ceiling. Feel the heat through the windows. Pretzels travel through the upper half of each oven for baking, slide down to reverse direction, and dry or become hard and deliciously crunchy during their journey in the lower half of the oven.

Cost: Free

Freebies: Product samples; outlet store discount coupon.

Video Shown: 15-minute video covers company history and pretzel-twisting, along with close-ups of production steps.

Reservations Needed: Yes

Days and Hours: Tue and Thur 10:00 AM and 2:00 PM.

Plan to Stay: 35 minutes, plus time in outlet store.

Minimum Age: None

Disabled Access: Yes, by special arrangement for factory-floor tour.

Group Requirements: Groups of 15 or more people should call 1 day in advance.

Special Information: No photography

Outlet Store: Sells 1-oz. vending machine bags to bulk 6-lb. cartons of pretzels, potato chips, and tortilla chips; 50-percent discount on bagged items. Also sells decorative gift tins and logoed clothing. Open Mon–Sat 9:00 AM–5:00 PM and Sun 12:00 PM–5:00 PM. Closed holidays. Catalog available by calling (800) 233-7125, ext. 1410.

Directions: From Pennsylvania Tpk., take I-83 South to Rt. 30 West. Take Rt. 116 West. Snyder's will be on your left. Check in for tour at outlet store counter.

Nearby Attractions: Utz Quality Foods potato chip tour in Hanover (see page 278); Harley-Davidson motorcycle tour (see page 261) and Wolfgang Candy (call 800-248-4273) both in York, about 1 hour away. Lancaster and Pennsylvania Dutch attractions about 1–1½ hours away.

Sturgis Pretzel House ⟨⟨ *pretzels*

219 East Main Street
Lititz, PA 17543
(717) 626-4354

Pennsylvania has many large pretzel manu-facturers whose tours will "wow" you with massive machines, fast-moving conveyor belts, and mind-boggling production num-bers. At Sturgis Pretzel House, though, pretzel making is more of a participatory art. The workers, many of whom are fifth- and sixth-generation relatives of the founder, proudly explain that Sturgis is the first commercial pretzel bakery in the U.S.A. (opened in 1861). Housed in a restored 200-year-old building, with displays of old pretzel-making equip-ment as well as modern mixers, extruders, and oven, the company makes the tour an integral part of its business.

Playing pretzel-maker is the most fun on the tour. As you stand in front of a rolling table, your tour guide will give you a small ball of dough. You'll roll the dough into a thin pencil, pick it up from both ends, cross it to form rabbit ears, then twist the ends and pull them back to rest on the loop. As you twist your pretzel, the guide explains that the monk who invented the pretzel in A.D. 610 wanted to make from dough the sign of the prayer, which involved crossing both arms with hands on the opposite shoulders. The three holes in a pretzel rep-resent the Father, Son, and Holy Ghost.

You won't get rich after you receive an "Official Pretzel Twister" certificate. In the days before automation, founder Julius Sturgis paid twisters about 25 cents per thousand pretzels. Now the company manu-factures most of its hard pretzels by machine. You can stand near the machine that automatically shapes the dough into pretzels and then bakes and salts them. While contemporary pretzel-making seems so easy, it doesn't compare to the dexterity shown by the Sturgis family member who hand-twists a soft pretzel as the tour ends.

Cost: $1.50. Children under 2, free.
Freebies: Small hard pretzel that doubles as your tour ticket; paper hat that you must wear during tour, and well-earned "Official

Pretzel Twister Certificate."
Video Shown: No
Reservations Needed: No, except for groups of 12 or more people.
Days and Hours: Mon–Sat 9:30 AM–4:30 PM, every 15–30 minutes. Closed Thanksgiving, Christmas, and New Year's.
Plan to Stay: 20 minutes for tour, plus time for gift shop.
Minimum Age: None
Disabled Access: Yes
Group Requirements: Groups of 12 or more should call ahead. Groups also receive free soft pretzels.
Special Information: It can be hot stand-ing near the pretzel-baking machine.
Gift Shop: Tour ends at small gift shop area. You enter the pretzel house through larger store that sells gift items and pretzels, in-cluding their unique horse-and-buggy-shaped pretzels. Special prices on multiple bags and large bags. Look for book entitled *The Pretzel Story*, which includes pho-tographs, company history, and explanation of evolving pretzel-making process. Open Mon–Sat 9:00 AM–5:00 PM. Catalog available.
Directions: From Lancaster, take Rt. 501 North to Lititz. Turn right on Main St. (Rt. 772). Sturgis Pretzel House is on left, with big pretzel in front. From the east, take Penn-sylvania Tpk. (I-76) to Exit 21. Go south on Rt. 222 and turn right onto Rt. 772 into Lititz. Follow above directions.
Nearby Attractions: Wilbur Chocolate Candy Americana Museum (interesting exhibits, including handmade candy demon-strations and video on chocolate-making, plus factory outlet, call 717-626-3249); Johannes Mueller House; Lititz Springs Park; Penn-sylvania Dutch sites and Lancaster attractions all within short drive.

U.S. Mint   ~~~   *coins*

5th and Arch Streets
Philadelphia, PA 19106-1886
(215) 408-0114

We all know that money doesn't grow on trees, but do you know where 50 percent of U.S. coins come from? A tour of the Philadelphia U.S. Mint, which currently strikes approximately 2 million quarters, 4.4 million dimes, 2.6 million nickels, and 20 million pennies each weekday, will show you just that. Encompassing an entire city block, the world's largest mint also houses a museum of rare coins, historic medals, and antique mint machinery.

In the lobby area, see all commemorative coin designs issued since 1892 and notice the 1901 Tiffany mosaics on the walls. Press on past the displays to the glass-enclosed observation gallery above the mint factory floor. From this 300-foot-long vantage point, you witness mere strips of metal and blanks being turned into money. An awesome array of machines heats, washes, dries, sorts, edges, stamps, inspects, counts, and bags the coins that are punched out of the metal strips.

You will better understand what you see on this self-guided tour if you refer to the diagram in the free pamphlet distributed at the beginning of the tour and press the buttons to hear the taped explanations. A new video system gives visitors a close-up view of coinage production, the designing and engraving processes, and of a special ceremony held in the mint's vault. From another area you can see medals and special collectors' coins produced by a process similar to that used for regular coins.

In the mezzanine area, additional displays of coins and artifacts include the original coining press used at the first mint in 1792. These displays appear more interesting than the earlier ones, probably because you just saw how such coins are made. Then hurry down to the gift shop to purchase your own coins and begin your collection. Or, of course, you can just admire your spare change with your newfound knowledge.

Cost: Free

Freebies: Brochure

Videos Shown: 7 videos show close-ups at each production stage.

Reservations Needed: No

Days and Hours: 9:00 AM–4:30 PM. September through April, Mon–Fri; May and June, Mon–Sat; July and August, Mon–Sun. Closed Thanksgiving, Christmas, and New Year's. No production on federal holidays or most weekends. Call above number for recording of schedule.

Plan to Stay: 45 minutes for self-guided tour and coin gallery, plus time for gift shop.

Minimum Age: None, but smaller children may not be able to see or understand all the displays.

Disabled Access: Yes

Group Requirements: None

Special Information: Read pamphlet before beginning self-guided tour. It also explains the sculptor-engravers' and die-makers' work not seen on public tour. Tours of U.S. Mint in Denver, CO available (see page 42).

Gift Shop: Sells commemorative coins and medals, as well as books on money, American history, and U.S. presidents. Mint your own souvenir medal in gift shop for $2. Open same days and hours as tour. For catalog information, call (202) 283-COIN.

Directions: From Pennsylvania, take Schuylkill Expwy. (Rt. 76 East) to Vine St. Expwy., exit right at 6th St. Go south 2 blocks and turn left onto Market St. Go 1 block and turn left onto 5th St. Go 1 block north to Arch St. Mint imposingly occupies entire right side of 5th and Arch Sts. From New Jersey, take Benjamin Franklin Bridge to Philadelphia. Take 6th St./Independence Hall exit on right, follow signs to 6th St. Turn left onto Market St. and follow above directions.

Nearby Attractions: Downtown Philadelphia attractions include Independence Hall, Liberty Bell, Betsy Ross' House, Christ Church, and Benjamin Franklin's grave.

Wendell August Forge   — *metal and crystal giftware*

620 Madison Avenue
Grove City, PA 16127-0109
(412) 458-8360 / (800) 923-4438

Wendell August Forge is the oldest and largest hand forge in the country. The company that Wendell August started in 1923 with making hand-forged architectural pieces (such as railings and gates) now makes beautiful metal giftware. This self-guided tour shows you the steps in producing their individually hand-crafted products, from the cutting of sheet metal to the final hammering and polishing of finished pieces.

Die engraving is the most intricate and time-consuming step. Master die engravers use only a hammer, chisels, and their own creative talents to engrave designs into steel slabs. The carved die design, sometimes taking eight weeks to complete, is the reverse of the actual image. Try to find the engraver's initials on the die; they're cleverly hidden in the design.

Your ears alert you to the hammering area. Watch craftspeople carefully clamp down a blank piece of aluminum or bronze over the design. They use specially designed hammers to force the metal into the die's carved-out portions, creating a raised image on the other side. One moment it's a flat piece of metal, and the next you see the detailed image of an eagle soaring gracefully over a rocky canyon.

After this initial hammering, the piece moves to an anvil to be flattened, anviled, and edged before the remarkable "coloring" process occurs. Each metal piece is placed face-down onto a specially grated screen and held over an open fire in an early-1930s forge. The fire's black smoke bakes onto the piece. After cooling, special polishing removes 97 percent of the baked-on smoke, leaving just enough color to highlight the design. Although Wendell August artisans never produce two identical pieces of giftware, their hallmark and company logo on the back of each item attest to its quality.

Cost: Free

Freebies: Brochure and map; catalog available upon request.

Video Shown: 7-minute video provides close-up view of production steps.

Reservations Needed: No, but recommended for groups of 15 or more.

Days and Hours: Mon–Thur and Sat 9:00 AM –6:00 PM, Fri 9:00 AM–8:00 PM, and Sun 11:00 AM –5:00 PM. Closed holidays. Production Mon–Sat 9:00 AM–4:30 PM. When not in production, see manufacturing process video in gift shop; may be able to view work area.

Plan to Stay: 20 minutes for self-guided tour, plus time for video and gift shop.

Minimum Age: None for families, above elementary-school age for groups.

Disabled Access: Yes

Group Requirements: Welcomes any size group. Recommends 1 week's advance notice for groups larger than 15. Insurance prohibits tours by groups of elementary-school-age children.

Special Information: You may talk with the craftspeople but, for your own safety, do not touch any metal in production. During busy seasons, Wendell Bear may greet you with a hug. New facility in Berlin, OH, heart of Amish Country, opened Summer 1994 (call 330-893-3713); features production tours, museum, and theater.

Gift Shop: Store and showroom display all Wendell August handmade items, including intricately designed coasters, plates, serving pieces, trays, and Christmas ornaments. Engraved crystal and glass, plus other unique gift items. Open same hours as above. Catalog available from numbers above. Gift shop also has LGB model train suspended overhead on 200 feet of track and authentic nickelodeon.

Directions: From I-79, take Exit 31. Follow blue and white signs. From I-80, take Exit 3A. Follow signs.

Nearby Attractions: Daffin's Chocolate Factory tour (call 412-342-2892); Troyer Farms Potato Chips tour (call 800-458-0485).

Website: www.wendell.com

Using hammer and chisel, die-cutters engrave designs at Wendell August Forge.

Showrooms display many of the works made at Wendell August Forge in Grove City, Pennsylvania, and Berlin, Ohio.

Utz Quality Foods   *potato chips*

900 High Street
Hanover, PA 17331
(717) 637-6644 / (800) 367-7629

The Hanover Home brand potato chips made by Salie and Bill Utz in 1921 at a rate of 50 pounds of chips per hour has evolved into a large regional snack-food company that produces up to 14,000 pounds of award-winning chips per hour. This self-guided tour allows you to view the entire 30-minute process that transforms a raw spud into a crunchy chip. An overhead observation gallery equipped with push-button audio and video stations lets you view the entire factory floor.

Potatoes roll and tumble like marbles past you into the peeling machine, which tosses them until the skin is removed. Peeled whole potatoes move along to the slicer, which is programmed to chop them into slices $^{55}/_{1000}$ths of an inch thick. The slices are bathed in 340° cooking oil, showered with salt, and dried on long conveyors while being inspected for discoloring. Flavorings (such as barbecue or sour cream and onion) are added just before packaging.

Notice the pipes running throughout the factory, along walls and over workers' heads. These pipes carry water and oil to and from the production floor. Utz's innovative in-house recycling program uses water to eliminate most of the discarded product waste, such as unused potatoes, skins, and damaged returns. The "waste" is then sold to local farmers for animal feed, while the oil is used to make soap.

As you walk through the observation gallery, you see several Utz products traveling in different directions until they reach the packaging area. Chips are poured into giant funnels, which dump precisely measured amounts into bags of all sizes. Workers pack the bags into boxes, and Utz's almost 300 trucks transport them all over the eastern U.S. Although your potato-chip trip ends above the loading area, don't forget to grab a "souvenir" bag on your way out.

Cost: Free

Freebies: Snack-size bag of potato chips.

Video Shown: 2 stations on tour show live camera shots.

Reservations Needed: No, except for groups larger than 10 people.

Days and Hours: Mon–Thur 7:30 AM–4:30 PM. If factory is in production on Fri, tours will be offered. Call above number in advance for Fri schedule. Closed holidays.

Plan to Stay: 20 minutes for self-guided tour, plus time for nearby outlet store.

Minimum Age: None

Disabled Access: Flight of steps to observation gallery; however, all visitors are accommodated, so call ahead for assistance.

Group Requirements: Groups of 10 or more should call 2 days in advance to schedule tour guide.

Special Information: Brochure available on recycling program.

Outlet Store: Located a few blocks east on the corner at the corporate offices, 861 Carlisle St. (Rt. 94). All Utz products, including chips, pretzels, and popcorn, available in several sizes; chips and pretzels in cans up to 96 ounces; also, decorator cans with Christmas and other designs. Look for special "Grandma Utz" Pennsylvania Dutch–style hand-cooked chips, and "gourmet" hand-dipped chocolate-covered chips and pretzels. Open Mon–Fri 8:00 AM–6:00 PM, Sat 8:00 AM –5:00 PM, Sun 12:00 PM–5:00 PM. Catalog available.

Directions: From Harrisburg, take I-15 South to PA 94 South into Hanover. Turn right onto Clearview Rd. (outlet store is on corner). Utz potato-chip factory is straight ahead at intersection of Clearview Rd. and High St. Tour entrance is on left side of building. From Maryland, take MD 30 North (becomes PA 94) to Hanover. Turn left onto Clearview Rd. and follow directions above.

Nearby Attractions: Snyder's of Hanover and Pfaltzgraff pottery tours (see pages 273 and 269); Martin's Potato Chips tour (call 717-792-3565); Gettysburg about 20 minutes away.

Bacardi 〜 *rum*
Route 165, Intersection Route 888
Cataño, Puerto Rico 00962
(787) 788-1500

BACARDI CORPORATION

After soaking up the Puerto Rican sun and rum, you'll want to cool off at a tour of the Bacardi Rum Distillery, the largest rum distillery in the world, near Old San Juan. Started in the 1860s by Don Facundo Bacardí, the company remains family-owned. When you drive onto the 127-acre complex along the palm tree–lined road and well-manicured grounds, you feel the presence of a successful company.

Relax and wait for the start of your tour by sipping mixed Bacardi cocktails in the pavilion shaded by the undulating roof, shaped like spread bat-wings. Since the bat is the company trademark, you'll see it reflected throughout the tour. The first stop on your tram ride is the towering white building known as "The Cathedral of Rum." Enter the cool first floor, stand in the replica of an old rum warehouse (complete with oak barrels), and notice the painted wall mural of Old San Juan.

At each stop a different guide will provide you with information about the company, such as the significance of the bat logo (symbol of good luck, prosperity, and tradition). At the Hall of Rum, displays include the maps and flags of all the distillers and bottlers of Bacardi Rum around the world, advertisements, photographs of the Bacardi family, and a diorama of the buildings on the complex.

While you don't see much of the distilling process, another hostess explains the four-step process of fermentation, distillation, aging, and blending. Board the tram to the bottling facility, where overhead signs explain the bottling process. The uncaser turns cartons upside down to remove empty bottles. The bottles do-si-do under the air cleaner, which cleans them with pressurized air and vacuum. Bottles rattle loudly and spin along five or six bottling lines, where filler machines use a vacuum system to fill them. After the capper machines apply tamper-resistant caps at a pre-set torque, the labeler glues on labels

and tax stamps. At the end of each line, a worker inspects the bottles as they glide by. You leave the tour with a wealth of company information and an opportunity to sample more of their drinks and stroll the peaceful grounds overlooking Old San Juan.

Cost: Free
Freebies: Mixed rum drinks, sodas and juice for minors.
Video Shown: 3-minute video, in English or Spanish, covers bottling process.
Reservations Needed: No, except for groups larger than 20 people.
Days and Hours: Mon–Sat 9:00 AM–10:30 AM and 12:00 PM–4:00 PM, every 20 minutes. No tours if special event, so call ahead. No bottling on Saturdays. Closed during the Christmas holidays and the last 2 weeks of May. Call for schedule for other holidays.
Plan to Stay: 1½ hours for tour and sampling.
Minimum Age: None, as long as accompanied by adult.
Disabled Access: Yes
Group Requirements: Groups larger than 20 people should call 2 days in advance. Ask for pavilion tour.
Special Information: No smoking during the tour, since highly explosive area.
Gift Shop: Rum 'N' Things sells logoed T-shirts and large assortment of gift packs of Bacardi rum. Open Mon–Sat 9:00 AM–4:00 PM. Closed Christmas and the last 2 weeks of May. Call regarding other holidays.
Directions: From Old San Juan, take ferry at pier #2 to Cataño. Take public bus to distillery. Driving from Old San Juan, take Rt. 1 South to Rt. 22 West. Take Rt. 165 North. Distillery on right at intersection with Rt. 888.
Nearby Attractions: Cabras Island; El Morro Castle in Old San Juan.
Other Caribbean Distilleries Tours: Virgin Islands Rum Industries makes Cruzan Rum in St. Croix (call 809-692-2280); Appleton Rum tour in Jamaica (call 876-966-9215).

See color photos, page 164

Vanguard Racing Sailboats ～ *racing sailboats*

16 Peckham Drive
Bristol, RI 02809
(401) 254-0960

As one of the leading builders of racing boats between 8 and 16 feet, Vanguard prides itself on being the exclusive supplier of Finn-class sailing dinghies for the 1992 Barcelona Olympics. This marked the first time in 25 years that a nonhost country won the job of building them. So no sailor will have an advantage, precision manufacturing drives Vanguard's boat-building process to ensure that the boats are identical. If you can tolerate the strong glue smell, you can walk along the plant floor, stand next to the workers, and observe all the stages in making the different Vanguard models.

Fiberglass boats are built from the outside in, starting from separate molds of the hull and deck. The molds are mirror images of these boat-body parts. The precision begins in the room where a band saw cuts stacks of fiberglass sheets according to an exacting pattern. In the spray booth, the bright gelcoat that's sprayed into the mold provides the boat's color.

In a process called "laying up fiberglass," workers use paint rollers to glue the strips down into the molds. You'll see them hand-lay the resin-soaked fiberglass sheets, reminding you of making papier-mâché dolls. To ensure that each boat weighs the same, the resin and fiberglass are carefully weighed before being laid into each boat; the hulls are specially measured against a template. The separately made hull and deck are also cored with PVC foam and vacuum-bagged.

In a nearby area, workers add hardware such as the cleats and mast step. Hanging from the ceiling are decks and hulls joined by glue and married together with huge pterodactyl clamps. As these flying dinosaurs are lowered, you realize that hidden inside is a sleek racing boat. Even if you're only an occasional sailor, you'll appreciate what's involved in building a high-performance racing boat.

Cost: Free
Freebies: Stickers
Video Shown: No
Reservations Needed: Yes
Days and Hours: Mon–Fri 9:00 AM–4:00 PM. Closed holidays.
Plan to Stay: 20 minutes for tour
Minimum Age: 10
Disabled Access: Yes
Group Requirements: No maximum group size as long as 5 days' advance notice is given.
Special Information: As with any fiberglass-boat manufacturing plant, there is a strong glue smell.
Gift Counter: Sells logoed T-shirts.
Directions: From Rt. 114, go over Mt. Hope bridge toward Bristol. Bear right on Rt. 136. Turn left at Gooding Ave. Turn right at Broad Common Rd., and left at Peckham Dr. Factory is 200 yards ahead on the right.
Nearby Attractions: Thames Glass tour in Newport is less than 1 hour away (call 401-846-0576); Herreshoff Marine Museum in Bristol; Colt State Park; Haffenreffer Museum of Anthropology; Newport's beaches, mansions, Naval War College Museum, Museum of Yachting at Fort Adams, Tennis Hall of Fame, and other attractions are 20 minutes away. (This area of Rhode Island has many sailboat manufacturers, but very few give public tours. However, if you own a boat made by a company in this region, or are considering the purchase of one, a tour probably could be arranged by calling the company or your local dealer directly.)

American Classic Tea *teas*

Charleston Tea Plantation
6617 Maybank Highway
Wadmalaw Island, SC 29487
(803) 559-0383 / (800) 443-5987

On a small island 25 miles south of Charleston, the last 11 rural miles along a dead-end road, lies the only commercial tea plantation in the U.S.A. Charleston Tea Plantation is a tea farm rather than an Old South plantation with white columns. Its entrance, however, through a 7-foot high chain-link fence (bearing only the number 6617) and long rows of perfectly manicured 3½-foot-high-by-5-foot-wide tea hedges, is just as enchanting. While factory tours are currently not available, a visit to Charleston Tea Plantation is an experience: part meeting the owners, who explain tea history, harvesting, and production; and part garden party.

Park between the tea hedgerows and check in at the reception area under a live, Spanish-moss-covered oak tree. Under an oak-trees-and-gardenias canopy, watch a video on tea history, harvesting, and processing. Then stroll along the paved walkway to where Mack Fleming, co-owner and president (in alternating years), stands in a tea field next to the 20-foot-long-by-12-foot-high mechanized harvester, a big green monster whose wheelbase straddles a tea row. Mack designed it when he was Director of Horticulture for Lipton. (Lipton operated a research facility at this site from 1963 to 1987, when Mack Fleming and Bill Hall purchased it.) The efficiency of this cross between a cotton picker and tobacco harvester allows the plantation to compete with inexpensive Far East manual-harvesting costs.

Farther down the path you'll meet Bill Hall, co-owner and third-generation English tea taster. He earned this honor through an apprenticeship in England, tasting 800 to 1,000 cups of tea five days a week for four years. Bill explains the processes that harvested tea leaves undergo in the factory. In a 5-foot-high bin, a fan blows air through them to reduce their moisture content. After 18 hours, the flaccid leaves are ground and spread out to oxidize in open air. The green leaves turn coppery orange. Next, in a 250° dryer, the leaves tumble back and forth among seven conveyors and turn from copper to black tea, which is then tasted, sorted, graded, and packaged. At the end of your tour, enjoy American Classic Iced Tea and Benne sesame wafers while relaxing under a white latticework gazebo.

Cost: Free
Freebies: Tea samples with Benne wafers.
Video Shown: 8-minute video overviews entire production process, from harvesting to factory.
Reservations Needed: No, except for school groups.
Days and Hours: First Sat of month from May through October only. 10:00 AM–1:30 PM; tours start every 30 minutes. Canceled in case of rain. Tour schedule subject to change. Call (800) 443-5987 for latest information.
Plan to Stay: 45 minutes, plus time for gift tent and relaxing on grounds.
Minimum Age: None
Disabled Access: Yes
Group Requirements: Tours can be arranged for school groups on selected weekdays during May by calling 2 months ahead.
Special Information: Wear comfortable shoes and clothing for this ½-mile outdoor walking tour.
Gift Shop: Awning-stripe tent offers tea bags, loose tea, ready-to-drink tea beverages, logoed T-shirts, tea jellies, and Charleston sweetgrass baskets (frequent basket-making demonstrations near tent). Open tour hours. Catalog available from 800 number above.
Directions: From Charleston, take Hwy. 700 (Maybank Hwy.) South directly onto Wadmalaw Island. Plantation entrance is 11 miles from Church Creek Bridge.
Nearby Attractions: Atlantic Littleneck Clam Farm tour (call 803-762-0022), 25 miles away; Angel Oak Park, 11 miles away; Kiawah Island Resort, 22 miles away.

BMW ~ *cars*
1400 Highway 101 South
Greer, SC 29651
(888) TOUR-BMW (888-868-7269)

BMW Zentrum

The bright new BMW Zentrum Visitors Center seems to appear out of nowhere as you approach it. The Zentrum (German for "center") sits in front of BMW's first manufacturing facility outside of Germany. Ten white flags wave in front of the white horseshoe-shaped building nestled on BMW's 1,139 acres. Opened in 1996, the 28,000-square-foot Zentrum gives you views of famous BMW race and art cars and a sneak preview of the experimental BMW cars of the future.

Follow a covered walkway from the Zentrum into the quiet factory that produces the sporty Z3 Roadster. In the Communications Plaza, the plant's "town center," the three main manufacturing areas—body, paint, and assembly—physically intersect.

The assembly of the car body requires more human involvement than most car factories; robots assist with only 25 percent of the BMW frame's construction. In the Body Shop, workers in green fire-resistant jackets weld the steel parts together at a marriage station, while bursts of sparks fly into the air.

The paint shop is 7 stories high (only 3 stories above ground), protected by a glass wall, and highly pressurized to keep debris from contaminating the paint environment. Cars pause at each station to be cleaned and coated with a sealant to reduce noise and water leakage before being primed, color-coated, and clear-coated.

In assembly, the painted bodies are placed on a rotating conveyor and tilted 90 degrees so workers can install the parts in the car's underbody without bending or stooping. Each car travels along the oval assembly line on an AABV (Automated Assembly Body Vehicle), a small platform run by electronic monorail under the floor. Associates install the interior parts, such as the engine, fuel lines, gas tank, dashboard, seats, and radio.

Finally the cars are rigorously tested. New cars are driven straight off the line onto a rough cobblestone road to check the handling, shifting, and braking. Afterwards, an eight-minute water test simulates heavy rain hitting at highway speeds.

Cost: Adults, $3.50; seniors and children under 12, $2.50.
Freebies: No
Video Shown: 17-minute movie "Ride the Line," virtual factory tour following the assembly line of a BMW Z3 Roadster. Shown every ½ hour in the surround-sound theater.
Reservations Needed: No, for Zentrum; yes, for the plant tour.
Days and Hours: Zentrum: Tue–Sat 9:30 AM –5:30 PM, Thur until 9:30 PM. Closed holidays. Plant tours: Tue–Thur 10:00 AM and 2:00 PM. Plant tours may be abbreviated or canceled due to new model development and unreleased automobile designs. No plant tours on holidays, July 4th week, and the week between Christmas and New Year's.
Plan to Stay: 1¼ hour for Zentrum, 45 minutes for tour, plus time in gift shop and café.
Minimum Age: None, for Zentrum; 12, for plant tour.
Disabled Access: Yes
Group Requirements: Groups over 20 people should fax request 1 month in advance to (864) 989-5527, or write BMW Manufacturing Corp., P.O. Box 11000, Spartanburg, SC 29304. Maximum group size: 20 people. BMW confirms reservations up to 90 days ahead. Group discounts available.
Special Information: No photography in plant
Gift Shop: Sells BMW memorabilia and BMW model cars. European-style café serves German beer, pretzels, and cappuccino. Open same hours as Zentrum.
Directions: From I-85, take Exit 60 for Hwy. 101 South. Turn left after 300 yards at 1-mile-long driveway. Follow signs for "BMW Visitors Center."
Nearby Attractions: Biltmore House in Asheville, NC, and Blue Ridge Mountains are 1 hour away.

See color photos, pages 166–167

Homestake Gold Mine ~ *gold*

160 West Main Street
Lead, SD 57754
(605) 584-3110

Not long after Custer's military expedition discovered gold in the Black Hills of South Dakota, prospectors rushed into the area of Deadwood Creek, panning the streams for the yellow nuggets they hoped would make their fortune. Once the gold in the stream had been "panned out," a few persistent individuals began the search for a site where they could mine the precious metal from rock. Among these were the Manuel Brothers, who, in 1876, discovered an outcrop of ore (called a "lead," pronounced "leed") and went on to extract $5,000 worth of gold from it by the end of that spring. That site became what is known today as Homestake Gold Mine, the oldest underground gold mine in the Western Hemisphere.

From the observation deck, view the awe-inspiring Open Cut surface mine, the site of the outcrop discovered by the Manuels. Watch miners drill holes and blast the surface with explosives, while trucks haul the ore away to be processed into gold. You then board a bus to the Yates Crusher Room, where a standard cone crusher and a gyratory crusher smash 4- to 6-inch rock chunks into pieces smaller than one inch. At your next stop, the Yates Shaft, you watch workers loading equipment and preparing to journey as much as 8,000 feet underground in a cage-like elevator. This elevator is raised and lowered by giant drums (hoists) connected to the elevator by a cable. These hoists, which you see in the Yates Hoist Room, hold 5,200 feet of cable and are run by enormous motors.

Next, ride through the Homestake's biological Wastewater Treatment Plant complex, a state-of-the-art facility comprising 20 buildings where cyanide and heavy metals are removed from the water used in ore processing. You arrive at the South Mill and enter a building dominated by 12-foot-long, six-foot-diameter revolving drums—the rod mills and ball mills. The ore passes through these horizontal cylinders as "pulp"—ore mixed with water—to be crushed. Once the ore is finely

ground, it's possible to separate gold particles from rock particles and to extract the gold. Nearly 400,000 ounces of gold is produced by Homestake Gold Mine each year.

Cost: Adults, $4.25; seniors, $3.75; students age 6–18, $3.25; under 6, free. Net proceeds are donated to local charities.
Freebies: Ore samples
Video Shown: 10-minute video shows the underground mining and refining process. A 30-minute video is also available for sale.
Reservations Needed: No, except for groups over 20 people.
Days and Hours: Visitor Center observation deck: Open year-round Mon–Fri 8:00 AM–5:00 PM; June through August, also open Sat and Sun 10:00 AM–5:00 PM. Closed major holidays. Mine Tour: May through September only. Tours leave every ½-hour during Visitor Center hours.
Plan to Stay: 1 hour for tour, plus time for gift shop.
Minimum Age: None
Disabled Access: There is access to the Visitor Center but not to the tour itself.
Group Requirements: Groups over 20 people should call 1 week in advance. Inquire about group rates.
Special Information: Hard hats must be worn on tour.
Gift Shop: Sells Homestake-logoed memorabilia, including T-shirts, sweatshirts, and mugs, plus belt buckles, books, and a video. Open same hours as Visitor Center. Catalog available by calling the above number.
Directions: From Deadwood, take Hwy. 85 North for 3 miles. You'll see signs for "Lead City Park" and a large surface mine.
Nearby Attractions: Mt. Rushmore Jewelry and Sioux Pottery and Crafts tours (see pages 284 and 285); Black Hills Mining Museum; Broken Boot Gold Mine; Mount Rushmore, 1 hour away.

Mt. Rushmore Jewelry   ⟿   *jewelry*

2707 Mt. Rushmore Road
Rapid City, SD 57701
(605) 343-7099 / (800) 658-3361

Black Hills Gold jewelry first appeared after the Black Hills Gold Rush of 1876. By law, in order to use the name "Black Hills Gold," companies must manufacture the jewelry in the Black Hills of South Dakota. To produce Black Hills Gold's characteristic green tint, 12-karat gold is alloyed with silver; alloying gold with copper creates a pink tint. This tour shows you the ancient "lost wax" method of casting used to manufacture all Black Hills jewelry.

Imagine a golden leaf, precise in form and detail and smaller than a contact lens. At Mt. Rushmore jewelry such minuscule foliage is commonplace. See workers with soldering needles "tack" tiny leaves and grapes onto the shanks of rings. At the "wriggling" station, watch a craftsperson wiggle a tool back and forth to etch ridges and veins into a leaf one-third the size of a cornflake. Artisans sit at rows of workstations equipped with small drills, jeweler's loupes, and plenty of tweezers.

All jewelry originates in the Design Room. Artists fashion rubber molds into which hot wax is shot. After the wax sets, the mold is pried apart, and the wax ring joins others on a wax "tree" about the size of a centerpiece. The tree is then dipped in plaster, and this plaster cast slides into a kiln. The wax melts, and liquid gold is injected into the resulting hollow cavity. When the metal has set, the hot cast is dunked in cold water. The plaster shatters, revealing an exact duplicate of the original wax model. This gold tree of rings is pruned, and each ring is ground, buffed, frosted, and polished. During busy holiday seasons, the company's 125 employees produce over 1,000 pieces of jewelry per day.

Cost: Free
Freebies: No
Video Shown: 7-minute video on company history, legend and history of Black Hills Gold, and production shown in showroom.
Reservations Needed: No, except for groups larger than 40 people.

Days and Hours: May through September: Mon–Fri 8:00 AM–3:00 PM, tours generally on the hour; October through April: tours by walk-in or reservation. Closed holidays and week between Christmas and New Year's.
Plan to Stay: 20 minutes, plus time in factory showroom.
Minimum Age: None
Disabled Access: Yes
Group Requirements: No maximum group size. Large groups will be split. Requests 1 day's advance notice for groups larger than 40 people.
Special Information: This family-run business is one of the few jewelry manufacturers' tours that allows visitors directly onto the production floor.
Factory Showroom: Sells entire 3,600-style line of Black Hills Gold jewelry. Rings are arranged in velvet cases among elegant watches, dishes, and crystal bowls. Open May through September, Mon–Sat 8:00 AM–8:00 PM, Sun 9:00 AM–5:00 PM; October through April, Mon–Sat 9:00 AM–5:00 PM. Closed Christmas, Thanksgiving, and Easter.
Directions: From I-90, take Exit 57. Turn left onto Omaha St. Turn right onto Mt. Rushmore Rd. Mt. Rushmore Jewelry is at intersection of Walpole Blvd. and Mt. Rushmore Rd. From Hwy. 79, travel west on Fairmont Blvd. to Mt. Rushmore Rd.
Nearby Attractions: Sioux Pottery and Crafts and Homestake Mine tours (see pages 285 and 283); video and observation booth at Landstrom's Black Hills Gold Creations (call 800-843-0009 or 605-343-0157); Mt. Rushmore; Reptile Gardens; the Ranch Amusement Park; Geology Museum at South Dakota School of Mines.

Sioux Pottery and Crafts ⟶ *pottery*
2209 Highway 79 South
Rapid City, SD 57701
(605) 341-3657 / (800) 657-4366

The red clay used at Sioux Pottery comes from Paha Sapa, the Black Hills area, and is considered sacred. This clay is carefully fashioned into vases and pots whose exteriors are then graced with Sioux Indian designs symbolizing the Sioux culture, environment, activities, and dealings. For example, crossed arrows represent Friendship, a zigzag of lightning stands for Swiftness, and a diamond wedged between two backwards Es connotes Horses Killed in Battle.

Along with the red clay, the craftspeople at Sioux Pottery also utilize a more secular variety from Kentucky. This white, elastic clay is used for certain pieces, such as those with handles, which are too delicate to withstand the pronounced shrinkage inherent in firing red clay. About ten artists can be seen working at any one time, each one seated at an old kitchen table. The floors of their workspace are powdered with dust; bootprints lead to a dank back room where the red clay exists as "slip" (earthy red liquid). From outside, the slip is piped into concrete vats, where it is mixed and strained, then turned into clay.

The artists employ three different methods for turning clay into pots: casting, wheel-throwing, and jiggering. In casting, slip is poured into plaster molds. The plaster absorbs the excess liquid, and the clay takes the shape of the mold. In wheel-throwing, potters bend over spinning pottery wheels, hand-forming original pieces from balls of clay. The third method, jiggering, is used for flat plates and bowls. As the wheel spins, a potter lowers a blade that cuts out the shape. White or red, all unfired pottery is called "greenware." You'll see shelves of greenware, all dull and smooth. The Indian artists paint freehand designs and proudly sign their names on each piece.

Cost: Free
Freebies: No
Video Shown: No
Reservations Needed: No, except for groups

larger than 12 people or to arrange tours outside regularly scheduled times.
Days and Hours: Mon, Wed, Fri 11:00 AM for guided tours Memorial Day through Labor Day. Self-guided tours any time during gift-shop hours. Best viewing days are Tue–Fri; not much produced on Mon or Sat. Closed holidays and week after Christmas.
Plan to Stay: 20 minutes, plus time in gift shop.
Cost: Free
Minimum Age: None
Disabled Access: Yes
Group Requirements: Call 2–3 days in advance for groups larger than 12 people. Groups larger than 20 will be split into smaller groups.
Special Information: A lot of clay dust in the back rooms' air.
Gift Shop: Sells handmade pots, bowls, and dishware, as well as mandalas, dance shields, painted cattle skulls, and sacred medicine wheels, all created locally by members of Sioux nation. Factory seconds available at 50-percent off. Open May through August, Mon–Fri 8:00 AM–5:00 PM, Sat 10:00 AM–4:00 PM, Sun 12:00 PM–4:00 PM; September through April, Mon–Fri 8:00 AM–5:00 PM, Sat 10:00 AM–2:00 PM except September Sat 10:00 AM–4:00 PM. Catalog available by mail for $5.
Directions: From I-90 bypass, take Exit 59 and go south on LaCrosse St. Turn left (east) on East North St. to Cambell St. Turn right (south) on Cambell to St. Patrick St. Turn right again (west) on St. Patrick to Hwy. 79 South Business Loop. Swing left onto Hwy. 79. Sioux Pottery is 2 blocks ahead on your right.
Nearby Attractions: Mt. Rushmore Jewelry and Homestake Mine tours (see pages 284 and 283); Black Hills National Forest; Mount Rushmore; Geology Museum at South Dakota School of Mines; Reptile Gardens; the Ranch Amusement Park.

Jack Daniel's Distillery ~ *whiskey and beer*

Lynchburg, TN 37352
(615) 759-4221

In the heavily vegetated, woodsy, hilly terrain of south-middle Tennessee, you feel you're visiting a national park rather than the world's oldest registered distillery (1866) when you tour Jack Daniel's. A babbling brook follows you through the entire tour. You learn from the tour guide that the water is no coincidence, that Jasper Newton (Jack) Daniel chose this property because of Cave Spring's iron-free water. This pure limestone water flows at 56° year-round and is one secret of Jack Daniel's fine whiskey.

Your tour begins with a short minivan ride up the hill to one of 45 aging houses. The large wooden structure's air is thick and musty with the smell of whiskey and wood. Your eyes take in only a small fraction of the 20,164 barrels of aging whiskey lined up seven stories high. Four years of warm days and cool nights inside these white-oak barrels gives Jack Daniel's whiskey its flavor and color.

In the rick yard, landmarked by a black smokestack, Moore County hard sugar-maple wood is burned to make charcoal. In charcoal mellowing vats the distilled, fermented whiskey seeps through 10 feet of charcoal and a wool blanket at a rate of less than six gallons an hour.

You'll see another interesting whiskey-making step in the hot, noisy mash room. Here, in large tanks called mash tubs, corn, rye, barley malt, water, and yeast ferment for four days. A panel measures the liquid's progress toward becoming 140-proof whiskey.

A wooden structure that resembles an old Southern country farmhouse is actually Jack Daniel's original office, which dates back to 1878. Still in its natural setting, it is filled with period furniture, old file cabinets, and ledgers that documented the company's financial transactions. What has been updated is an old whiskey bottling house, now used to brew 1866 classic oak-aged beers.

Cost: Free

Freebies: Ice-cold glass of lemonade in White Rabbit Saloon after tour.

Videos Shown: Video at tour's beginning explains Jack Daniel's and whiskey-making. Video at end of tour shows bottling process (not on tour).

Reservations Needed: No, except for groups larger than 30 people.

Days and Hours: Mon–Sun 8:00 AM–4:00 PM. Brewery tour is optional at end of distillery tour. Closed Thanksgiving, Christmas, and New Year's. On Saturdays, Sundays, and during 2-week July shutdown, you follow standard tour route, even though distillery isn't in production.

Plan to Stay: 1 hour for videos and tour.

Minimum Age: None

Disabled Access: Yes. Specially designed van tour for people in wheelchairs.

Group Requirements: Groups larger than 30 should call on Thursday of week before visit.

Special Information: Lots of walking, so wear comfortable shoes. Tour booklets available in major foreign languages. Distillery is designated a National Historical Landmark. Brewery offers exhibit of Southern brewing history.

Gift Shop: Just about every store in Lynchburg sells Jack Daniel's souvenirs but no whiskey. Lynchburg Hardware and General Store has largest selection, including old-time saloon mirror, wooden whiskey chest, stoneware jugs, and playing cards. Catalog available at above number.

Directions: From Nashville, take I-24 South to Exit 111 (Hwy. 55 West). As you enter Lynchburg, visitors center parking lot entrance is off Hwy. 55 next to Mulberry Creek Bridge. From Chattanooga, take I-24 North to Exit 111. Follow above directions.

Nearby Attractions: Lynchburg is filled with Southern charm and hospitality. Visit courthouse and Miss Mary Bobo's Boarding House (Southern-style food served). Worth tour in Tullahoma (see page 290).

Nissan ～ *cars and pickup trucks*

983 Nissan Drive
Smyrna, TN 37167
(615) 459-1444

Imagine 89 football fields side-by-side and back-to-back, all under one roof! That would be an unfathomable size for a sports complex, but it is the actual size of Nissan's first U.S. manufacturing plant, which employs nearly 6,000 people. Since it began production in 1983, the unemployment rate in Rutherford County has been cut in half. You are shuttled through the enormous production plant on an endless network of concrete polyurethane mini-thruways which covers the entire plant. All around you, everywhere you look, there are light trucks, Sentras, and Altimas being assembled, painted, and inspected.

Zigzagging through the massive welding operation, you feel as if you are on a Stephen Spielberg movie set. Look up at what seems like a conveyor system suspended from the ceiling as sparks fly from tentacle-like robot arms welding together the main body parts of the vehicle shell. This mixture of automation and computerization is called the Intelligent (or "smart") Body Assembly System (IBAS). IBAS robots replace the conventional jigs that hold steel panels together during the initial welding of the vehicle's body. The computerized capabilities of the "smart" system allow for more than one model of vehicle to be manufactured on each line and use lasers to check accuracy.

As your tour guide maneuvers the shuttle along the maze of conveyers, the unmistakable smell of fresh paint begins to fill your nostrils. Gazing through the glass that encloses the conveyer belt, you see employees clothed in what resembles surgical garb. You are now cruising through the paint facility. Here, in a precise and lengthy process, layers of primer and paint are intermittently applied and inspected by robots and humans. Employees carefully check each automobile's finish as part of the quality control system. Heat engulfs you as you pass the enclosed paint-bake oven and air blower zones where the cars are dried.

On yet another line you are reassured of the human touch when you see technicians, heads bowed in concentration and fingers flying, manually assembling Sentra and mini-van engines. It's fun to witness the finishing touches in the final production stages, such as workers adding seats and catalytic converters to some of the over 450,000 vehicles produced here each year.

Cost: Free
Freebies: No
Video Shown: 10-minute overview of Nissan and manufacturing at Smyrna plant.
Reservations Needed: Yes. Maximum of 55 people per tour, whether individuals, families, or groups. Occasional last-minute cancellations, so it's worth a call to see if you can fit into tour.
Days and Hours: Tue and Thur at 8:30 AM, 10:00 AM, and 1:00 PM. Closed holidays, week between Christmas and New Year's, and 2 weeks in July.
Plan to Stay: 1 1/2 hours for video and tour.
Minimum Age: 10 (5th grade)
Disabled Access: Yes
Group Requirements: Maximum number of 55 people per time period if no other tours scheduled. Reservations accepted up to 3 months in advance.
Special Information: No photography or shorts.
Gift Shop: No
Directions: From Nashville, take I-24 East toward Chattanooga. Take Exit 70 (Almaville Rd.) and turn left toward Smyrna (Almaville Rd. becomes Nissan Dr.). Nissan is about 3 miles ahead on right. Enter Gate 1.
Nearby Attractions: Sam Davis Home; attractions in Murfreesboro (geographic center of Tennessee) include Stones River Battlefield, Oakland Mansion, and antique stores. Nashville's attractions, including Purity Dairies tour (see page 288) and Grand Old Opry, are 20 miles away.

Purity Dairies 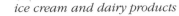 *ice cream and dairy products*

360 Murfreesboro Road
Nashville, TN 37224
(615) 244-1900

A cheery ice-cream parlor welcomes you to Purity Dairies' ice-cream plant. In the tour room, the 50-something-year-old company shows a film about milk and the manufacturing of their dairy products. Then the big blue curtain opens, revealing a huge window with a panoramic view of the ice-cream factory.

Seeing the production of ice-cream sandwiches is almost like watching a live theater performance, with each player taking a specific role. The show is a continuous interaction of machinery, humanity, and ice cream. In the foreground, two women handle the sandwich machine. One feeds chocolate wafers into the machine, which squirts out the exact amount of vanilla ice-cream filling for each sandwich. The other worker boxes the sandwiches after they have been automatically wrapped. A complicated labyrinth of overhead piping, frosty and dripping with condensation, runs throughout the plant. A milk-based mixture is pumped to various stainless-steel machines, where it is flavored, transformed into ice cream, and shot into individual cartons. The cartons are automatically shrink-wrapped and sent to the freezer for hardening.

A short walk outside takes you to the milk plant, with more overhead pipes everywhere. The daily production of 10,500 pounds of cottage cheese causes a natural sour odor in the room where Purity makes Little Miss Muffet's curds and whey. An enormous stainless-steel tub filled with the white lumpy stuff comes into view, and your guide explains the intricacies of separating curds and whey to produce cottage cheese.

In another part of this facility, Purity manufactures its own plastic milk containers. It takes 7,754 plastic beans to make a gallon jug. At the end of the tour, visitors convene at the weigh station and the group is collectively weighed. Here the Purity trucks are also weighed before heading out to make deliveries. The loud moo you might hear is the horn on one of Purity's special home-delivery trucks, painted white with large black spots that resemble a . . . guess what? (The horn is a hint.)

Cost: Free

Freebies: Children receive ice-cream sandwiches; adults receive frozen yogurt, premium ice cream, sherbet, and gift pack of cottage cheese and other items.

Video Shown: 17-minute movie about Purity's milk and other products.

Reservations Needed: Yes. Individuals and families must join scheduled group tour. Tours may fill years in advance, but individuals or families should ask about available space on existing group tours.

Day and Hours: Tues, Thur, Fri. Children's tours, 10:00 AM, 11:15 AM, and 12:30 PM. Adult tours, 10:00 AM–12:00 PM for tour and 12:00 PM–2:00 PM for complimentary lunch for out-of-state visitors.

Plan to Stay: 2 hours for video and tour, plus time for lunch (adult tour).

Minimum Age: 4

Disabled Access: Yes

Group Requirements: Adult tours need at least 4 months' advance reservations; children's tours, 8 weeks ahead. At press time, company said group tours are booked far in advance. Maximum kids' group size is 50; maximum for adults is 40.

Special Information: Because company has expanded marketing territory, tour is very popular. Book as far ahead as possible.

Gift Shop: No

Directions: From the south, take I-65 to Fesseler's Lane exit. Turn right at end of exit, then take first right on Elm Hill Pike. Purity is at intersection with Murfreesboro Rd. From the north, take I-65 to Murfreesboro Rd. exit. Turn left at end of exit. You'll see signs and Purity logo.

Nearby Attractions: Nissan tour (see page 287); Grand Old Opry; Opryland.

Saturn ~ *cars*

Welcome Center
100 Saturn Parkway
Spring Hill, TN 37174
(615) 486-5440 Welcome Center / (800) 326-3321 Plant Tour

To many Americans, the Saturn car represents the rebirth of U.S. automobile manufacturing. Since the first General Motors Saturn rolled off the line in 1990, these import-fighting cars have earned a reputation for their high quality, the no-haggle sales approach by retailers, and enthusiastic customers. The manufacturing plant began offering regular public tours in the summer of 1997. A horse barn has been renovated into the new Saturn Welcome Center. The Welcome Center's theme is the "Saturn Difference" and consists of interactive displays and exhibits on the Saturn story.

This highly integrated manufacturing complex includes the power train, general assembly, and body systems buildings. Saturn's Spring Hill site sits on approximately 2,400 acres of what was previously farmland—in fact, the company currently farms approximately 1,200 acres of land, raising corn, wheat, soybeans, and hay. The Saturn manufacturing plant has been built and painted to blend into the countryside, so very little of the plant can be seen from the highway or the Welcome Center. To see the manufacturing plant, you will need to register for a plant tour and take a ten-minute bus ride from the Welcome Center to the plant.

Near the entrance to the Welcome Center is a kiosk that gives you a short introduction to the company. The displays are arranged in eight horse stalls that can be viewed by starting at either end of the barn. The history stall contains mementos from the site and the founding of Saturn. Other stalls contain videos and memorabilia on teamwork, owner's letters, and community activities. Three of the stalls are dedicated to the manufacturing story, where you can see the polymer beads that make up Saturn body panels and view a display that explains the lost-foam process used in making Saturn engines.

Cost: Free
Freebies: Saturn Welcome Center brochure and product brochures.

Video Shown: 15-minute video entitled "One Car at a Time" covers Saturn production.
Reservations Needed: No, for Welcome Center; yes, for plant tour. Occasional last-minute cancellations allow walk-in visitors to take a plant tour. Call (800) 326-3321 for information and reservations.
Days and Hours: Welcome Center: Mon–Fri 8:00 AM–5:00 PM, Sat 9:00 AM–3:00 PM. Plant Tour: Factory tour program is new. Days and hours in flux, but no weekend tours. Plant closed holidays, including the day after Thanksgiving, the week between Christmas and New Year's, Good Friday, and 2 weeks in July. Call Welcome Center for hours during holiday weeks.
Plan to Stay: 2 hours for Welcome Center and plant tour, plus time for gift shop.
Minimum Age: 6, for plant tour; none, for Welcome Center.
Disabled Access: Yes, for Welcome Center. Call above number for accommodations on plant tour.
Group Requirements: No maximum for Welcome Center, although advance notice appreciated. Maximum 30 people per plant tour time period. Reservations accepted up to 3 months in advance.
Special Information: No photography in plant. Visitors must wear safety glasses on tram tour. No shorts.
Gift Shop: Saturn Stuff Store sells Saturn-logoed items, including shirts, hats, key chains, jackets, and videos. Hours are same as the Welcome Center.
Directions: From Nashville, take I-65 South. Exit at Rt. 396, Saturn Pkwy. West. Take Hwy. 31 South. Watch for sign.
Nearby Attractions: Natchez Park; Nashville's attractions, including Purity Dairies tour (see page 288) and Grand Old Opry, about 40 minutes away. Local area around Spring Hill and Columbia includes many antebellum homes and Civil War sites.

Worth ~ *softballs, baseballs, bats, and accessories*

2100 North Jackson Street
Tullahoma, TN 37388
(931) 455-0691

From its small beginnings in 1912 making leather harnesses and horse collars, Worth has become the U.S.'s largest manufacturer of baseballs and softballs and has successfully diversified into bats, gloves, and bags. The Parish brothers now run the company, making them the family's fourth generation to be in charge. The tour through their Tullahoma factories is a mecca for softball and baseball players.

After a brief talk in Parish Hall about all the company's products and its colorful history, the ex-ballplayer tour guide takes you through the ball-making area. The company is proud of the "reduced injury factor" baseballs and softballs it invented. They use a polyurethane core that makes the balls softer than the traditional yarn-wound or cork and latex balls, but just as lively. Watching the core-making process reminds you of bread rising in the oven. Liquid chemicals are pumped into round metal molds and then spun around on a machine that looks like a big lazy Susan. The reaction between the chemicals causes them to expand and harden into the proper shape and weight. Watch a few workers hand-stitching the covers on balls (most of the covers are sewn on at another plant) and maybe even test your dexterity by sewing a few of the 88 stitches in a softball.

The high-end aluminum-bat factory, which is a few miles away (you need to drive), introduces you to the loud, pounding swaging machines. The bats start as hollow silver metal tubes. The machines hammer away at each tube to shape the bat's barrel, taper, and handle. Then the bat is cut to the proper length. The plug, which adds the weight, is snapped into the end of the barrel, and the cap is applied at the bottom of the handle. The colorful bats look like candy canes rolling around when the grips are spun onto the handle.

Near the tour's start is the accessories area. In this cut-and-sew operation workers make sports bags, including the popular U-Tote Softball Equipment Bag to store all the balls and bats you saw made on the tour.

Cost: Free
Freebies: No
Videos Shown: Sometimes, based on time of year and tour schedule. Videos range from company history to product demonstrations.
Reservations Needed: Yes
Days and Hours: Wed 8:00 AM and 10:00 AM. Tours moved to another day if Wednesday is holiday or plant closed. No tours between Christmas and New Year's and usually the week before or of July 4th. (Call for details on summer shutdown.)
Plan to Stay: 1½ hours for tour, plus time for company store.
Minimum Age: None, but would not recommend babies in bat-making factory.
Disabled Access: Yes, for Parish Hall, ball plant, and accessories. Bat plant more difficult.
Group Requirements: Maximum size is 25 people; 1 month's advance notice suggested.
Special Information: No photography. Hot in summer and always loud in bat factory.
Company Store: Sells seconds and inventory close-outs on balls, bats, and accessories, and logoed T-shirts, and jackets. Open Mon–Fri 8:00 AM–3:30 PM. Closed holidays. Consumer catalog available at above number.
Directions: From Nashville, take I-24 East to State Hwy. 55 (Exit 111 for Tullahoma and McMinnville). At exit-ramp stop sign, turn left onto Hwy. 55 West to Tullahoma and Manchester. In Tullahoma, turn right on U.S. Hwy. 41A (Jackson St.) and follow the road through town. Worth is approximately 5 miles ahead on right after lanes narrow. Enter the building with "Worth, Inc." sign. From Atlanta and Chattanooga, take I-24 West and follow the same directions. Company can fax map.
Nearby Attractions: Jack Daniel's Distillery tour (see page 286); George A. Dickel Distillery tour (call 931-857-3124); Staggerwing Museum, a unique aviation museum for the "Lear Jet of the '30s."

American Airlines C.R. Smith Museum

4601 Highway 360 at FAA Road *air travel*
Fort Worth, TX 76155
(817) 967-1560

You'll recognize the American Airlines C.R. Smith Museum, named after the man who served as company president for most of the years between 1934 and 1973, by the fully restored DC-3 (the *Flagship Knoxville*, which flew for American from 1940 to 1948) in front. The Grey Eagles, a group of mostly retired American pilots, bought the *Knoxville*, and a team of American mechanics restored it to its current glistening condition. Opened in July 1993, this 25,000-square-foot corporate museum contains informative interactive displays and video presentations.

The circular glass History Wall in the center of the open floorplan highlights company developments and memorabilia from the first airmail service (1918) to today, including a 767 maintenance manual on CD-ROM. Some of the oldest items, including a letter Charles Lindbergh carried on his first airmail flight from Chicago to St. Louis, bring American's heritage to life. Beyond this section is an "American Family" display, with lifelike mannequins representing American employees and videos describing their jobs and teamwork.

"Working in the Air," "Working on the Ground," and "Maintaining the Fleet" exhibits detail the equipment and procedures used in airline operations. You can sit in a cabin mockup and feel like a pilot or flight attendant. You'll also get an up-close look at a jet engine, aircraft landing gear, and an air traffic control system. The "Flightlab" has a wind tunnel, test equipment, and simulators that teach the basic principles of flight. Near these more technical displays are brass-plate etchings of four different American Airline planes. Put a piece of paper on your chosen plate and rub it with a crayon to make a souvenir. If only flying a real plane and running an airline were this easy!

Cost: Free
Freebies: Brass rubbings (see above).
Movie Shown: 14-minute film, *Dream of Flight*, runs every ½-hour. Theater's all-around sound system and panoramic screen give you the feeling of flying on an American Airlines' jet. Also, touch-screen videos throughout museum.

Reservations Needed: No, but recommended for groups larger than 10 people.
Days and Hours: Tue 10:00 AM–7:00 PM, Wed–Sat 10:00 AM–6:00 PM, Sun 12:00 PM–5:00 PM. Call for holiday hours.
Plan to Stay: 1½–2 hours for displays, videos, and film, plus time in gift shop.
Minimum Age: None
Disabled Access: Yes
Group Requirements: Reservations requested for groups larger than 10 people for guided tour and film.
Special Information: Special-event rental of museum available (call 817-967-5910). Summer educational day camp (call 817-967-1560). With the museum's open floorplan, the Map and Guide provide a helpful overview of the numerous displays.
Gift Shop: Unique aviation-related items, such as models, crystal and porcelain eagles, clocks, mobiles, toys, and books. Also, museum and American Airlines–logoed items. Closes ½ hour before museum.
Directions: From Dallas/Fort Worth Airport (3 miles away), take south exit and follow signs for Hwy. 360 South. Exit at FAA Rd. Turn right at stop sign. Museum is on right. From Hwy. 183 East, take FAA Rd./Hwy. 360 South exit. Turn right at stop sign. Museum is on right.
Nearby Attractions: Mrs Baird's Bread tour and Mary Kay factory tour and company museum (see pages 302 and 300); Studios at Las Colinas tour (call 972-869-3456); Six Flags Over Texas; Fort Worth Zoo and Fort Worth Museum of Science and History about 20 miles away; Downtown Dallas attractions, including JFK Museum, about 15 miles away.

Blue Bell Creameries 〜 *ice cream*

1000 Horton Street
Brenham, TX 77833
(409) 830-2197 / (800) 327-8135

This "Little Creamery in Brenham" maintains its small-town image through its advertising and girl-and-cow logo. At its headquarters, the nineteenth-century red-brick schoolhouse offices, 1930s-replica refrigerated delivery truck, country store, and ice-cream parlor further that country feel. In the visitors center see photos of Blue Bell and Brenham, and the company's original wooden time clock.

In the plant, look down through glass windows at the production floor's maze of stainless-steel pipes and various shaped tanks. Almost everything happens inside the tanks, so your tour guide explains the process. Base-mix ingredients are blended, homogenized, and pasteurized, then cooled and piped into refrigerated holding tanks. The tanks' huge round doors resemble ship portholes. Liquid flavorings are added in the rectangular flavoring tanks.

The mailbox-shaped freezer barrels whip and freeze the mixture to milkshake consistency. The ice cream and "dry" ingredients (fruit, cookie chunks, cookie dough, etc.) meet in the white pipes before traveling into containers. If the flavor of the day is banana split, workers peel and slice bananas in the behind-the-scenes kitchen. In the filler machine, empty, open, half-gallon round cartons spin to mix ice cream and ingredients as they flow into the cartons. Colorful lids slide down to cover the filled cartons.

Another room offers more movement as 3-ounce Dixie cups are filled. Cups resting in a circular disk are filled two at a time; the disk rotates after every two are filled. You will be mesmerized by the repetitive spin-fill, spin-fill process. Nearby, ice-cream sandwiches start as chocolate wafers sliding down a V-shaped holder. Two wafers converge, and a hardened ice-cream slice drops between them. Paper quickly wraps around the sandwich and helps maintain its shape. The sandwiches travel single-file until they're mechanically pushed into cardboard boxes. All this whets your appetite for the samples you'll enjoy in the ice-cream parlor.

Cost: Adults, $2; children 6–14, $1.50; under 6, free.

Freebies: Ice-cream serving in the parlor; logoed paper hat.

Videos Shown: 7-minute film, "Blue Bell Creamery: Then and Now," on company's early history. If no plant production, watch 6-minute film of ice-cream-making process.

Reservations Needed: No, except for groups of 15 or more people. Everyone must make reservations for spring break and Easter tours.

Days and Hours: Mon–Fri 10:00 AM–2:30 PM, every 30 minutes in summer. Fall and winter tour schedule varies; call for exact tour times and days. Closed holidays.

Plan to Stay: 40 minutes, plus time in visitors center, ice-cream parlor, and Country Store.

Minimum Age: No

Disabled Access: Only for films, ice-cream parlor, and country store. Stairs in plant.

Group Requirements: Groups of 15 or more should call at least 2 weeks in advance. Call 1 month ahead for spring and summer tours. Maximum group is 50 people.

Special Information: March and April are busiest tour months because bluebonnets, the Texas State Wildflower, are in bloom. No photography in plant. Since theater holds 50 people, allow some waiting time during summer.

Country Store: Sells logoed items, Texas handicrafts and cookbooks, miniature delivery tractor-trailer, jellies, and hot sauces. Items gift-wrapped in ice-cream containers. Open Mon–Fri 8:00 AM–5:00 PM, Sat 9:00 AM–3:00 PM. Closed holidays. Catalog available from 800 number.

Directions: Take U.S. 290 to FM 577 North. Blue Bell is 2 miles ahead on right.

Nearby Attractions: Monastery of St. Claire; Rose Emporium; Historic Downtown Brenham; annual Maifest; Washington County Fair.

Collin Street Bakery   *fruitcake*

401 West 7th Avenue
Corsicana, TX 75110
(903) 874-7477 / (800) 504 1896

COLLIN STREET BAKERY

Collin Street Bakery (1896) is the oldest fruit-cake bakery in the U.S.A. The family-owned company's history is as colorful as the cherries, pineapples, papaya, and pecans on its cakes. The Deluxe Fruitcake has circled the earth aboard an Apollo spacecraft and adorned the tables of royalty, famous entertainers, sports legends, and politicians.

A glass-windowed, metal door opens from the lobby onto a small elevated platform. (Tell someone in the Bake Shop that you want a tour; they'll admit you to the baking area and explain the action. Otherwise, you can watch through the window—minus the aroma and sounds.) From October to mid-December, what you see is one of the most memorable sights of any in this book. A sea of workers, standing in small stalls on both sides of at least three production lines, hand-decorate fruitcakes' tops with pecans and candied fruit. The cakes, at this point only dough in round baking pans, flow in from the left. Each worker grabs a cake, decorates it with pecans, then places it back on the line headed for the ovens.

Another worker races about with a big scoop, keeping each decorator's holding bin filled with pecans. During this busy period the staff increases from around 80 employees to over 650, and workers decorate over 30,000 Original Deluxe Fruitcakes each day, making more than 1.5 million each year. Workers have been known to burst into their own classic holiday song—"I've Been Working on the Fruitcake."

From the platform, look toward the back of the production area at a highly automated bakery operation. To the left, pecan-filled batter is mixed in vats, and dough is automatically deposited into baking tins and leveled by hissing machines. To the right, an oven consumes long trays of up to 2,800 cake pans in one swallow. The dough-filled tins travel a precisely timed journey through the long oven and cooling tunnel. As a

testament to the fruitcake's quality, hanging from the back of the production area are flags from some of the 200 countries to which Collin Street ships (Japan is the top fruitcake importer).

Cost: Free

Freebies: Small samples and 10¢ coffee; postcards.

Video Shown: Optional 10-minute video on production process, shown in lobby area.

Reservations Needed: No, except for groups of 8 or more.

Days and Hours: Mon–Fri 8:00 AM–5:00 PM. Closed holidays. October 1 through mid-December, you watch fruitcake production from small landing just inside production area. Other times, take guided tour through baking machinery. Any time of year, need to ask for tour in adjoining Bake Shop.

Plan to Stay: 10 minutes for viewing, plus time for video and Bake Shop.

Minimum Age: None

Disabled Access: Yes

Group Requirements: Requests 1 week's advance notice for groups of 10 or more. No maximum group size, although only 10 people can watch from landing at one time.

Special Information: No photography

Bakery Shop: Sells over 136 different baked items, including Deluxe Fruitcake, rum cake, pecan pie, and pecan bread. Ask about unboxed factory-second fruitcakes. Also sells logoed T-shirts, caps, and baskets. Open Mon–Thur 7:00 AM–5:30 PM, Fri–Sat 7:00 AM–6:00 PM, and Sun 12:00 PM–6:00 PM. Fruitcake catalogs available from (800) 248-3366 and Cryer Creek Kitchens food items available from (800) 468-0088.

Directions: From I-45, take exit for Hwy. 31 West; becomes 7th Ave. in Corsicana. Bakery is on your left.

Nearby Attractions: Navarro Pecan Co. group tours available through Chamber of Commerce (call 903-874-4731); Pioneer Village; Richland-Chambers Lake.

Dr Pepper Bottling   ~ *soda*
221 South Patrick
Dublin, TX 76446
(817) 445-3466

In 1885 Wade Morrison named his newly developed soft drink after his sweetheart's father, Dr. Charles T. Pepper, hoping to win approval of his marriage proposal. This Dr Pepper plant is the world's oldest (opened in 1891), and still cranks out bottles of D.P. with 1940s machinery. Owner Bill Kloster, a plant employee since 1933, has many stories to tell and proudly displays his extensive collection of Dr Pepper memorabilia. His grandson Mark now helps run the business.

During D.P. bottling, an Amaretto-like aroma fills the air. Reusable glass bottles slowly and noisily shake, rattle, and roll past on old, gray machinery. Gears turn, and bottles rise, drop, and turn like amusement-park carousel horses, then do-si-do and waddle single file down conveyor belts. Since parts are no longer available, many of these vintage machines are held together with ingenuity and baling wire. Compared to the speed of current bottling lines (500 per minute), these machines seem to move in slow motion (32 per minute).

The filling process begins as bottles clatter through the 37-foot-long bottle-washer. They pass under the syruper for a squirt of syrup, under 20 valves that fill them with pure carbonated water, and under the crowner for their metal caps. The mixer turns the bottles over in three somersaults, then a worker grabs two bottles in each hand and sets them into bottle-shaped cut-outs on a lightboard for inspection. After twirling each bottle to ensure consistent color (shows proper mixing) and crack-free bottles, the worker stacks 24 bottles into the slats of each red or yellow wooden crate. People travel great distances to load their cars with these wooden crates of Dr Pepper, made with Imperial Holly pure cane sugar (most bottlers use corn syrup).

In the museum rooms, Bill's artifacts trace Dr Pepper's heritage from its beginnings in an 1885 Waco, Texas, drugstore to the present. His collection includes Dr Pepper signs, billboards, advertisements, every calendar from 1944 to the present, and clocks. His prized possessions are a life-size cardboard cut-out of the red, white, and blue saluting Patriotic Girl, and attention-grabbing motion displays like the carousel with three airplanes bearing the numbers *10*, *2*, and *4* (representing the times you should drink Dr Pepper for some extra "pep").

Cost: Adults $1.50; children 6–12, 50 cents; under 6, free.
Freebies: Ice-cold Dr Pepper
Video Shown: No
Reservations Needed: No, except for groups larger than 10 people.
Days and Hours: Mon–Fri 9:00 AM–5:00 PM. Sat 10:00 AM–5:00 PM, Sun 1:00 PM–5:00 PM. No tours 12:00 PM-1:00 PM. Closed Thanksgiving, Christmas, and New Year's. Bottling only on Tuesday from 9:00 AM–11:30 AM and 1:00 PM –3:30 PM. Other days, a bottling simulation is shown.
Plan to Stay: 30 minutes for tour and museum area, plus time in gift shop.
Minimum Age: None
Disabled Access: Yes
Group Requirements: Groups larger than 10 should call 1 week in advance. Groups over 20 people will be split.
Special Information: Dr Pepper Museum, located in a 1906 bottling plant in Waco, TX, (90 miles away), chronicles history of soft-drink industry and includes Dr Pepper memorabilia, old television commercials, soda fountain, seasonal exhibits, and classroom. Call (817) 757-1024.
Gift Shop: Old Doc Soda Fountain and Gift Shop sells logoed items including T-shirts, jewelry, towels, and limited-edition watches with old Dr Pepper designs. Can purchase Dr Pepper by case. Working soda fountain mixes soda right in your drinking glass. Open same hours as plant and museum.
Directions: From Fort Worth, take Hwy. 377 South to Dublin. Plant is on left 1 block past center of town.
Nearby Attractions: Just for Dolls Factory (call 817-445-2650); Proctor Dam and Parks.

The Dulcimer Factory — *dulcimers*

715 South Washington Street
Fredericksburg, TX 78624
(210) 997-6704

The dulcimer, a stringed folk instrument that originated in West Virginia's Appalachian Mountains in the 1800s, is truly an American instrument. John and Shirley Naylor brought this mountain music to Texas Hill Country in 1986, when they started making dulcimers in their San Antonio garage and selling them at fairs, arts-and-crafts shows, gun shows, rattlesnake roundups, and chili cook-offs. Now their factory and store make and sell eight styles of dulcimers in pecan, walnut, maple, cherry, and cedar. In an industry that's comprised of mostly individual artisans, this company is probably the biggest manufacturer.

Your tour begins in the playing room, where dulcimers hang from the walls. The tour guide demonstrates how easy it is to play a dulcimer. You learn that the body shape and wood type determine the instrument's sound. Three basic designs evolved: Appalachian hourglass, said to represent a woman's figure (deepest tone, greatest volume); teardrop (bluegrass); and flat, fish-like shape (soft, higher pitch). The number and pattern of holes carved in the body also give each instrument a unique sound. Using a scroll saw with a jeweler's blade, John skillfully carves sound holes in such delicate shapes as hummingbirds, vines, hearts, and flowers, and then wood-burns them.

After admiring the finished dulcimers, you visit the woodshop to see how the process begins. Through windows, you may see 12-foot rough planks being machine-sawed, planed, and sanded into ⅛-inch-thick parts—heads, tails, sides, and bottoms. These thin parts are stacked on shelves, and the potent cedar aroma fills the air. Next is the building room where parts are glued together. You may see a fret board glued to a top, jigs and clamps securing parts, or clothespins holding a thin wooden strip to a dulcimer's inside. This "bracing" provides more surface area for gluing the top and bottom to the sides.

The curvaceous sides are formed when, after the thin wood pieces soak in a water tank, a worker clamps each part around a mold with a heater beneath it. When dry, the wood retains the curves. Workers hand-sand the dulcimers. With your new appreciation for dulcimer-making, try your hand at playing one in the strumming room at the end of the tour.

Cost: Free
Freebies: Information sheet on mountain dulcimer history.
Video Shown: No
Reservations Needed: Recommended for individuals. Required for groups larger than 8 people.
Days and Hours: Mon–Fri 10:30 AM–12:00 PM and 1:00 PM–3:30 PM every ½ hour. Closed holidays.
Plan to Stay: 10–15 minutes, plus time in gift shop.
Minimum Age: None
Disabled Access: Yes
Group Requirements: Groups larger than 8 should call 1 week in advance. Groups larger than 30 will be split into smaller groups. Large-group tours last 40 minutes.
Special Information: Depending on day you visit, you'll see different processes.
Gift Shop: Can purchase dulcimers from factory. Retail store a few blocks away (155 E. Main St.) sells kits as well as finished Broomstick, Hill Country, and Appalachian Mountain dulcimers; books, accessories, and listening tapes. Open Mon–Sat 10:00 AM–5:30 PM, Sun 11:00 AM–5:00 PM. Slightly shorter hours in winter. Closed holidays. Catalog available from above number.
Directions: From San Antonio, take Hwy. 87 into Fredericksburg. Factory is on right just before town.
Nearby Attractions: In Kerrville, 25 miles away, Mooney Aircraft tour (see page 301) and James Avery Craftsmen (jewelry-making video and observation window; call 210-895-1122); Enchanted Rock; Nimitz Museum; Lady Bird Johnson Park; Willow City Driving Loop; Old German stone houses.

Imperial Sugar Company ~~~ *sugar*

198 Kemper Street
Sugar Land, TX 77478
(281) 491-9181

IMPERIAL SUGAR COMPANY

Imperial has refined sugar in Sugar Land (a small town just outside Houston) for over 150 years, making Imperial the oldest continuing commercial enterprise in Texas. On the original site of the 1843 mill and surrounding sugarcane fields now stands a large industrial complex that produces more than 3½ million pounds of refined cane sugar a day. This tour shows you what's involved in making all that sweet stuff.

In the warehouse, which can store 40 million pounds of raw sugar, watch workers use small front-end loaders to remove the raw sugar from open boxcars. A conveyor-belt system carries the raw sugar to the top of the warehouse, where it rains down to form light-brown hills on the floor below.

For safety reasons, the only other refining steps you see are in the Melt House, where centrifugal machines noisily spin and wash the raw sugar to remove molasses and impurities. Overhead pipes then move the washed raw sugar to large, enclosed melt tanks, where it is mixed with warm syrup and hot water to form sugar liquor. The guide's explanation at the beginning of the tour helps you better understand what you see, as the hiss and rumble of the machines make it hard to ask questions.

The sugar goes through many more refining steps than you might expect before you see it again in the packaging room. For example, in the Char House (the factory's towering, eight-story red-brick landmark), the sugar liquor is gravity-filtered through long cylinders that contain cattle-bone charcoal. Most of the remaining color and impurities are absorbed by the bone char. In the packing room, you'll stand next to machines that fill, weigh, and package sugar into containers from single-serving packets to 100-pound bags. The sweet-smelling air, the rhythmic machines, and the constant movement of colored bags and boxes have an almost hypnotic effect.

Cost: Free

Freebies: Brochure explains processing of raw sugar into refined cane sugar.

Video Shown: No, however tour guide's detailed explanation of refining process in visitors building starts the tour.

Reservations Needed: No, except for groups of 10 or more.

Days and Hours: Mon–Fri 10:00 AM and 2:00 PM. Closed holidays. Calling first is recommended; refinery occasionally operates on 4-day work schedule.

Plan to Stay: 1 hour for presentation and tour, plus time in gift shop.

Minimum Age: 3rd grade for school groups. No minimum for children with their parents.

Disabled Access: Refinery has old buildings with steps throughout.

Group Requirements: Groups of 10 or more should call 2 weeks in advance. Maximum group is 60 people.

Special Information: No photography. Any jewelry above waist (including watches and rings) must be removed, along with all items from top shirt pocket. Tour involves short bus ride and outdoor walking. On rainy days, tour does not visit raw-sugar warehouse. Commemorative markers on refinery grounds note its unusual history.

Gift Shop: Sells logoed items including caps, T-shirts, mugs, aprons, and golf items. Also sells Imperial Sugar cookbooks, a company tradition since 1915. Open after tours.

Directions: Take I-59 South to Hwy. 6 exit in Sugar Land. Turn right (north) onto Hwy. 6. At Alt. 90, turn right and then left onto Ulrich. Tour building is on right immediately after railroad tracks.

Nearby Attractions: Frito-Lay tour (call 713-342-0951); George Ranch; Confederate Museum; Fort Bend Museum. Houston's attractions, 15–30 miles away, include Space Center Houston tour (call 713-244-2100).

Jardine's Texas Foods

Texas-style foods

Jardine Ranch
Buda, TX 78610
(512) 295-4600

After touring Austin and Texas Hill Country sites, Jardine's authentic Texas-style foods round out a Texas gastronomic experience. The graceful live oak trees, restored chuck wagon, gazebo, and oak rocking chairs on the wide front porch of the company's headquarters all welcome you to the Jardine ranch and invite you to "set a spell."

Head honcho Dan, often clad in cowboy boots and western hat, his wife, Lisa, and their grown children make you feel at home at this family-run company. A visit to Jardine's combines ranch relaxation, a warm homey feeling, and an opportunity to view the bottling and packaging of hot sauce, barbecue sauce, chili, and jalapeño peppers through windows in the limestone ranch-house "factory."

Legend has it that after many years of cooking for cowboys on trail drives, D.L. Jardine settled in Texas Hill Country. As a chuck-wagon "cookie," he added various combinations of chiles, peppers, and spices to beans, meat, and cornbread. Since 1979, D.L.'s nephew Dan and his family have produced foods based on these early recipes—initially packaging them in the family's garage and now on this peaceful 30-acre ranch. To develop new recipes, Dan researches the history and culture of foods that characterize Texas heritage.

As you stroll outdoors under the sloped, ridged-tin roof and awning, look through several windows into a small section of the factory. If they're making Jardine's popular Chisholm Trail Texas Chili Bag O' Fixin's, watch hair-netted workers hand-fill reusable cloth bags with cellophane-wrapped spice packets. Seated at a long table, they grab packets from red plastic bins, insert them into the cloth bags, and pull a string to tighten each bag shut.

In the next area, items are hand-packed. Workers stuff jalapeños, olives, or pickles into glass jars. Through the last window, you'll see the horseshoe-shaped automatic filling line. Sauces, such as barbecue and picante, simmer in the three kettles to the left. The sauce passes through a pipe and a funnel into the bottles, which are capped, suction-sealed, labeled, and sent along a conveyor belt to the shipping warehouse. You leave craving the nearest Texas-style restaurant or your own kitchen so you can whip up some of these specialties.

Cost: Free

Freebies: Bottle of Texas Champagne brand hot pepper sauce; mail-order catalog.

Video Shown: No

Reservations Needed: Preferred; required for groups larger than 10 people.

Days and Hours: Mon–Fri 9:00 AM–4:00 PM. No production during 12:00 PM–1:00 PM lunch break. Closed holidays.

Plan to Stay: 15 minutes for tour, plus time for grounds, historic graveyard, and gift display case.

Minimum Age: None

Disabled Access: Yes

Group Requirements: Groups larger than 10 should call 2 days in advance. Food tastings are arranged for groups.

Special Information: Picnic tables and open-pit barbecue available on request.

General Store: Sells Jardine's authentic Texas-style foods, including salsas, condiments, spices, and other ranch-style recipes. Open Mon–Fri 9:00 AM–4:00 PM. Closed holidays. Catalog available from (800) 544-1880.

Directions: From I-35, take Exit 221 for Loop 4 toward Buda. Travel 1.1 miles and turn right just past the D.L. Jardine's sign. Turn right onto Chisholm Trail, which leads to the offices. Park on left.

Nearby Attractions: Manny Gammage's Texas Hatters tour (see page 299); Austin's attractions, including the State Capitol, Lyndon B. Johnson Library & Museum, and 6th Street, are 11 miles away.

JCPenney Museum ⟿ *retail stores and catalogs*

6501 Legacy Drive
Plano, TX 75024
(972) 431-TOUR

JCPenney

In 1902 James Cash Penney opened "The Golden Rule" cash-only dry-goods store in the small mining town of Kemmerer, Wyoming. With 36 stores in 1913, the company was renamed J.C. Penney Company and the "Penney Idea," seven mission-statement principles that guide the company today, was formulated. Now the company has over 1,200 stores nationwide and a thriving catalog and drugstore business. You can take a guided tour of its state-of-the-art home office and also visit the company's historical museum.

In the central rotunda at the heart of this 125-acre complex is a larger-than-life bronze sculpture of Mr. Penney. A replica of the first Golden Rule store is carved into his desk. A small, open museum area displays well-worn, yellowed early advertisements through recent catalog covers. A replica of the first Kemmerer store—including shopkeeper, dry goods, and original wooden counter—lines one wall. Other displays illustrate company development, including credit cards (1957) and the first electronic point-of-sale system (1960s).

You will be most impressed with the expansiveness of this three-story glass-atriumed megastructure. With a portion of the profits from selling its 45-story New York City skyscraper (company headquarters 1964 to 1987), Penney purchased 429 acres in rural Plano, Texas. This 1.9-million-square-foot office unites over 3,300 corporate "associates," Mr. Penney's name for his first employees, who worked "with" rather than "for" him.

The open floorplan and walkway seating areas facilitate communication between associates. Company day-care services and fitness facilities promote employee morale. A robotic mail-delivery system and on-site direct video broadcast system connecting over 1,200 stores enhance productivity. After seeing many of its features, you'll agree that this futuristic home office—located on Legacy Drive—is a legacy to the founder and to the company's associates.

Cost: Free

Freebies: Museum brochures

Videos Shown: Small theater shows short nostalgic films, including 1950s interviews with Mr. and Mrs. Penney. 9-screen video wall flashes commercials and building construction videos.

Reservations Needed: No, for museum. Yes, for Home Office tour (individuals and groups call 2 weeks in advance).

Days and Hours: Museum: Mon–Fri 8:00 AM–5:00 PM. Tour: Tue–Thur 10:00 AM and 2:00 PM. Closed holidays.

Plan to Stay: 20 minutes for museum (1 hour for guided tour and museum) plus time for lunch in company cafeteria, where curved glass walls frame a waterpool with fountain.

Minimum Age: None

Disabled Access: Yes

Group Requirements: For Home Office tour, groups should call 2 weeks in advance. Groups over 25 will be split into smaller groups. Other tour times may be requested.

Special Information: Guided tours of museum and company archives can be arranged for individuals and groups 2 weeks in advance; call 972-431-7925.

Gift Shop: JC's, down the escalator from museum, sells logoed clothing, pictures of building, and other items. Open Mon–Fri 8:00 AM–3:00 PM.

Directions: From Dallas, take Dallas Tollway North to Legacy Dr. exit. Turn left onto Legacy Dr., then right onto Communications Pkwy. Turn left onto Headquarters Dr. Park in North or South garage. Tours meet at Mr. Penney's statue in center of building (main rotunda).

Nearby Attractions: Mary Kay factory tour and company museum (see page 300); American Airlines C.R. Smith Museum (see page 291); Studios at Las Colinas tour (call 972-869-3456); Dallas' downtown attractions, including Dealey Plaza and JFK Sixth Floor Museum, are 20–30 miles away.

Manny Gammage's Texas Hatters

5003 Overpass   *Western-style hats*
Buda, TX 78610
(512) 295-4287 / (800) 421-4287

By such titles as "Dr. of Mad Hattery," "Wizard of Lids," and "A 'Manny' of Many Hats," you know that Manny Gammage was no ordinary hatmaker. One of the few custom Western-style U.S. hatmakers left, he hatted such personalities as Ronald Reagan, Howard Cosell, Jerry Jeff Walker, Burt Reynolds, and Willie Nelson. Now his wife and daughter carry on his legacy. Photographs, many autographed by the famous people wearing Manny's hats, form a collage on the shop walls. Baseball caps, each with its own story, hang from the ceiling's wooden beams.

Once inside the small store, make your way over to the wooden counter and take a stool. Ask Joella, Manny's daughter and third-generation hat-maker, to guide you through the wooden saloon-door marked "Employees Only," into the small production area. Be careful not to touch anything as you work your way through the cramped quarters to the back.

Hats start as unshaped hat-bodies made of beaver and hare's hair. From cubbyholes lining the walls, a worker selects the correct solid wooden block for the desired hat style and the wearer's head shape. After steam-heating the hat, he uses his muscles to stretch it over the heavy block. With an iron that weighs 15 pounds in the morning but feels like 45 pounds by evening, the worker irons and hand-sands the brim in circular stroking motions. He also irons out the crown as it slowly rotates on a contraption clamped to the wooden work table. These processes are repeated and fine-tuned to correctly shape each hat.

As you squeeze your way into the next area, Joella explains that there are "too damn many steps" involved in making a hat. Study the well-worn poplar-wood disks, or "flanges," stored in slotted shelves. Look for the LBJ flange—you'll recognize it by the letters LBJ on the side. Sandbags are lowered onto a wooden flange to flatten the hat's brim. In the next small area, an old Singer sewing machine puts bindings in the brim; leather sweatbands and satin linings are sewn in by hand. More personality comes from the hatband—elephant hide, snakeskin, lizard, leather, and feathers. Even if you don't buy a hat, you'll leave with some great stories.

Cost: Free
Freebies: A token souvenir
Video Shown: No
Reservations Needed: Yes
Days and Hours: Tue–Sat 9:30 AM–5:30 PM. Closed holidays and week of July 4th.
Plan to Stay: 20 minutes
Minimum Age: None. Children require adult supervision.
Disabled Access: Yes; however, difficult maneuvering in tight quarters.
Group Requirements: Groups larger than 10 will be split into smaller groups and need to call at least 1 week in advance.
Special Information: Best time to watch workers is in the morning. Hot in summer.
Retail Store: Sells custom-made hats for 1-week delivery. Most popular styles are high-roller and hunter, both in black. Open same hours as above. Catalog available from 800 number.
Directions: Take I-35 to Exit 220. Exit puts you on Overpass Rd. Look for 45-foot-high hat sign.
Nearby Attractions: Jardine's Texas Foods tour (see page 297); Austin's attractions, including Sixth Street, Lyndon B. Johnson Library and Museum, and Capitol Building, are 11 miles away.

Mary Kay

cosmetics and skin-care products

16251 Dallas Parkway
Dallas, TX 75248
(972) 687-5720

Inscribed at the entrance to the company museum is Mary Kay Ash's motto: "You can do anything in the world that you want to do if you want it badly enough and you are willing to pay the price." This determination and Mary Kay's ability to motivate and reward her (mostly female) sales force has made Mary Kay, Inc.—founded in 1963 by Mary Kay and her son Richard—into one of America's most admired companies.

Drive from corporate headquarters to the aromatic manufacturing facility, where 38 lines fill and package over 200 Mary Kay products. On the eye-shadow line, pink plastic bottoms, clear tops, and eye-shadow refills merge on a freeway system that, together with human hands, packages approximately 65,000 per ten-hour shift. Once mascara, concealer, or lip-gloss tubes are filled, workers manually insert applicators with a gentle twist. It's fun to follow a bottle through the fragrance line—filling, manually inserting straws and atomizer tops, stamping down lids, and hand-packing perfume bottles.

The tour highlight, however, is the waxy-smelling lipstick line. Liquid lipstick—wax, emollients, and color—is pumped into oblong metal molds, which are stacked onto an iced cooling table to solidify. Workers manually insert each lipstick bullet into its tube. Upright tubes march into a glass-enclosed oven, where flames melt the outer layer to give the lipstick a shine. The next time you apply (or watch someone apply) lipstick, you'll appreciate this labor that enhances women's beauty.

The corporate tour's highlight is Mary Kay's personal office at the corporate headquarters, with its crescent-shaped pastel sofa and her desk. Afterwards, take a self-guided tour of the Mary Kay Museum: Dreams Come True in the corporate office lobby (reservations not required). Its art deco white, pink, and black granite floors and brass-trimmed dark wood cases display mannequins wearing the director's suits since 1963, Mary Kay product lines, and many photographs and awards.

Cost: Free

Freebies: No

Video Shown: Several videos in museum cover company history, manufacturing process, company career opportunities, and annual seminars.

Reservations Needed: No, for museum. Yes, for corporate and manufacturing facility tours. Individuals, call (972) 687-5720 at least 2 days in advance. Groups, see below.

Days and Hours: Museum: Mon–Fri 9:00 AM –5:00 PM. Manufacturing headquarters tours: Mon–Thur 10:30 AM and 2:00 PM. Corporate tours: Tue–Fri 9:00 AM–4:30 PM. Closed holidays.

Plan to Stay: 45 minutes for museum and corporate tour; 1 hour for factory tour.

Minimum Age: None

Disabled Access: Yes, for corporate building and most of factory tour (call ahead for arrangements for 1 flight of stairs).

Group Requirements: Groups larger than 25 must call at least 1 week in advance for reservations. Groups larger than 15 will be split into smaller groups.

Special Information: Photography allowed in museum and office, but not in plant.

Gift Shop: No

Directions: To corporate headquarters: From Lyndon B. Johnson Frwy. (I-635), take Dallas Tollway North exit at Westgrove/ Keller Springs. Follow service road through Keller Springs and turn left at Westgrove. Turn left back onto service road going south. Mary Kay is first big building on right. To manufacturing facility: from Stemmons Frwy. (I-35), take Regal Row exit. Head south on Regal Row. Plant is 2 blocks ahead on left.

Nearby Attractions: American Airlines C.R. Smith Museum (see page 291) and JCPenney headquarters and museum (see page 298) 20–30 miles away; downtown Dallas attractions include JFK Museum, Dallas Museum of Art, Museum of the Americas, and West End Marketplace.

Mooney Aircraft ～ *light airplanes*

Louis Schreiner Field
Kerrville, TX 78208
(210) 896-6000

Established in 1948, Mooney is one of the few single-engine, light-airplane manufacturers left in the U.S.A. The high cost of product liability insurance has forced many manufacturers out of the market and cut production to about 10 percent of 1960s output. Mooney prides itself on making planes that rival the speed and performance of larger craft. The walking tour through the plant gives you a close-up view of light-plane construction.

Your tour begins in the pre-flight building, a modified hangar where the planes receive their instrument panels, seats, and other cabin accessories. Since planes are not painted until they're completely built and tested, most of them still wear their naked aluminum skin. Peek inside a plane—it looks like a mangle of wires and tubes with the "yoke" (steering wheel) sticking out.

Walk along the concrete floor into the appropriately named "hammer house," where you'll see and hear everything from a basic hand-held hammer to a 2,500-ton press used to shape pieces of metal and aluminum into parts for Mooney and other major commercial aircraft manufacturers. The big green presses are as deep below the surface as they are high above the ground. Workers grind and smooth the edges of the parts on buffers, adding to the industrial cacophony.

The plane is built in the cavernous assembly building. No conveyors or automated assembly lines are used to form the plane or transport parts. Your tour guide takes you through the subassembly stations, where you'll watch a wing constructed in one area and the tail section in another. Jigs (the frames that hold parts together while they are being worked on) are everywhere. Discover how workers stretch the aluminum skin around the steel-tube frame that is the skeleton of all Mooneys. When the wings are married to the fuselage, with workers rolling around underneath the plane to bolt and fasten them together, the silver bird finally looks like it will fly.

Cost: Free
Freebies: Product literature
Video Shown: No
Reservations Needed: No, except for groups larger than 10 people.
Days and Hours: Tue–Fri 10:00 AM. Closed holidays. Usually closed the week between Christmas and New Year's, and 1 week in July or August.
Plan to Stay: 45 minutes for tour, plus time for gift counter.
Minimum Age: 8
Disabled Access: Yes
Group Requirements: Groups larger than 10 people should make reservations 2 days ahead. No maximum group size.
Special Information: Photography allowed only in final assembly area. No air conditioning, so hot in summer. Mooney Aircraft Pilots Association Annual Homecoming, second weekend in October. Mooney also subcontracts for several large aerospace companies. Wear comfortable shoes for this indoor and outdoor walking tour.
Gift Counter: Sells logoed items, including hats, T-shirts, mugs, and jackets. Product list available at above number. Open after tour upon request. Information on purchasing planes available from (800) 456-3033.
Directions: From I-10, take Hwy. 27 towards Comfort. Go through towns of Comfort and Centerpoint. Immediately after Kerrville Airport is Al Mooney Rd. Turn right and follow road around to company's offices. Park in lot past security station.
Nearby Attractions: James Avery Craftsmen (visitors center has jewelry-making video and observation window; call 210-895-1122); the Dulcimer Factory tour (see page 295), about 25 miles away, in Fredericksburg; Texas Hill Country attractions include Cowboy Artist America Museum and Y.O. Ranch tour with exotic and native animals (call 210-640-3222).

Mrs Baird's Bakery ~ *bread*

7301 South Freeway
Fort Worth, TX 76134
(817) 293-6230

Discover the bakery that introduced sliced bread to Texas. Now one of the most modern bread bakeries in America, Mrs Baird's started as a home-kitchen operation in 1908. Although the Baird children once delivered bread to the neighbors in baskets, a fleet of delivery trucks now journey the vast highways of Texas and the surrounding region. One thing has not changed since Mrs. Baird began baking in her home five generations ago: "Family pride" is still the final ingredient.

After donning your own paper baker's hat, embark on a voyage into the bakery. Notice the smell of yeast permeating the air around you. Compare your own pantry to this fantastic food warehouse. Bags stacked high on metal shelves around you contain up to 2,000 pounds of ingredients, such as salt and powdered milk. Each of these "super sacks" of ingredients will eventually end up sifted together in the 25-foot-tall sifter and then moved to the mixers to become part of the bread dough. The company uses 100,000 pounds of flour each day to make up to 140,000 loaves of bread.

As you move out of the ingredient area and closer to the ovens, the aroma changes to that of fresh-baked bread. Machines drop fistfuls of dough for hamburger buns into baking pans. Turn around to see larger portions of dough for making loaves of bread fall into place. In the afternoon, witness Mrs Baird's specialty, hand-twisted white bread, the only exception to full automation in the plant. Watch the baker twist two long ropes of dough together like a braid to form one loaf. The dough is then placed in the pans and taken by conveyor to rise.

Gaze upward at a bumper-to-bumper highway of bread and hamburger buns traveling by on cooling tracks above your head. The depanner machine removes the fresh-baked bread from the pans with rows of suction cups. Blades, sharpened every five minutes, slice the 107° bread. Then the fresh bread is popped into the bags you see in the store.

Cost: Free

Freebies: Logoed paper hat, hot slice of bread, pencil, activity pamphlet for children, and a sweet baked goodie, freshly baked at the cake plant next door (cake plant is not open for tours).

Video Shown: 7-minute video on the nutritional importance of bread, the company history, and the baking process.

Reservations Needed: Yes, reservations should be made at least 3 weeks in advance. Call (817) 293-6230 and ask for the tour coordinator or call (817) 615-3050 to leave a voice-mail message.

Days and Hours: Mon and Wed 10:00 AM–4:00 PM, Fri 10:00 AM–6:00 PM. Closed holidays.

Plan to Stay: 45 minutes

Minimum Age: 6

Disabled Access: Yes

Group Requirements: Maximum group size is 25 people. Larger groups will be divided. One adult is required for every 10 children.

Special Information: No photography. It's warm in the bakery, so dress comfortably. Hand-twisting can be seen only on afternoon tours. Other Mrs Baird's Bakery facilities offering tours include Dallas (214-526-7201) and Houston (713-690-3227). Days and hours vary at each location; call for details.

Gift Area: No

Directions: From downtown, take I-35W South to Sycamore School Rd. Turn left under the highway overpass. Take an immediate left onto the service road. Turn right into the bakery and follow "Tour Visitors" signs.

Nearby Attractions: American Airlines Museum and Mary Kay cosmetics tour and museum (see pages 291 and 300); *Ft. Worth Star-Telegram* newspaper tour (call 817-551-2212); Studios at Las Colinas tour, about 45 minutes away (call 972-869-3456).

Nocona Athletic
208 Walnut Street
Nocona, TX 76255
(817) 825-3326

*baseball gloves
and football equipment*

Nocona, Texas, is the leather goods capital of the Southwest. Nocona Athletic Goods Company started making Nokona baseball gloves and other sporting goods during the Depression. While U.S. sporting-goods companies began shifting labor-intensive baseball-glove production overseas in the early 1960s, Nocona proudly stayed at home. (Current imports represent 98 percent of glove sales nationwide.) The Nokona ball glove is one of three glove lines still made in the U.S.A., and the plant tour gives you the chance to see all of the production steps. While workers have some help from machines, you'll notice that the process is far from automated.

Making baseball and softball gloves begins with selecting the correct leather, which Nocona does on site, not overseas. The tour guide passes around pieces of cowhide and kangaroo leathers so you can feel the contrasting textures, and explains the differences between leather used in today's gloves compared to that of previous decades. Each glove's 14 to 18 leather pieces are die-cut from big leather sheets. Workers lay a metal frame in the shape of a hand on the correct spot and use a press to cut out a piece. They use experience gained from guiding patterns here for the past 50 years.

After stamping the name and logo on the leather, workers meticulously sew the pieces together. Up to this point the glove has been built inside-out, so it's turned right side out one finger at a time on a hot iron. Workers then weave a long needle in and out of the glove to lace the leather together before stretching it on hot irons and applying leather-conditioning oils. You'll be tempted to pick up a glove and play catch in the middle of the factory.

From the aroma of leather, move to the smell of glue in the department that assembles football equipment, such as shoulder pads and helmets. Workers construct this equipment mostly from pre-molded plastic parts and shock-absorbing pads. Don't forget

to visit the company's small collection of old leather baseball mitts and football helmets, conjuring images of Ty Cobb and Knute Rockne in the years of day games, grass gridirons, and U.S.A.-made sporting goods.

Cost: Free

Freebies: Product catalogs used for whole-sale trade.

Video Shown: No

Reservations Needed: Preferred

Days and Hours: Mon–Fri 8:00 AM–12:00 PM and 1:00 PM–4:00 PM. Closed holidays, 2 weeks at Christmas, and 2 weeks around July 4th.

Plan to Stay: 1 hour

Minimum Age: None

Disabled Access: Yes

Group Requirements: No minimum. Maximum group size is 30 people with 1 day's advance notice.

Special Information: Glue smell may initially bother some people.

Gift Shop: Nocona Boot Company Factory Outlet (6 blocks away on Hwy. 82) sells first- and second-quality Nokona gloves.

Directions: From Dallas, take I-35 to Hwy. 82 West exit in Gainesville. Stay on Hwy. 82 West into Nocona, turn right at Clay St., and left on Walnut. Company is in big red-brick building on right.

Nearby Attractions: Nocona Boot Company tour (call 817-825-3321); Nocona Belt Company tour (call 817-825-3271); Justin Park; Lake Nocona.

Kennecott Utah Copper ⌒ *copper mine*
Kennecott's Bingham Canyon Mine Visitors Center
Bingham Canyon, UT 84006
(801) 322-7300

If you moved Chicago's Sears Tower to the bottom of the Bingham Canyon Copper Mine, it wouldn't even reach halfway to the top of the mine. In fact, at over 2½ miles across and a ½-mile deep, this mine is the deepest human-made excavation on earth. In 1906 steam shovels began eating away at a mountain that divided Bingham Canyon. Today huge rotary drills and electric shovels have replaced steam shovels, and an open pit has replaced the mountain. Kennecott is still mining copper from Bingham Canyon, which has yielded over 14 million tons of copper—more than any other mine in history.

Your visit begins with an unbelievable view of the mine from an overlook. The view encompasses hundreds of millions of years of the earth's history and lots of brown dirt in a circular pattern. Look down at the workers and machines who remove about 300,000 tons of material daily, knowing that soon you will learn exactly how miners remove the copper ore from this canyon.

Inside the Visitors Center, eight exhibits teach you everything from the mine's history to the daily uses of copper and how Kennecott protects the environment through reclamation and revegetation projects. For those especially interested in history, one exhibit tells how the surrounding area of Utah developed and prospered along with the copper industry. You will also learn about the people of Kennecott and the company's community efforts.

In the center's 80-seat theater, watch a video which provides a condensed explanation of the entire copper-mining process, as well as some of the history behind the mine and its neighboring communities. As you drive away from the Bingham Canyon Mine, be sure to glance back at the mountainside you saw as you drove in; you now have a new appreciation of the mining industry, copper, and Bingham Canyon.

Cost: $3 per vehicle, $2 for motorcycles, with all funds going to local charities.
Freebies: Company brochures
Video Shown: 13-minute video explaining mine history and operation.
Reservations Needed: No, but call at beginning and end of season to verify Visitors Center is open.
Days and Hours: Open April through end of October, weather permitting. Mon–Sun 8:00 AM–8:00 PM. Closed holidays.
Plan to Stay: 1 hour
Minimum Age: None
Disabled Access: Yes
Group Requirements: None. $30 entrance fee for tour buses. Booklet available for educators and tour guides.
Special Information: Tour does not permit you to go down into the mine. However, observation deck and exhibits offer views of it.
Gift Shop: Sells souvenirs, T-shirts, and postcards, as well as educational books, small rocks, and minerals. Shop is operated by local Lions Club, and is not part of Kennecott. Open same hours as Visitors Center.
Directions: From Salt Lake City, take I-15 South to 7200 South exit, and turn right. Turn right onto 7800 South, which turns into Bingham Hwy. Take Bingham Hwy. toward Copperton. Mine is visible on mountainside ahead. Follow signs to Kennecott's Bingham Canyon Mine.
Nearby Attractions: Geneva Steel Mill tour in Orem, 30 miles away (call 801-277-9178); Salt Lake City's attractions, including Salt Lake Temple, Great Salt Lake, and ski resorts, are about 25 miles away; Mormon Church headquarters.

Ben & Jerry's   *ice cream and frozen yogurt*

Route 100
Waterbury, VT 05676
(802) 244-TOUR

Given Ben & Jerry's down-home image, you'd expect to see hundreds of workers using individual churns to make its ice creams and yogurts. Instead, from a glass-enclosed, temperature-controlled mezzanine area you look down at a state-of-the-art ice cream factory that can turn out 180,000 pints per day. The grounds are filled with whimsical interactive displays and games, like the "Wheel-O-Flavor," that let you experience ice cream-making and ease the waiting time for this very popular tour.

Your guide goes down onto the factory floor to identify the different equipment and explain the process, with most of the action happening inside enclosed machines. Ice cream and frozen yogurt begin with an unflavored base mix stored in the 36° tank room. The mix travels to the labeled flavor vat, to the freezer (where it gets the consistency of soft-serve), into the fruit and chunk feeder, to the special automatic pint-filler that handles "chunk intensive" flavors, to the pint bundler, and finally to the spiral hardener. In this last step, the ice cream freezes solid at a temperature of -60°.

On the production area's back wall, a giant banner announces an impressive statistic, like the number of pounds of cookie dough used during the past year in making their top-selling flavor. Rock music blares down on the factory floor, courtesy of the Joy Gang. Every half-hour a quality control worker grabs pints from the freezer, slices them open with a machete, and inspects for the proper number of chunks per bite (among other things). On the way out, you may get to watch this inspection. Make sure you peek into the flavor laboratory to see new flavors in development, and look at the Hall of Fame's colorful pictures, posters, and paraphernalia that humorously document the company's proud, offbeat history.

Cost: $2.00 per person; 10 percent of the proceeds go to community and Vermont non-profit groups. Children 12 and under, free.

Freebies: A sample of ice cream, frozen yogurt, or sorbet, and Ben & Jerry's button.

Video Shown: Funky 8-minute movie on how 2 childhood friends turned what they learned from a $5 correspondence course on ice-cream-making into a multimillion–dollar business that shares its success with its employees and the community.

Reservations Needed: No, except for groups of 10 or more people.

Days and Hours: Mon–Sun 10:00 AM–5:00 PM (until 8:00 PM in summer). Tours at least every 30 minutes, with tickets given out on a first-come, first-served basis. No production on Sundays, holidays, or company celebration days, although tours see video of the production line operation. Call tour hotline number for up-to-date schedules.

Plan to Stay: 30 minutes for tour and movie, plus time for the wait, grounds, displays, and gift shop. Grounds are a low-key family ice-cream park.

Minimum Age: None

Disabled Access: Yes

Group Requirements: Reservations for groups of 10 or more people suggested. Call (802) 244-5641, ext. 2289. No reservations accepted for tours during July, August, and holidays.

Special Information: Afternoon tours fill up quickly, particularly in summer.

Gift Shop: Scoop Shop features all Ben & Jerry's flavors. Gift shop, with piped-in folk music, offers Vermont gifts, logoed clothes, MeMOOrabilia (like cow socks and floating farm Moobile), and other stuff. Open Mon–Sun 10:00 AM–6:00 PM (until 9:00 PM in summer). Catalog available from (802) 651-9600.

Directions: Take I-89 to Exit 10. Go north on Rt. 100 toward Stowe. Factory is about 1 mile ahead on left. Look for giant picture of Planet Earth outside factory at top of hill.

Nearby Attractions: Cabot Creamery Annex Store; Stowe and Sugarbush ski areas; Cold Hollow Cider Mill; Mt. Mansfield.

Cabot Creamery 〜 *cheese*

Main Street
Cabot, VT 05647
(802) 563-2231

On a hillside in Vermont, sparkling white 130,000-gallon milk silos emblazoned with the red-and-green Cabot Creamery logo overlook the entrance to the visitors center and plant, where some of the nation's best sharp cheddar cheese is made (winner of U.S. Championship Cheese Contest). This guided tour shows you how the cooperative creamery converts milk from local farms into famous Vermont cheddar cheeses, and also how it packages its yogurts, cottage cheese, and sour cream.

You'll peer through glass windows into the packaging and processing rooms, where workers fill large cooking vats with quality-tested, heat-treated milk and a starter culture. The curd that forms is cut with stainless-steel knives that help separate the curd from the whey. Once the whey is separated and drained off, workers vigorously mix the curd on huge metal finishing tables to "cheddar" it until the correct pH level is reached.

In overhead towers, the curd is then pressed into 42-pound blocks or round stainless-steel frames to create cheese wheels. Every 90 seconds another block emerges from a tower and enters an airtight cellophane bag for proper aging (nine months for sharp cheddar, 14 months for extra-sharp). With the cheese-making process in various stages of production, your ten-minute walk captures the five hours needed for every vat of milk to become cheese (33,000 pounds of whole milk in each vat yields approximately 3,500 pounds of cheese).

Cost: $1 donation supports various Vermont causes and projects. Children under 12, free.
Freebies: Cabot cheese and dip samples under the "Grazing Encouraged" sign in gift shop. Cabot Critters coloring book, 1 per family.
Video Shown: 10-minute video on history of Vermont farming and dairy industry, development of Cabot Cooperative Creamery in 1919, and highlights of processes used to make different Cabot products.

Reservations Needed: No, except for groups larger than 40 people.
Days and Hours: June through October, Mon–Sun 9:00 AM–5:00 PM; November through May, Mon–Sat 9:00 AM–4:00 PM. Tours run every ½-hour. Last tour is 30 minutes before closing. Call ahead for cheese-making days.
Plan to Stay: 30 minutes for tour and video, plus time to nibble in the gift shop.
Minimum Age: None
Disabled Access: Yes
Group Requirements: Groups larger than 40 should call at least 1 week in advance.
Special Information: Cabot Creamery Annex store (near Ben & Jerry's factory on Rt. 100) shows cheese-making video and sells Cabot products, Vermont specialty foods, beer, and wine.
Gift Shop: Sells all Cabot products, including such specialty cheddars as garlic dill. Offers selected factory specials and other Vermont-made food products and gifts. Open same hours as tour. Cheese catalog available from (800) 639-3198.
Directions: From I-89, take Exit 8 for Montpelier. Head east on Rt. 2 and turn left onto Rt. 215 East in Marshfield Village. Cabot Creamery is 5 miles ahead on right. From I-91, take St. Johnsbury exit. Head west on Rt. 2 and turn right on Rt. 215 to Creamery.
Nearby Attractions: Maple Grove Farms and Ben & Jerry's tours (see pages 307 and 305); bird- and wood-carvers, family farms (Cabot Visitor's Center has information on carvers and farms); Goodrich's Sugarhouse (call 800-639-1854). For more information on cheese factory tours, call Vermont Department of Agriculture, Food, and Markets (802-828-2416).

Maple Grove Farms 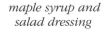   *maple syrup and salad dressing*

167 Portland Street
St. Johnsbury, VT 05819
(802) 748-5141 / (800) 525-2540

The company that two women started in 1915 is now one of the world's largest packagers of maple syrup and manufacturers of maple products. Maple Grove Farms has also developed a full line of natural fruit syrups and gourmet salad dressings, with its honey-mustard dressing a top-selling New England gourmet dressing.

This guided factory floor tour has a small-town feeling. You'll watch bottles of pure maple syrup or salad dressing filled, labeled, and packed on the assembly line. Downstairs in the "kitchen," workers on one side boil and mix maple syrup for making candy; on the other side, it's salad dressing or fruit syrup. Your nostrils will battle over the conflicting smells, with fruit syrups (especially raspberry) usually the clear winner.

A vintage 1930s candy depositor pours the maple candy mix into rubber sheet molds. The mixture cools for about an hour before the "ladies," as the tour guide calls them, shake the candy out onto padded mats. The candies are placed into metal baskets for an overnight bath in a crystallizing mixture of sugar and syrup, a natural preservative. Look through the glass window at carts filled with candy air-drying on metal trays, and at the quick-moving hands that individually pack the maple candies into boxes (3,000 to 4,000 pounds per day).

Cost: $1; children under 12, free.
Freebies: Small sample bag of maple candies. Gift shop offers free tastes of different maple syrups and the salad dressing of the day.
Video Shown: Tour begins with 8-minute video highlighting maple syrup–making process, company history and manufacturing. When factory tour not operating, this video plays in Cabin Store
Reservations Needed: No, except for groups of more than 40 people.
Days and Hours: Mon–Fri 8:00 AM–11:45 AM and 12:30 PM–4:30 PM, year-round. Tour runs about every 12 minutes. Closed holidays.

Plan to Stay: 25 minutes, including tour, video, Maple Museum, and gift shop. Maple Museum is an authentic sugarhouse with all tools and equipment used by Vermont sugar-makers, and complete explanation of evaporation process.
Minimum Age: None
Disabled Access: Only on bottom floor of factory, but company does not encourage it because floor can be slippery.
Group Requirements: Tours for groups of more than 40 people require reservations.
Special Information: Production stops around 3:30 PM. While syrup and dressing are filled and packed daily, candy not made every day during winter.
Gift Shop: Cabin Store sells many maple products, such as maple butter, maple crunch, and maple drops. Also offers company's gourmet dressings and fruit-flavored syrups, along with standard Vermont tourist items. Look for factory seconds in seconds area. Cabin Store and Maple Museum open Mon–Sun 8:00 AM–5:00 PM, from beginning of May until late October. During winter, store is in factory and open same hours as tour. Catalog available from (802) 748-3136.
Directions: From I-91, take Exit 20 for Rt. 5 North. Take Rt. 2 East. Factory is about 1 mile from center of town. From I-93, take Exit 1 in Vermont, turn onto Rt. 18 towards St. Johnsbury, then turn left onto Rt. 2 West. Factory is a few miles ahead on left.
Nearby Attractions: Cabot Creamery tour (see page 306); Goodrich's Sugarhouse (call 800-639-1854); Fairbanks Museum and Planetarium; New England Maple Museum, about 1½ hours away in Pittsford.

Crowley Cheese ~~ *cheese*

Healdville Road
Healdville, VT 05758
(802) 259-2340 / (802) 259-2210

When most cheese factories call their cheese "handmade," they usually mean that machines did the processing with a little human involvement. At the U.S.'s oldest still-operating cheese factory (established 1882), "handmade" means what it says. Except for modern sanitation and refrigeration techniques, Crowley's cheese-making tools are from the 1800s.

The outside of this three-story brown clapboard building, a National Historic Place, looks more like a house than a cheese "factory." But inside, the solo cheese-maker (formerly a practicing lawyer who took over the business from his father) proudly enjoys showing visitors how to make old-style Colby cheddar using nineteenth-century techniques. You can stand near the 1,000-gallon sterile vat that looks like a large bathtub filled with milk. Steam flows through the hollow walls to heat the milk.

The cheese-maker adds the culture and, later, rennet (a milk-coagulating enzyme). Once the mixture has a yogurt texture, it is "cut" into small cubes, which separate from the whey and become the curd. Watch how the cheese-maker uses the cheese rake to gently stir the curd. This keeps curd particles separate and helps them cook evenly.

Once the whey is drained, the curds look like mounds of popcorn. The cheese-maker works the curds by hand, rinsing them with fresh spring water before placing them into cheesecloth-lined metal hoops. Overnight, old crank presses remove excess whey. Then the cheese wheels age at least two months for "mild" and over a year for "extra-sharp." After looking at the pictures on the walls, listening to the cheese-maker's explanation, and watching traditional cheese-making techniques, you leave saying the Little Miss Muffet nursery rhyme.

Cost: Free
Freebies: Cheese
Video Shown: 9-minute video on history of company and cheese-making process, usually shown when not in production.

Reservations Needed: No, except for groups over 25 people.

Days and Hours: Mon–Fri 8:00 AM–4:00 PM. Closed holidays. Since small operation, call ahead about cheese production schedule.

Plan to Stay: 15 minutes for tour, plus time for gift shop and duck pond.

Minimum Age: None. Tour is very popular with young children; "Sesame Street" filmed feature on cheese-making at Crowley.

Disabled Access: Yes

Group Requirements: Groups larger than 25 should call a few days ahead.

Special Information: Best time to see production and talk to cheese-maker is 11:00 AM to mid-afternoon. When no one is in factory, calls to above number may not always be answered. Don't despair, just call back or try contacting gift shop at (802) 259-2210.

Retail Store: Located 1½ miles away on main Rt. 103; sells mild, medium, and sharp Crowley Cheese in 8-oz. bars, 2.5- and 5-pound wheels, smoked bars, and spiced (caraway, dill, garlic, hot pepper, onion, and sage) bars; Vermont specialty foods and gifts. Open Mon–Sat 10:30 AM–5:30 PM, Sun 11:00 AM–5:30 PM (suggest calling to check if open). Closed Christmas and New Year's. Call above number for order form.

Directions: From I-91, take Rt. 103 North. At split with Rt. 100, stay on Rt. 103 for 3 miles. Pass Crowley Cheese Shop, turn left onto Healdville Rd. for factory. From Rutland, take Rt. 7 South to Rt. 103 South. Then go 10¾ miles to flashing yellow light at Belmont Rd. in Mt. Holly. Continue on Rt. 103 South for about 3 miles and turn right onto Healdville Rd.

Nearby Attractions: Cerniglia Winery tour (call 800-654-6382); Vermont Marble Exhibit (call 802-459-3311 ext. 436); Weston (a lovely small New England village); Coolidge Family Homestead; Okemo ski area.

Photo © 1991 Crowley Cheese, Inc.

Kent Smith, owner and cheesemaker, hand-rakes the curd at Crowley Cheese in Healdville, Vermont.

Photo © 1991 Crowley Cheese, Inc.

Crowley Cheese is the oldest cheese factory in the United States.

Simon Pearce ⟋ *glass and pottery*

Route 5, Windsor, VT 05089
(802) 674-6280
The Mill, Quechee, VT 05059
(802) 295-2711

SIMON PEARCE

Simon Pearce, originally trained as a potter, apprenticed in Sweden before opening a glassblowing factory in Ireland in 1971. Because of high energy costs, Simon moved his business to the U.S. in 1981. Simon housed his first U.S. factory in a historic, 200-year-old red-brick woolen mill next to the Ottauquechee River in Quechee, Vermont. In 1993 Simon designed a brand-new manufacturing facility 9 miles away in Windsor, Vermont.

Both facilities offer self-guided tours. From Windsor's raised catwalk viewing gallery, you can observe the entire glassblowing process. The doors of the large furnace in the room's center open automatically when a worker steps on a floor mat to gather glass from the furnace. Workers may appear to be wandering around, but each has a specific mission as part of a two- or three-person team.

The glassblower chooses a blowpipe from the warmer (glass adheres well to warm blowpipes), gathers the appropriate amount of glass from the center furnace, and blows it into a wooden mold. The apprentice opens the mold and gathers glass onto a pontil iron, which holds the piece during hand-finishing of the rim. The cross underneath each piece, made by this pontil iron, has become the Simon Pearce trademark.

In Quechee, you can watch glass and pottery production. Stairs at the back of the extensive, well-displayed showrooms lead you down to a smaller, more intimate operation. From behind a wooden railing, you observe a glass-blowing team only a few feet in front of you.

In the pottery area, a potter hand-throws pottery on a wheel and a decorator hand-paints a dinner plate, lamp base, or vase. Feel free to ask about the processes, from throwing or slipcasting to decorating and firing. Both facilities will impress you with the skill and craftsmanship involved in handmade pottery and glass.

Information below applies to both facilities unless otherwise noted.

Cost: Free
Freebies: No
Video Shown: No
Reservations Needed: No, except for groups.
Days and Hours: Mon–Sun 9:00 AM–5:00 PM. Closed Christmas and Thanksgiving.
Plan to Stay: 30 minutes each, plus time in gift shops and Simon Pearce Restaurant in Quechee (802-295-1470 for reservations).
Minimum Age: None
Disabled Access: Yes, at Windsor. No wheelchair access to production in Quechee, but gift shop and restaurant are accessible.
Group Requirements: While Quechee discourages bus tours, Windsor easily accommodates buses. Groups larger than 50 should call 1 month in advance.
Special Information: Facilities can get warm because of furnaces.
Retail Shops: Sell first- and second-quality Simon Pearce pottery and glass. Windsor open Mon–Sun 9:00 AM–5:00 PM. Quechee open Mon–Sun 9:00 AM–9:00 PM. Catalog available from (800) 774-5277.
Directions: To Windsor: from western Massachusetts, take I-91 North to Exit 9, bear right onto Rt. 5. Simon Pearce is 1 mile ahead on left. From New Hampshire, take I-89 to I-91 South. Follow above directions. To Quechee: from western Massachusetts, take I-91 North to I-89 North to Exit 1. Take Rt. 4 West. Turn right at first blinker after Quechee Gorge. Follow signs. From New Hampshire, take I-89 North to Exit 1 in Vermont. Follow above directions.
Nearby Attractions: For Windsor: New Catamont Brewery (call 802-296-2248); American Precision Museum (call 802-674-5781); Vermont State Craft Center; Constitution House. For Quechee: quaint town of Woodstock; Billings Farm; Killington Ski Resort.

See color photo, page 161

Website: www.simonpearce.com

Simon Pearce attaches a handle to a pitcher in his studio at The Mill, Simon Pearce Glass.

The Quechee pottery and glassmaking factory was converted to its present state from an historic 200-year-old wool mill.

Vermont Teddy Bear   ～ *teddy bears*

2236 Shelburne Road
Shelburne, VT 05482
(802) 985-3001 / (800) 829-BEAR

A plain little teddy belonging to a boy named Graham was the inspiration for Vermont Teddy Bears. When Graham's father discovered that none of Graham's stuffed animals—not even that most American of toys, the teddy bear—were made in the U.S., he decided to make an American teddy bear. In 1995 the company moved to its new 57-pastoral-acre site. You'll drive down its long, winding drive toward the airport hangar–shaped shipping building, the hexagonal retail store (each panel a different color), and the multi-colored barn silo topped with a beanie—complete with propeller.

After hearing a brief history of the company in the Bear Lab, you head for the workshop, a magical place that enchants young and old. Moving through the brightly painted workshop, you'll expect Santa's elves to appear at any moment. The enthusiastic tour guides ("Bear Ambassadors"), workers, and bears do everything in their power to make sure you have fun.

Follow the paw prints to the cutting table. With cookie-cutter dies, a hydraulic press stamps out bear parts from 12 to 14 layers of soft fur. Workers at several stations sew together bear limbs, torsos and heads, inside-out so seams are hidden. Bears are then turned right side out and pumped full of stuffing with 130 pounds of air pressure. Limbs are joined to torsos, and eyes are placed. (The plastic eyes are supplied by the last U.S. company that produces them.)

Bears are dressed as everything from artists to veterinarians and carefully packed with an inflated "bair" bag, holding a board game (so the bear won't be bored while traveling), a picture of the bear's family, and a personalized message.

After the tour you'll want to go back to the Make A Friend for Life fun shop to stuff your own teddy bear. Select your hungry (that is, unstuffed) bear from the Cub House. Spin the dial to choose the bear's filling—dreams, happiness, love, giggles. Step on the gas pedal of the colorful stuffing machine. After the teddy is stitched up, you'll receive its birth certificate.

Cost: Tour: Adults, $1; children under 17, free. Make a Friend for Life (stuff your own bear): $24.50.

Freebies: Fuzzy little "Button Bear" that fits over shirt button.

Video Shown: "Make a Friend for Life" video stars Gary Burghoff, formerly Radar O'Reilly on TV's MASH. Shown in lobby. Sold in Bear Shop.

Reservations Needed: No, except for groups of 10 or more people.

Days and Hours: Mon–Sat 10:00 AM–4:00 PM, Sun 11:00 PM–4:00 PM. Limited weekend production; however, tours are still fun. Closed holidays.

Plan to Stay: 20 minutes for tour, plus time for Bear Shop and Make a Friend for Life fun shop.

Minimum Age: None (but must bring the kid inside you).

Disabled Access: Yes

Group Requirements: Groups over 10 people should call (800) 829-BEAR (829-2327), ext. 1358, 1–2 weeks in advance. Maximum group size is 40 people.

Gift Shop: Bear Shop is stocked with bears waiting to go home with you. Carries logoed T-shirts, fleece pullovers, and sweatshirts. Open Mon–Sat 9:00 AM–6:00 PM, Sun 10:00 AM–5:00 PM. For more information on Bear-Grams and catalog, call (800) 829-BEAR.

Special Information: Special events include Celebration Days on the first weekend of August and OctoBEAR Fest the first weekend in October.

Directions: From I-89, take Exit 13 onto I-189 West. When I-189 ends, turn left onto Rt. 7 South through town of Shelburne. Factory located ½ mile past Shelburne Museum.

Nearby Attractions: Ben & Jerry's Ice Cream factory tour (see page 305); Champlain Chocolate Company viewing windows (call 802-864-1807); Shelburne Museum.

See color photos, page 177

The Candle Factory ⟿ *candles and soap*

Williamsburg Soap & Candle Company
7521 Richmond Road
Williamsburg, VA 23185
(757) 564-3354

In 1964 the Barnetts of Williamsburg opened a gift shop along busy Richmond Road. They soon added candle-making as a tourist attraction, and the scent of their 10-inch bayberry tapers lured visitors inside. While the Candle Factory now produces over 13 million candles a year in more than 70 different shapes, colors, and scents, the fragrant aromas of rose, pine, lemon, jasmine, and bayberry still beckon travelers.

The process begins when paraffin is brought to the factory in a specially designed truck. The truck's holding tank is surrounded by steam coils that keep the paraffin hot. Steam coils also keep the paraffin in liquid form in the holding tanks behind the factory and in the pipes that bring it to the production area.

Most of the Candle Factory's production area, where candles are made by dipping, pouring, and molding, is visible through the large observation-booth window. Scents and dyes are stirred into the 180° wax, and parallel rows of hanging wicks are dipped over and over into the bubbling vats. To ensure that the candles are evenly shaped, they are dipped 42 times. Although a machine does the dipping, dexterous workers must then trim the wicks, put the candles in a die-cut mold to shape the bases, and polish and box them. The factory can produce over 1,000 of these tapers in two hours. Each year the factory uses 1 million pounds of wax and 6 million feet of wick.

Poured candles are made by pouring hot wax into a ceramic or glass container with a wick inside. Since the wax shrinks as it cools, a second pouring is needed to fully fill the container. For molded candles, wax is poured twice into a cylindrical mold. Once removed from the mold, the new candles must be trimmed, straightened, polished, and boxed. The largest molded candles must be shaped by hand.

Cost: Free

Freebies: No

Video Shown: A button in observation booth starts informative 9-minute video that describes candle- and soap-making and Candle Factory history. Shows processes not seen from booth.

Reservations Needed: No

Days and Hours: Mon–Fri 9:00 AM–4:00 PM. Candle Factory is in production Mon–Fri but video in observation room is available same hours and days as gift shop. Closed Thanksgiving, Christmas to New Year's, and July 4th week.

Plan to Stay: 20 minutes for self-guided tour from observation room, plus time for gift shops.

Minimum Age: None

Disabled Access: Yes

Group Requirements: No advance reservations needed. Tour buses welcome. No maximum group size; however, only 30 people can fit in room at one time.

Retail Store: Candle Factory sells wide selection of candles and soaps, candle accessories (such as holders and sconces), factory seconds, and market test runs. Open Mon–Sun 9:00 AM–5:00 PM. Call for extended summer and fall hours. Closed Thanksgiving, Christmas, and New Year's. Other shops on premises include Barney's Country Store, Quilts and Needlework Shop, Emporium, and Christmas House.

Directions: From I-64, take Exit 231A (Norge exit). Take Hwy. 607 in the direction that exit lets you off. Turn left onto Richmond Rd. (Rt. 60). Candle Factory is on right. From I-95, take I-295 South to I-64 East. Follow above directions.

Nearby Attractions: Williamsburg Pottery Factory tour (see page 317); Williamsburg Doll Factory tour (see page 316); Anheuser-Busch (Budweiser) Brewery tour (call 757-253-3039); Colonial Williamsburg; Busch Gardens; James River Plantation; Richmond Road, "the Discount Boulevard of Virginia."

Levi Strauss   ～ *jeans*

Highway 3
Warsaw, VA 22572
(804) 333-4007 / (804) 333-6112

Following their creation in the California gold fields in the 1850s, jeans' popularity spread in the 1930s, as Easterners visited Western dude ranches and saw Levi's jeans in action. In the 1950s the Levi's craze was reborn after James Dean and Marlon Brando wore jeans in two popular movies. In search of a factory to supply the East Coast, the company operated a small pilot plant in the Telephone Company garage in rural Warsaw, Virginia, for two years before building a permanent, modern facility in 1953. This plant, which has grown from 40 employees to about 300 today, produces children's sizes, from Little Levi's up to Student.

The jeans-making process changed in 1991. Before that, it took seven to eight days to make a pair of jeans from start to finish. Cut bundles of fabric had to travel as a group to every department in the plant. On any given day, numerous pairs of jeans were at various stages of production. Under the alternative manufacturing system instituted in 1991, individual teams complete jeans daily. Denim enters as fabric at 8:00 AM and voilà! it comes out as jeans at 4:30 PM the same day. On a tour you'll watch as seven four 75-member teams produce a total of about 13,000 jeans per day.

One highlight is the plotter room, where stencil designs arrive by computer. The plotter machine seems to just take off and start drawing designs onto long rolls of white paper. These pattern sheets are known as "markers." The denim is spread out onto long tables by an automatic spreader machine or manually by a worker walking back and forth along a table's length to unwind the bolt of fabric. Notice the rows of tables with denim stacked 60 layers high (enough for 60 pairs of jeans). The plotter machine's markers are spread across the fabric and stapled to the top layer. With a hand-held band saw, workers follow the markers to cut the denim.

The fabric is cut and ticketed, ensuring that every part of one pair of pants has the same number. Then parts such as loops, flies, and pockets go to the parts department, and the balance go to the other teams. After the parts, or "feeder," team is finished, the other teams complete each pair of jeans. These seven teams all do the same tasks, including sewing leg panels together, front pockets on, and front and back rise. Check the next pair of Levi's youth jeans you buy or wear. If the plant number is 581M, you know they were made right here in Warsaw.

Cost: Free
Freebies: No
Video Shown: No
Reservations Needed: Yes
Days and Hours: Tue–Thur 8:00 AM–4:30 PM (winter) and 7:00 AM–3:30 PM (summer). Closed holidays, week of July 4th, week after Easter, and week of Christmas.
Plan to Stay: 45 minutes
Minimum Age: None
Disabled Access: Yes, except steps to plotter room.
Group Requirements: Groups larger than 10 people should call 2 weeks in advance for reservation. No maximum group size.
Special Information: Check photography restrictions at tour time. Flat shoes recommended since floor tiles can be slippery. Tours also available at Levi's older, less automated San Francisco plant (see page 26).
Gift Shop: No
Directions: From Washington, D.C., take I-301 South to Hwy. 3 East toward Warsaw. Factory is on right, before town. From Richmond, take I-360 East to Warsaw. Turn left onto Hwy. 3. Factory is 2 miles ahead on left.
Nearby Attractions: Historic homes such as Stratford (Robert E. Lee's home) and Wakefield (George Washington's home); Westmoreland Park.

Rowena's

758 West 22nd Street
Norfolk, VA 23517
(800) 980-CAKE

pound cakes, jams, jellies, cooking sauces, and gifts

For a taste of Southern hospitality and mouth-watering pound cake, stop by Rowena's in Norfolk. Rowena's began in 1983, when friends and family urged Rowena Fullinwider to sell her jams and cakes, which were already favorite gifts and charity-bake-sale items. Today, Rowena's is a million-dollar business that ships its foods nationwide and as far away as Guam and Finland.

Your tour begins in Rowena's retail store. Within the maze of its compact operation, you'll see every stage of production. As you enter the kitchen, enjoy the sweet smell of Carrot Jam (a Rowena's specialty) or the zesty scent of Cooking and Barbecue Sauce. Watch a cook drain jam from the mixing bowl by turning a faucet at the bottom, or stir up a Lemon Curd Sauce with a three-foot whisk.

Your appetite will be further whetted in the next room, where cakes are made. Most of the equipment will be familiar to anyone who cooks, but on a grander scale. You could curl up in one of the two extra-large mixers (originally they belonged to the Cruiseship U.S.S. *United States*), and you could make a meal licking one of their huge beaters. Rowena's cooks are especially proud of the two enormous six-shelved rotating ovens. Look inside the window and watch 25 large cakes or 250 small loaf cakes take an hour's ride on the Ferris-wheel racks.

After baking and cooling, the cakes are hand-wrapped and decorated with ribbon. Workers also label all sauce and jam jars with flowery stick-on labels. While this room may be quiet when you visit, it's a scene of round-the-clock action during the busy holiday season. Finally you'll be able to taste any of Rowena's foods available. As you savor pound cake with Raspberry Curd or sample Peach Orange Clove Jam, you will appreciate the TLC that goes into Rowena's products.

Cost: Free

Freebies: Paper tour hat, samples, and a "color me" placemat for children.

Video Shown: No

Reservations Needed: Yes

Days and Hours: January through September only: Mon–Wed 9:00 AM–3:00 PM. Closed holidays.

Plan to Stay: 30 minutes, plus time in gift shop.

Minimum Age: Rowena's prefers that children be of school age.

Disabled Access: No stairs; however, inquire when making reservations.

Group Requirements: Maximum group size is 25 people. Call 1 week in advance.

Special Information: Factory gets hot during warm months.

Gift Shop: Sells Rowena's entire line, including Almond, Lemon, and Coconut Pound Cakes, Lemon Curd Sauce, and Heavenly Curry Sauce. Offers foods produced for Colonial Williamsburg. Look for seasonally updated recipe leaflets and two children's story cookbooks, *The Adventures of Rowena and the Wonderful Jam and Jelly Factory* and *The Adventures of Rowena and Carrot Jam the Rabbit*. Open year-round Mon–Fri 8:30 AM–5:00 PM. Catalog available from 800 number.

Directions: Since street names change frequently, please pay close attention to directions. From Virginia Beach Expwy., take I-64 or I-264 to Waterside Dr. (becomes Boush St.). Turn left on 22nd St. Rowena's is on right at the end of the street. From Richmond, take Granby St. exit. Pass the Virginia Zoological Park on the left and follow Granby St. when it veers to the right. Take a right on 22nd St. Rowena's is at the end of 22nd St. on right.

Nearby Attractions: Chrysler Museum of Art; Waterside; Nauticus Maritime Museum; Norfolk Botanical Garden; Virginia Zoological Park; Hunter Victorian and Hermitage Museums; Virginia Beach and Colonial Williamsburg are 30–45 minutes away.

See color photo, page 190

Williamsburg Doll Factory ~ *porcelain dolls*

7441 Richmond Road
Williamsburg, VA 23188
(757) 564-9703

Williamsburg Doll Factory's showroom instantly transports you to a fanciful world of Victorian weddings and Civil War–era Southern teas. You'll recognize Bonnie Blue, from *Gone With The Wind*, gaily riding a carousel in her blue velvet dress. This is the world of Margaret Anne Rothwell and her Lady Anne porcelain dolls.

Margaret Anne's mother taught her to make doll clothing as a child in Belfast, Ireland. When she moved to the U.S., she made dolls for her own daughters. Friends and family urged her to go into business and, in 1977, she began making dolls in her home. Her first business milestone came when her dolls were accepted by theme parks such as Busch Gardens and Disney World. In 1980 she began making porcelain dolls that became very popular; to meet the demand, she moved to her present location. A recent deal with the QVC shopping network has led to even more success.

Margaret Anne designs each doll's concept. The dress is most important because it determines the doll's complexion, hair color, and style. In the porcelain department, Margaret Anne's son David and other artists create molds, mix porcelain slip, paint, and kiln-fire heads and body parts. Through an observation window, you'll watch them carefully sculpt delicate hands and paint doll faces. Completed doll parts are strung with elastic to allow joint-like movement.

Some dolls have porcelain bodies as well as heads and limbs, while others have a "composite" body of latex and clay (a modern version of the glue-and-papier mâché composite of antique dolls). Every material used in Lady Anne dolls, except some wigs and eyes, is made in the U.S.A.

You can also observe the finishing department operations. Watch a craftperson glue individual eyelashes onto a doll's face, fit a doll's dress, or crown a doll with a wig of golden curls. After being dressed and inspected, these enchanting dolls are matched with a certificate of authenticity and shipped to a collector who will treasure their quality and beauty.

Cost: Free
Freebies: No
Video Shown: No
Reservations Needed: No, unless groups larger than 30 people want guided tour.
Days and Hours: Mon–Fri 9:00 AM–5:30 PM except during 12:00 PM–1:00 PM lunch. Factory does no weekend production; however, you can view workstations. Closed Thanksgiving, Christmas, and New Year's.
Plan to Stay: 20 minutes for self-guided tour through observation windows, plus time in retail store.
Minimum Age: None, but children must be kept off doll displays.
Disabled Access: Yes
Group Requirements: Groups larger than 30 should call 1 week in advance to arrange for tour guide, maybe even Margaret Anne herself.
Special Information: No photography
Retail Store: Sells limited-edition Lady Anne and other collectible dolls, and doll parts for hobbyists. Open Mon–Fri 9:00 AM–5:30 PM (6:00 PM in Summer), Sat 9:00 AM–6:00 PM, Sun 10:00 AM–5:00 PM. Closed Thanksgiving, Christmas, and New Year's.
Directions: From I-64, take Exit 231A (Norge exit). Take Hwy. 607 in the direction that exit lets you off. Turn left onto Richmond Rd. (Rt. 60). Doll Factory is on right. From I-95, take I-295 South to I-64 East. Follow above directions.
Nearby Attractions: Williamsburg Pottery and the Candle Factory tours (see pages 317 and 313); Anheuser-Busch (Budweiser) self-guided brewery tour (call 757-253-3039); Colonial Williamsburg; Busch Gardens; James River Plantations; Richmond Road, "the Discount Boulevard of Virginia."

Williamsburg Pottery Factory

Route 60
Lightfoot, VA 23090
(757) 564-3326

*pottery, wood,
floral design,
and plaster*

Williamsburg Pottery Factory is a sprawling, 200-acre monument to America's love of discount shopping, annually attracting over 3.5 million visitors—more than Colonial Williamsburg and Busch Gardens combined. Within the 32 buildings and outlet stores you'll find everything and anything: jewelry, gourmet foods, Oriental rugs, furniture, shoes, plants, imports from around the world, lawn Madonnas, cookware, and pottery. You can also tour the four main factories—pottery/ceramics, woodworking, floral design, and cement/plaster.

The Pottery's nearly 2 million square feet of factory and retail space took nearly 60 years to complete—and it's still growing. It all began in 1938 when James E. Maloney, still active in the business, bought the first half-acre of land, dug a well, built his kiln and a one-room shack for his young wife and himself, and set up his roadside pottery stand. "Jimmy," as he's always been known in these parts, is first, last, and always a potter. He worked closely with Colonial Williamsburg's archeologists and ceramics experts during that colonial capital's restoration by John D. Rockefeller. In 1952 The Pottery became licensed to make and sell replicas of CW's eighteenth-century salt-glaze and redware. This helped The Pottery grow.

In the pottery/ceramics factory, potters create thousands of pots and decorative home accessories by hand and with molds. Eighteenth-century-style salt-glaze and slipware is made, glazed and fired here in the giant kiln. Highlights include seeing old-fashioned clay "tavern pipes" and the famous Williamsburg "Bird Bottle" birdhouses being made. Although signs posted in the workshop provide the basics, the craftspeople are happy to explain their work.

While The Pottery was once known mostly for its pottery, many other things are now made here. In floral design production, designers create arrangements of native Williamsburg dried flowers and plants grown right at The Pottery. At the cement/garden-ware factory building, you can watch fabrication of lawn and garden benches, birdbaths, and fountains. A tour of the plaster factory takes you from mold-making through the drying and trimming of plaster wall plaques, statues, containers, and other decorative objects. Among the numerous retail stores are greenhouse, potpourri, cactus, silk-flower arranging, and lamp production areas. You leave feeling that you've had a potpourri of experiences.

Cost: Free

Freebies: No

Video Shown: No

Reservations Needed: No

Days and Hours: Pottery/ceramics factory: Mon–Fri 8:00 AM–4:30 PM. Grounds: Mon–Sun "sunup to sundown." Closed Christmas.

Plan to Stay: 1 hour for 4 self-guided tours, plus hours for shopping.

Minimum Age: None

Disabled Access: Yes

Group Requirements: Group tours available by advance arrangement with Marketing Department.

Special Information: Wear comfortable walking shoes and watch where you walk.

Outlet Shops: Pottery's shops sell nearly everything. Shops rustic, but prices are great. Open Sun–Fri 8:00 AM–6:30 PM (opens later on Sundays), Sat 8:00 AM–8:00 PM. Shorter hours January through April. Closed Christmas.

Directions: From I-64, take Exit 234A for Lightfoot. Turn right on Hwy. 199. Turn right at first traffic light. After first stop sign, go through back entrance to grounds. Follow driveway around. Pass nursery. After second stop sign, ceramic factory will be on your right. From I-95 South, take I-64 East; follow above directions.

Nearby Attractions: The Candle Factory and Williamsburg Doll Factory tours (see pages 313 and 316); Anheuser-Busch (Budweiser) Brewery self-guided tour (call 757-253-3039); Colonial Williamsburg; Busch Gardens; James River Plantations.

Boehms Chocolates ⌒ *chocolates*
255 N.E. Gilman Boulevard
Issaquah, WA 98027
(425) 392-6652

A visit to Boehms tells a story, taking you through Julius Boehm's artifact-filled Austrian Alpine home, the candy factory he founded, and the chapel dedicated to mountain-climbers. A climber himself, Boehm was lured to Washington's Cascade Mountains, "America's Alps." He was considered the oldest man, at age 81, to climb 14,000-plus-foot Mt. Rainier. A lover of art and music, he filled his home with such items as a marble replica of Michelangelo's *David*, a wind-up music box, and a potpourri of Bavarian Old World artifacts.

Downstairs from Boehm's home is the candy factory. The pungent chocolate smell fills the air. Depending on the day, different sweets simmer in the kitchen. Mixers' metal blades stir Victorian creams. A worker with a wooden paddle stirs a truffle or peanut-brittle mixture in a copper cauldron before pouring it onto a steel cooling table and spreading it to the thickness of the steel bars at the long table's edges.

Women, trained in the art of hand-dipping chocolate, roll out the day's soft filling into round strips. With one hand they pinch off a portion, gently tossing it to the other hand, which continuously swirls the chocolate around on a marble slab to maintain the desired temperature. It coats the filling and decorates the top. Other varieties of centers pass through the enrober's chocolate waterfall to get their chocolate coating. After traveling through a cooling tunnel, all chocolates are hand-packed into gift boxes for distribution to Boehms' retail stores.

Next visit the Luis Trenker Kirch'l, a replica of a twelfth-century Swiss chapel near St. Moritz. Boehm built this masculine church with a boulder inside as a dedication to mountain climbers who died attempting to reach their mountains' summits. Current Boehms owner Bernard Garbusjuk, trained as a pastry chef in his German homeland, proudly boasts that your tour isn't too commercialized since it ends in the chapel and not at the gift shop.

Cost: Free
Freebies: Chocolate samples
Video Shown: No
Reservations Needed: Yes, for guided tour; no, for self-guided tour.
Days and Hours: Factory floor guided tours available for individuals and families mid-June to end of September only. Mon–Fri (except Wed) 10:30 AM and 1:00 PM. Guided group tours available year-round. Weekend tours may be available. Self-guided viewing through windows available year-round including weekends. Closed holidays.
Plan to Stay: 45 minutes for factory, home, and chapel tour, plus time for gift shop and grounds.
Minimum Age: None, for families. Children in groups must be 5 years or older with one adult for every 5 children.
Disabled Access: Yes, for factory and chapel. Difficult for home.
Group Requirements: Minimum group size is 15; maximum is 50. Groups should call 1 month in advance.
Special Information: Limited production weekends. Foreign-language tours arranged with advance notice. Chapel available for rental.
Gift Shop: Sells all 160 luscious Boehms candies including Boehms' specialties, Mozart Kugeln (marzipan and filbert paste center double-dipped in chocolate), and Mount Rainier (caramel fudge and cherry center dipped in chocolate). Open year-round Mon–Sun 9:00 AM–6:00 PM with extended summer weekend hours. Closed Christmas and New Year's. Mail-order brochure available.
Directions: From I-90, take Exit 17. Follow Front St. to Issaquah. Turn left onto Gilman Blvd. Two candy canes mark entrance.
Nearby Attractions: Lake Sammamish State Park; Snoqualmie Falls; Gilman Village; Salmon Days Festival in September. Seattle's downtown attractions, including Pike's Place Market and the Space Needle, 13 miles away.

See color photo, page 163

Website: www.forsuccess.com/chocolate/boehms

Tempting nut clusters are hand-dipped at Boehms Chocolates in Issaquah, Washington.

Once founder Julius Boehm's house, this Austrian Alpine chalet is now Boehm's Candy Kitchen.

Boeing ⌒ *commercial aircraft*

Tour Center
Highway 526
Everett, WA 98206
(425) 544-1264 / (800) 464-1476

Touring Boeing's 747, 767, and 777 aircraft plant is like visiting the Grand Canyon. You oversee the assembly areas from a third-story walkway, marveling at the enormity of the facility (world's largest-volume building; 11 stories high, 98 acres) while attempting to grasp the details of the process. As with the Grand Canyon, it's best to just take in the vastness, listen to your tour guide, and be awed by it all.

A short bus ride from this 1,000-acre complex's visitor center, a long brisk walk though an underground tunnel, and an elevator ride take you to the open-air mezzanine observation deck. Gaze out over the subassembly floor as different airplane parts slowly come to life. The loud rivet-guns' spattering fills the air, as earmuffed workers assemble plane wings, passenger bays, and nose cones. Overhead, cranes zigzag back and forth with plane parts.

You may see up to thirteen 747s, 767s, or 777s on the final assembly floor at any one time. Don't expect to watch an entire plane created before your eyes. A new 747 rolls out about every five days, helping Boeing capture nearly 60 percent of the global commercial aircraft market. Notice the true colors of the jumbo jet's shiny metals and materials, the miles of wiring, the electronic components, and the other plane innards you take for granted at 30,000 feet. As the bus travels back to the tour center, you'll pass the paint hangar. Sitting nearby on the runway waiting for flight tests are freshly painted jets headed for airlines around the world.

Cost: Free
Freebies: Postcard set
Video Shown: 20-minute film on Boeing history, from its 1914 start (when lumberman Bill Boeing took his first aircraft ride) to its current projects.
Reservations Needed: No, except for groups larger than 10 people. In future, factory plans to switch to a reservation system.

Days and Hours: Mon–Fri 9:00 AM–11:00 AM, and 1:00 PM–3:00 PM, on the hour. Call for additional tour times during peak season (May through October). Closed holidays, week between Christmas and New Year's, and for special events. Same day tickets available from 8:30 AM and may sell out by 12:00 PM.
Plan to Stay: 90 minutes for video and tour, plus time for gift store and wait.
Minimum Age: Children must be 50 inches tall.
Disabled Access: Yes
Group Requirements: Groups of 10 or more people need advance reservations—at least 3–6 months in advance for summer tours. Maximum group is 45 people. Group-tour times differ from public tour times. Reservation fee, $6 per person. Call (800) 464-1476 for group reservations.
Special Information: No photography allowed on Boeing property. GrayLine of Seattle also offers tour with guaranteed entrance.
Gift Store: The Flight Line Gift Store sells souvenir and gift items with Boeing logo, including clothing, miniature airplanes, postcards, and aviation books and posters. Open Mon–Fri 9:00 AM–5:00 PM. Closed holidays and for special events. Catalog available from (800) 671-6111.
Directions: Located 25 miles north of Seattle. Take I-5 to Exit 189. Go west on State Hwy. 526 and follow signs to Boeing Tour Center.
Nearby Attractions: *Seattle Times* North Creek tour (call 425-489-7015); Everett Center for the Arts; Animal Farm; Firefighters Museum; Kasch Park; Walter E. Hall Park and Golf Course; Silver Lake Park. Museum of Flight at Boeing Field in Seattle (call 206-764-5700). Tour Center desk has Everett Visitor's Guide, which includes all local attractions, accommodations, restaurants, and map.

Boise Cascade ～ *lumber and plywood*
Timber and Wood Products Division
805 North 7th Street
Yakima, WA 98901
(509) 453-3131

This mill began producing lumber in 1904 as the Cascade Lumber Company, which later merged with Boise Payette Lumber Company to become Boise Cascade Corporation. The Yakima facility has two sawmills and a plywood plant. Over 70 million board feet of lumber, 5 million panels of plywood, 2,700 rail cars of woodchips, and 30,000 dry tons of shavings are produced annually. Plant retirees toss off these impressive statistics, along with the mill's history and details of its operation, during your guided tour.

The Douglas fir and ponderosa pine logs arrive at the mill on trucks. Once sorted by size, they go to the large log mill, small log mill, or plywood plants. A world of endlessly moving belts and chains takes the logs through all production stages. No wood is wasted in the production of plywood or lumber, as all trim and bark are used in the powerhouse boiler or shipped to a pulp mill.

In the sawmills, the process starts when logs travel through the debarker. While you may not get a chance to work the huge spinning ring that removes the logs' bark, you can sit in the cage with the person who does the cutting. The whirling saws sing as they seem to gobble up the logs. Every four hours the blades are removed for sharpening.

The logs must then be squared on either two or four sides in what's called the "headrig." Another set of band saws reduces the squared logs into boards and lumber. Edger saws complete the squaring of the piece before it is scanned for defects and trimmed to length. Machines automatically sort and stack the lumber by thickness and length before drying in the steam-heated kilns.

Logs at the plywood plant are cut and then peeled down to 2½-inch diameters in the core lathe. This state-of-the-art machine peels up to four logs per minute. The ⅛-inch-thick veneer produced at the lathe travels via belt conveyors to a clipper and is cut into 4-foot widths. On the automatic layup line, sheets of veneer are glued together and placed in the hot press to make plywood. The process produces enough plywood panels to stretch from Seattle to New York and back, with some to spare.

Cost: Free
Freebies: No
Video Shown: No. Video highlighting plywood production and sawmill available for purchase.
Reservations Needed: Yes
Days and Hours: Mon–Fri 9:00 AM; 12:30 PM tour available upon request. Closed holidays.
Plan to Stay: 2 hours
Minimum Age: 8. Tour popular with elementary-school children. All Yakima 4th-graders take this tour.
Disabled Access: Stairs and catwalks throughout facility. Can arrange auto tour of mill with advance notice.
Group Requirements: Can handle groups up to 25 people with 3 weeks' advance notice.
Special Information: Noisy. Must be able to wear provided protective lenses, earplugs, and helmets. Tour of forestry and logging operations available (call 509-925-5341). No video cameras.
Gift Shop: No
Directions: Take I-82 to Yakima Ave. exit. Turn right onto Seventh St., which leads to plant.
Nearby Attractions: Yakima Indian Nation Cultural Center; Yakima Historical Museum; Yakima Greenway (4½-mile walk along Yakima River); Toppenish City of Murals (28 murals—longest is 110 feet; call 509-865-6516); Yakima Valley wine tours (call 509-248-2021 for brochure).

Frito-Lay   *snack foods*

4808 N.W. Fruit Valley Road
Vancouver, WA 98660
(360) 694-8478

In 1932 two entrepreneurs unaware of each other set out on similar paths that would eventually lead to Frito-Lay, Inc. In Texas, Elmer Doolin and his mother, Daisy, cooked Fritos brand corn chips in her kitchen at night. By day, he sold them from the back of his Model-T Ford. Meanwhile, in Tennessee, Herman W. Lay sold potato chips from the back of his Model A. In 1945 the two companies began selling each other's products; they merged in 1961 and became part of PepsiCo in 1965.

After your guide shows you the color-coded oil- and corn-holding tanks behind the plant, peek through the entranceway into the Fritos, Doritos brand, and Tostitos brand tortilla chips "kitchen" area. Corn is ground between large milling stones to form *masa*, a golden dough. An extruder flattens ribbons of masa, and whirling blades cut them. These raw Fritos fall into a precisely heated blend of oils, where they curl up as they cook. For Doritos and Tostitos, masa is pressed into a thick sheet and fed through rollers. Large cutters then stamp it into triangles or circles. As the shapes flash-bake in large, 700° toaster ovens, flames create golden flecks and small "bubbles" in them. The proofer equalizes their moisture content, then all three products are salted and seasoned.

At least 7 million pounds of potatoes arrive daily at 40 Frito-Lay plants across the nation. Employees hand-inspect the washed, peeled potatoes, which then drop into a round, spinning tub. Centrifugal force helps straight blades slice Lays brand potato chips; blades shaped like tambourines with rippled edges cut Ruffles brand potato chips. After the slices cook in hot oil, they're salted or seasoned and cooled in a rotating drum. Before packaging, they pass through the potato-chip sizer, which sorts out small chips for small bags and large chips for large bags.

Visit the Cheetos brand cheese-flavored snacks area. Stone-ground cornmeal is kneaded into a smooth, hot, elastic dough, which is then pressed through an extruder's tiny holes. The change of pressure and temperature when the bits of hot dough leave the extruder causes them to expand and begin to pop and bounce. A sharp blade cuts these nuggets of popped cornmeal before oven-baking or frying. You'll be amazed by the giant, hollow, spinning cylinder in which the pale-yellow Cheetos bounce around to receive a real cheese coating, emerging bright orange.

See the highly automated packaging process before visiting the large warehouse, which can store only 1½-days' output. You'll leave filled with tastes of all the freshly made Frito-Lay products—and now you know how Ruffles get their ridges.

Cost: Free
Freebies: Fresh samples during tour
Video Shown: No
Reservations Needed: Yes. Individuals and families must join scheduled group tour.
Days and Hours: Tue and Thur 10:00 AM and 11:15 AM. Summer schedule may vary. Closed holidays.
Plan to Stay: 1 hour
Minimum Age: 5
Disabled Access: No; floors can be dangerously slippery.
Group Requirements: Minimum group is 8 people; maximum is 30. Call 2–3 weeks in advance.
Special Information: No photography. No jewelry, shorts, or open-toed shoes. Can be quite warm in summer. Frito-Lay once had national tour program; now only a few factories still give tours, mostly to local groups.
Gift Shop: No
Directions: From I-5, take 4th Plain exit. Go west on 4th Plain Blvd. Turn right onto Fruit Valley Rd. Factory is about 1 mile ahead on left.
Nearby Attractions: Fort Vancouver; Officer's Row.

K2 ⟳ *skis and snowboards*

19215 Vashon Highway S.W.
Vashon, WA 98070
(800) 426-1617

Like a ski run down a mountain, a tour of K2 traverses you through ski- and snowboard-making from top to bottom. In 1961, using borrowed skis as a pattern, Bill Kirschner made himself a pair of fiberglass skis. These became his prototype for the launch of K2, named after both the world's second-highest mountain and the two Kirschner brothers.

The ski-making process involves more steps than you might imagine, and this tour shows almost all. Start your trail through the largest U.S. snow-ski manufacturer at "top making." An automated squeegee slides across plastic sheets to silk-screen them with bright graphics. The sheets then slither along the conveyor through the drying oven. Once cooled, they are returned to the screener on a white hospital bed. This process is repeated until eight to 12 layers of bright graphics decorate each plastic sheet, wide enough for four ski tops. They are baked and cooled, then cut into individual ski-tops by the die-cut (or "Rambo") machine. Look through the glass window at the UV-cured coating area. Here, a clear waterfall of liquid protectant coats the tops. As in a tanning room, UV lights dry and harden the coating.

Several different procedures are used in making ski cores. The "big braider" feeds threads of fiberglass, Kevlar (used in bullet-proof vests), and carbon through 64 frantically do-si-do-ing bobbins. In a braided pattern, these threads wrap around the wooden cores of high-performance skis. Different braiding patterns ("recipes") alter the ski's stiffness. The pressroom makes molded ski cores ("blanks"). Workers wet-wrap a wooden or foam core in colorful epoxy and fiberglass layers. As if making a fajita, a worker places toe and tail protectors, shock-absorber strips, the wooden or foam core, and more inside these resin-drenched layers, wraps it all up, and places it into a mold. The worker lowers the 200° press, applying 1,200 pounds-per-square-inch of pressure. In the sanding room,

excess resin is sanded off the blanks. The Bostik wheel-topper glues tops and blanks together. Once sprayed with rubber cement, the Bostik rolls over, or "peels" the top onto the blank.

A special multi-stage process is required for bending, hardening, and sharpening the ski's steel edges. Although the tour doesn't follow the 35 steps in order, by the time you've zigzagged into all the different production rooms, you will understand how skis are made. After watching the ski parts finally get sandwiched together (up to 2,400 pairs per day), you'll search for the nearest mountain to try them out.

Cost: Free

Freebies: Ski tops, posters, and stickers.

Video Shown: No

Reservations Needed: Yes. K2 prefers groups. Individuals and families join scheduled group tour.

Days and Hours: Mon–Fri 10:00 AM and 1:00 PM. Closed holidays and 2 weeks starting around Christmas, so employees can go skiing and test out the skis. *Tours have been temporarily suspended.*

Plan to Stay: 1 hour

Minimum Age: 3

Disabled Access: Yes

Group Requirements: Maximum group is 50 people. Call 1 day in advance for reservations. Some larger groups can view 10-minute videos on manufacturing process, skis, and skiing, and hear presentations from K2 employees. Request this when you make reservations.

Special Information: Parts of tour have noise, heat, and strong fumes.

Gift Shop: No

Directions: Take ferry from Seattle or Tacoma to Vashon Island. Vashon Hwy. is main street off ferry. K2 is in center of town.

Nearby Attractions: Seattle's Best Coffee tour (see page 328); Vashon Island beaches and peaceful biking roads.

Liberty Orchards ⟳ *fruit candies*

117 Mission Street
Cashmere, WA 98815
(509) 782-4088 / (800) 231-3242

The story of Liberty Orchards is the story of two Armenian immigrants striving to succeed in the U.S.A. After failed attempts at running a yogurt factory and an Armenian restaurant, in 1918 they purchased an apple orchard, which they called Liberty Orchards to honor their new homeland. Aplets and Cotlets fruit candies, originally known as "Confections of the Fairies," grew out of a use for surplus fruit.

A guided tour of Liberty Orchards, now in its third generation, shows you how they create these natural fruit-flavored candies. Start your tour in the nut-sorting room, where California walnuts and Hawaiian macadamia nuts are sorted. Visit the Old-World kitchen where concoctions of fruit juices, fruit purees, pectin, sugar, and cornstarch cook at 230° in stainless-steel kettles large enough to produce 256 pounds of candy. As the candy boils, steam emerges from the kettles, and a fruity, perfumed aroma fills the air. With long metal paddles, the cook stirs the bubbling concoction and then tastes it for correct consistency—a tough job but someone has to do it. The cook's helpers pour the hot candy into smaller kettles and add nuts and natural flavoring. Then they pour the candy into long, plastic-lined wooden trays, roll it flat, and cover it for a day's rest in the cooler.

In the factory, workers flip the slabs of cooled candy out of their trays and coat the candy with cornstarch, which acts as a natural preservative to keep moisture inside. Candy-cutters cut the candy into bite-size cubes. Tumblers coat the sides of the cubes with cornstarch and then cover them with powdered sugar. Nimble-fingered packers hand-pack the candies into plastic trays at a rate of 4,000 to 5,000 per hour per packer. Fortunately the tour guides pass out free samples of these chewy treats, or you would be tempted to reach into the packing bins.

Cost: Free

Freebies: 3 different flavors of candies.

Video Shown: No, but you can purchase colorfully illustrated 20-page booklet called "The Story of Aplets & Cotlets," which covers family history, product and packaging development, and production process.

Reservations Needed: No, but preferred for groups larger than 12 people.

Days and Hours: April through December, Mon–Fri 8:00 AM–5:30 PM, Sat–Sun 10:00 AM–4:00 PM. Occasional weekend production. No production during 11:00 AM–11:30 PM lunch break and after 4:00 PM. January through March Mon–Fri 8:30 AM–4:30 PM. Tours run every 20 minutes, stopping ½ hour before closing. Closed New Year's, Christmas, Thanksgiving, President's Day, and Easter.

Plan to Stay: 15 minutes, plus time for Country Store.

Minimum Age: None. Children under 16 must be accompanied by adults.

Disabled Access: Yes

Group Requirements: Groups larger than 12 people will be split into smaller groups. Call 2 days in advance.

Special Information: Floor can be slippery. Production generally Mon–Fri, plus occasional weekends. Liberty Orchards is in heart of Washington's apple industry, which produces 5 billion apples per year—half of all the apples eaten in America.

Gift Shop: Country Store sells all Liberty Orchards fruit and nut candies (such as Aplets and Cotlets), apple gifts, and Northwest products. Open same hours as tour. Catalog available from (800) 888-5696.

Directions: From Seattle, take U.S. 2 East. Take Cashmere exit, which puts you on Division St. Follow Aplets & Cotlets signs. Turn left onto Mission St. Liberty Orchards is on left.

Nearby Attractions: Boeing Everett plant tour (see page 320); October Apple Days festival; Nearby Cascade loop attractions include Leavenworth Bavarian Village, Ohme Gardens, and Rocky Reach Dam.

Microsoft Museum ⟋ *personal computers and software*
One Microsoft Way
Redmond, WA 98052
(206) 703-6214

This highly interactive museum is a journey through the history of computer development—from the introduction of the first portable digital computer to the Information Superhighway. Unfortunately, access to this museum is restricted to Microsoft employees and their guests.

A quick study of the timelines on the museum's outer doors and inner corridor reveals events throughout the history of the world that led to the growth of the software industry and the creation of Microsoft, such as the introduction of the Altair 8800 (one of the company's first computers) and the installation of the Microsoft Mouse. It's surprising to see that items on display—many of which were designed only in the past ten years—are already considered archaic. They provide a sense of just how quickly the computer industry has evolved. Visitors gravitate toward exhibits of their own first computers, and marvel at how old-fashioned they now appear. In fact, if you can remember when the movie *Jaws* first hit the big screen, then you have an idea of when the first portable computer hit the retail market!

The history of hardware and operating systems illustrates in detail the transformation of digital computer to high-tech, on-line programs. Observe the process firsthand in one of the museum's video kiosks, where guests can select and view short films about Microsoft Windows, CEO meetings with Bill Gates, or Jay Leno's introduction of Windows '95 on "The Tonight Show." Other interactive stations include company trivia information, new products for children, and previews of forthcoming DreamWorks titles.

A corner devoted to the typical Microsoft office brims with artifacts, from photos to moving boxes, and even a rubber-band gun one employee uses to relieve tension. Trash, trinkets, and empty soda cans litter the desk and floor, while product-release information and international contact lists hang from a corner bulletin board. Employees will update the "office" throughout the year, each adding his or her own personality and sharing with visitors a slice of company life. With facts, history, and a sense of humor (check out the list of company pranks), the museum thoroughly captures Microsoft's distinctive culture, revealing the personalities "behind the screens."

Cost: Free

Freebies: Museum pin and car sticker, e-mail access, and the opportunity to comment on the museum at their on-line station.

Videos Shown: Video "kiosks" throughout the museum highlight company culture and related events.

Reservations Needed: Museum visits are scheduled during museum hours by employee recommendation only.

Days and Hours: Mon–Fri 10:00 AM–4:00 PM. All visitors must be invited and escorted by an employee of Microsoft.

Plan to Stay: 45 minutes–2 hours

Minimum Age: None

Disabled Access: Yes

Group Requirements: Tours are not available to the general public. Any groups interested in arranging a tour must have an employee sponsor.

Gift Shop: The company store is not open to the general public.

Directions: Take SR 520 East and exit on N.E. 51st St. Turn right on N.E. 51st St. Turn right on 156th St. Turn left on N.E. 40th St. Turn right on 159th. Go through the 4-way stop and take the first left into the parking area. Go to Bldg. 14 on the northeast side of the parking lot.

Nearby Attractions: Lake Washington; Seattle's attractions, including Pacific Science Center, Pike's Place Market, and Space Needle, 13 miles away.

Redhook Ale Brewery ~~~ *beer*

3400 Phinney Avenue North
Seattle, WA 98103
(206) 548-8000

Founded in 1981, Redhook Ale Brewery has become one of the most respected regional breweries in the Northwest, which has the highest per-person beer consumption in the country. Its classic pub-style Ballard Bitter and full, rich Redhook E.S.B. ale have a loyal following in the region.

Both the building that houses the brewery and the technology used in brewing make your visit more memorable than the standard brewery tour. Since 1988 Redhook has occupied the historic home of the Seattle Electric Railway, located in Seattle's Fremont district. The beautifully restored red-brick, green-trimmed trolley-car barn sets it apart from the standard industrial look of most other breweries. It also belies the state-of-the-art technology you'll see inside that produces the company's draft beers.

A century-old German company designed Redhook's brewing equipment, making it one of the most technically advanced breweries. You'll notice computer control panels monitoring the amounts of malted barley, hops, yeast, and water. The rows of polished stainless-steel fermentation tanks, with their maze of pipes and valves, have special automatic mechanisms to regulate temperature and pressure. The equipment even allows brewers to transfer batches from vessel to vessel without manual labor. Although high-tech equipment may play a big role in Redhook's beer-making, one sip and you'll taste the "craft" of beer brewed in the European tradition.

Cost: $1
Freebies: Samples of Redhook ales and tasting glass.
Video Shown: No
Reservations Needed: No, except for groups larger than 20 people.
Days and Hours: Mon–Fri 1:00 PM, 3:00 PM, and 5:00 PM; Sat and Sun 12:00 PM–5:00 PM on the hour. Closed major holidays. Limited production on weekends.

Plan to Stay: 40 minutes for tour and beer sampling, plus time to drink and eat at Trolleyman Pub.
Minimum Age: None, however minors may need supervision.
Disabled Access: Yes
Group Requirements: Groups larger than 20 should call 1 week in advance.
Special Information: Redhook has a new brewery and tour facility in Woodinville (N.E. 145th St.) that brews and packages its bottled and draft beers. The brewery is modeled after a Bavarian brewery in Andechs, Germany. The 24-acre site includes Public House, beer garden, and visitors center. Call (425) 483-3232 for tour times. The company has an architecturally similar brewery in Portsmouth, NH. Call (603) 430-8600 for tour times.
Gift Shop: Trolleyman Pub sells shirts, beer mugs, posters and other accessories with Redhook logo or picture of brewery, along with light, catered menu and full section of Redhook beers. Open Mon–Thur 10:00 AM–11:00 PM, Fri 10:00 AM–midnight, Sat 11:00 AM–midnight, Sun 11:00 AM–7:00 PM. Catalog available from above number.
Directions: From I-5 North, take 45th St. exit. Turn left onto 45th St. and left onto Stoneway. Turn right onto 34th St. and right onto Phinney Ave. From I-5 South, turn right onto 45th St., then follow directions above.
Nearby Attractions: *Seattle Times* North Creek tour (call 206-489-7015); Rainier Brewing Co. tour (call 206-622-2600); Woodland Park; University of Washington; Lake Washington Ship Canal and Government Locks.

Website: www.redhook.com

Nighttime at the Beer Garden and Cataqua Public House at Redhook Ale Brewery in Portsmouth, New Hampshire; you'll see a similar facility in Woodinville, Washington.

Visitors to Redhook Ale Brewery follow a path through the brewing equipment.

Seattle's Best Coffee ⌒ *coffee*

19529 Vashon Island Highway
Vashon, WA 98070
(800) 722-3190

The birth of America's love of gourmet coffee started in the Pacific Northwest, and Seattle's Best Coffee has been a key player. Founded by James Stewart in 1970, Seattle's Best Coffee has sprouted into a national retail store chain and mail-order operation. You can visit SBC's small specialty- and certified organic-roasting facility (one of two the company uses to roast its coffee) on bucolic Vashon Island.

Before you enter this two-story 1914 converted country store (originally a dance hall over a dry-goods store), relax on the porch chairs. Inside the tasting room, your tour guide explains that roasting, the hands-on art that unlocks the coffee's flavor, is the most important process in coffee-making. Learn that the longer coffee beans are roasted, the darker they become, resulting in richer, stronger coffee.

You may be lucky enough to observe a professional tasting in action. Seated at the heavy granite cupping table, which spins like a lazy Susan, master roaster Peter Larsen, founder Jim Stewart, and director of quality assurance Dave Wickberg taste and evaluate different coffees. Observe them as they sample a small spoonful of coffee, rapidly inhaling the coffee, forcing it to spray over their tongue while drawing in air. They swirl the coffee in their mouths and discard it into the two-foot high aluminum spittoons positioned at their feet. The cuppers evaluate each coffee for its aroma, acidity, body, and flavor.

Walk along the weathered wooden floor to the museum area. Illuminate an interactive world map showing the world's coffee-growing regions, and see coffee packages from Japan, Germany, and Saudi Arabia. Notice the collage of unusual items SBC has found over the years in the burlap bags of coffee beans it receives—soccer and lottery tickets, cigarette packages from Indonesia, belt buckles, and other common objects (coins, nails, etc.)—all screened out during the production process.

Look down over the balcony railing at the red German Probat Roaster. Several times a week, it roasts 132-pound batches of organic coffee for approximately 20 minutes. Afterwards, they cool in a stainless-steel pan at the lower side of the roaster. You'll leave with a new appreciation for the cup of coffee you drink every morning.

Cost: Free
Freebies: 4-oz. sample of the day. On front porch, coffee available for 50 cents per cup.
Video Shown: No
Reservations Needed: No, except for groups over 4 adults. Call the day you plan to visit to see if they will be roasting.
Days and Hours: Mon–Fri 10:00 AM–3:00 PM. Closed major holidays. Since tours are rather informal here, you'll need to ask the person working behind the retail counter to give you a tour.
Plan to Stay: 15 minutes, plus time in store.
Minimum Age: None
Disabled Access: Yes, for retail store and museum area. Tight quarters for tasting room.
Group Requirements: Groups over 4 adults should call 1 week in advance. Groups over 12 people will be split into smaller groups.
Special Information: Roasting process is loud.
Retail Store: Sells SBC bulk and pre-packed coffees, coffee- and espresso-makers, thermoses, logoed ceramic and plastic tumblers, as well as latte bowls and chocolate-covered espresso beans. Open Mon–Fri 7:00 AM–6:00 PM, Sat 9:00 AM–4:00 PM. Also open Sun 9:00 AM–4:00 PM, in summer. Catalog available from (800) 962-9659.
Directions: Take ferry from Seattle or Tacoma to Vashon Island. Vashon Hwy. is the main street off ferry. SBC is in the center of town.
Nearby Attractions: K2 Skis used to give tours (call 800-426-1617 for an update); Maury Island Farming Co. viewing windows (call 206-463-9659); Vashon Island beaches and peaceful biking roads.

Blenko Glass ~ *glass*

Fair Grounds Road
Milton, WV 25541
(304) 743-9081

BLENKO GLASS COMPANY, INC.

At Blenko Glass, you will see a 3- to 4-inch diameter "gob" of molten glass transformed into a foot-high water vase or pitcher right before your eyes. This self-guided tour allows you to stand behind a wooden railing and observe glassmaking for as long as you want. Only a few yards away workers hold yard-long blowpipes, or "punties," with red-hot glass at the end. You'll feel the heat gushing out of the furnaces. Although there are no signs to explain the glassblowing process, you will quickly figure out the steps by their artful repetition.

It takes six people and about five minutes to initially shape each item. A "gatherer" delivers a glass gob to a blower seated at a workbench. The blower, who has eight years of experience, rolls the punty along the arms of his workbench with his left hand and cups the glass into a wooden scoop-shaped block held in his right. The blower constantly twirls the punty to keep the glass from sagging. Then he lowers it into a hand-carved cherrywood mold and blows air into the punty's opposite end so the glass fills up the mold. Another craftsperson then gently kicks the mold's clamps open and, with a two-pronged pitchfork, carries the translucent object to the finisher. After several more steps, which require reheating, the finished piece is allowed to cool.

In the second-floor museum, which you walk through on the way to and from the observation area, learn about Blenko's history. The company started in 1893 to manufacture stained glass for windows but has since diversified. Exhibits include some of Blenko's custom products, such as green and crystal glass buttons made for Miss West Virginia in the 1960s, a paperweight commemorating George Bush's inauguration, and the Country Music Award Trophy. In the Designer's Corner, stained-glass windows made by nine leading American studios glow in the sunlight.

Also in the sunlight, the outdoor "Garden of Glass" affords a relaxing stroll along a gravel walkway lined with stone benches and a menagerie of glass animals. Walk over the wooden footbridge, alongside a fountain, to a peaceful 3-acre lake. You'll want to end your tour at the adjacent outlet store, which offers great values on Blenko glass.

Cost: Free

Freebies: No

Video Shown: No

Reservations Needed: No, except for groups larger than 50 people.

Days and Hours: Mon–Fri 8:00 AM–12:00 PM and 12:30 PM–3:00 PM to watch craftspeople. Plant is closed for 2 weeks beginning around July 1 and week between Christmas and New Year's.

Plan to Stay: 30 minutes for self-guided tour and museum, plus time for outlet store.

Minimum Age: None, but children must be supervised.

Disabled Access: Yes, for outlet store and "Garden of Glass." However, flight of stairs leads to museum and observation gallery.

Group Requirements: Groups larger than 50 should call ahead to avoid time conflicts with other groups.

Special Information: Due to furnaces, observation deck is hot in summer.

Factory Outlet/Museum: Store's tables are crammed with various colored vases, seconds, discontinued items, and bargains. Store and museum hours: Mon–Sat 8:00 AM–4:00 PM and Sun 12:00 PM–4:00 PM. Catalog available at above number.

Directions: Take I-64 to Exit 28, then Rt. 60 West. Turn left at traffic light onto Fair Grounds Rd. Follow signs to Blenko Glass Visitor Center.

Nearby Attractions: Gibson Glass, makers of multicolored paperweights, offers self-guided tour (call 304-743-5232); October West Virginia Pumpkin Festival; Camden Park; Berryhill House and Gardens & Craft Center.

Brooke Glass 〜 *glass*

6th and Yankee Streets
Wellsburg, WV 26070
(304) 737-0619

Brooke

Brooke Glass is the last surviving glass factory in a town that once had many. The company's buildings have been used by glassmakers since 1879, originally by Riverside Glass. Primarily making pressed-glass products through the years, the company adapted its product lines to the times. In the 1930s and '40s, it made taillights for cars and railroad lantern globes. Today it makes popular Victorian-style and art deco lamp and lighting fixture parts, candle glass, and other giftware items.

The guided tour begins in the mold room, where various size cast-iron molds are repaired and cleaned, awaiting their use. These intricate molds can cost thousands of dollars and become the temporary home for molten hot glass. In the main production area, the two ovens glow from the tremendous heat needed to melt together the components that form glass. A worker uses an iron rod with a ceramic or stainless-steel ball on the end to gather an orange glob of glass, which is then placed into the mold. The excess molten glass is snipped off. Sometimes the mold is then put into a machine that spins it at such a high speed that the glass pattern seems to grow out of the mold.

Quickly the mold is placed under an air compressor, where it cools enough to solidify the glass. The mold is then opened. What was glowing orange molten glass only a few seconds earlier is now a clear-colored light fixture or vase. A second worker gently removes the piece from the cast-iron mold and puts it into the fire polisher for a few seconds before it heads off for cooling. This two-person process continues at a rapid, mesmerizing rate.

You'll hear drills putting holes into the tops of the solid glass lighting fixtures and notice workers dipping the clear glass pieces into a special acid bath that frosts them. In the art department, the cool, peaceful artistry contrasts nicely with the other parts of the factory. The artists sit around a big wooden table, with racks of glass pieces waiting for their decoration. Each artist gracefully dips her brush into a paint palette wheel before applying the colors of a floral pattern or nature scene, or perhaps customizing a glass giftware item for a wedding party.

Cost: Free

Freebies: No

Video Shown: 15-minute video available for viewing in gift shop upon request or when factory not in production.

Reservations Needed: No, except for groups of 15 or more people.

Days and Hours: Mon–Fri 10:00 AM and 2:00 PM. Extra times available for groups. Closed holidays and first 2 weeks in July.

Plan to Stay: 25 minutes for tour, plus time for gift shop.

Minimum Age: No, but could be hot and noisy for young children.

Disabled Access: A few steps lead up to the factory and gift-shop buildings.

Group Requirements: Groups of 15 or more people should call at least 3 days in advance. No maximum group size.

Special Information: No photography. Occasionally do glassblowing, but mostly pressed and, sometimes, spun glass.

Gift Shop: Sells first-quality Brooke Glass items, including lamp and lighting fixtures, candleholders, and bells. Can etch names and other designs to personalize glass pieces. Matching and restoration of antique glass shades available. Open Mon–Sat 9:30 AM–5:00 PM. Closed major holidays.

Directions: From I-70, take West Virginia Rt. 2 North towards Wellsburg. Turn left at Sixth St. in Wellsburg. Park in gift shop parking lot. Tour starts in store.

Nearby Attractions: Creegan Company tour (see page 235); Weirton Steel tour (call Weirton Transit at 304-797-8597 to arrange tour); Brooke County Museum; Wheeling's attractions, including Oglebay 15 miles away.

Homer Laughlin China   *china*

6th and Harrison Streets
Newell, WV 26050
(304) 387-1300 / (800) 452-4462

Since its beginnings in 1871, Homer Laughlin has grown into the nation's largest manufacturer of restaurant china. Their bright-colored Fiesta tableware is the most collected china pattern in the world (first introduced in 1936). On this tour of one of the most automated pottery factories in the U.S., you observe three ways of shaping clay, plus the glazing, firing, and decorating processes.

Your tour starts with a talk in the museum room. Glance at the displays on the walls showing discontinued patterns, including Virginia Rose scalloped-edge plates.

As you walk through this mile-long factory, notice the maze of pipes along the ceiling, the tracks along the floor on which the kiln cars travel, and the row upon row of gray stacked plates, cups, and bowls waiting to enter the kiln. Hear the sounds of dishes rattling together. Watch as automatic jiggers form round plates at a rate of 400 to 500 dozen per day. Ram presses squeeze slabs of clay between two plaster dyes to create such irregular shapes as slanted sides, squared corners, and ovals. The top die is pressed into the bottom die under 2,200 pounds-per-square-inch of pressure. In the casting process, liquid clay known as "slip" is poured into plaster molds. The slip dries in the shape of the mold. Cup handles are formed in tree molds of six to eight handles. A machine trims and prepares them for individual hand attachment to each cup.

A spray machine showers liquid glaze onto the dry pottery called "greenware." Once glazed, each piece is loaded by hand onto the shelves of a kiln car. Robotics are used to stack a filled kiln car automatically into the largest fast-fire kiln in the industry.

After the short 11-hour journey (it used to take 48 hours) through this 2,400°, 350-foot-long tunnel kiln, the computer directs each kiln car back to its initial workstation. Presses stamp the Homer Laughlin trademark onto the bottom of each piece. In the decorating department, pattern decals are hand-applied. Workers slide the water-soaked decals onto individual cups and plates and push out air bubbles with small hard rubber squeegees. Decorative lines are painted on by hand or machine, using a silk-screen pattern, before another firing in the decorating kiln, this time for only 59 minutes. Pieces are shipped out as soon as they're finished, to the tune of 500,000 pieces of china per week.

Cost: Free
Freebies: Souvenir ceramic tray
Video Shown: No
Reservations Needed: No, except for groups larger than 20 people.
Days and Hours: Mon–Fri 10:30 AM and 1:00 PM. Closed holidays.
Plan to Stay: 1 hour, plus time in outlet store.
Minimum Age: None
Disabled Access: Yes, for most of tour.
Group Requirements: Groups larger than 20 people should call 1 week in advance. No maximum group size.
Special Information: Photography allowed in museum only. Areas near kilns are quite warm in summer.
Outlet Store: Sells first- and second-quality of entire product line, including Fiesta dinnerware and flatware and Lyrica dinnerware. Also offers close-out patterns and colors. Open Mon–Sat 9:30 AM–4:50 PM, Sun 12:00 PM–4:50 PM. Closed major holidays.
Directions: From Pittsburgh, take Rt. 30 West to Chester, WV. Turn left at end of exit ramp and then left onto Rt. 2 South for 2 miles; factory is on right. From Youngstown, take Rt. 11 South to East Liverpool. Follow signs to Newell Toll Bridge. Once on bridge, follow signs to Homer Laughlin.
Nearby Attractions: Brooke Glass, Creegan Animation, and Hall China tours (see pages 300, 235, and 237); East Liverpool Museum of Ceramics; Mountaineer Park Racetrack and Resort.

Fenton Art Glass *glass*

420 Caroline Avenue
Williamstown, WV 26187
(304) 375-7772

In western West Virginia, rich in mountains, sand, and natural gas, the ancient art of glassmaking is kept alive by a handful of artisans and factories. Fenton Glass began in 1905, when two Fenton brothers pooled $284 to build their Williamstown plant. Now in its fourth generation of family ownership and management, Fenton Glass continues this art in the U.S. The tour takes you from the extreme heat and speed of the blow/press shops to the decorating area's exacting calm.

After a brief chemistry lesson (sand is glass' main ingredient), follow your guide onto the blow/press shop floor. Gatherers, handlers, and carriers dodge around you with "gobs" of red-hot glass, handles, and freshly blown or pressed pieces. Each worker, trained by apprenticeship, has a specific function in the team effort of creating each item. To produce a bowl, the "gatherer" rolls the long pole ("punty") inside the 2,500° furnace to gather a "gob" of glass, which is put into a bowl-shaped mold. The "presser," one of the most experienced craftsmen in the shop, lowers a lever with exacting pressure, squeezing molten glass into a decorative bowl.

Downstairs, in an enclosed room, fresh-air-masked artisans paint crushed 22-karat gold onto glass eggs. Elsewhere in the decorating area, artists paint designs on glass using crushed-glass pigments. When applying floral designs, an artist first paints the flowers' blossoms on a dozen pieces, returning later to add leaves and stems. You gain an appreciation for the steps involved in producing tomorrow's heirlooms.

Cost: Free
Freebies: Brochure on glassmaking
Video Shown: "The Making of Fenton Glass," 23-minute video in museum theater, covers production, how specific glass items are made, company history, and hand-carving of cast-iron molds.
Reservations Needed: No, except for groups larger than 20 people.

Days and Hours: Mon–Fri 8:30 AM–10:00 AM and 11:30 AM–2:30 PM. Call for exact tour times, as factory work schedule changes. Closed holidays. No factory tours for 2 weeks starting end of June or beginning of July.
Plan to Stay: 1½ hours, including tour, video, and museum, plus time for gift shop. Museum emphasizes first 75 years of Fenton Glass (1905–1980), and other Ohio Valley companies' glass. Museum has same hours as gift shop.
Minimum Age: 2. Supervise children carefully since you get very close to the hot glass.
Disabled Access: Blowing/pressing area and gift shop are accessible. Stairs to decorating department and museum.
Group Requirements: Groups of 20 or more need advance reservations.
Special Information: Wear close-toed, thick-soled shoes. Glassblowing area is well ventilated but hot during summer. Watch where you walk.
Gift Shop and Factory Outlet: Sells Fenton's 400-item first-quality line. Only outlet for preferred seconds and first-quality discontinued glass collectibles. Also carries Royal Doulton, Lenox, and other giftware and collectibles. Museum sells glassmaking history books. Annual February Gift Shop Sale and July 4th sale. Year-round, open Mon–Sat 8:00 AM–5:00 PM, Sun 12:15 PM–5:00 PM. Additional hours: April through December Mon–Fri open until 8:00 PM. Closed New Year's, Easter, Thanksgiving, and Christmas. Catalog available from above number.
Directions: From I-77, take Exit 185; follow blue-and-white signs to gift shop. From Rt. 50, take I-77 North. Follow directions above.
Nearby Attractions: Lee Middleton Doll Factory tour (see page 240); Blennerhassett Island; Historic Marietta, Ohio, across Ohio River.

Website: wvweb.com/www/fenton_glass

An array of art glass is made at Fenton Art Glass in Williamstown, West Virginia.

A glass worker shapes molten glass during factory tour.

Pilgrim Glass   *glass*

Airport Road
Ceredo, WV 25507
(304) 453-3553

By experimenting with different products and positioning itself in the upper end of the glass market, Pilgrim Glass has prospered. In addition to being the world's largest producer of cranberry glass (made of 24-karat gold fused with lead crystal), Pilgrim produces a limited-edition sand-carved cameo and etched art glass collection.

From an elevated observation deck you can see the entire glassmaking production area. Even at this height you feel the heat from the furnaces. Watch the creation of Pilgrim art glass. Notice the round assembly line of bowls immediately below you. Workers gather and blow glass while swinging and twirling their punties to prevent the molten glass from sagging. Glass animals, like all art glass, begin as a gob of molten glass. With forceps, workers pull shapes from the center. They stretch, turn, shape, clip, and score the shapeless gob into a glass animal. Only the artisan knows whether it will become a porpoise, cat, or unicorn.

The cameo glassmaking process begins with the blowing of up to 11 layers of molten glass on top of each other. All layers must be the identical expansion coefficient to ensure the same rate of expansion and avoid shattering. When the glass has cooled, workers sandblast away one layer at a time until the initial layer of colored glass is exposed. Each individual pattern is used only once and is destroyed in the carving of a single layer. Many of these multicolored relief designs depict West Virginia's natural beauty, with such names as "Morning Mist," "Clearing in the Forest," and "Silhouetted Trees." Although you cannot see any of the detailed steps in making cameo glass, you will appreciate the skill involved by viewing the cameo collection in the gift gallery.

Cost: Free
Freebies: No
Video Shown: Optional 8-minute video shown in sale room gives close-up view of art-glass production. Recommends watching video before taking tour.
Reservations Needed: No
Days and Hours: Since tour is self-guided, plan to visit during following production times: Mon–Fri 8:00 AM–10:00 AM, 10:30 AM–2:30 PM, and 3:00 PM–6:00 PM. May not be in production on Fridays. Closed holidays, 3 weeks from end of June to July, and 2–3 weeks around Christmas and New Year's.
Plan to Stay: 20 minutes for tour and video, plus time for Glass Gallery.
Minimum Age: None
Disabled Access: Yes, for video and first-floor of gallery. Stairs lead to second floor of gallery and observation deck.
Group Requirements: None
Special Information: Furnaces keep observation deck warm. Speaker system on observation deck allows the foreman to narrate activities on the shop floor to viewers.
Retail Store: Glass Gallery displays Pilgrim's art glass in sunlit sections containing same-color bowls, pitchers and vases. Cameo glass in display cases. Second-floor gallery showcases more intricate and valuable cameo glass. Factory outlet room sells second-quality and first-quality discontinued glassware at reduced prices. Two cases display historical pieces made at Pilgrim Glass, on loan from master blower Robert McKeand, a Pilgrim Glass employee since 1959. Open Mon–Sat 9:00 AM–5:00 PM and Sun 1:00 PM–5:00 PM. Catalog available from above phone number.
Directions: Take I-64 to Exit 1 in West Virginia. Follow signs to Tri-State Airport. Pilgrim Glass is on left. Signs in parking lot invite you to "See It Made."
Nearby Attractions: Huntington Art Museum.

Allen-Edmonds ～ *shoes*

201 East Seven Hills Road
Port Washington, WI 53074
(414) 284-3461

Allen-Edmonds' shoes cushion some of the most famous feet that tread the globe. Visitors to Allen-Edmonds will see the shoes worn by three U.S. presidents. You can even touch the size 24 EEEEEEs handcrafted for a teenager in Seattle, the brown-and-white spectators worn by the U.S. Men's Olympic team in 1992, and a pair of alligator golf shoes with gold-plated spikes. For added color, there are the red, white, and blue clown shoes worn by Oscar- and Emmy-winning actor Ernest Borgnine.

Walk into the atrium gallery of Allen-Edmonds Corporate Center in Port Washington, Wisconsin, and you'll see shoes worn by the well-heeled from all over the world. It's the Allen-Edmonds Shoe Revue, a distinctive collection of men's footwear worn by presidents, kings, sports celebrities, and film stars. There's even a pair of brown cordovan loafers presented to the Pope by Allen-Edmonds' president and owner John Stollenwerk. Along the atrium viewing gallery are movie posters with displays of the Allen-Edmonds shoes featured in major films. You'll see the footwear worn by Clint Eastwood in *In the Line of Fire*, Danny DeVito in *Hoffa*, and Dustin Hoffman and Andy Garcia in *Hero*.

From glass windows along the atrium walkway, notice how shoes in the Bottoming department progress down a conveyor belt like ducks waddling along a three-tier shooting gallery. Workers pull unfinished shoes off the conveyor to perform various procedures. One worker guides a shoe through a machine that stitches all around the insole. This 360-degree welting process has been a tradition since the company was founded in 1922. Visitors may see worn Allen-Edmonds being re-crafted into almost-new condition (they re-craft more than 1,000 pairs each week).

Between a video and what you can see from the atrium windows, you will learn the entire handcrafting process. Each pair of Allen-Edmonds shoes requires 212 production steps—from the inspection of the leather to the final shine. Willie, a 56-plus-year veteran who started at 30¢ per hour, can supposedly do all 212 steps himself!

In the finishing department in the back, each new pair is blanketed in soft burgundy flannel and tucked into a sturdy black box. They await shipment to a major department store, shoe salon, or the Shoe Bank, a 75,000-pair on-site shoe store that will undoubtedly be your final destination.

Cost: Free
Freebies: Catalog
Video Shown: 12-minute video includes shoe production and clips of Allen-Edmonds in the news.
Reservations Needed: No, except if groups over 6 people want a tour guide.
Days and Hours: Mon–Sun 8:00 AM–5:00 PM. Tour guides available only Mon–Fri. No productions on weekends.
Plan to Stay: 25–30 minutes for atrium gallery and video, plus time in Shoe Bank.
Minimum Age: None
Disabled Access: Yes
Group Requirements: Groups over 6 people should call 1–2 days in advance to arrange for a tour guide. For groups over 25 people, subgroups may begin their tour at the Shoe Bank.
Outlet Store: The Shoe Bank offers full line of Allen-Edmonds first-quality men's and women's shoes at 25 percent off standard price. Open Mon–Fri 7:00 AM–9:00 PM, Sat 9:00 AM–9:00 PM, Sun 9:00 AM–6:00 PM. Re-crafting services available. Annual July Tent Sale is a big event. For catalog and dates of July Tent Sale, call (800) 235-2348.
Directions: From Milwaukee, take I-43 North to Exit 100. Look for big American flag at Allen-Edmonds entrance.
Nearby Attractions: Kohler Design Center and tour (see page 340); Lake Michigan; Cedarburg.

See color photos, page 178

Carr Valley Cheese *cheese*

S3797 County G
La Valle, WI 53941
(608) 986-2781 / (800) 462-7258

Named after its location, Carr Valley Cheese is one of the few companies that produces cheddar cheese the old-fashioned way. Many Wisconsinites remember the 1930s and 1940s, when, as kids, they snacked on fresh curd from cheese factories that dotted Wisconsin's countryside every few miles. You can taste fresh, warm curd that squeaks against your teeth and observe how it is turned into cheese.

In the retail store, a glass wall runs the length of the production area, where you may see owner Sid Cook, a fourth-generation cheese-maker, clad in bib overalls. Since each of the four 19-foot-long stainless-steel vats is at a different production stage, it helps to review the picture board and audiotape before taking your self-guided tour. Each day 52,000 pounds of pasteurized milk are filtered from holding tanks into cheese vats, which resemble single-lane lap-swimming pools. A large whisk (an "agitator") twists and turns as it travels the length of a vat and back. A culture (begins ripening process and tastes like sour milk) and rennet (causes milk to solidify) are added, and a wire harp cuts the mixture into small curds. As the whey (liquid) is removed, a separator extracts the cream. The cheese remains in the vat.

Once solid, the cheese is cut into 20-inch-by-2-inch slabs. While they're stacked like slices in a loaf of bread, excess moisture drains from the slabs. The curd mill chops them into small chunks, and workers fill small black metal buckets with 25 pounds of curd. You can see curds weighed, poured into forms, and pressed into wheels.

Walk around to the back of the plant to see wheels waxed and packaged. In the wax room, a rack of cheese wheels is lowered into a 2-foot-deep vat of 200° clear, red, or black wax (color depends on cheese's age). The wax seals out air and protects the cheese from mold as it cures in the warehouse for up to two years (longer aging means sharper cheddar).

Cost: Free
Freebies: Samples of curds and cheeses.
Video Shown: No, however picture board and 4-minute audiotape in retail store explain cheese-making.
Reservations Needed: No, except for groups larger than 30 people.
Days and Hours: Mon–Sat 8:00 AM–12:00 PM. Best time is 10:00 AM. Closed Thanksgiving, Christmas, and Easter.
Plan to Stay: 30 minutes for self-guided tour and retail store.
Minimum Age: None
Disabled Access: Yes, however difficult to get into wax room.
Group Requirements: Groups larger than 30 should call 1 day in advance to schedule tour guide; will be split into smaller groups.
Special Information: Can watch video and some production of European cheeses at their other facility, Wisconsin Pride, in Mauston (call 608-847-6998).
Retail Store: Sells full line of Carr Valley cheese. Wheel sizes: 3-pound "gem," 5½-pound "favorite," up to 23-pound "daisy," and 72-pound "cheddar" (once the industry standard). Also sells cut cheese, curds, sausages, and Wisconsin-made jams, jellies, and honey. Sells cheese production video. Open Mon–Sat 8:00 AM–4:00 PM. Catalog available from (800) 462-7258.
Directions: From I-90/94, take Hwy. 12 South. Take Hwy. 33 West through Reedsburg (look for Carr Valley Cheese signs) to La Valle. Go straight onto Hwy. 58 South through Ironton. After 1 mile, turn left onto County G. Brick plant is 2 miles ahead on right.
Nearby Attractions: Wisconsin Dells casinos and boat cruises, about 25 miles away. For complete list of Wisconsin cheese plants, write: Cheese Plants, Wisconsin Milk Marketing Board, 8418 Excelsior Drive, Madison, WI 53717.

Case Corporation ⟿ *tractors*
24th and Mead Streets
Racine, WI 53403
(414) 636-7818

Jerome Increase Case started his company in 1842 in western Racine County to manufacture threshing machines. He moved the business to Racine in 1844 to take advantage of Racine's proximity to Lake Michigan and its abundance of skilled labor. Case, until recently a 100-percent owned Tenneco subsidiary, has become a leading worldwide producer of agricultural and construction equipment. (Tenneco also purchased the agricultural asset of International Harvester in 1985.)

The tractor plant is one of three Case plants in Racine and is the only factory worldwide in which Case builds the two-wheel-drive Magnum series tractor. Magnum has appeared on *Fortune* magazine's list of 100 products America makes best and has received highest recognition from the Society of Agricultural Engineers. This guided walking tour covers almost half of the 1.5-million-square-foot plant to show tractor-building from start to finish. The facility is huge, which isn't surprising considering the tractor's size—it weighs as much as 8 tons, with tires as tall as people.

When Case launched the Magnum line in 1987, it completely rebuilt the old assembly line and installed the most current manufacturing equipment and procedures. Among the new assembly line's important features are automated handling systems, a robotic wash and paint system, and computerized diagnostic testing. As you move between the subassembly areas, your Case-retiree tour guide points out special production features, such as the bar code identification system. Each tractor and cab is identified and tracked with a bar code from the moment the assembly process starts.

After the cab's metal pieces are welded together, it moves down its own line. Workers add components such as glass, fenders, seat, fuel tank, and roof. When cab and body come together, it finally looks like the well-known bright red Case International tractor. Just before the tractor receives its tires, a two-member team determines whether it meets Case quality standards. If it does, the workers place a decal bearing their signatures on the cab threshold. This certifies that the tractor is ready to begin its working life and symbolizes the commitment of the Case/UAW Employee Involvement Program.

Cost: Free
Freebies: No
Video Shown: 18-minute slide show on history of Racine, Case, and the transmission, foundry, and assembly plants.
Reservations Needed: Yes
Days and Hours: Tue and Thur 9:00 AM and 12:30 PM, Wed 9:00 AM. Case focuses on customer tours but tries to give public tours when time available. Closed holidays, week between Christmas and New Year's, and plant maintenance shutdowns.
Plan to Stay: 1½ hours for slide show and tour, plus time in gift shop.
Minimum Age: 12
Disabled Access: Yes
Group Requirements: Make reservations 2 weeks in advance. Maximum group is 100 people.
Special Information: No photography. Tours also available at Case foundry and transmission plants in Racine (call above number). Other Case tours at combine and cotton picker plant (East Moline, IL; call 309-752-3000) and construction equipment plant (Wichita, KS; call 316-941-2235).
Gift Counter: Sells logoed T-shirts and caps, and scale model Case tractors and construction machines. Open after tours.
Directions: From I-94 exit at Hwy. 11. Follow Hwy. 11 East to the junction with Sheridan Rd. (Hwy. 32). Turn left onto Sheridan Rd., then take the first right. Follow the sign for parking.
Nearby Attractions: SC Johnson Wax Golden Rondelle Theater and Administration Building tour (see page 346); Racine Zoo; Museum of Fine Arts; Racine County Historical Museum; Engine House No. 3.

Consolidated Papers ⟿ *paper*

4th Avenue
Wisconsin Rapids, WI 54494
(715) 422-3789

The forests of the Upper Midwest help make Wisconsin the nation's leading producer of paper. In the middle of the state lies Wisconsin Rapids, home of Consolidated Papers, North America's largest manufacturer of the coated printing papers used in magazines, catalogs, annual reports, and brochures. Set inside a concrete and brick building several stories high and stretching five city blocks, Consolidated's largest machine produces enough paper to create a 19-foot-wide strip from Chicago to New York City every day.

At the headbox, the start of the paper machine, a mixture of 99 percent water and 1 percent wood fiber is sprayed onto a rotating mesh screen. A combination of gravity and suction drain much of the water as the sheet of paper forms on the wire. The remainder of the water is removed by squeezing the sheet between giant rollers and then drying it with steam-heated dryers. Five hundred feet away, the newly formed paper wraps onto giant spools at the end of the paper machine. If you time it right (about every 40 minutes), you can see a "turn-up," where a new reel of paper is started without ever slowing down or stopping the process.

The 20,000-pound reels of paper move on to a 475-foot machine that applies two separate layers of coating to each side of the sheet. The next stop is the supercalenders, which iron and polish the sheet to a high gloss. Finally the reels of paper, now weighing as much as 33,000 pounds, are taken to the rewinder, where they are cut into smaller rolls for shipment to customers or conversion to sheets.

Your guide will then escort you to Consolidated's Converting Division. Computer-controlled automated guided vehicles (AGVs) transport rolls of paper across 7,000 feet of predetermined routes in the floor. At the facility's sheeters, rolls of paper are cut to size, packaged, and labeled. The AGVs take the finished paper to a cavernous warehouse that can store more than 20 million pounds of paper.

Cost: Free

Freebies: Small writing pad, brochure, postcard, and fact card.

Video Shown: 7-minute overview of the mill's operation, including pulp-making and forestry program.

Reservations Needed: No, except for groups of 5 or more people.

Day and Hours: Wed, Thur, and Sat at 10:00 AM. Other times by prior arrangement. Closed some holidays.

Plan to Stay: 1½ hours for tour and video.

Minimum Age: None. Parents are discouraged from bringing infants since noise level in mill may disturb them. Children under 12 must be accompanied by an adult.

Disabled Access: Yes. Advance notice requested, so adequate number of guides can be available.

Group Requirements: Groups should call at least 1 week in advance. For specially arranged tours, minimum group size is 4 people. Maximum group size is 75 people.

Special Information: Wear comfortable, flat shoes. Company also offers forest tour nearby. Paper mill tour at subsidiary in Duluth, MN (call 218-628-5100).

Gift Shop: No

Directions: From Madison, take I-90/94 West to I-39 North (Exit 108). Take Hwy. 73 West and turn right on Hwy. 13 North. Cross the Wisconsin River. Turn right onto West Grand Ave. Turn left on 4th Ave. Mill tour entrance is 1½ blocks on right.

Nearby Attractions: Wisconsin Dairy State Cheese tour (see page 349); Wausau Papers tour (see page 348) about 1 hour away; Wisconsin Rapids Paper Mill tour (call 715-422-3789); Steven Point Brewery tour (call 715-344-9310). Wisconsin Paper Council publishes a brochure of Wisconsin paper tours (call 414-722-1500).

General Motors *sport-utility vehicles and pickups*

Truck & Bus Group
1000 Industrial Avenue
Janesville, WI 53546
(608) 756-7681

General Motors has been building vehicles in Janesville since the Samson Tractor in 1919. Through the years this plant has produced a range of vehicles including Chevys, Buick Skyhawks, and now the popular Suburban, Yukon, Tahoe, and medium-duty trucks. During WWII the factory made artillery shells. With the factory's long history, it's no surprise that this plant and the retiree who leads your walking floor tour exude a sense of pride. It's also one of the few automotive tours that individuals and families can take without advance reservations.

You'll see plenty of robots assisting the workers. In the Suburban body shop, over 160 robots perform about 70 percent of the welds. These robots, which look more like bird beaks, bend over from their bases to apply spot-welds. The colorful shooting sparks make you realize how much safer it is for robots to perform this task than workers, who mostly program, monitor, and repair this equipment.

Once the steel body-frame is assembled, it moves through a dimensional vision system that uses laser beams to check the frame parts' sizes against their ideal measurements. In other parts of the factory, robots also apply the base-coat paint in enclosed booths, and put the prime and urethane on the window glass before workers pop it into place. While the body frame is being constructed, other lines build the chassis. Workers assemble the underneath part first, and a turnover hoist flips the chassis over like a pancake.

In the final assembly lines, an overhead hoist lowers the vehicle body onto the chassis, and workers bolt them together. To the music of air tools, parts such as fenders and grills seem to arrive from every direction for attachment. You will see the dynamic vehicle-test area, where the vehicles sit on rollers and accelerate to 60 mph so major features can be tested. At this point the assembly process is complete, and you're tempted to hop in and hit the road.

Cost: Free

Freebies: Key chain; brochure with pictures of tour highlights; historical timeline that traces plant's lineage.

Video Shown: 9-minute pre-tour video, which overviews the plant history and vehicle production.

Reservations Needed: No, except for groups of 10 or more people.

Days and Hours: Mon–Thur 9:30 AM and 1:00 PM. Closed holidays, week between Christmas and New Year's, and 2 weeks in July.

Plan to Stay: 1½ hours for video and tour.

Minimum Age: None, although children under 5 may be frightened by noise and sparks.

Disabled Access: Yes

Group Requirements: Groups of 10 or more should make reservations as early as possible—tours fill quickly, especially in spring and summer. Maximum group is 100 people.

Special Information: No photography. Vehicle-painting by robots is not on tour, but you see plenty of robots perform other tasks.

Gift Counter: Sells numerous logoed items, including T-shirts, jackets, hats, and scale models. Open only after tours.

Directions: From I-90, take Hwy. 351 West. Turn right at stop sign and proceed north on Hwy. G (Beloit Ave). Turn left at Delavan Dr. and left at plant. Enter through doors in center of building, directly under flagpole on roof. From Hwy. 14 West, go straight onto O, which becomes Delavan Dr., then turn left at plant. Call above number for maps to plant from other directions.

Nearby Attractions: Wisconsin Wagon group tours (call 608-754-0026 or 608-757-3160); Rotary Gardens; Palmer Park; Tallman House; Milton House.

Kohler ~ *bathtubs, whirlpools, toilets, and sinks*

Design Center
101 Upper Road
Kohler, WI 53044
(920) 457-3699

A visit to Kohler is more than just a tour of the world's largest plumbingware manufacturer. The factory tour begins and ends at the Kohler Design Center, a three-level showcase of products and bathroom layouts that are so attractive you'll want to move in. The Design Center also houses the company museum, which chronicles Kohler history since 1873, and Kohler's own colorful "great wall of china."

Guided by a company retiree, your tour begins in the pottery building's molding area, a humid place where bare-chested men smooth wet clay toilets with large sponges. Next come the kilns: long, brick ovens that bake glazed clay fixtures into "vitreous chinaware." Stroll among glossy stacks of Thunder Grey sinks and Innocent Blush commodes. Watch inspectors "ping" the chinaware with hard rubber balls and listen for cracks.

Next, enter Wisconsin's largest iron foundry—its electric melt system eliminates the smoke and fumes previously associated with foundries. It's still an imposing place, full of molten metal, warning lights, and hissing machinery—a highly memorable industrial experience. Here you'll discover how they make molds to form cast-iron tubs, sinks, and engine blocks. The concrete floor shudders with the heave and thud of massive presses that create sand molds. You'll feel the heat from the "ladles" of glowing molten iron traveling by on forklifts. Deeper inside the building, an automated production line turns out one bathtub casting every 30 seconds.

In the enamel building, workers gingerly remove red-hot bathtubs, lavatories, and kitchen sinks from ovens. Enamel powder that melts into porcelain is quickly sifted onto each fixture. Finally, pass into the whirlpool-bath section, where up to seven tubs bubble serenely. After three hours of touring this enormous plant, you may be more than a little tempted to flop into the water and relax.

Cost: Free

Freebies: Product-line books in Design Center.

Video Shown: 20-minute video in Design Center shows Kohler history and Kohler Village highlights.

Reservations Needed: Yes, for plant tour. No, for Design Center.

Days and Hours: Factory tour: Mon–Fri 8:30 AM. No tours on holidays, week between Christmas and New Year's, last week of July, or first week of August. Design Center: Mon–Fri 9:00 AM–5:00 PM and Sat, Sun, and holidays 10:00 AM–4:00 PM.

Plan to Stay: 2–3 hours for factory tour, plus time for video, museum, and Design Center.

Minimum Age: 14, for tour; under 18 must be accompanied by adult. None for Design Center.

Disabled Access: Discouraged for tour, because of stairs. Design Center is fully accessible.

Group Requirements: Kohler requests that you call for complete group information. Groups larger than 8–10 people will be split.

Special Information: No photography on tour. Up to 2½ miles of walking, including some outdoors. Be careful where you walk. During tour you'll see examples of works produced by artists in the Arts/Industry Residency program.

Gift Counter: Design Center sells postcards, polo shirts, and Kohler replica trucks.

Directions: From Chicago and Milwaukee, take I-43 North to Kohler exit. Follow signs into Kohler—the company is the town. Stop at Kohler Design Center for orientation information and start of plant tour. From Madison, take I-94 East to Milwaukee, then I-43 North. Follow above directions.

Nearby Attractions: Shops at Woodlake Kohler; The American Club "five diamond" resort hotel; Blackwolf Run championship golf courses; Waelderhaus, replica Austrian chalet in style of Kohler family's ancestral home; Kohler Village tour (May–October).

Miller Brewing  *beer*

Visitors Center
4251 West State Street
Milwaukee, WI 53208
(414) 931-BEER

In 1855 Frederick Miller took over the Plank-Road Brewery. Surrounded by woods, the small operation was no bigger than a Victorian house. Today a replica of the Plank-Road Brewery stands in "Miller Valley," the world of pipes, warehouses and loading docks that comprise the mighty Miller brewery.

After a dazzling video, you walk outdoors and upstairs to the packaging-center balcony. See all the cans roaring along conveyor belts that wind through wet machinery, packing up to 200,000 cases daily. Employees lube the gearworks with soapy water; no oil or grease is allowed. At each viewing station, TV monitors offer tourists inviting close-ups of the scenes before them. The mammoth distribution center covers the equivalent of five football fields. As you look out across its half-million cases of beer, notice the train track that rolls right into the warehouse; a clean boxcar waits, looking like a toy, dwarfed by the high ceiling.

The brewhouse is where Miller Brewing Company makes its beer, up to 8½ million barrels annually. Climb 56 stairs to look down on a row of towering, shiny brew kettles where "wort," a grain extract, is boiled and combined with hops. Stroll through Miller's historic Caves Museum, a restored portion of the original brewery where beer was stored before the invention of mechanical refrigeration. It features a collection of authentic 1800s brewing equipment. In the Bavarian-style Miller Inn, you and fellow tourists have plenty of time to relax and sample Miller's various beers or a soft drink. Take a few minutes to inspect the impressive collection of antique steins. In the summer, enjoy your beverage in an adjoining beer garden enlivened by music.

Cost: Free
Freebies: Beer, soda, and postcards.
Video Shown: 15-minute video shows brewing process and overview of Miller's history.

Reservations Needed: No, except for groups of 15 people or more.
Days and Hours: Mon–Sat 12:00 PM–3:30 PM. Closed holidays and week between Christmas and New Year's.
Plan to Stay: 1 hour for video and tour, plus time for beer tasting and gift shop.
Minimum Age: Under 18 must have adult supervision.
Disabled Access: Tour Center (includes video), Miller Inn, and Caves Museum are accessible. Plant not yet accessible.
Group Requirements: Groups of 15 or more, call ahead for reservations (414-931-2467). Maximum of 90 people per group. No reservations for Saturday tours.
Special Information: Best time to see production is weekdays.
Gift Shop: Sells full line of clothes, mugs, steins, caps, mirrors, clocks, draft handles, and other beer paraphernalia featuring familiar Miller emblems. Look for popular "Girl-in-the-Moon" jewelry and clothes. Open Mon–Sat 10:00 AM–4:30 PM.
Directions: From Chicago, take I-94 West to 35th St. Turn right (north). Turn left (west) onto State St. Pass through "Miller Valley" (well marked) to last building on left, Miller Tour Center and Gift Shop. From Madison, take I-94 East to Hwy. 41 North to the exit for State St. Follow signs to right, down hill to traffic light. Turn left onto State St. Tour Center is 1 block ahead on right.
Nearby Attractions: Quality Candy/Buddy Squirrel factory tour (see page 344); Milwaukee County Zoo; Mitchell Park Horticulture ("The Domes"); Milwaukee County Museum; Milwaukee Art Museum; Boerner Botanical Gardens; Cedar Creek Winery. Miller Tour Center front desk has directions to many local attractions.

See color photo, page 190

Natural Ovens   *breads and cereals*

4300 County Trunk Circle
Manitowoc, WI 54221
(920) 758-2500 / (800) 558-3535

Paul Stitt founded Natural Ovens in 1976, after discovering that many food companies were adding appetite stimulants to their products to increase sales. A biochemist, Paul believes food should be good for you, filling, and satisfying. Now he and his wife, Barbara, supply fresh breads to over 1,200 grocery stores in a handful of states. When you tour the facility, you'll notice that in their employee cafeteria, junk food has been replaced by delicious foods made with fresh vegetables, fruits, and grains, some even grown on company grounds.

Your tour begins in the huge lobby in front of a 11-by-17-foot stained-glass window depicting the farm and museum, as well as the growing and harvesting of flax. In 1986 Paul rediscovered flax, which has been proven beneficial in lowering cholesterol and reducing the risk of heart disease. Flax is used in almost all of the bakery's products.

View the bakery through a series of windows. The bakers arrive at 2:00 AM to begin mixing the "sponge," the base of the dough made with flour, yeast, and water. The bakery uses three semi-truckloads of flour a week—60 acres of wheat! After the sponge rises for three hours, it's put into the mixer and the rest of the ingredients are added to make enough dough for 550 loaves. You may gasp as the enormous blob of dough is dumped out of the mixer. After the dough has risen twice and been mixed three times, the huge mass goes through the dough divider, making more-manageable 2-pound pieces. The smaller clumps look like little rabbits as they flop from the divider into the molder, where they're kneaded and shaped into loaves.

After rising, the dough moves to the 106-foot-long oven, made of 60 tons of steel and 25 tons of brick. In just one hour 3,000 loaves will travel from one end of the oven to the other. Smell the heavenly aroma as you watch thousands of golden loaves emerge right under your nose. Within 16 hours, those same loaves will be sitting on a grocery shelf somewhere far away from Manitowoc.

Cost: Free

Freebies: Hot samples of baked goods.

Video Shown: 8-minute video provides close-up look at the mixing and baking process. Shown when no production.

Reservations Needed: No, except for groups larger than 10 people.

Days and Hours: Tours: Mon, Wed, Thur, Fri 9:00 AM, 10:00 AM, and 11:00 AM. The baking is completed by 2:00 PM. No baking on Tue. Self-guided viewing of bakery when lobby is open, Mon–Fri 8:00 AM–5:00 PM, Sat 8:00 AM–3:00 PM. Museum: Mon–Sat 9:00 AM–3:00 PM. Both are closed Thanksgiving, Christmas, and New Year's.

Plan to Stay: 1–1½ hours for bakery tour, self-guided tour of Farm and Food Museum, including antique buildings and machinery, and friendly animals to pet, including Prince the llama, known for his hugs and kisses.

Minimum Age: None

Disabled Access: Yes, though parts of farm and museum are more difficult to access.

Group Requirements: Groups over 10 people should call at least 4–6 weeks in advance. Maximum group size 55 people.

Special Information: When in season, pick berries on the farm grounds.

Gift Shop: The lobby of the factory sells a complete selection of Natural Ovens products, plus unique specialty items including books, vinegars brewed locally, almond butter, aprons, and maple syrup. Open lobby hours. Catalog available from above number.

Directions: From the south, take I-43 North to Exit 144. Turn right on Hwy. C. Turn left on CR. Bakery is 2½ miles ahead on left. From the north, take I-43 South to Exit 149. Turn left onto Hwy. 151 East. Turn right onto CR. Bakery is 1 mile ahead on right.

Nearby Attractions: Wisconsin Maritime Museum; Rahr West Art Museum; West of the Lake Gardens (open May–October); Lake Michigan Car Ferry.

This huge blob of dough pouring out of the mixer will make 550 loaves of Natural Ovens bread.

The beautifully manicured grounds of Natural Ovens in Manitowoc, Wisconsin, include the bakery and the Farm and Food Museum.

Quality Candy/Buddy Squirrel

1801 East Bolivar Avenue   *chocolates and popcorn*
Milwaukee, WI 53207
(414) 483-4500

This factory tour is actually two tours in one. In 1916 immigrants Joseph and Lottie Helminiak opened Quality Candy Shoppes in Milwaukee's popular Mitchell Street shopping district. In the early 1950s, Buddy Squirrel combined forces with Quality Candy. Today, the two product lines are housed in a 45,000-square-foot factory and warehouse, and the family-owned company operates more than 20 stores in two states. This joint tour allows you to see how Quality Candy makes award-winning chocolate candies and how Buddy Squirrel processes popcorn products.

Your tour begins in the Quality Candy kitchens. Here, candy-makers prepare and mix the ingredients for the chocolate candies' centers. Centers, made from scratch in these kitchens, include caramel, creams, toffee, cordials, marshmallow, and nougat. From a viewing corridor, you see the centers embark on a short journey to the enrobing room, where they are engulfed in a fountain of either milk or dark chocolate before going through the cooling tunnel. One of the highlights of the tour is watching over 80 seasonal solid chocolate moldings being made, varying in sizes from ¾-oz. to a 67-pound rabbit. All the candies then travel to the packing area to be boxed and sent off to a Quality Candy store or wholesaler.

The Buddy Squirrel segment adds some "pop" to the tour. Tons of corn kernels dive into giant poppers, in which they become popcorn. The popcorn is then seasoned with butter, cheese, caramel, and other flavorings. Once again, your taste buds are tempted by the scents in the air. The popcorn meets up with the nuts (also made by Buddy Squirrel but not seen on tour) in the packing room, and the goodies are prepared for their voyage to candy and nut stores all over the region.

Cost: Free

Freebies: Samples of candy and popcorn.

Video Shown: No

Reservations Needed: Yes. Individuals and families need to join scheduled group tour or form group of at least 10 people.

Days and Hours: Tue–Thur 10:30 AM and 1:00 PM. No tours on holidays, November and December, 4 weeks before Easter (except for Annual Open House), and 1 week at the beginning of July and August.

Plan to Stay: 45 minutes, plus time for Kitchen Store.

Minimum Age: 10

Disabled Access: Yes

Group Requirements: Groups of at least 10 people should call 4 weeks ahead. Maximum group size is 50 people.

Special Information: Annual Easter Open House (the two Sundays before Easter from 10:00 AM–4:00 PM) features Mr. & Mrs. Easter Bunny and special factory tours.

Retail Store: Kitchen Store sells all Quality Candy/Buddy Squirrel products, including chocolates, award-winning Butter Almond Toffee, Pecan Caramel Tads, popcorns, and nuts. Open Mon–Sat 9:00 AM–4:30 PM (closes at 2:00 PM on Saturdays in summer). Closed holidays. Catalog available from above number.

Directions: Take I-94 to Layton Ave. exit. Turn left onto Brust, then right on Whitnall. Make a quick left on Kansas St. Quality Candy/Buddy Squirrel factory is on right. Enter under bright red awning on south side of building.

Nearby Attractions: Miller Brewery tour (see page 341); Milwaukee County Zoo; Mitchell Park Horticulture ("The Domes"); Milwaukee County Museum; Milwaukee Art Museum; Boerner Botanical Gardens; Cedar Creek Winery.

Trek   ⟿   *bicycles*
801 West Madison Street
Waterloo, WI 53594
(920) 478-2197 / (800) 879-8735

When does a bike start to look like a bike? At the Trek plant, not until it reaches final assembly. Here the lean frame, little more than a wisp of painted geometry, meets pedals, cables, handlebars, and wheels, which are then boxed together for shipment to bike stores worldwide.

You'll see how Trek, which started in 1975 with four employees building frames for midwestern bicycle dealers, has innovated bike production. Metal frames take their form in the welding area. Thousands of metal pipes and joints, looking like bins of plumbing fixtures, are arranged precisely on steel tables and soldered together. It's a crackly, clattery region made brilliant with spits and stripes of green flame from the welding torch. Trek's frames of carbon fiber, a lightweight, almost ethereal compound, are built in an adjoining area. Workers hustle around the mounted carbon frames, spreading the fast-drying glue before it stiffens and sets. These newly glued frames are baked in an oven, then sanded smooth.

All frames, metal or carbon—about 1,000 a day—go to the paint department. They hang like coats on conveyor hooks that trundle toward large sheet-metal closets: the painting booths. Meanwhile, robots in a nearby department join rims to hubs, creating the wheels that will eventually meet up with the frames. On the glossy floor, heaps of fresh black tires, with the incarnate odor of a bike shop, are stacked hundreds deep. See the spokes bending and weaving into position and the "hop and wobble" process of computer-monitored "rim truing." On your way out, notice the "Employee Parking" area, an indoor rack some 50 yards long that's crowded with colorful bikes. If you drive your car to Trek, the largest manufacturer of quality bicycles in the U.S., you'll find a large gravel lot with plenty of places to park!

Cost: Free

Freebies: Promotional posters and catalogs

Video Shown: No

Reservations Needed: Yes

Days and Hours: Tue–Fri 9:30 AM. Closed holidays. Closed for 2 weeks around the end of June and beginning of July.

Plan to Stay: 45 minutes for tour.

Minimum Age: None

Disabled Access: Most of tour is wheelchair accessible.

Group Requirements: Groups larger than 12 people must call 1 week in advance. Maximum group size is 15 people. Does not want traditional bus tours.

Special Information: No video cameras. Photography restricted in some areas.

Gift Shop: No

Directions: From I-94, take Marshall/ Deerfield exit. Travel north on Hwy. 73 toward Marshall. Turn right at Hwy. 19 (Main St. in Marshall). Trek plant is 4 miles ahead on right.

Nearby Attractions: In Waterloo, inquire locally about tour of local pickle factory; John Deere lawn tractor plant tour in Horicon (call 414-485-4411); Madison's attractions, including Arboretum, Vilas Park Zoo, and State Capital tours, about 40 minutes away.

SC Johnson Wax

1525 Howe Street
Racine, WI 53403-2236
(920) 260-2154

*specialty
home-cleaning products*

In 1886 S.C. Johnson (at age 53) created and marketed a paste wax formula to sell as a sideline to his parquet flooring business. It became so successful that he expanded his line to introduce wood dyes, dance wax, and paints. In 1939 SC Johnson Wax Company moved into a building designed by Frank Lloyd Wright and eventually branched out to manufacture such familiar products as Glade, Edge Gel, and Raid.

In the company's corporate display room, pictures, products, and descriptions illustrate the company's unique development. The unfaltering dedication to business is depicted in the presented histories of the company's four generations of chairmen. See a display of various SC Johnson Worldwide consumer products. Learn how other countries contribute ingredients to products. In the Golden Rondelle lobby, see some of the prestigious awards presented to the company for marketing environmentally friendly products.

Strolling through the company's world headquarters, you will be dazzled by the interior of the Administration Building. Wright built this massive, futuristic "Great Workroom" using 21-foot columns that shoot up and expand outward as they reach the ceiling, resembling the stem and base of upside-down wineglasses. Illuminated Pyrex glass tubing wraps around the building, giving the impression of natural sunlight, yet not one real window exists! Equally impressive in its shape is the Research Tower, rising over 150 feet into the air. Designed using the cantilever principle, which is similar to the root, trunk, and branch system of a tree, the tower appears to hang suspended in the air.

Although not on the tour, the company's nearby production facility, "Waxdale," covers nearly 43 acres. Waxdale's aerosol lines can fill up to 500 units per minute. As the company's primary U.S. manufacturing plant, it is one of the most modern and efficient production, warehousing, and shipping centers in the world.

Cost: Free

Freebies: Brochures on Frank Lloyd Wright and his architecture.

Videos Shown: Golden Rondelle Theater shows 3 videos at varying times Fri between 9:15 AM and 3:00 PM. *On the Wing* is a 35-minute exploration of natural and mechanical flight; *Living Planet* features a 38-minute aerial view of Earth. There is also a 10-minute feature on Frank Lloyd Wright.

Reservations Needed: Yes

Days and Hours: Fri 9:15 AM, 11:00 AM, 1:15 PM, and 3:00 PM. Closed holidays and week between Christmas and New Year's Day.

Plan to Stay: 30 minutes for building tour, plus up to 2 hours for all films.

Minimum Age: None, but children under 14 must be accompanied by an adult.

Disabled Access: Yes

Group Requirements: Groups should call 2 weeks to 2 months in advance. Maximum group size is 40 people.

Gift Shop: No

Directions: Take I-94 to Hwy. 20 East (Washington Ave.). Continuing east for about 8 miles, Hwy. 20 East curves left. Do *not* take curve but go straight (east) onto 14th St. Golden Rondelle Theater is 3 blocks ahead.

Nearby Attractions: Case tractor tour (see page 337); Wustum Art Museum; Racine Zoo.

Website: www.scjohnsonwax.com

The futuristic "Great Workroom" was designed by Frank Lloyd Wright.

SC Johnson Wax produces a wide variety of well-known products.

Wausau Papers   ~~~ *paper*

2nd Street
Brokaw, WI 54417
(715) 675-3361

Heavily forested North Central Wisconsin is perfect for papermaking. Wausau Papers, established in 1899, is one of the industry's largest independent paper manufacturers. Every day 15,000 8-foot aspen logs are chopped, washed, chipped, and "deligni-fied," or turned into steamy pulp in the digesters. In the beater room, a humid, wet-towel-smelling place, workers dump clays and fillers into vats loaded with this pulp. See the whole dizzying mass swirl like a tor-nado 2,000 gallons deep. Your retiree tour guide explains that this mixture, or "furnish," is then dyed by a computerized coloring sys-tem and becomes "stock."

In the machine room, the wet stock (99 percent water) hits the wire section of the paper machine and begins to shed its water, then swiftly coheres as it rockets through the press section and around a series of roaring dryers. At the far end of the papermaking machine, a football field away, a drum reel gathers 10,000 pounds of fresh, warm paper. Over 485 tons of paper spin off the four massive paper machines every day. This new paper is continually tested for quality. In the testing room, you'll see a half-dozen curious gadgets, all poking and stretching the newly made paper. Over 50 samples are scrutinized from each shift.

Hundreds of rolls of paper sit in the cut-ter room. The rolls are so huge that while passing among them, you will glow with the reflection of their many hues. All around the cutter room are machines slicing and stack-ing, reaming and wrapping. Some machines combine into one smooth operation a cut-sheeter, wrapper, packager, and palletizer. In a 24-hour period these computerized sheet-feeders can transform rolls of paper into 44 million sheets of 8½ x 11 paper.

Your guided tour ends in shipping and receiving, an immense room that reaches four stories to an aluminum ceiling. Each day 25 trucks leave the docks for all parts of the country. As you stroll the aisles, notice the vast selection of vibrant colors, ranging from the typical reds and blues to the amus-ingly named Fireball Fuchsia, Planetary Purple, or Liftoff Lemon.

Cost: Free
Freebies: Writing pad of colored paper and welcome book.
Video Shown: 10-minute overview of mill's operation.
Reservations Needed: Yes. Prefers that indi-viduals and families join scheduled group tours.
Days and Hours: Mon–Fri 9:00 AM–3:00 PM. Closed holidays.
Plan to Stay: 2 hours for video and tour.
Minimum Age: 12
Disabled Access: Steps throughout plant.
Group Requirements: 5 days' advance notice required. No maximum group size.
Special Information: Best time to see pro-duction is before 1:00 PM. Wear comfortable, flat shoes. Loud and quite hot in places.
Gift Shop: No
Directions: From Madison, take I-51 North through Wausau to Brokaw exit. Turn right at stop sign and drive down slope to mill.
Nearby Attractions: Consolidated Papers tour about 1 hour away (see page 338); Hsu's Ginseng Farm tour (call 715-675-2325); Rib Mountain; Leigh-Yawkey Woodson Art Mu-seum; Marathon County Historical Museum; Andrew Warren Historic District. Wisconsin Paper Council publishes a brochure of Wis-consin paper tours (call 414-722-1500).

Wisconsin Dairy State Cheese *cheese*

Highway 34 & C
Rudolph, WI 54475
(715) 435-3144

The Dairy State Cheese plant, owned for generations by the Moran family, is fronted by a busy little shop. Look through the bank of windows either upstairs or downstairs from the shop, and you'll see a vast room filled with stainless-steel pipes, vats, and tables. A few workers move about in hair nets and rubber boots, but much of the "Stirred Curd Cheddar" process you're watching is highly automated. Given the size of the production room, the near absence of people is conspicuous, a testimony to the efficiency of state-of-the-art cheese-making equipment.

Off to your left rise several immense silos filled with thousands of gallons of pasteurized and cultured milk. Ten pounds of milk are used in producing every pound of cheese. A network of pipes carries the milk from the silos to four vats, each one longer than a school bus. All day the upright enclosed vats are filled and emptied. The curds and whey are pumped over to long tables. A "forker" swirls as it drifts up and down the length of the long narrow vat, beginning the process of separating the liquid (whey) from the milk solids (curd).

When the whey is drained off, what remains is a warm mass of glossy curds. The final step is to salt the curds. The fresh curds are automatically fed into presses, where they are compacted into 700-pound blocks of brand-new cheese. The massive orange or white blocks are then sealed into wooden boxes for aging. After about one month, the cheese is shipped to Kraft for cutting. When your tour ends, be sure to return to the shop and browse among the coolers stocked with 85 varieties of cheese. Buy yourself a bag of curds so fresh they'll squeak on your teeth.

Cost: Free
Freebies: Cheese samples
Video Shown: Optional 23-minute film promotes Wisconsin cheese and details manufacturing process.

Reservations Needed: No, except for groups larger than 25 people.
Days and Hours: Mon, Tues, Thur, and Fri 8:30 AM–5:15 PM, Sat 8:30 AM–5:00 PM. Production ends around 3:00 PM. Sun 9:00 AM–12:00 PM, but no production. Call to confirm holiday hours.
Plan to Stay: 15 minutes for self-guided viewing, plus time for video and cheese shop.
Minimum Age: None
Disabled Access: Yes
Group Requirements: Groups larger than 25 should make reservations 2 days in advance. Ice-cream cones and cheese samples provided for school tours.
Special Information: Guide available by request with 2 days' notice.
Retail Store: Cheese shop sells wide selection of cheeses, sausage, and locally made ice cream. Open Mon–Fri 8:30 AM–5:15 PM, Sat 8:30 AM–5:00 PM. Sun 9:00 AM–12:00 PM. Call about holiday hours. Catalog available from above number.
Directions: Take U.S. 51 North to the Hwy. 73 exit at Plainfield. Turn left (west) on Hwy. 73 to Hwy. 13. Turn right (north) and go through Wisconsin Rapids, following signs for Hwy. 34 North. Enter town of Rudolph, and Dairy State Cheese is on right.
Nearby Attractions: Consolidated Papers tour (see page 338); Wisconsin Rapids Paper Mill tour (call 715-422-3789); Stevens Point Brewery tour (call 715-344-9310); Rudolph Grotto Gardens and Wonder Cave. For complete list of Wisconsin cheese plants, write: Cheese Plants, Wisconsin Milk Marketing Board, 8418 Excelsior Drive, Madison, WI 53717.

Rocky Mountain Snacks 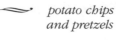   *potato chips and pretzels*

1077 Road 161
Pine Bluffs, WY 82082
(307) 245-9287

When Dr. Richard Canfield visited Wyoming, he noticed Pine Bluffs' numerous potato fields. From this observation, Wyoming's only potato-chip manufacturer was born. Having owned a similar business in Pennsylvania, Canfield found a deserted factory and spent months cleaning, moving in, and repairing used equipment. Rocky Mountain Snacks began production in December 1986 with one kettle. Today, with five kettles, Rocky Mountain makes about 50,000 pounds of potato chips each week.

The first thing you encounter when you enter the brick factory building is a 12-foot-tall-by-8-foot-wide stainless-steel storage hopper holding 2,600 pounds of potato chips. In fact, you'll quickly realize that all of the equipment is stainless steel. With the production manager as your tour guide, you'll walk right onto the factory floor—next to the kettles. Notice the clouds of steam that rise into the exhaust fans above each kettle. Smell hot oil and frying potatoes, along with the seasoning of the day.

Native Wyoming potatoes, peeled, washed, and sliced, dive into 220-gallon rectangular stainless-steel cooking kettles filled with 305° oil. In these 8-foot-long-by-4-foot-wide kettles, raw potato slices sizzle in hot oil. Surrounded by steam, "self stirrers" (Teflon-coated metal rakes designed and built by the company's maintenance man) automatically rake the potatoes back and forth. The steam subsides as the cooking cycle ends. After 15 minutes, the rakes raise the chips onto a conveyor. They sit there while another batch cooks, allowing excess oil to drip back into the kettle. Due to the potatoes' water content, each batch of 90 to 100 pounds of raw potatoes yields only 23 pounds of chips.

Workers hand-inspect for dark chips; then the chips travel along a vibrating table underneath a seasoning box, which sprinkles such flavorings as barbecue, jalapeño, or chicken. Each packaging line has a 12-hopper carousel that weighs and releases the correct amount of chips into the bagging machine. Bags are formed over a tube and heat-sealed shut in this order: bottom, back, and top. Workers then hand-pack the potato-chip bags into cardboard boxes for storage or shipment to nearby states or Canada.

Recently the company started making pretzels, to the tune of 600 pounds per hour. You can watch them making thins, minis, sticks, Bavarians, rods, nuggets, and bullets.

Cost: Free

Freebies: 1-ounce bag of potato chips.

Video Shown: No

Reservations Needed: Preferred for individuals. Required for groups (see below).

Days and Hours: Mon 10:00 AM–3:00 PM. Closed holidays.

Plan to Stay: 45 minutes

Minimum Age: 6, with 1 adult required for every 5 children.

Disabled Access: Yes, however floors can be slippery.

Group Requirements: Groups larger than 5 people should call at least 2 days in advance. Groups larger than 15 will be split into smaller groups.

Special Information: Factory is loud and can be quite warm near kettles in summer. Floor gets slippery.

Gift Shop: No, but can buy individual bags or cases of potato chips and pretzels from office. Open Mon-Fri 8:00 AM–4:30 PM.

Directions: From I-80, take Pine Bluffs Rest Area exit. Follow signs toward Pine Bluffs. At dead end, turn left onto Hwy. 30. After ¾-mile, turn right at airport sign. Cross railroad tracks, go 2½ miles, and turn left onto Rd. 161 (if you come to dirt road, you've gone too far). Factory is about 1 mile ahead on left.

Nearby Attractions: Texas Trail Museum; Pine Bluffs Rest Area; Cheyenne's attractions, including Cheyenne Frontier Days Museum, Wyoming State Museum, Wyoming Capitol, and Wyoming Game and Fish Visitors Center, are 40 miles away.

Itinerary Planners and Vacation Ideas

Factory tours and company visitors centers/museums are free or inexpensive highlights you can add to a family vacation or business trip. This section helps you plan trips based on your favorite products and regions of the U.S.A. Factory tours allow you to watch workers and machines in action, so you'll see most production Monday through Friday during normal business hours (some companies' tours are offered only on specified days or at certain times of year). Company visitors centers/museums usually also have weekend and holiday hours. Most of the tours listed in this section require minimal advance planning; however, many require reservations, so plan accordingly.

Please refer to the full write-ups in the book for more information. Check the Nearby Attractions sections to round out these itineraries. Call the destinations to verify times and directions between locations. We also suggest that you use a detailed map of the region you are visiting and plan your trip carefully. AAA offers members a route-planning service, highlighting the best roads and highways that lead to your destination.

A. Day Trips

Atlanta's Pride
CNN (television news), page 56.
World of Coca-Cola Atlanta (soda), page 58.

Chicago Area for Fun
Haeger Potteries (artwork pottery) in East Dundee, page 70.
Motorola Museum (electronics) in Schaumburg, page 75.
Revell-Monogram (plastic model kits) in Morton Grove, page 76.

Chicago on Business (Try to squeeze one in during your next trip)
Chicago Board of Trade (grain and financial futures and options), page 68. (See the
    Nearby Attractions under Chicago Board of Trade for more sites related to
    finance.)
Chicago Mercantile Exchange (livestock and financial futures and options), page 68.
Chicago Tribune (newspaper), page 67.

Traveling to or from O'Hare International Airport:
McDonald's Museum (fast food) in Des Plaines, page 73 or
Motorola Museum (electronics) in Schaumburg, page 75.

Dallas/Ft. Worth Area's Corporate Leaders
JCPenney Museum (retail stores and catalogs) in Plano, page 298.
Mary Kay (cosmetics and skin-care products) in Dallas, page 300.

Traveling to or from Dallas/Ft. Worth Airport:
American Airlines C.R. Smith Museum, page 291.

Detroit Transportation
Henry Ford Museum and Greenfield Village (cars) in Dearborn, page 145.
Lionel (model trains and accessories) in Chesterfield, page 149.

Fort Wayne Food (David Letterman's home state)
Perfection Bakeries (bread), page 86.
Sechler's (pickles) in St. Joe, page 87.
Seyfert's (potato chips and pretzels), page 88.

Lake Michigan Coast (Western Michigan)
Brooks Beverages (7-Up, Canada Dry, and other sodas) in Holland, page 141.
DeKlomp/Veldheer (wooden shoes and delftware) in Holland, page 143.
Original Wooden Shoe Factory (wooden shoes) in Holland, page 150.

Las Vegas—Beyond the Casinos (Henderson Factory Four)
Cranberry World West (Ocean Spray products), page 202
    and color photos page 169.
Ethel M Chocolates (chocolates), page 203 and color photos page 165.
Favorite Brands International (marshmallows), page 204.
Ron Lee's World of Clowns (clown and animation figurines) page 205.

Louisville Charm
American Printing House for the Blind (Braille and large-type publications and

audio books), page 96.
Colonel Harland Sanders Museum (KFC fast food), page 100.
Hillerich & Bradsby (Louisville Slugger baseball bats), page 104.
Louisville Stoneware (pottery), page 106 and color photo page 181.

Minnesota—Winter Sports
Arctco (Artic Cat snowmobiles) in Thief River Falls, page 152.
Christian Brothers (hockey sticks) in Warroad, page 154.
Polaris (snowmobiles) in Roseau, page 158.

New York City on Business (Try to squeeze in at least one during your next trip)
NBC Studios (television programs), page 219.
New York Stock Exchange (stocks and bonds), page 220. (See Nearby Attractions
    under NYSE for more sites related to finance.)
Radio City Music Hall (live entertainment), page 224.

Traveling to or from LaGuardia Airport:
Steinway & Sons (pianos), Friday mornings only, in Long Island City, page 225.

Northern Indiana—RV Capital of the World
Coachmen in Middlebury, page 80.
Holiday Rambler in Wakarusa, page 82.
Jayco in Middlebury, page 84.
RV/MH Heritage Foundation Museum and local Convention & Visitors Bureau
    lists other RV company tours (see Nearby Attractions under Holiday Rambler).

Northern Michigan—Chocolates and Cherries
Amon Orchards (cherries and cherry products) in Acme, page 139 and color
    photos, page 162.
Kilwin's Chocolates (fudge, chocolates, and ice cream) in Petoskey, page 148.

Oregon Coast
Oregon Connection/House of Myrtlewood (wood items) in Coos Bay, page 252.
Tillamook Cheese (cheese) in Tillamook, page 255.

Traveling to or from Portland:
Rodgers Instrument (organs) in Hillsboro, page 254 and color photos page 189.

B. Multiple-Day Trips

Auto Factory Adventure (2–4 Days)
Day 1: Toyota in Georgetown, Kentucky, page 112.
   Ford Explorer plant in Louisville, Kentucky, page 102.
Day 2: Corvette in Bowling Green, Kentucky, page 101.
Day 3: Nissan in Smyrna, Tennessee, page 287.
   Saturn tour and visitor center in Spring Hill, Tennessee, page 289.
Day 4: BMW in Greer, South Carolina, page 282 and color photos pages166–167.
   OR
Day 4: Mercedes-Benz in Vance, Alabama, page 4 and color photos page179.
   OR
Day 2: Navistar International (trucks) in Springfield, Ohio, page 244.
   Honda Visitor Center in Marysville, Ohio, page 239.

Boston and Beyond (2–3 Days)
Day 1: Boston Beer (Samuel Adams beer), Thur–Sat only, page 129.
   National Braille Press (Braille publications), page 135.
   Wm. S. Haynes (flutes), page 137.
Day 2: Cape Cod Potato Chips (potato chips) in Hyannis, Massachussetts, page 130.
   Cranberry World (Ocean Spray products) in Plymouth, Massachussetts, page 131
      and color photos page 168.
   Pairpoint Crystal (glass) in Sagamore, Massachussetts, page 136.
   OR
Day 2: Stonyfield Farm (yogurt) in Londonderry, New Hampshire, page 210.
   Top of the Tree (apple pie) in Londonderry, New Hampshire, page 211.
Day 3: Anheuser-Busch (Budweiser beer) in Merrimack, New Hampshire, page 206
      and color photos page 171.
   Castle Springs (bottled spring water and beer) in Moultonborough, New
      Hampshire, page 208 and color photo page 187.
   Hampshire Pewter (pewter tableware and gifts) in Wolfeboro, New Hampshire,
      page 207.

Bourbon Bounty in Kentucky (2 Days)
Day 1: Rebecca-Ruth Candies (chocolates and Bourbon Balls) in Frankfort, page110.
   Old Kentucky Candies (bourbon candy) in Lexington, page 108.
   Wild Turkey Distillery in Lawrenceburg, page 114 and color photos page 174.
Day 2: Maker's Mark Distillery in Loretto, page 105.
   Additional places of interest for bourbon lovers: Heaven Hill Distillery; Oscar
   Getz Museum of Whiskey History; Jim Beam's American Outpost; Annual
   Bardstown September Bourbon Festival. (See Nearby Bourbon-Related
   Attractions under Maker's Mark.)

Central Colorado (3 Days)
Day 1: Denver
   Stephany's Chocolates (chocolates and toffee), page 41.
   U.S. Mint (coins), page 42.
Day 2: Boulder Area
   Celestial Seasonings (tea), page 36.
   Coors (beer) in Golden, page 37.
Day 3: Colorado Springs
   Current (cards, wrapping paper, and catalog), page 38.

Simpich (dolls), page 40.
Van Briggle (pottery), page 43.
OR
Day 3: Estes Park
   Michael Ricker Pewter (pewter sculptures) in Estes Park, page 39.

China, Glass, and Pottery in Eastern Ohio Area (2 Days)
Day 1: Brooke Glass in Wellsburg, West Virginia, page 330.
   Homer Laughlin China in Newell, West Virginia, page 331.
   Hall China in East Liverpool, Ohio, page 237.
   Side trip to Creegan (animated characters) in Steubenville, Ohio, page 235.
Day 2: Mosser Glass in Cambridge, Ohio, page 243.
   Robinson Ransbottom Pottery in Roseville, Ohio, page 245.
   Roseville-Crooksville pottery communities attractions and annual July pottery
      festival featuring tours of other pottery factories. (See Nearby Attractions
      under Robinson Ransbottom.)
   Side trip to Longaberger (baskets) in Dresden, Ohio, page 241.

Colonial Williamsburg Area (2 Days)
Day 1: Rowena's (pound cakes, jams, cooking sauces, and gifts) in Norfolk,
      page 315 and color photo page 190.
Day 2: Williamsburg Doll Factory (porcelain dolls), page 316.
   The Candle Factory (candles and soap), page 313.
   Williamsburg Pottery Factory (pottery, wood, and plaster), page 317.

Disney World and Beyond (3 Days)
Day 1: Magic of Disney Animation Studios (animated features) in
      Lake Buena Vista, page 51.
Day 2: Nickelodeon Studios (television shows) in Orlando, page 52.
Day 3: Correct Craft (Ski Nautiques water-ski boats) in Orlando, page 47.
   E-One (fire trucks) in Ocala, page 48.

Food and Festivity in Louisiana (2 days)
Day 1: New Orleans area
   Blaine Kern's Mardi Gras World (parade floats) in New Orleans, page 115
      and color photos page 172.
Day 2: Cajun Country
   Konriko (rice and Cajun seasonings) in New Iberia, page 118.
   McIlhenny Company (Tabasco brand pepper sauce) on Avery Island, page 120
      and color photo page 192.
   Tony Chachere's (Creole seasonings and rice mixes) in Opelousas, page 122.

Gastronomic Tours in Texas (4 Days)
Day 1: Collin Street Bakery (fruitcake) in Corsicana, page 293.
Day 2: Imperial Sugar Company (sugar) in Sugar Lane, near Houston, page 296.
   Blue Bell Creameries (ice cream) in Brenham, page 292.
Day 3: Jardine's Texas Foods (Texas-style foods) in Buda, near Austin, page 297.
Day 4: Dr Pepper Bottling (soda), bottling on Tuesdays, in Dublin, page 294.
   Dr Pepper Museum in Waco (see Special Information under Dr. Pepper).
   Mrs Baird's Bakery (bread) in Fort Worth, page 302.

Glassblowing in West Virginia (2 Days)
Day 1: Fenton Art Glass in Williamstown, page 332.
   Side trip to Lee Middleton Original Dolls in Belpre, Ohio, page 240.

Day 2: Blenko Glass in Milton, page 329.
   Gibson Glass factory (see Nearby Attractions under Blenko Glass).
   Pilgrim Glass in Ceredo, page 334.

Hawaii—Off the Beaches (2 Days)
Day 1: Oahu
   Maui Divers of Hawaii (jewelry) in Honolulu, page 62 and color photos page 183.
   Royal Hawaiian Mint (commemorative gold coins) in Honolulu, page 64.
Day 2: Hawaii (the Big Island)
   Big Island Candies (chocolate-covered macadamia nuts) in Hilo, page 60.
   Mauna Loa (macadamia nuts and chocolates) in Hilo, page 63.
   Holualoa Kona Coffee (coffee) in Holualoa, page 61.

Milwaukee—Beer and Beyond (4 Days)
Day 1: Miller Brewing, page 341 and color photo page 190.
   Quality Candy/Buddy Squirrel (chocolates and popcorn), page 344.
Day 2: Allen-Edmonds (shoes) in Port Washington, page 335 and
     color photos page 178.
   Kohler (bathtubs, whirlpools, toilets, and sinks) in Kohler, page 340.
Day 3: SC Johnson Wax (specialty home-cleaning products) in Racine, page 346.
   Case (tractors) in Racine, page 337.
Day 4: Natural Ovens (breads and cereals) in Manitowoc, page 342.
   OR
Day 4: General Motors (sport-utility vehicles and pickups) in Janesville, page 339.
   Trek (bicycles) in Waterloo, page 345.

Musical Instrument Mecca (3 Days)
Day 1: Wm. S. Haynes (flutes and piccolos) in Boston, Massachusetts, page 137.
Day 2: Steinway & Sons (pianos) Friday mornings only, in Long Island City, New
   York, page 225.
Day 3: Martin Guitar in Nazareth, Pennsylvania, page 266 and color photo page 175.

Niagara Falls (2 Days)
Day 1: (depending on your direction of travel in New York State to Niagara Falls):
   Corning Glass Center in Corning, page 215 and color photos page 191.
   OR
   George Eastman House (photography) in Rochester, page 216.
Day 2: Choose two of the following:
   The Original American Kazoo Company in Eden, page 221.
   Perry's Ice Cream in Akron, page 222.
   QRS Music (player-piano rolls) in Buffalo, page 223.

Pretzels and Potato Chips in Pennsylvania (2–3 Days)
Day 1: Herr's in Nottingham, page 262 and color photos page 186.
   Anderson Bakery in Lancaster, page 258.
   Sturgis Pretzel House in Lititz, page 274.
Day 2: Utz Quality Foods in Hanover, page 278.
   Snyder's of Hanover in Hanover, page 273.
   (On the way to Utz and Snyder's, visit Harley-Davidson in York, page 261,
     or Pfaltzgraff in Thomasville, page 269.)
   OR
Day 2: Chocolate Diversion
   Hershey's Chocolate World in Hershey, page 263.
   Pennsylvania Dutch Candies in Mt. Holly Springs, page 268.

Day 3: Utz Quality Foods in Hanover, page 278.

San Francisco with Kids–Fun for Adults, Too! (3 Days)
Day 1 (May need to choose only two):
  Basic Brown Bear Factory (teddy bears) in San Francisco, page 14
    and color photos page 184.
  Fortune Cookie Factory in Oakland, page 20.
  Dreyer's and Edy's Grand Ice Cream in Union City, page 18.
  (Consider side trip to Intel Museum in Santa Clara for science-oriented
    children, page 24.)
Day 2: Herman Goelitz (jelly beans) in Fairfield, page 22 and
    color photos page 182.
Day 3: Hershey's Visitors Center in Oakdale, page 23 and color photos page 180.

St. Louis and Kansas City—Bud and Beyond (3 Days)
Day 1: McDonnell Douglas Museum (airplanes, missiles, and spacecraft)
    in St. Louis, page 200.
  Chrysler (minivans and pickup trucks) in Fenton, page 194.
  Anheuser-Busch (Budweiser beer) in St. Louis, page 193 and
    color photos pages 170 and 171.
Day 2: Purina Farms (pets and farm animals) in Gray Summit, page 198.
Day 3: Hallmark Visitors Center (greeting cards) in Kansas City, page 195
    and color photos page 185.

Studios of Southern California (2–3 Days)
Days 1 and 2: Paramount Pictures in Hollywood, page 31.
  Warner Bros. Studios in Burbank, page 35.
  NBC Studios in Burbank, page 29.
Day 3: Universal Studios Hollywood in Universal City, page 34.

Sweet Tooth Tour—East Coast (3 Days)
Day 1: Moore's Candies in Baltimore, Maryland, page 126.
Day 2: Pennsylvania Dutch Candies in Mt. Holly Springs, Pennsylvania, page 268.
  Hershey's Chocolate World in Hershey, Pennsylvania, page 263.
Day 3: Sherm Edwards (chocolates) in Trafford, Pennsylvania, page 272.

Sweet Tooth Tour—West Coast (3 Days)
Day 1: Phoenix
  Cerreta's Candy in Glendale, Arizona, page 9.
Day 2: Las Vegas
  Cranberry World West in Henderson, Nevada, page 202 and
    color photos page 169.
  Ethel M Chocolates in Henderson, Nevada, page 203 and color photos page 165.
  Favorite Brands International in Henderson, Nevada, page 204.
Day 3: San Francisco Area (fly to San Francisco). Choose one:
  Herman Goelitz (jelly beans) in Fairfield, California, page 22 and color photos
    page 182.
  Hershey's Visitors Center in Oakdale, California, page 23 and color photos
    page 180.
  OR
Day 3: Seattle Area (fly to Seattle)
  Boehms Chocolates in Issaquah, Washington, page 318 and
    color photo page 163.

Vermont—Beyond Ben & Jerry's (3 Days)

From the South:

Day 1: Crowley Cheese in Healdville, page 308.
   Simon Pearce (glass and pottery) in Windsor and Quechee, page 310
      and color photo page 161.
Day 2: Maple Grove Farms (maple syrup, salad dressing) in St. Johnsbury, page 307.
   Cabot Creamery (cheese) in Cabot, page 306.
Day 3: Ben & Jerry's (ice cream) in Waterbury, page 305.
   Vermont Teddy Bear in Shelburne, page 312 and color photos page 177.

Washington State (2 Days)

Day 1: Boeing (commercial aircraft) in Everett, page 320.
   Boehms Chocolates in Issaquah, page 318 and color photo page 163.
   Redhook Ale Brewery (beer) in Seattle, page 326.
Day 2: Liberty Orchards (fruit candies) in Cashmere, page 324.
   Boise Cascade (lumber and plywood) in Yakima, page 321.

Company Index

Product Index

About the Authors

Bruce Brumberg and Karen Axelrod traveled across the U.S.A. to "kick the tires of the American economy." This husband-and-wife team journeyed from the massive Boeing plant in Everett, Washington, to the ranch-like factory of Jardine's Texas Foods in Buda, Texas (pictured above). During their travels, Bruce earned an "Official Pretzel Twister" certificate, while Karen was awarded an "Honorary Brewmaster" title and "Official Candymaker's Diploma." Fascinated by how things are made and companies grow, they visit factories for fun, business ideas, and free samples. When not traveling, they live with their daughter, Hilary, near Boston, Massachusetts. Bruce owns a legal and financial publishing company. Before writing this book, Karen was a buyer for 10 years for major retail and catalog companies.

AVALON
TRAVEL
publishing

BECAUSE TRAVEL MATTERS.

AVALON TRAVEL PUBLISHING knows that travel is more than coming and going—travel is taking part in new experiences, new ideas, and a new outlook. Our goal is to bring you complete and up-to-date information to help you make informed travel decisions.

AVALON TRAVEL GUIDES feature a combination of practicality and spirit, offering a unique traveler-to-traveler perspective perfect for an afternoon hike, around-the-world journey, or anything in between.

WWW.TRAVELMATTERS.COM

Avalon Travel Publishing guides are available at your favorite book or travel store.

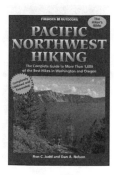
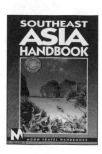

FOR TRAVELERS WITH SPECIAL INTERESTS

GUIDES

The 100 Best Small Art Towns in America • Asia in New York City
The Big Book of Adventure Travel • Cities to Go
Cross-Country Ski Vacations • Gene Kilgore's Ranch Vacations
Great American Motorcycle Tours • Healing Centers and Retreats
Indian America • Into the Heart of Jerusalem
The People's Guide to Mexico • The Practical Nomad
Saddle Up! • Staying Healthy in Asia, Africa, and Latin America
Steppin' Out • Travel Unlimited • Understanding Europeans
Watch It Made in the U.S.A. • The Way of the Traveler
Work Worldwide • The World Awaits
The Top Retirement Havens • Yoga Vacations

SERIES

Adventures in Nature
The Dog Lover's Companion
Kidding Around
Live Well

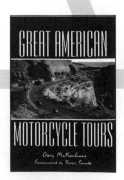